Trouble in the Camera Club

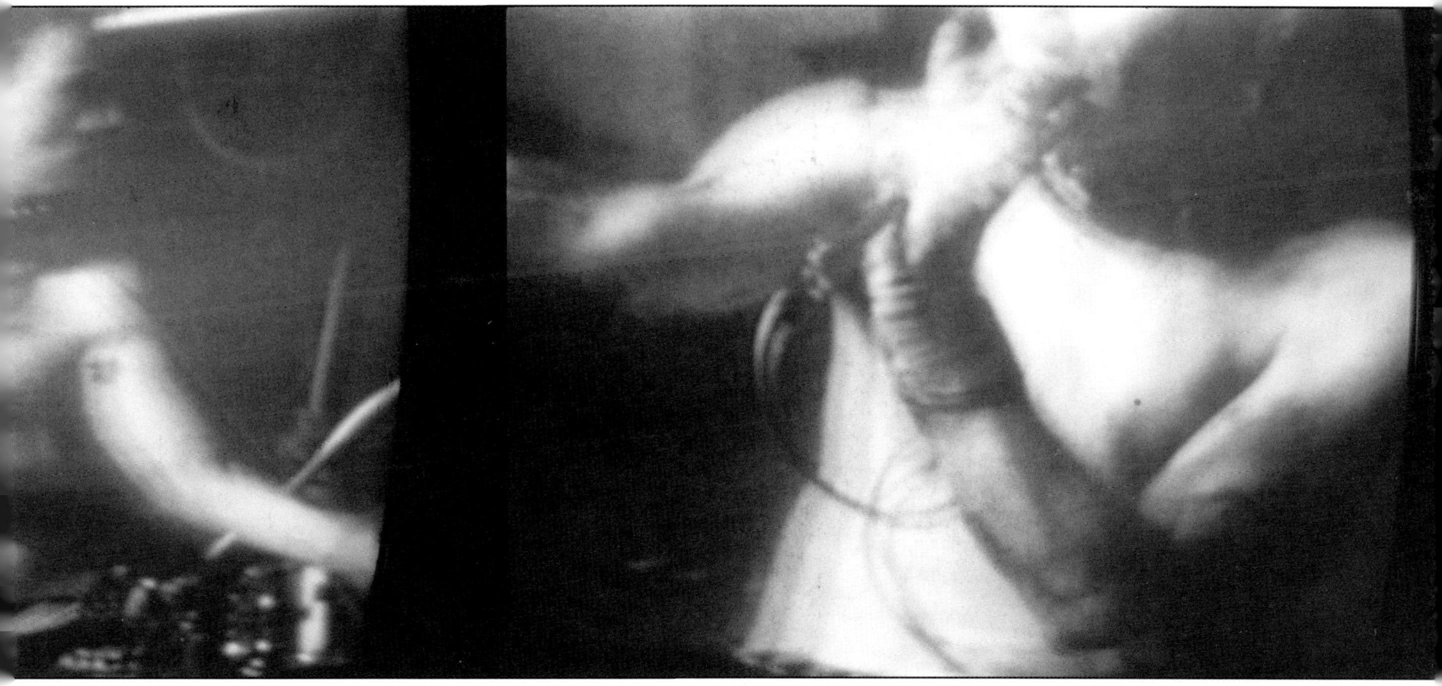

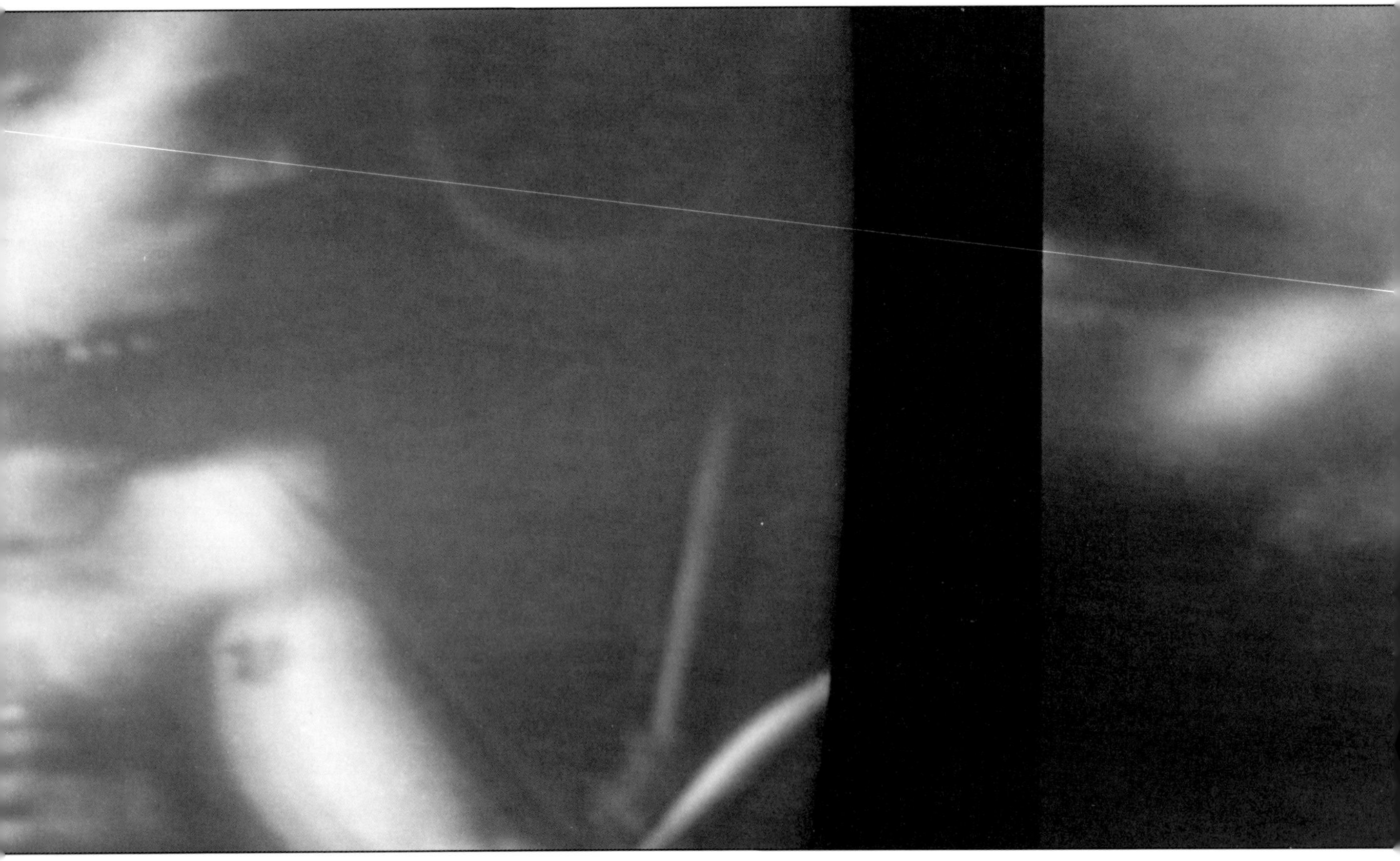

Trouble in the Camera Club

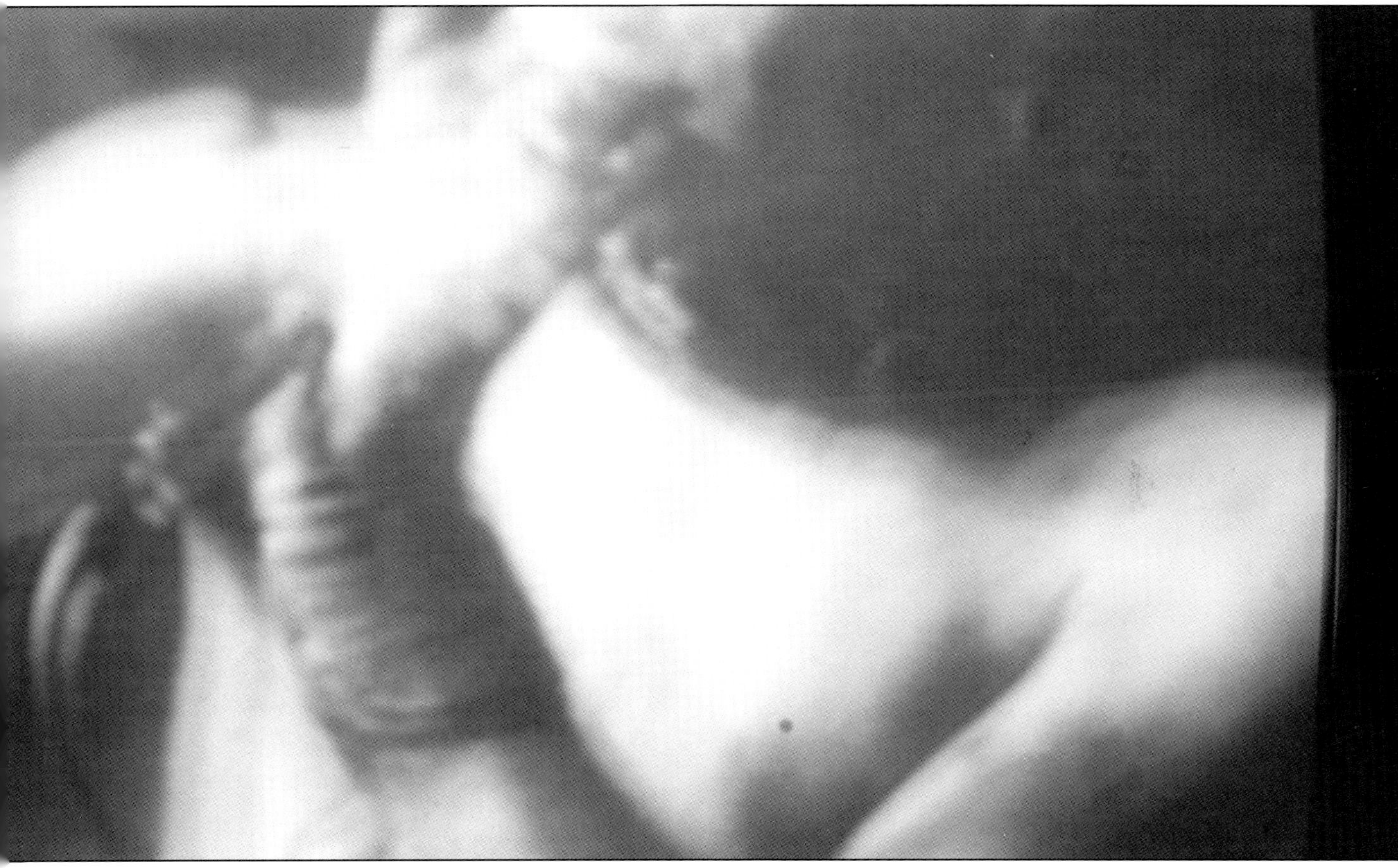

Don Pyle

ECW Press

Published by ECW Press
2120 Queen Street East, Suite 200, Toronto, Ontario, Canada M4E 1E2
416.694.3348 / info@ecwpress.com

All images from the collection of Don Pyle except where noted. Damned LP courtesy of Dallas Good.
Spray-paint images used in folio design courtesy Eduard Piél.

LIBRARY AND ARCHIVES OF CANADA CATALOGUING IN PUBLICATION

Pyle, Don, 1961-
Trouble in the camera club : a photographic narrative of
Toronto's punk history 1976-1980 / Don Pyle.

ISBN 978-1-55022-966-0

ALSO ISSUED AS:
ISBN 978-1-55490-966-7 (PDF)

1. Punk rock music—Ontario—Toronto—Pictorial works. 2. Punk rock music—Ontario—Toronto—History and criticism. I. Title.

ML3534.6.C2P996 2011 782.4216609713541 C2010-906725-8

Developing editor: Jennifer Hale
Cover design: David Gee
Interior layout and design: Rachel Ironstone
Production: Troy Cunningham
Printing: Wai Man Book Binding 1 2 3 4 5

The publication of *Trouble in the Camera Club: A Photographic Narrative of Toronto's Punk History 1976-1980* has been generously supported by the Canada Council for the Arts which last year invested $20.1 million in writing and publishing throughout Canada, by the Ontario Arts Council, by the OMDC Book Fund, an initiative of the Ontario Media Development Corporation, and by the Government of Canada through the Canada Book Fund.

ONTARIO ARTS COUNCIL
CONSEIL DES ARTS DE L'ONTARIO
Canada
Canada Council for the Arts
Conseil des Arts du Canada

PRINTED AND BOUND IN CHINA

Foreword

Strange. Well built young men, some of them have exploited your worlds. Equipped with frightening voices, and several dangerous talents, they are sent into town to take it from behind, tricked out in disgusting luxury.
Paradise of Violence, of grimace and madness.
(One day in the future, these poets will exist.)
— Arthur Rimbaud, in a letter to his mentor, *Parade* (1872)

1977 — now is the time of the assassin.

I will give you a gang, one you wished a gang really looked like, where Cinema was our language, Violence our currency . . . History ours to steal! Otherwise known as PUNK ROCK.

PUNK is timeless. Time, and society, didn't see it coming. Rimbaud did . . . over 100 years ago. And then, it hit the seers who put it on the stage in Toronto, London, New York. And to think, there are *still* bands, three full decades after the first and only assault that mattered, calling themselves PUNK, but they can never be — they are only Elvis impersonators . . . for cynicism only hardens with time.

Not all the true visionaries were musicians; in the beginning most of it could not have been done without *the* first PUNK promoters, Gary Topp and Gary Cormier — true heroes. Another who sensed it in the air from the very start is the artist who took these pictures — Don Pyle, who at the age of 14 started on his journey of documenting *real* first-generation PUNK. I'm proud to be among his collection.

Steven Leckie VILETONES — PUNK /2010

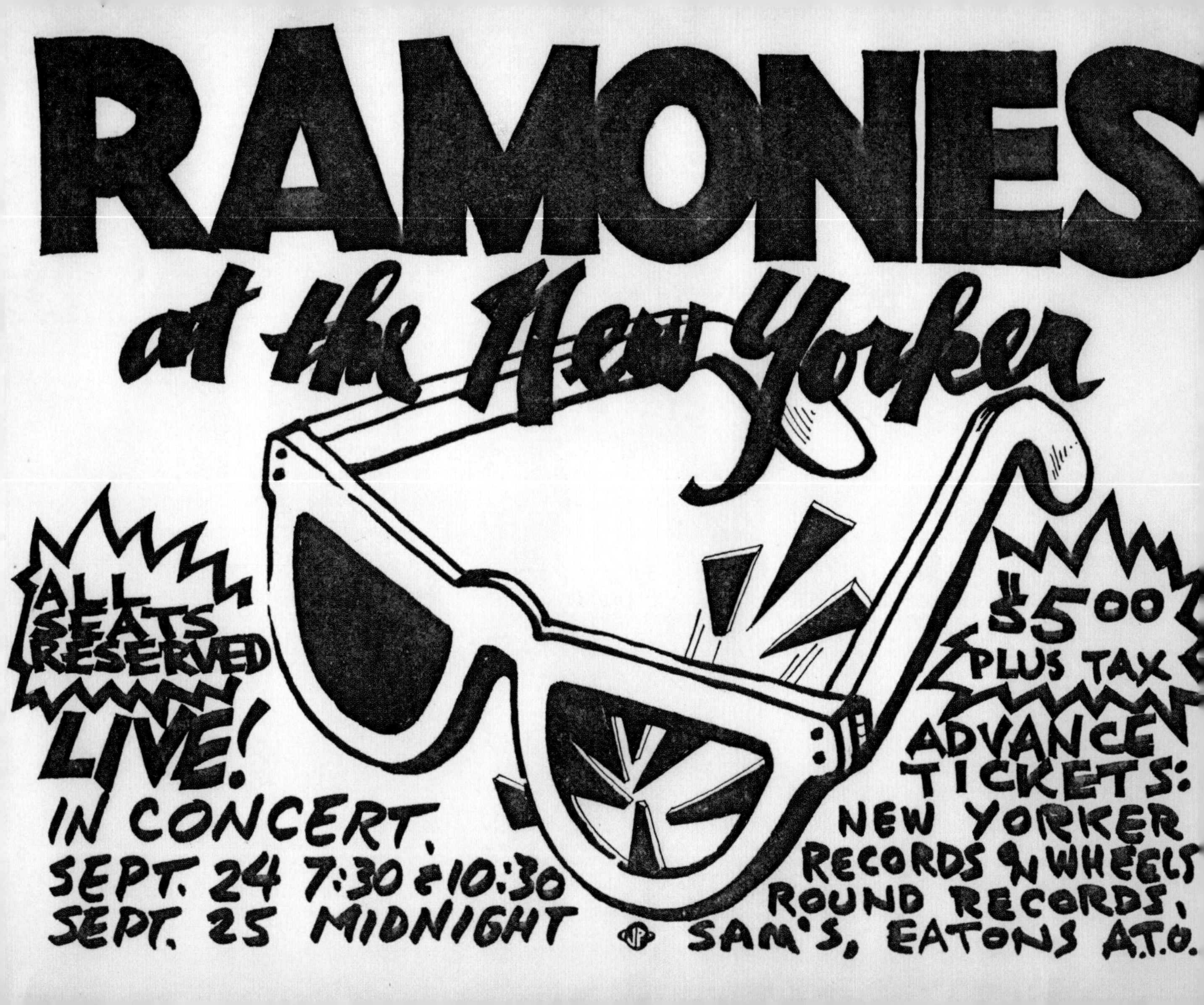
RAMONES
at the New Yorker
ALL SEATS RESERVED
LIVE!
IN CONCERT.
SEPT. 24 7:30 & 10:30
SEPT. 25 MIDNIGHT
$5.00 PLUS TAX
ADVANCE TICKETS:
NEW YORKER
RECORDS 'N WHEELS
ROUND RECORDS,
SAM'S, EATONS A.T.O.

Ramones, New Yorker Theatre, 1976

This was it, the beginning of so many things to come that couldn't have been imagined before this day. Everything from the 1910 Fruitgum Company to The Stooges had coagulated to form this most perfect creation. At this moment the Ramones were the fastest and loudest band in the world and had just put out their immaculate first LP, a masterpiece sleeved in the greatest album jacket ever made. To me, they remain absolutely perfect and self-contained: pure art created by examining one thing over and over again, working within a strictly defined set of parameters.

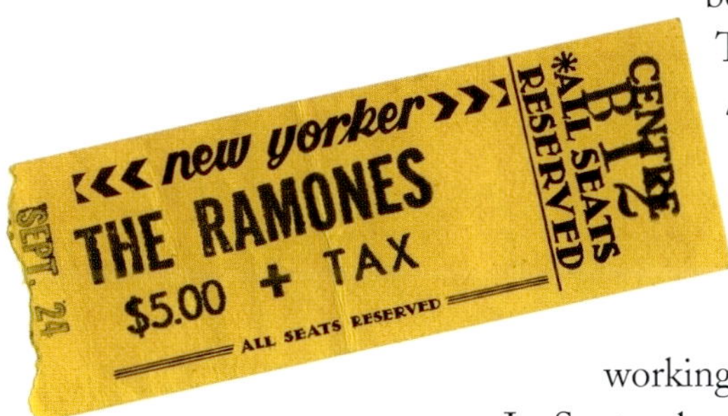

In September 1976, their first Toronto show at the hallowed New Yorker Theatre was, as corny as it may sound today, a defining moment and needless to say, at 14 years of age, my mind was blown wide open. There were not even any other "punk" bands to enlist as opening act. The opener, Johnnie Lovesin in Adidas T-shirt and sweatpants, illustrated the clear before-and-after we experienced in that moment. Wailing away on solo guitar, he was flanked by two homemade wooden boxes, each of which concealed a person pushing up a poster of a wincing Hendrix that had been stapled to a piece of wood, revealed through a cloud of dry ice.

My friend Roger and I were beyond excited to see the Ramones. My mother had an 8 mm movie camera gathering dust in her closet that she had bought for her honeymoon in 1946 and had not used since. I took it with me and Roger filmed three minutes of the concert but without proper lighting all that was visible were glints of chrome and Joey's knee jerking in the darkness to the beat. My cheap cream-colored plastic Instamatic camera was all I had to take pictures with and the disappointing results encouraged me to save up for a 35 mm camera.

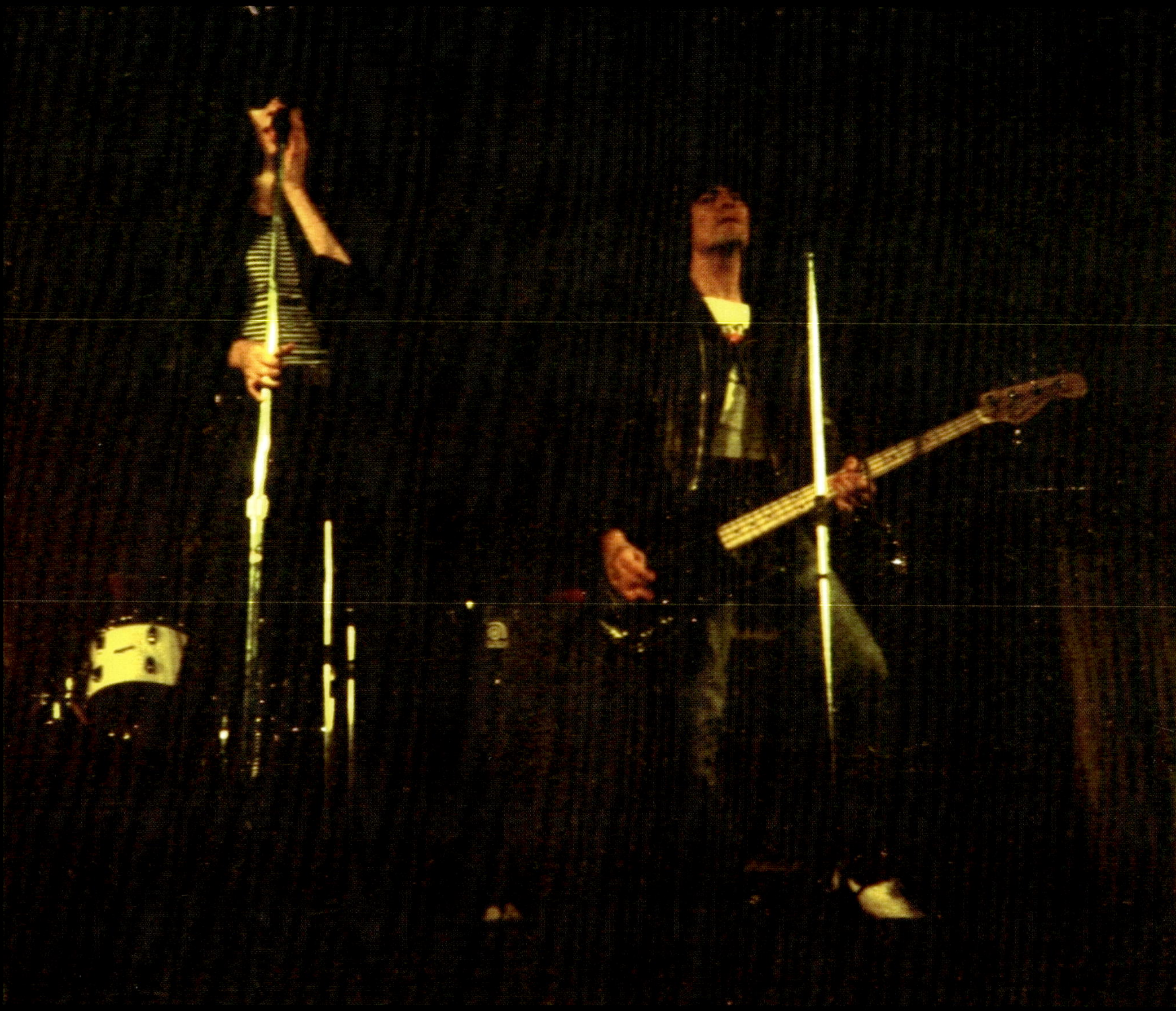

I had taken the jacket of their LP with me to try and get them to sign it, and before the show, we spotted the Ramones walking together down Yonge Street. I stopped them and asked them to please sign my album, and as they passed the cover around, they continued with the argument they were clearly having before I ran into them. Skipping and sputtering, my ballpoint pen barely registered Joey's signature so he took out his own black marker and patiently retraced his signature. Tommy took the cover last, and when he reached the end of his name, he continued gouging the cover with the marker, his voice rising with every swirl as it embodied the anger he was spewing at the others, until I had to yank it out of his hands.

From this moment on, everything in my life would be different.

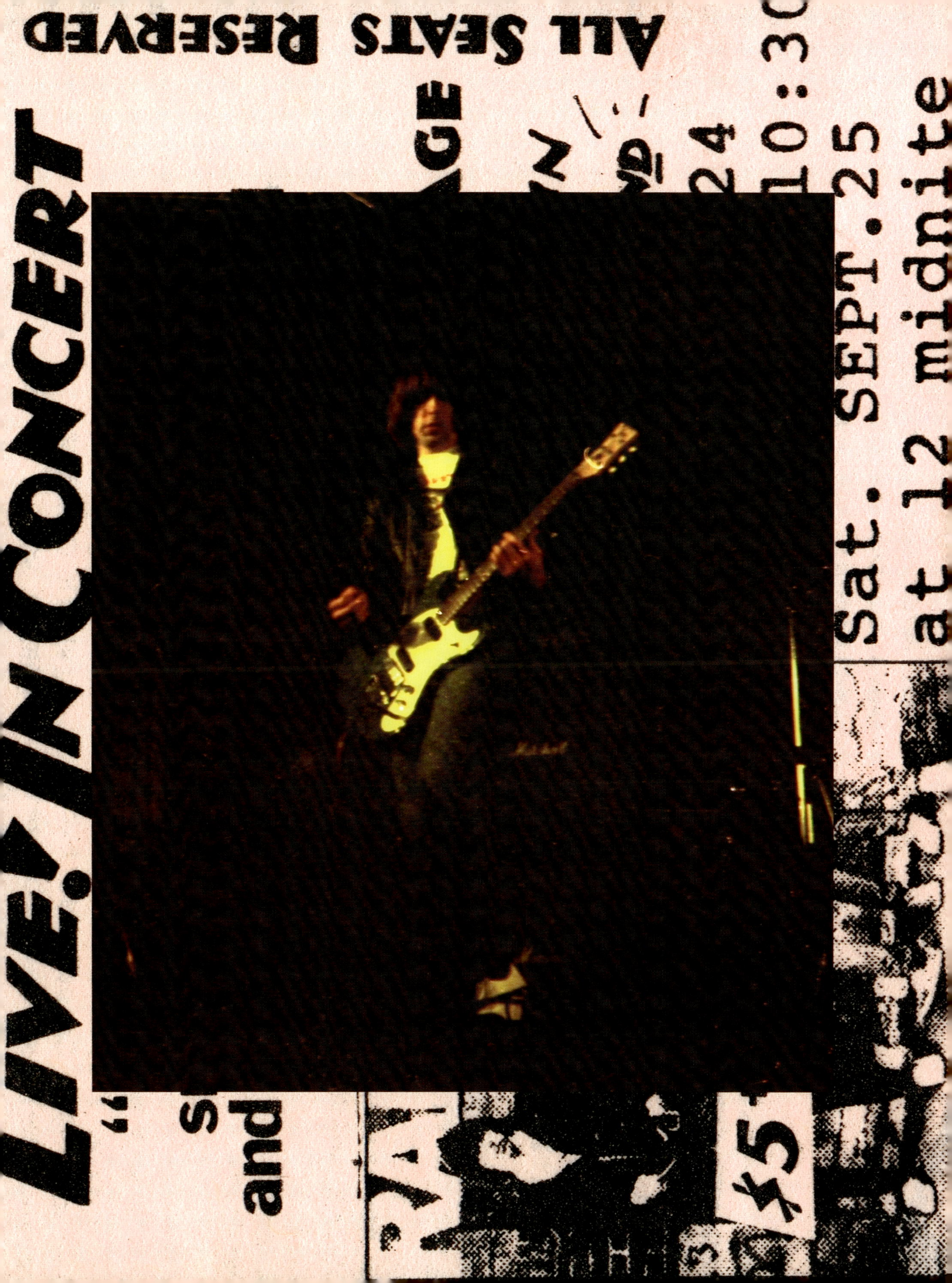
LIVE! IN CONCERT
ALL SEATS RESERVED
Sat. SEPT. 25
at 12 midnite

CN Tower, 1976

Emblematic of Toronto's wish to be noticed, the boldly ridiculous CN Tower neatly divided time as the city joined the modern age. In this image, the tower is more or less complete and a couple of months away from allowing visitors to clamber over the construction debris to go up for a look, its layers of new concrete clearly visible like an oversized portion of Jell-O 1-2-3. But the surrounding lands reveal railway yards that had not yet been redeveloped into ugly condos, and large plots that are impossibly open compared to the same concentrated area today. There is no convention center, no domed stadium, only this new structure that couldn't help but be closely attached to the psyche of the citizens it loomed over. Shiny and new, the tower coincided with "punk" and was given its due in 1977 on the debut single by The Poles.

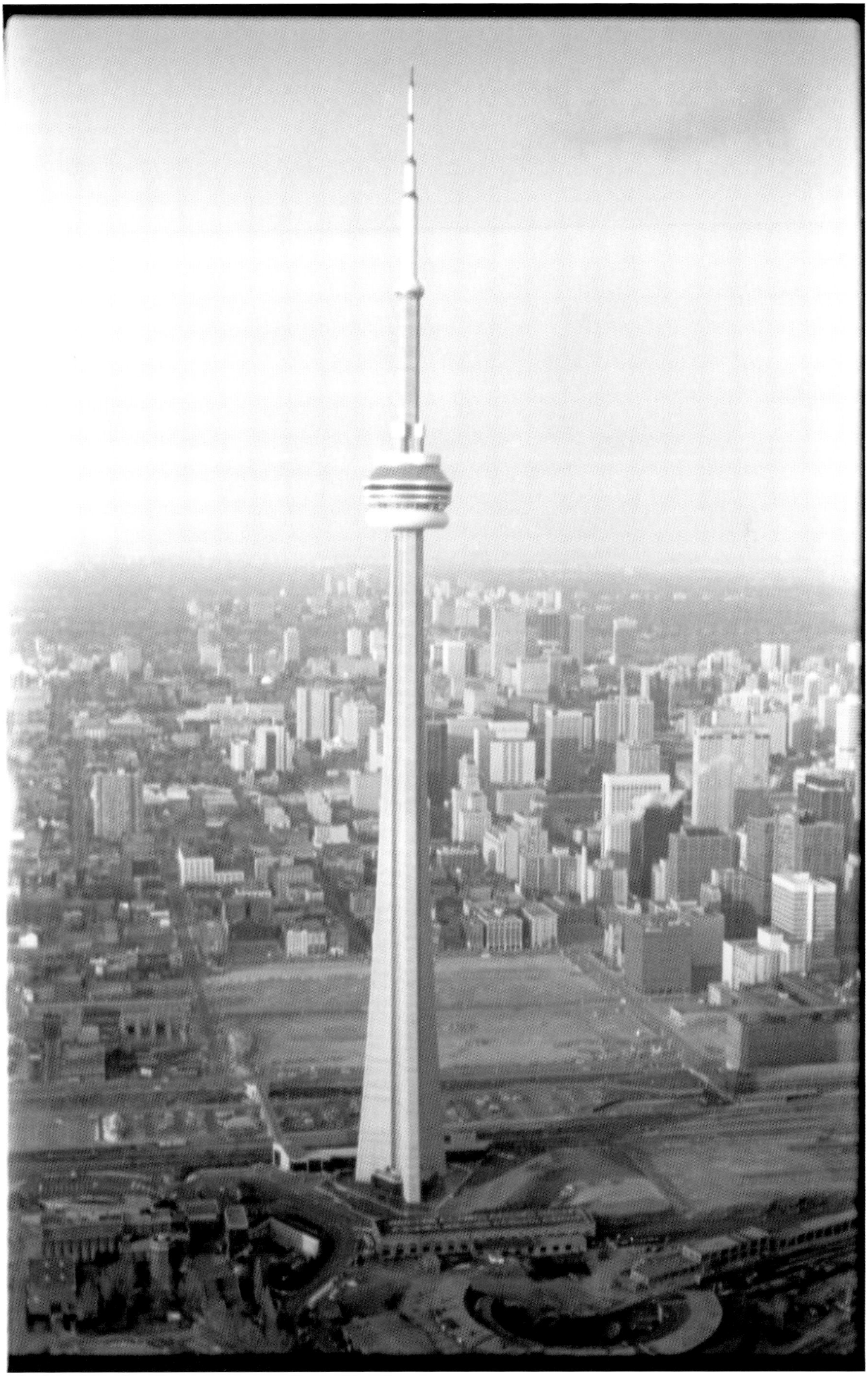

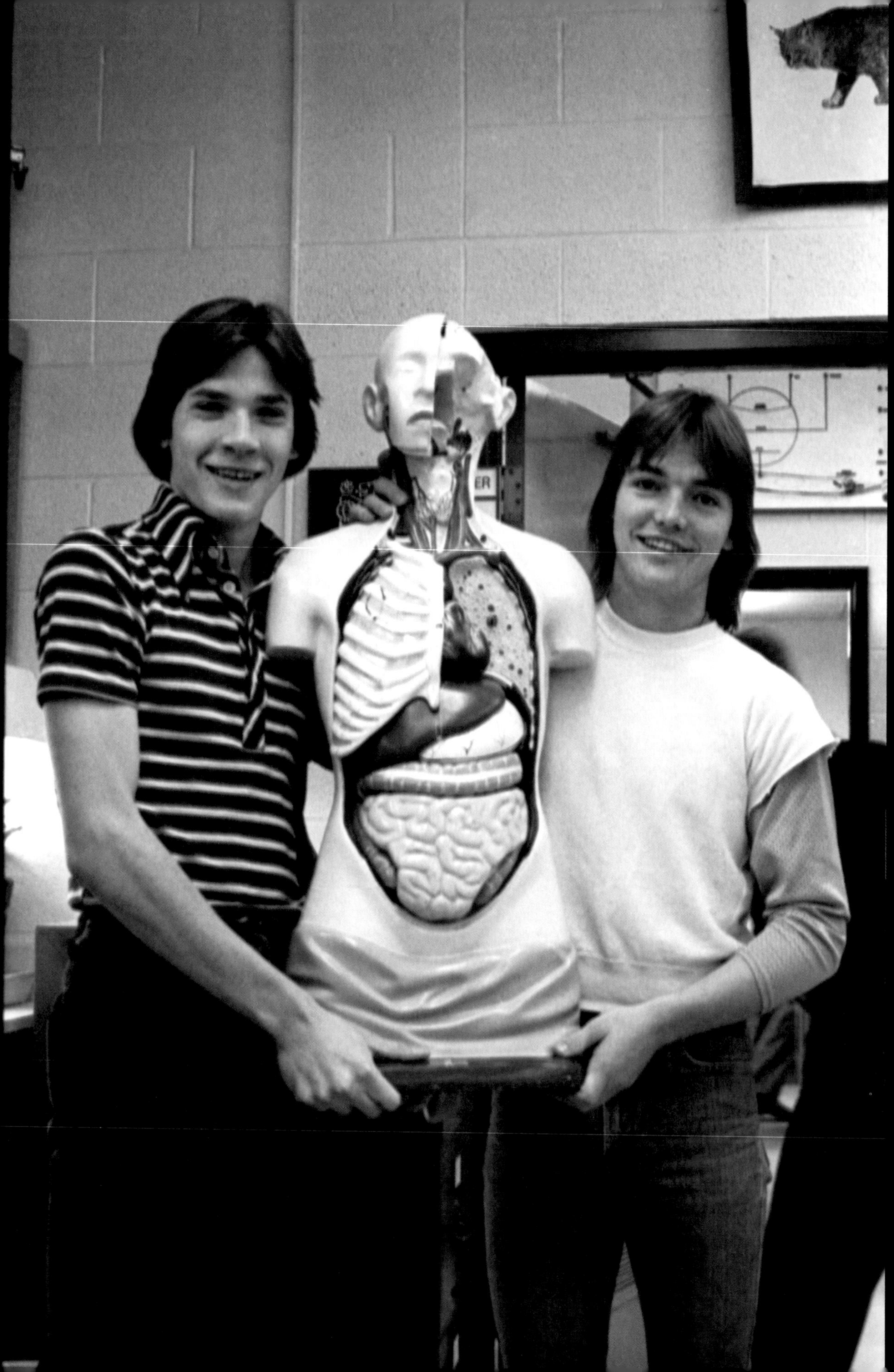

Trouble in the Camera Club

Trouble in the Camera Club documents my perspective of the golden-moment birth of the revolution, of what became known as punk rock. Anything I say is as true as I remember it to be. These were not the good old days, this wasn't the time-of-your-life — but it was as great as any day that happens today.

I saved money from my flyer delivery route to buy a stereo, but when the big bucks started to roll in from my after-school job as a stock boy at our neighborhood drugstore, my next major purchase was a Canon AT-1 manual 35 mm SLR camera with a standard 55 mm lens. I joined my high school's camera club to learn how to develop and print, and to get free chemicals. In exchange for taking photos of teenagers eating French fries or team pictures of adolescents in ill-fitting uniforms, I could use the darkroom at any time. Having to take photos for the school yearbook was a good way to get out of class and also provided two refuge rooms — the yearbook office and the darkroom — to avoid having to lunch with the jocks and other teenagers that I felt so alienated from, who were working toward careers in accounting or had aspirations of starting a family.

I would buy black-and-white film by the foot and wind my own canisters so I could have more frames to shoot, trying to squeeze 40 frames onto one spool, causing the sprockets to become disengaged, sometimes to pretty cool effect. My camera case was a plastic grocery store bag, just something to protect it from the rain and snow.

Runnymede Collegiate, 1978

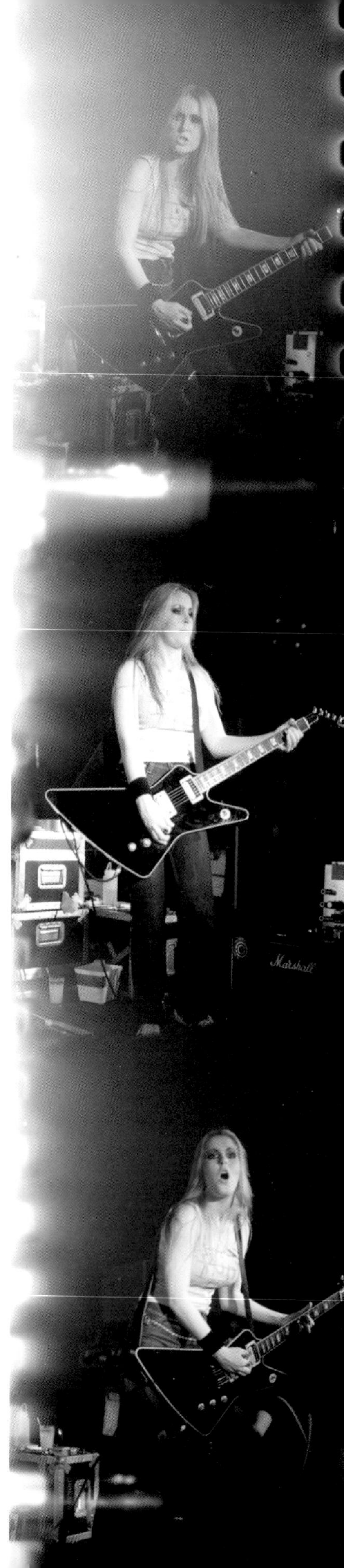

The Runaways, Lita Ford, El Mocambo, 1977

The school provided bags of powdered developing solution and stop fluid chemicals that the two or three others who used the darkroom and I would have to stretch beyond their intended lifespan. The enlargers were old and clunky with jagged negative holders from years of student abuse, but we didn't know any better — they did the job. We could borrow school enlargers on weekends, and this gave me the excuse I needed to avoid having to go to the family cottage. Instead, I'd cover the windows with black garbage bags, tape up the bottom of the door and turn my mother's bathroom into a darkroom for the weekend, printing pictures in the day and going out to explore at night.

Coincidental with this were the first grumblings of the punk rock explosion about to happen around the world. From age 14 to about 18, I took my camera to many of the gigs I was attending — needing to capture and retain every spastic gesture of my new experiences. Shooting with ambient lighting, bad eyesight and thick, heavy glasses, manual focus and long shutter times, resulted in a trial-and-error schooling in photography. I have severe astigmatism and have worn glasses since second grade and by the time I was 16, I began going through a series of ill-fitting hard contact lenses that improved my self-esteem . . . if not my vision. My contact lenses would constantly drift out of place, and without autofocus, many of my photos would be blurry. I considered pursuing a career as a photographer, but without encouragement or support for higher education, my vision problems made me decide on other options.

I loved using Ilford 400 ASA film because of its rich blacks and exaggerated grain, or sometimes Kodak Tri-X, which had better tonal gradations and could be pushed to high speeds with less grainy results. I never thought about what would be best for these photos 30 years later. I was interested in experimenting with shutter speeds and with pushing film to such high speeds that I could shoot with very little light. Overdeveloping film would often result in grays being an overexposed flare of white, and grain being large enough to make regular film look like Kirlian photographs. Even though I had some kind of camera since the time I was four years old and was always taking photos, it was when I began to develop and print my own that I started to shoot a lot more. These photos were my education in the process.

Primitive darkroom conditions and the fact that I was still learning left me with overexposed and underexposed, scratched, dusty and watermarked negs. Because of limited funds, I was only able to print a few images from each roll of black-and-white film. Eventually, my binders of negatives became these objects overlooked because of familiarity: artifacts from the past to be packed and unpacked as I moved from place to place. When I began scanning my negatives in 2007, I saw what I had for the first time, shocked by not only the quality of the images, but by the fact they

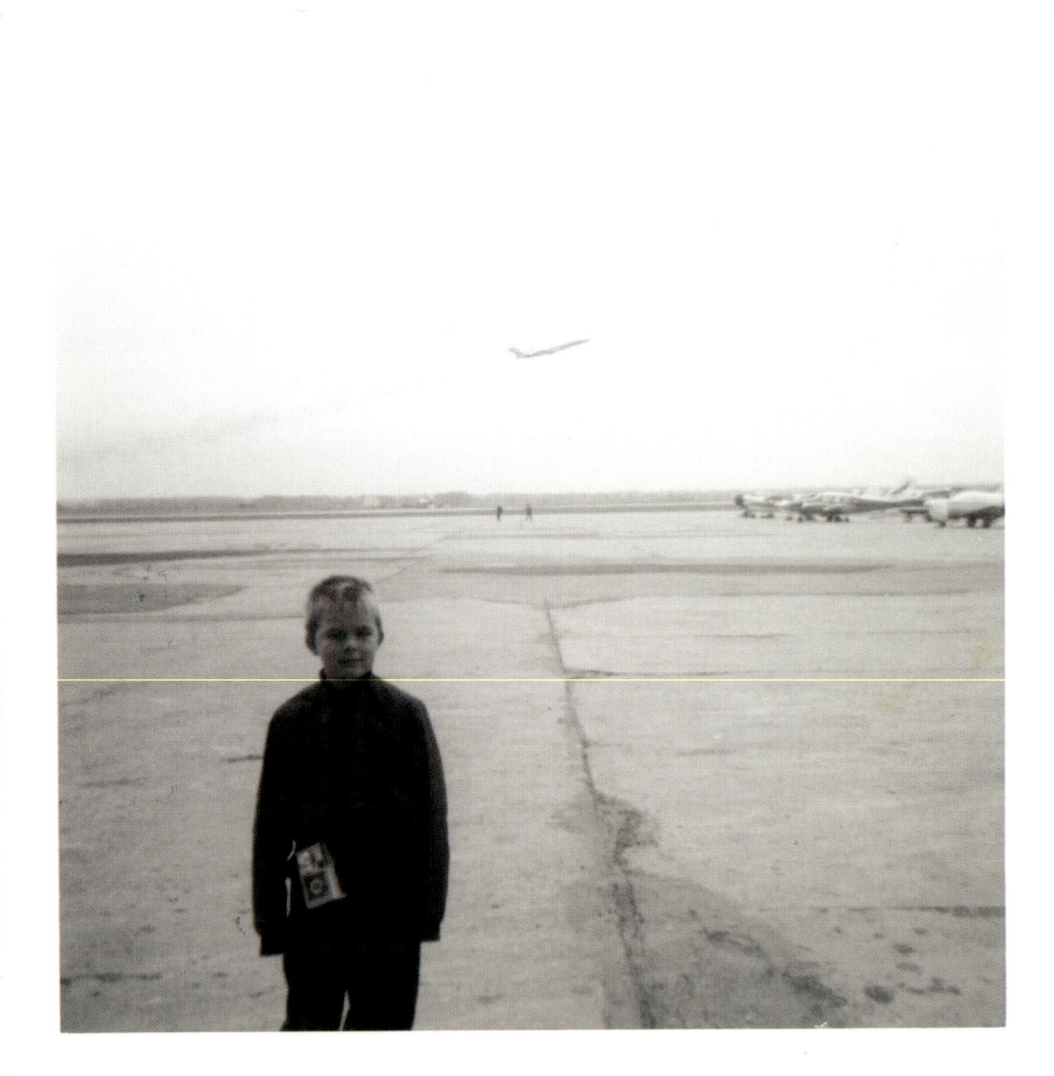

DP, 1967

had been made by someone so young — a kid I hardly recognized. Most of the images contained in this collection were printed for the first time when I prepared to exhibit them in spring 2007, restored and in some cases, the decaying beauty and chemical blobs left intact, seeming to visually interpret the shards of sound and pure mania of the moment. In a color world, it's easy to forget the gorgeous play of light and silver that happens with black-and-white film. Over time, the black areas and the white areas retreated from each other in chemical reaction with gray, undecided where to go.

My mother worked at Queen and Yonge Streets, at Simpson's department store. I would go visit her, and by age nine or 10, I was exploring Queen Street West, scouring the used bookshops that were concentrated there. Long before chain shops moved in and the only music venue was country and western bar the Horseshoe Tavern, Queen West was seedy and run-down. Where once there were porno shops with orange painted windows and Hasidic men pushed racks of clothing through streets of beautiful old factory sweatshops, the street is now putrid with the stink of bath bombs and condos. Around 1975, when flyers appeared on telephone poles for "underground" gigs and art school events, I related to them immediately and knew they connected to a particular undefined aesthetic embodied in music I was already listening to, like New York Dolls and Sparks.

Before punk rock was punk rock, there was a scene happening in Toronto, even though it had yet to be defined or gain a focus. I had an awareness of it, but was too young to know that I was already participating in it. When I'd go see Rough Trade, Iggy Pop, Alice Cooper, The Tubes, Blue Öyster Cult, David Bowie or The Dishes, many of the same people would be there. We were probably all "reading" *Rock Scene* and *Trouser Press*, taking style tips from Wayne County and buying mail order records from weirdo bands that advertised their releases in the classified sections, like Half Japanese and The Nerves. I know I was.

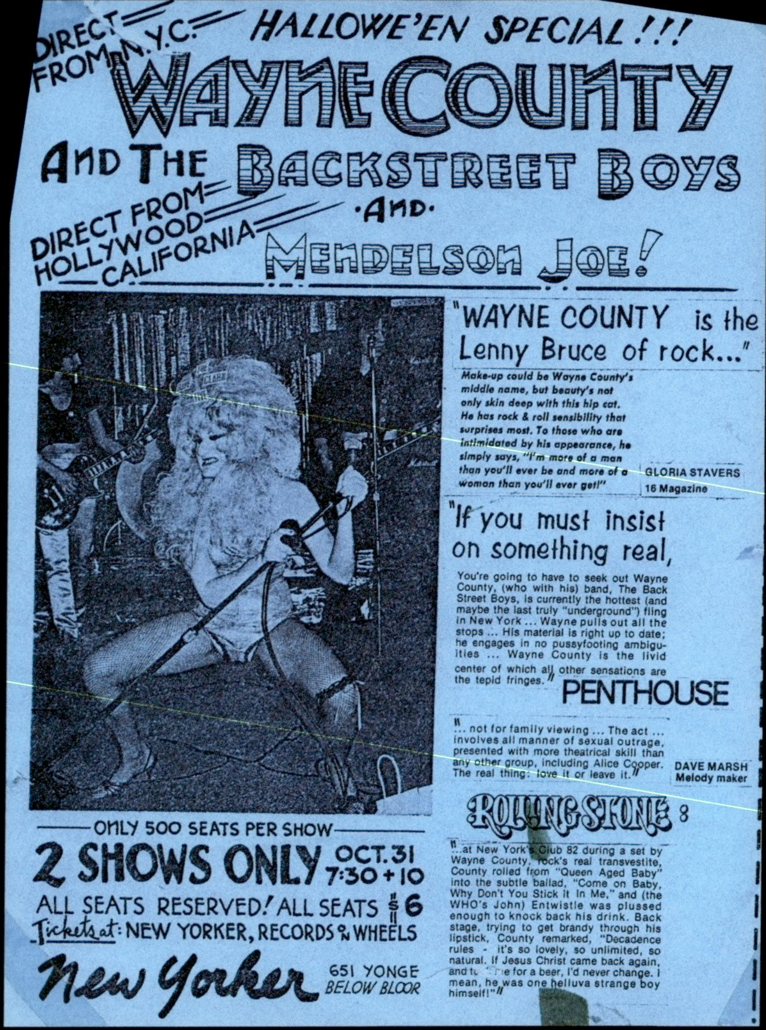

It was an easy time to get a great education in music as all the revered LPs that are now acknowledged as laying the bedrock of punk could be had for next to nothing. I bought my first Velvets album for 99 cents at the discount grocery store Knob Hill Farms, and one shop on Yonge Street, Kelly's Stereo Mart, had so many copies of Lou Reed's *Berlin* that dozens of boxes of the LP were used as legs for the clearance cassette bin — no one was interested in them, even at 29 cents each. There was some kind of psychic communion happening among the disparate cast of characters, who met in rep theatres like the Roxy and the New Yorker for screenings of John Waters and Alejandro Jodorowsky films, and who haunted secondhand record shops looking for used Seeds and Troggs albums, and 45s of R & B tracks covered by the New York Dolls. David Bowie and Roxy Music pointed out new portals of discovery for me. Jacques Brel, Velvet Underground, Mott the Hoople, Iggy Pop, Scott Walker and tons of other incredible artists were revealed in liner notes, album sleeves, and interviews. Everything was already happening and evolution had already occurred before it was branded as "punk rock."

Among the *Rock Scene* snaps of Patti and Johnny were photo sequences of a new band called Ramones, shopping for guitars and hanging out. There was something completely captivating about them: they wore sunglasses at night and leather jackets at a time when your mother would cry, as my mother did, if you came home with one. I was instantly excited about them and knew exactly what they'd sound like. One afternoon I was flipping through the delete bins in the back of a Yonge Street record shop when this music came on over the stereo. In a wave of goose bump rush, I hurried to the front to confirm what I already insti[...] was the first Ramones album.

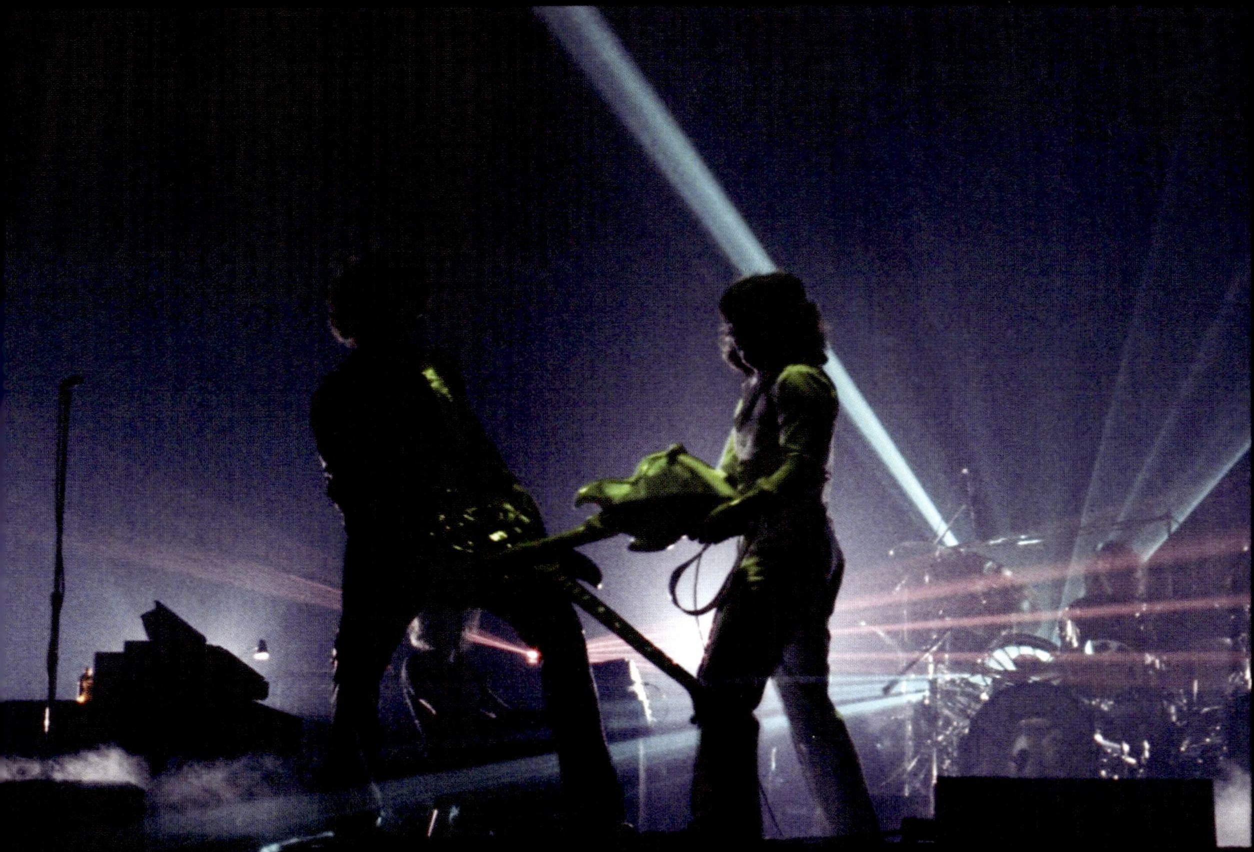

Blue Öyster Cult, Maple Leaf Gardens, 1977

I was a music-obsessed kid, spending all of my allowance on records and later, concerts. My best friend Roger and I spent all of our time playing records, staring at their covers for hours on end. On weekends we worked our way through the bins and bins of alphabetized vinyl at Sam the Record Man, regularly looking at every single album and 45 on the main floor and in the upper floors' clearance racks. I recall a sleepover where we saw the Dolls perform "Trash" on TV. Totally wired from that performance, I could barely sleep, and the next morning we were waiting for Sam the Record Man to open so we could both buy it. We shared similar obsessions and often strategized our purchases so we could buy and hear more things; one would buy *Horses* and the other would buy *Born to Run*. We didn't really understand "mainstream" or "underground" because we'd look at *Circus* magazine and David Bowie would be on the cover. We thought the bands we listened to were popular because they were in magazines, but we didn't know any other people that liked them. As a child, I would go to see any band I could, just to see live music. I resented not being able to see the bands I wanted because you had to be over 18. And when the New York Dolls played a bar called the Queensbury Arms in 1975, I phoned and begged to be allowed in, promising not to drink. When I told the manager I was 13, of course he said no.

In October 1975, The Tubes played a midnight show at Massey Hall on the eve of my 14th birthday. This was the first time my mother let me go downtown all night and it opened the floodgates. The first "bar" I went to was the Crash 'n' Burn where my worries about being asked for ID disappeared as the door person took my money without question or a second notice. Emboldened by passing on my first attempt at underage entry, I began to go to bar gigs any night I could. That there were only 10 or 40 people in the audience gave no indication that history was being made as I witnessed and sometimes photographed the earliest gigs of Toronto bands including the Viletones, The Diodes, The Ugly, The Curse, and The Dishes, and visiting ambassadors of the new wave, The Vibrators, The Clash, The Runaways, The Heartbreakers, Dead Boys and of course, the Ramones.

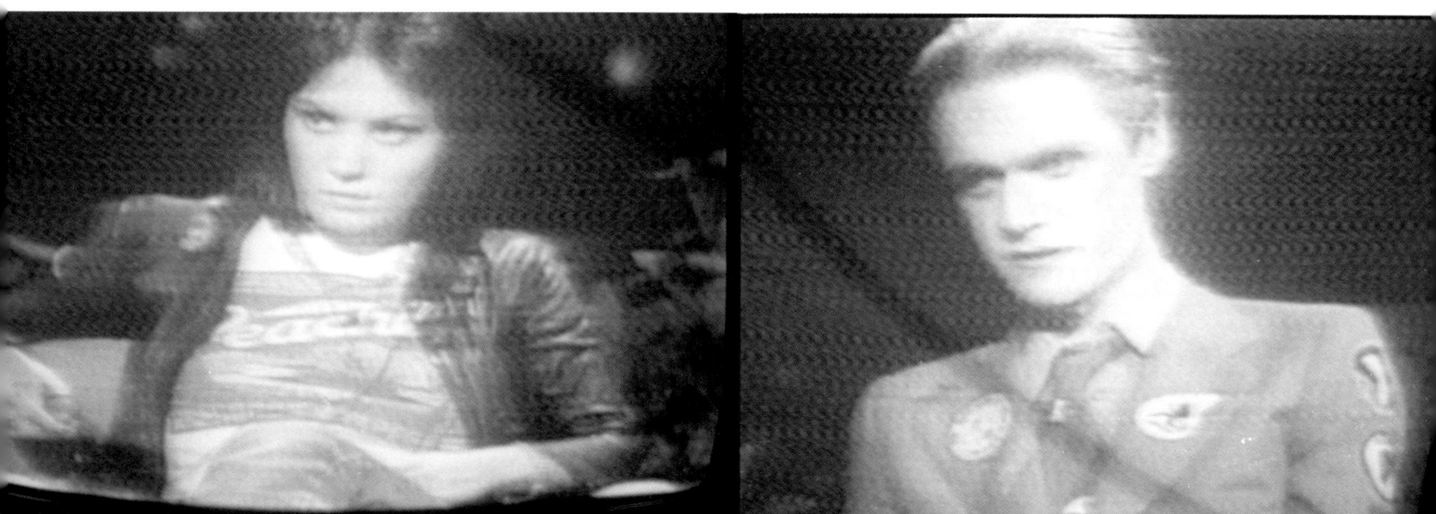

Joan Jett and Kim Fowley, 1977

In 1976, Yonge Street was the power center of local music, where union-controlled bars and cover-version-heavy five-sets-a-night gigs enforced the formal sameness of bands that played there. Original music was rare and only for the top-draws, like local emerging act Rush, or Goddo and Moxy. The earliest venues for the hard new sounds happening were Yonge Street venues like the New Yorker Theatre and the Colonial Tavern. There were few other options. As the virus spread, A Space Gallery, David's, the Hotel Isabella, the Beverly Tavern, the Ontario College of Art's auditorium and the Crash 'n' Burn became the spaces where hot new ideas were set on fire, where a band who had started playing their instruments three weeks previous could excite an audience starved for the tsunami we thought would wipe away Establishment dinosaurs.

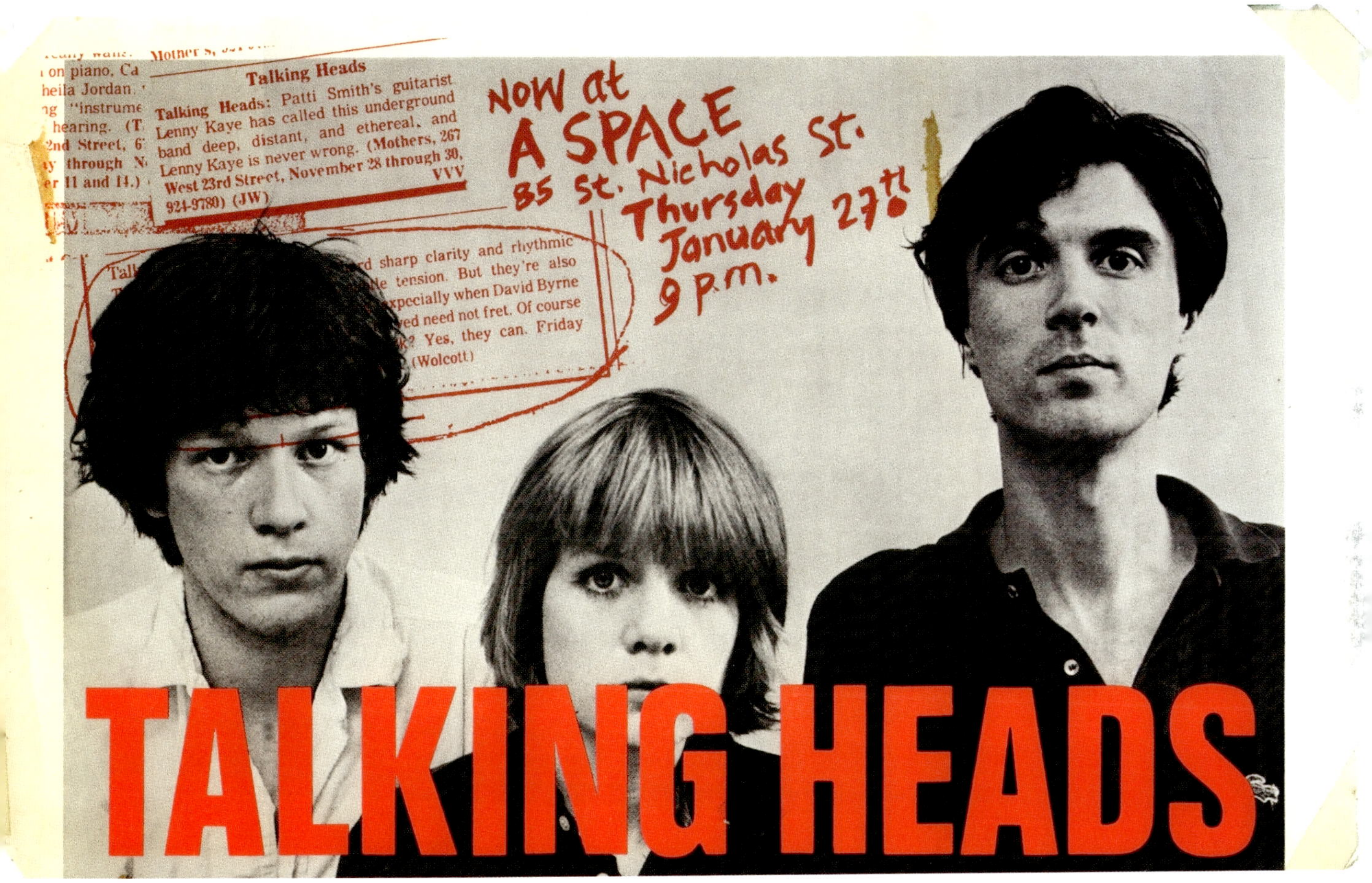

Many of the earliest punk venues were places where mold grew, the toilets were broken and only old men whose main priority was cheap draft would hang out. The Turning Point and the basement of Hotel Isabella were still infinitely preferable to established "legendary" spaces like the El Mocambo, where a bouncer might throw you down the second-floor stairs for not sitting down, or for dancing. Even though the El Mo hosted The Runaways, The Damned, Elvis Costello, The Undertones (undeveloped negatives of whom remained in my developing tank for ten years

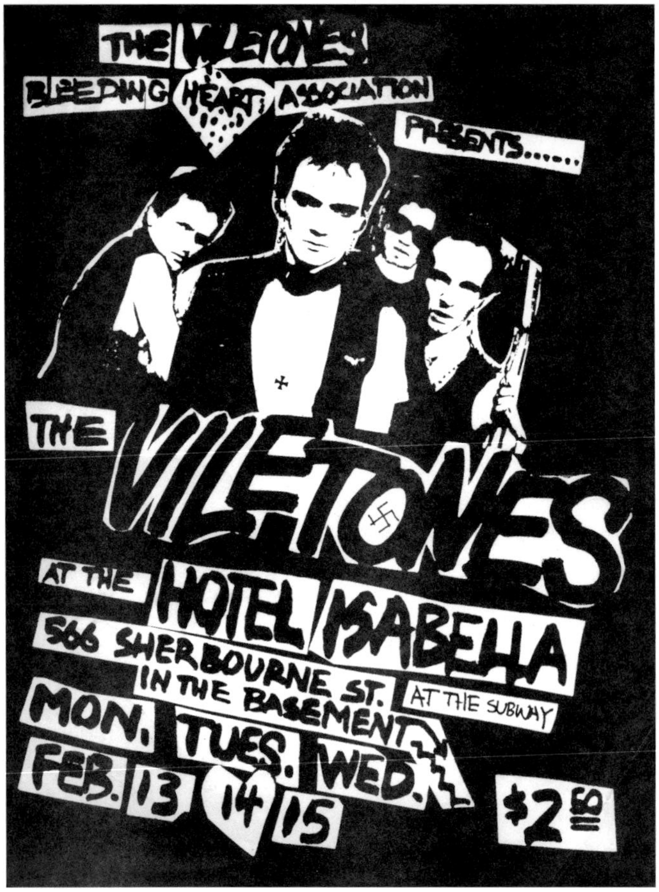

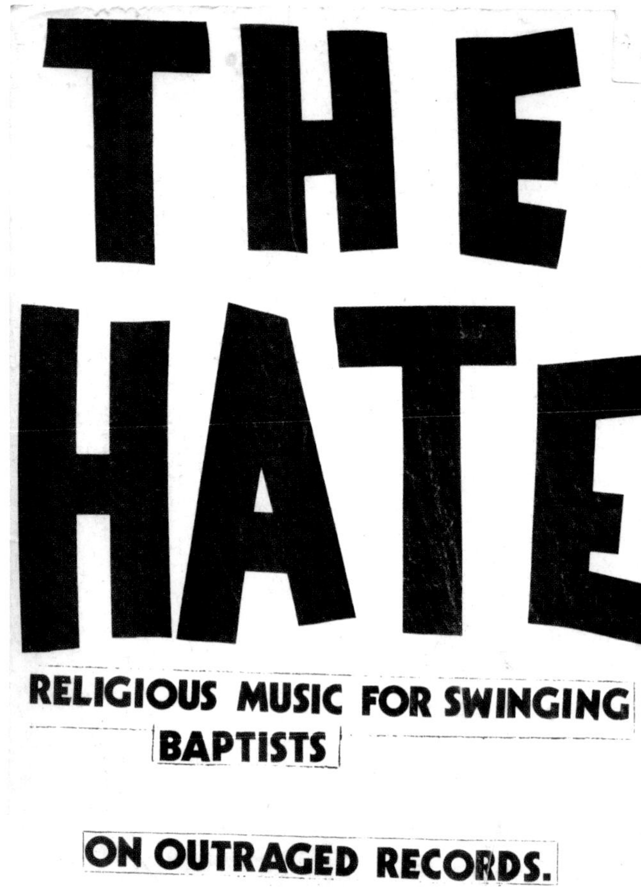

before it was broken) and tons of other great shows, it was an oppressive joint on a power trip: a bar with little respect for audiences and a long-haired fear of the new. The people who worked at the New Yorker and the Horseshoe were totally different — they *were* the audience for the bands that played there and mostly let the crowds govern themselves, knowing that our thrashing and strangling was an ecstatic response to the sound, not a prelude to a bar fight. At both the New Yorker and the Horseshoe, the bouncer (and "bodyguard" to the Viletones) everyone knew was Tank, as cuddly as he was intimidating, a big boy who no one wanted to be on the bad side of.

About five blocks from the Horseshoe, the Crash 'n' Burn was lit with bare bulbs; the bar was a door laid flat, with beer on ice in a bathtub or galvanized basin. There was no decor that I can remember, just gray or white brick walls, a few hardware store floodlights and people and a PA — everything you needed. David's was a down-and-out gay disco with frayed carpets and a winding staircase with white wrought-iron railings that encircled a cast-molded, long-dried-up fountain of its Michelangelo namesake, and the waiter wore a T-shirt with his name in iron-on letters — "Mr. Shit." (I later became acquainted with Mr. Shit, aka Randy. The band he started, The Hate, performed one of the most memorable gigs I witnessed at the Turning Point as singer Angie Ignorant stormed the stage with his cock impaling a photo of Pierre Trudeau, urine spraying the audience from what looked like Pierre's mouth). The few customers that came to these stellar early gigs were welcomed and ID was never an issue for this underage kid and the new underage friends I was making. I was big for my age and imagined that at 15 they really believed I was 18, but it's obvious when I see photos of myself then that I looked my age. These two venues contained great emotional power for me then and now: I recall passing in the world of adults at a licensed venue for the first time at the C 'n' B, and as a closeted young gay boy being in a gay bar for the first time, at David's.

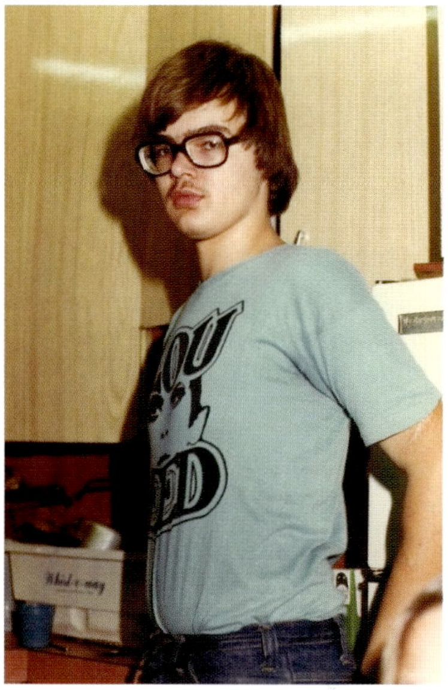

DP, 1975

The Toronto music scene was quite incredible at that time and is often underrated. Fantastic new groups like Swollen Members and The Sophisticatos came and went in flashes of white heat. There was no excuse not to do it, whatever it was. The Dents, a cadre of 16- and 17-year-old suburban brats, were an enormous inspiration to me. My favorite local bands were comprised of adults compared to The Dents, a group closest to my age. Then, I never felt that any of the bands were unjustly ignored by the media; there was almost no media to ignore them. I didn't expect to see The Ugly on the CBC network, rife as it was with friendly sing-along shows like *Don Messer's Jubilee* and with a smirky and square dismissive tone for any mention of punk. Future Diodes and Crash 'n' Burn manager Ralph Alfonso had a scene column in a free newspaper called *Cheap Thrills*, and Steven Davey — later of The Dishes and The Everglades — wrote reviews of cool records like Mick Ronson's *Slaughter on 10th Avenue* album in Canadian music magazine *Beetle*. There was precious little to inform you of the new local resistance movement.

Being the music snob I already was, I didn't want everyone to know about my secret underground; I was quite happy for most people at school to wallow in their Ted Nugent misery and be oblivious to the real excitement happening downtown in their own city. The idea of "star" was relative. To me, the Diodes and Viletones were stars — the ones who eventually put out records, who looked and acted their role full-time, who played regularly and were always the headliners. In this star system, they were the brightest constellations. Without weekly publications or widely distributed magazines, how would anyone outside of the city borders know about The Curse? It's easy to see London and New York as having more vital music cultures, but this is only a mirage created by lack of media representation in Toronto. Any Torontonian who saw gigs at legendary venues like the Marquee

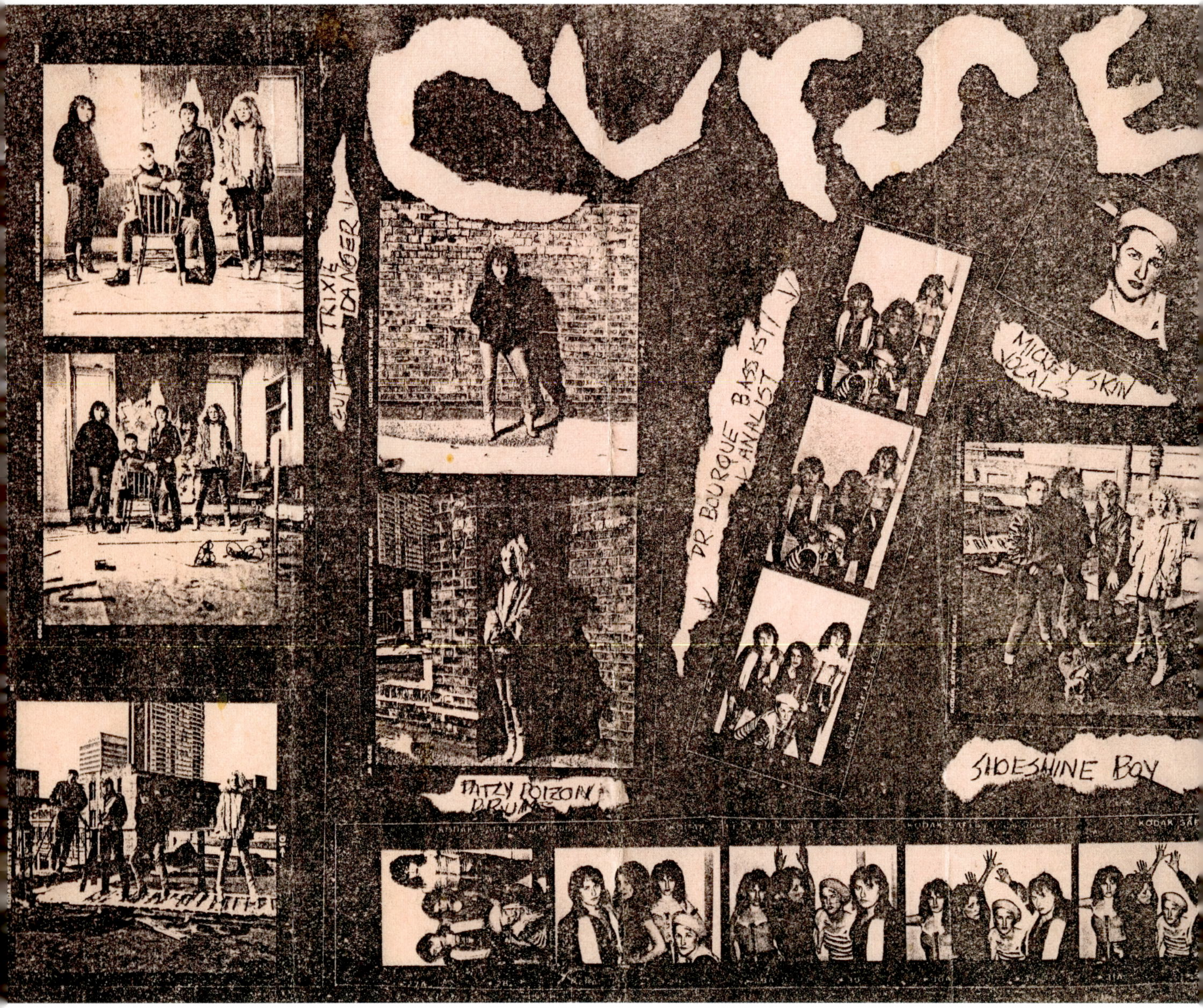

in London and Max's Kansas City in New York City knew that the insurgence happening at home was at least as great.

The other obvious reason for the disproportionately small amount of international attention paid to Toronto's early punk scene is the minimal vinyl output from the best bands at their peak, and the inability of any of the bands to sustain momentum beyond a couple of short years. The Diodes made one fantastic 45 and one album before their Top 20 aspirations drained them of their most original aspects. "Screamin Fist," the first song on the first single by the Viletones, is perfection in its goose bump–inducing heaviness — the bass playing sixteenths on one note, then one big guitar chord, a furious drum roll and then the whole band pounding one dirty chord. The record's dynamic production and intensity were never matched again. The band only released one more comparatively limp sounding EP before imploding and dividing. Teenage Head put out one 7-inch that captured the blistering speed and attack they had live, followed by a washed-out LP on which Gord Lewis's crunchy guitar is bled of all tension and fire. The Curse had one amazing single and were gone. The original and best version of The Ugly never managed even one single, the 45 they did put out being an anemic studioized interpretation of the band. Cardboard Brains produced only a couple of singles — one of which a friend insisted sounded like Wishbone Ash — before disappearing. The mystical kitsch of The Poles' totemic anthem, "CN Tower" — itself a blatant symbol of Toronto's futuristic aspirations and a significant divider of new and old Toronto — gave way to an album of insipid attempts at mainstream bubblegum.

Every local band I can think of who flashed brilliance in their earliest days succumbed to the compromises that almost seemed necessary for someone to put out an album in Canada. The Demics, ditto. There was no PiL or The Fall, none that flourished or developed in new ways. Artists that were attached to but on the periphery of the punk scene, like Nash the Slash and Martha and the Muffins, were who ended up enduring and gaining international attention. Amazingly diverse and talented artists were not supported by local benevolent millionaires, as so many British artists had been by Virgin Records founder Richard Branson. Hell, it was Branson who brought Nash and the Muffins to the rest of the world!

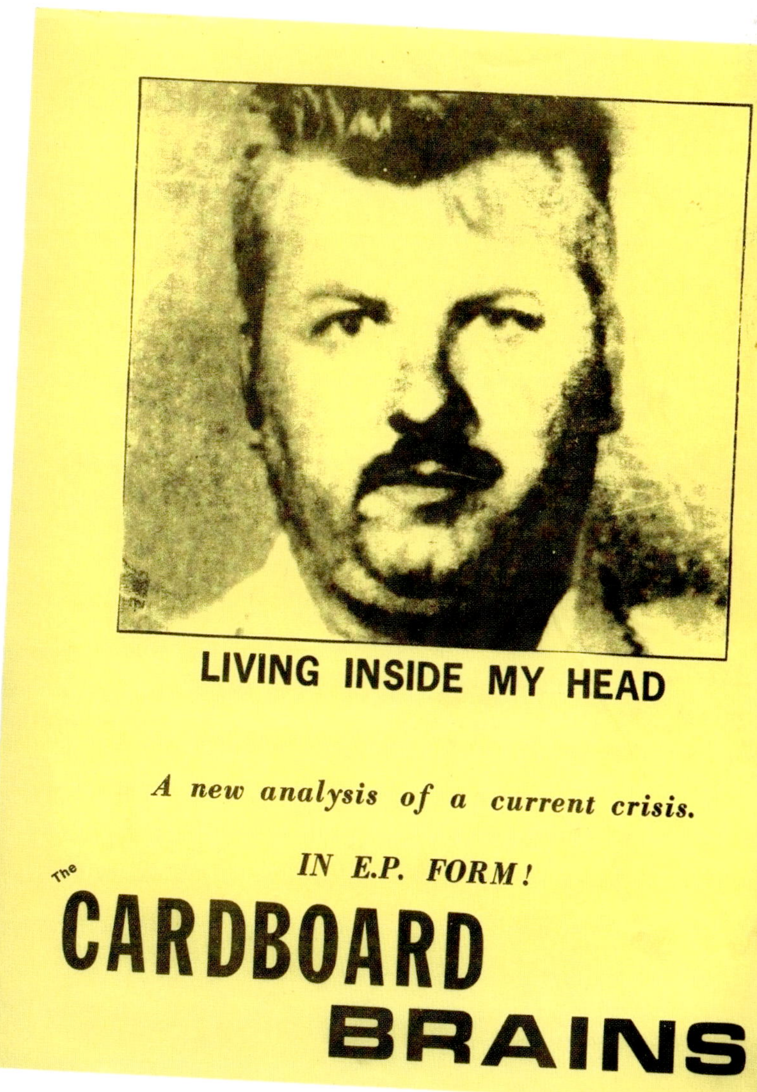

Despite where any of the bands represented here ended up, The Curse, Viletones, The Diodes, Teenage Head, The Dents, The Demics and so many others that came and went were shocking and nothing less than amazing. Like every scene before or since, you really had to be there for it to make sense. And being 16 or 23 was as essential an ingredient to the magic as the bands, the people, the beer or the drugs. So many people have a desire to be given a finite definition of punk, but so much is left out of the true story. Imagine a thousand embers sparking at once but all separate from each other — but *of* the same thing. When all those points suddenly came into awareness of each other, it became a movement, the thing that got called punk. If you were of a particular disposition, there was no need to explain the connection between Cheap Trick, Alice Cooper, Milk N' Cookies, Suzi Quatro, the Faces, Brownsville Station, and Nazi Dog or Johnny Rotten. It seems obvious in retrospect that something was being built; we just didn't know what it would look like until it arrived and was subsequently dismantled.

Canada was in its earliest days of cultural transformation from colonial outpost to whatever you might describe it as today, and few other places cared what was happening in Toronto or Vancouver. Bands from the United Kingdom would follow the historical precedence of Giovanni Caboto by adopting a stage name (John Cabot) and come to try to conquer Canada; fortunately for us, their invasion often began and ended in Toronto. So we got to see XTC, The Slits, The Stranglers, Gang of Four and Billy Fury. It's hard to imagine in the information age, but sometimes the only thing you might know about a non-local band was gleaned from one fuzzy black and white photo in the back pages of some cheap magazine; my attraction to them could be as simple as the font used to spell the band's name. Some of what was so powerful about these bands' image is what we *didn't* see, with the backstory totally created by our imaginations. The Fast, or The Nerves could only be read about in *Rock Scene* or *Trouser Press*. The dearth of available photographic documentation I'm sure contributed to my impulse to take pictures. It was not until around 2000 that I even saw moving pictures of artists as famous as Velvet Underground.

Toronto seemed sleepy, even though I had little to compare it to. Almost nothing was open on Sunday and on that day it would not be unusual to stand at the corner of Yonge and Bloor — the major intersection of the biggest city in Canada — and not see a single other person. Most of downtown was made up of old, low-rise Victorian-period buildings. Row houses, small businesses and pinball arcades with shooting galleries stood where there are now office towers, malls and nightclubs. Folk-club-turned-punk venue the Turning Point and vinyl retailer Round Records (the first store to carry *Never Mind the Bollocks*) sat on what is now the most expensive commercial real estate in Canada. You couldn't buy a beer without buying a meal, something one club got around by selling sandwiches made

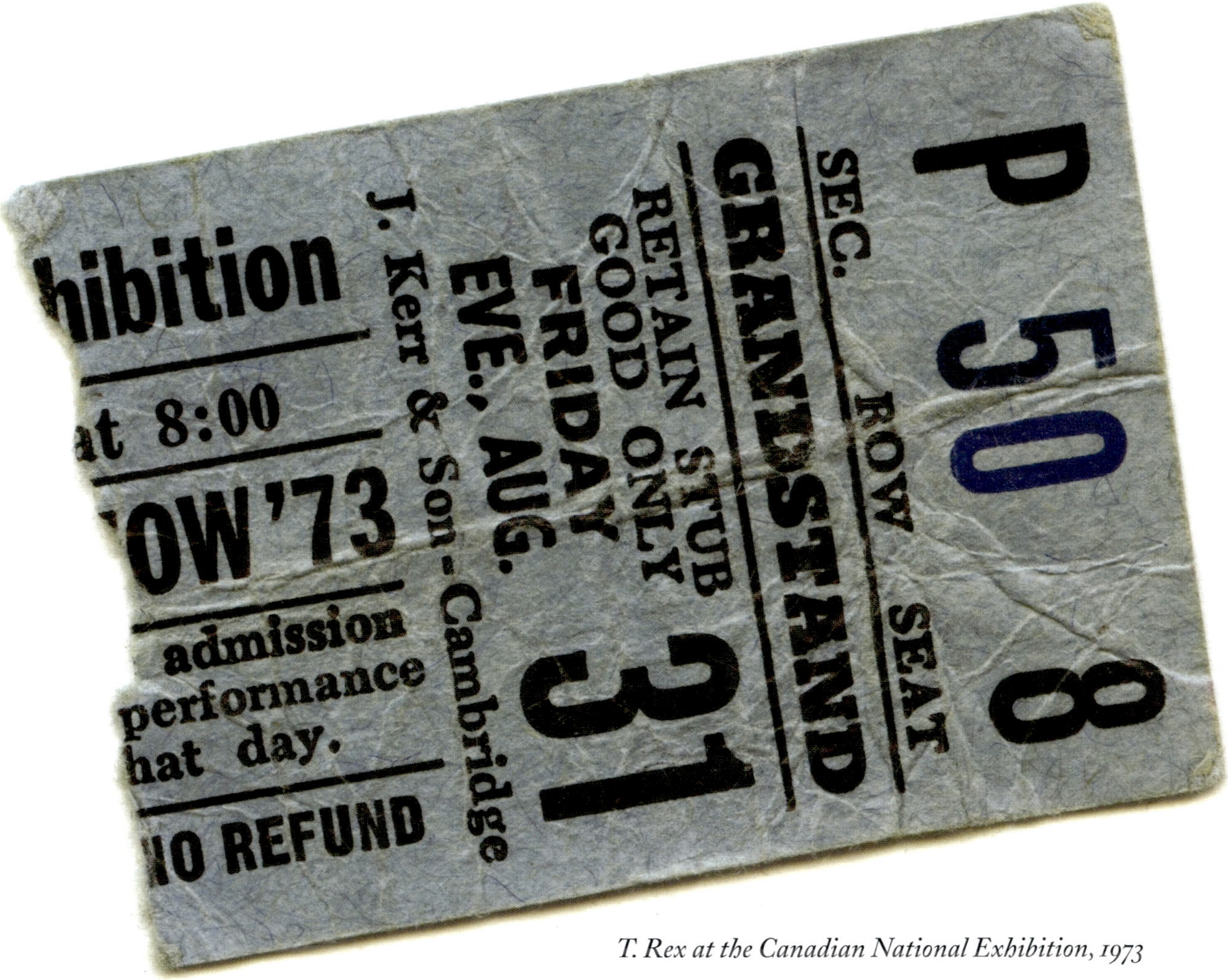

T. Rex at the Canadian National Exhibition, 1973

out of wood. Somehow, the performance of putting something that resembled food on the table in front of you (and recyclable to the next customer!) fell within the set of ridiculous legal definitions laid out by the Liquor Control Board of Ontario. But there was also beauty in the unlit laneways and side streets. Unlike today, everything was not illuminated, examined and exploited with every vacant or derelict plot built up. Unexplored and empty streets held all kinds of possibilities with darkened doorways in alleys leading to sexual adventure or an after-hours party; places to conduct forbidden activities were easy to find. The pockets of adventure had to be searched for, but vibrant life existed below the snoozy surface.

In Canada, T. Rex was not playing with The Damned, as they had in the U.K. Instead, they were sandwiched between April Wine and Three Dog Night at a fairground. If you wanted to know about the crusty and dangerous, leather-jacketed fringe beyond what was presented in *Circus* magazine you had to really search it out. The first shops in Toronto to sell punk records usually had one box of maybe 20 to 40 titles — practically every single "punk" record released at the time. I recall seeing an EMI copy of Sex Pistols' "Anarchy in the U.K." at Art Metropole

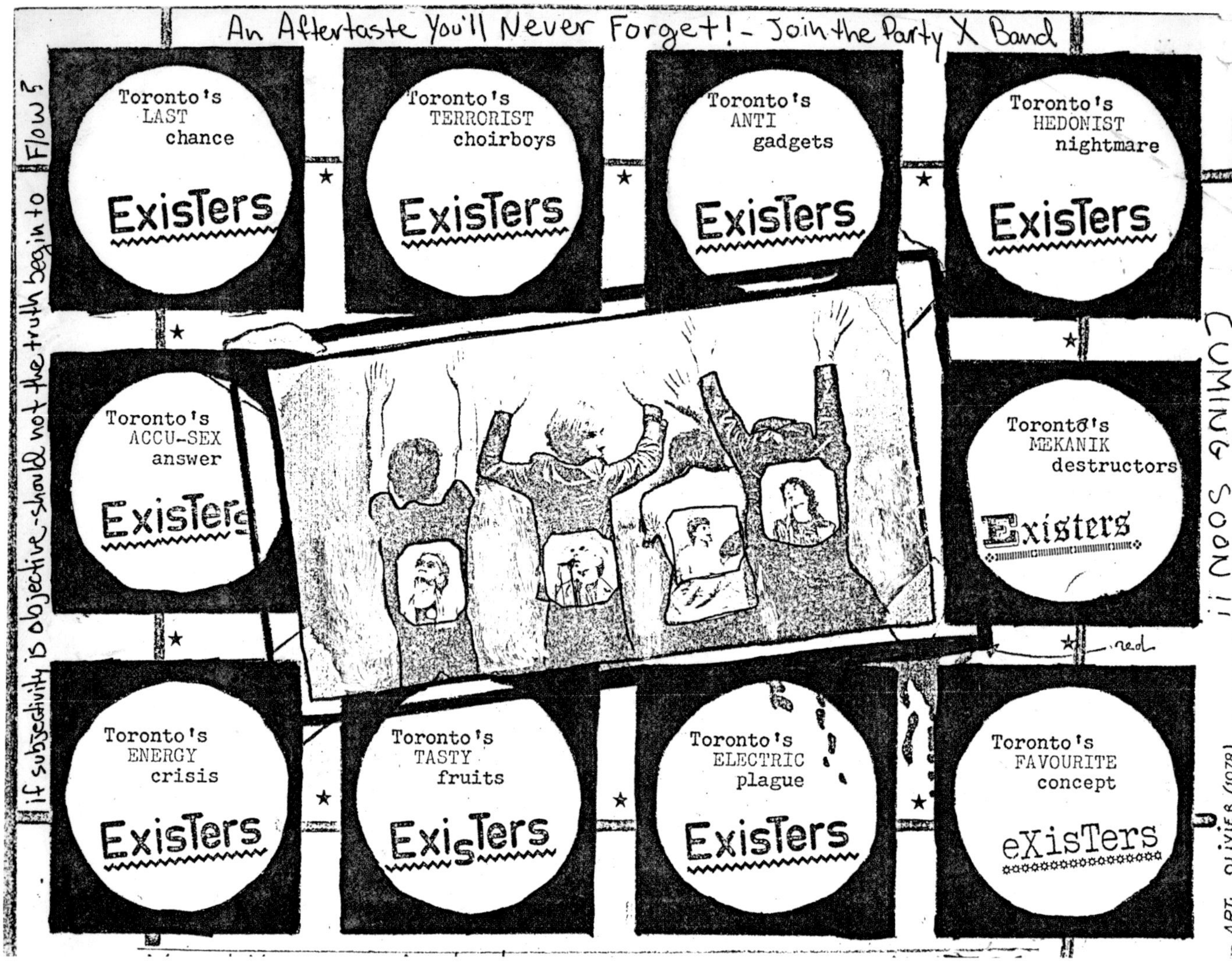

on Yonge Street among a handful of singles that someone had brought back from a trip to London; I passed it up because it didn't have a picture sleeve.

Posters stapled to wooden telephone poles, and handbills put up in the couple of used-clothing shops where you could buy out-of-fashion narrow-leg jeans and 1950s shirts, were missives from this secret society — coded transmissions that could only be comprehended by those tuned to the same frequency. Cheap photocopies were a new thing and their sloppy grays and washed-out tones were perfectly instant, just like the bands whose performances they heralded. The photocopier and punk rock were made for each other. Many people I've met since say they nabbed flyers whenever they saw them so they usually didn't last long. Sometimes it really was about waiting for the streetcar at the right corner at the right moment to see an ad for a gig before it was gone.

The images contained in this collection represent many levels of discovery for me. My camera gave a shy and awkward kid something to hide behind. I could avoid detection as I passed in the world of adults for the first time. It also gave

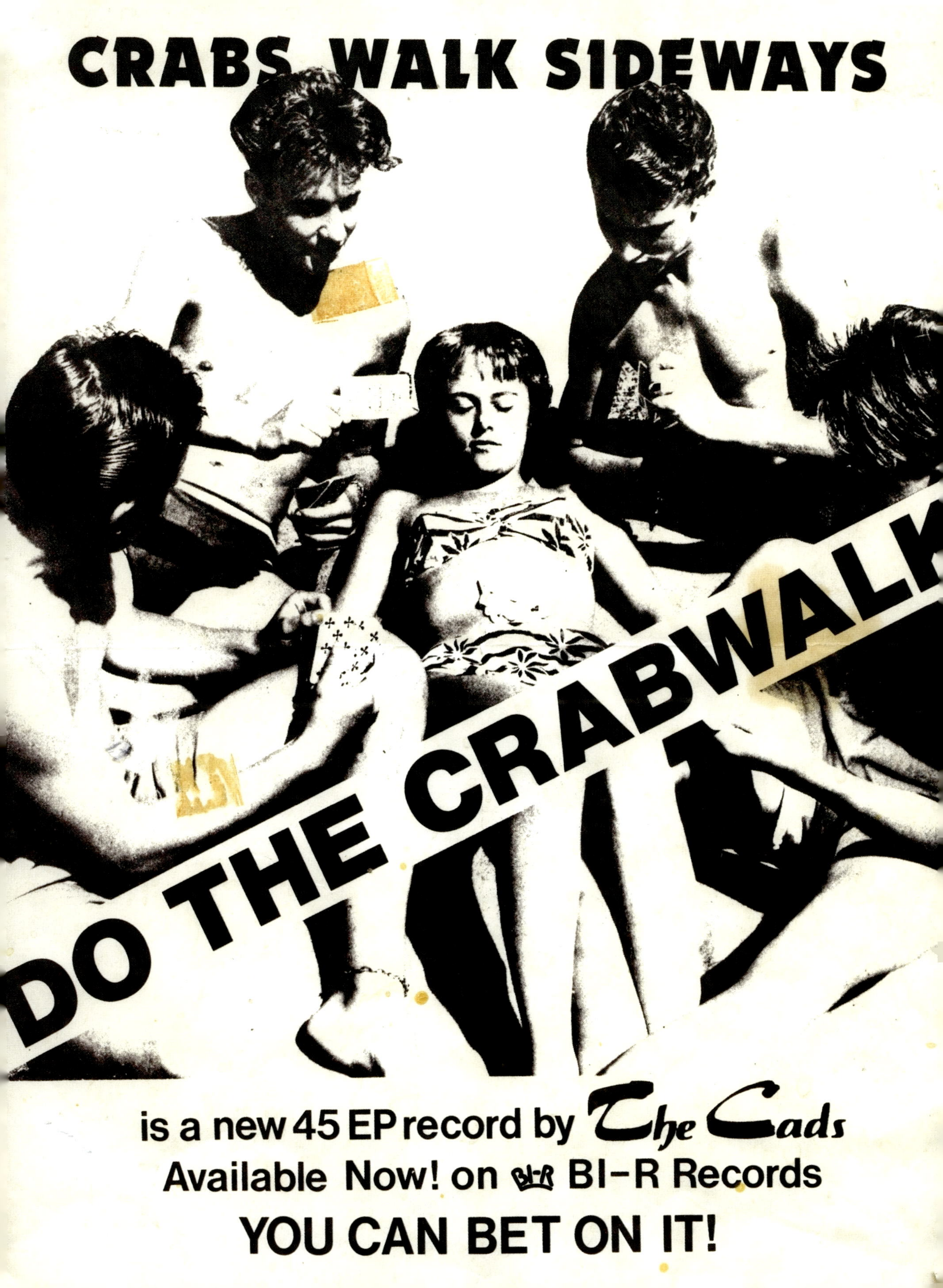
CRABS WALK SIDEWAYS
DO THE CRABWALK
is a new 45 EP record by The Cads
Available Now! on BI-R Records
YOU CAN BET ON IT!

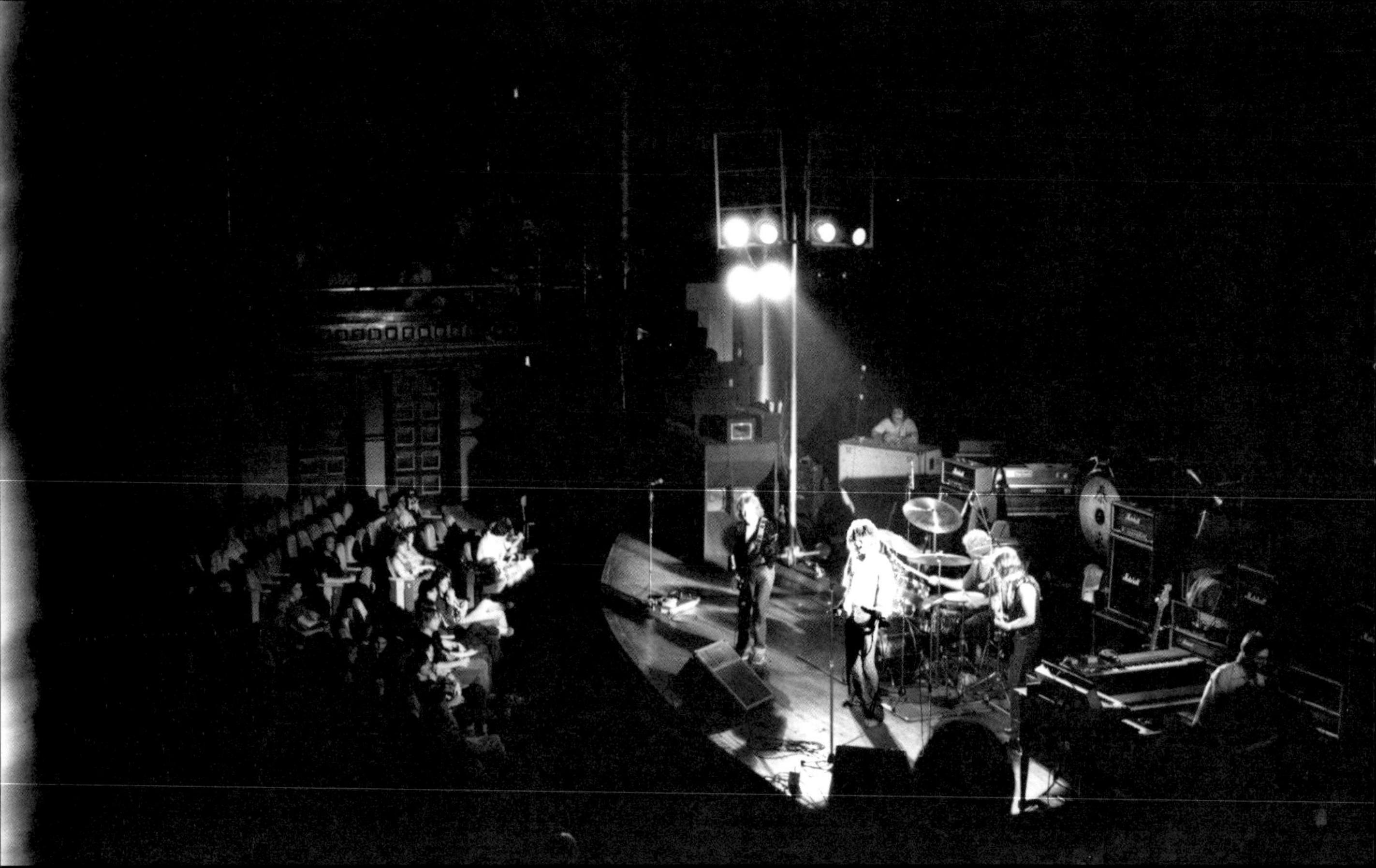

me something to do, a way to participate before I was in a band. I loved being at the front, at the loudest and most intense spot possible, and suffered bloody shins numerous times as the result of waves of people knocking me into the wooden edge of the Horseshoe stage. I borrowed a zoom lens once for a David Bowie show at Maple Leaf Gardens, and used a friend's flash a couple of times, but most of my photos are close up and eliminate the audience because that is where I was. When Blondie played the El Mocambo, I had to lean back to focus because Deborah Harry was inches away, sometimes supporting herself on my shoulder to see over the heads of the audience.

These pictures also represent the formation of a personal belief system. The ethics of punk, as I saw it, embodied a spirit of radical innovation, community, equality and fairness: of being motivated to create, regardless of skill or ability and of ideas trumping chops. "Punk" was a utopian ideal of a new society untethered from the rules set down by parents and "authority" — in more ways than I realized at the time, almost identical to the ideals of the teenagers in *Rebel Without a Cause*, the beatniks and the hippies the newly defined punks acted out hating so much.

Examining my negatives in extreme close-up while retouching them was sometimes like social archaeology. Stubbie beer bottles litter the stage, and in many of my photos from '76 to '77, there are roadies in the background with shag haircuts and droopy moustaches; the looks on their faces seem to say they know something has happened around them but they aren't quite sure what it is. On the same strip of negatives as Bryan Ferry are photographs of opening band Rough Diamond, the new group led by ex–Uriah Heep knob, David Byron. The before-and-after feeling that punk had brought was evident as a walrus-stached and poodle-haired Byron pranced about in a sheer jumpsuit, making ridiculous rock gestures that had worked so well only two or three years previous. That he was a casualty of the new sensibility was obvious in the stony reaction of the crowd. Even Peter Gabriel wore a black leather jacket at his 1977 first post-Genesis gig in Toronto, that simple bit of fashion making him seem somehow contemporary and considered for relevancy. The guy at Records on Wheels who always sneered unwanted comments about my purchases ("*Cockney Rebel*? What are you buying *that* for?") suddenly traded the rainbow shag haircut he'd worked for years, like Todd Rundgren on the cover of his *Todd* album, for a flaming orange spiked Johnny Rotten do.

Rough Diamond, Massey Hall, 1977

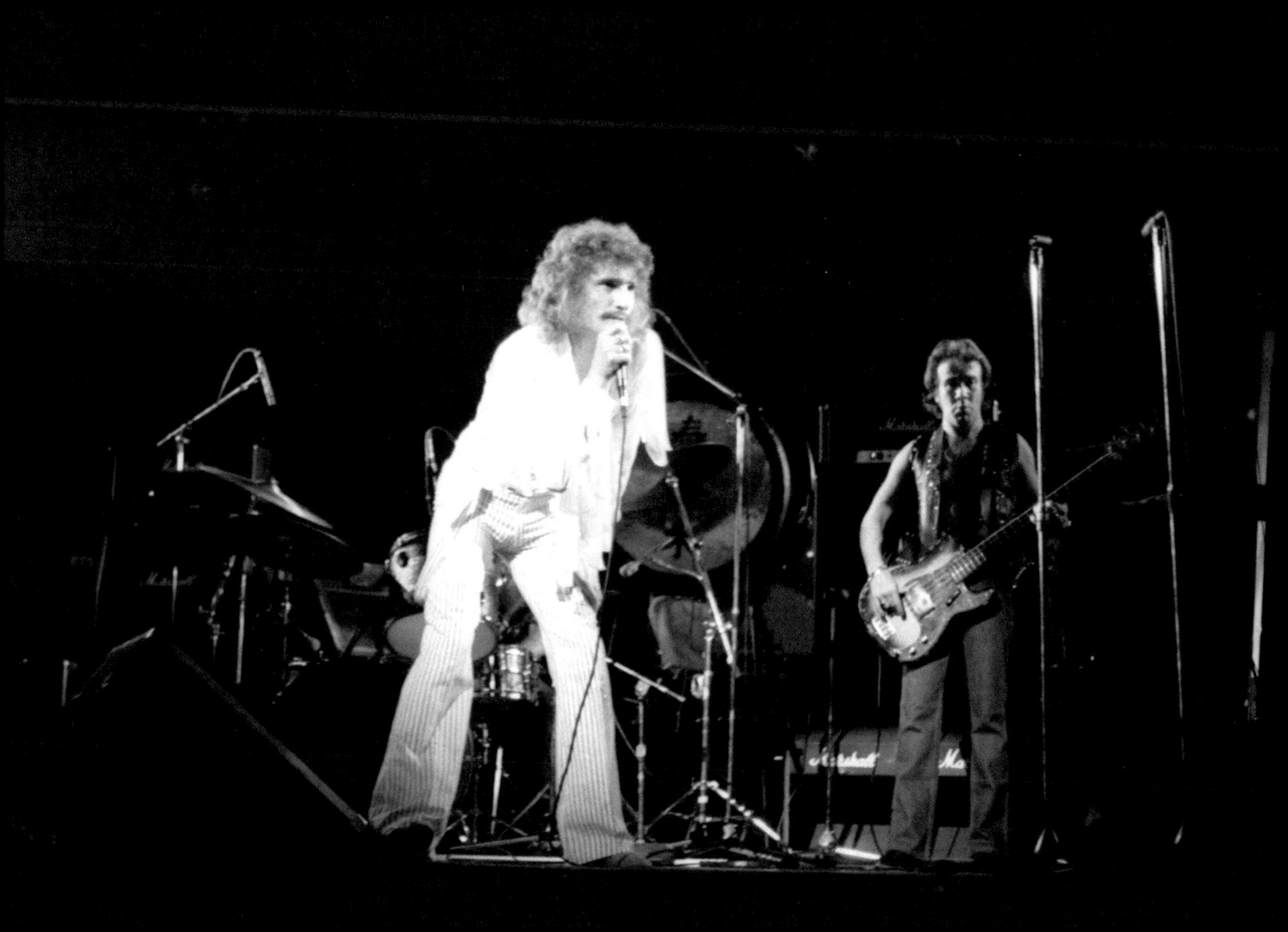

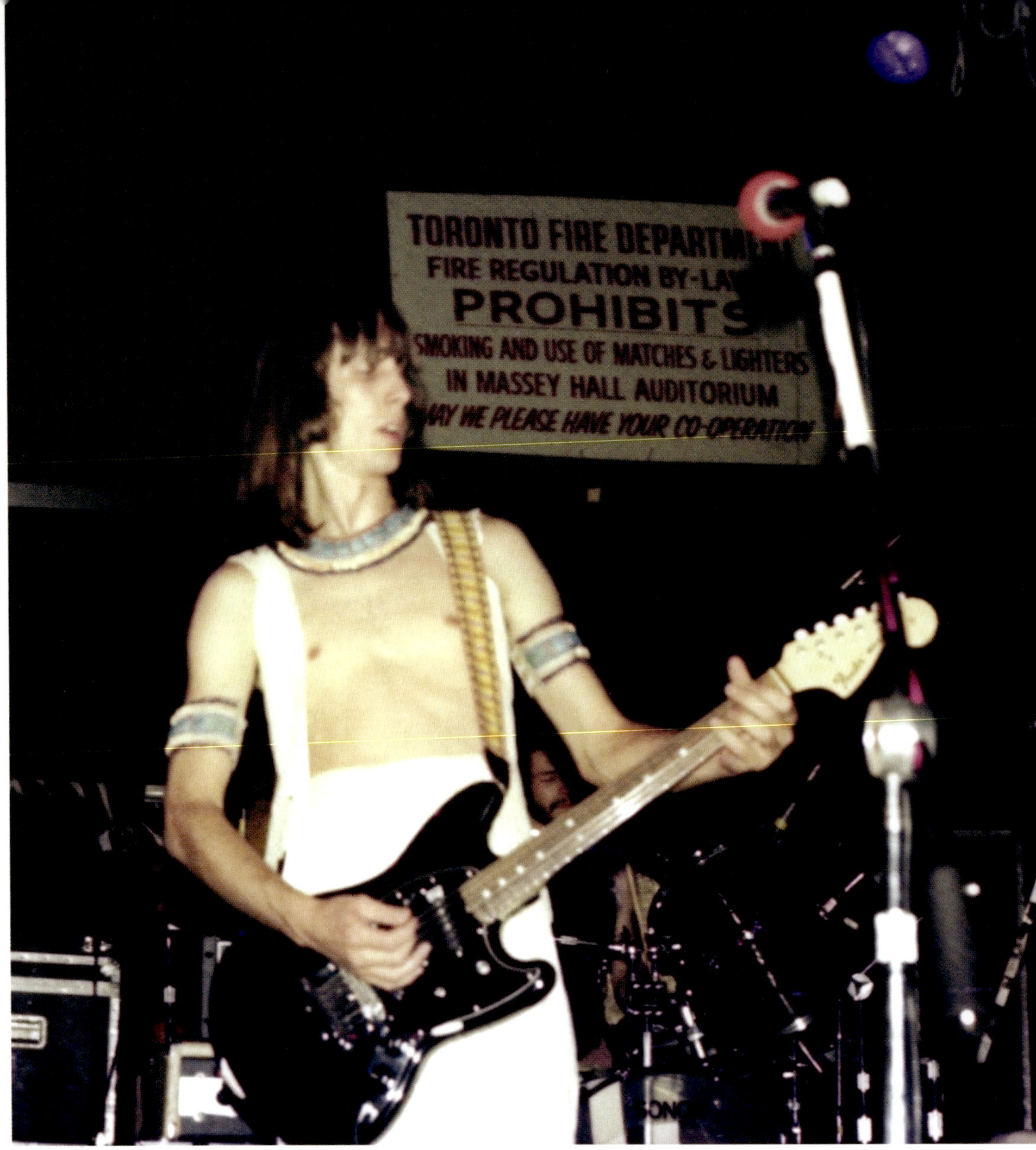

Todd Rundgren, Massey Hall, 1976

Like every teenager who feels they are the first to have any experience, it was an empowering and freeing period. In retrospect, I see aspects of how conservative punk was. Long hair and wide pants were not allowed, women were rarely equal and "faggots" were often reviled, even though the origins of the scene were in gay discos and with homo art-school cliques. In so many cases, the new gestures and poses playing out were still firmly rooted in traditional images of rock stardom and bad-seed mythology, despite the cleansing effect we dreamed punk would have on the old vision. The short window, before a uniform Sid-ness pervaded the scene, was hugely about invention and independence. By 1978, any illusions about

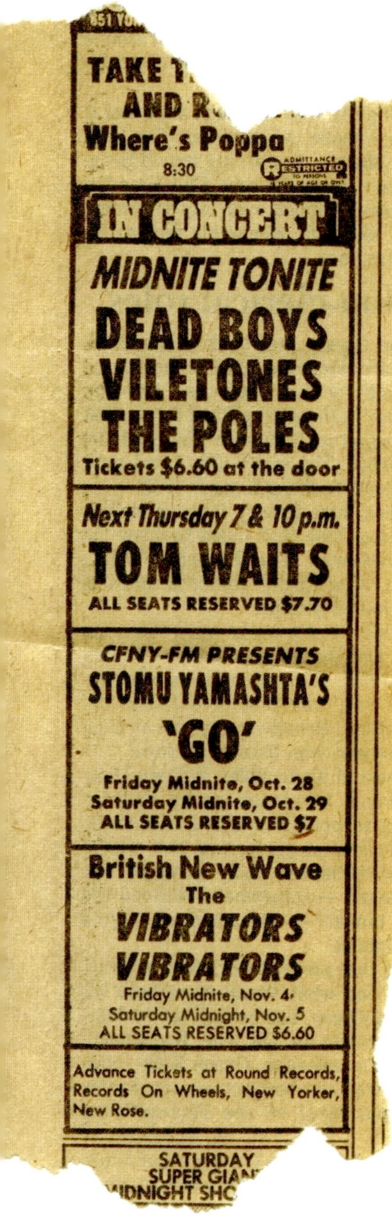

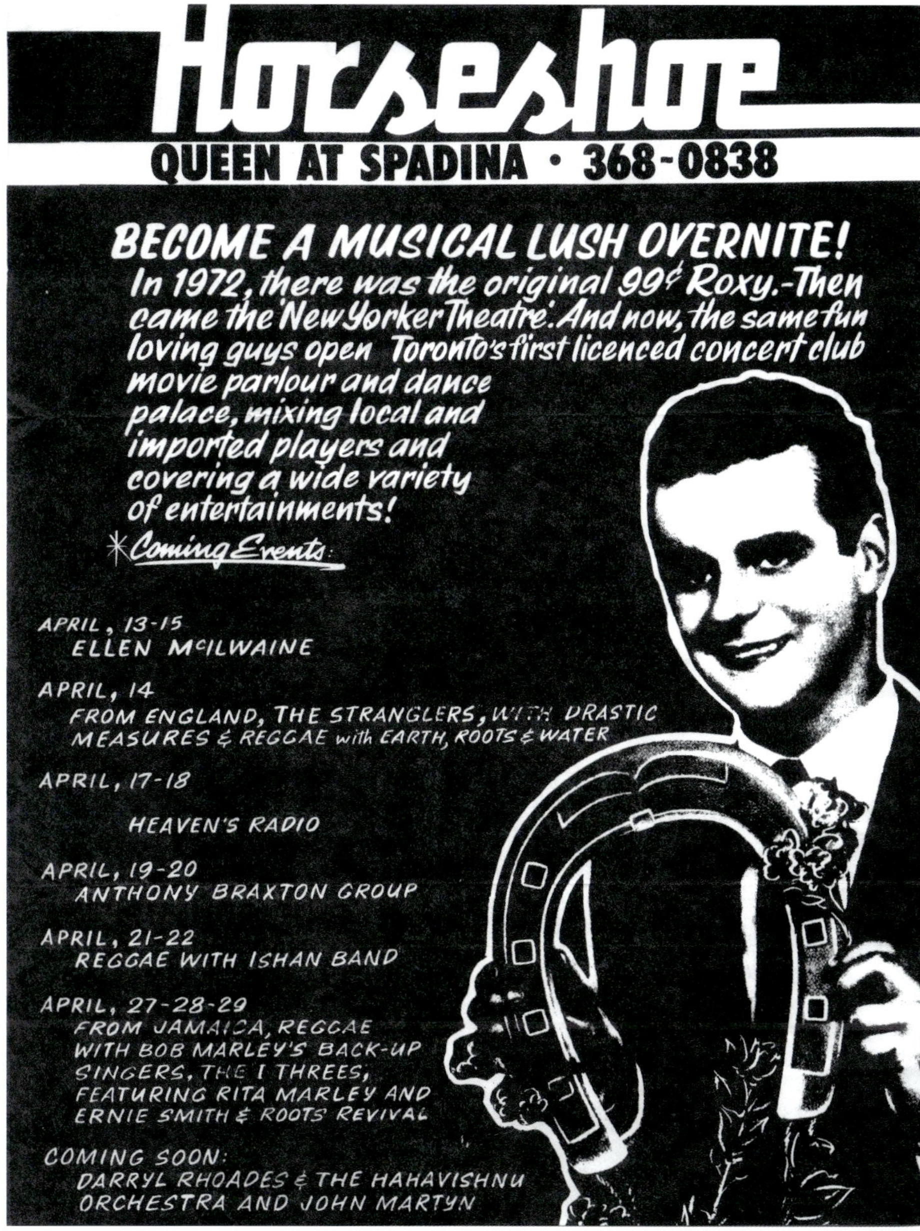

punk clearing the psychic slate of everything that sucked about music and society crumbled, as splintered factions laid the groundwork for today's segregationist approach to self-identity. Only one or two years before, the "punks" I knew were thrilled to sneak into a Donna Summer concert at Maple Leaf Gardens, and were buying used Tim Buckley and Culture albums. To me, and most of my friends, disco wasn't the enemy — the Steve Miller Band and The Doobie Brothers were.

I dread to think what this city's music scene would have been like without the New Yorker, the Horseshoe Tavern and the Edge, the three clubs booked by Gary Topp and Gary Cormier. We were able to witness the first appearances of ideological

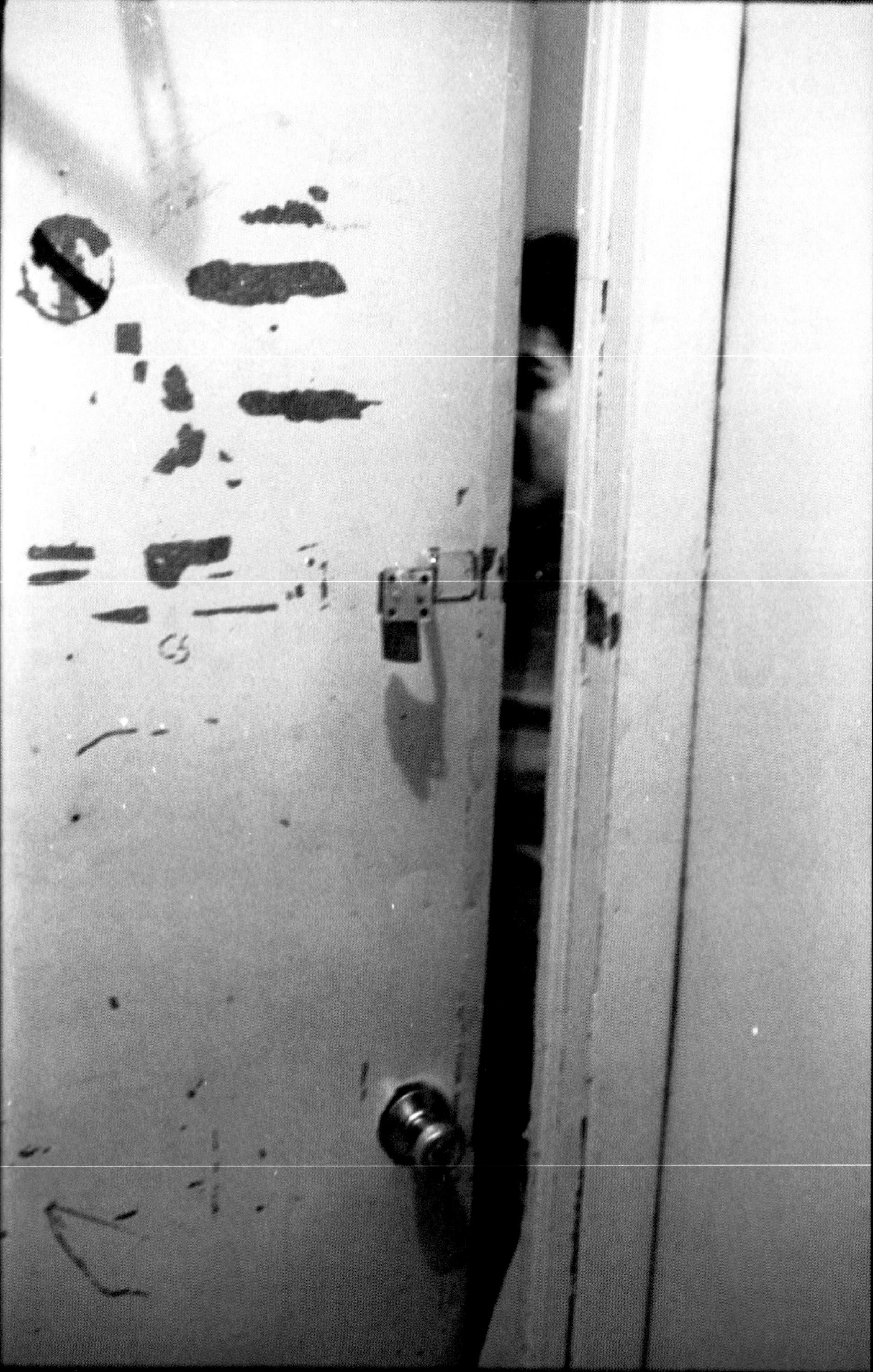

comrades because of the Garys' foresight and brilliant curatorial adventurousness in booking Wayne County, John Cale, Modern Lovers, Ramones, Dead Boys, Lewis Furey, The Vibrators and thousands of other bands that followed. Their scope was not limited to the new wave; Etta James, John Renbourn, The Flying Burrito Brothers, Maneige and John Martyn all graced the stages of the venues they booked, offering a vibrant and diverse feast for audiences. Respect to both of them for making Toronto an extraordinary place to be; this city's music scene would have been radically different without them and enough cannot be said about how important they were in creating Toronto's cultural history. Their choices in the bands and films they presented inspired musicians and artists in a ripple effect that is still apparent today. When I look at this collection of photos, the majority of them are from shows booked and presented by Gary Topp and Gary Cormier.

My friends and I gave the Garys all the money we had, but were not above pooling our resources to pay for one person to go in, get a stamp on their hand and then come out to show us the stamp so we could copy it with magic marker on our own hands. We'd meet in the apartment on Parliament Street at Carlton that various combinations of them shared at different times, or at a run-down rooming house on Glen Road (across the street from a spot where we once watched The B-Girls posing for a photo session!). Every Albertan transplant seemed to be required to live in that house when they moved here, drinking before the gig because we could often only afford admission and bus fare home on the all-night bus.

It's easy to wish I'd taken more photographs than I did — of Suicide taunting and attacking a confused audience, of The Slits' Ari Up shrieking with such intensity that my left eardrum popped, affecting my hearing for months afterward, or Richard Hell and the Voidoids with the great guitarist Robert Quine, and the cartoon horror of synthesizer punks The Screamers or The Cramps at their most brutal and primitive. Cardboard Brains may not have made such a lasting impression on me if I had been occupied with my camera, and as is the case in so many barely remembered nights, specific images imprinted on my memory originate from my negatives. I wish I'd taken more photographs of my friends, not realizing at the time what a huge component of the music experience they were. In fact, I recall trying to do what is obvious now when I see my photographs — I tried to eliminate all people other than the band, deeming the performers to be the most important thing in the frame. I would go see any band from New York, California or the United Kingdom and the price of admission was enough of an enticement. We were lucky to see The Damned for $5, and The Undertones for $3. I even went to see a new band with just one 45 out called The Police because they were from

The Parliament and Carlton apartment, 1979

England and it was only $2 to get in. At that price, it was easy to walk out when the irritating guitarist brought out a blow-up doll that he recited a love poem to. A friend once said to me that of all the hundreds of people that claim to have seen The Police before a tiny audience at the Horseshoe Tavern, I was the only one he believed — because I was the only one who said they were crap. I even wish I'd photographed that show.

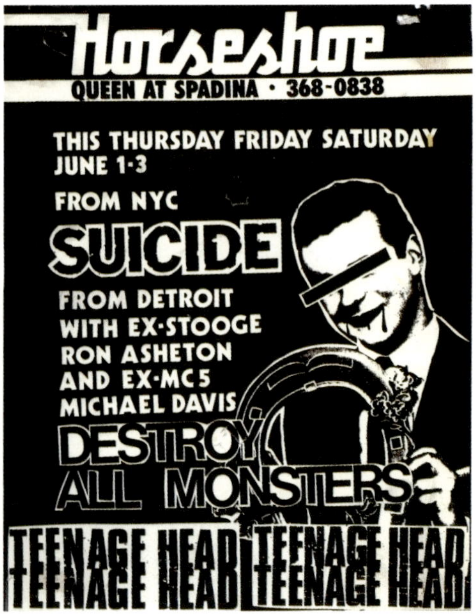

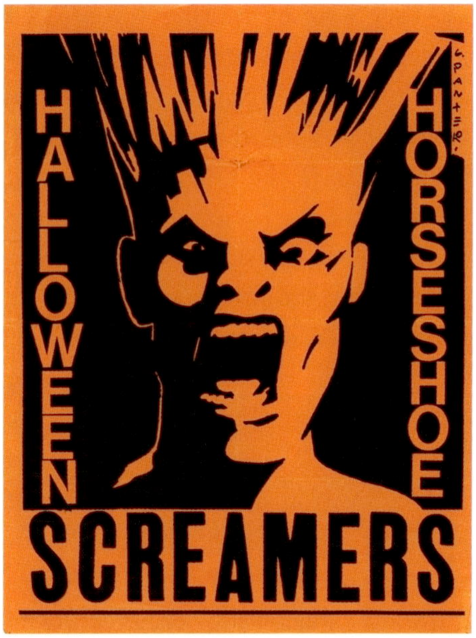

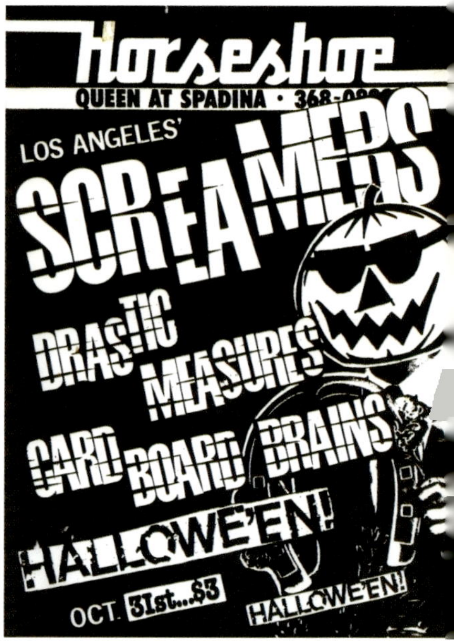

Some of the images revive sensory memory of the rush of volume and speed, and the absolute thrill of being crushed against the stage seeing The Stranglers. Bouncers pushing the crowd back, creating waves of human movement like wheat in the wind, is more palpable than my memory of the set-list. I remember spraying my friends' Virlana and Cram's apartment hallway with a fire extinguisher, but forget specific details of The Ugly show we went to see afterward. The memory of Teenage Jesus and The Jerks' drummer Bradley Field passing out on the sidewalk in front of the Horseshoe and then being shoved in the back of a police car equals that of the band's disengaged and disaffected performance. It was the perfect time to be a teenager and discover the city at night. Walking around a deserted downtown with Draga or Roger was as much a part of my new freedom as the gigs we went to see.

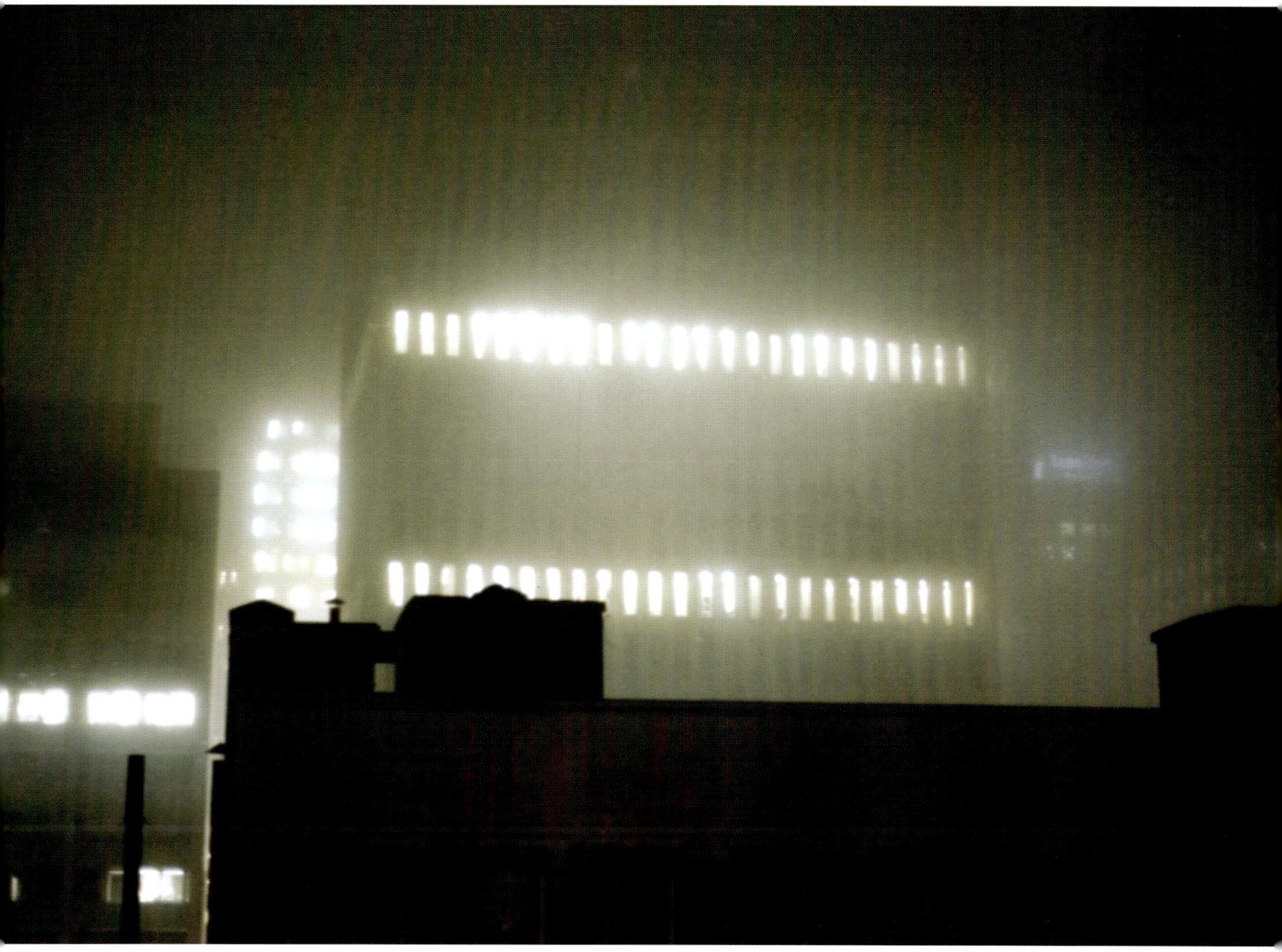

Temperance Street at Yonge looking south

On the northeast corner of Church and Gerrard Streets stood the Edge, an old house that was once probably a private residence, its stage cozied by a fireplace on one of the side walls, evidence of its past life as a living room. One night when going to see The Cramps there, my friend Reid and I climbed the fence around the demolition site next to the Edge, where similar Victorians were being torn down to make way for high-rise condos. We looked through the remnants of the lives of the people who had lived there, odds and ends like reel-to-reel tapes and an oversized Blue Mountain pottery sculpture of angelfish left behind to be crushed by the wrecking ball. I took the fish sculpture and gave it to The Cramps before the show. Lux carried the thing onstage with him and picked it up occasionally, singing to the fish and making kissy-lips with it. My memory of the decayed splendor of that ghostly torn-down basement seems so symbolic now of a transitional moment in the about-to-be-gentrified downtown core, of seeing the beauty hidden in the empty city at night — and it's every bit as memorable as the runs in Ivy's stockings or Bryan Gregory flipping his lit cigarette with his tongue to put the ember end inside his mouth. As snoozy as Toronto was, it was a wonderful place to be; punk was also the dividing line between old and new Toronto, of a new sense of modernism not connected to the down-home goodness of the CanCon iconography of Gordon Lightfoot or Valdy. Old, grand and opulent wood and marble edifices like Eaton's Queen Street department store were torn down to make way for the new glass and steel multiplexed and food-courted Eaton Centre.

More than 30 years later, seeing many of these images for the first time, they can't help but take on new meaning as historical document and memorial. That so many of the people I photographed have died imbues these pictures with melancholy for me, and some sense of tragedy to counterpoint the initial blast of youthful beauty, self absorption and the thrill of this new invention we'd created.

If you were cut out of the frame of a photograph or you think your band was better than The Diodes, I have to say that while these may be archival images, this is not a history book. This is a totally inaccurate snapshot of a particular part of Toronto at a particular time. In not depicting Cardboard Brains, Swollen Members, Drastic Measures, The Cads, The Wads, The Sophisticatos, The Dents, The Scenics, Nash the Slash, The Points, The Poles, The Androids, etc., this book doesn't begin to give a true picture of what fantastic bands there were here. However dysfunctional it was, there was a real sense of community among the bands and fans.

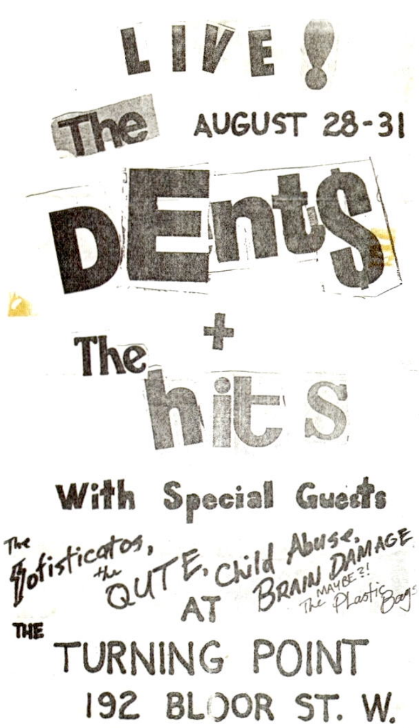

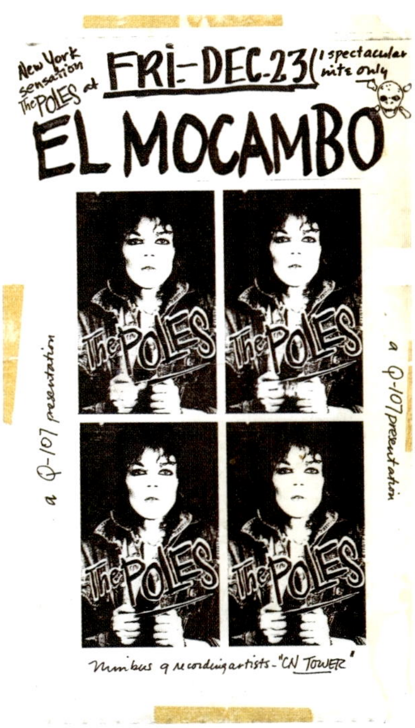

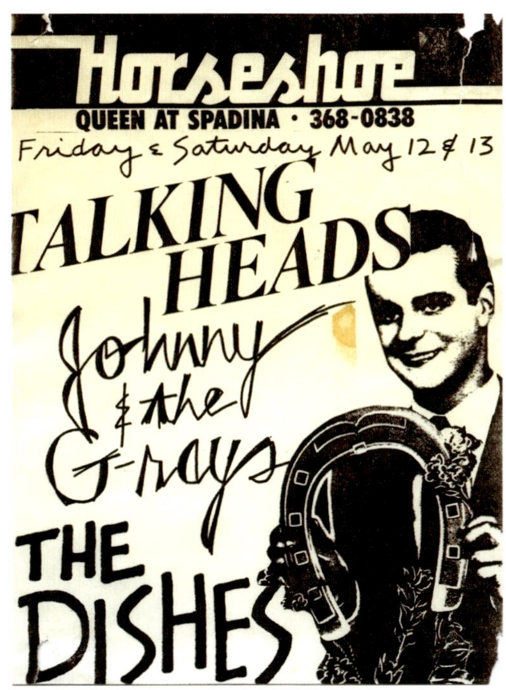

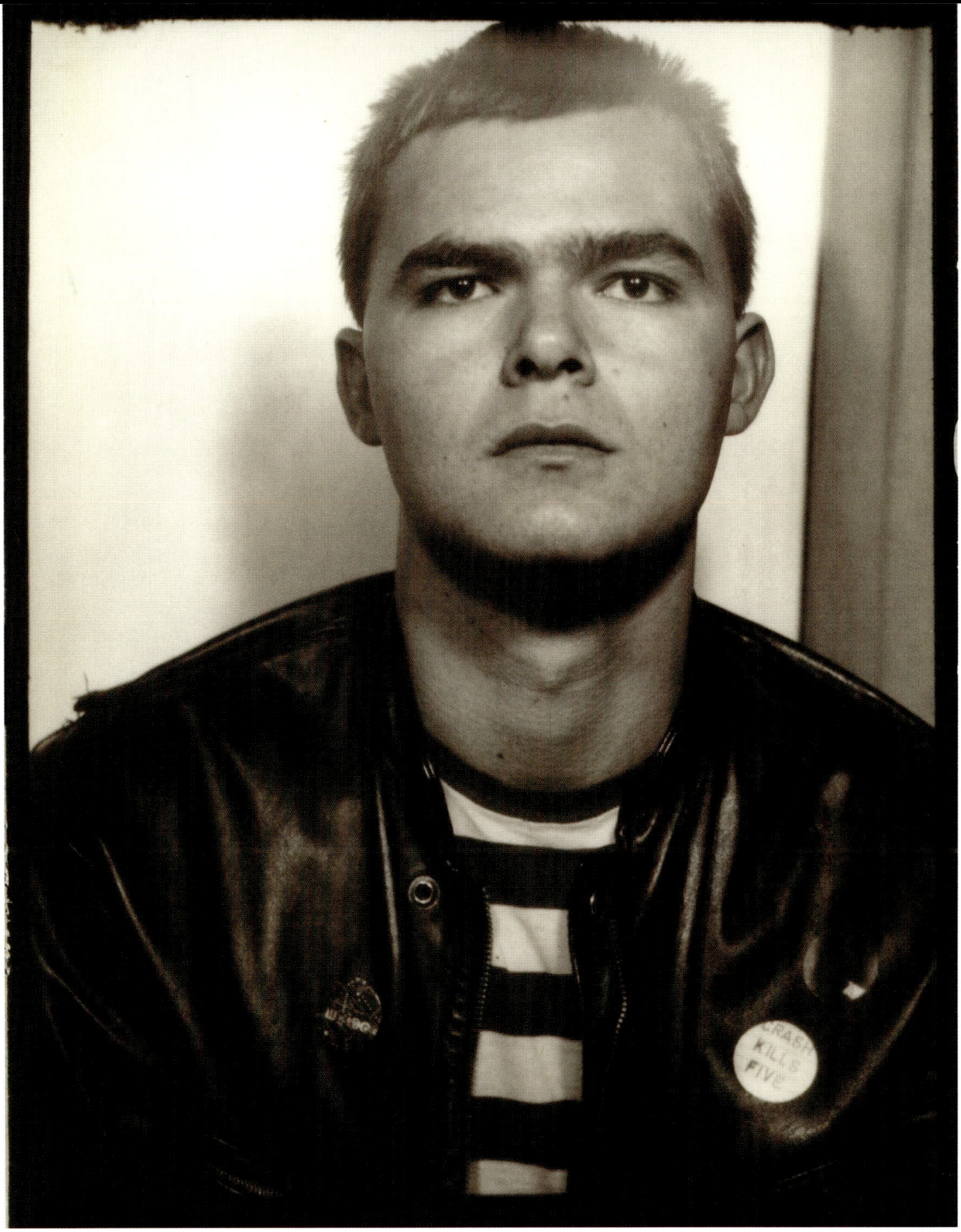

DP, 1979

This is what I shot. Maybe I didn't have my camera that night or was preoccupied talking with my friends. By 1979, my camera started to feel like a burden rather than an essential part of my experience. I turned my attentions more to making music and chasing men. I took photos at some shows, but not with the same fervor. Who knows, people may someday be itching to see my rare live photos of Soft Cell.

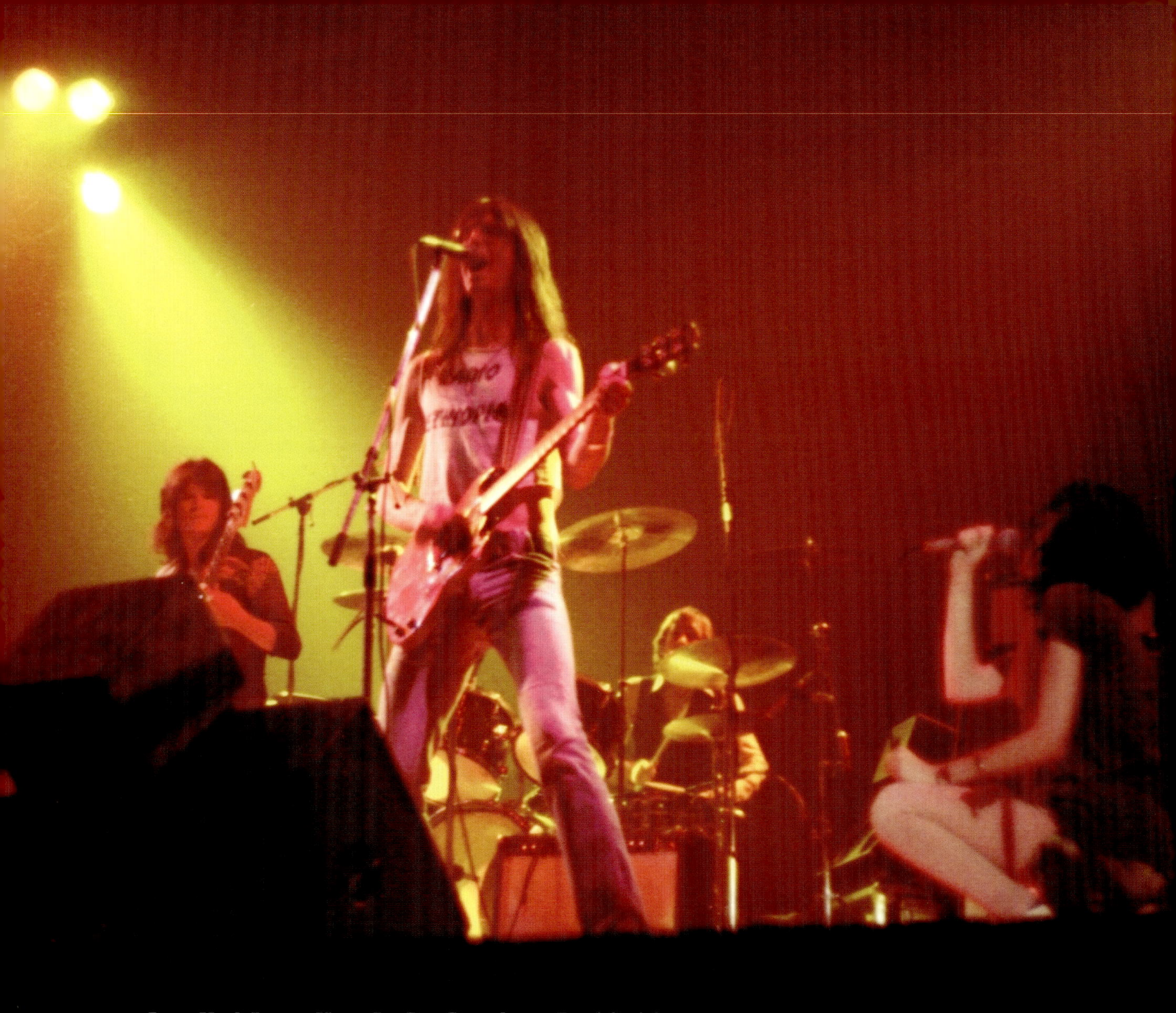

Ivan Kral, Lenny Kaye, Jay Dee Daugherty, Patti Smith

Patti Smith Group, Field House (Seneca College), 1976

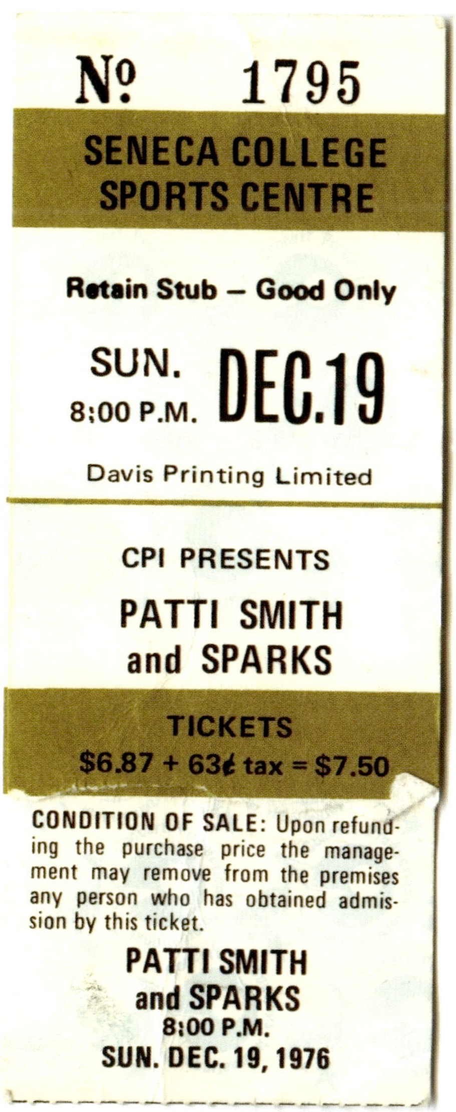

Patti Smith was touring for the just-released *Radio Ethiopia*, with Sparks opening in support of *Big Beat*. I don't recall why I didn't shoot Sparks since I loved them as much as I loved Patti. This was my almost disastrous first and last attempt at processing color film, something I look back on in disbelief, but this was how I could afford to take the number of pictures I did. This is what I was taking pictures of, and the only way to learn was to do it. I was heartbroken when the film came out of the developer awash in shades of purple and pink.

Patti wet her pants at some time during the show, the wet spot spreading across her satin shorts as she fell to the ground in front of me, ripping and torturing the strings off her guitar.

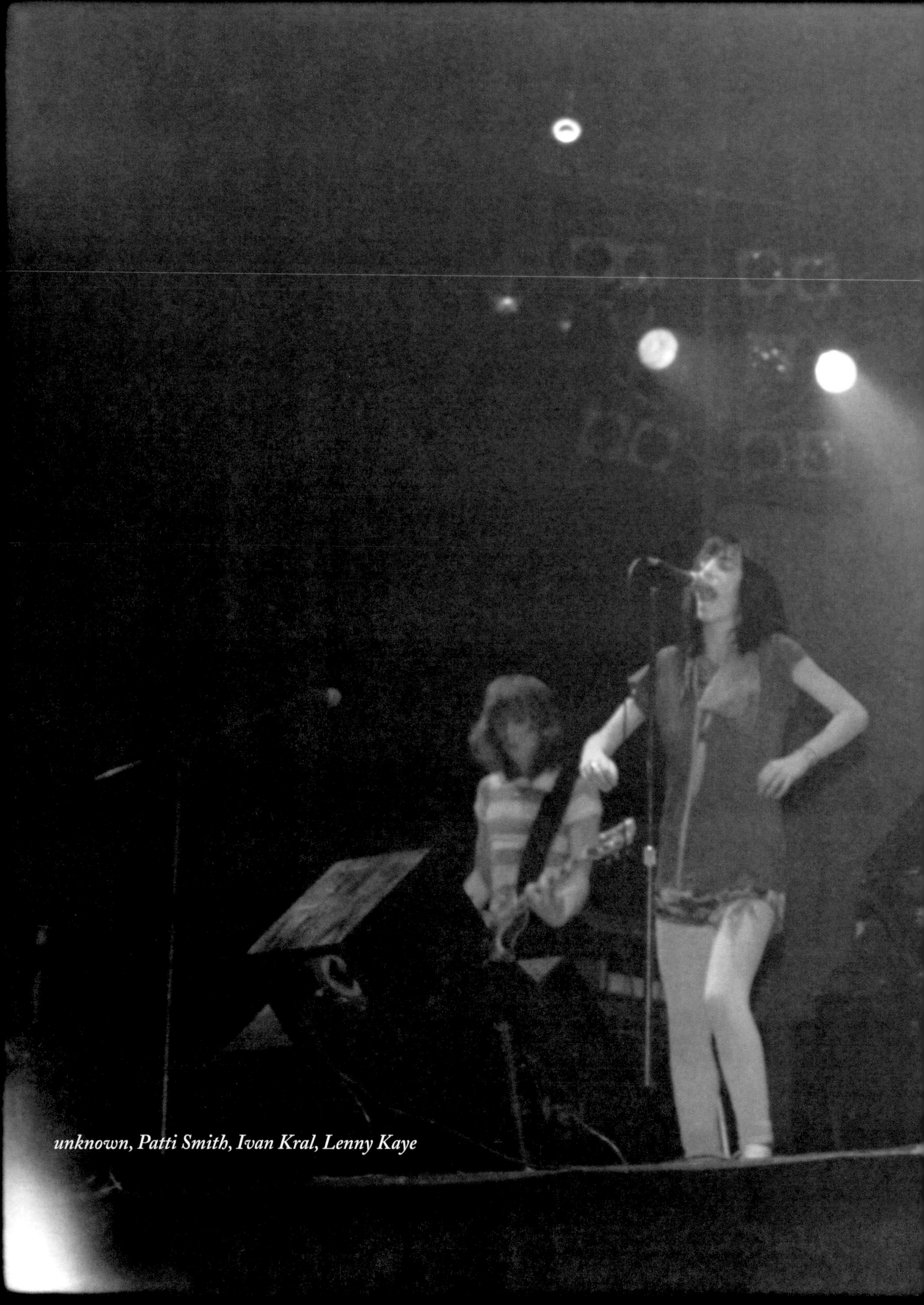

unknown, Patti Smith, Ivan Kral, Lenny Kaye

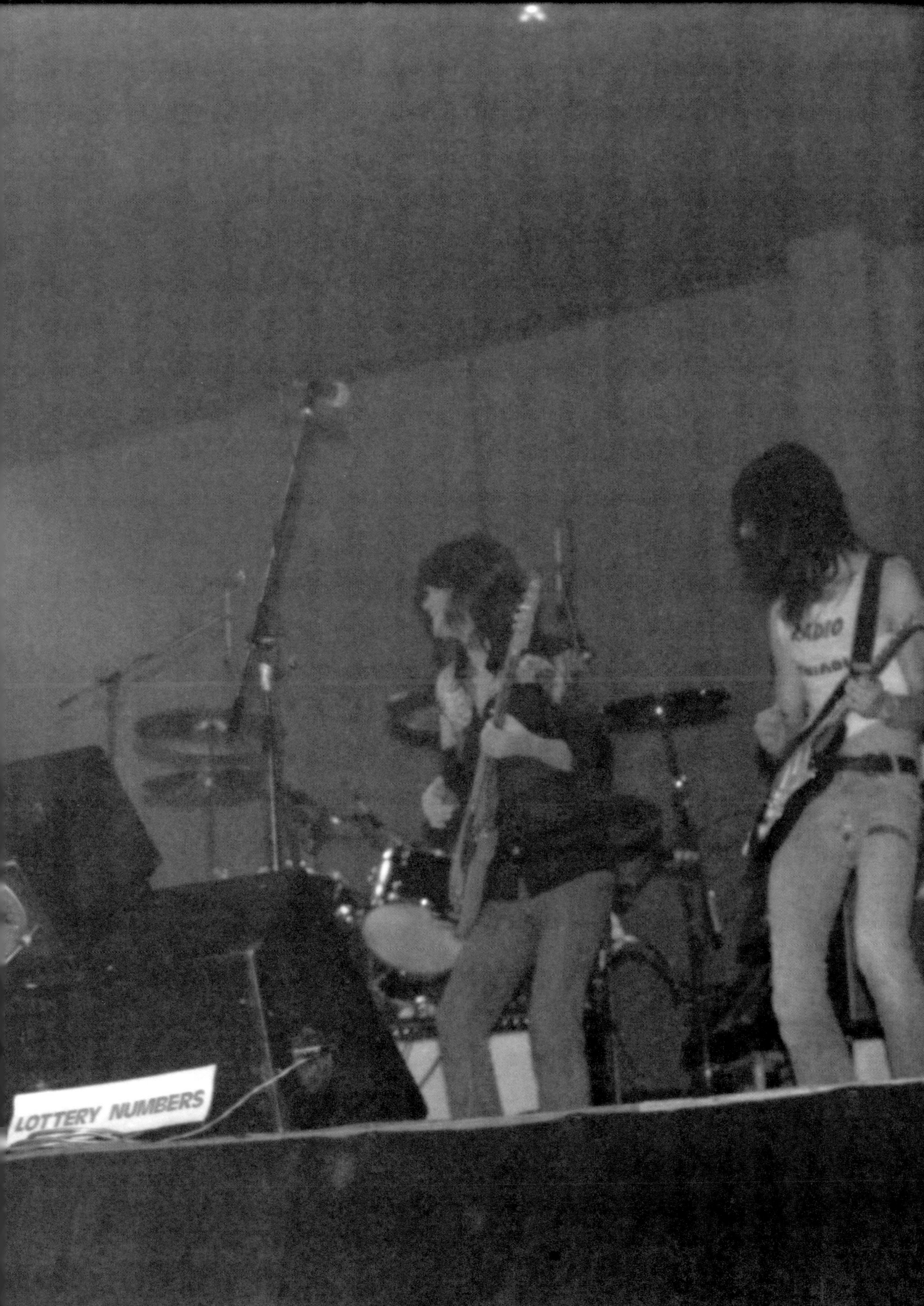
LOTTERY NUMBERS

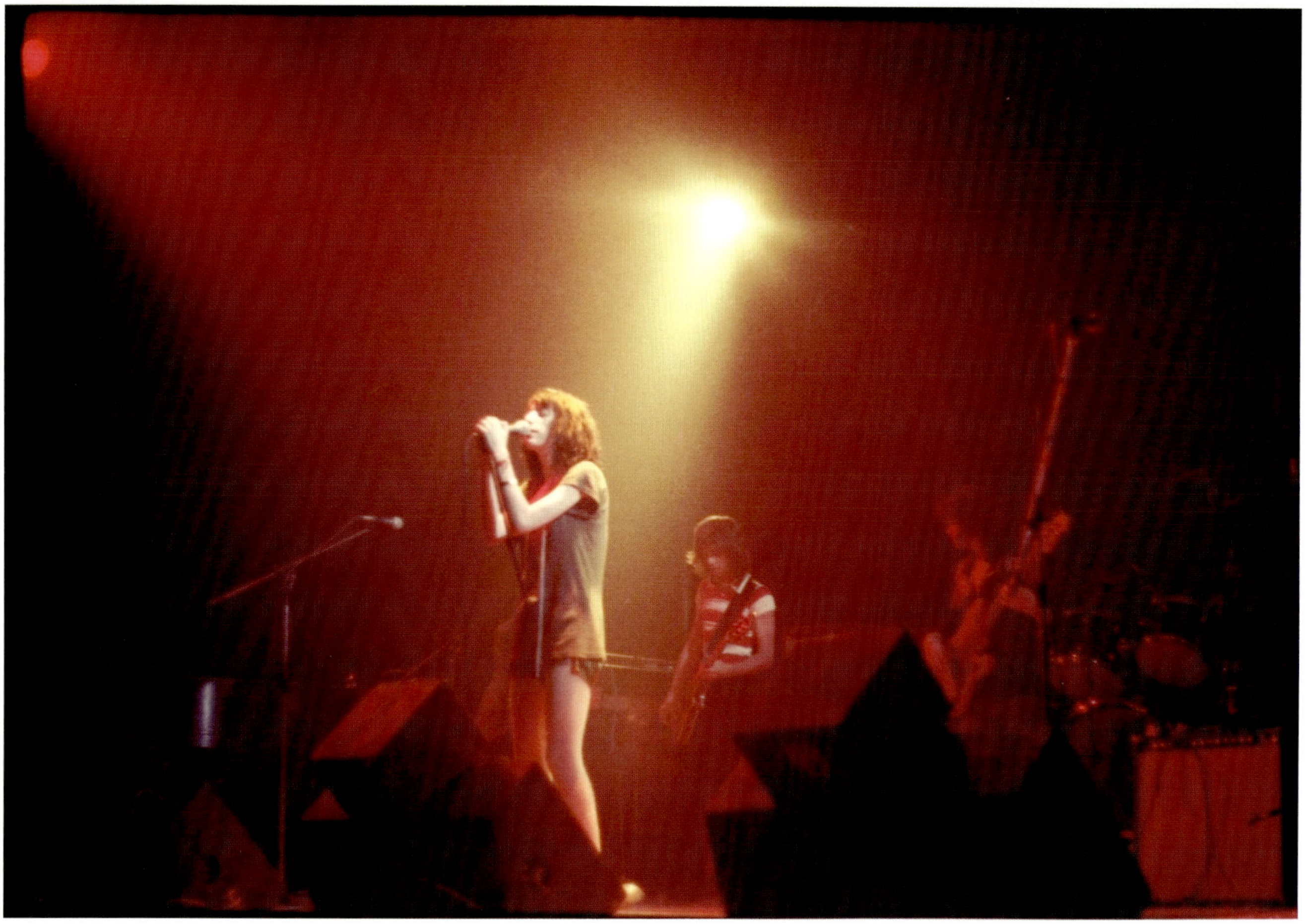

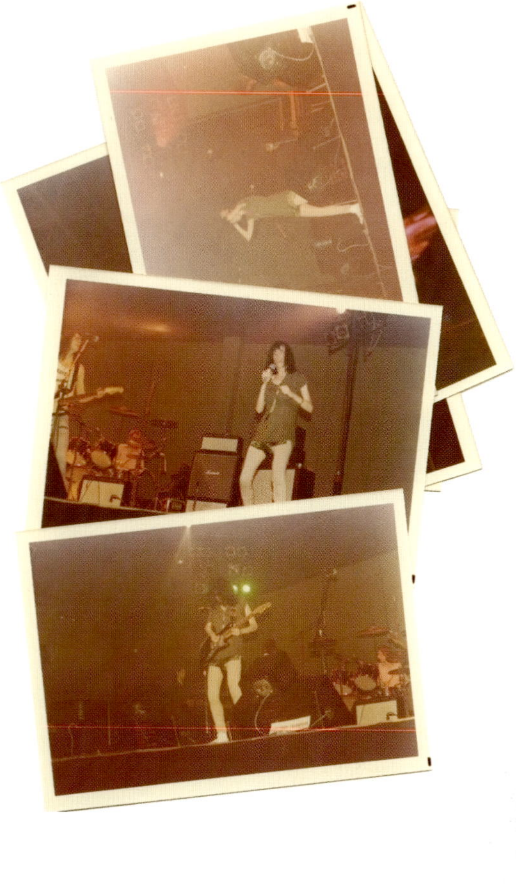

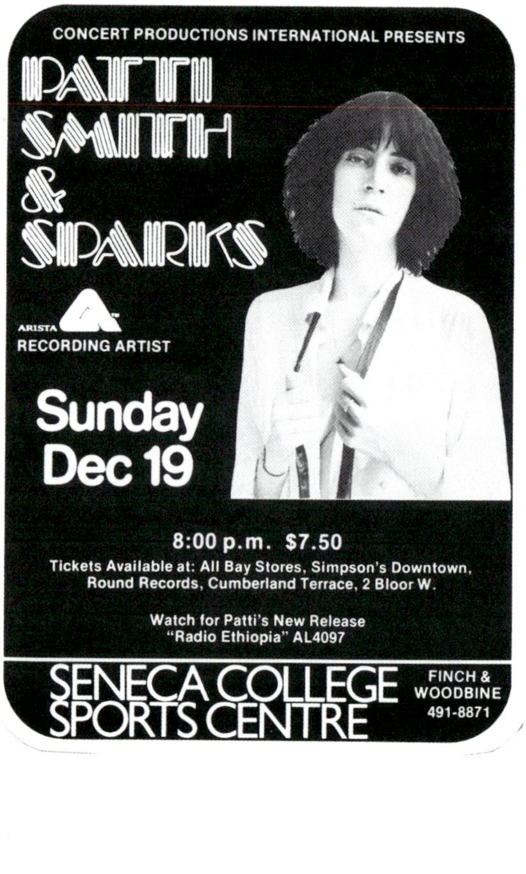
CONCERT PRODUCTIONS INTERNATIONAL PRESENTS
PATTI SMITH & SPARKS
ARISTA
RECORDING ARTIST
Sunday Dec 19
8:00 p.m. $7.50
Tickets Available at: All Bay Stores, Simpson's Downtown, Round Records, Cumberland Terrace, 2 Bloor W.
Watch for Patti's New Release "Radio Ethiopia" AL4097
SENECA COLLEGE SPORTS CENTRE
FINCH & WOODBINE
491-8871

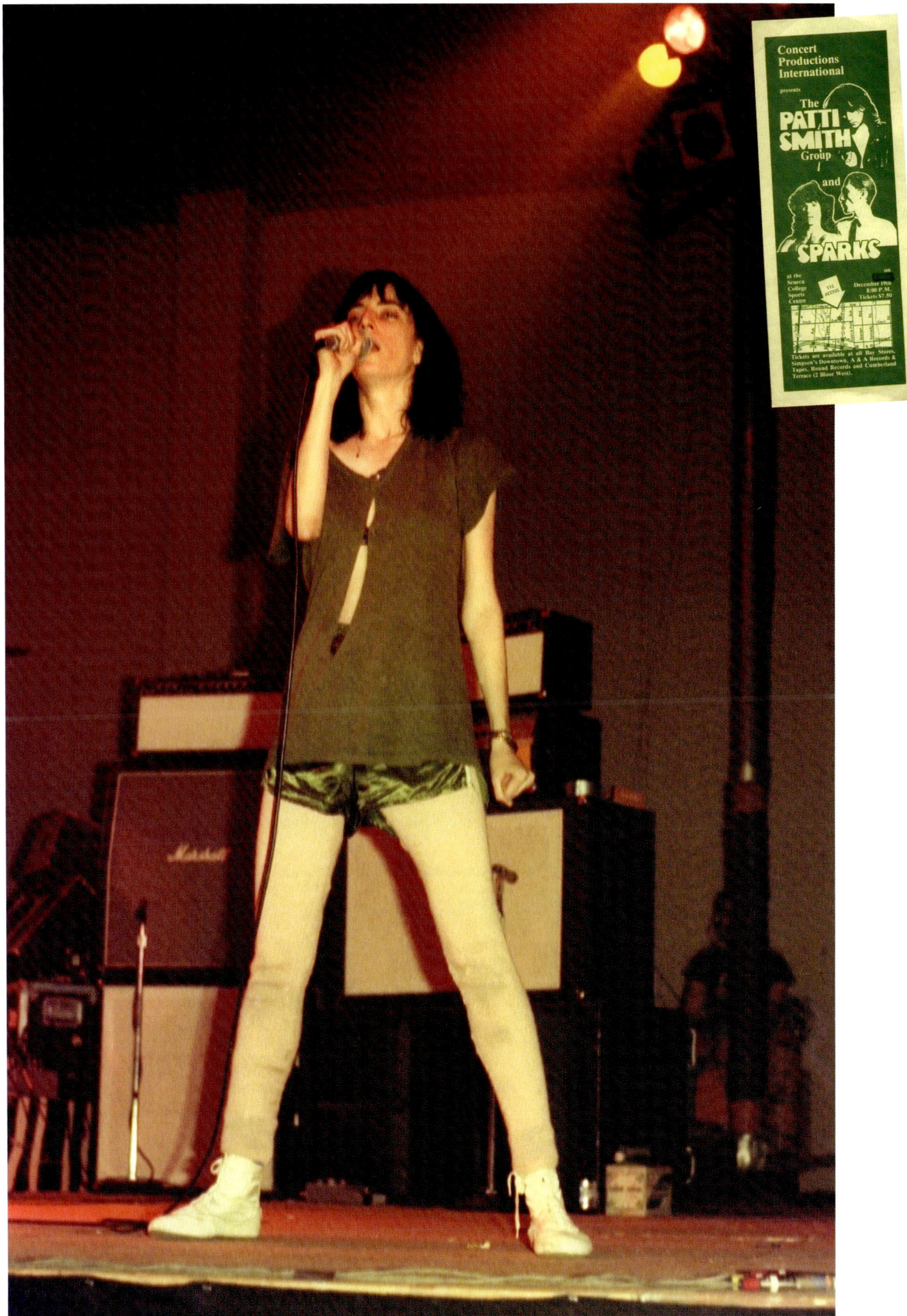
Concert Productions International
presents
The PATTI SMITH Group
and
SPARKS
at the Seneca College Sports Centre
on
December 19th
8:00 P.M.
Tickets $7.50
TTC ACCESS
Tickets are available at all Bay Stores, Simpson's Downtown, A & A Records & Tapes, Round Records and Cumberland Terrace (2 Bloor West).

Iggy Pop, Field House, Seneca College, 1977

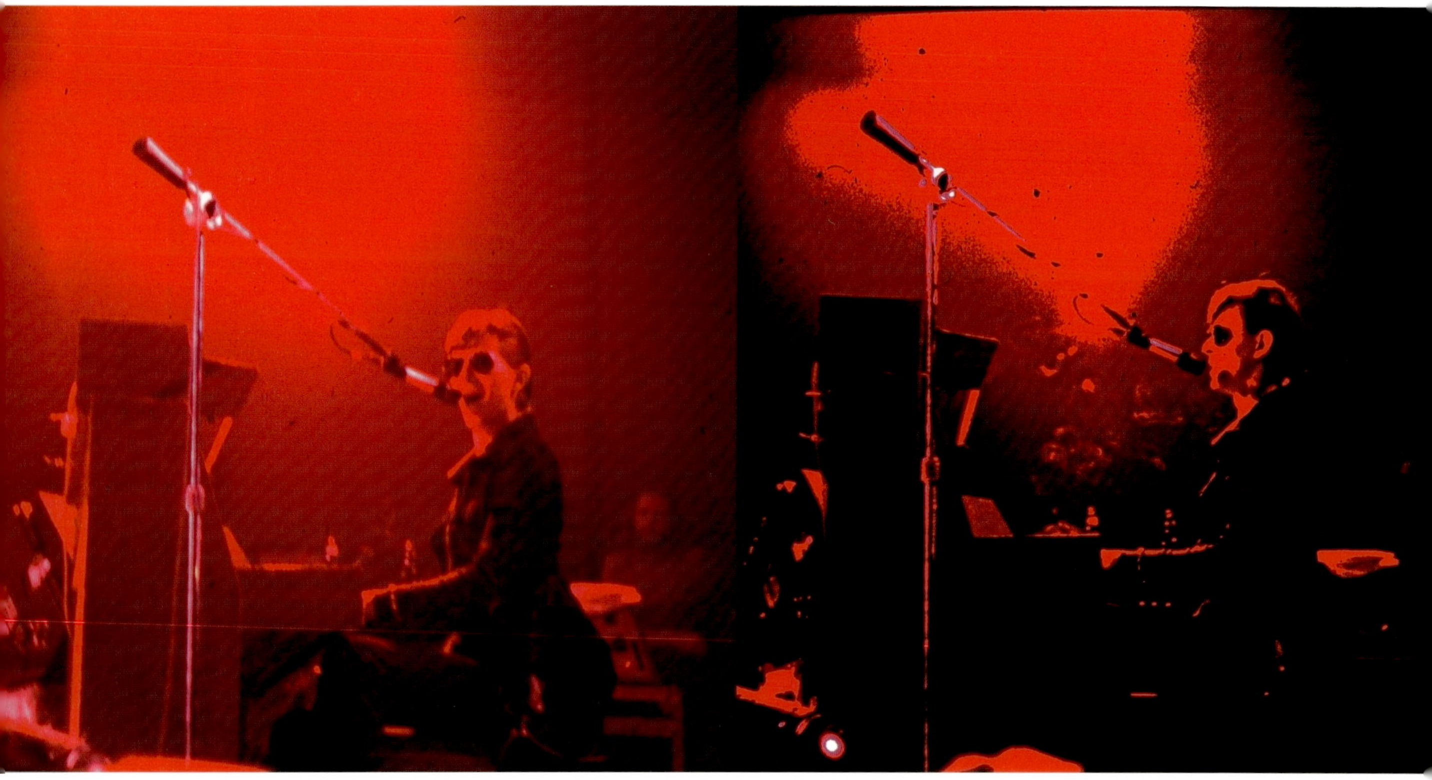

After disappointment with my Instamatic photos of the Ramones, I borrowed a 35 mm camera to shoot Iggy and David. My friend Roger and I skipped school to go early and get in line for the general admission show. Bowie, who had produced Iggy's awesome new album *The Idiot*, was playing keyboards, practically sending us into paroxysms of excitement. This was only Iggy's third post-*Idiot* solo show and featured *Kill City* and *Lust for Life* rhythm section (and future Tin Machine members!) Hunt and Tony Sales. When the doors opened, we tried to run to the front, but our feet had become numb from the long wait in the cold. Everyone who'd been waiting for hours hobbled as quickly as possible to get a spot at the front of the stage, with those who had just arrived rushing past us.

Blondie opened the show, adrenalized from the release of their first album — a record I knew I'd love from the cover photo alone. When I bought it, the guy behind the counter gagged, saying they were terrible. "They won't warm you up, they'll cool you down." I loved Blondie, totally digging the Farfisa-driven go-go pop and bassist Gary Valentine's scene-stealing showboating.

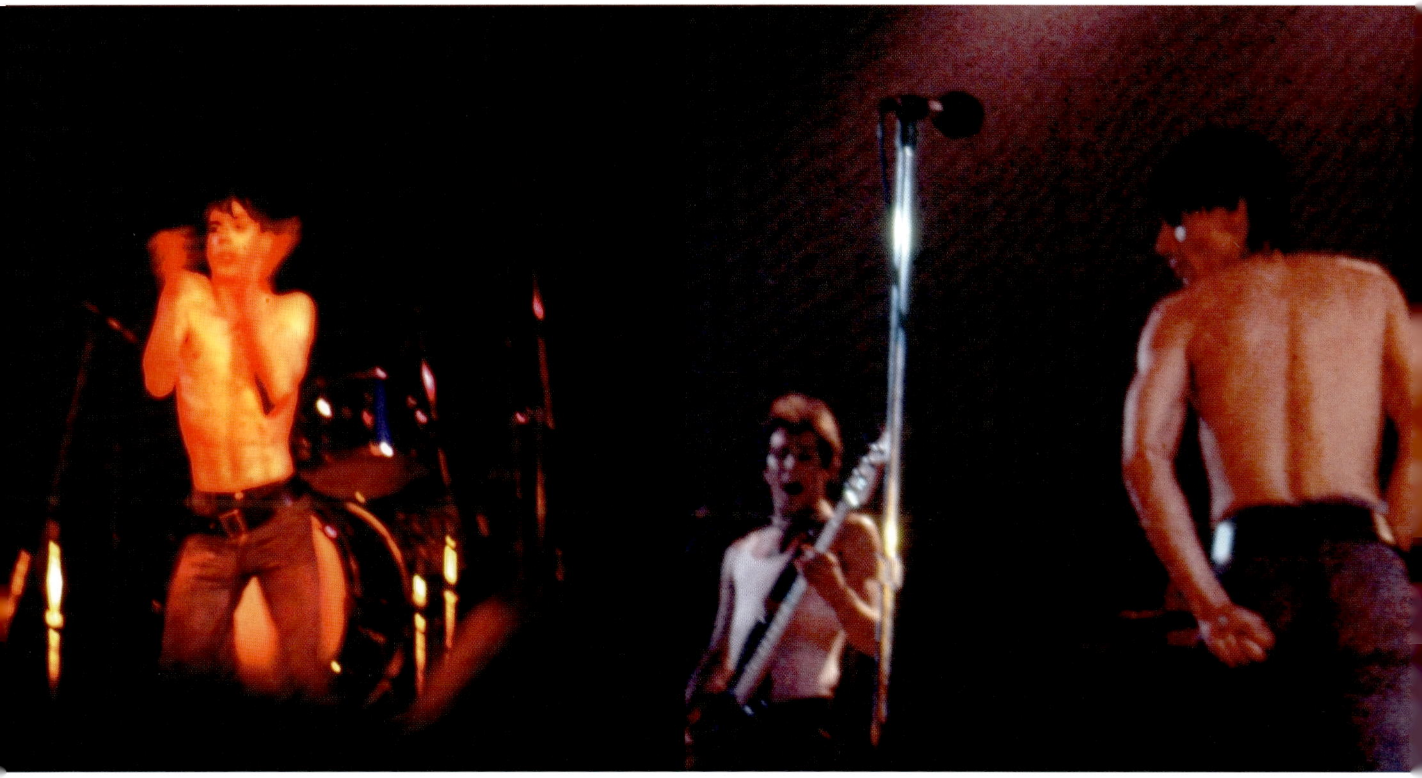

Iggy Pop, David Bowie, Tony Sales

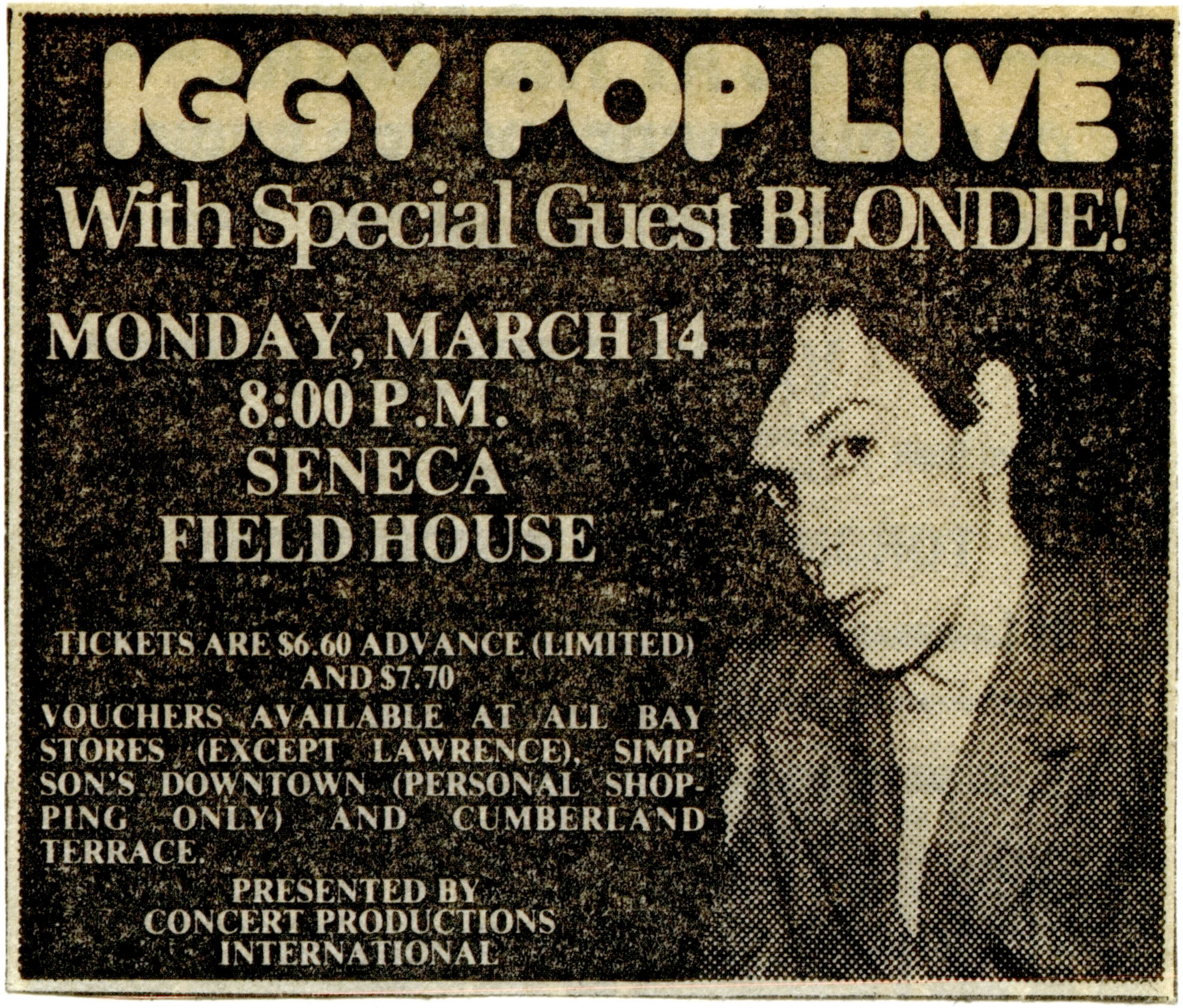

I wanted the best pictures possible so I naively asked at the camera shop what had the best color and they sold me two rolls of slide film. I shot a whole roll of Blondie, opening the camera at the end of the set to change the film. Confused at seeing it still in the sockets and not rolled back into the cartridge, like my Instamatic did, I couldn't figure out how to get the film out and asked the guy next to me if he knew how a camera worked. "You ruined the film, man," he said, showing me how to rewind it into the canister. Consequently, Iggy and David followed Blondie as the first artists I shot with 35 mm.

At 11 years old, my first obsessive musical freakout was to David Bowie via *Ziggy Stardust*. I subsequently devoured Lulu singles, Mott the Hoople and Dana Gillespie albums he produced, Velvets songs he covered, Anthony Newley LPs he mentioned in interviews, Mick Ronson solo records — anything David touched. This was the closest we had ever been to our pre-teen idol, crushed against the stage in front as he chain-smoked his way through the set.

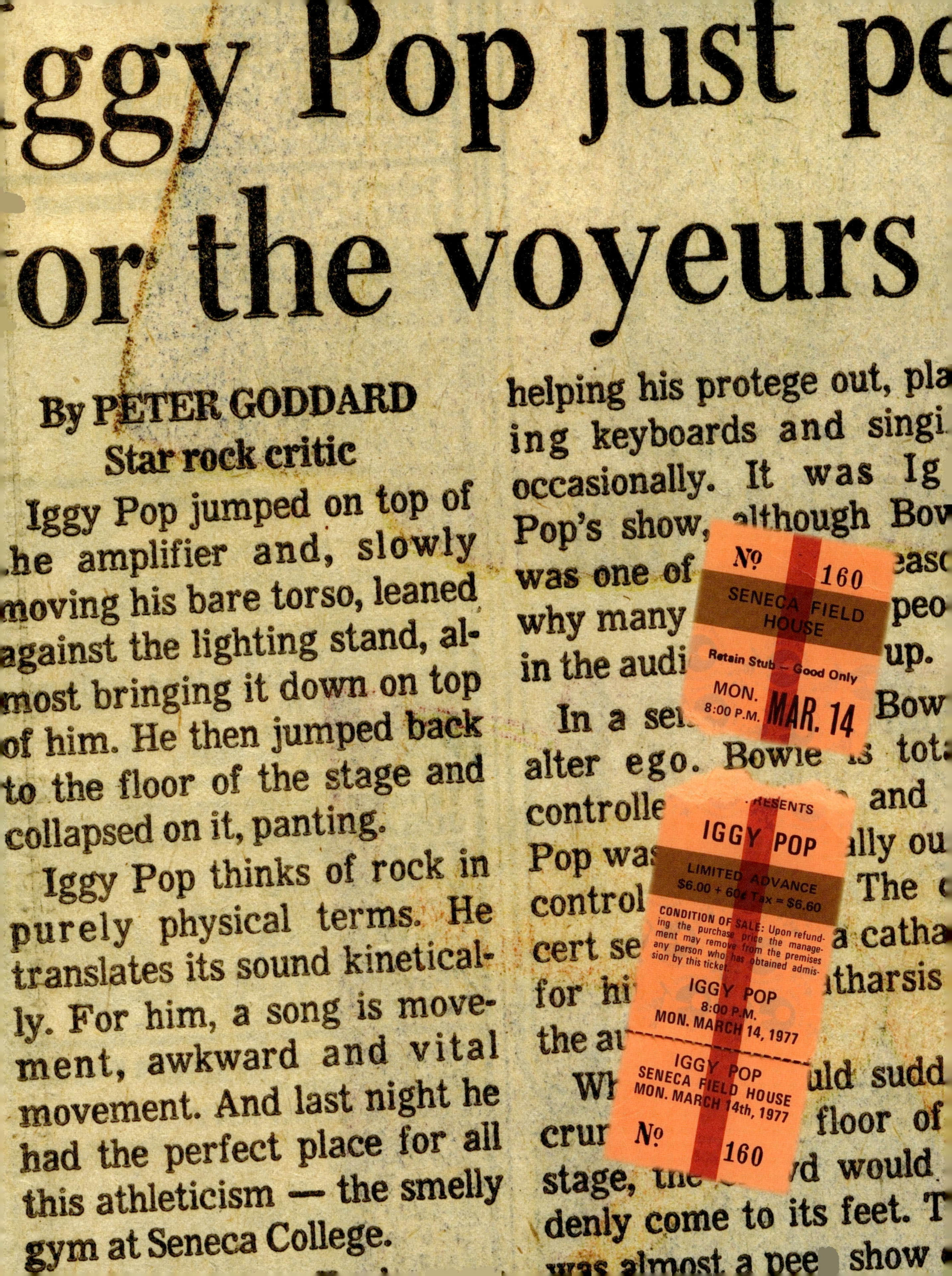

ggy Pop just pe or the voyeurs

By PETER GODDARD
Star rock critic

Iggy Pop jumped on top of he amplifier and, slowly moving his bare torso, leaned against the lighting stand, almost bringing it down on top of him. He then jumped back to the floor of the stage and collapsed on it, panting.

Iggy Pop thinks of rock in purely physical terms. He translates its sound kinetically. For him, a song is movement, awkward and vital movement. And last night he had the perfect place for all this athleticism — the smelly gym at Seneca College.

helping his protege out, pla ing keyboards and singi occasionally. It was Ig Pop's show, although Bov was one of … easo why many … peo in the audi… up.

In a se… Bow alter ego. Bowie is tot controlle… and Pop was… ally ou control… The cert se… a catha for hi… atharsis the au…

Wh… uld sudd crun… floor of stage, the … d would denly come to its feet. T was almost a pee show

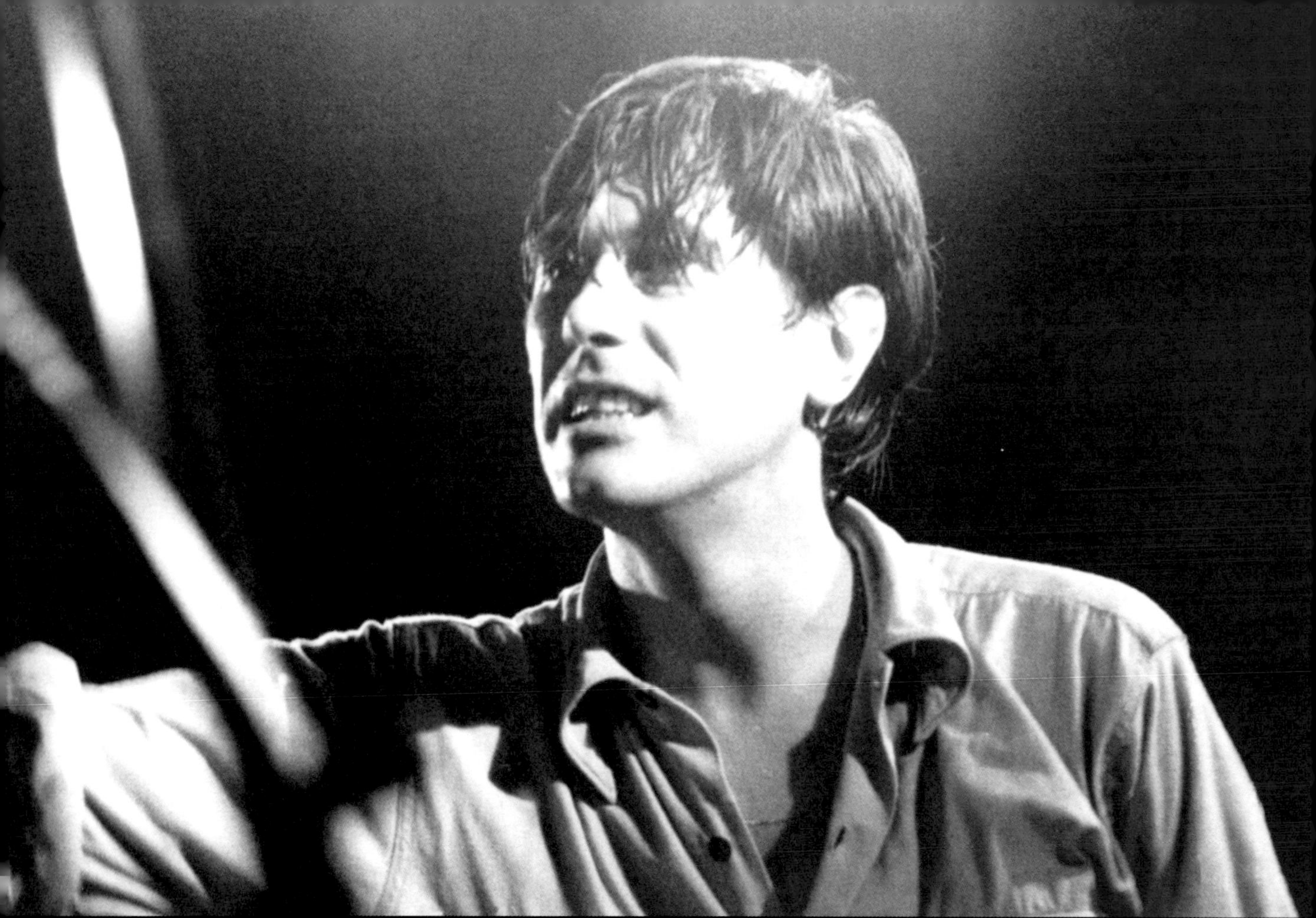

Bryan Ferry, with Chris Spedding (opposite page)

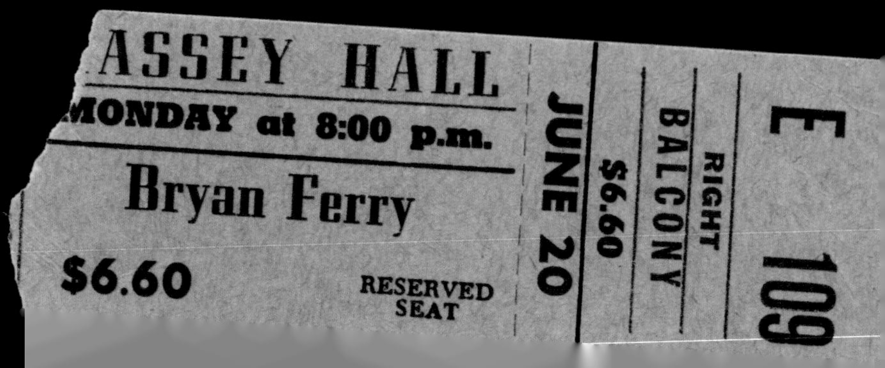

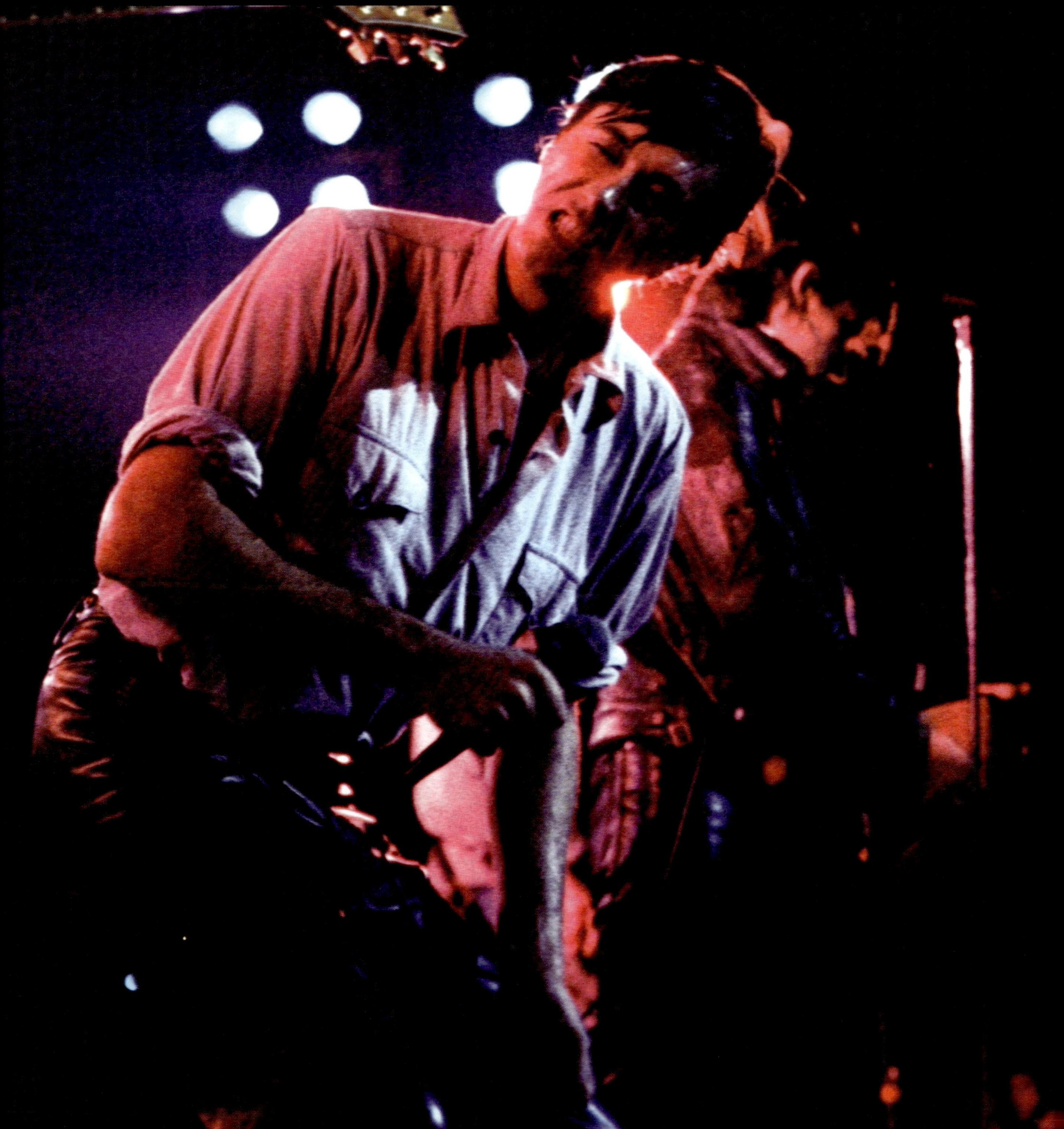

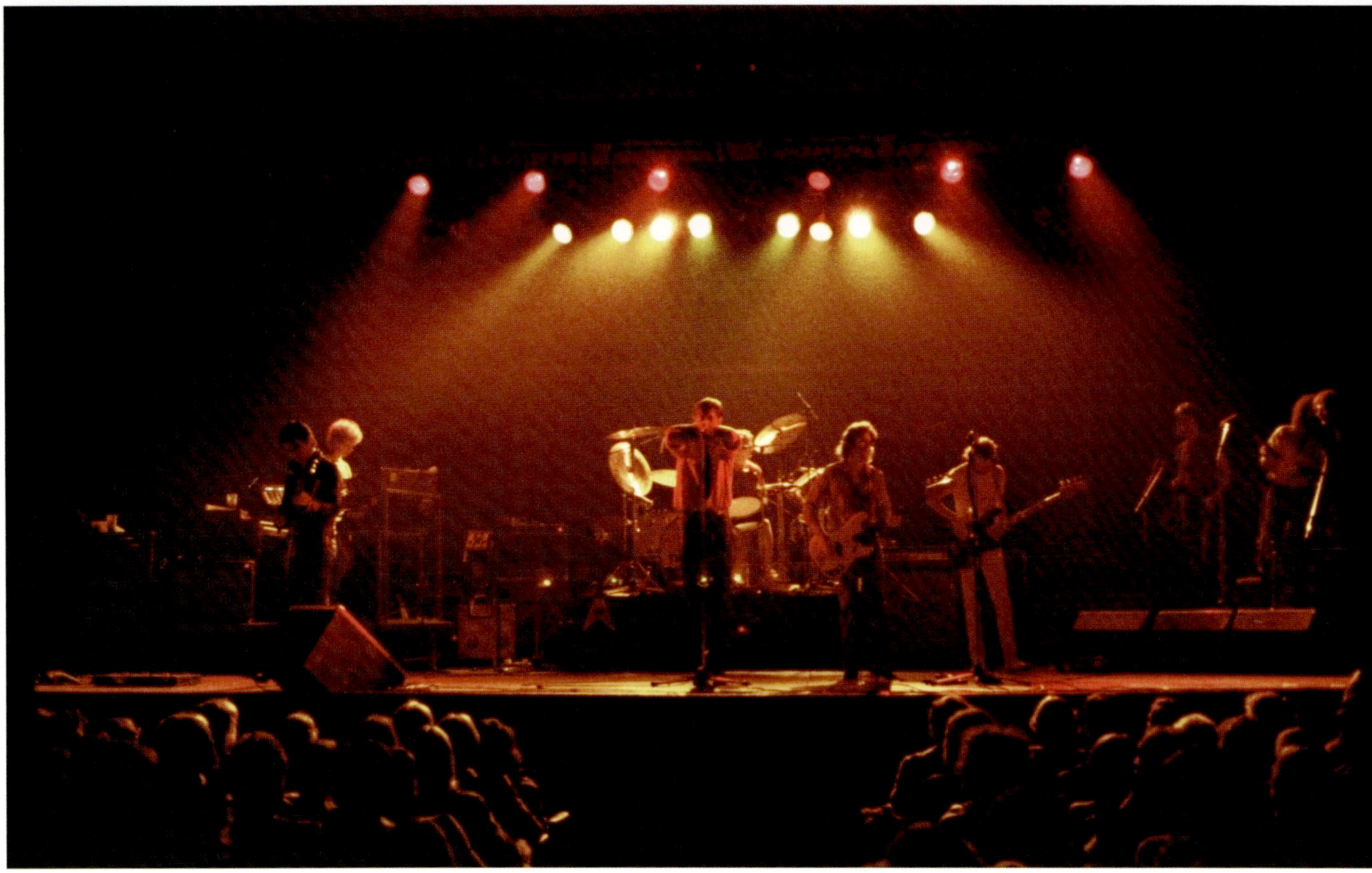

Chris Spedding, Ann Odell, Bryan Ferry, Paul Thompson, John Wetton, Phil Manzanera, Mel Collins, Martin Drover, Chris Mercer

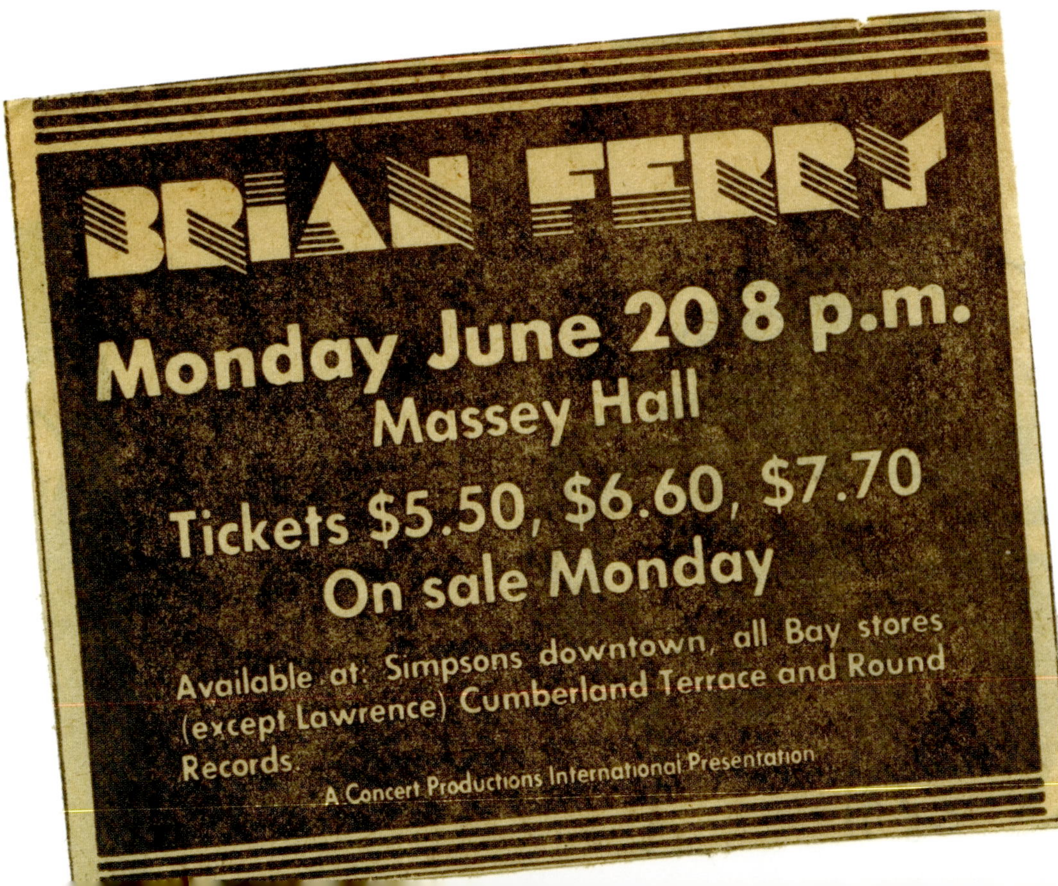

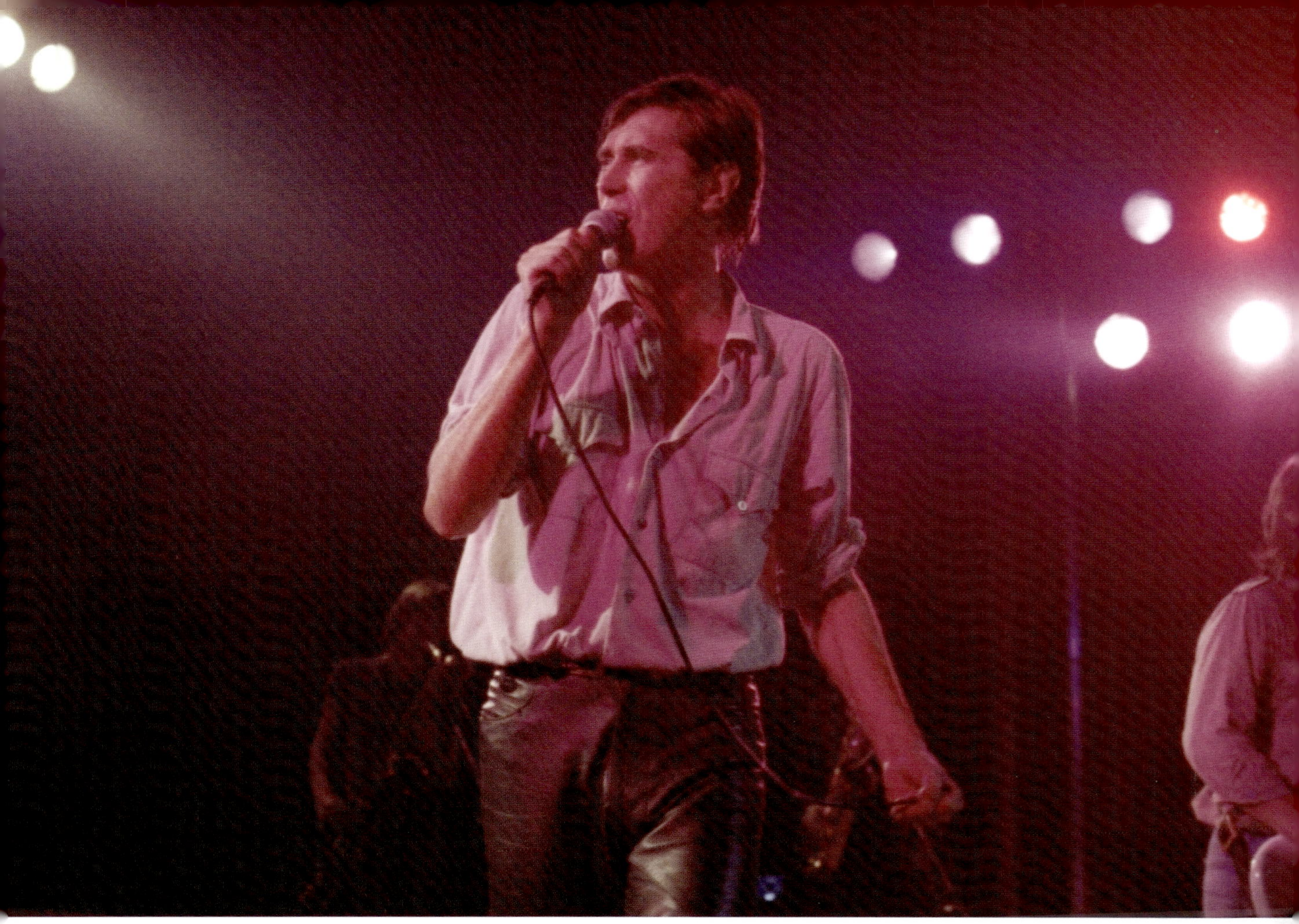

Bryan Ferry's first solo show in Toronto featured Roxy Music's Phil Manzanera and Paul Thompson, and guitarist Chris Spedding. Ferry's third solo album, *Let's Stick Together*, had just come out and the future of Roxy Music was in question. But at least they'd have burned out brilliantly at the end of their string of five incredible albums, the most recent having been *Siren*. Pre-'76, the periods most romanticized were Hollywood's glamour of the '40s and the cabaret scenes of Germany's 1920s Weimar Republic. When Alice Cooper vamped it was in imitation of Mae West; when Deaf School called for "Cocktails at Eight," they were drawing from a similar well as Roxy's space-age-jet-set-meets-sophisticate-social-scene nostalgia. Roxy created the template that locally was lifted wholesale by The Dishes. The new music mutiny, for all its seizure-of-power stance, was a fairly predictable generational shift in which nostalgia was now for the 1950s' *The Wild One* and the 1960s' *Wild in the Streets* instead. I thought that Ferry, as one of the foremost arbiters of style, acknowledged the shift simply by wearing leather pants and a skinny leather tie.

All heads turned to spot members of Blue Öyster Cult as the buzz went around that they — in town to play the following night at Maple Leaf Gardens — were standing at the back of the hall.

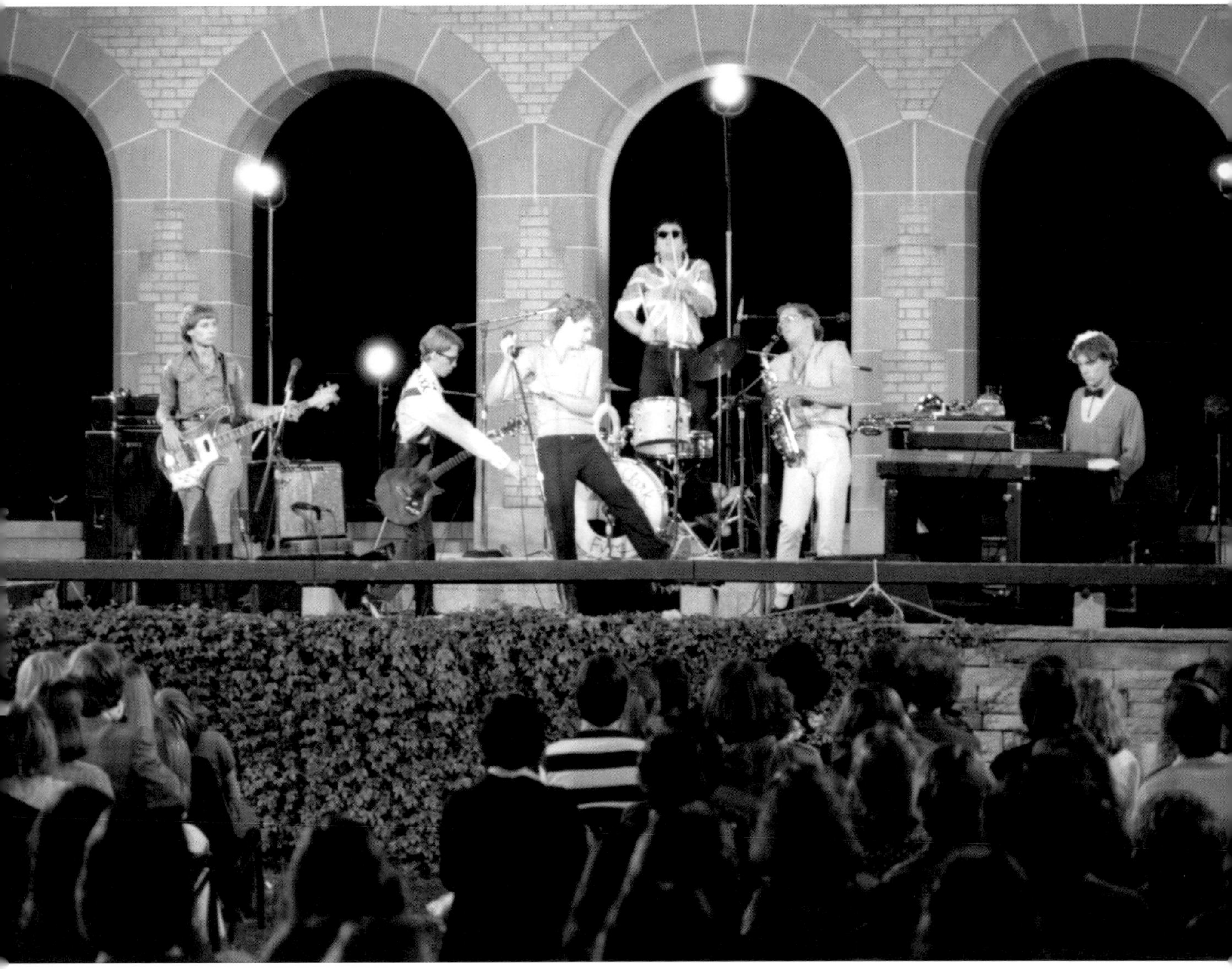

Ken Farr, Scott Davey, Murray Ball, Steven Davey, Michael Lacroix, Glenn Schellenberg

The Dishes, Hart House Quadrangle, University of Toronto, 1977

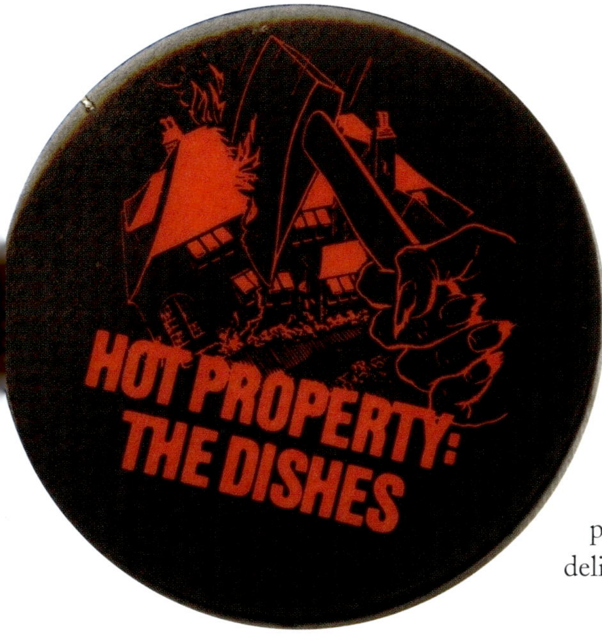

The Dishes played an outdoor concert at the University of Toronto, which was videotaped and broadcast on a local cable access channel. For about two years it seemed to be in a perpetual 2 a.m. broadcast cycle. Like Rough Trade before them, art school fashion plates The Dishes were the last transition point before arty and clever music was pigeonholed as "new wave" and fast and heavy bands as "punk."

The guy who sat next to me told me that the saxophone player was really a male model and that he wore glasses to deliberately look unattractive.

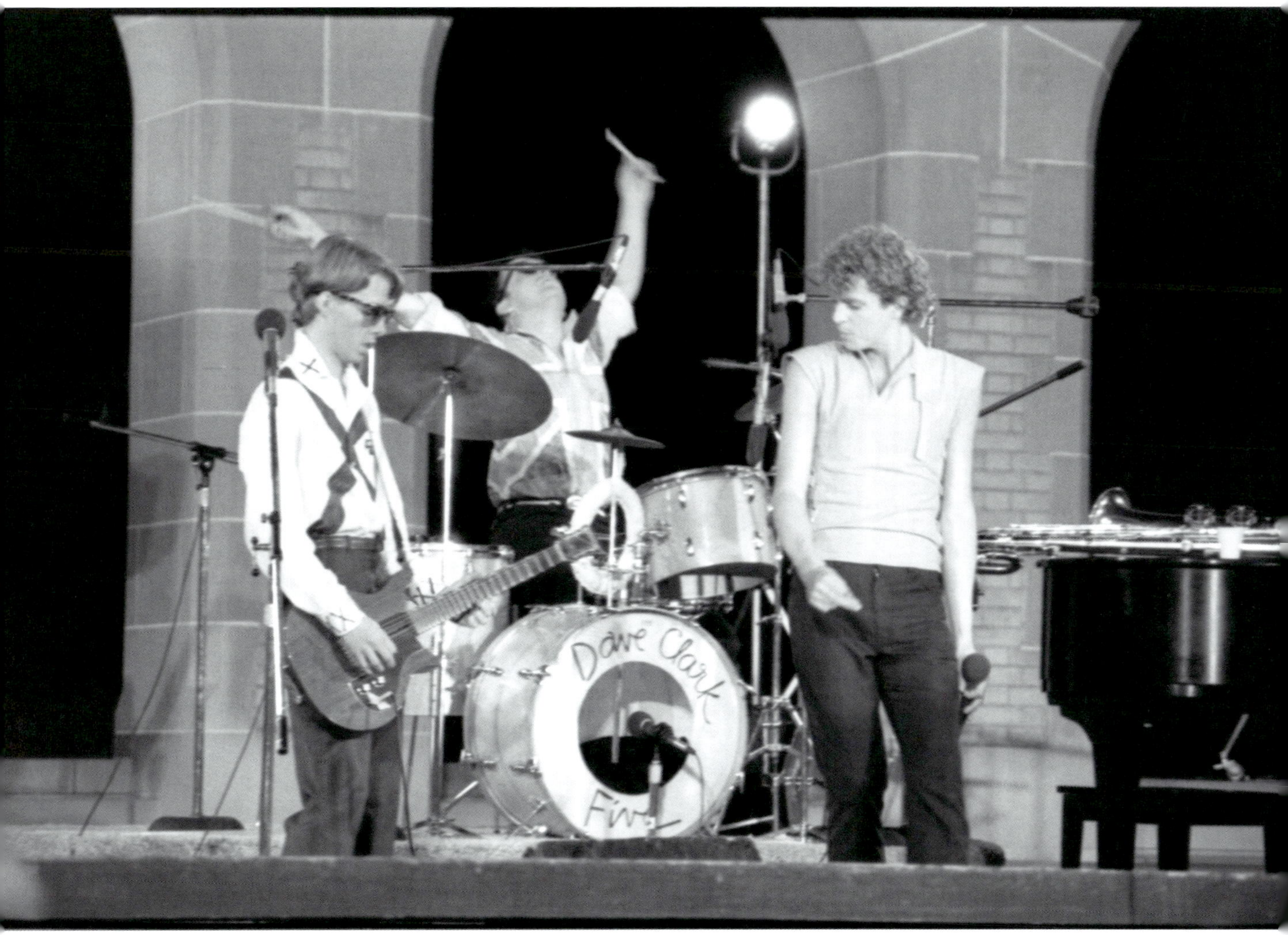

AGIT POP

Agitation-Popaganda

Fri/Sat 24&25 June, 1977.

DISHES JUBILEE SHOCKER!

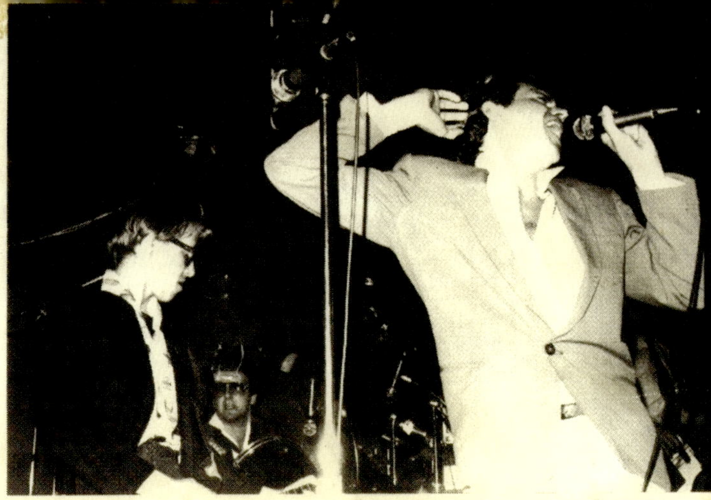

FASHION PLATE: Murray belts it out at the Chimney......

photo: Isobel Harry

by · Demand

THE DIS il celebrate ie ilver Jubilee of Her Majesty Queen Elizabeth 2 by a duo of Royal Performances on the Sovereign's birthday. As well, THE DISHES will be joined by GEEK/CHIC stylist, DAVID BUCHAN and FASHION BURN.

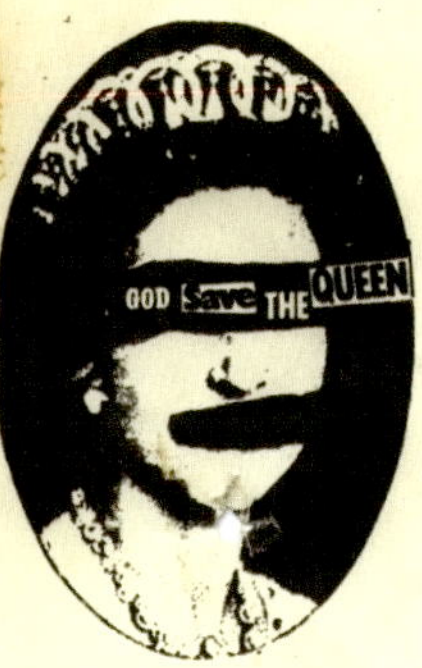

25 Years At Number One

THE DISHES are Toronto's foremost new wave combo and have been widely acclaimed...

"Avant-garde rock.... utterly unromantic, urban, and dryly witty."....Peter Goddard, Toronto Star

"Each of their songs are little bon-bons with poisonous centres fatal only to those from the suburbs"....Noah James, Nightout

"A must for the progressive minded" David Farrell, Record Week

"Too good and too inteligent"....R.Baegga, Toronto Entertainment Weekly

"There is a big sink to fill, and led by Bobby Vee/Bryan Ferry vocals of Murray Ball, the Dishes have got the liquid"....Clive Robertson,

IS THE NEW WAVE A PERMANENT WAVE?

WHAT GIVES?

The Dishes' will commence their World Tour, Summer 1977 at Crash N Burn, Toronto's trendiest Wreck Room. The C'N'B is located behind the Royal Alex, between Adelaide and King Streets. Performance at 9pm.

Admission $2.50

Crash N' Burn
15 Duncan St
24 & 25 June 1977

fold

"Their lyrics are often clever and mildly satirical and their stage wear includes short hair, straight pants, and skinny ck ties."....

Hopkins, Macleans

"The self-evident darlings of the Art Set"... erald Levitch, ronto Sun

"The nation's newest hitmakers!"....FILE Megazine

"The Dishes' music is reminiscent of old Looney Tune soundtracks as interpretted by the American International horrorchestra"....Lorne MacDonald, Varsity

"The Dishes attempt to use culture phen-

PLUS... FASHION BURN!

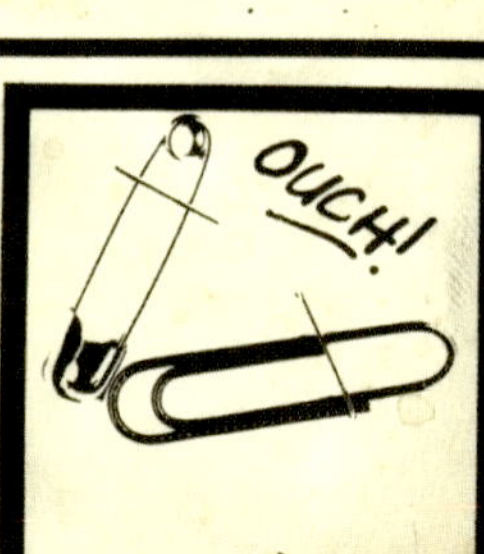

PUNK ROCK FASHION PARADE by TORONTO WARDROBE ARTIST– DAVID BUCHAN

Featuring: LUCASTA LUANDA CALLAA MYRANA ROCHAS

and MUCH, MUCH MORE!!

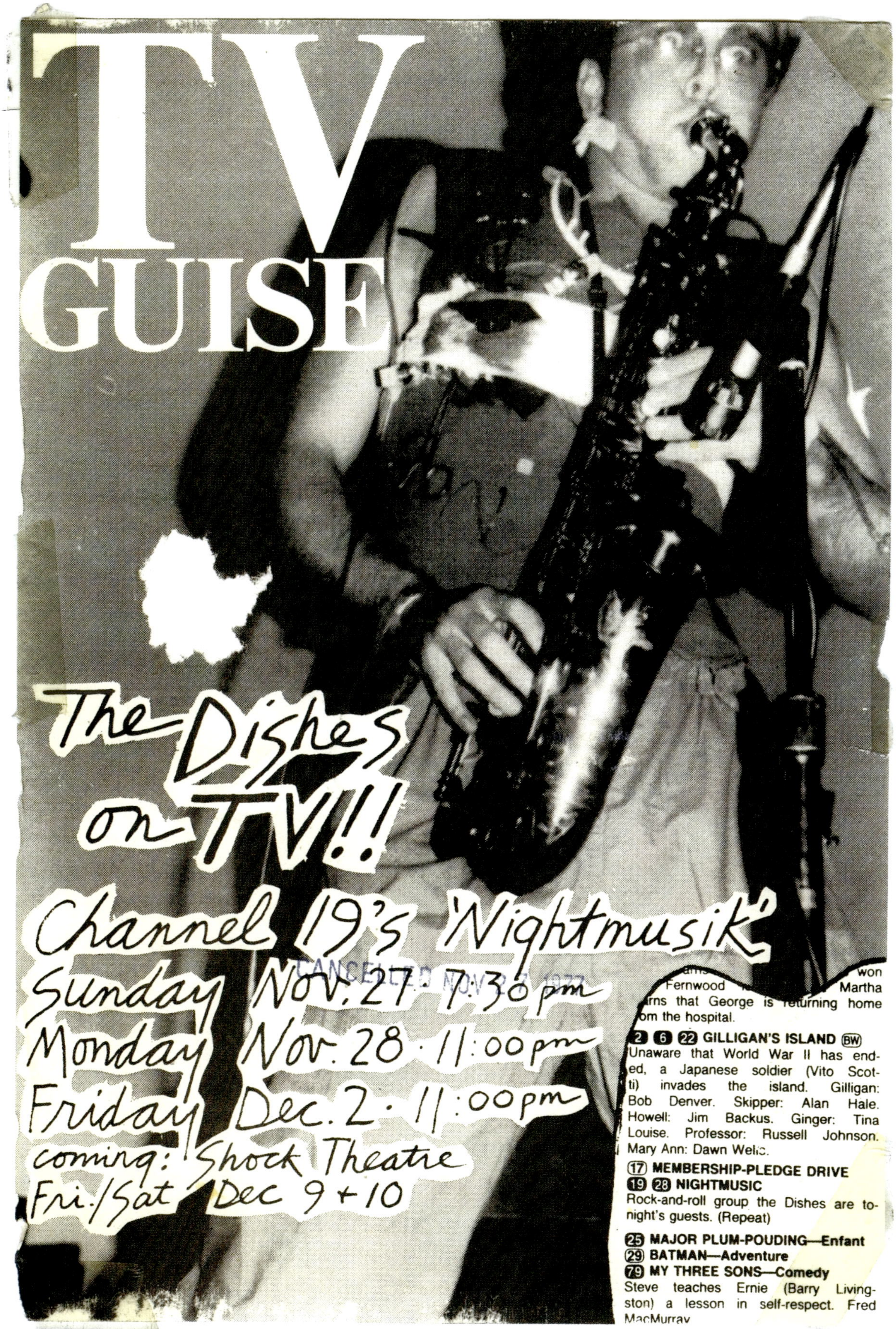
TV
GUISE
The Dishes
on TV!!
Channel 19's 'Nightmusik'
Sunday Nov. 27 7:30 pm
Monday Nov. 28 11:00 pm
Friday Dec. 2 11:00 pm
coming: Shock Theatre
Fri./Sat Dec 9 + 10
CANCELLED
Fernwood Martha
rns that George is returning home
om the hospital.
2 6 22 GILLIGAN'S ISLAND BW
Unaware that World War II has ended, a Japanese soldier (Vito Scotti) invades the island. Gilligan: Bob Denver. Skipper: Alan Hale. Howell: Jim Backus. Ginger: Tina Louise. Professor: Russell Johnson. Mary Ann: Dawn Wells.
17 MEMBERSHIP-PLEDGE DRIVE
19 28 NIGHTMUSIC
Rock-and-roll group the Dishes are tonight's guests. (Repeat)
25 MAJOR PLUM-POUDING—Enfant
29 BATMAN—Adventure
79 MY THREE SONS—Comedy
Steve teaches Ernie (Barry Livingston) a lesson in self-respect. Fred MacMurray

The Diodes, Crash 'n' Burn, 1977

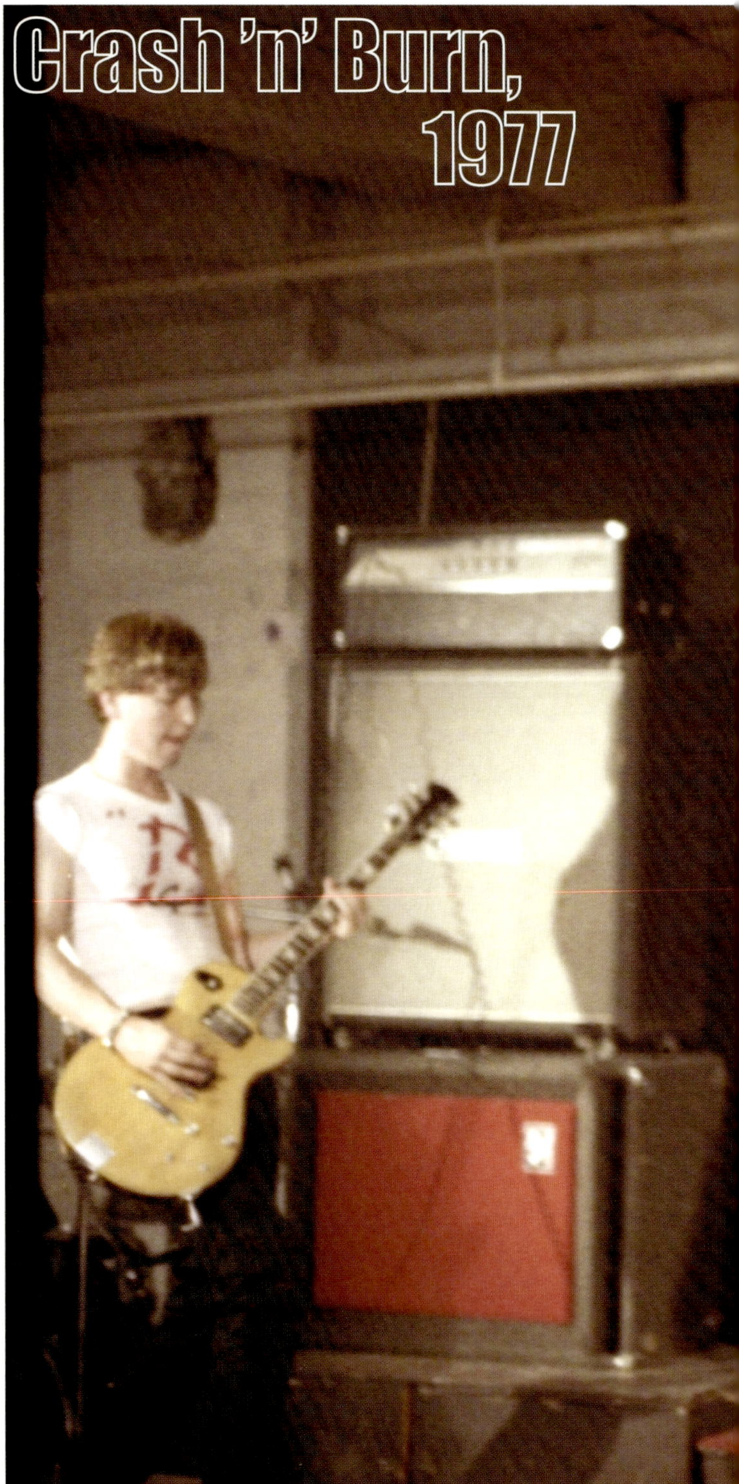

John Catto, Paul Robinson,
John Hamilton, Ian Mackay

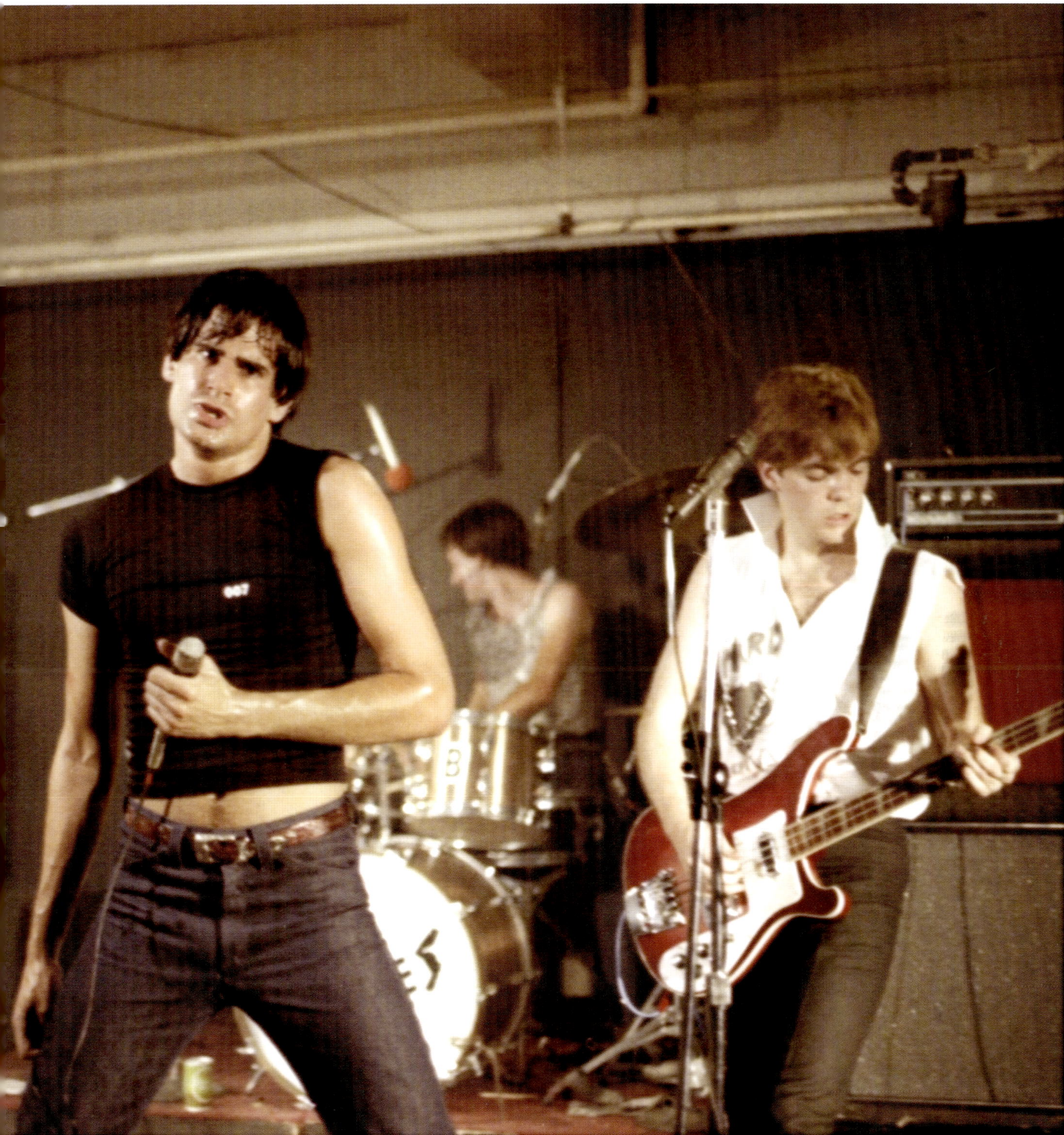

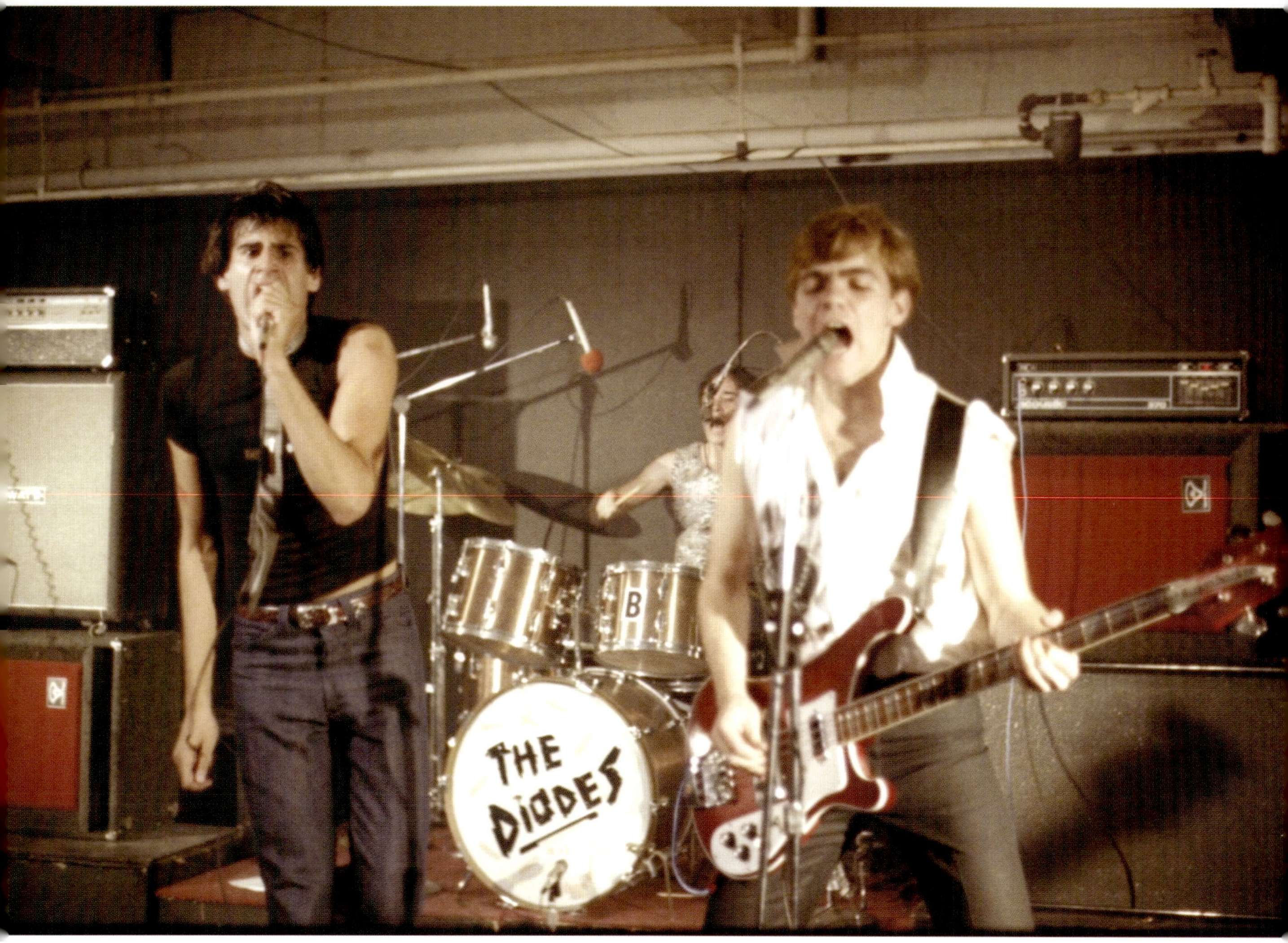

The Diodes seemed to play every show I saw at the C 'n' B.

Crash 'n' Burn felt like a dangerous place to me, partly because it was in a downtown warehouse district basement where the streets were completely empty at night, but also because it was the first time I was able to go into a bar. The seeming lack of rules was in stark contrast to the union-controlled club circuit where I would never have been allowed in, a place where everyone displayed their reinvented selves, with new names and haircuts.

The early Diodes were a fantastic mix of klutz and chaos, hard rock and bubblegum, and their blatant ambitiousness made it no surprise that they were the first local "punk" group signed to a major label. Songs about Karen Ann Quinlan, a young woman who'd od'd and then lived for years in a vegetative state after being taken off life support in 1976, and Anissa Jones, the child actor who played Buffy on the late-'60s TV show *Family Affair* and died at 18 of a drug overdose, were more petulant and self-consciously clever than the deliberately offensive Viletones singing "Auschwitz Jerk."

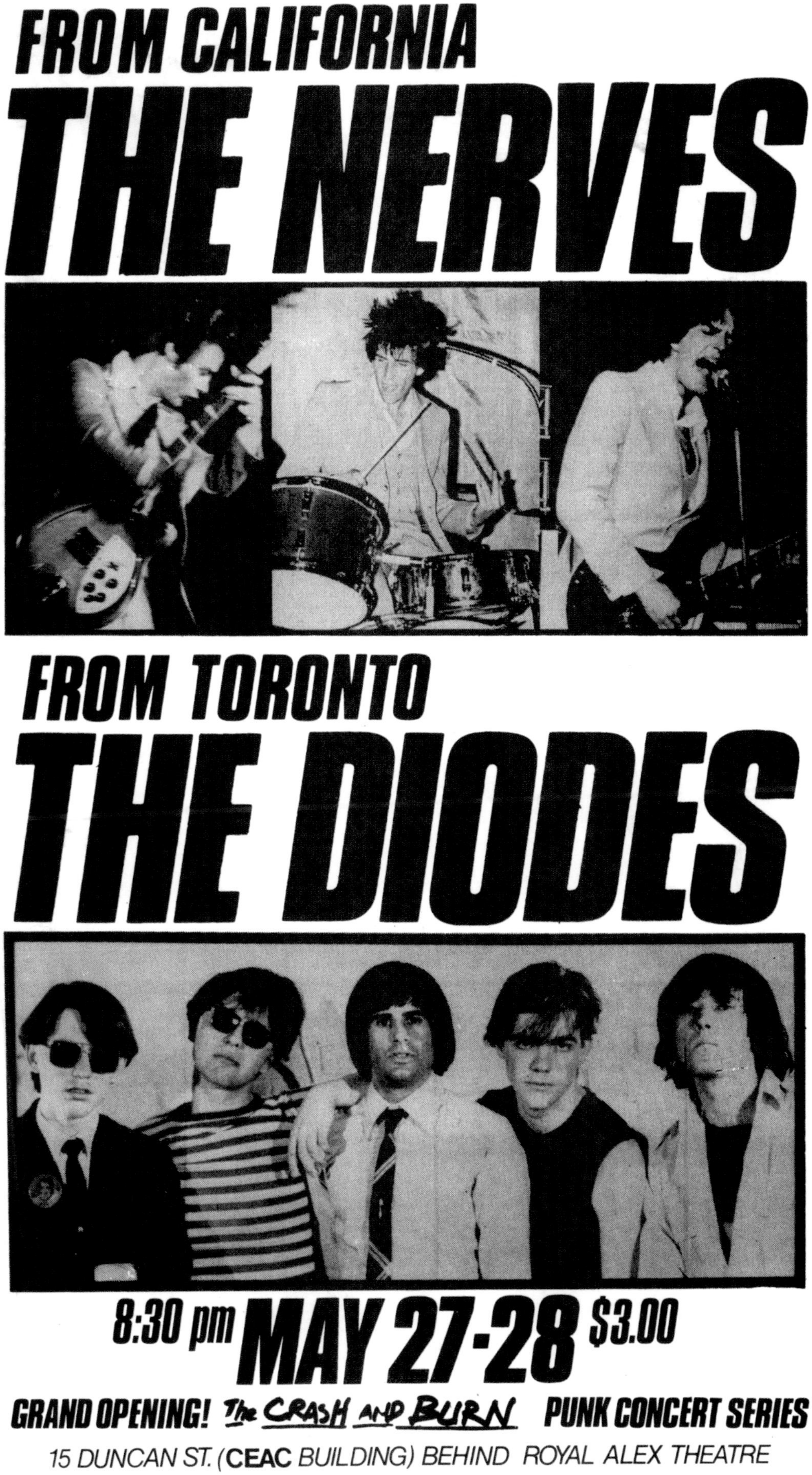
FROM CALIFORNIA
THE NERVES
FROM TORONTO
THE DIODES
8:30 pm MAY 27-28 $3.00
GRAND OPENING! The CRASH AND BURN PUNK CONCERT SERIES
15 DUNCAN ST. (CEAC BUILDING) BEHIND ROYAL ALEX THEATRE

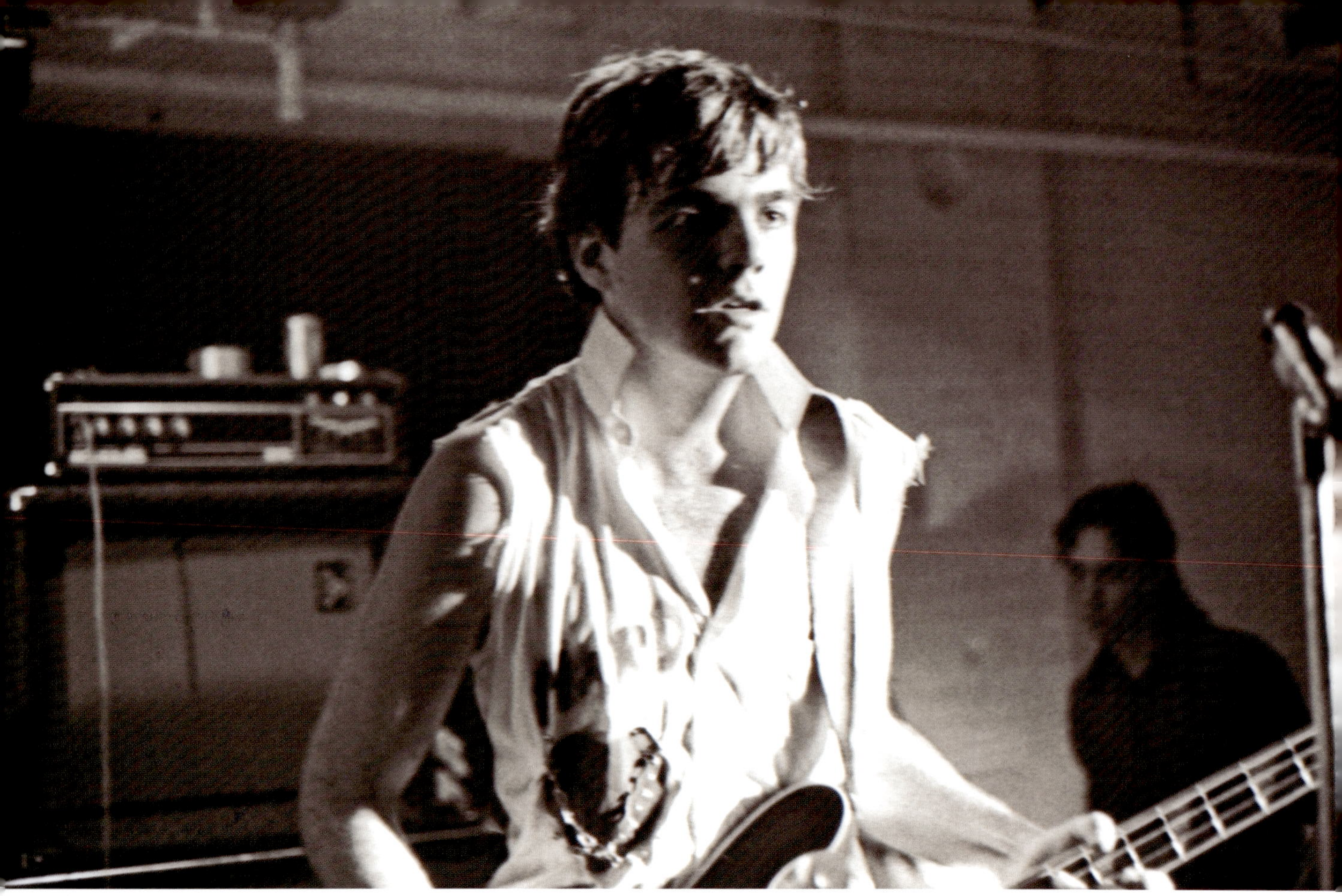

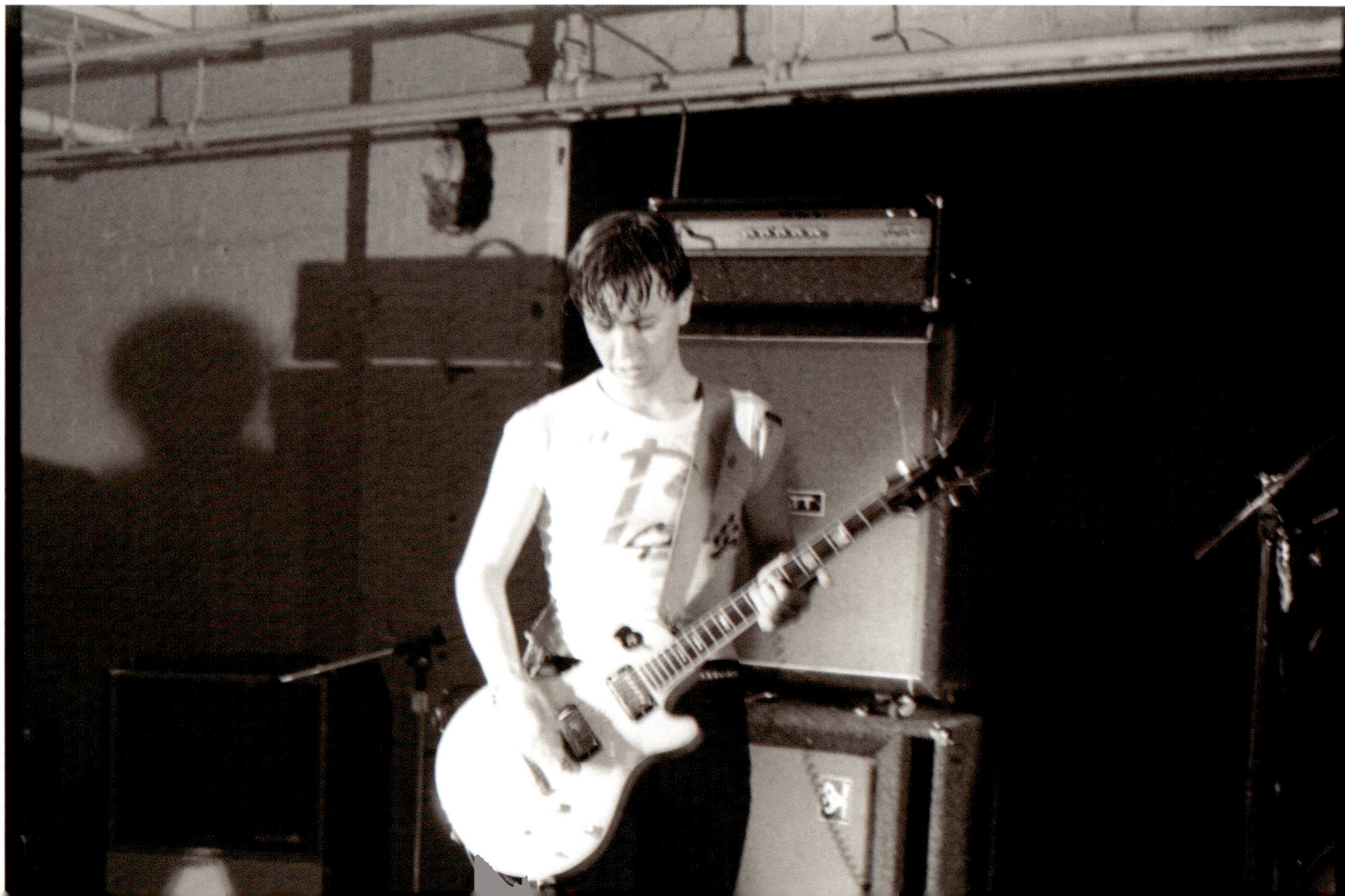

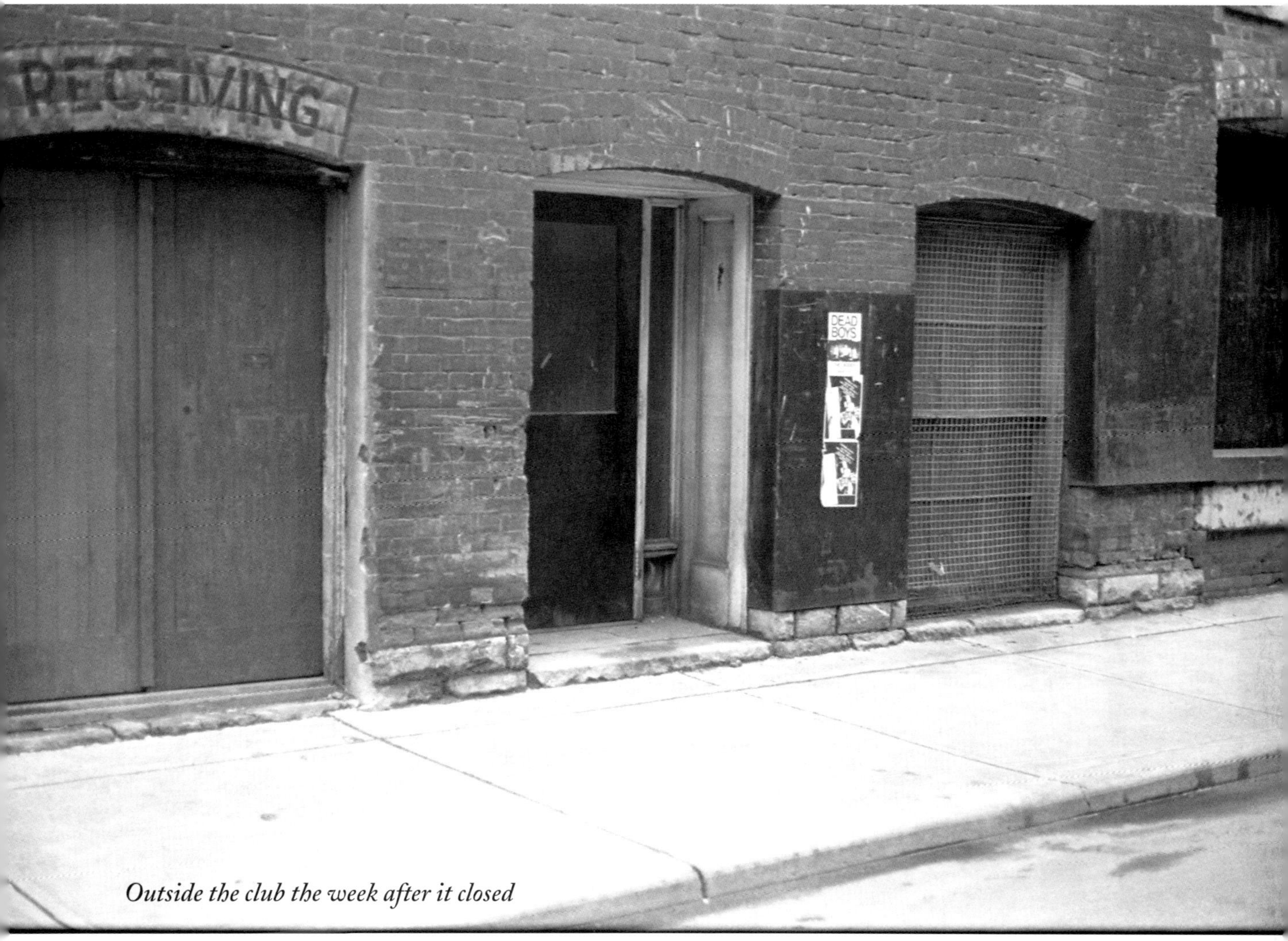

Outside the club the week after it closed

I took the New York Dolls patch I'd needlepointed off the back of my navy corduroy jacket and replaced it with a new patch I stitched that read "DIODES DIODES DIODES." The Viletones were more seemingly dangerous and cool to like, so I embraced The Diodes as a minor act of rebellion against the local hierarchies being established, it being expected for you to choose allegiance to one band or the other. While the Viletones clearly loved Teenage Head (even doing their song "Disgusteen" for a while) and were allied aesthetically with The Ugly, Steven Leckie would let few opportunities to ridicule The Diodes pass. And I don't recall that The Diodes ever did a show with Teenage Head or the Viletones, rivals even at this scale.

But ambition and diplomacy of The Diodes benefitted everyone as it was them, their manager Ralph Alfonso and the friends they rallied who created the Crash 'n' Burn series of concerts, and who cleaned the blood and beer off the floors the morning after a show there.

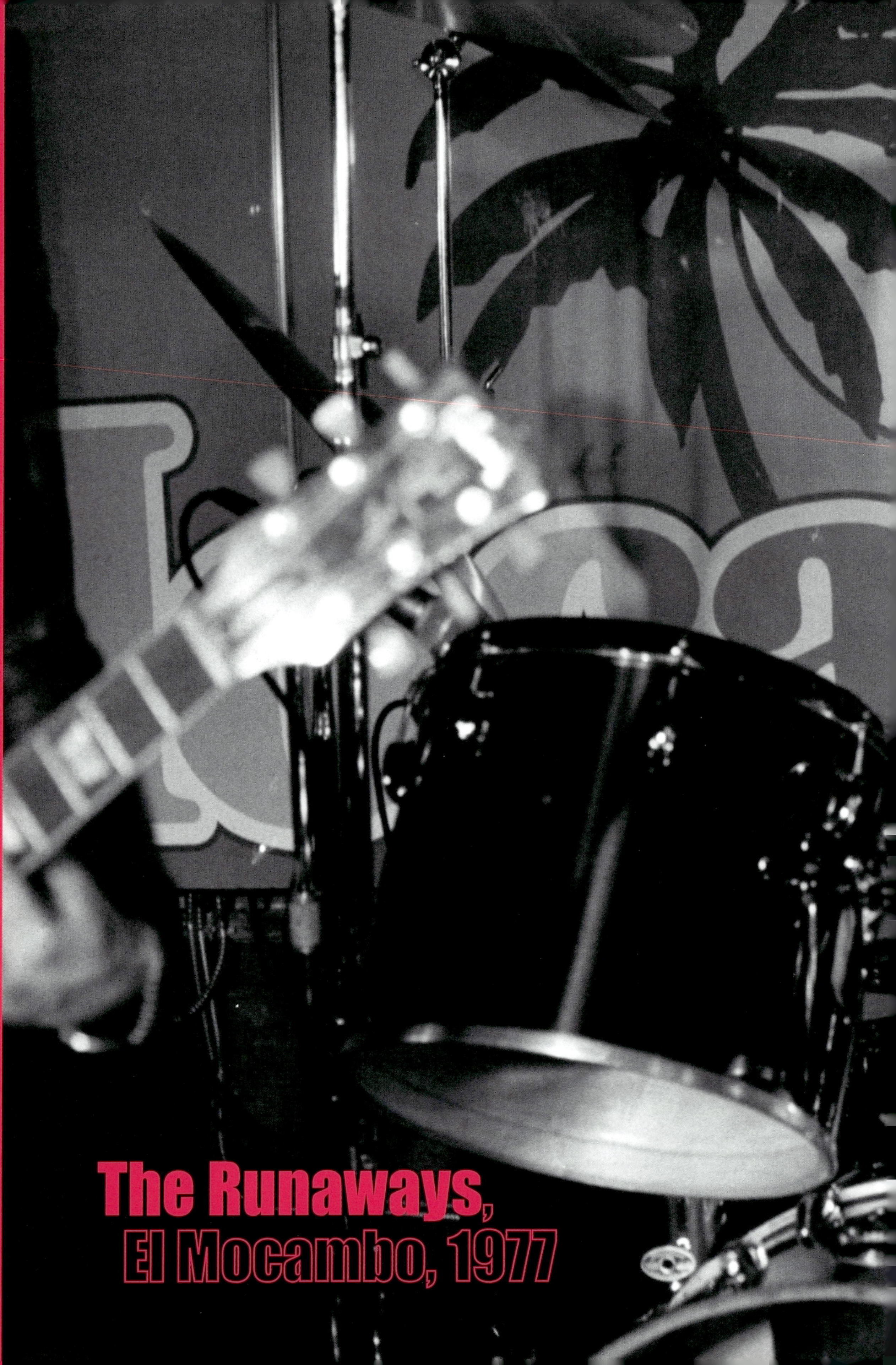

The Runaways,
El Mocambo, 1977

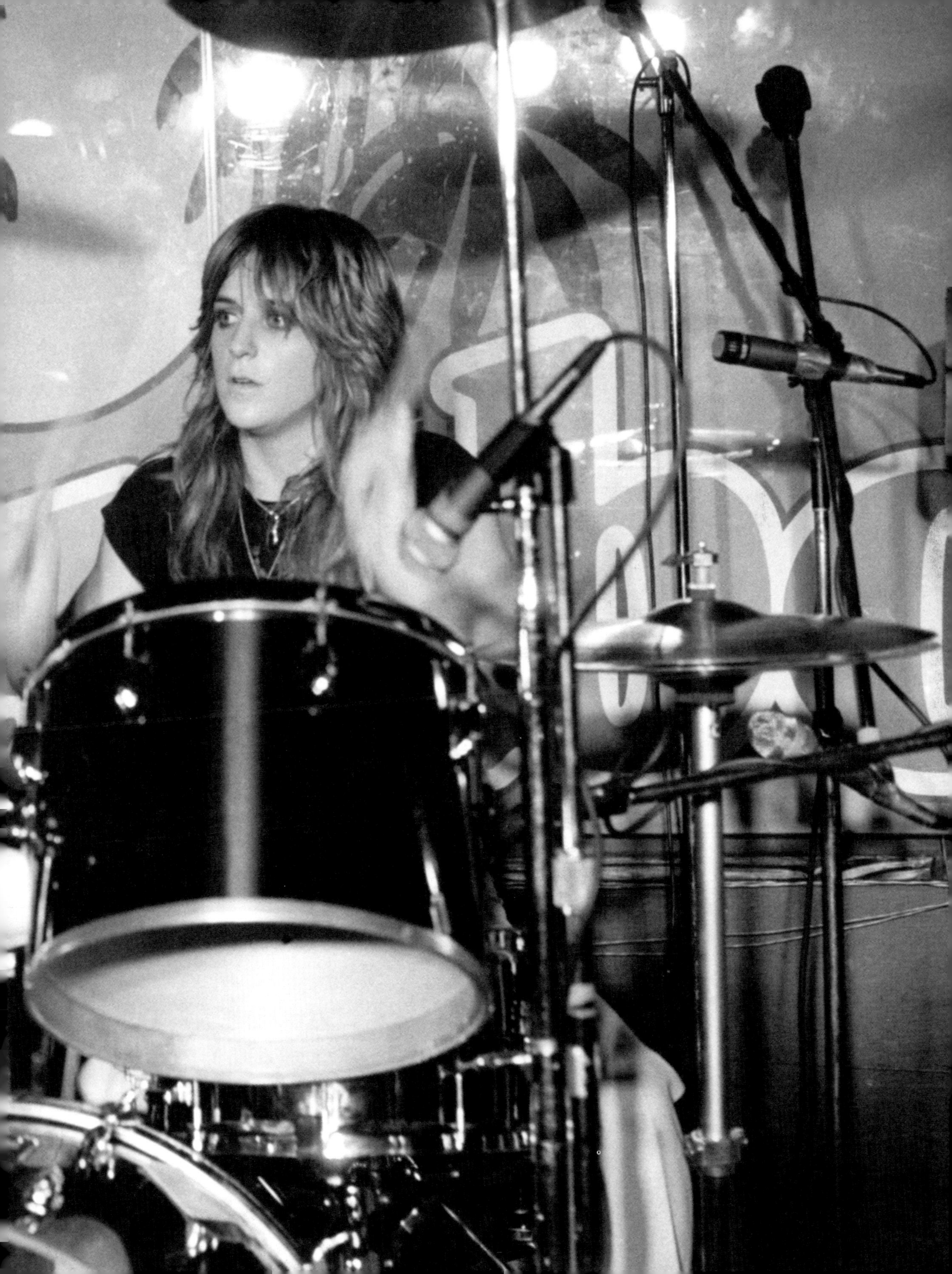

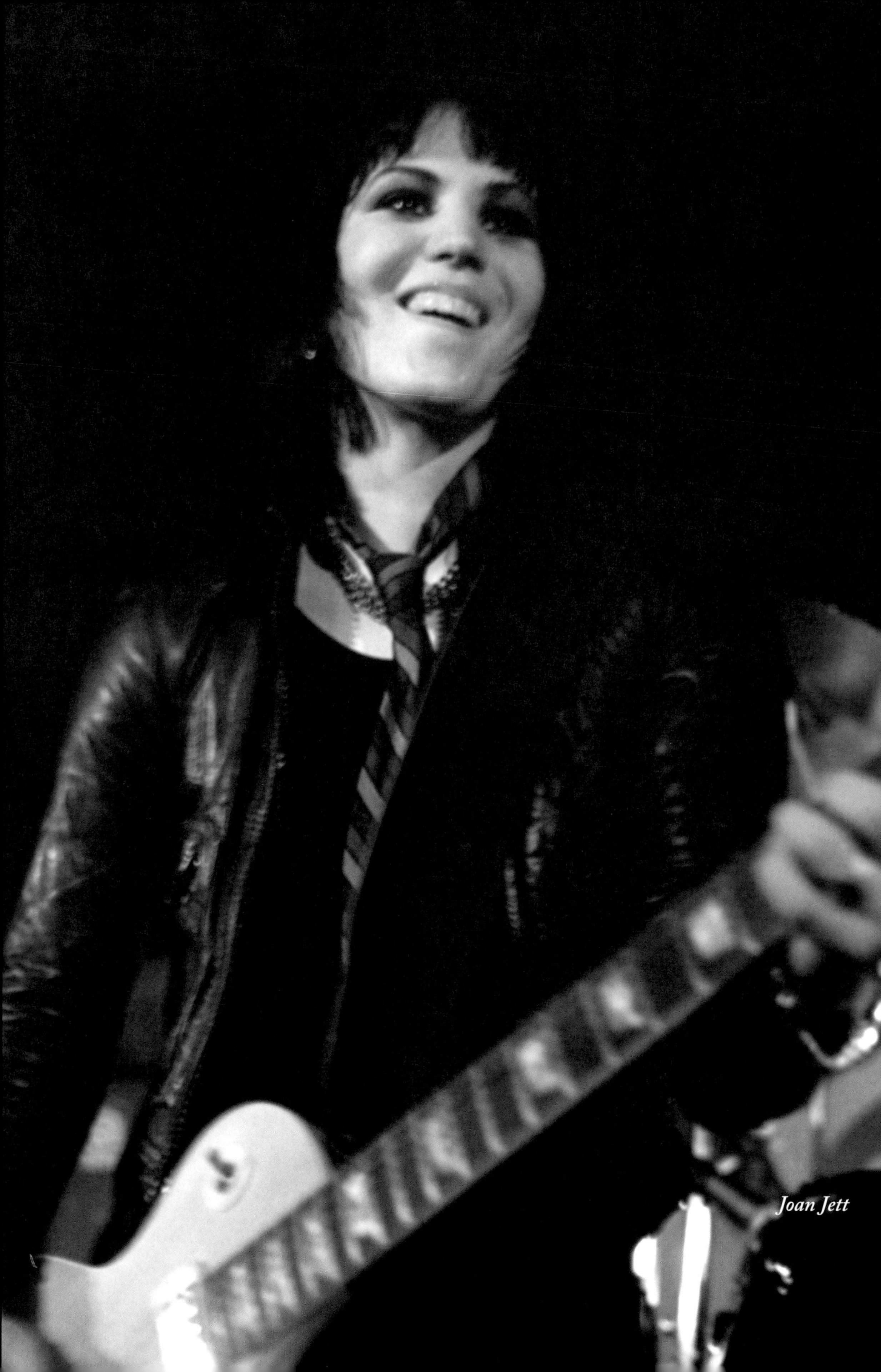

Joan Jett

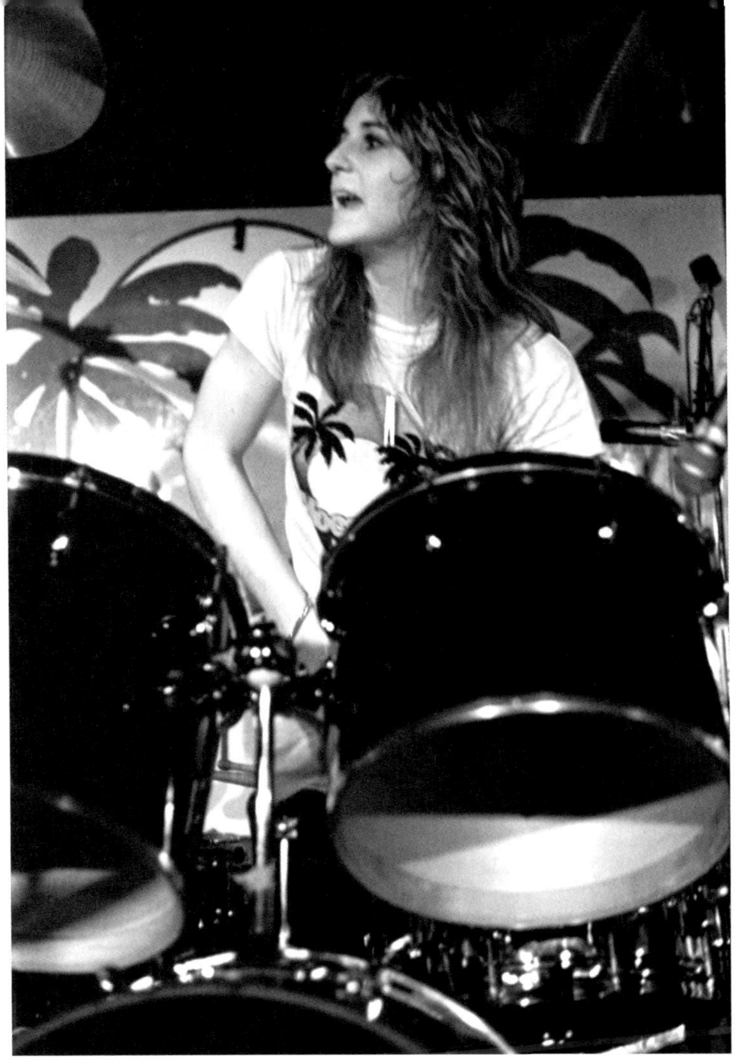

Sandy West

The Runaways were hugely inspirational to me. I loved that not only were they women in a band I loved — at a time when there were almost no all-female bands — but they were almost my age. Their first album came out when I was 14 so I was enthralled that the youngest of them was only 15. Labeled "punk" by some when the definition was still pretty slippery, their bubblegum-meets-metal-glam sound and hot pants rebellion totally appealed. That they were so mocked made me love them even more, and the argument that they couldn't play their instruments was obviously a misogynist slight never leveled at all-male bands. An older friend of mine blew up when I told him I thought The Runaways' *Live in Japan* album was a better and more relevant record than The Who's *Live at Leeds*, something I still believe today.

Seemingly unaware that they were not doing two shows but rather two sets, The Runaways returned to the stage and played the same set as their first, with almost the same stage patter.

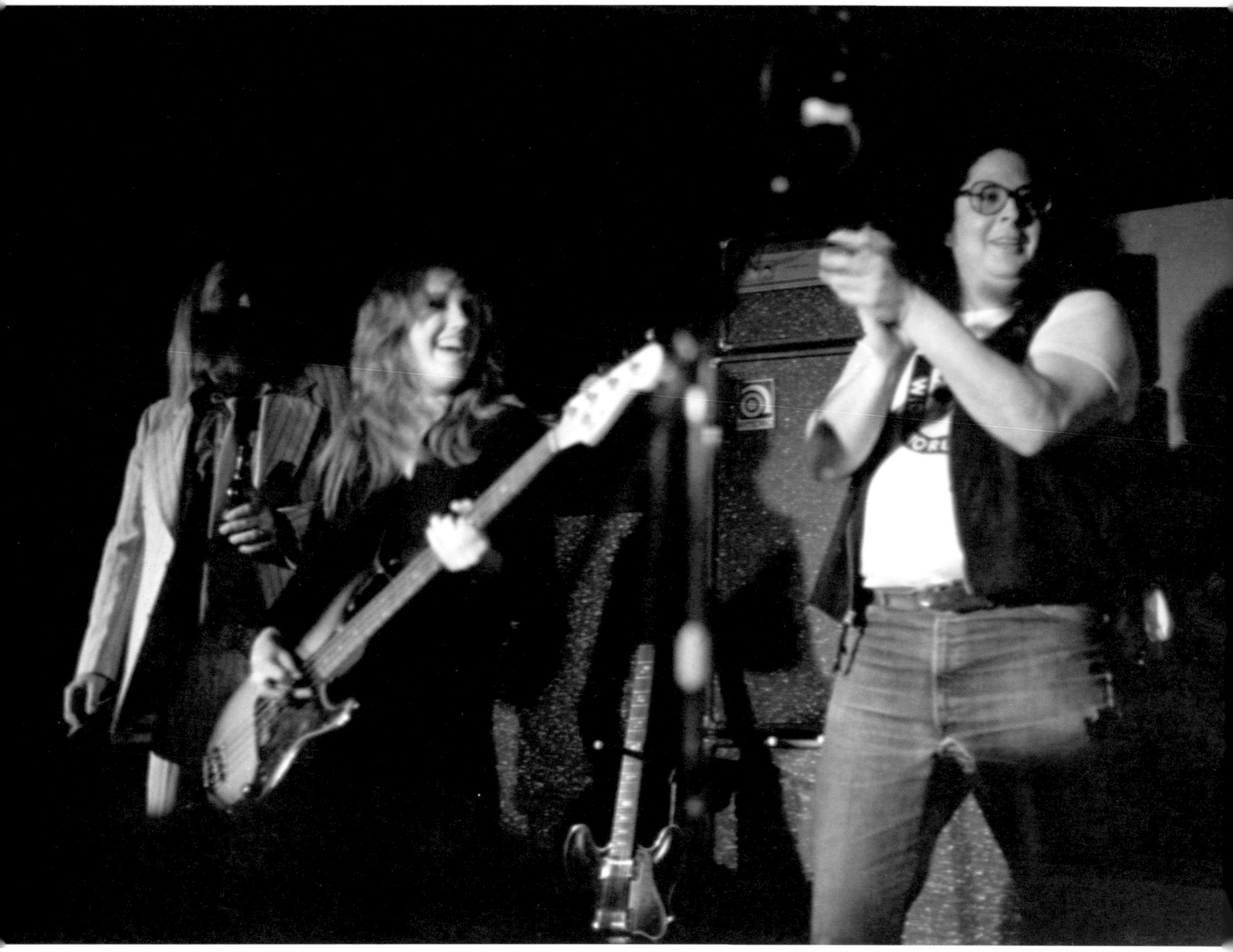

Joan and Sandy's butch-femme personas are now easily read as dyke, but then I believed that no good bands could be queer. That half the band was lesbian was clearly something I unconsciously recognized and which endeared them to me even more.

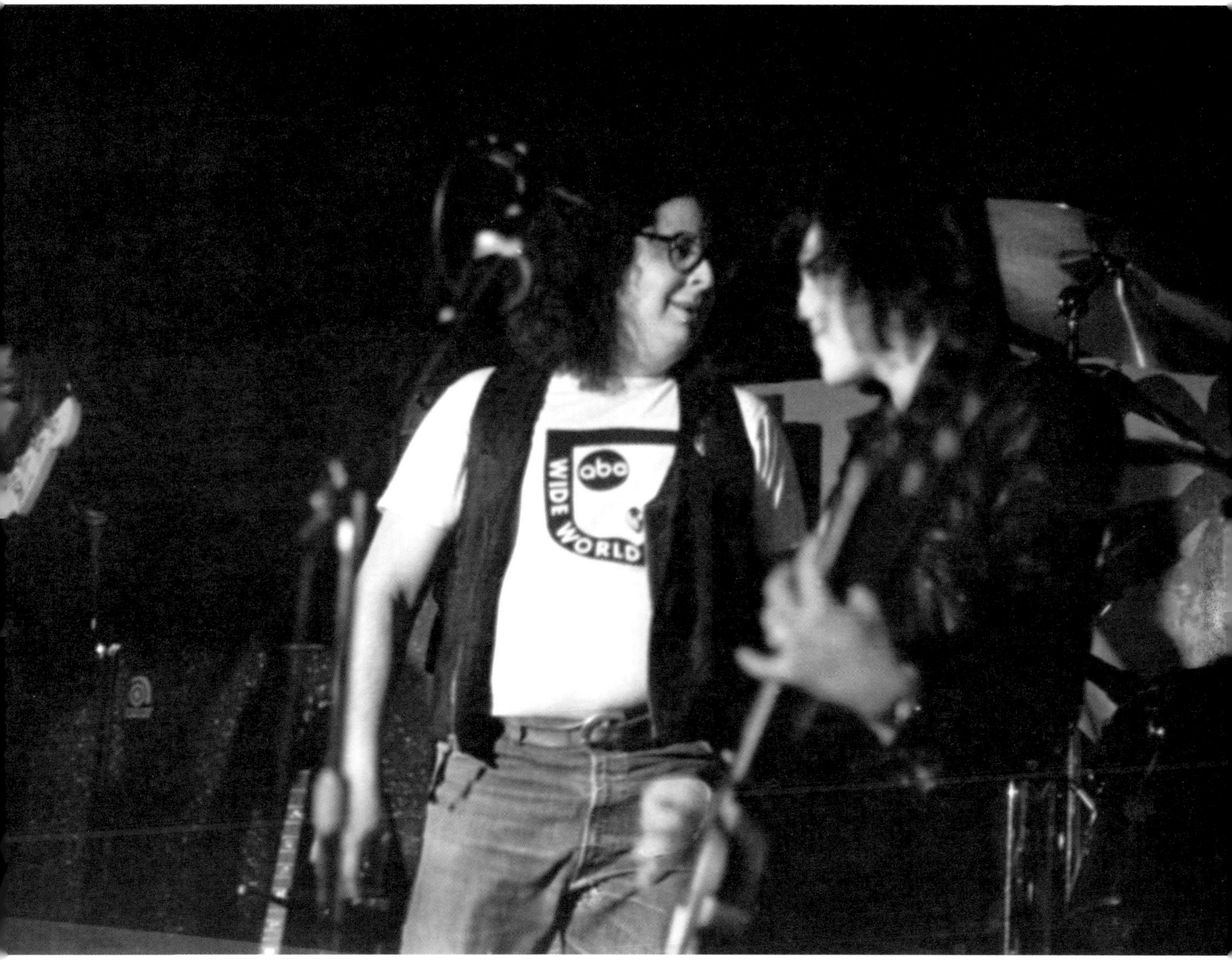

Howard "Eddie" Kaylan, Vicki Blue, Mark "Flo" Volman, Joan Jett

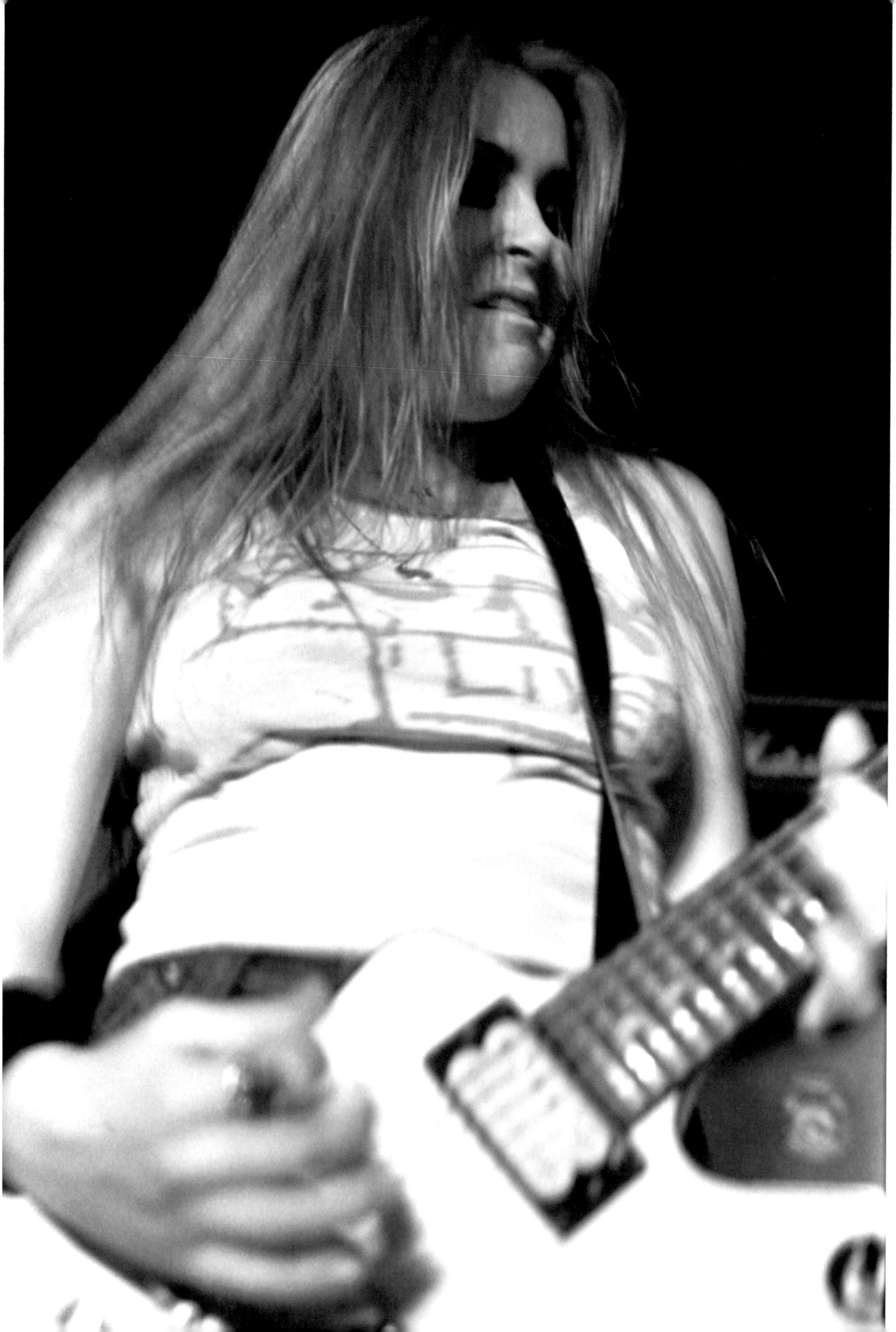

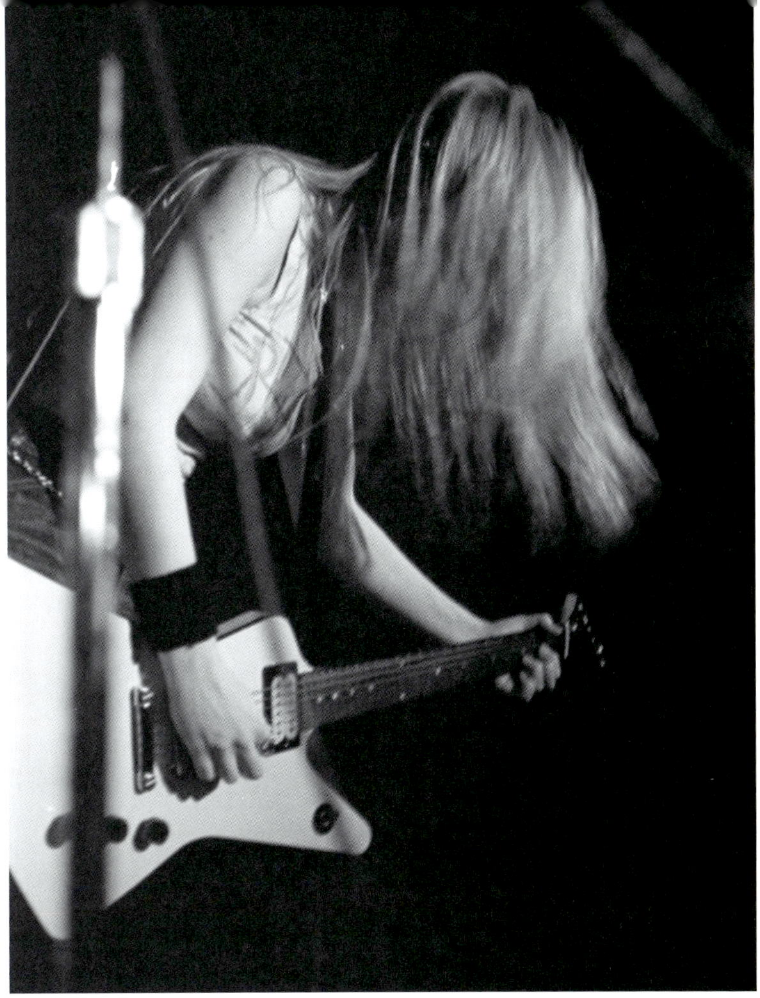

Lita Ford

Lita's pick

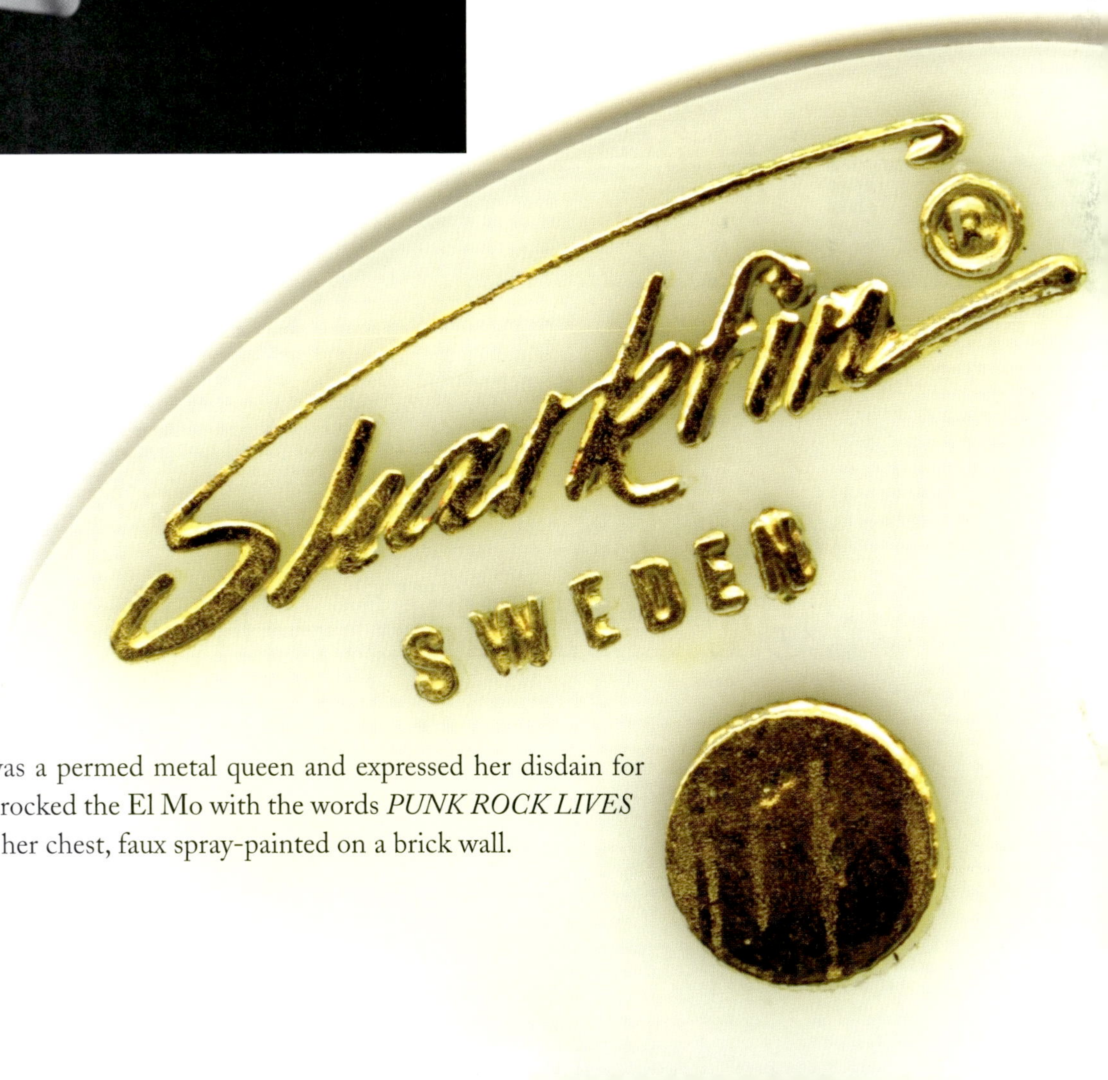

Before she was a permed metal queen and expressed her disdain for punk, Lita Ford rocked the El Mo with the words *PUNK ROCK LIVES* stretched across her chest, faux spray-painted on a brick wall.

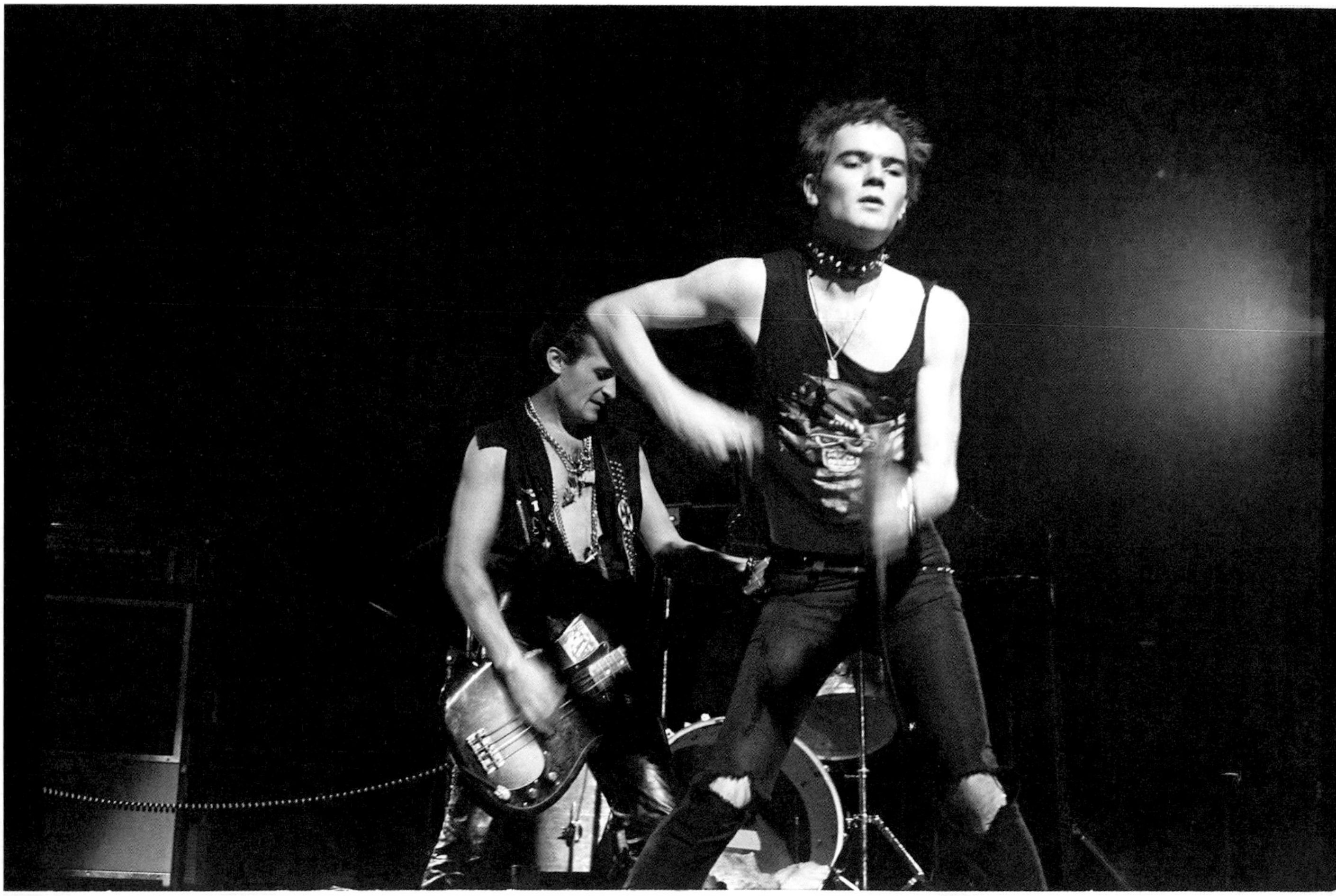

Chris Haight, Steven Leckie

Viletones, New Yorker Theatre, 1977

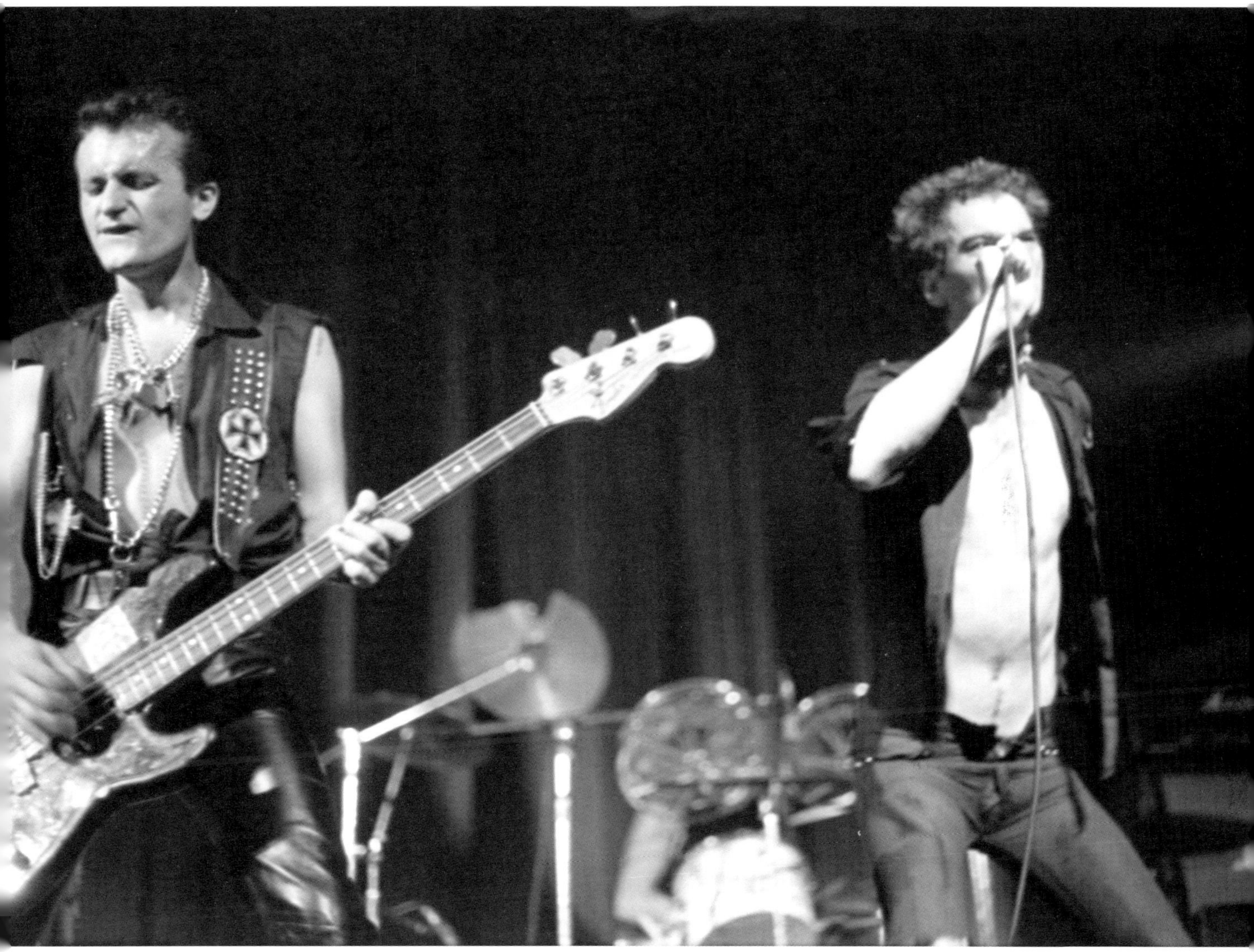

Maybe they had something to prove the night they opened for The Dead Boys at the New Yorker, one of a couple of shows pictured here, but the Viletones were more together than usual. This time no one drunkenly fell over the drum kit. Opening for the Ramones' second stint at the New Yorker, Dead Boys had shocked me with blisteringly loud guitars and Stiv acting out the most crazed Iggy interpretation. Months later they were the headliner and the Viletones could not be outdone by out-of-towners. I don't know that the Viletones had even opened for anyone else at this point — they were top-billed from day one.

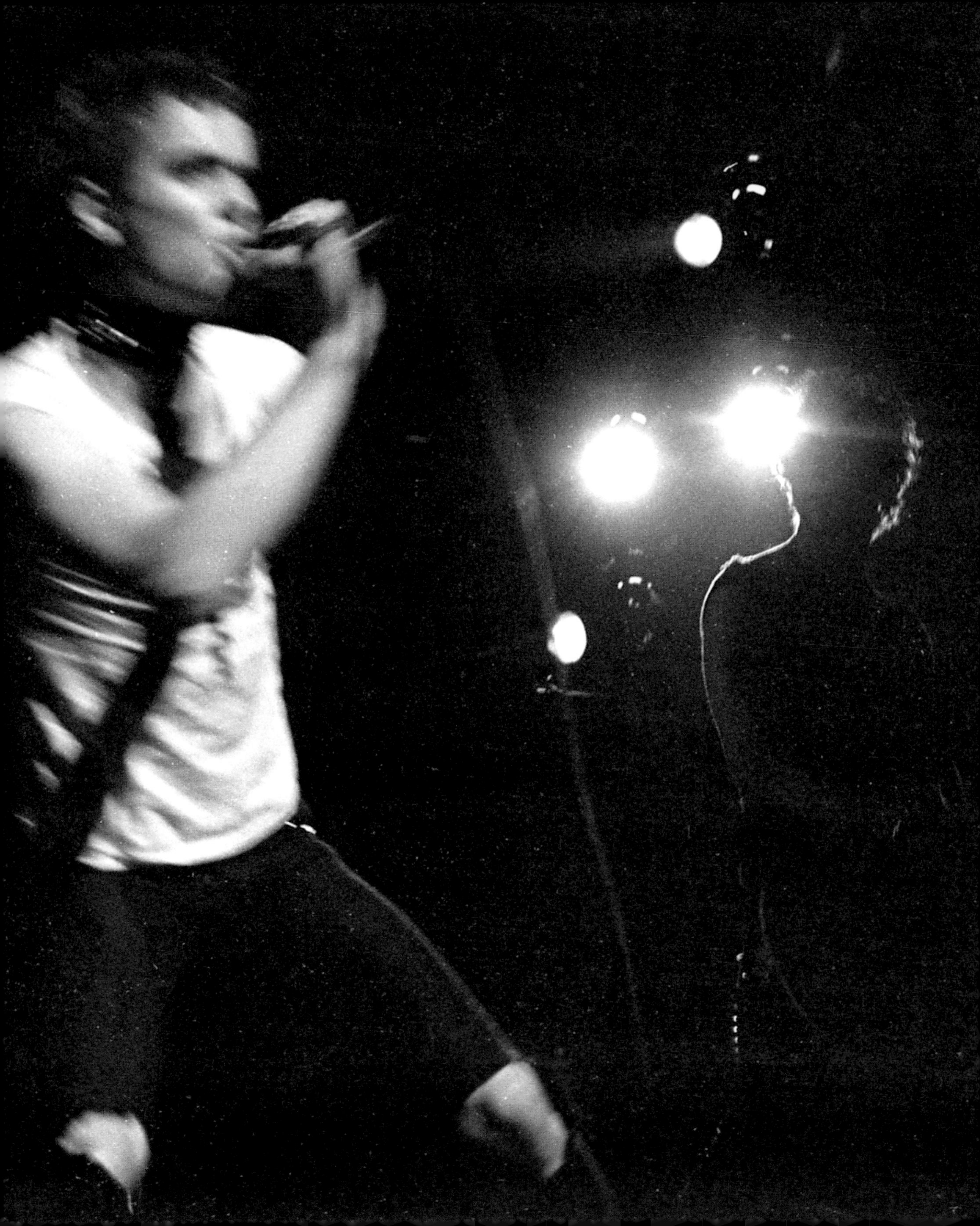

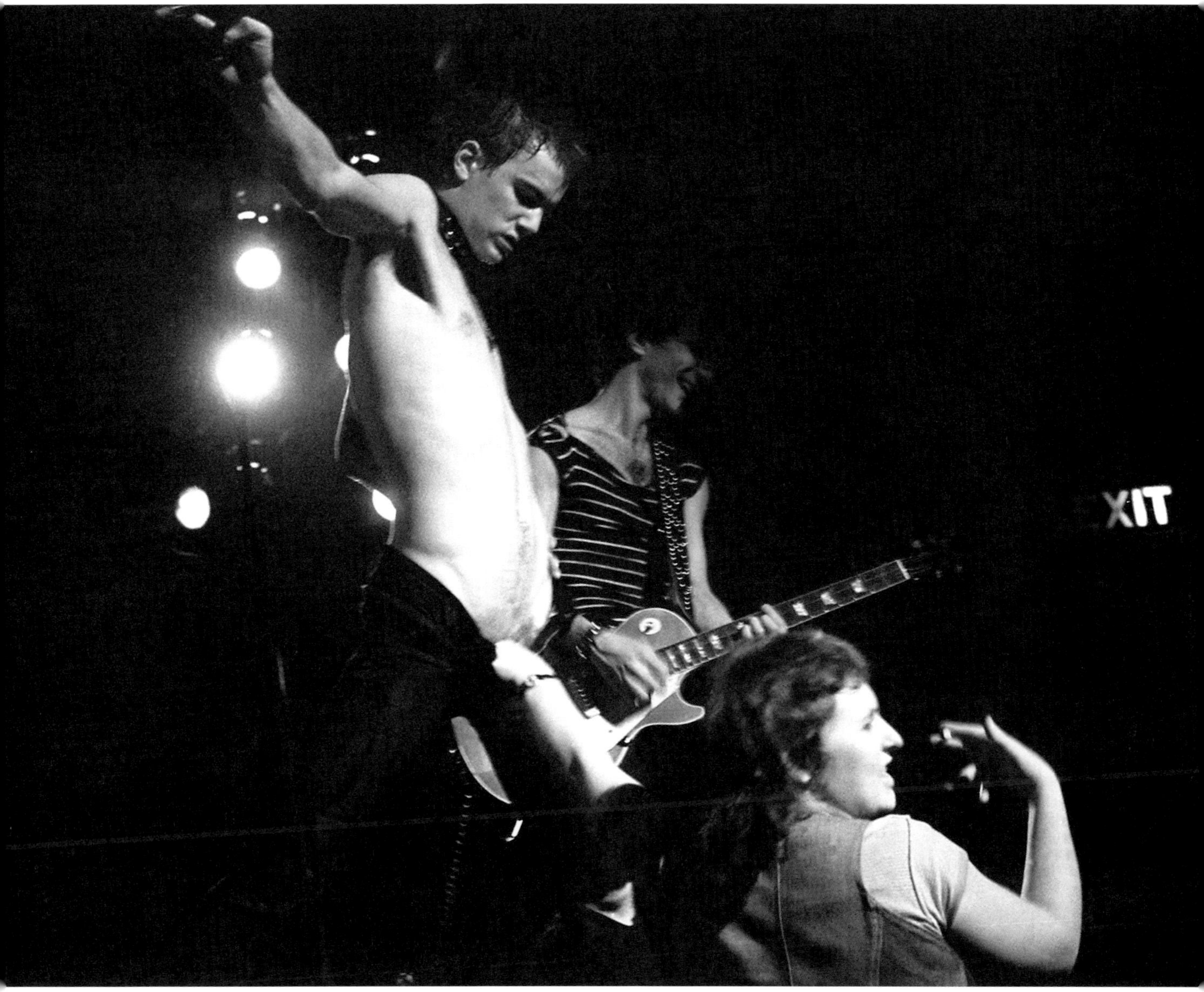

Steven Leckie, Freddy Pompeii, Dr. Bourque

Heckling the band, The Curse's Anna "Dr." Bourque came down to the front and Leckie stood, legs spread, at the edge of the stage thrusting his crotch out to her, daring her to do something with it. She undid his pants, looking back at her friends and laughing as if to ask "Should I?" before taking Leckie's cock out, jacking it a bit and then stuffing it back in his pants as the rest of the band looked on, laughing at her audacity.

Steven Leckie, Freddy Pompeii

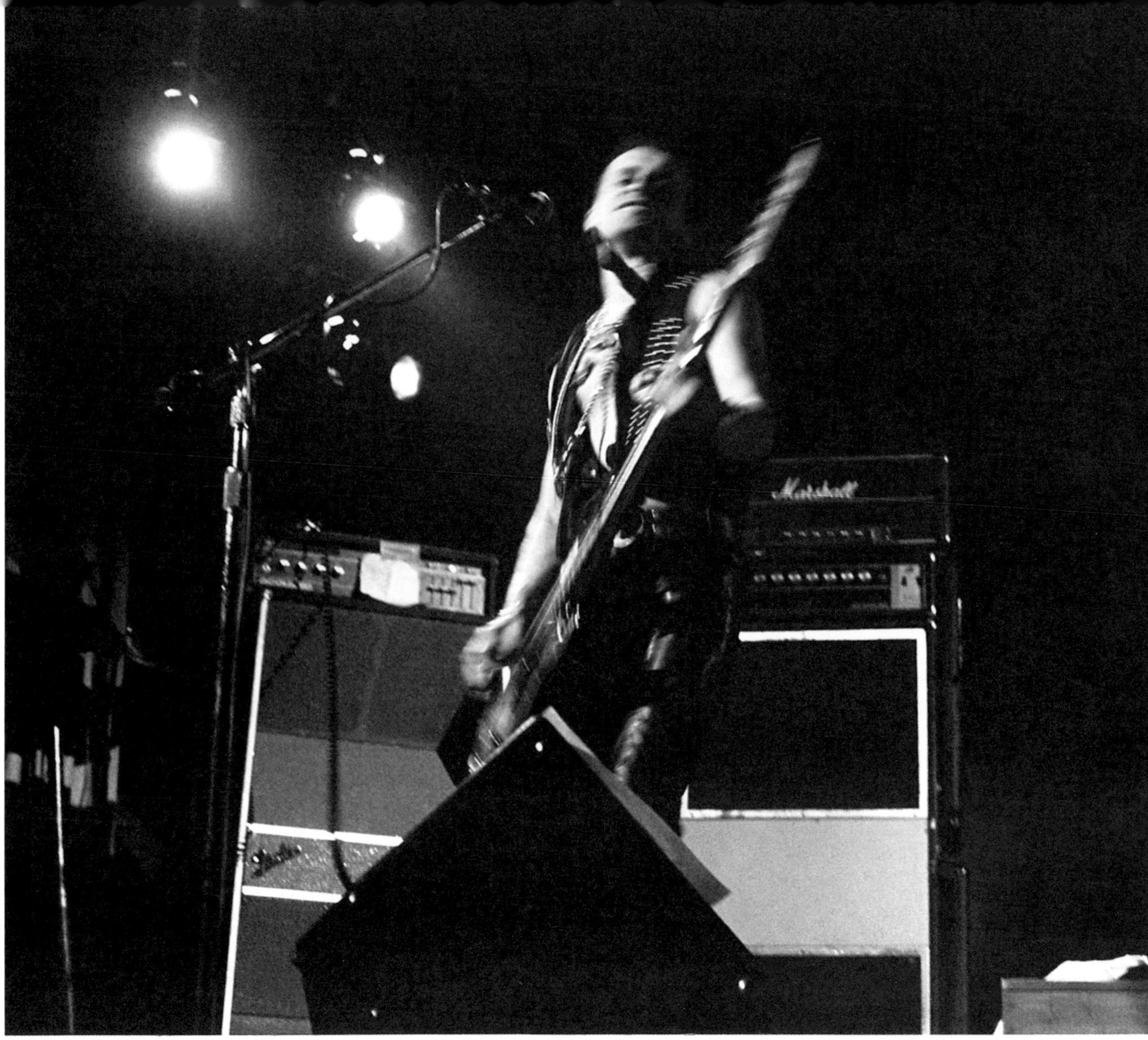

Chris Haight

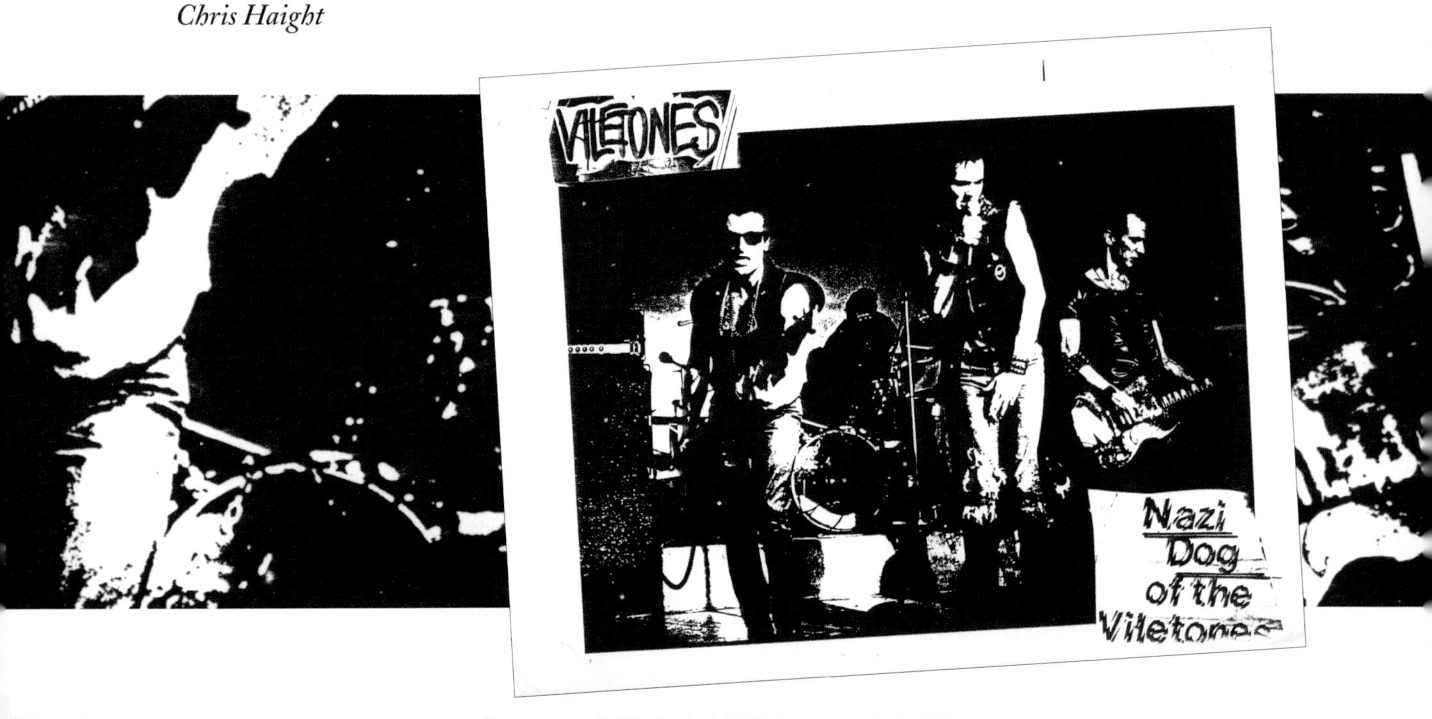

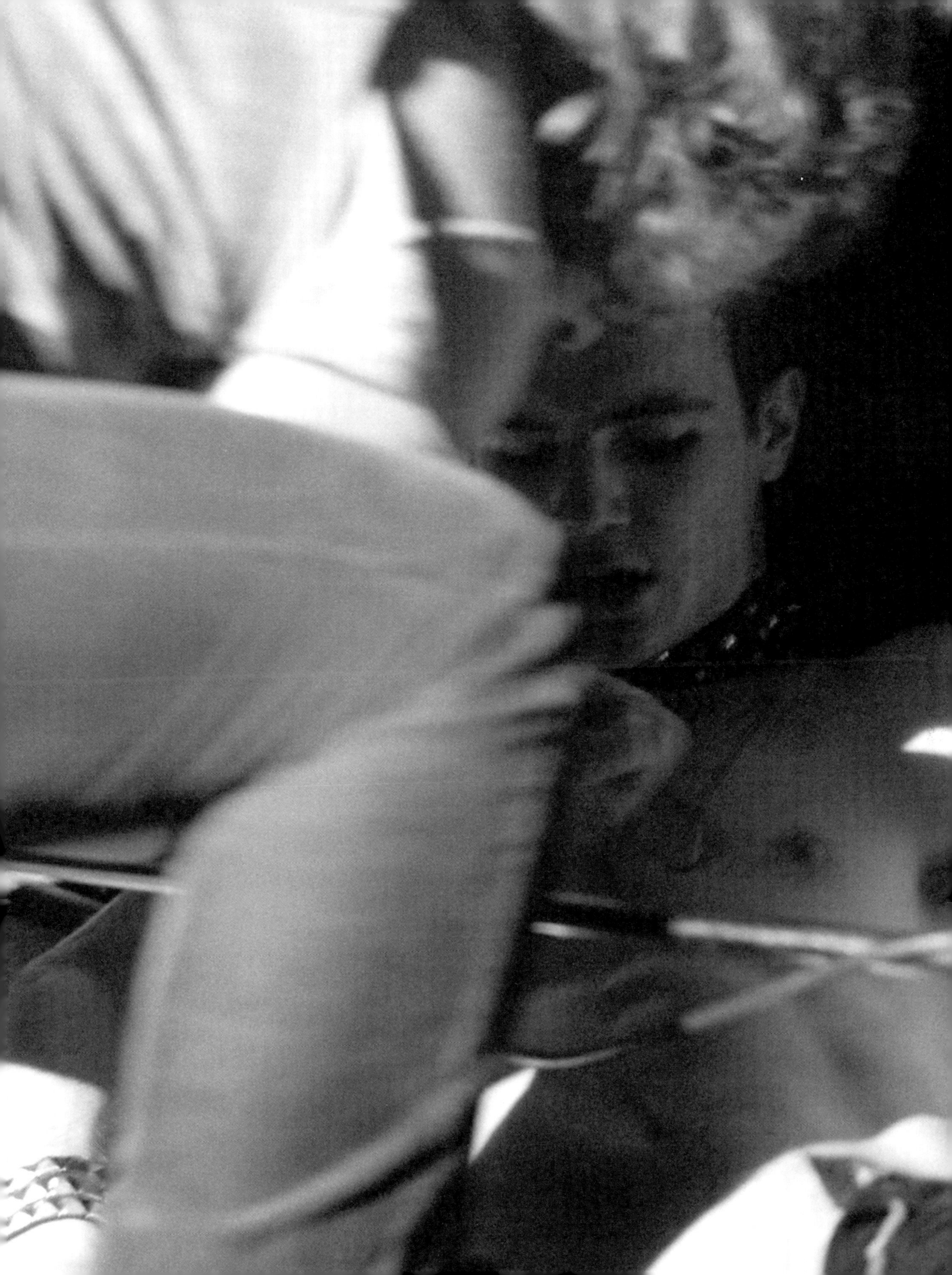

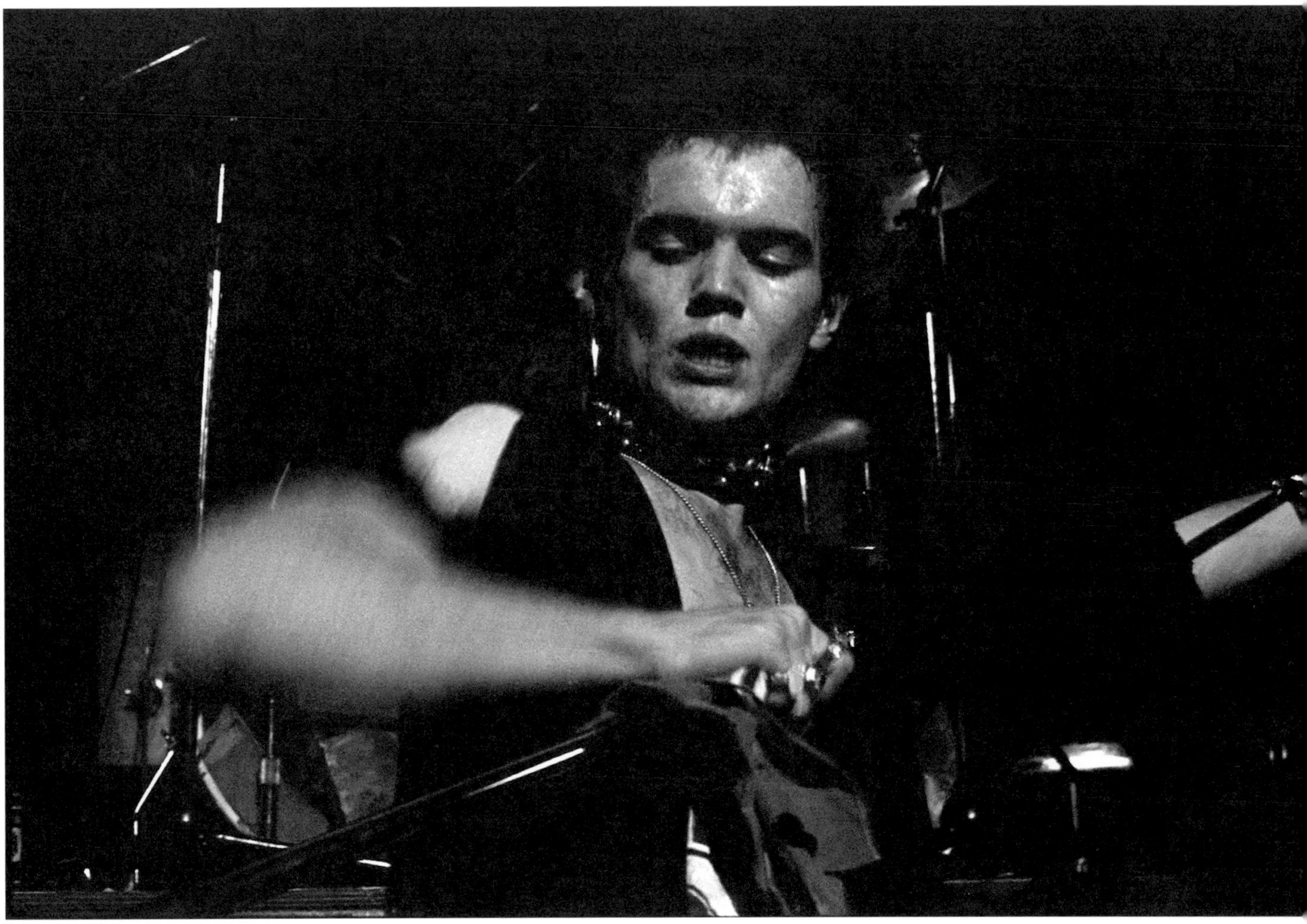

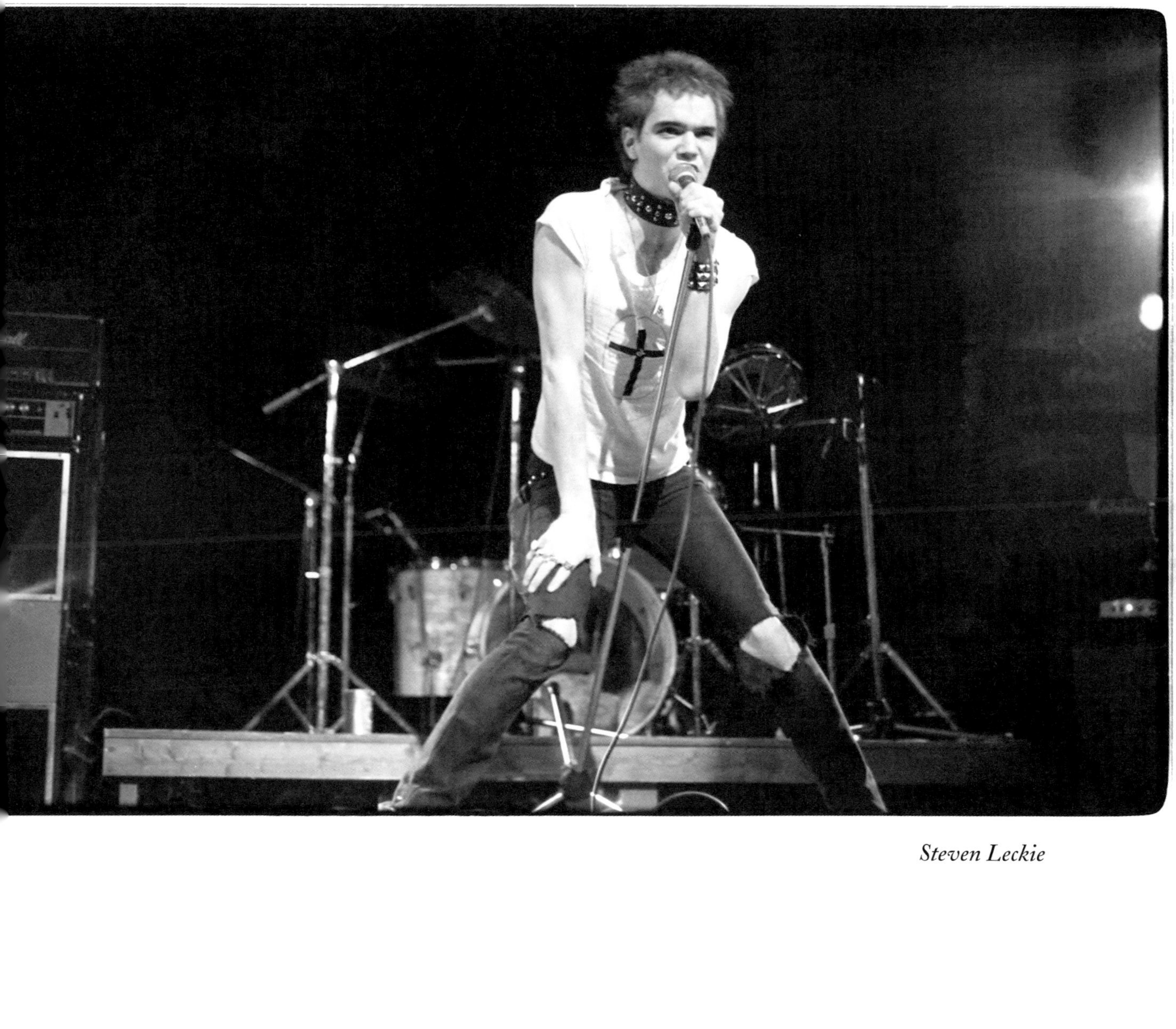

Steven Leckie

Dead Boys,
New Yorker Theatre, 1977

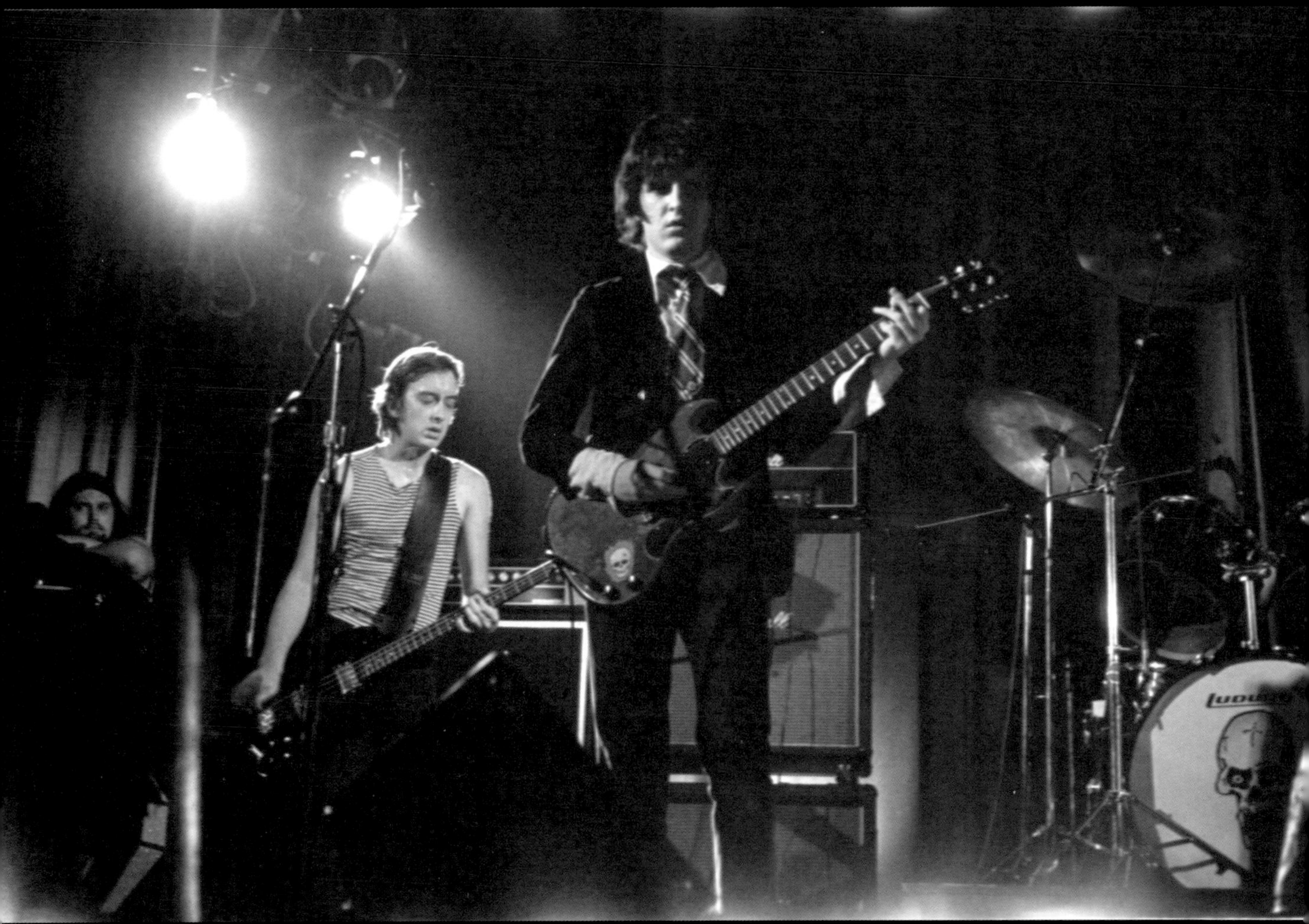

unknown, Jeff Magnum, Jimmy Zero, Johnny Blitz

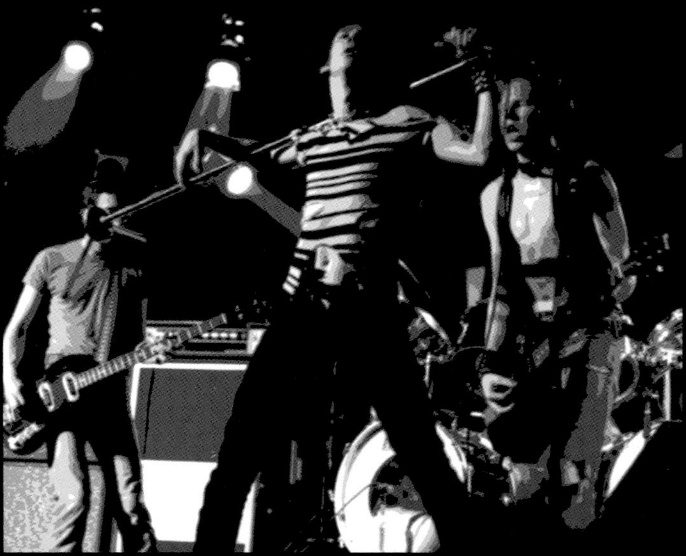

Jeff Magnum, Stiv Bators, Cheetah Chrome

Jimmy Zero, Stiv Bators

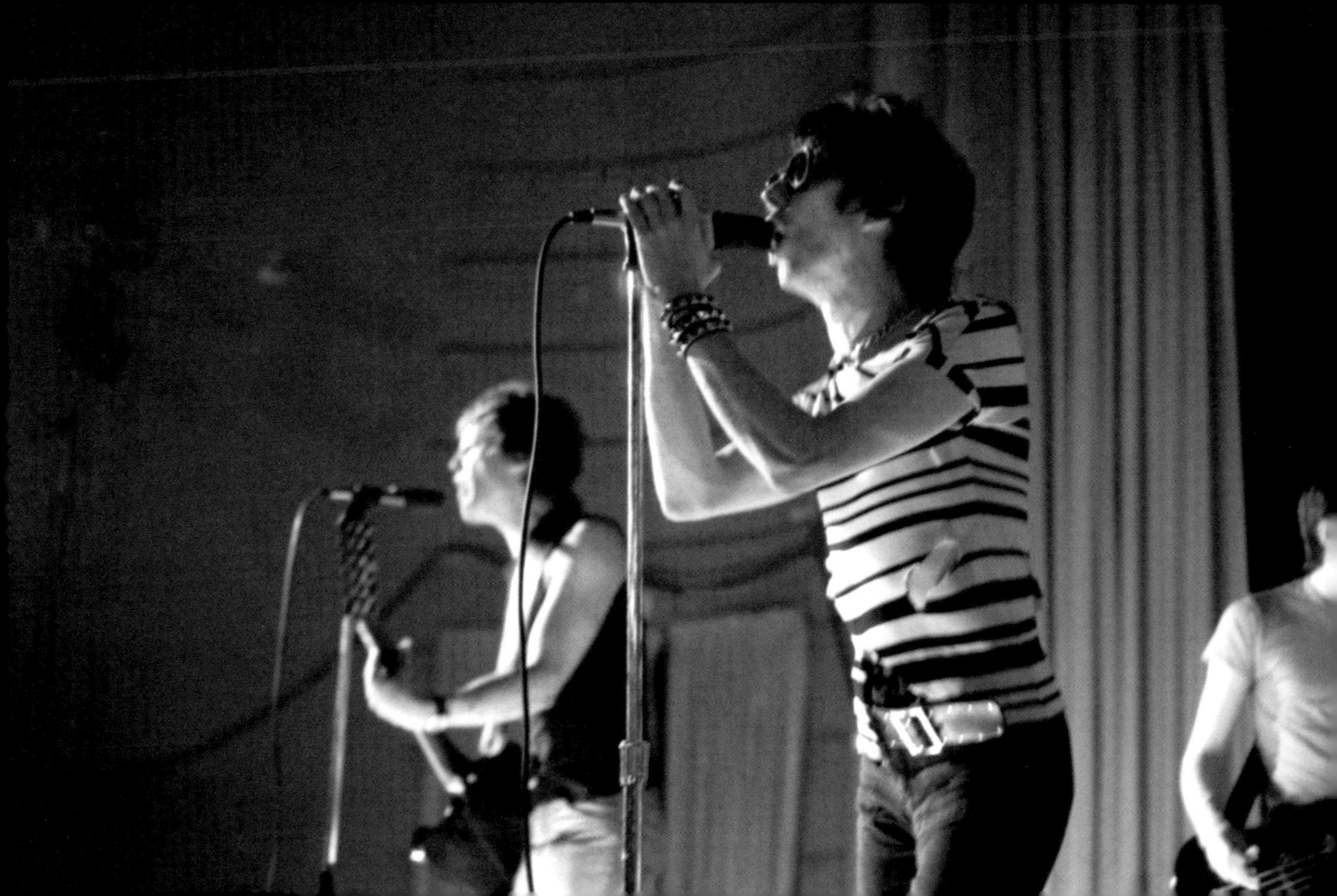

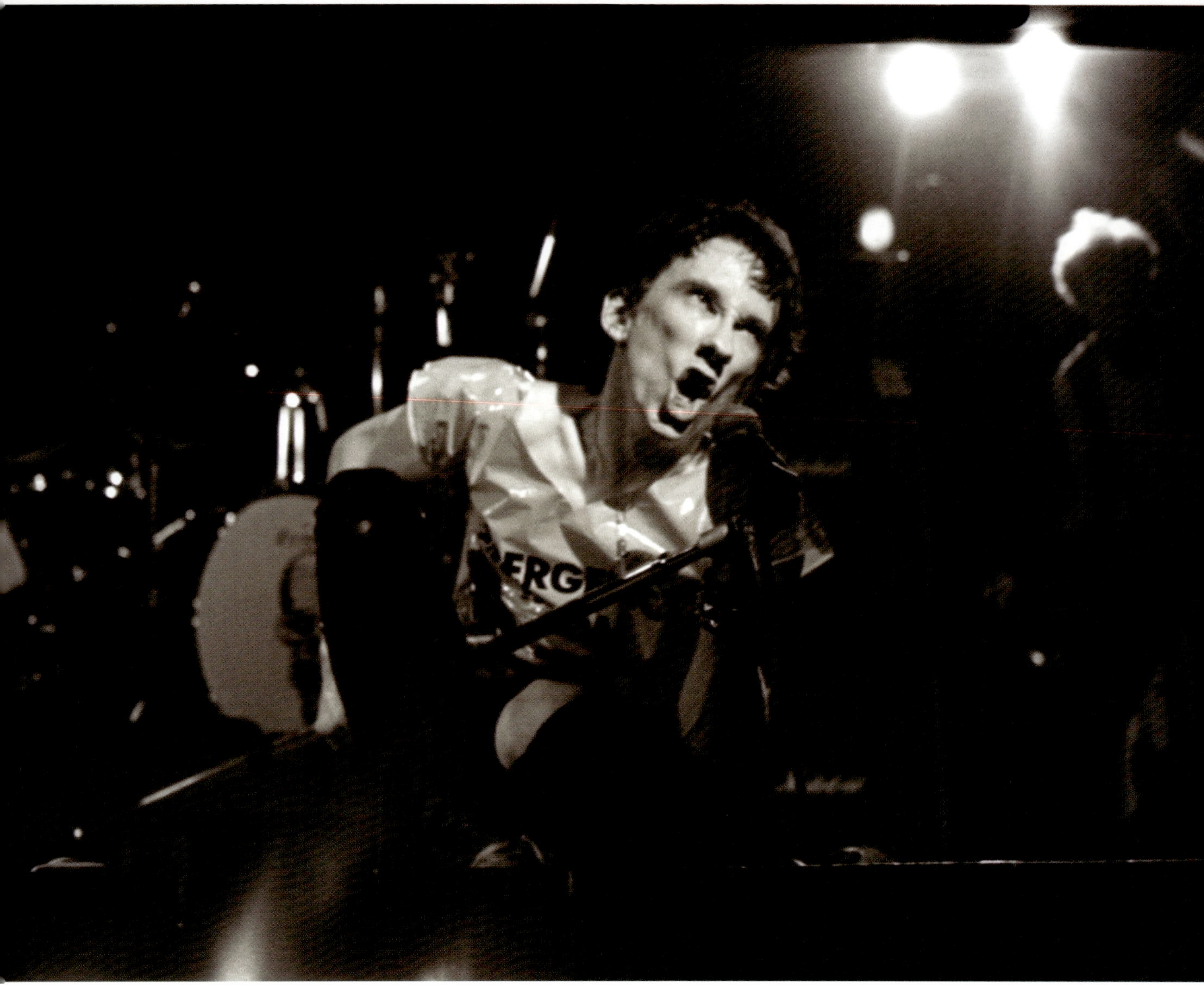

Stiv Bators

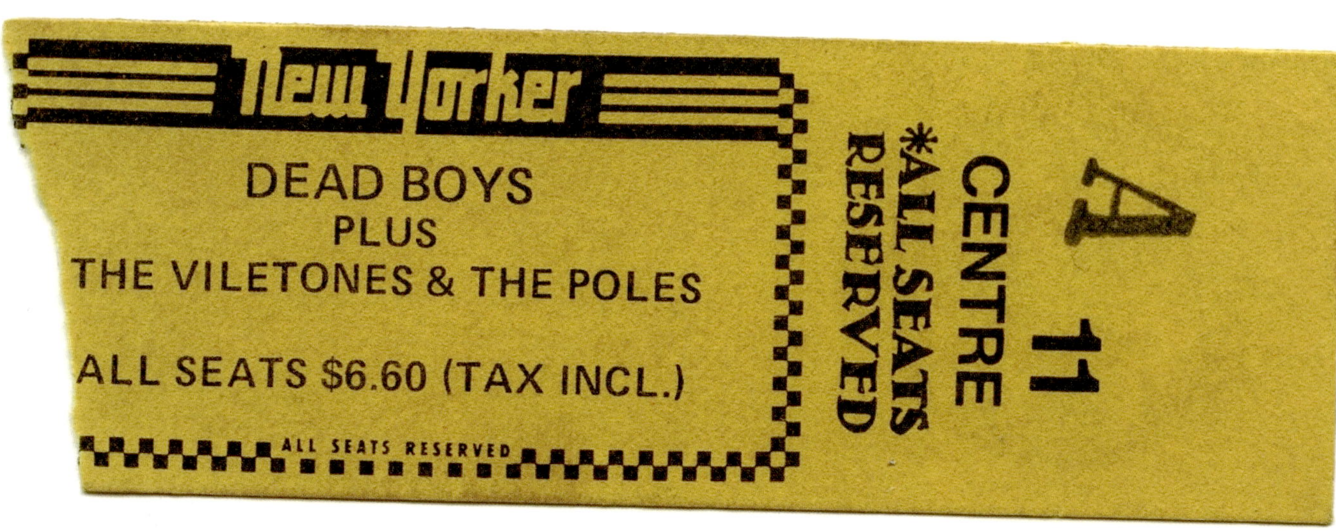
New Yorker
DEAD BOYS
PLUS
THE VILETONES & THE POLES
ALL SEATS $6.60 (TAX INCL.)
ALL SEATS RESERVED
*ALL SEATS RESERVED
CENTRE
A
11

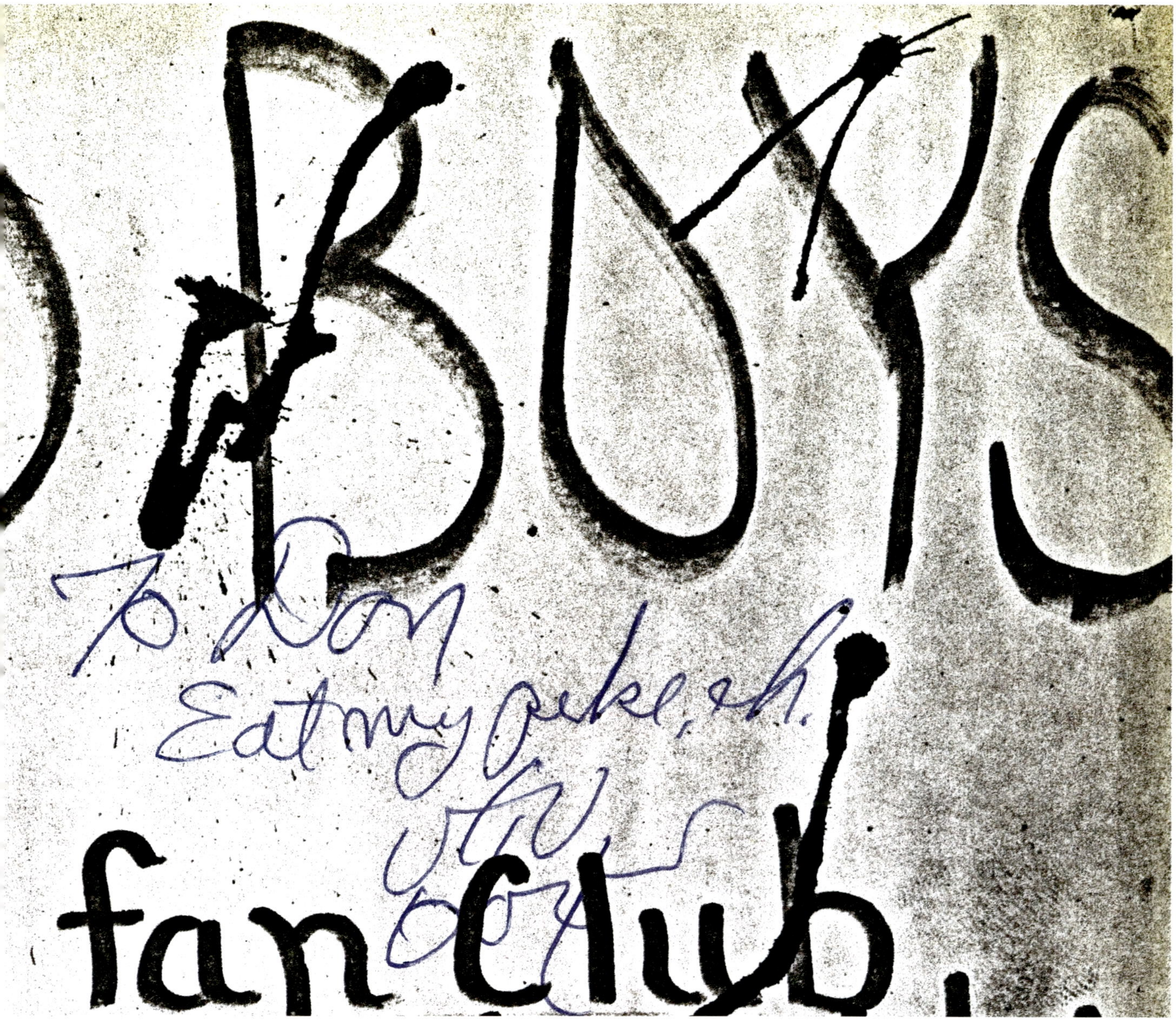

These images are from two shows: Dead Boys opening for the Ramones' second New Yorker appearance, and their own headlining show months later. Stiv took the stage wearing a "shirt" he'd made by cutting arm holes in a red plastic bag used for patients' possessions, with "EMERGENCY ROOM" printed on it in large letters. I thought it was cute that Stiv (from Ohio) had Canadianized his autograph to me on the fan club application form they were passing out, signing it "Eat my puke, eh." At this point I had never heard a band louder than The Dead Boys, and I still believed that stage personas were representative of what artists were really like as people. As they hung around after the show, I was taken aback at how chatty and friendly these monsters seemed.

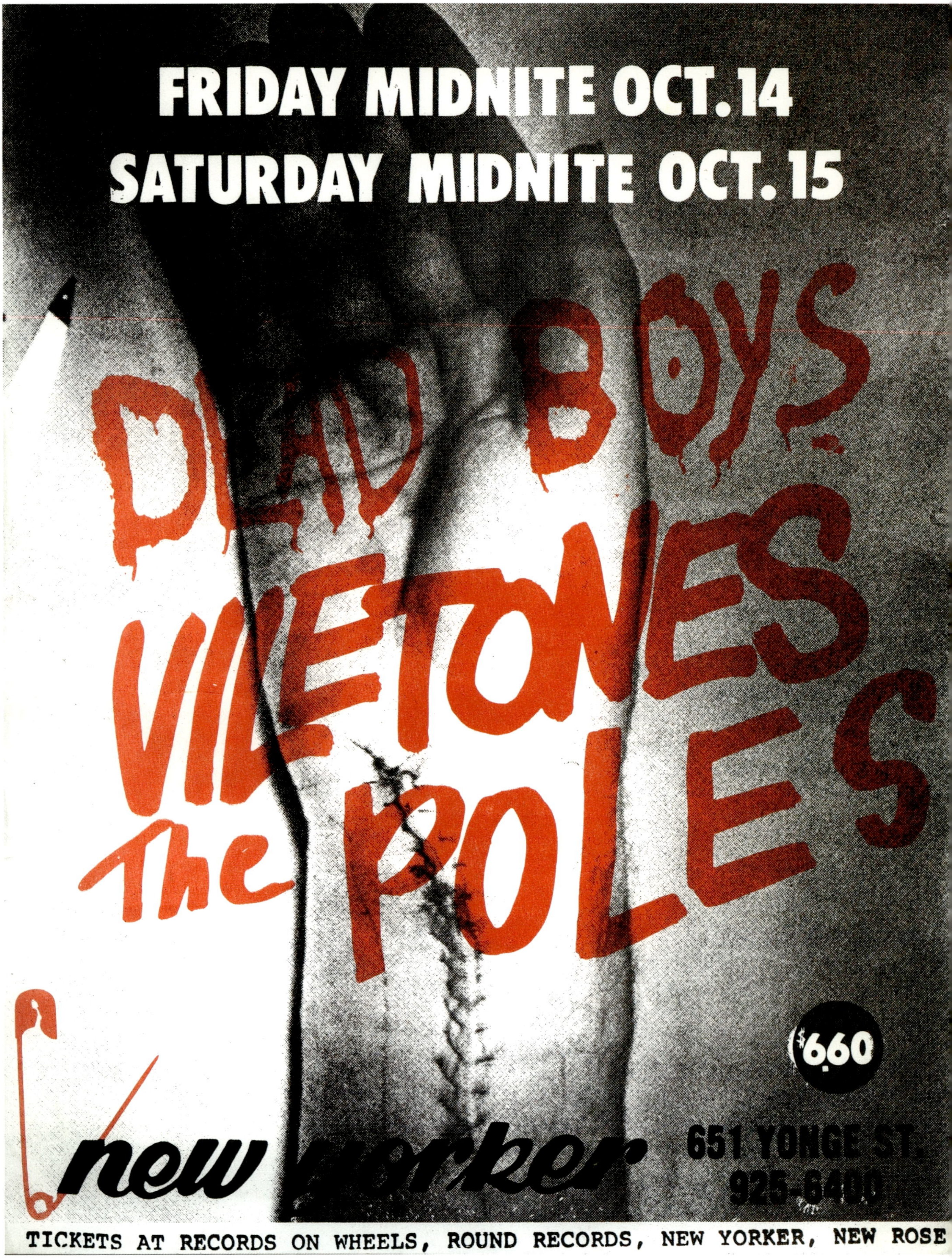
FRIDAY MIDNITE OCT. 14
SATURDAY MIDNITE OCT. 15
DEAD BOYS
VILETONES
The POLES
$6.60
new yorker
651 YONGE ST.
925-6400
TICKETS AT RECORDS ON WHEELS, ROUND RECORDS, NEW YORKER, NEW ROSE

Dead Boys,
Crash 'n' Burn, 1977

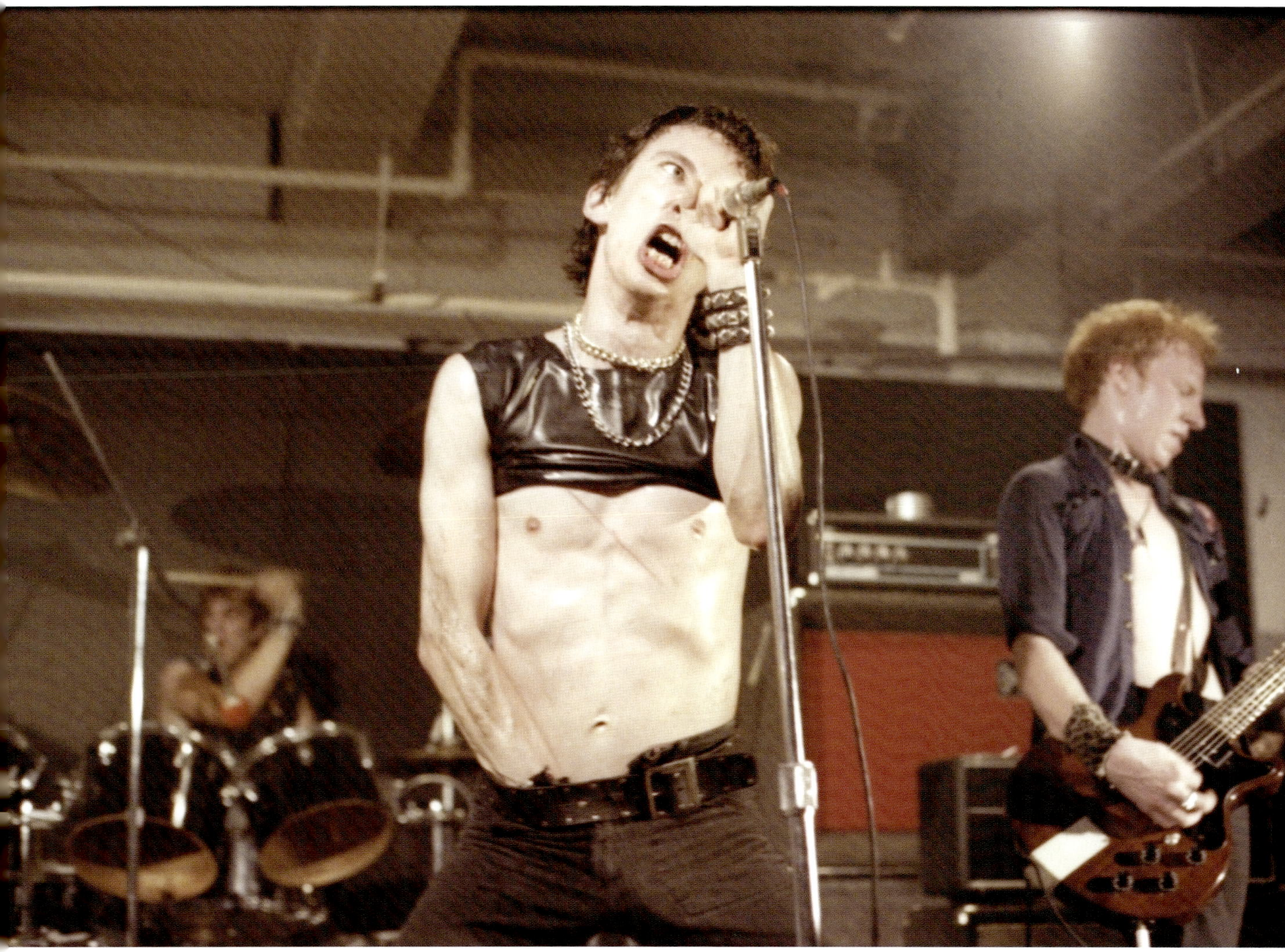

Johnny Blitz, Stiv Bators, Cheetah Chrome

The last weekend of the Crash 'n' Burn concert series is also captured beautifully in the stunning Ross McLaren film named after the club. Stiv stuck his head in the kick drum, swung from rafters, did some knife play on his stomach and arms, snarling and drooling in cartoon-terror pantomime. Pulling out the waistband of his jeans, Stiv puked into his pants then scooped some chunks out and stuffed them back in his mouth.

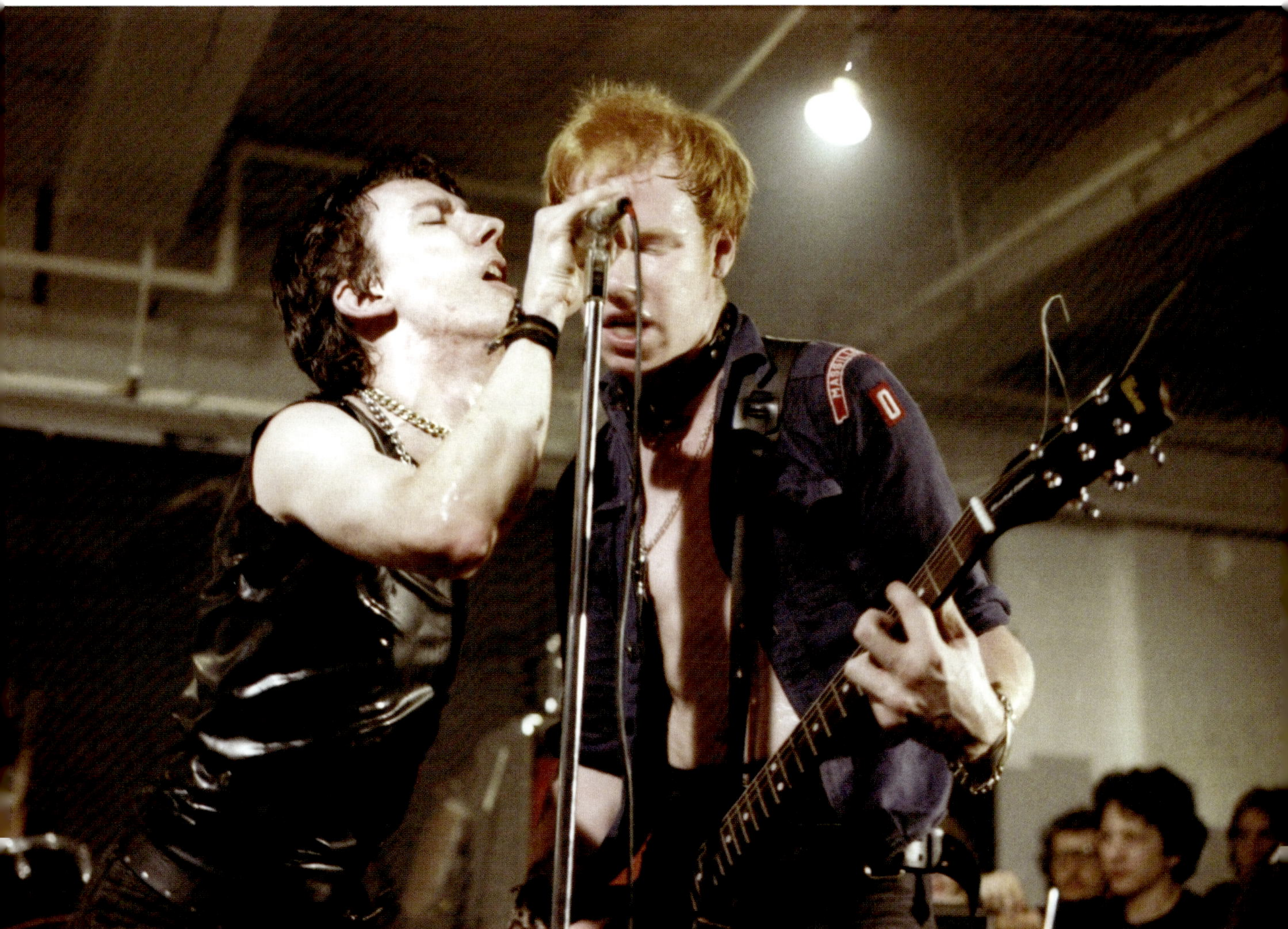

Stiv Bators, Cheetah Chrome

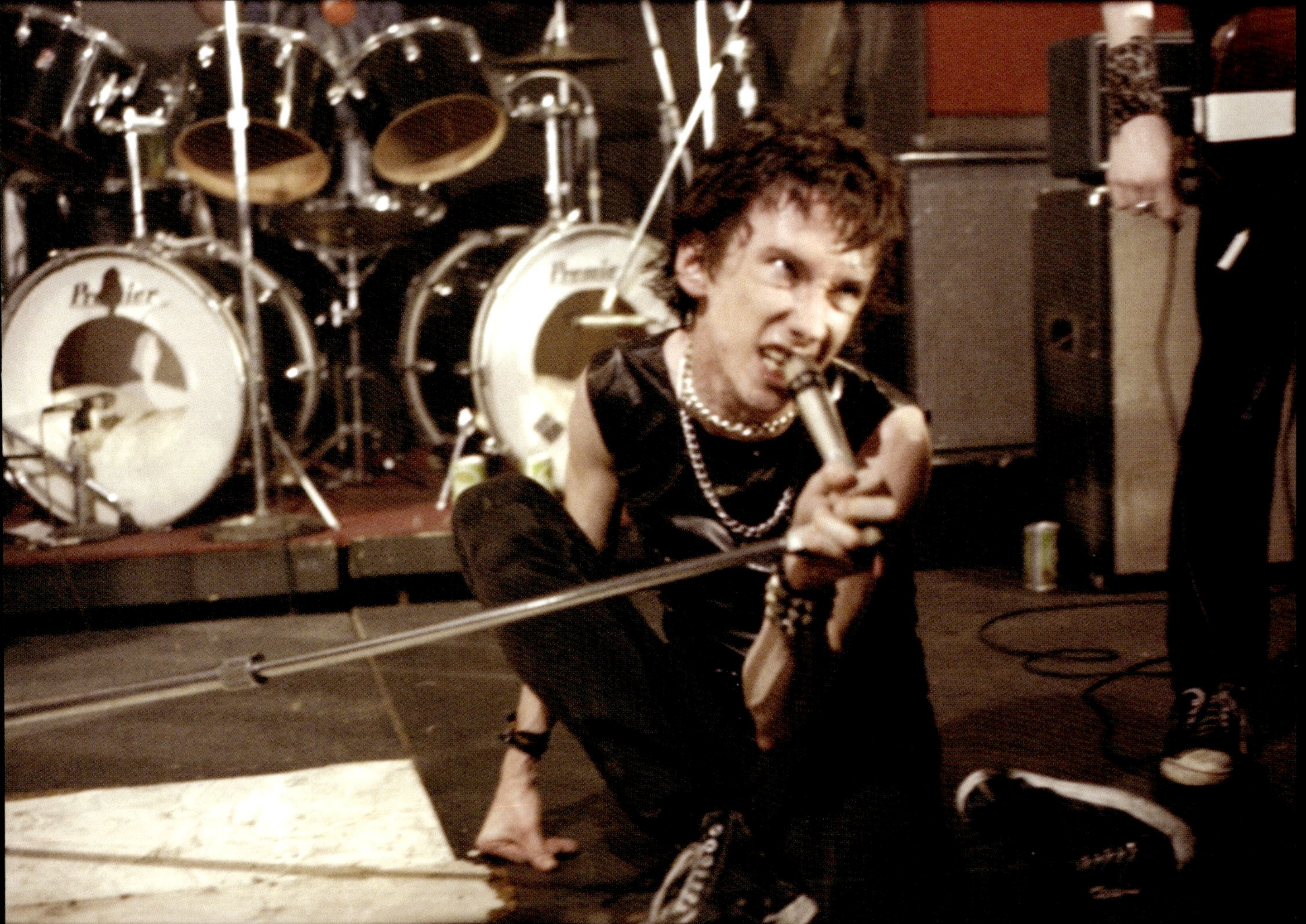

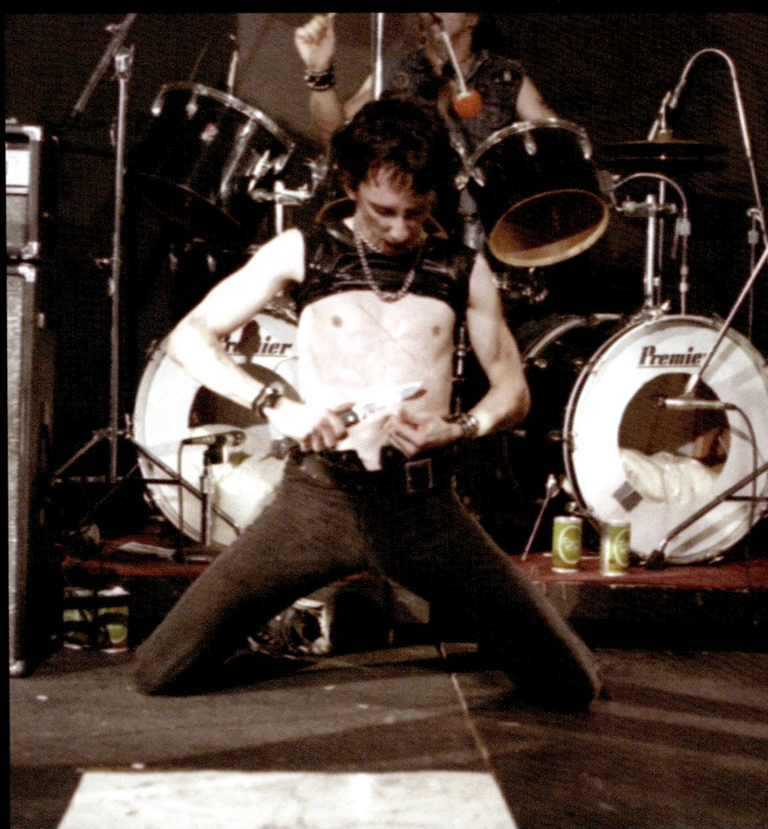

Stiv Bators

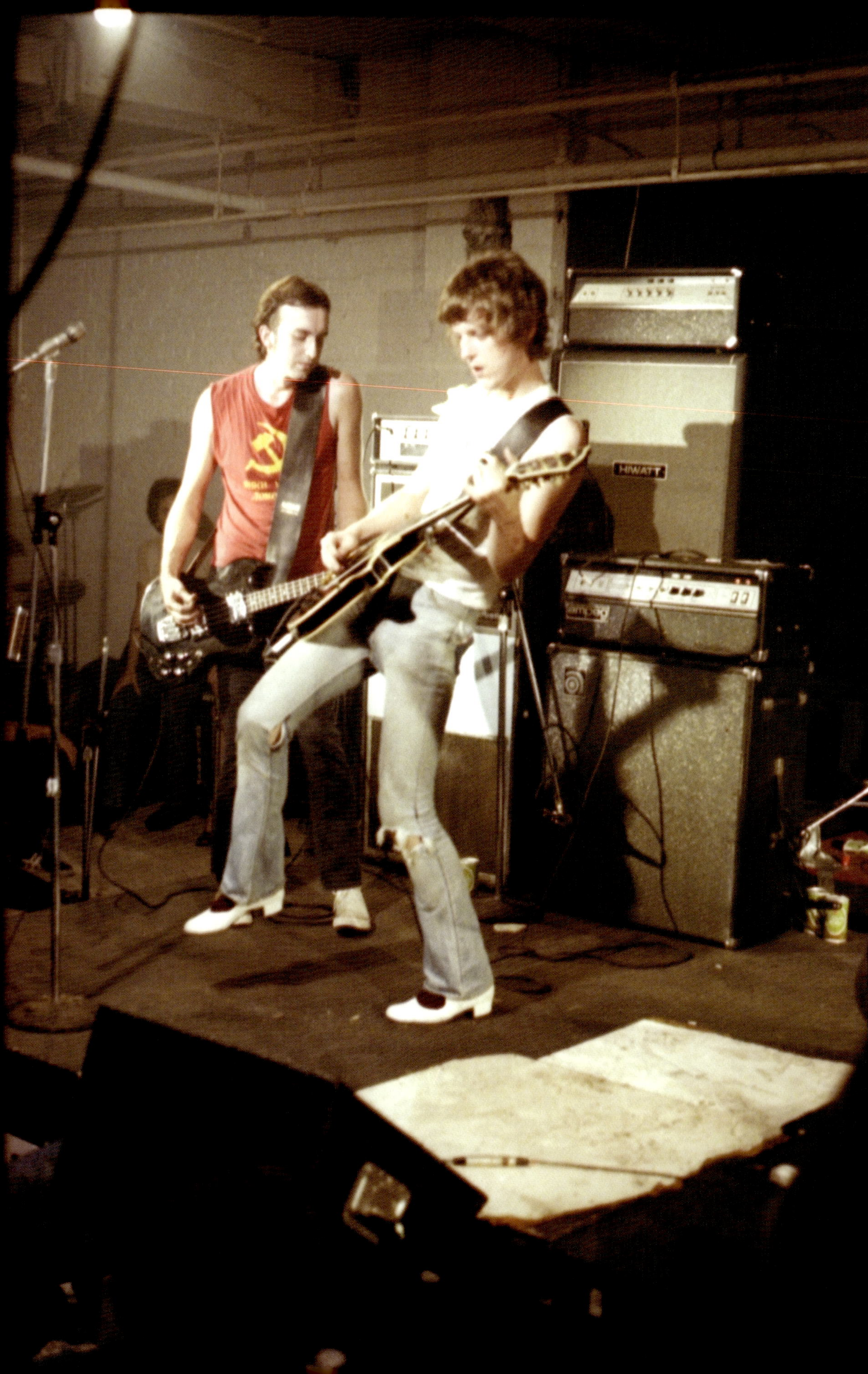
HIWATT

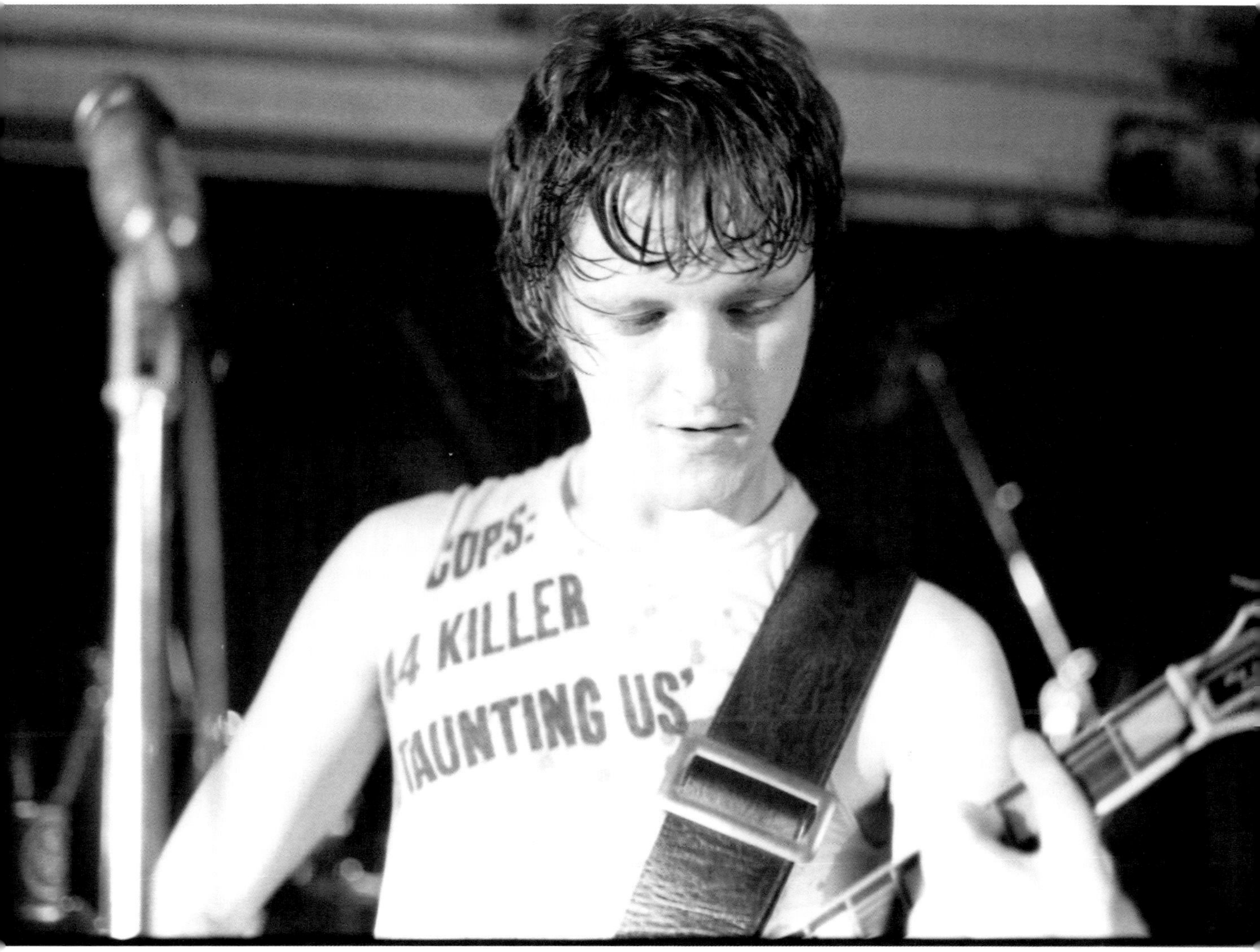

Jimmy Zero

Zero's shirt refers to the Son of Sam, David Berkowitz, the serial killer shooting people in New York City as punk was festering. In the thrill-seeking new regime, Berkowitz was canonized for his value at disturbing those who weren't ready for the black humor and offensive-at-all-costs sensibility.

Jeff Magnum, Jimmy Zero

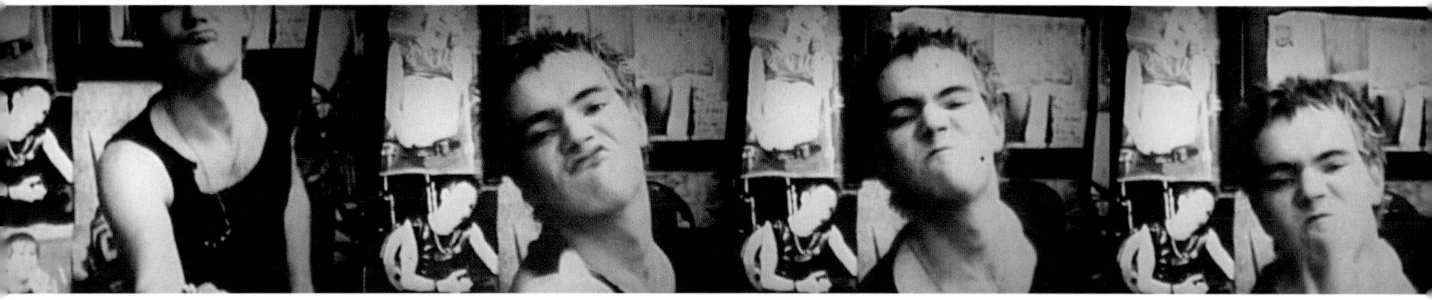

From the 1978 Suzanne Naughton film Afternoon with the Viletones at New Rose, *courtesy of Suzanne Naughton*

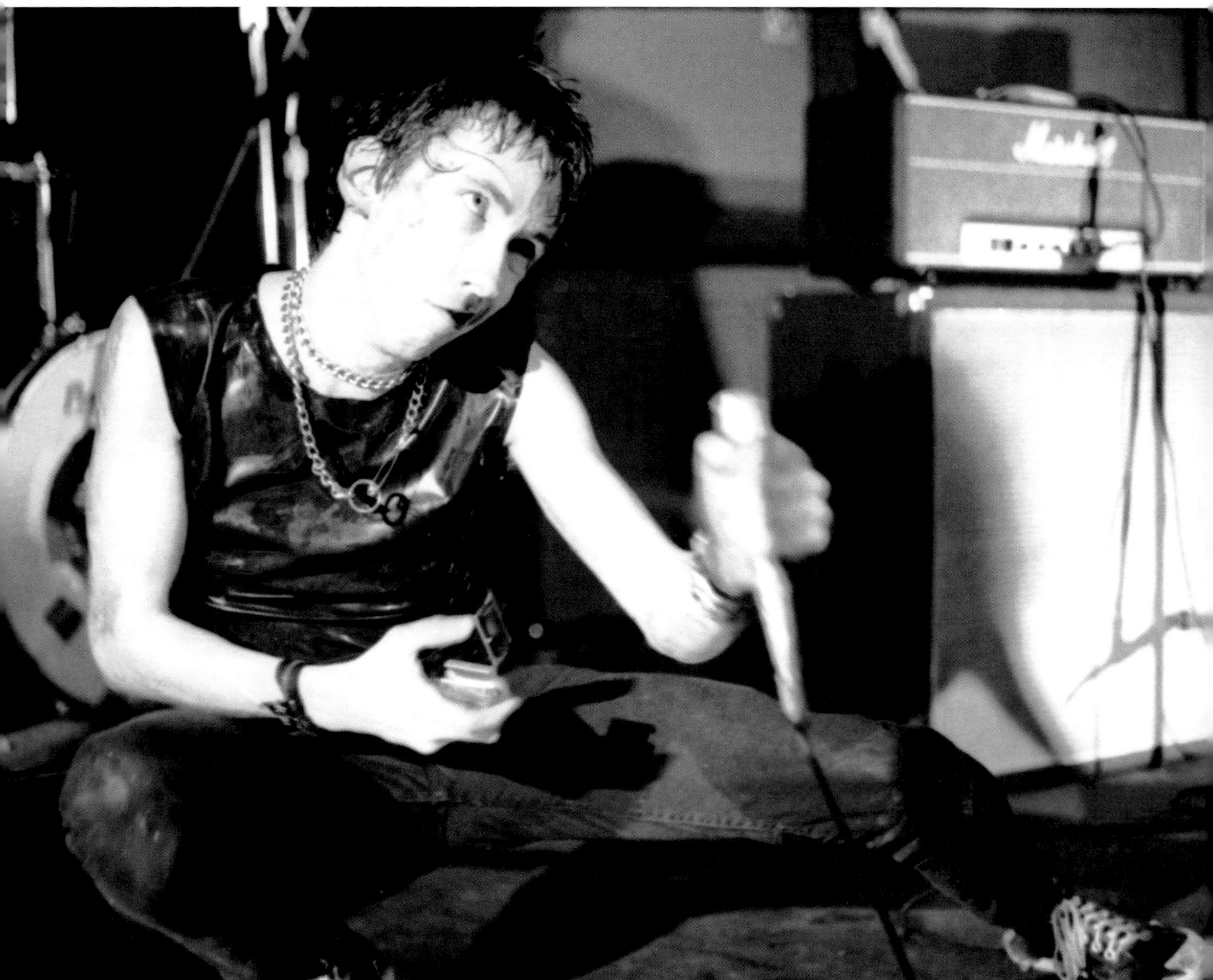

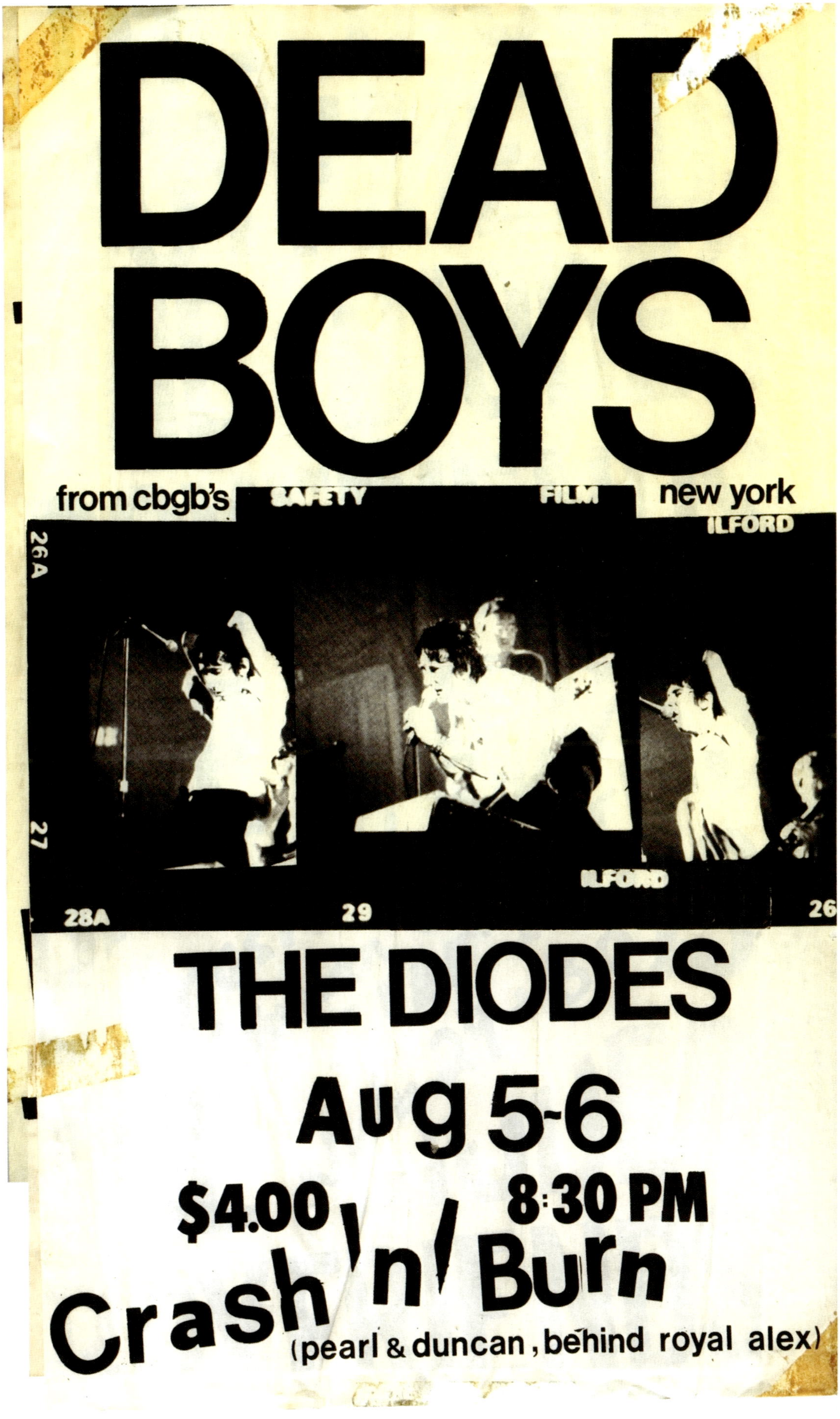
DEAD BOYS
from cbgb's
SAFETY
FILM
new york
ILFORD
26A
27
ILFORD
28A
29
26
THE DIODES
Aug 5-6
$4.00
8:30 PM
Crash 'n' Burn
(pearl & duncan, behind royal alex)

Roger's bedroom, 1977

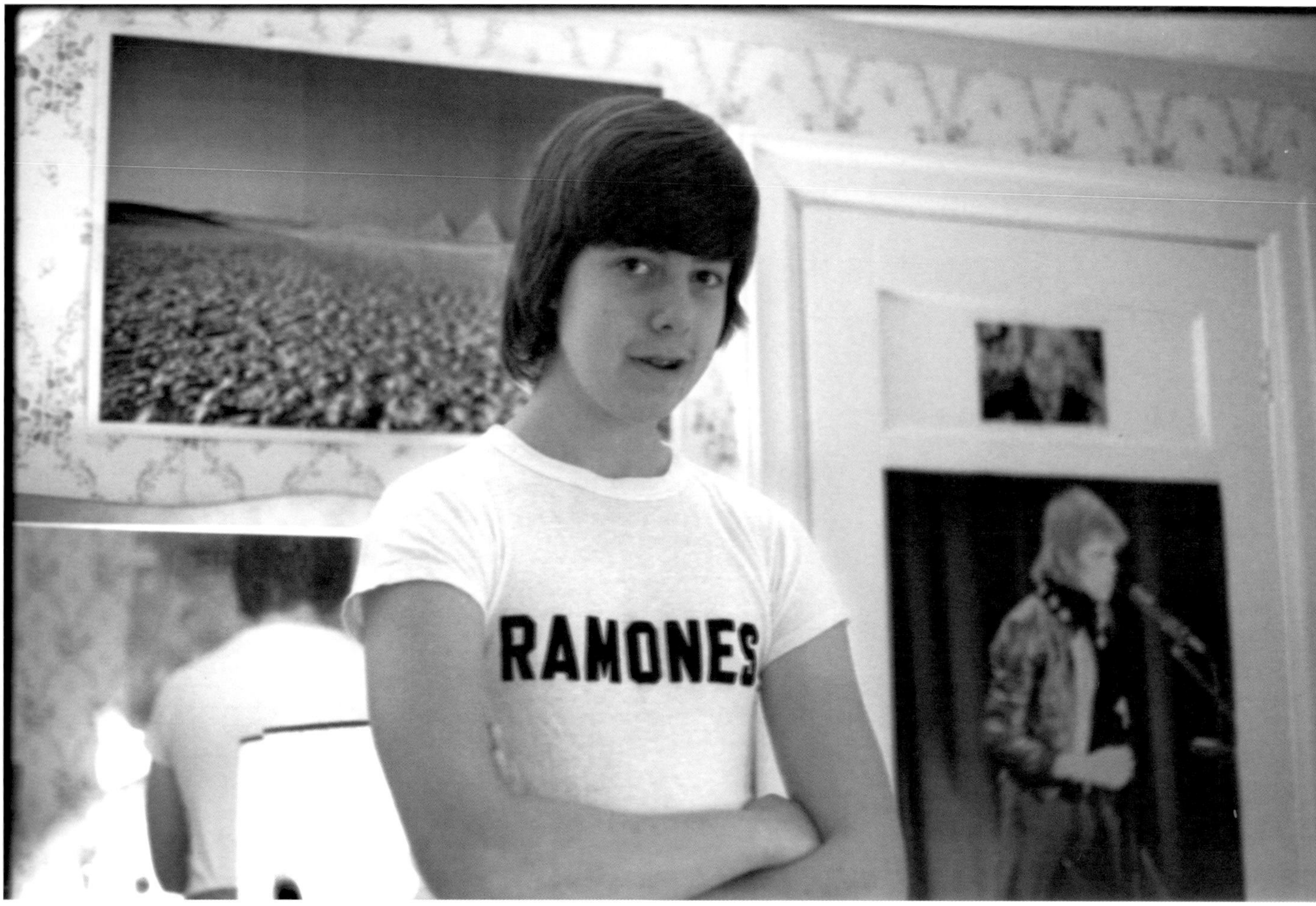

Roger was my best friend through many years of voracious music devouring and cultural exploration. He and I were in kindergarten together, went to our first concerts together and it was with him that I first explored the downtown nightlife. This image captures so much of the transformative moment that was happening, when we were obsessed with David Bowie and there were no manufactured Ramones T-shirts. I was covetous of this shirt he made with iron-on letters, similar to one we'd seen pictures of the Ramones wearing. The *Dark Side of the Moon* poster stands out as symbolic of the end of one epoch and Roger and his fantastic homemade top the beginning of another.

Ramones, New Yorker Theatre, 1977

Dee Dee, Johnny, Joey

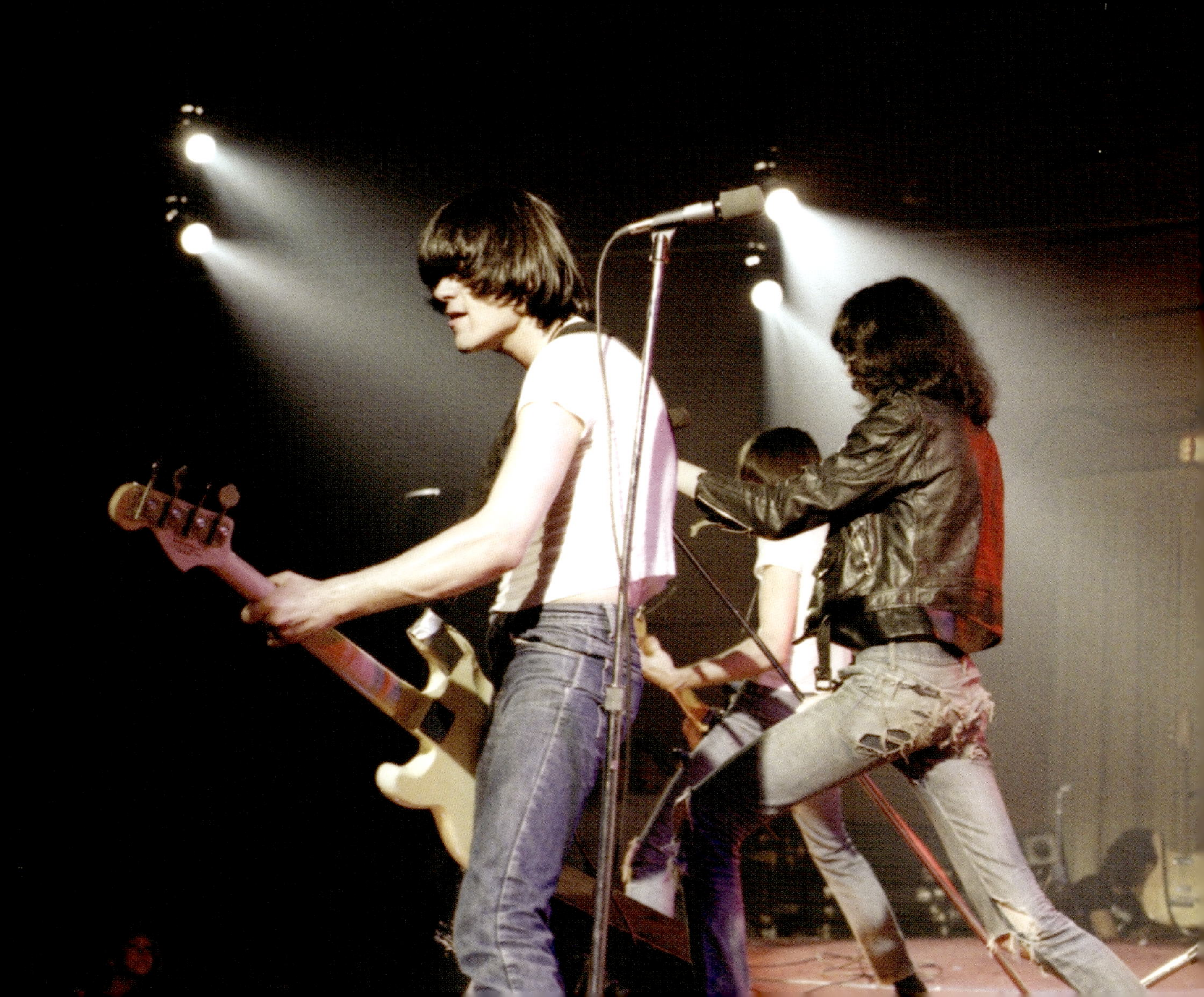

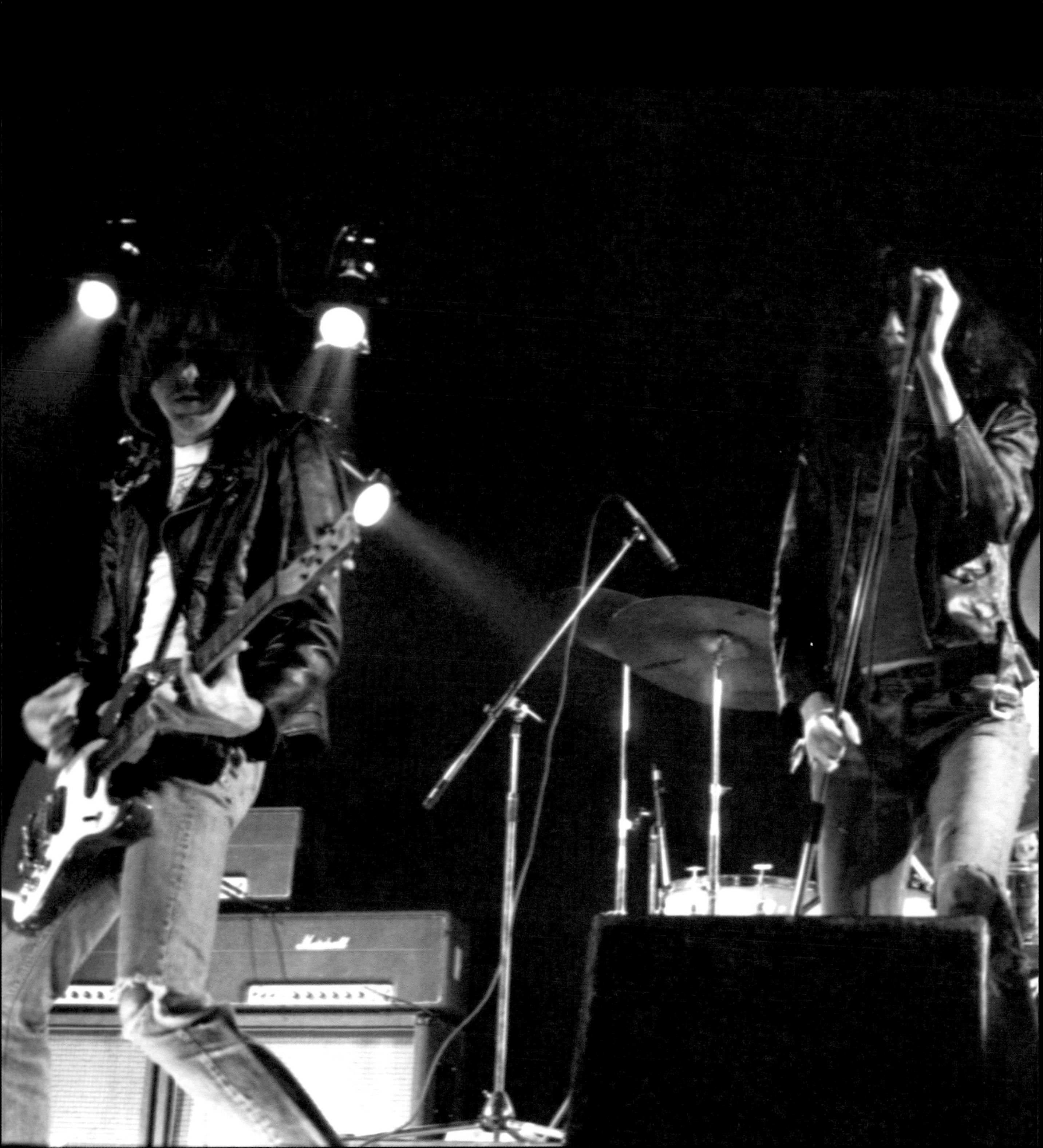

The Ramones' second Toronto show happened shortly after *Leave Home* was released, the cover of which caused some hometown pride as a result of Dee Dee wearing a New Yorker Theatre T-shirt.

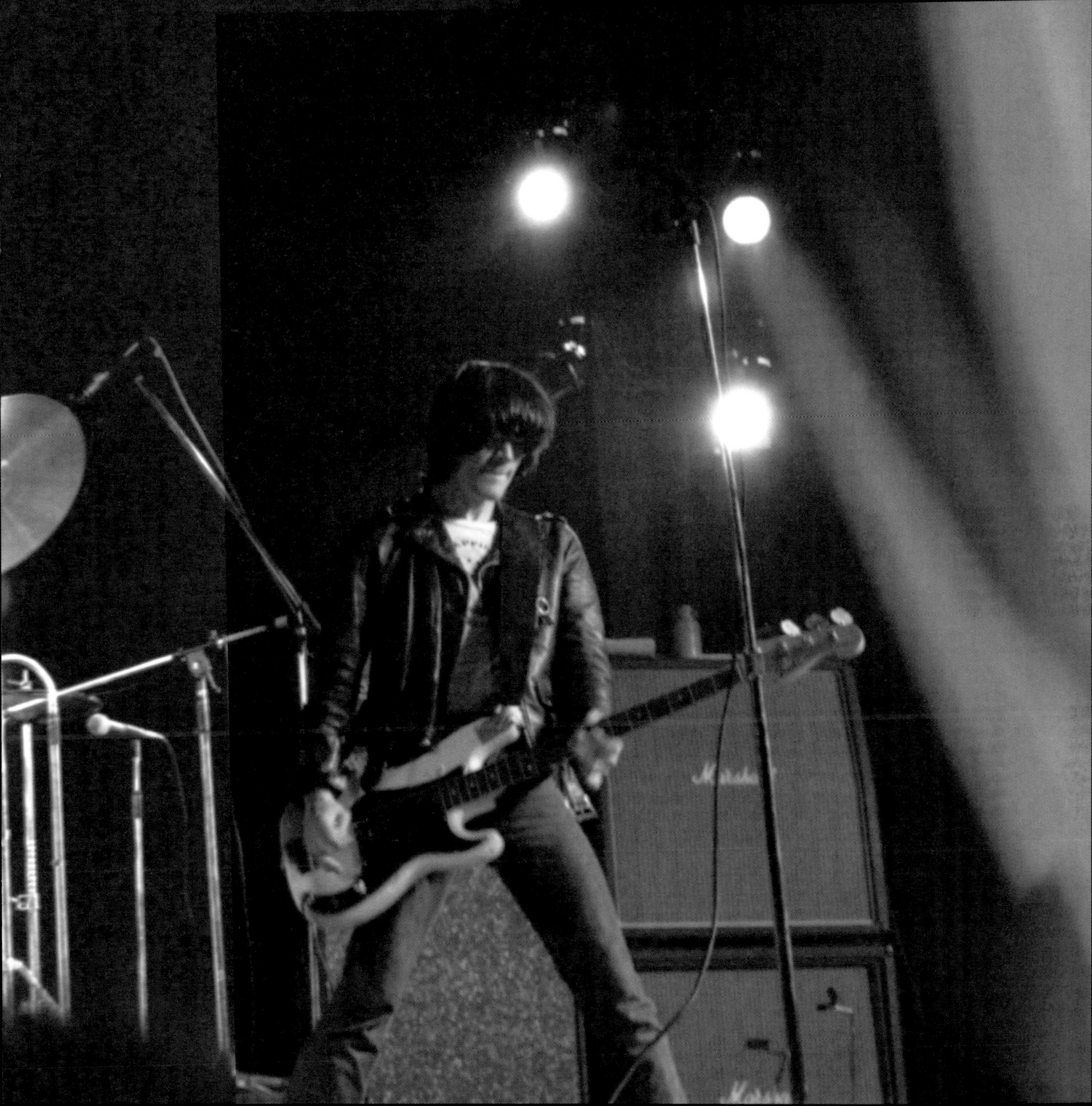

Johnny, Joey, Dee Dee

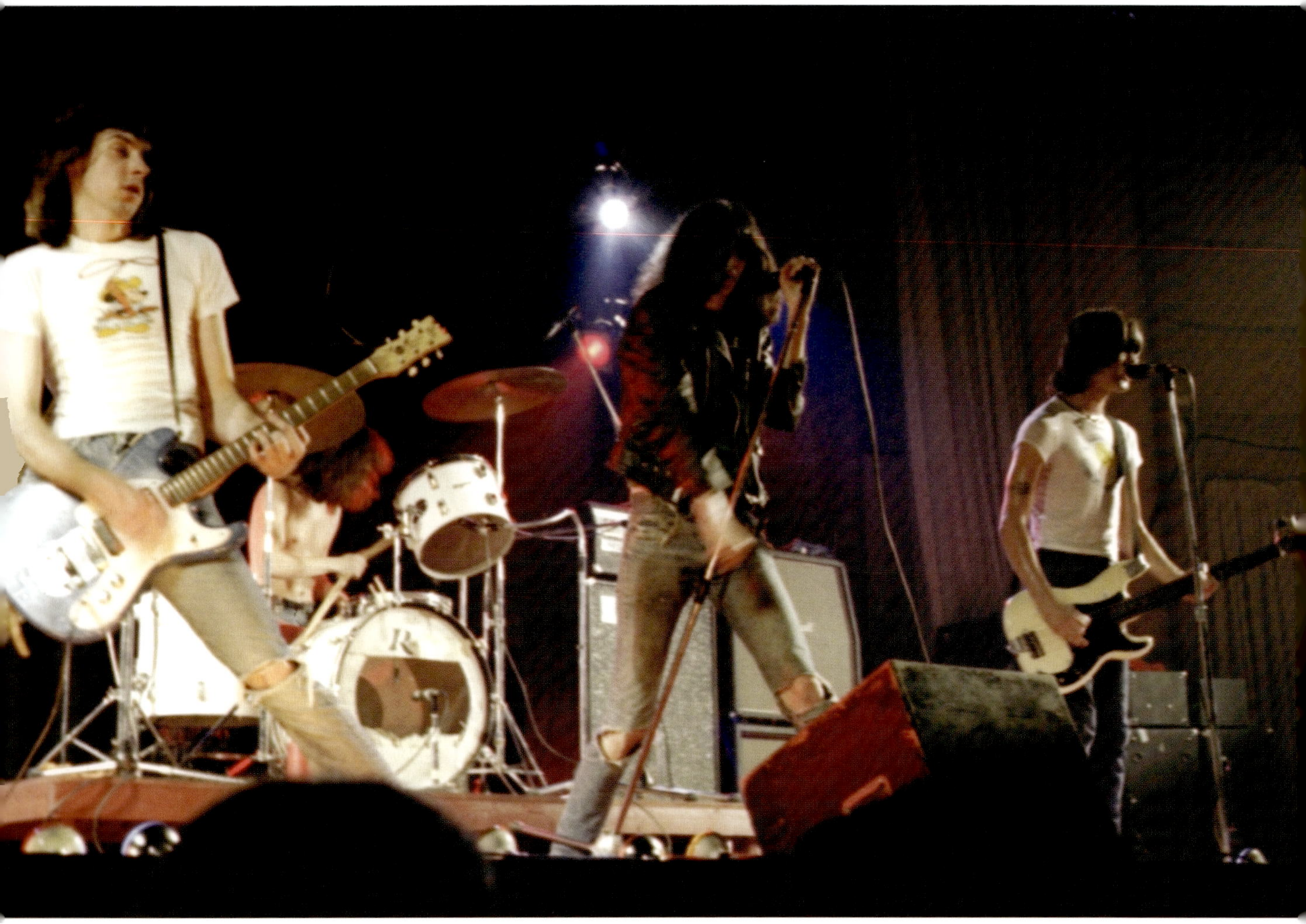

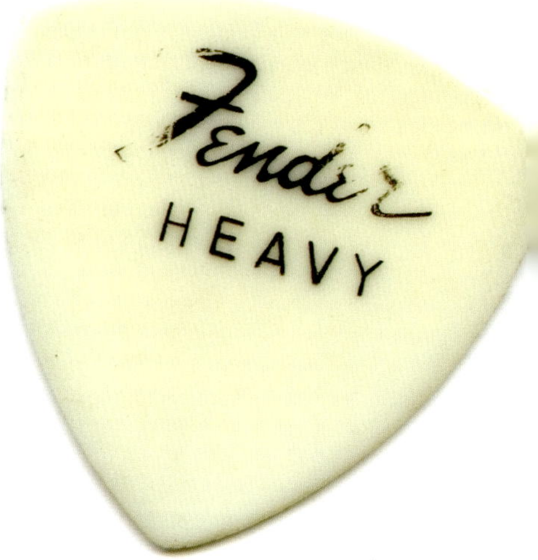

Johnny's pick

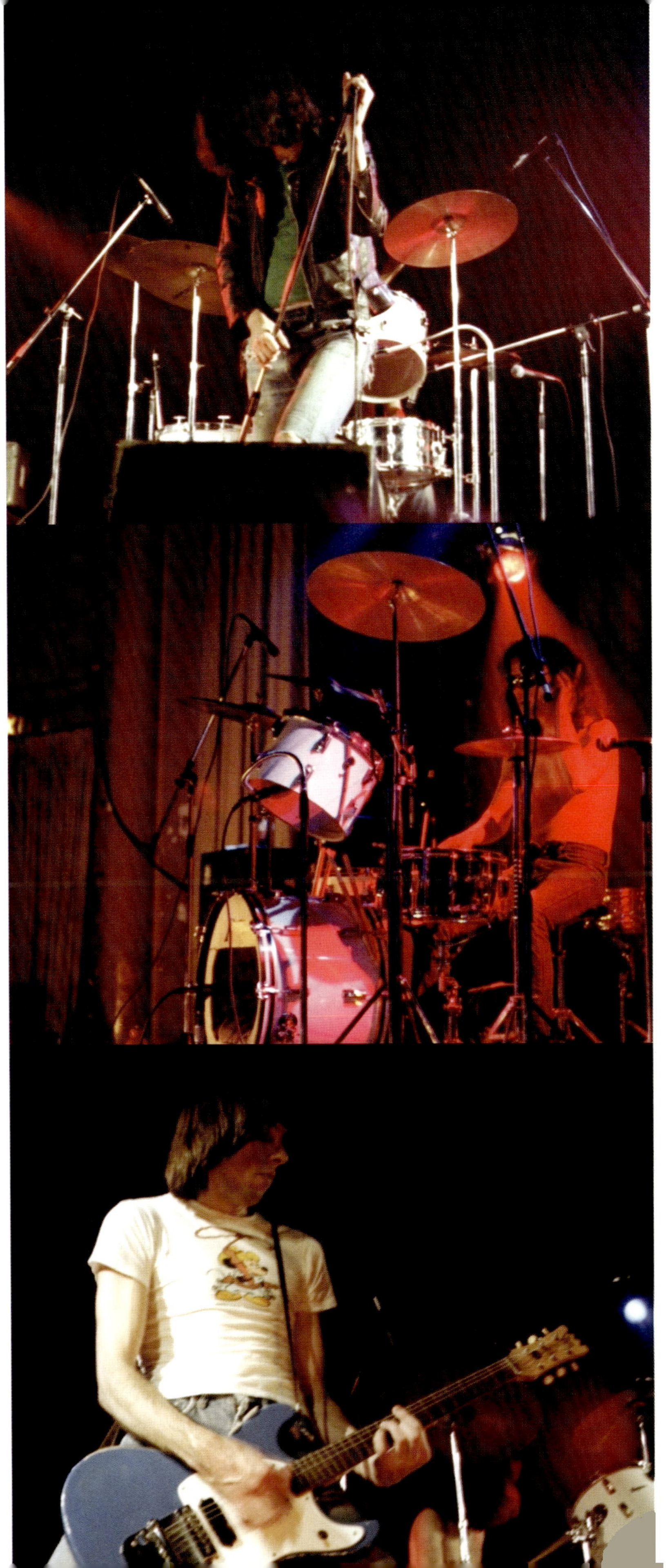

Joey, Tommy, Johnny

Ramones,
Masonic Temple, 1977

Opening for Iggy Pop on his Lust for Life tour.

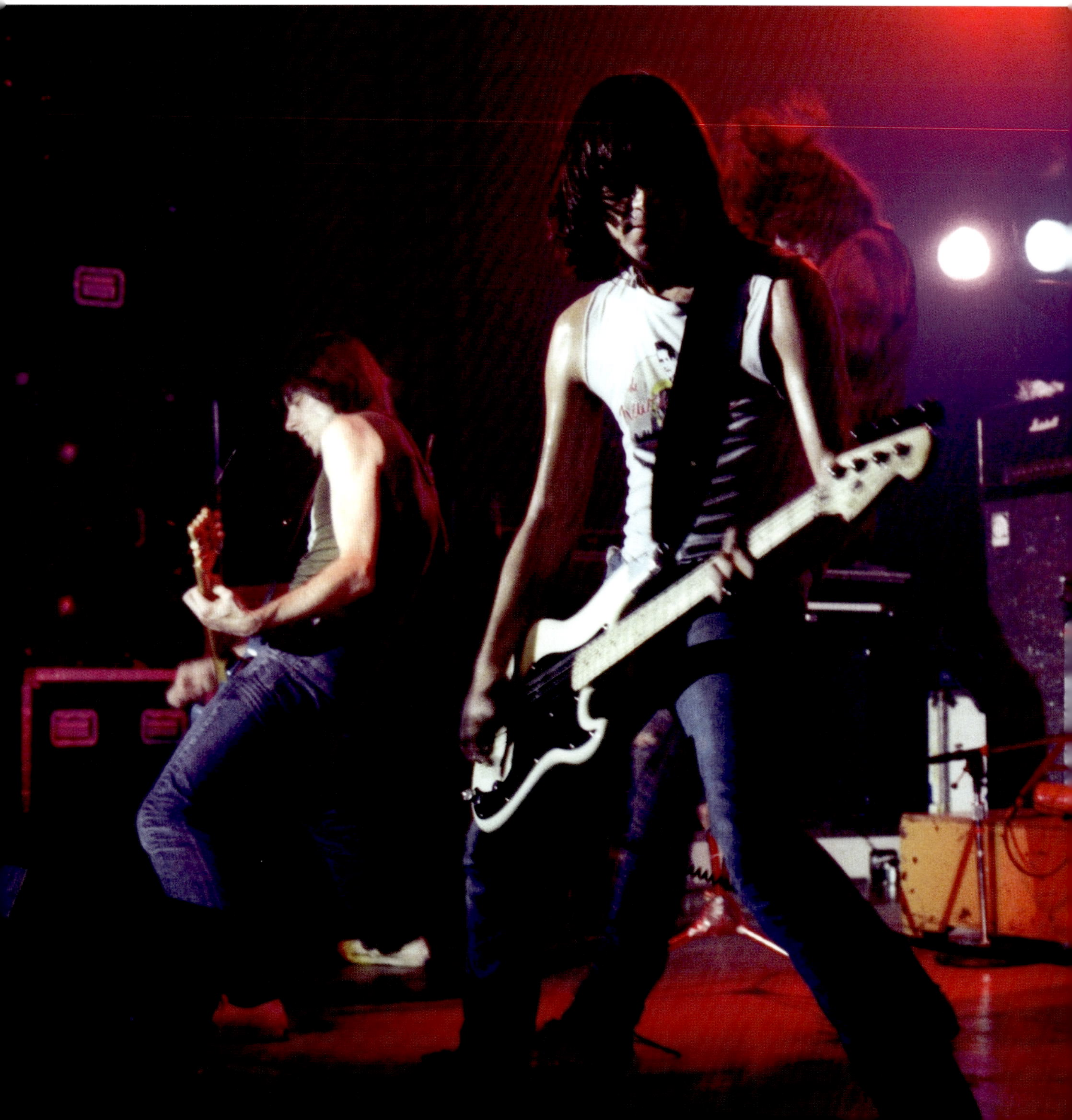

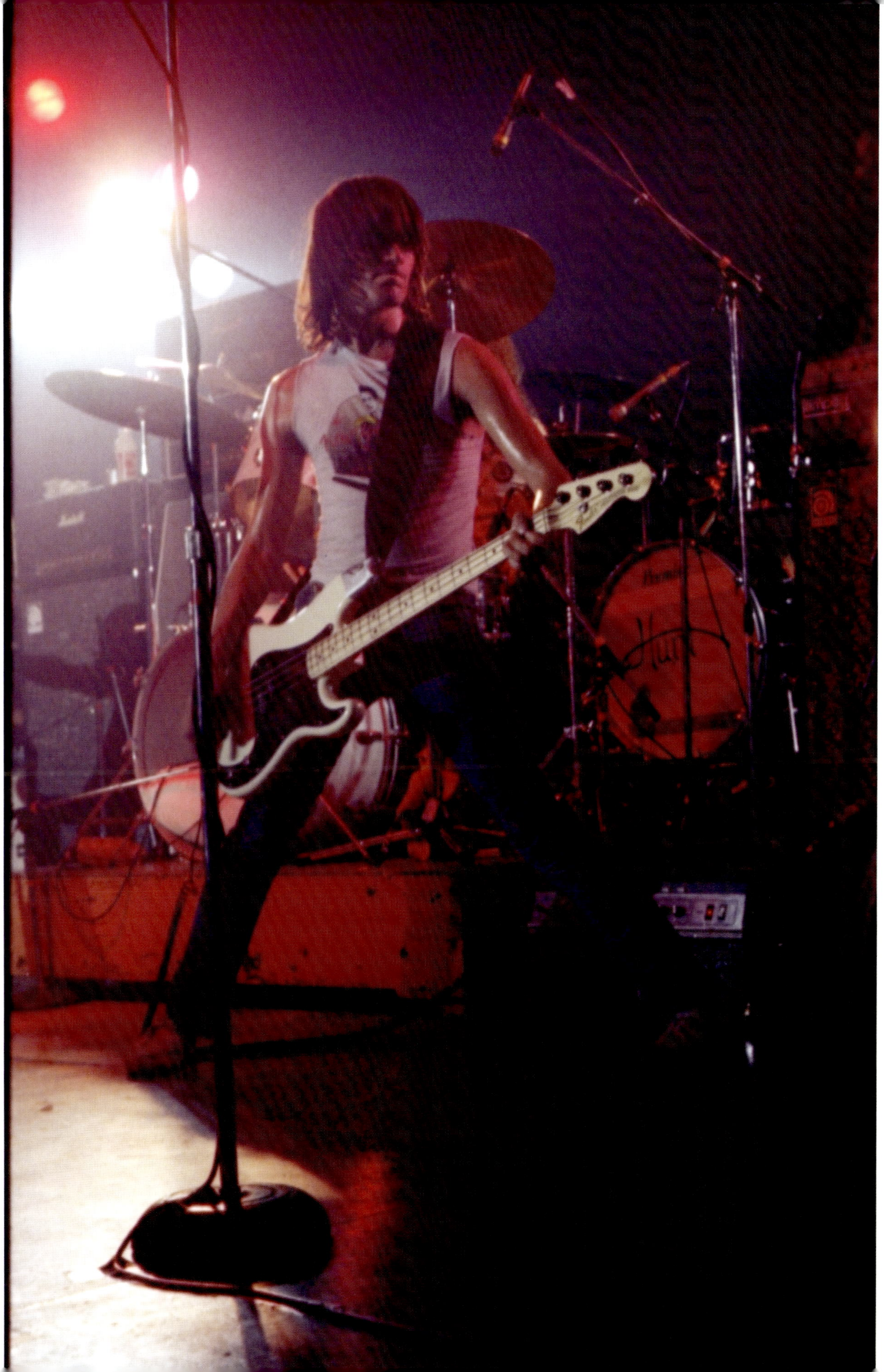

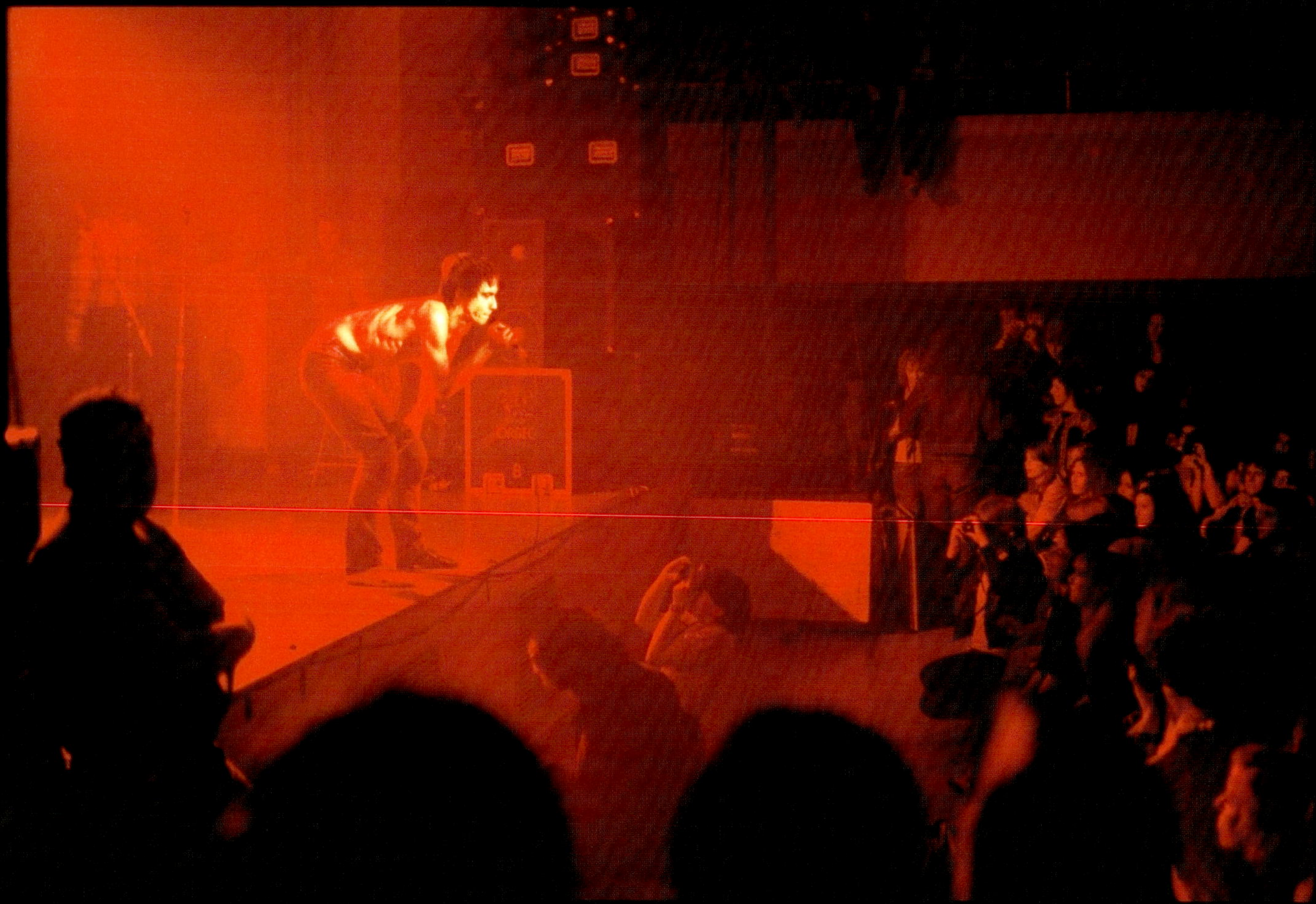

Iggy Pop, Masonic Temple, 1977

Iggy's second solo return to Toronto featured the same core band as The Idiot tour, minus David Bowie. Many people have looked at this image and commented about how security were keeping the audience back. They are perplexed by the lack of barricades. It's actually the sheer power of Iggy and probable fear in the audience that is creating the gap. Faced with a distant audience politely sitting in chairs, Iggy immediately got as close as he could to the small crowd. Even with the Ramones as the opening band, at this time Iggy could not fill the small hall.

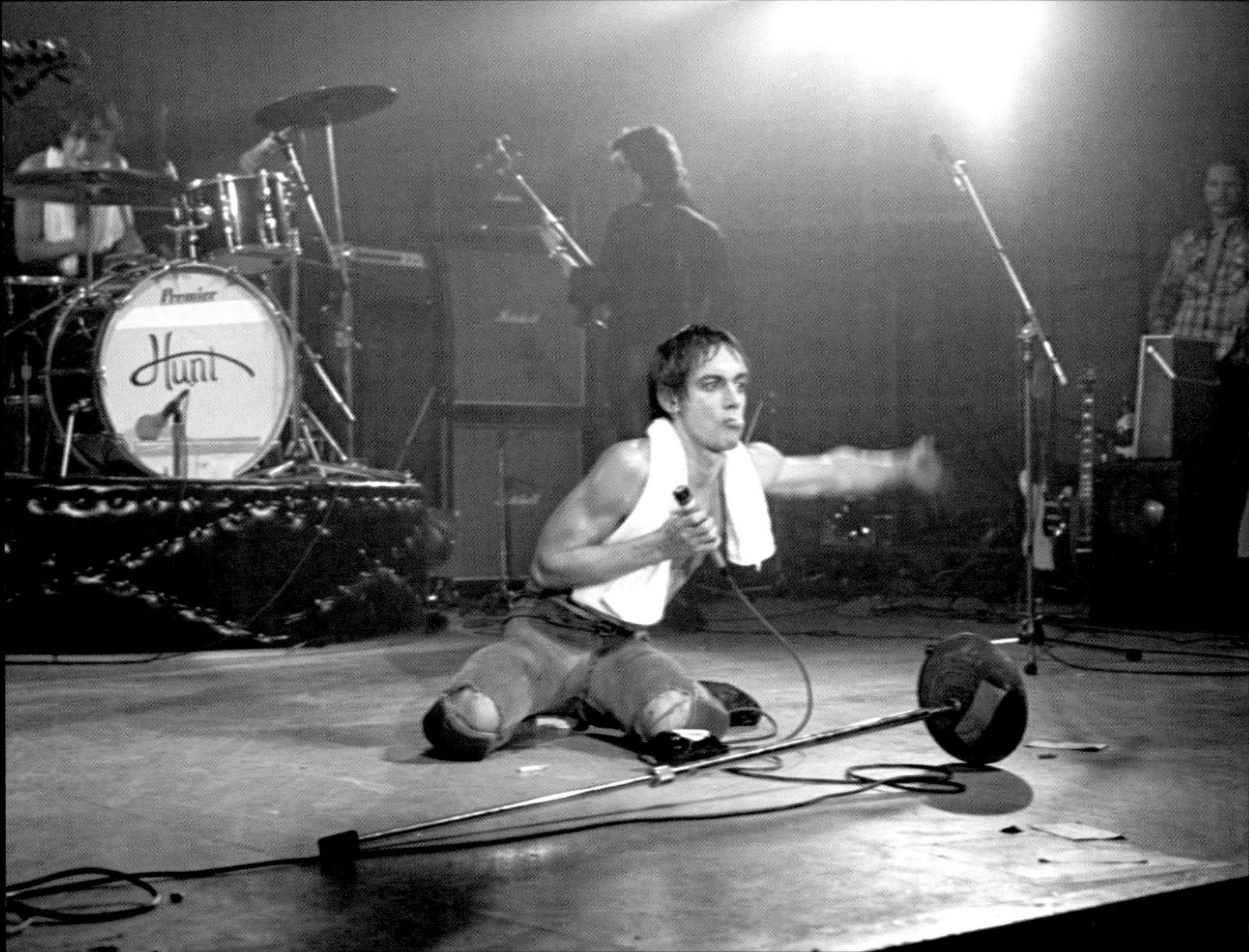

Hunt and Tony Sales, Iggy Pop

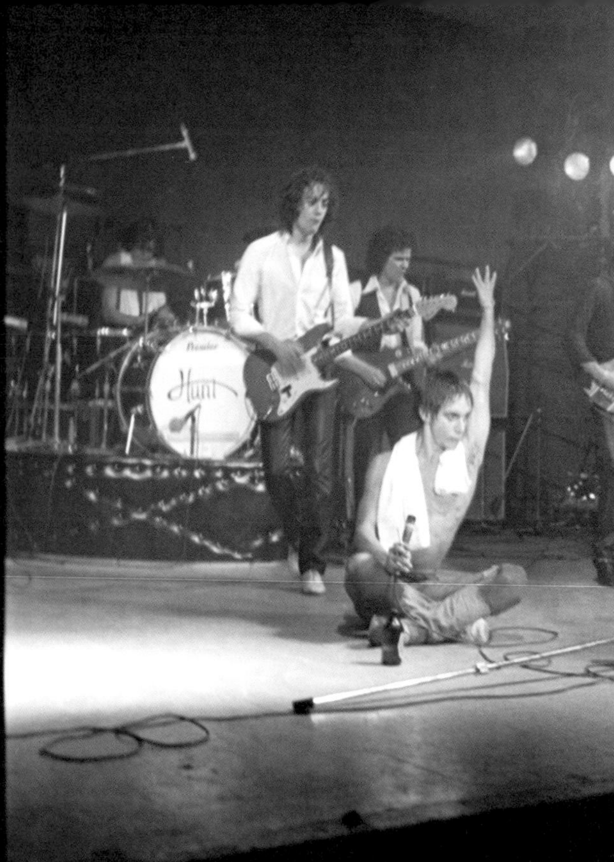

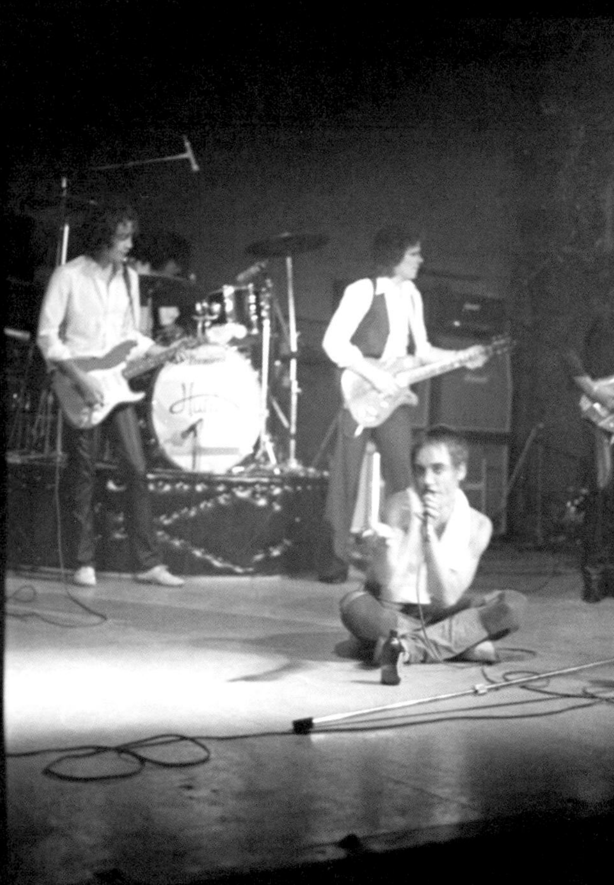

Scott Thurston, Iggy Pop, Tony Sales, Stacy Heydon

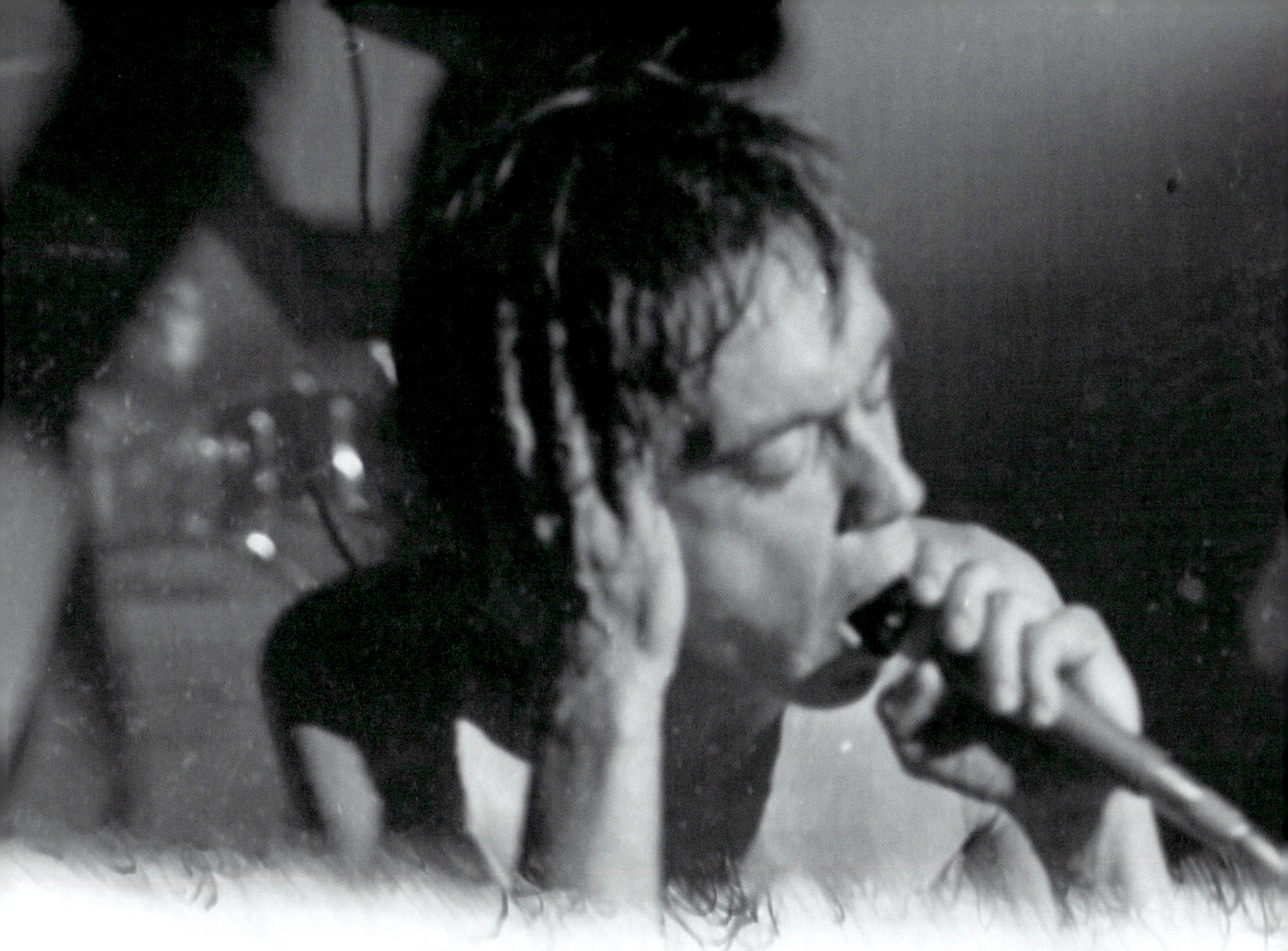

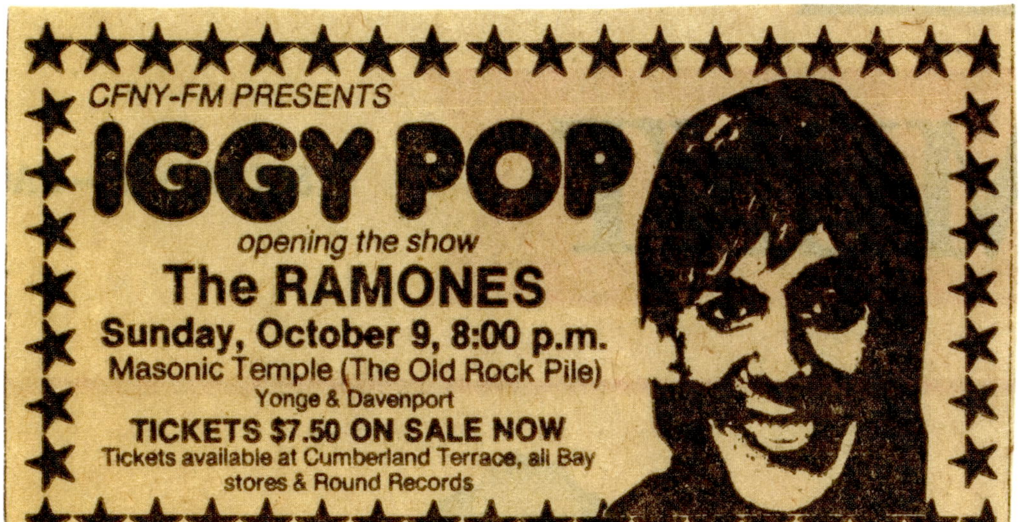
CFNY-FM PRESENTS
IGGY POP
opening the show
The RAMONES
Sunday, October 9, 8:00 p.m.
Masonic Temple (The Old Rock Pile)
Yonge & Davenport
TICKETS $7.50 ON SALE NOW
Tickets available at Cumberland Terrace, all Bay stores & Round Records

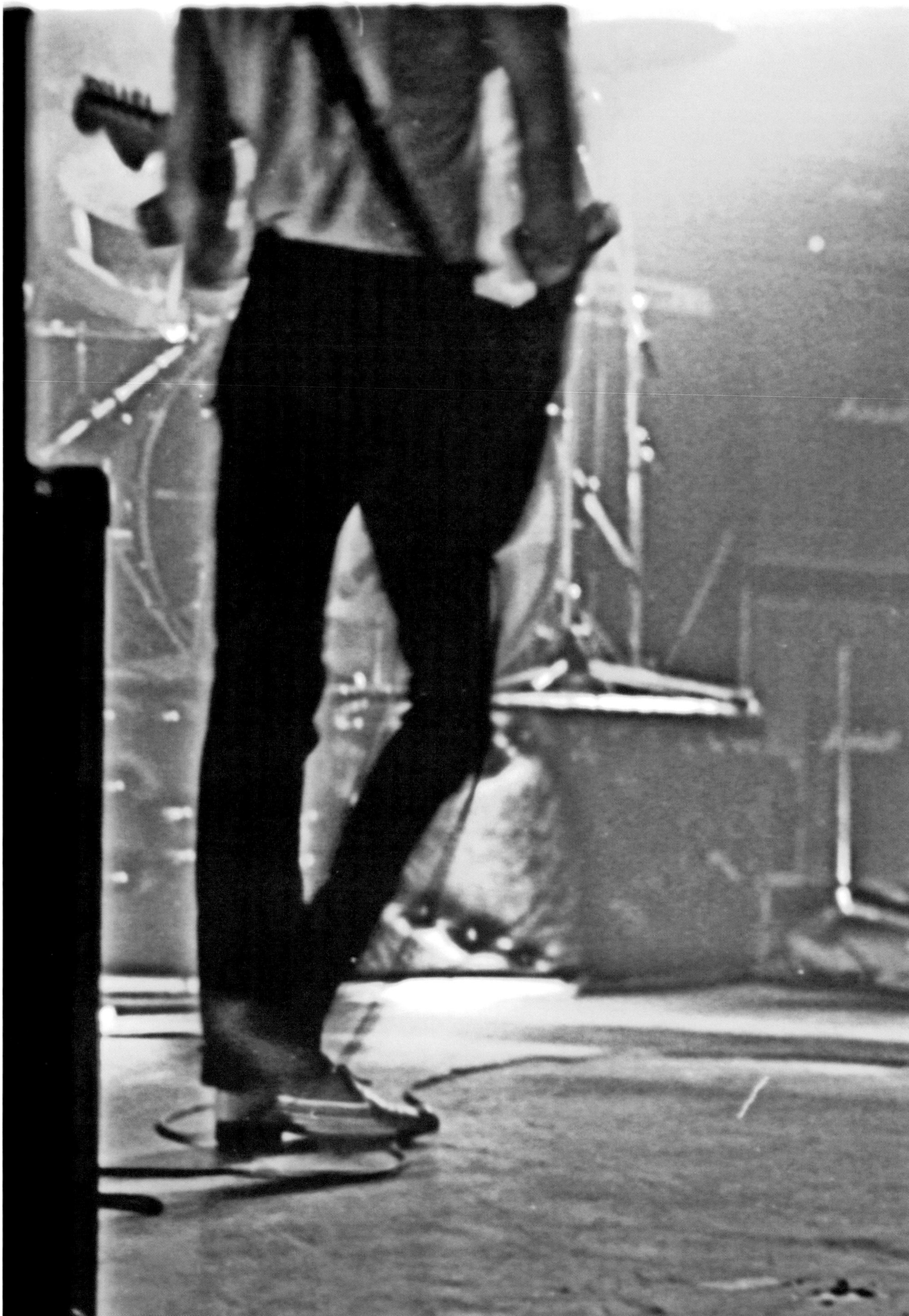

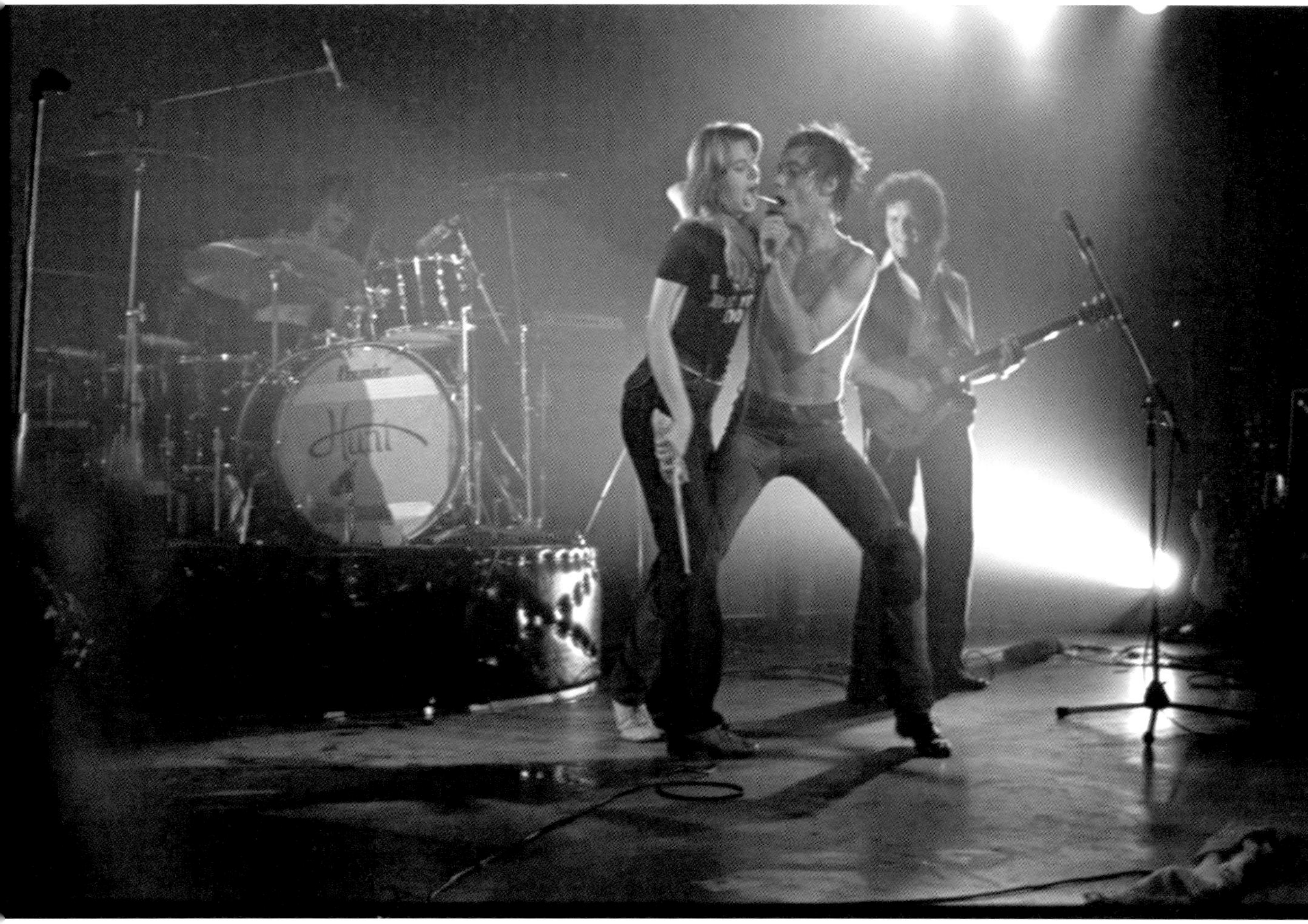

A woman pressed herself to the edge of stage, wearing a dog collar with leash, and a T-shirt reading "Iggy I Want To Be Your Dog." Waving the leash at him for several songs, Iggy ignored her until he eventually grabbed the leash and dragged the unprepared dog onto the stage for the song named on her top. Completely ignoring her, Iggy continued flailing around the stage, climbing up the PA, dragging the girl behind him as she tried to maintain her cool and her footing. Near the end of the song, he acknowledged her by shoving the mic in her face to sing the chorus.

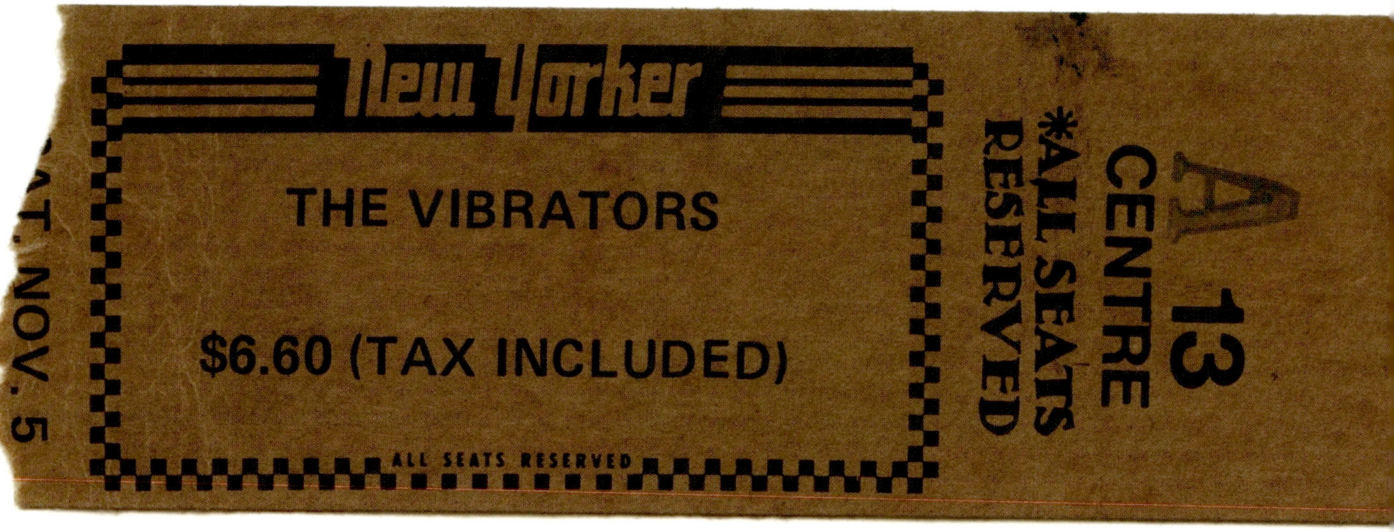
New Yorker
THE VIBRATORS
$6.60 (TAX INCLUDED)
ALL SEATS RESERVED
NOV. 5
A 13
CENTRE
*ALL SEATS RESERVED

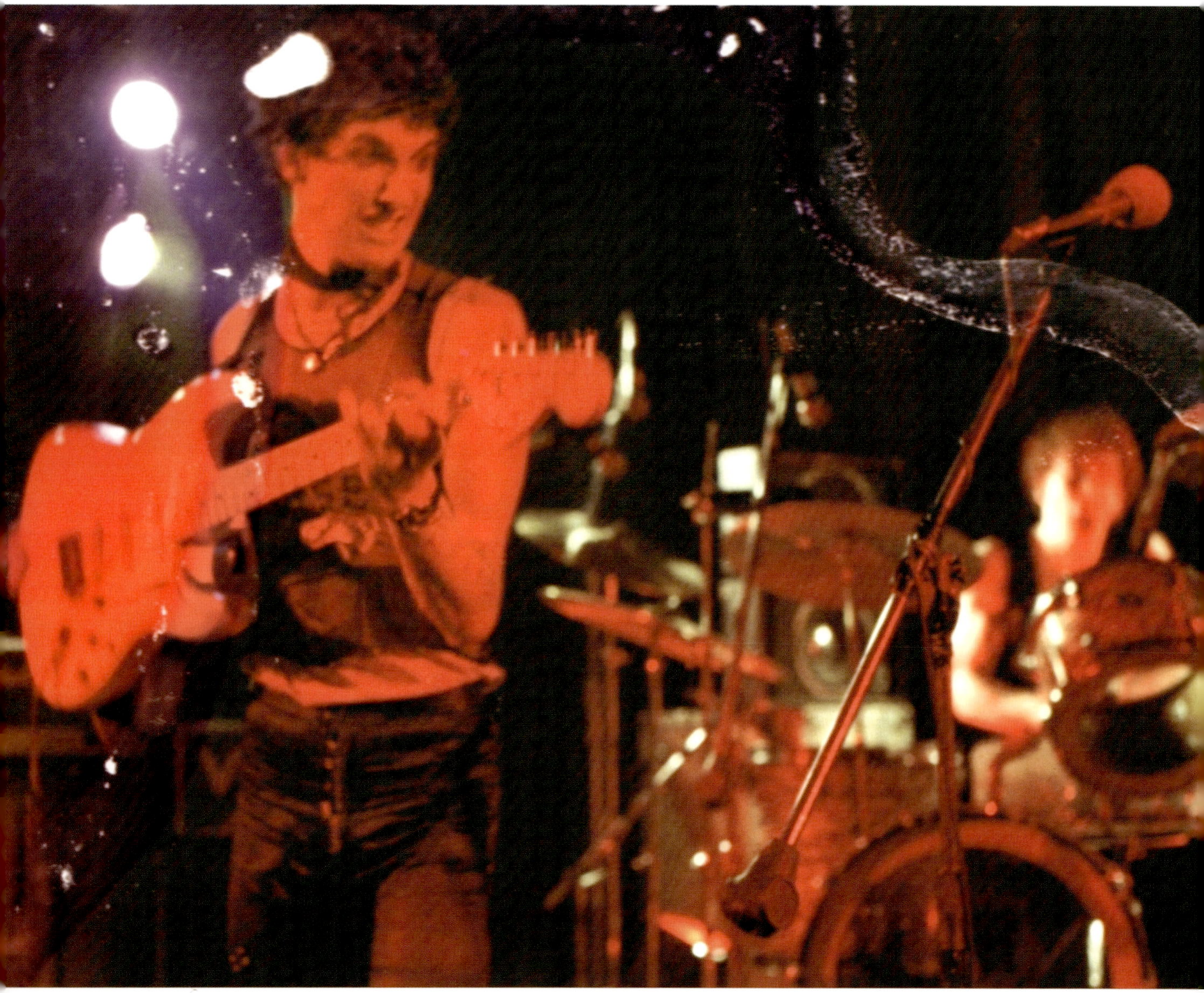

The Vibrators, New Yorker Theatre, 1977

Even at this early date, The Vibrators, with one great album to their credit, looked cartoonish and exaggerated, with pogo dancing, safety pins and requisite snarl. Still, they were exciting live and maybe even the first of the U.K. punks to play here. The singer of Toronto bar band Goddo was showing up at Crash 'n' Burn gigs, and his band was clearly trying to survive into the next generation. It was still a surprise though, with the proliferation of new bands, that Goddo was to be the opening band for The Vibrators. Anxious to see any live music, I watched them as

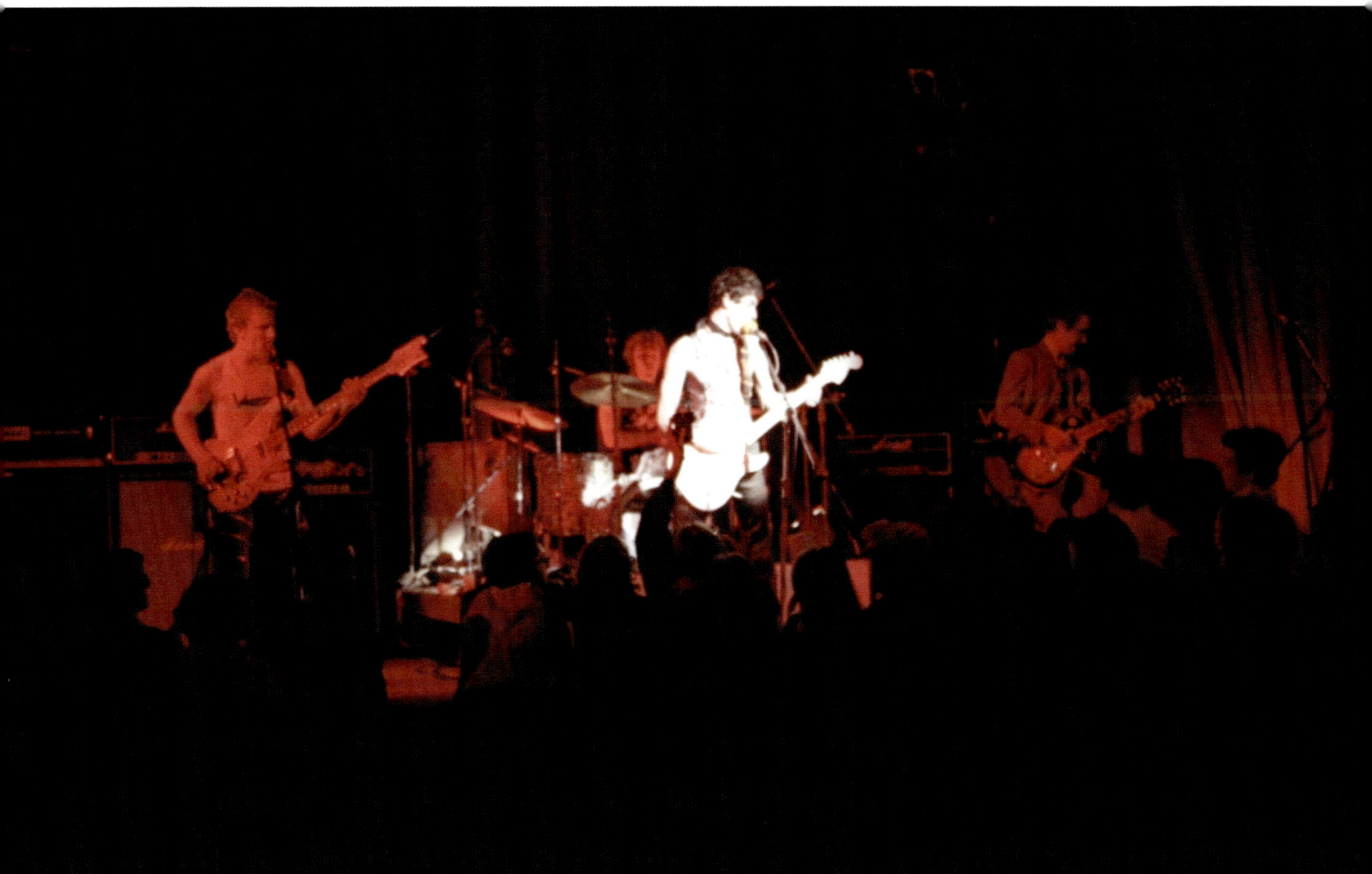

Gary Tibbs, Eddie Edwards, Knox, John Ellis

Knox, Eddie Edwards

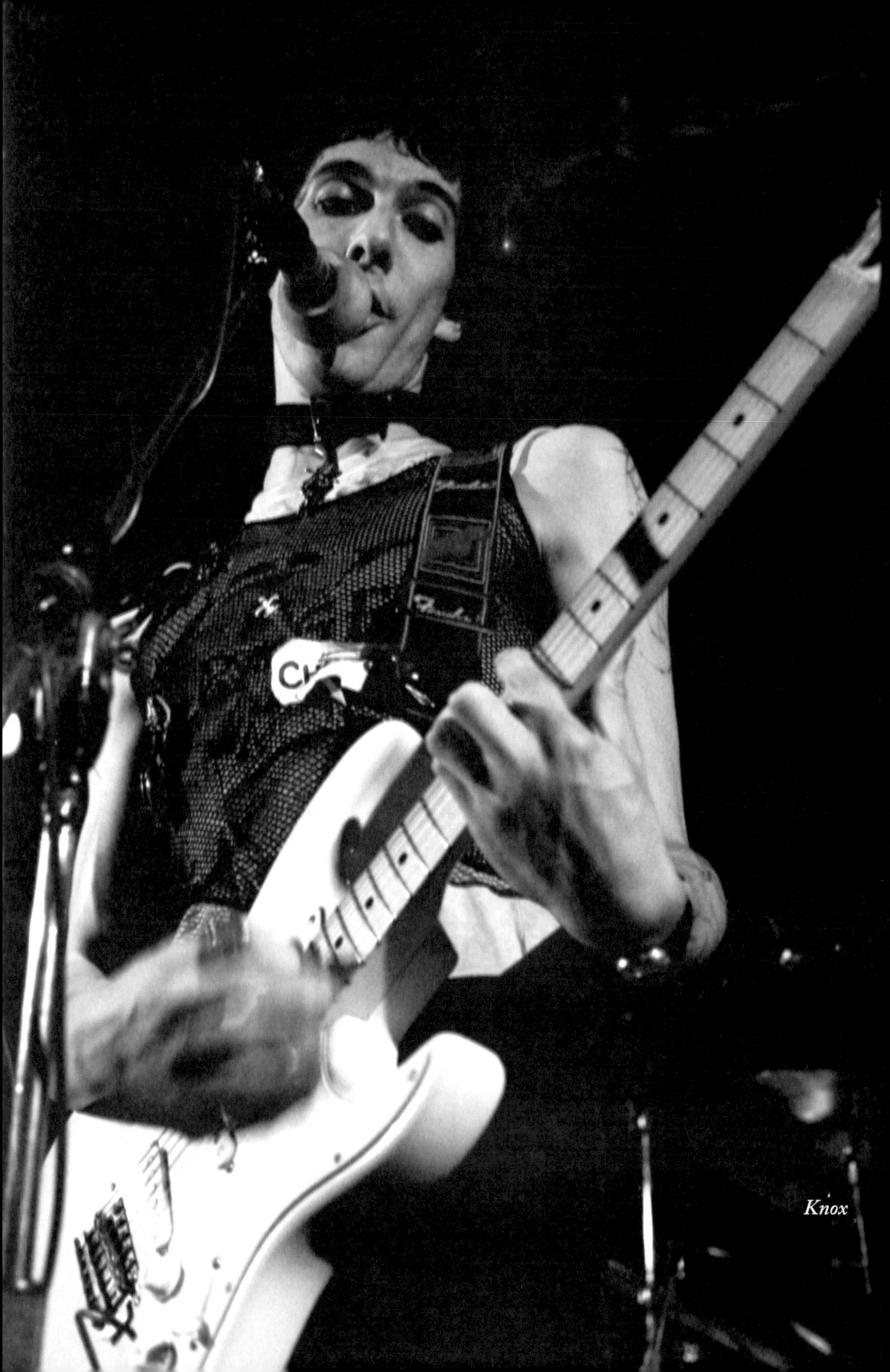

Knox

the place emptied of an audience no longer willing to tolerate these representatives of the oppressive bar scene we were happy to see die — satin pants, cock-rocket guitar posturing, shag haircuts and all. By the end of Goddo's set, maybe a dozen or so people remained, scattered throughout the small theater. Someone who had fled to the lobby later told me that singer Greg Godovitz huffed into the lobby directly from the stage and shouted, "Thanks a lot, Toronto."

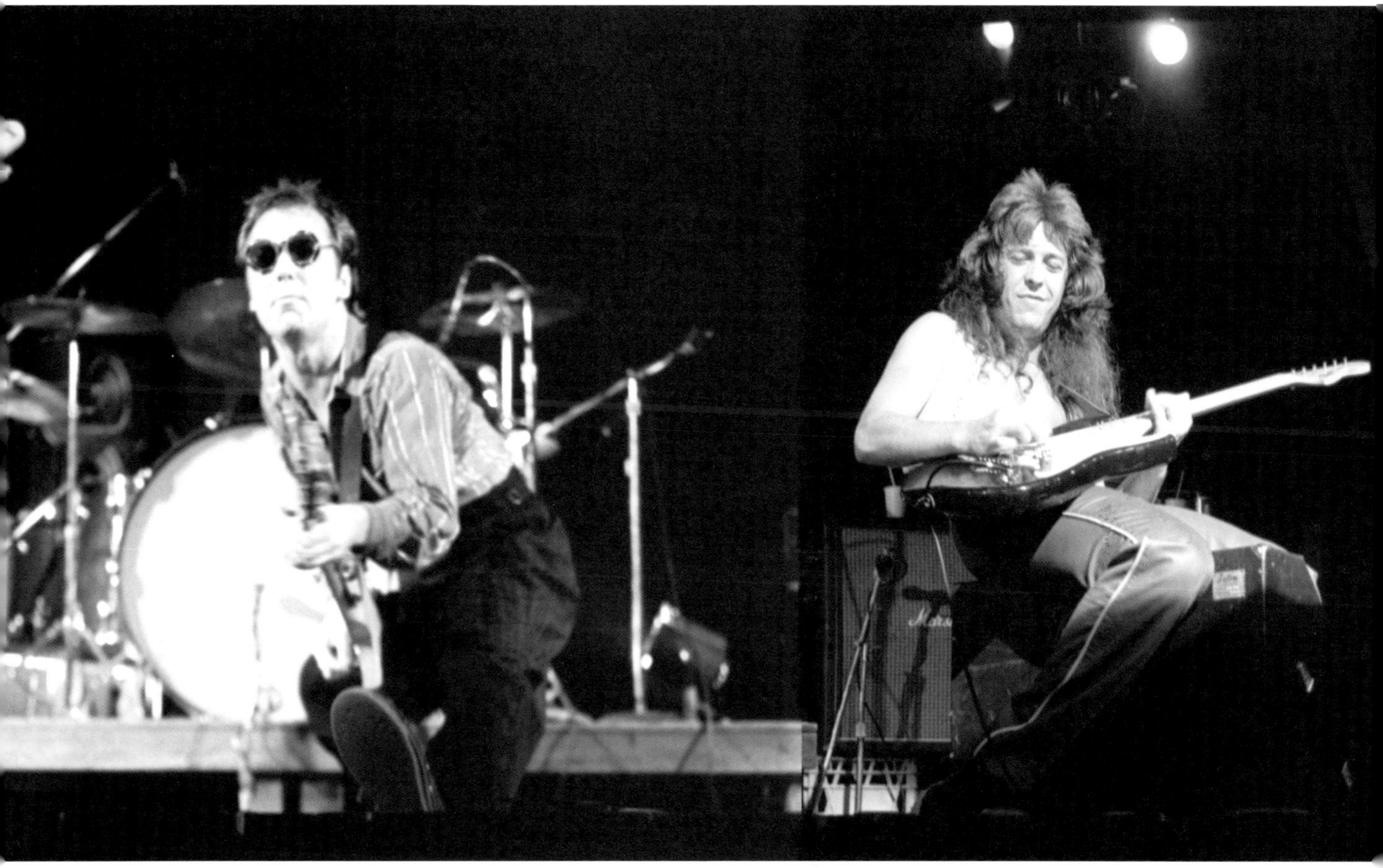

Greg Godovitz, Gino Scarpelli

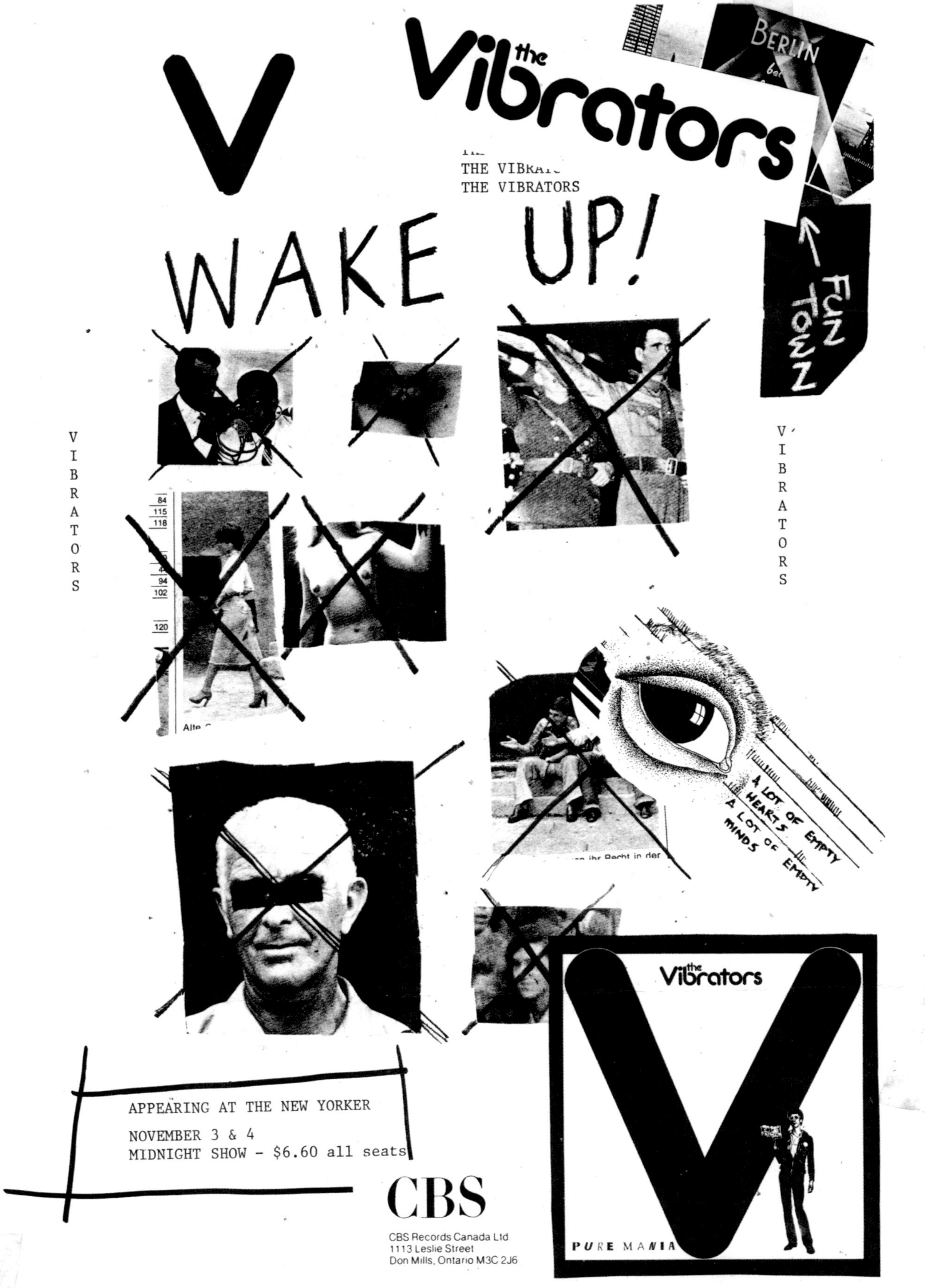
V
the Vibrators
BERLIN
THE VIBRATORS
WAKE UP!
FUN TOWN
VIBRATORS
VIBRATORS
A LOT OF EMPTY HEARTS
A LOT OF EMPTY MINDS
APPEARING AT THE NEW YORKER
NOVEMBER 3 & 4
MIDNIGHT SHOW - $6.60 all seats
CBS
CBS Records Canada Ltd
1113 Leslie Street
Don Mills, Ontario M3C 2J6
the Vibrators
PURE MANIA

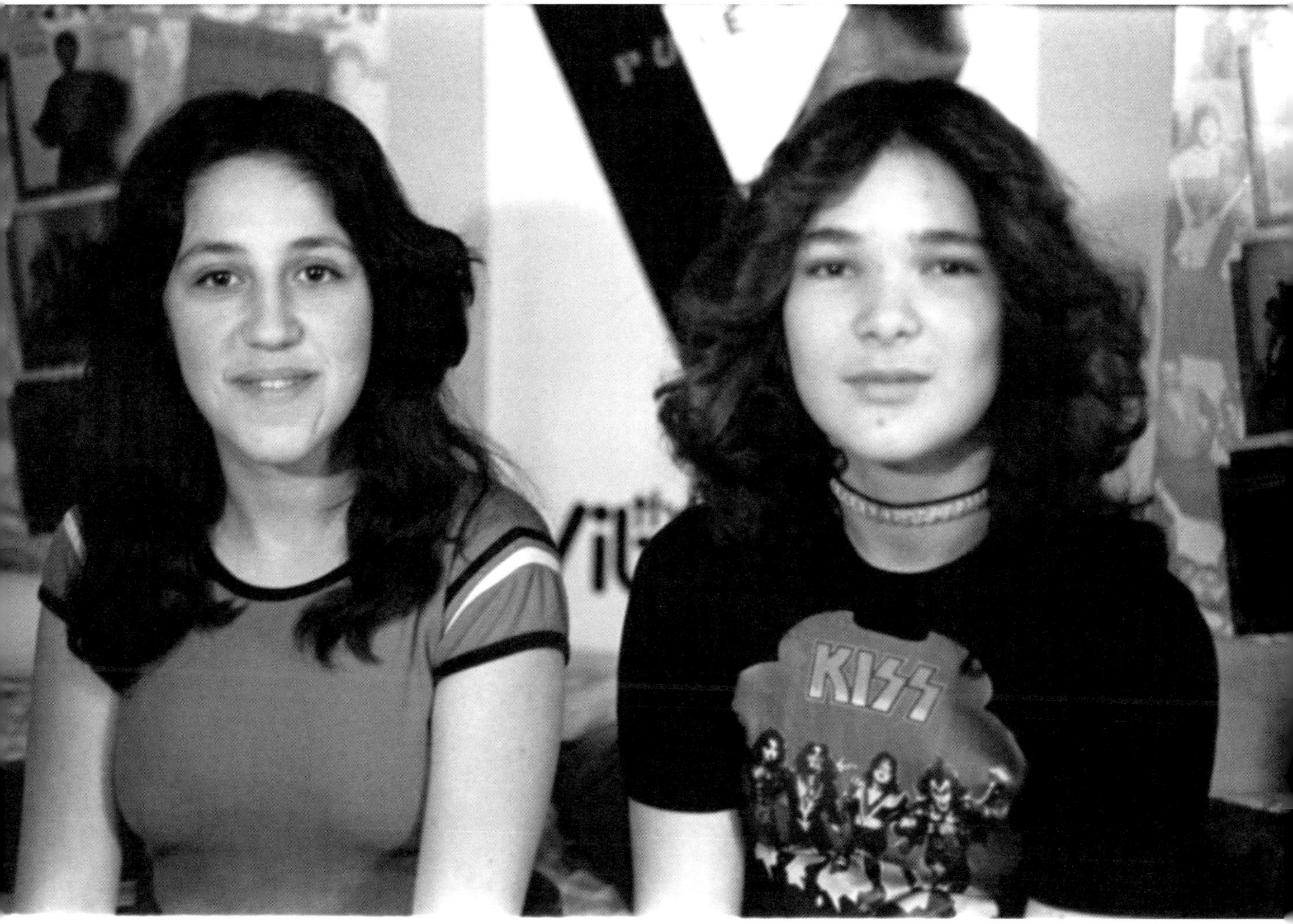

Sonia and Joanne

The Ugly, Turning Point, 1977

The Ugly looked like car thieves and gas station robbers, the kind of guys you couldn't ever picture taking their moms to lunch or pulling weeds in their garden while wearing sweatpants. In other words, they looked like a band. Or a gang. Sexy and sensual, vicious and visceral, the original band was a far greater thing than the one 45 they left behind.

When I saw this photograph for the first time, I was struck by the modesty of the tattoo on Nightmare's arm that reads "Rock 'n' Roll." It seemed so formal and polite, a sweet contradiction in ink. Nightmare reminds me of a bound Saint Sebastian riddled with arrows.

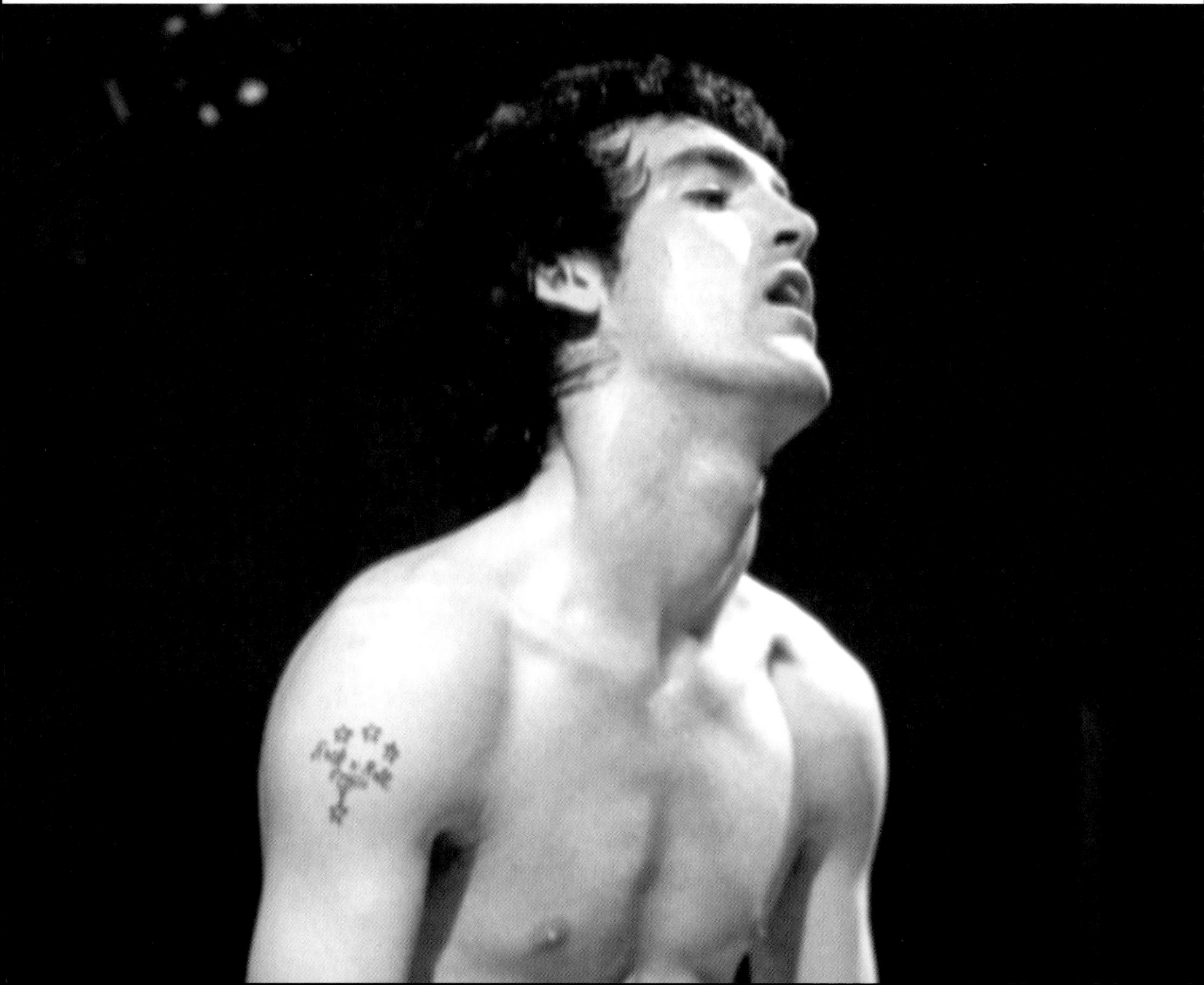

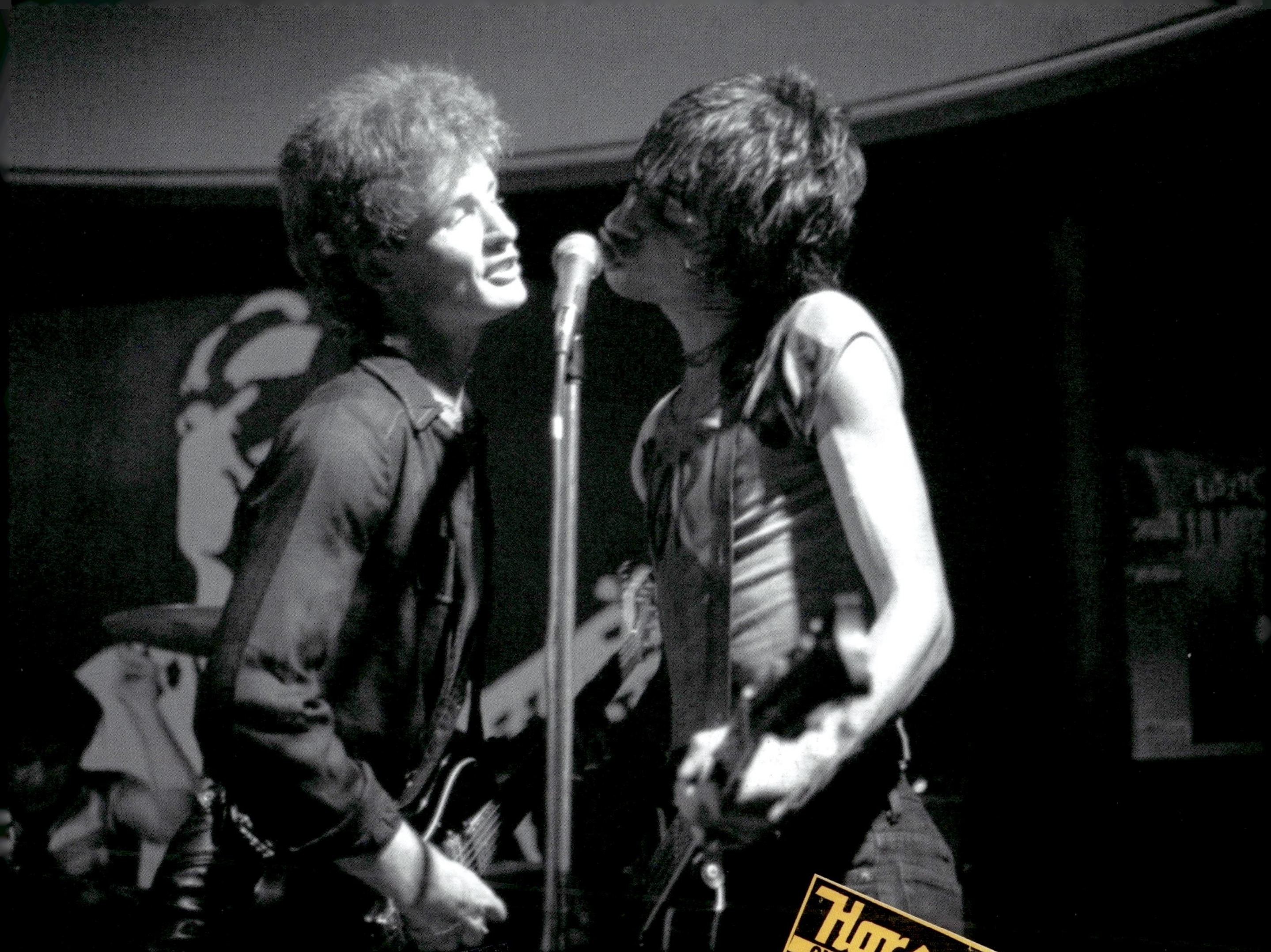

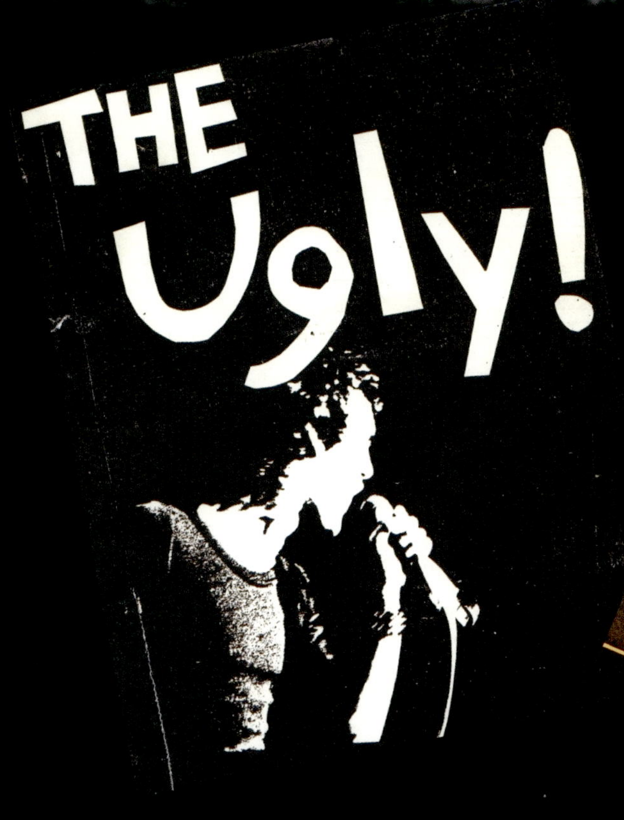
THE
Ugly!

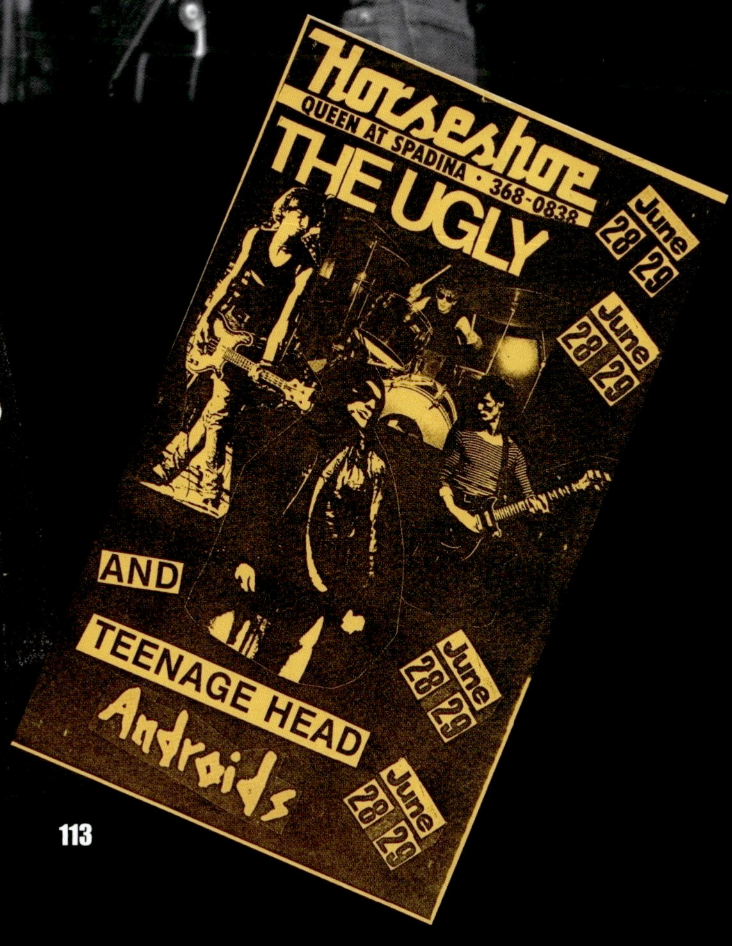
Horseshoe
QUEEN AT SPADINA · 368-0838
THE UGLY
June 28 29
June 28 29
AND
TEENAGE HEAD
June 28 29
Androids
June 28 29

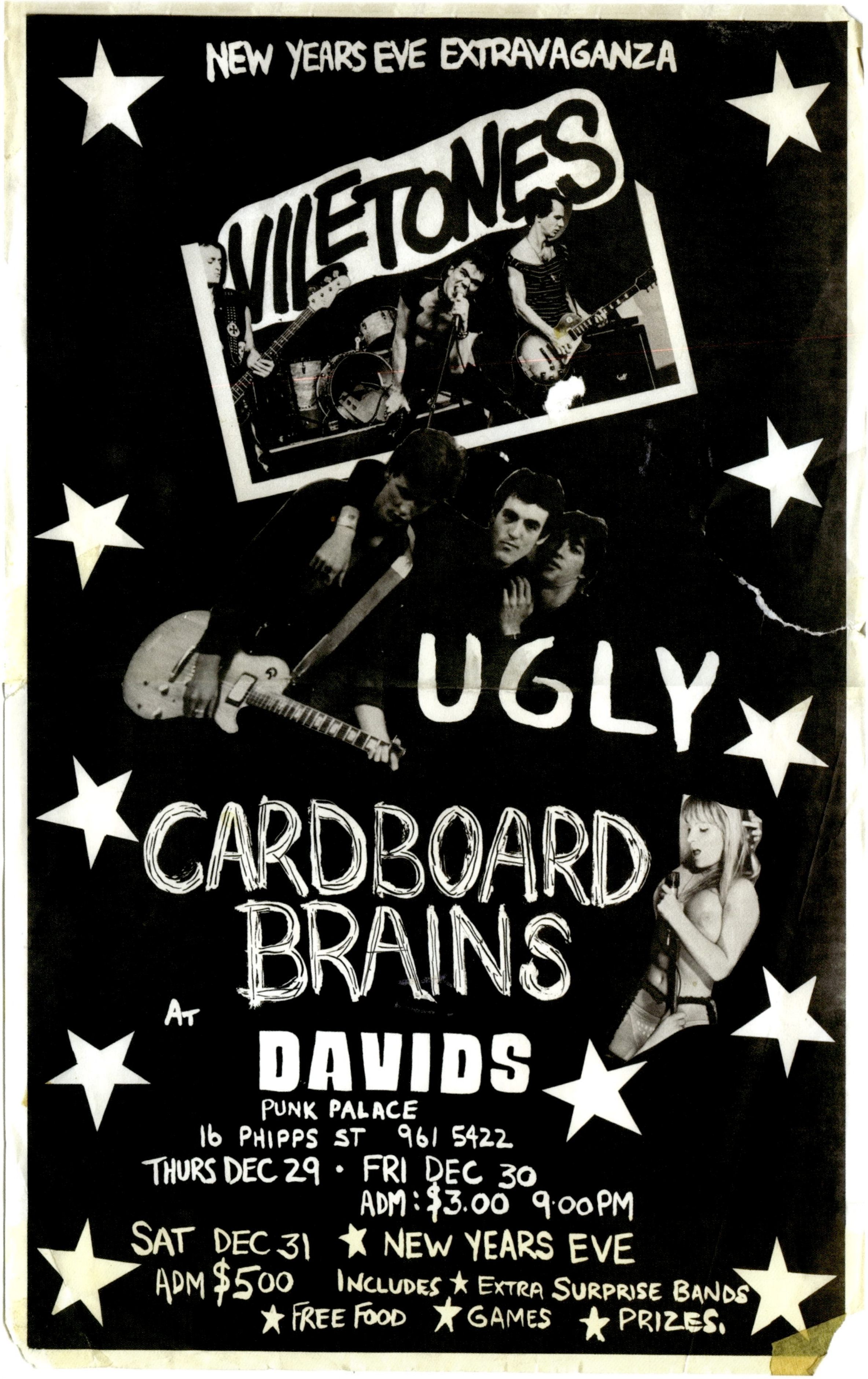
NEW YEARS EVE EXTRAVAGANZA
VILETONES
UGLY
CARDBOARD BRAINS
AT
DAVIDS
PUNK PALACE
16 PHIPPS ST 961 5422
THURS DEC 29 • FRI DEC 30
ADM: $3.00 9.00PM
SAT DEC 31 ★ NEW YEARS EVE
ADM $500 INCLUDES ★ EXTRA SURPRISE BANDS
★ FREE FOOD ★ GAMES ★ PRIZES.

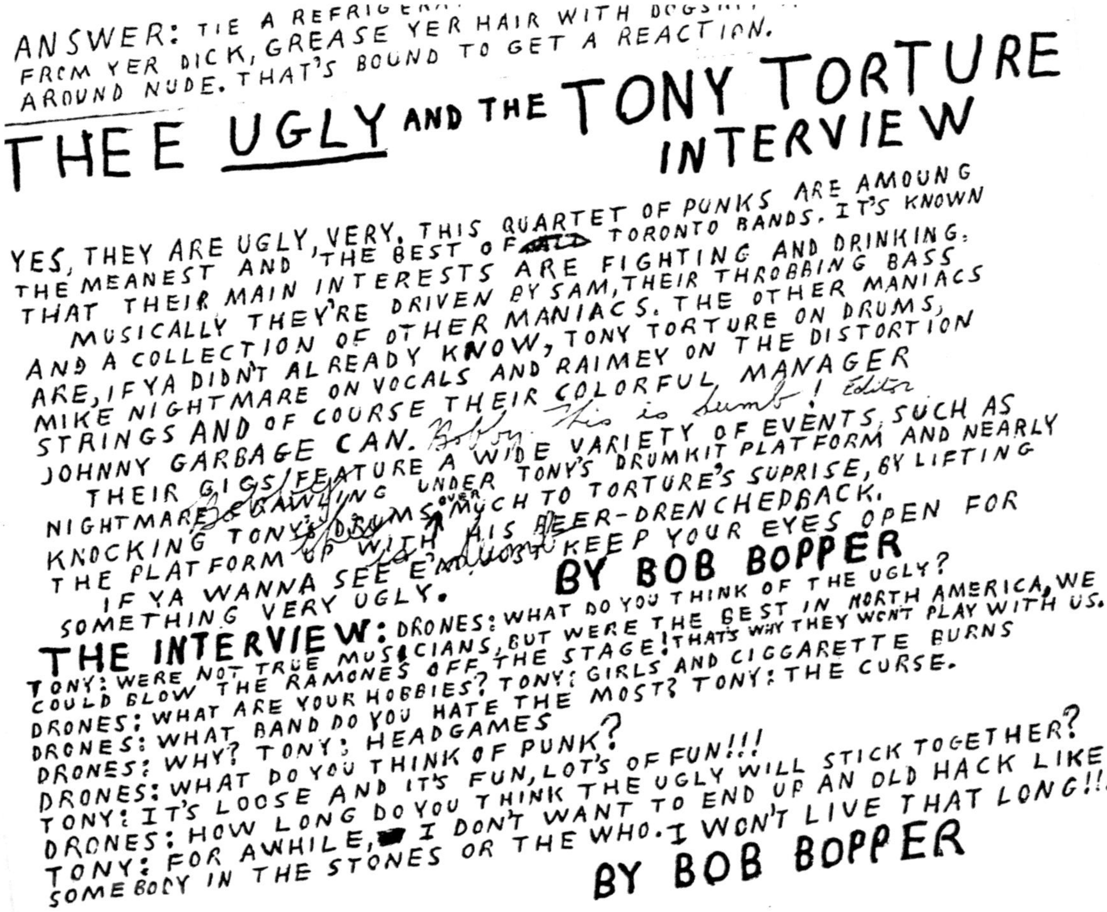

ANSWER: TIE A REFRIGERA... FROM YER DICK, GREASE YER HAIR WITH DOGSHIT ... AROUND NUDE. THAT'S BOUND TO GET A REACTION.

THEE UGLY AND THE TONY TORTURE INTERVIEW

YES, THEY ARE UGLY, VERY. THIS QUARTET OF PUNKS ARE AMOUNG THE MEANEST AND THE BEST OF TORONTO BANDS. IT'S KNOWN THAT THEIR MAIN INTERESTS ARE FIGHTING AND DRINKING. MUSICALLY THEY'RE DRIVEN BY SAM, THEIR THROBBING BASS AND A COLLECTION OF OTHER MANIACS. THE OTHER MANIACS ARE, IF YA DIDN'T ALREADY KNOW, TONY TORTURE ON DRUMS, MIKE NIGHTMARE ON VOCALS AND RAIMEY ON THE DISTORTION STRINGS AND OF COURSE THEIR COLORFUL MANAGER JOHNNY GARBAGE CAN. THEIR GIGS FEATURE A WIDE VARIETY OF EVENTS, SUCH AS NIGHTMARE CRAWLING UNDER TONY'S DRUMKIT PLATFORM AND NEARLY KNOCKING TONY'S DRUMS OVER, MUCH TO TORTURE'S SUPRISE, BY LIFTING THE PLATFORM UP WITH HIS BEER-DRENCHED BACK. KEEP YOUR EYES OPEN FOR THEM IF YA WANNA SEE SOMETHING VERY UGLY.

Bobby This is dumb! Editor

BY BOB BOPPER

THE INTERVIEW: DRONES: WHAT DO YOU THINK OF THE UGLY?
TONY: WERE NOT TRUE MUSICIANS, BUT WERE THE BEST IN NORTH AMERICA. WE COULD BLOW THE RAMONES OFF THE STAGE! THAT'S WHY THEY WON'T PLAY WITH US.
DRONES: WHAT ARE YOUR HOBBIES? TONY: GIRLS AND CIGGARETTE BURNS
DRONES: WHAT BAND DO YOU HATE THE MOST? TONY: THE CURSE.
DRONES: WHY? TONY: HEADGAMES
DRONES: WHAT DO YOU THINK OF PUNK?
TONY: IT'S LOOSE AND IT'S FUN, LOT'S OF FUN!!!
DRONES: HOW LONG DO YOU THINK THE UGLY WILL STICK TOGETHER?
TONY: FOR AWHILE, I DON'T WANT TO END UP AN OLD HACK LIKE SOMEBODY IN THE STONES OR THE WHO. I WON'T LIVE THAT LONG!!!

BY BOB BOPPER

I wish I could remember what the advertised "Games and Prizes" were for a Viletones/The Ugly/Cardboard Brains 1977-into-1978 New Year's Eve gig at Club David's. What I do remember is the "buffet," a vestigial formality of what might be expected at a "real" New Year's Eve party. Cold cuts and tomato slices flew and at least a few ended up down Mike Nightmare's pants. At the end of The Ugly's set, Nightmare swung his mic in circles above his head before sending it flying into the audience, where it landed at my feet. Noticing that everyone was still watching the last song erupt onstage, I unplugged it and tucked it into my jacket pocket. This was our cue to exit and go see The Cramps, who were playing across the road at the New Yorker.

When I got home, I looked at the mic and saw it had "NIGHTMARE" scratched into it. That scared me a little, clear evidence of my thievery, but I was also thrilled that now I had a microphone; I had all I needed to be a singer in a band. I was relieved the next day when news got to me that David's had burned down and all the band's equipment had been destroyed, thus hiding what I'd done. I was also relieved when the mic, like a cursed voodoo doll, was in turn stolen from me.

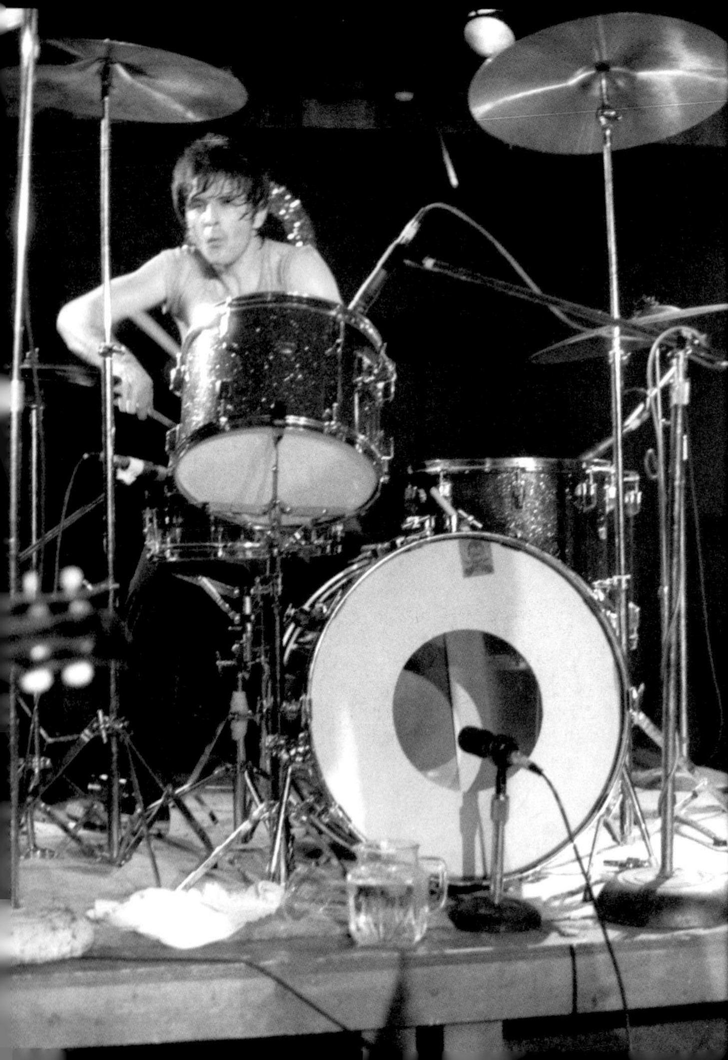

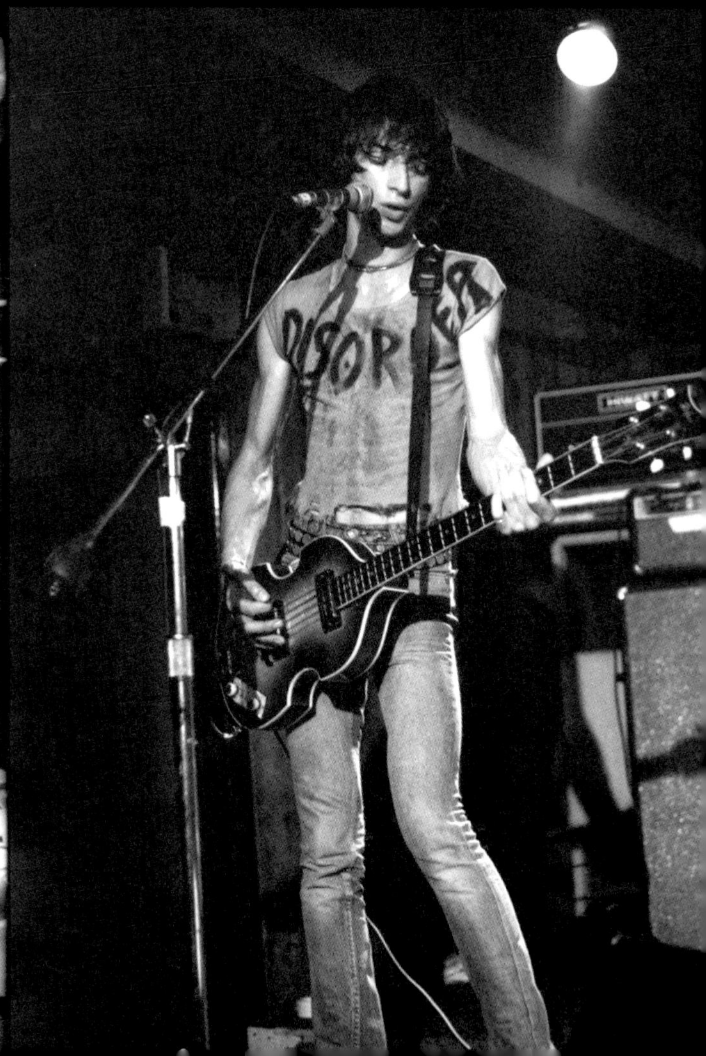

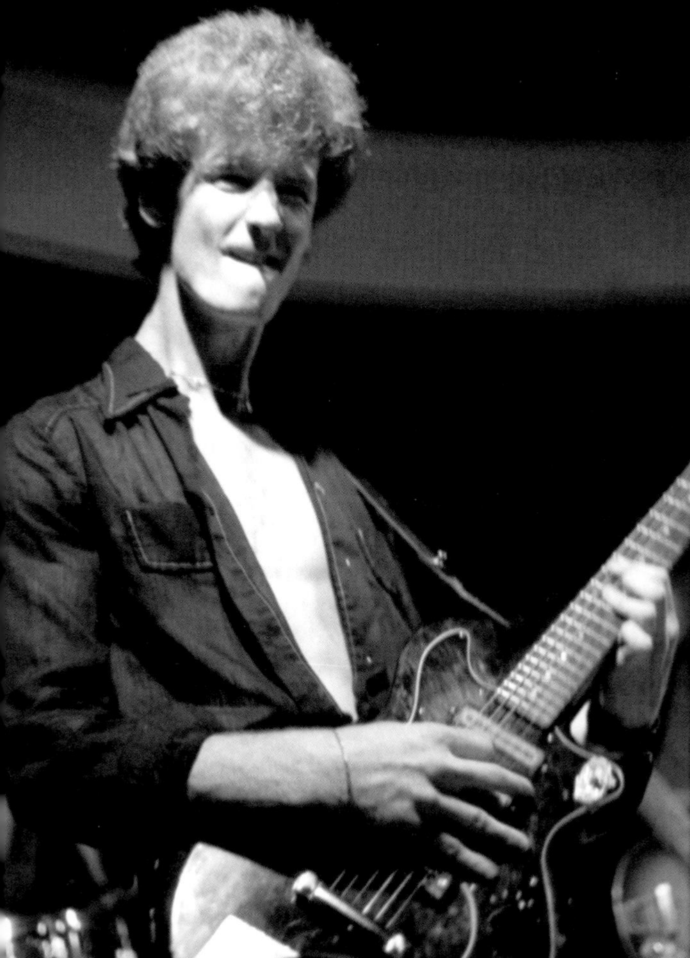
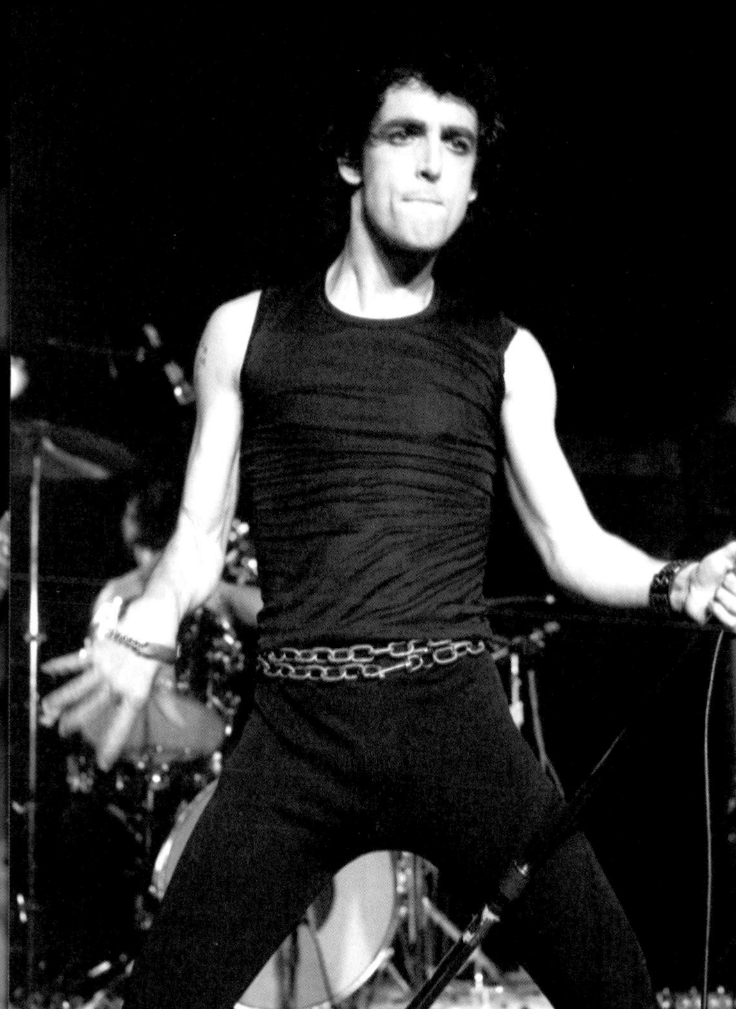

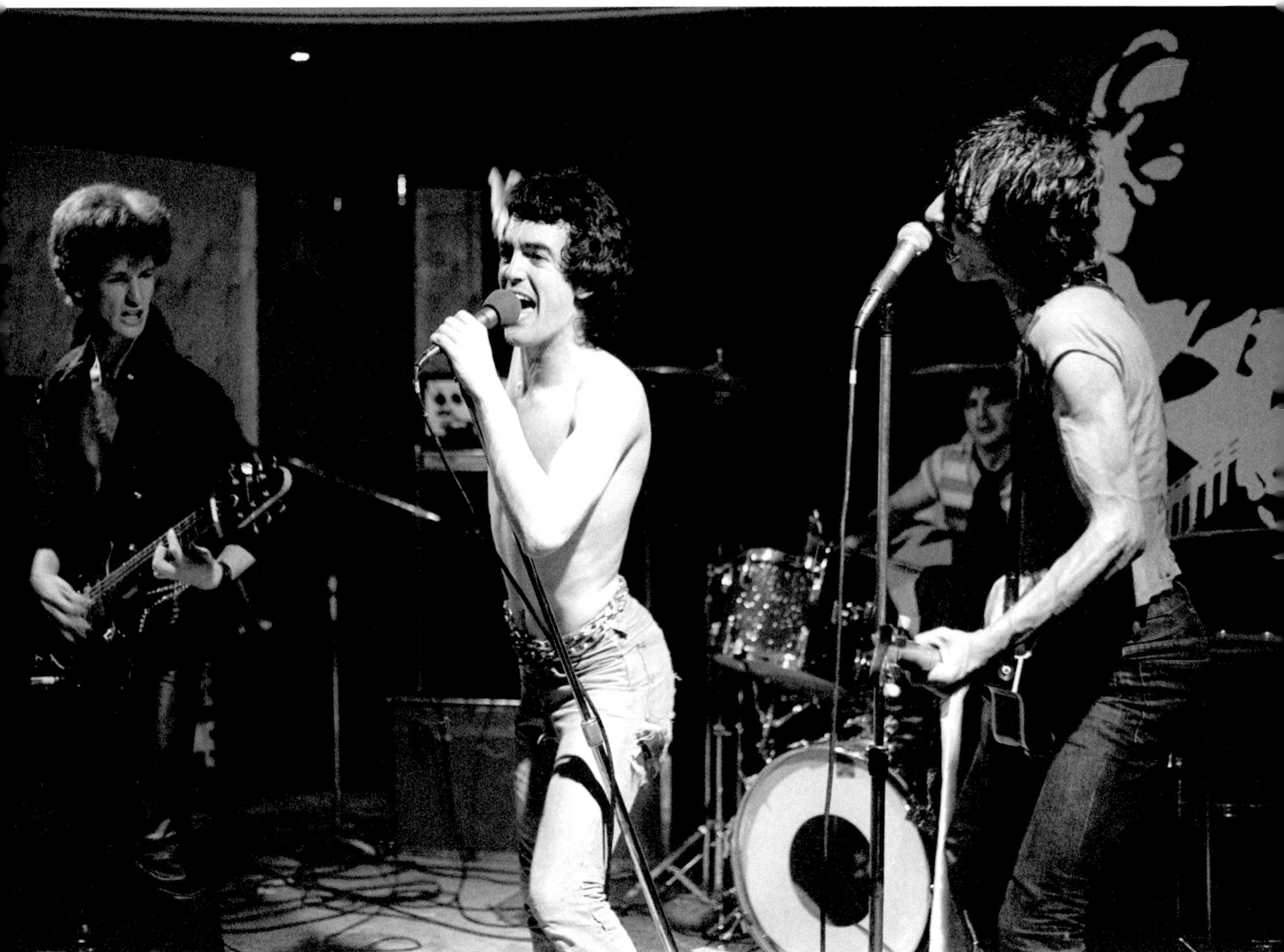

Raymi Gunner, Mike Nightmare, Tony Torcher, Sam Ugly

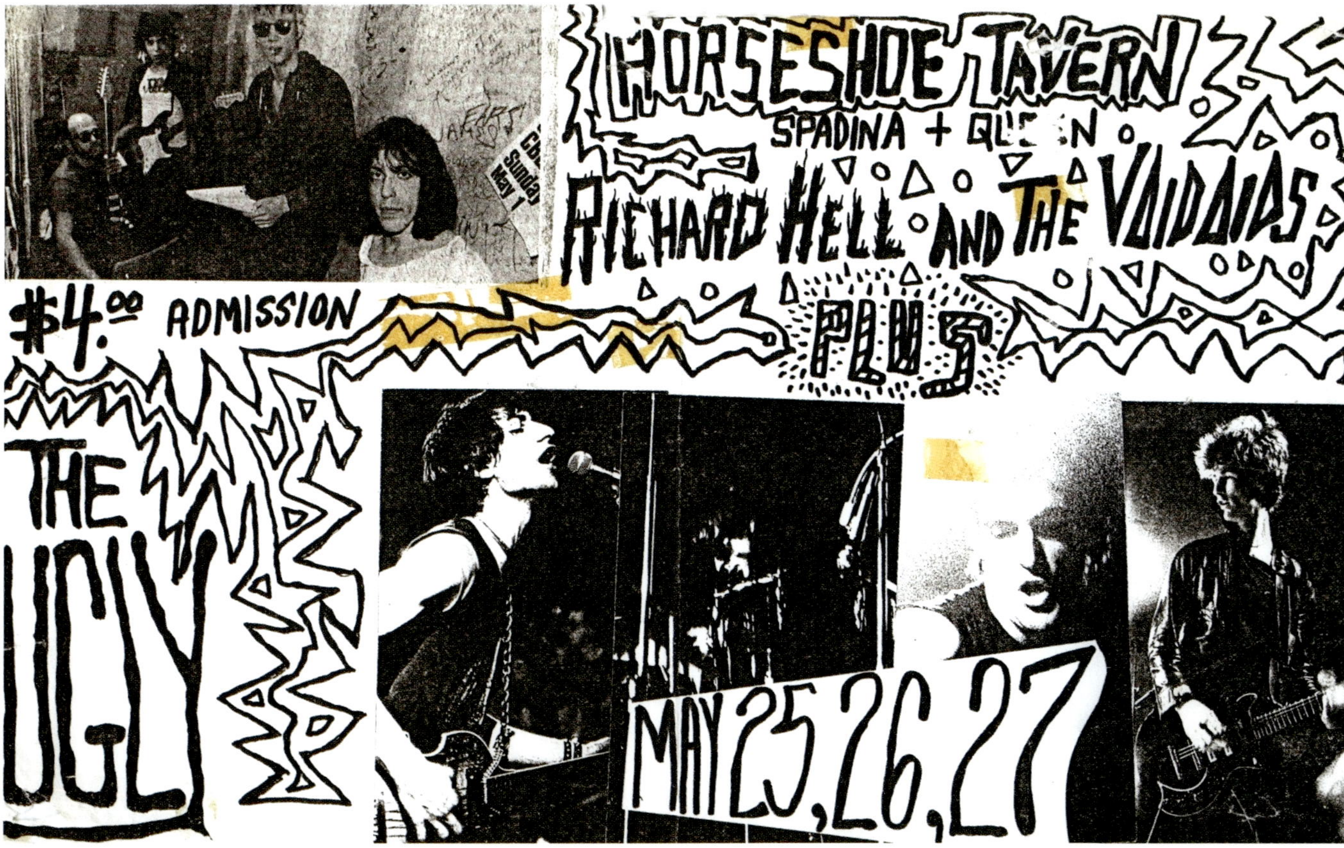
HORSESHOE TAVERN
SPADINA + QUEEN
RICHARD HELL AND THE VOIDOIDS
$4.00 ADMISSION
PLUS
THE UGLY
MAY 25,26,27

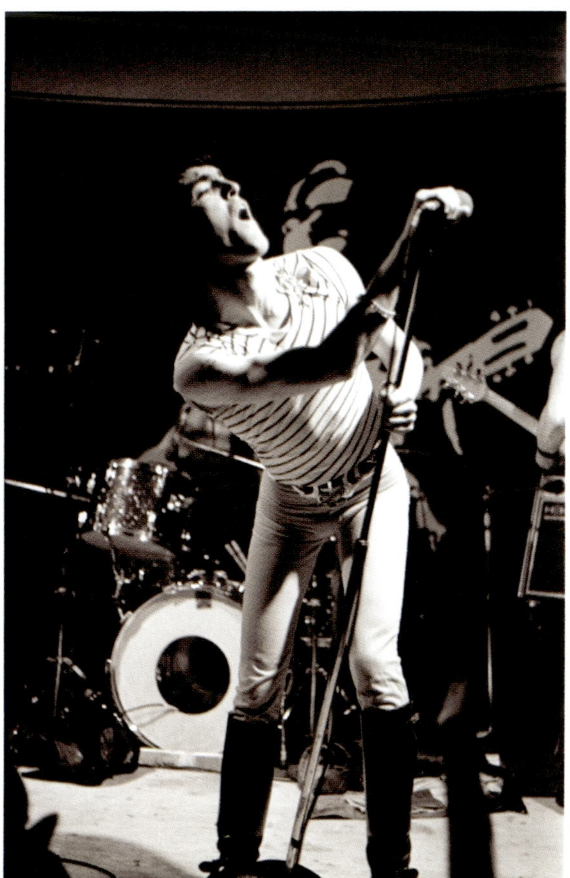

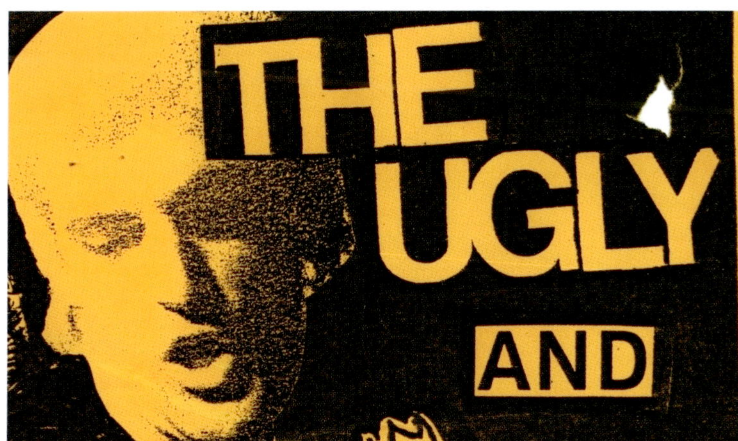
THE UGLY
AND

THE UGLY
THE UGLY
THE UGLY

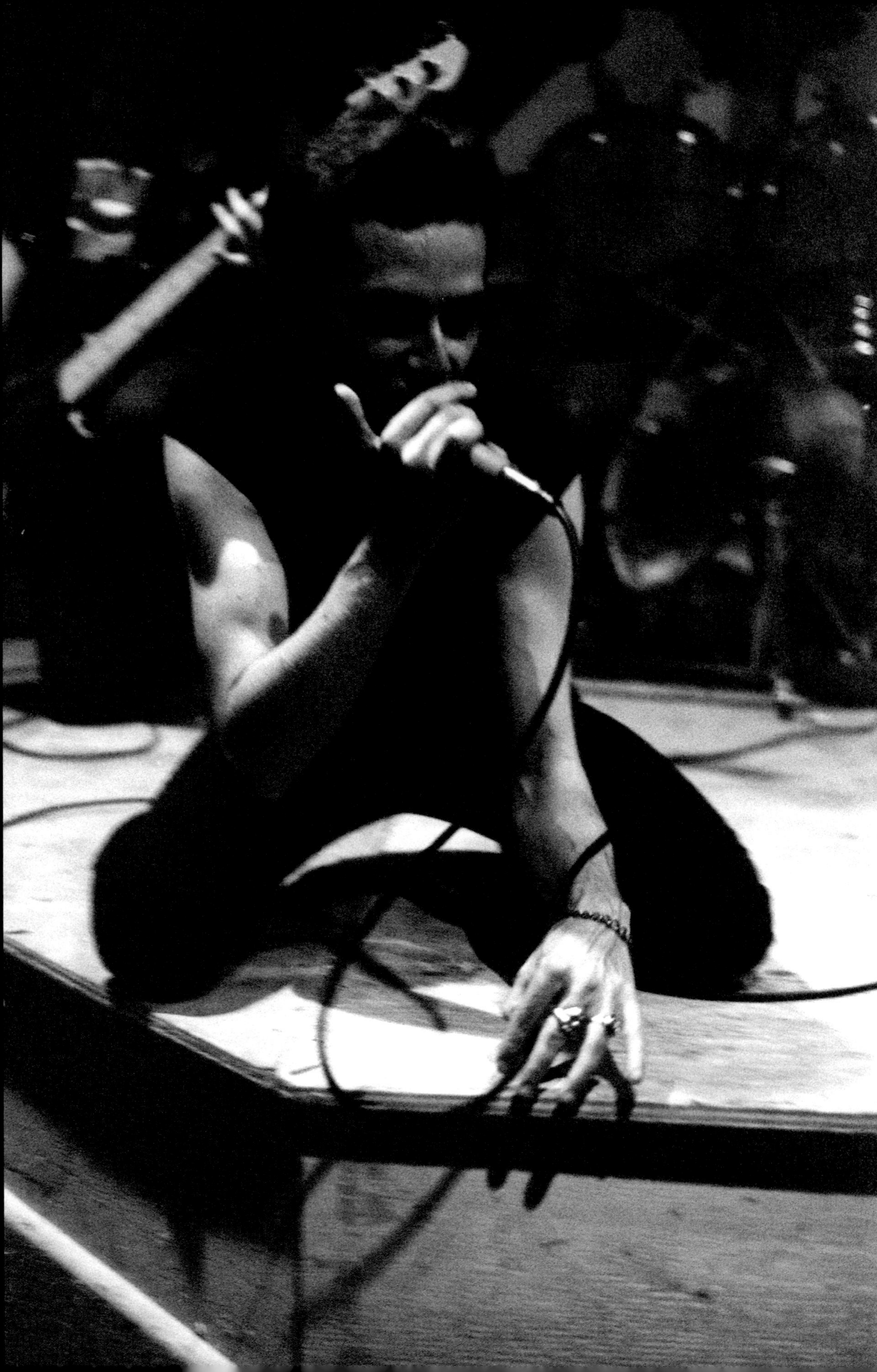

Arson,
Turning Point, 1978

Arson was a band that included Steve Goode from The Poles and Chick Parker, one of the guitarists in the second version of The Ugly. I saw singer Rudi Tuesdai arrive at the show in a Moxy/Streetheart-style wide-leg pale blue denim jumpsuit and then duck behind the curtain. He emerged a few minutes later in tight black punk clothes and then later flapped around the stage doing Iggy's moves exactly.

Viletones, Turning Point, 1977

Light was often very low at gigs so I'd experiment shooting 400 ASA film pushed to 1,000 or more ASA. Images would end up blurry, grainy and in extreme contrast. Preferring to use available light usually meant only taking pictures of whoever or whatever was lit. It was rare to capture drummer Motor Mike as most of the places the Viletones played were lit by a household lightbulb mounted in an institutional tomato can.

Their shows felt intense and unpredictable. Anything could happen but more often than not the threat of violence was contained in the music and performance, not in actual fighting. Sometimes, Steven Leckie would start a scrap with someone in the audience and then leave it to his fans, or their sometimes soundman Johnny Garbagecan, to finish the job. A bottle would be broken, with Leckie dragging the sharp glass down his arms threatening to cut himself more often than actually doing it. But there was blood. The original "classic" lineup, meaning the four-piece version that existed after their first couple of shows, would dwell for long stretches of time on one thrilling ominous chord as Leckie threw himself about, flailing and instigating fights. Unparalleled at turning even a cold Monday night into an event, the Viletones were epic and heroic — the hot central light of the explosive flare.

Steven Leckie, Freddy Pompeii

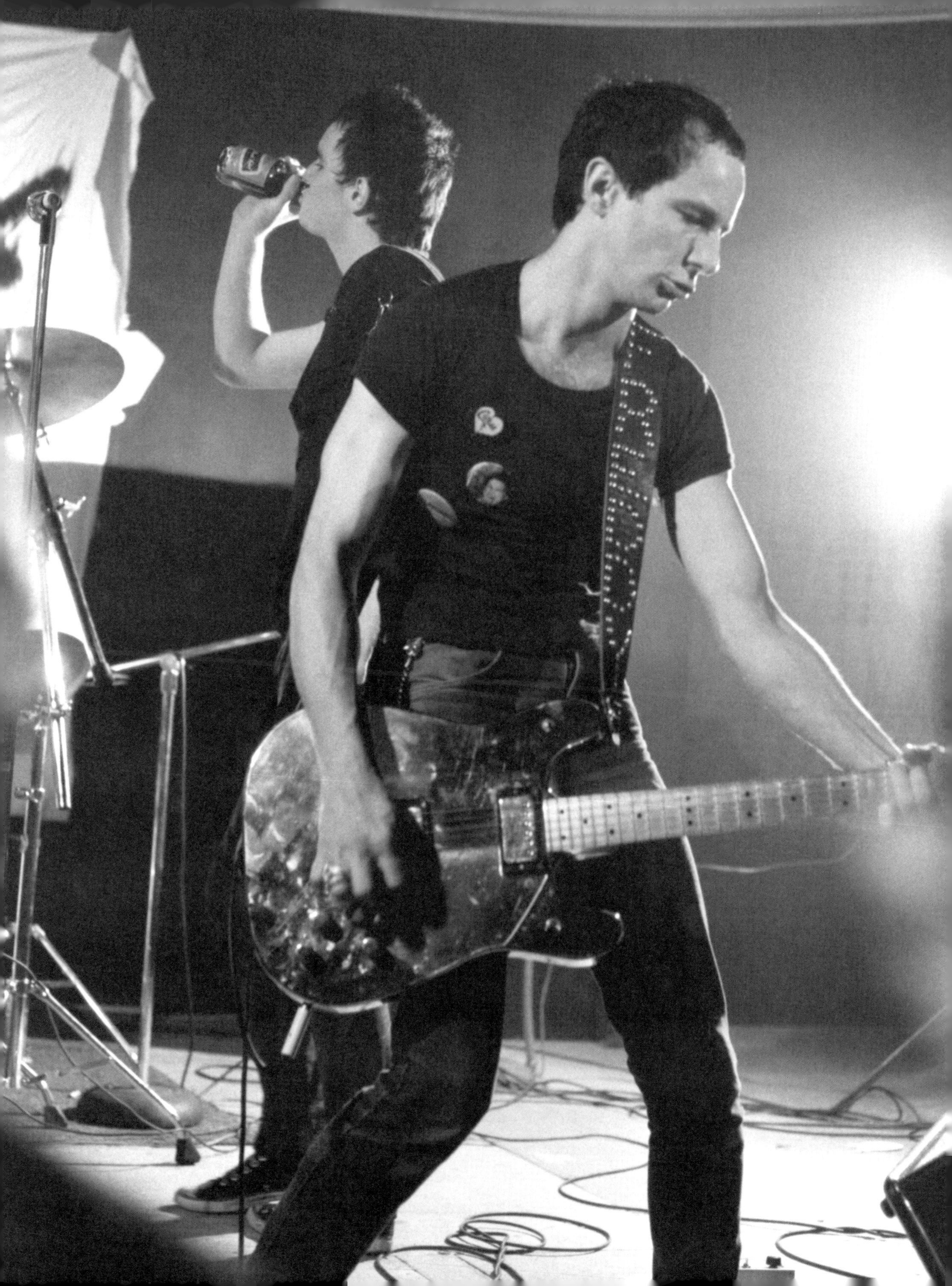

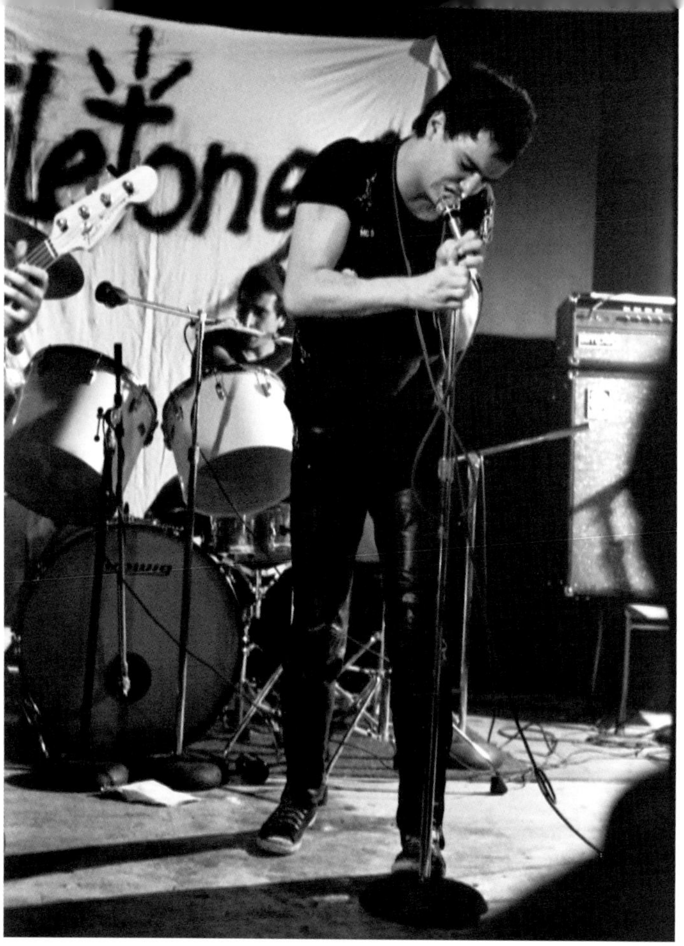

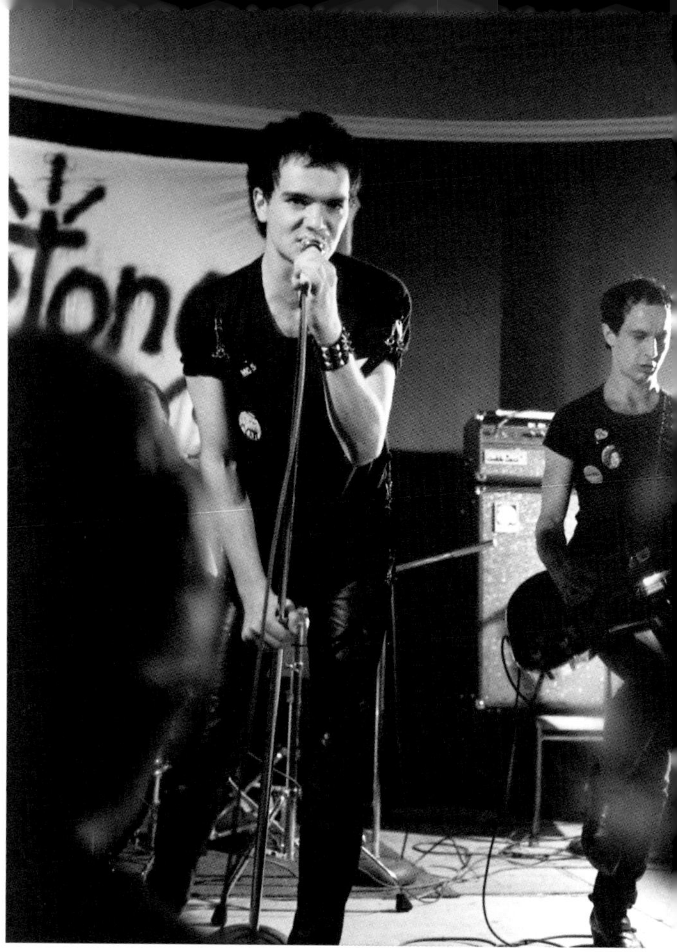

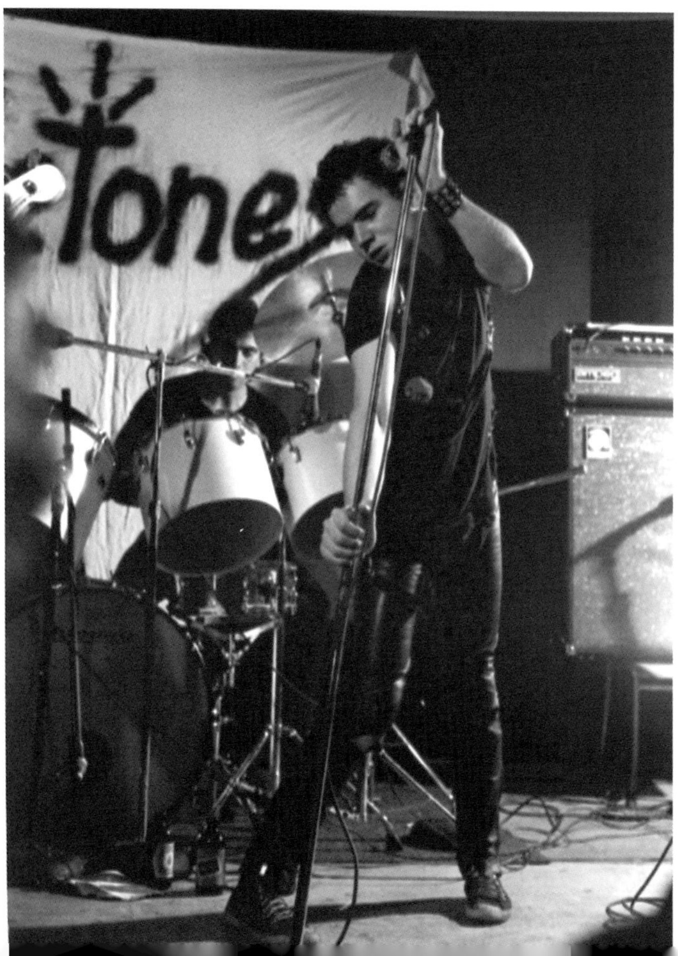

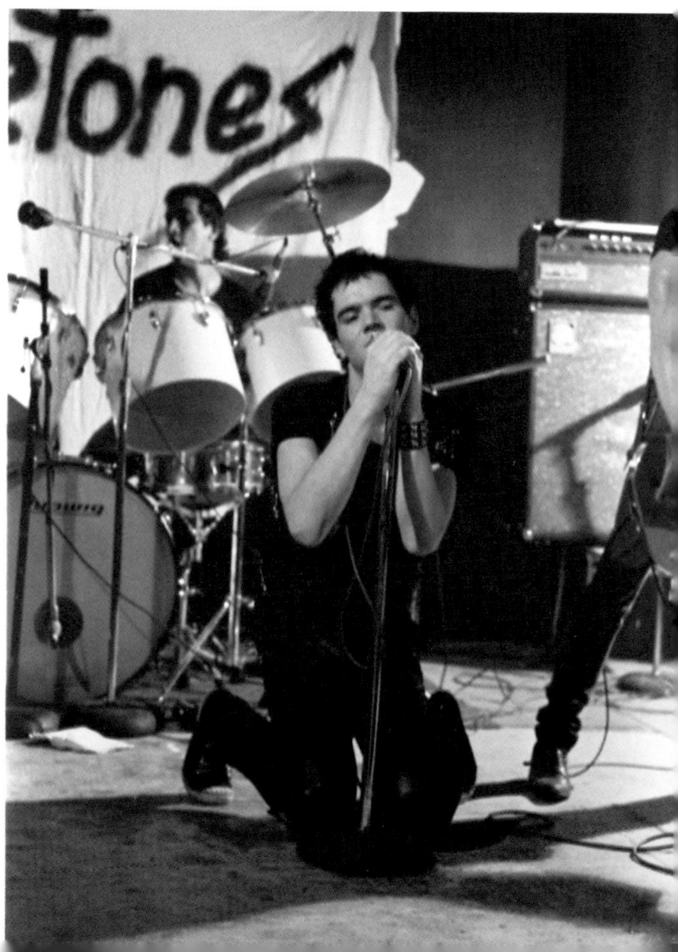

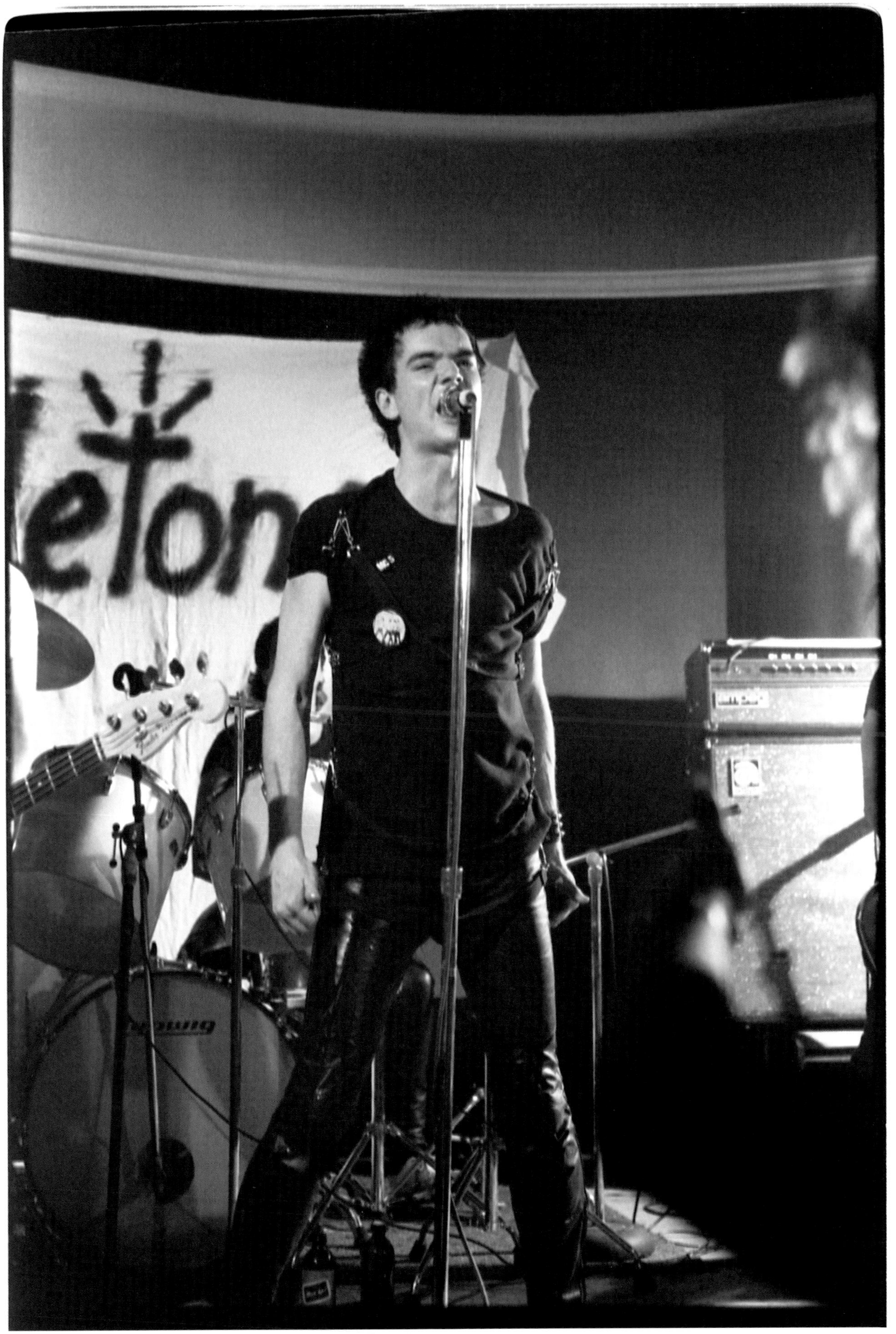

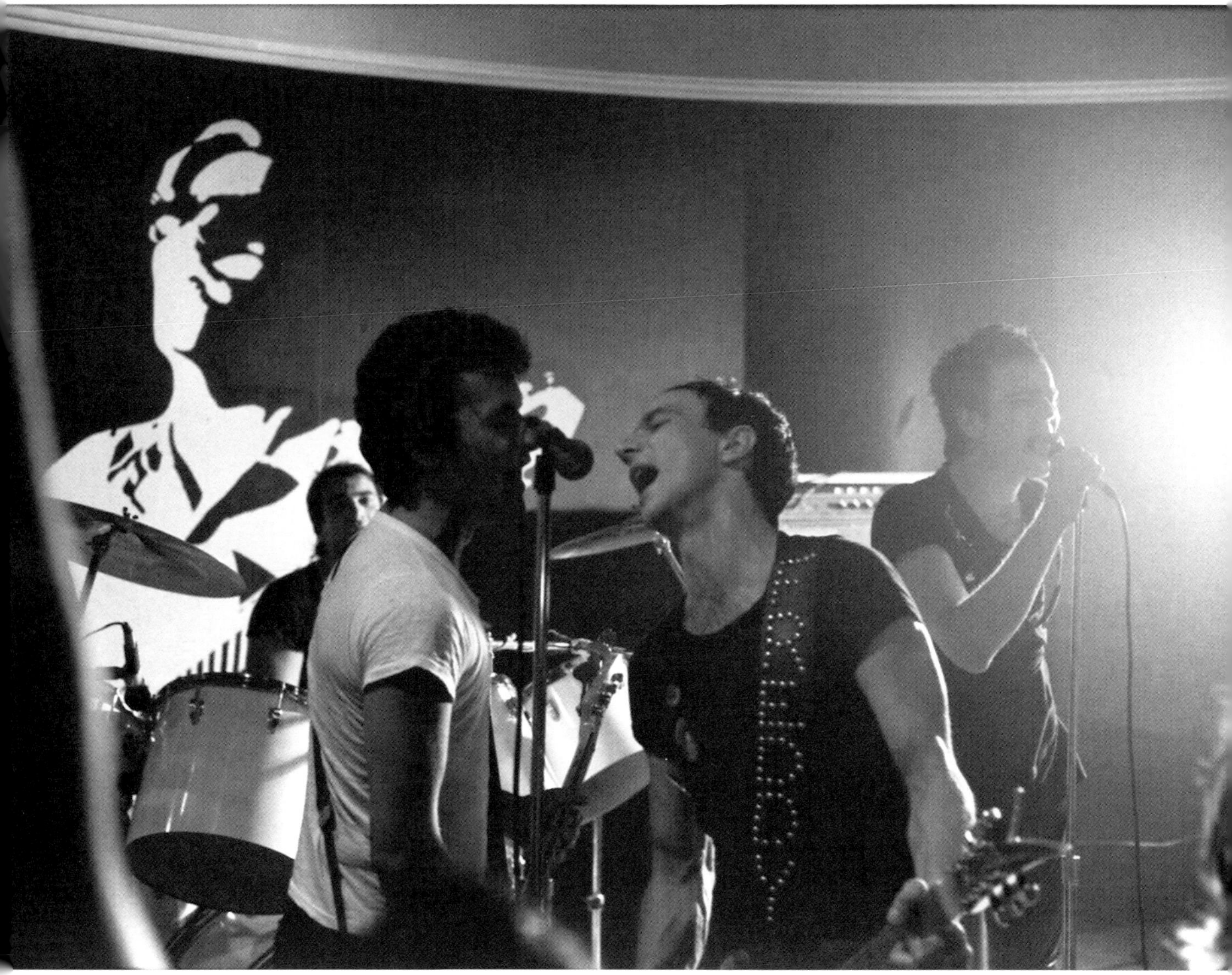

Mike "Motor X" Anderson, Chris Haight, Freddy Pompeii, Steven Leckie

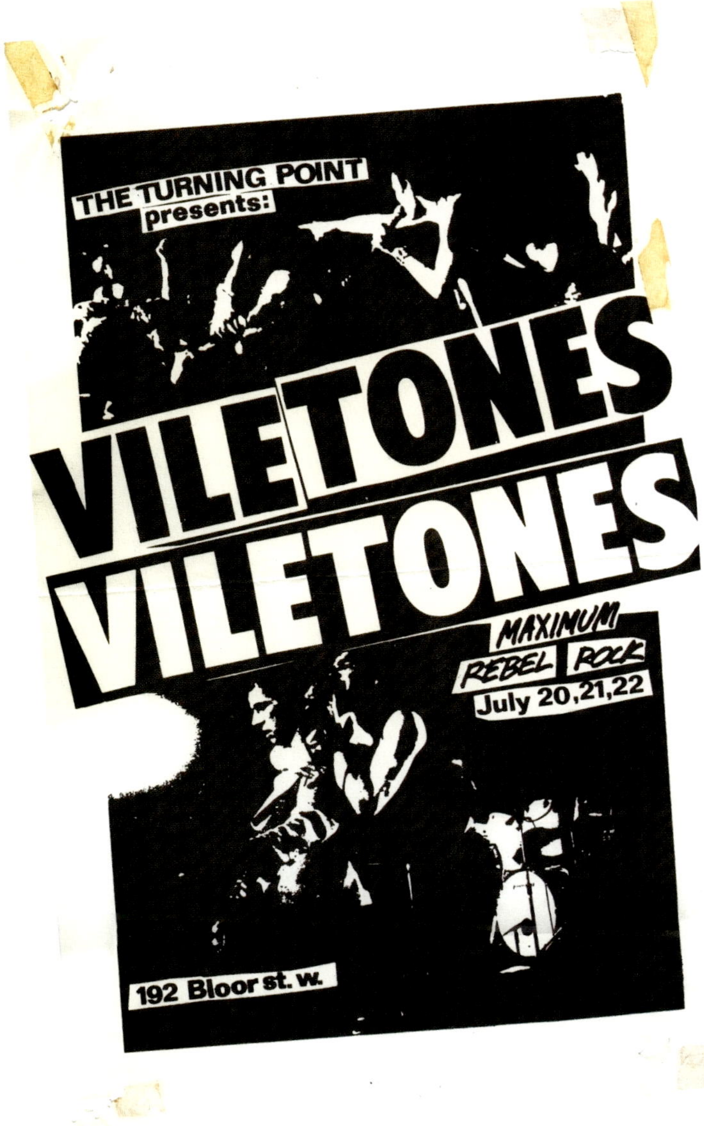

Freddy Pompeii pointed me in a direction that ended up being a very significant life situation. Freddy and his partner, Margarita, ran a little shop and ersatz Viletones clubhouse at Queen Street East and Parliament. It was called New Rose and sold T-shirts, badges and 45s. They were both somewhat protective of me, even as they gave the underage kid beer. One day, while delivering T-shirts I had made for them, I mentioned I was going to Calgary to visit my brother. Freddy said they'd just received a fan letter from Calgary and suggested I write to the guy. I did, telling him I was coming and asking if there were any punk bands in Calgary. He immediately wrote back warning me not to come; he couldn't wait to get out of Calgary and the only thing close to a punk group was his brother's band. Steve and his brother Alex and I became pen pals, something that today seems as quaint as doilies. Steve Koch moved to Toronto, followed soon after by Alex and his bandmates, Brian Connelly and Reid Diamond. Freddy's prompting resulted in Alex, Reid, Brian and I forming a band called Crash Kills Five, and, over the next 20 years, Shadowy Men on a Shadowy Planet with Brian and Reid, and Phono-Comb with Reid.

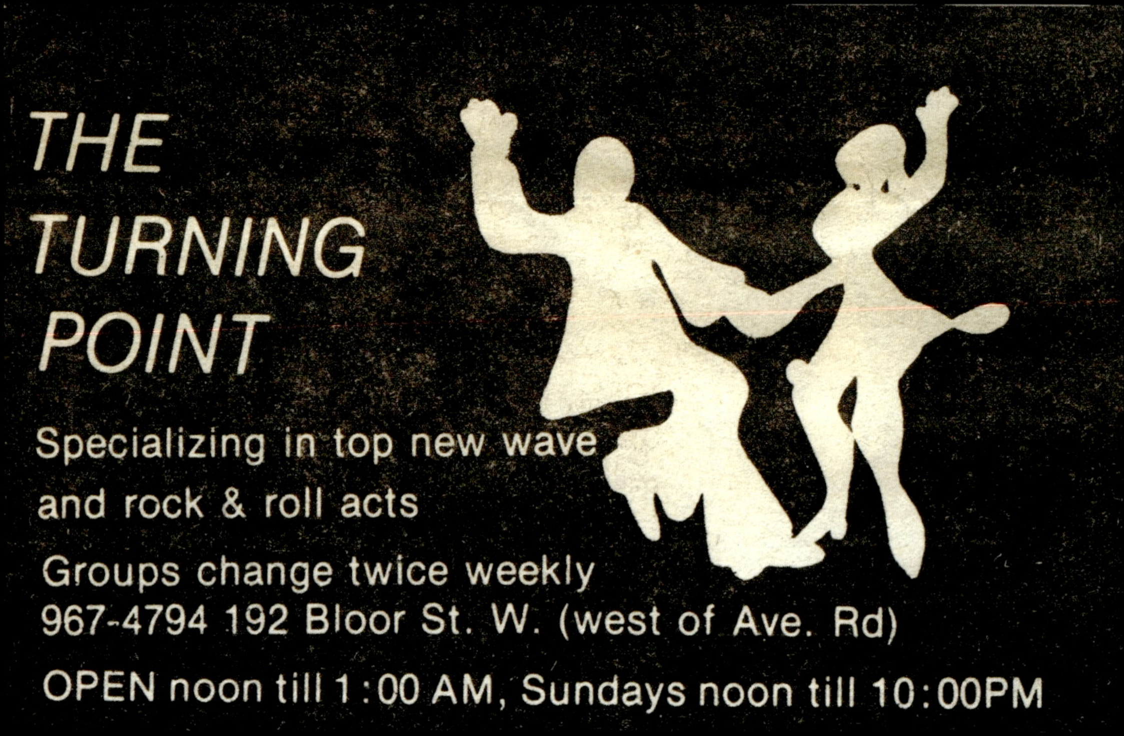

Besides being a totally captivating performer, Freddy was a real sweetheart and contrary to what you may have heard, is alive somewhere in Pennsylvania.

Whenever anyone mentions The Turning Point, they inevitably laugh about the giant mural of José Feliciano that graced the wall behind the stage. I recall gazing at José many times during gigs there, thinking how cool he looked in sunglasses — the detached observer of this music so at odds with his own.

The club was run by Joe and Anne, an elderly Irish couple grateful for the new audience that had found their venue. They had no qualms about underagers, as long as you were buying beer. My 14-year-old sister even worked the door there a few times. Joe would try to lure audiences back, drawing on the short list of bands he knew to be popular, telling people fibs like, "The Clash are going to be doing a surprise show here next Tuesday."

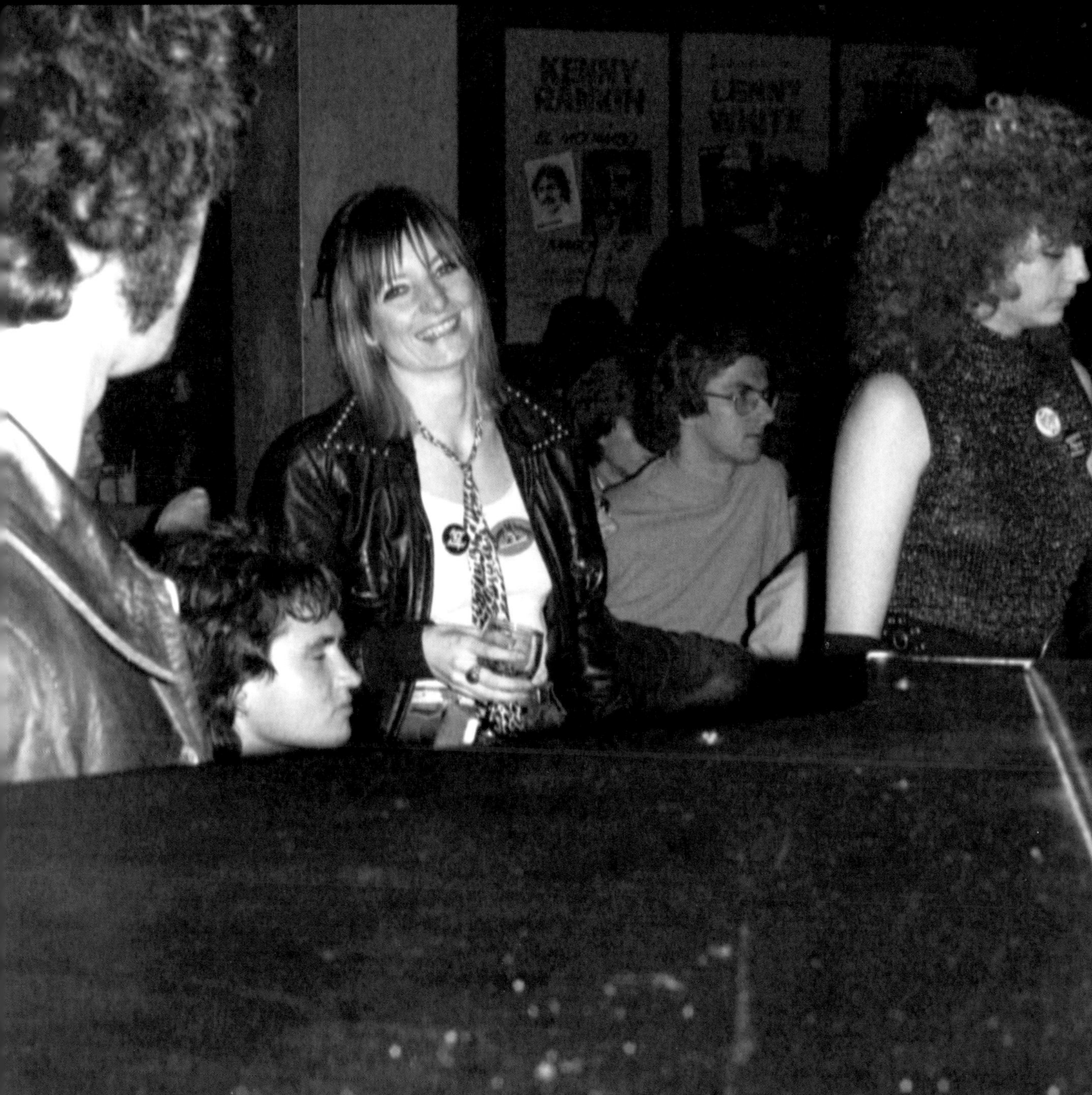

Margarita Passion

Other People

I sometimes took photographs of my friends and other people I was at gigs with, usually on the sidewalk after the show as we figured out where to go next or just hung out talking.

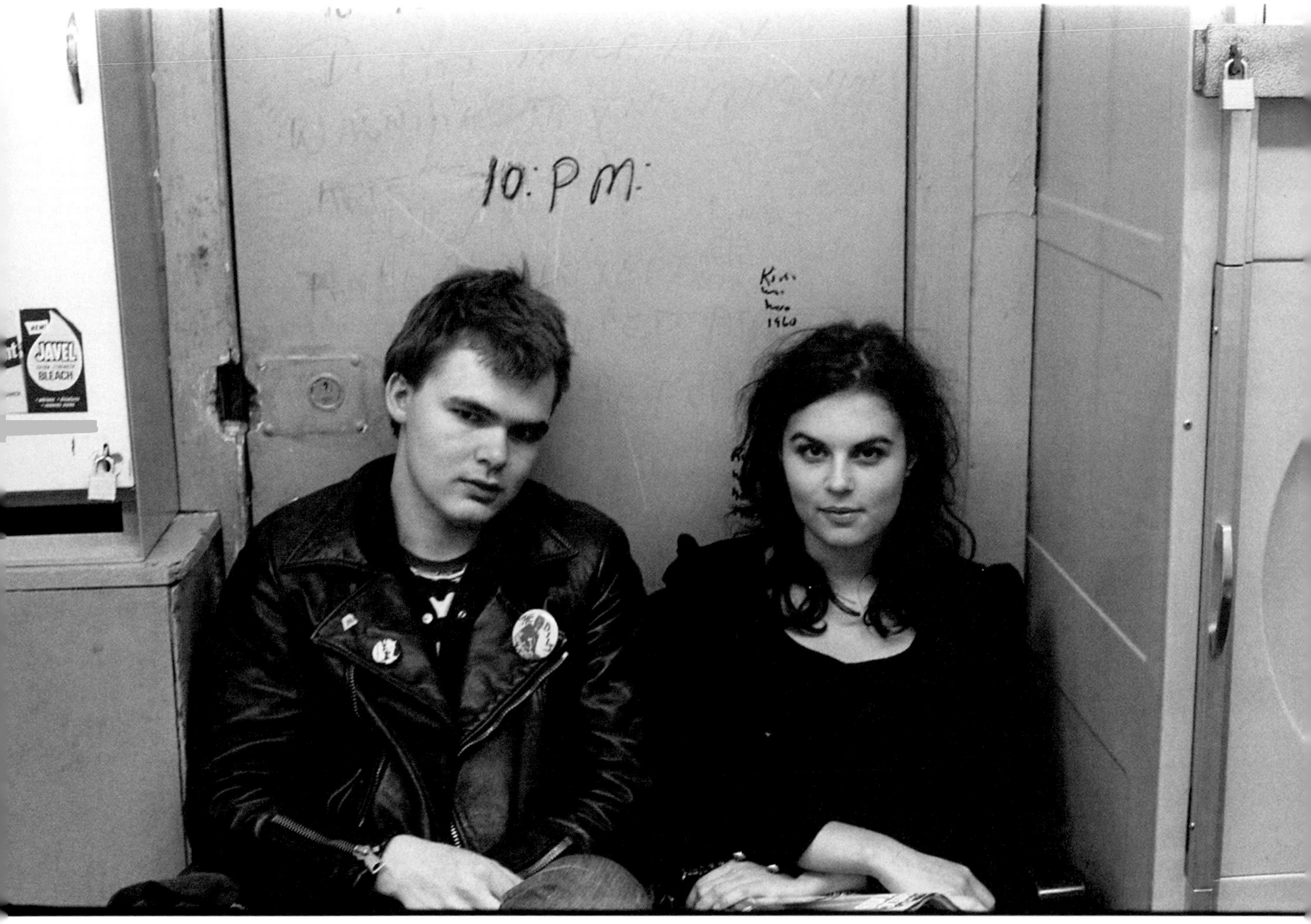

Virlana and I at a Laundromat on Carlton Street at Parliament. I placed my camera on the washing machine adjacent to us and shot it using the timer

Virlana in the same Laundromat, which also offered "Bachelor Service"

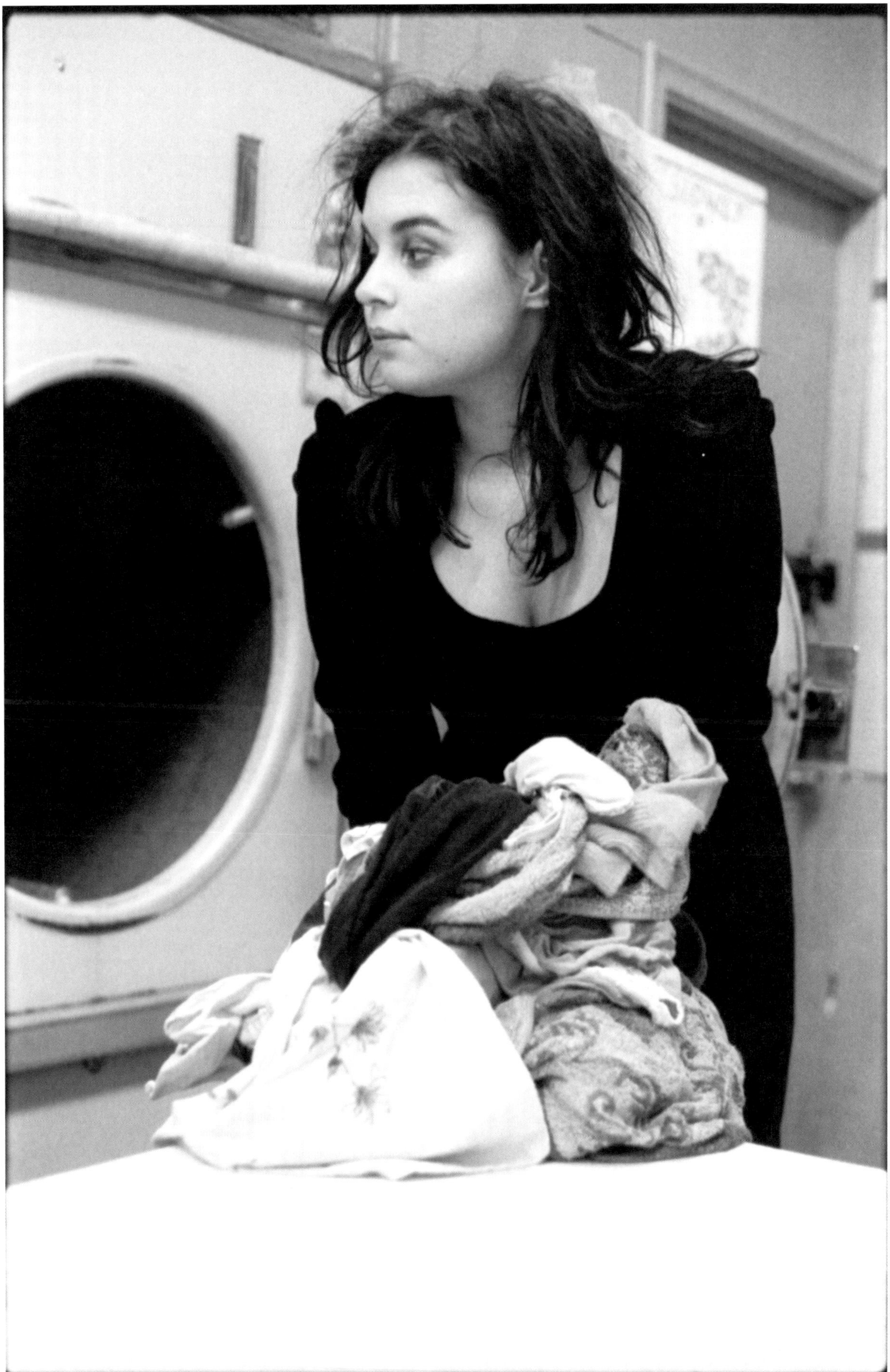

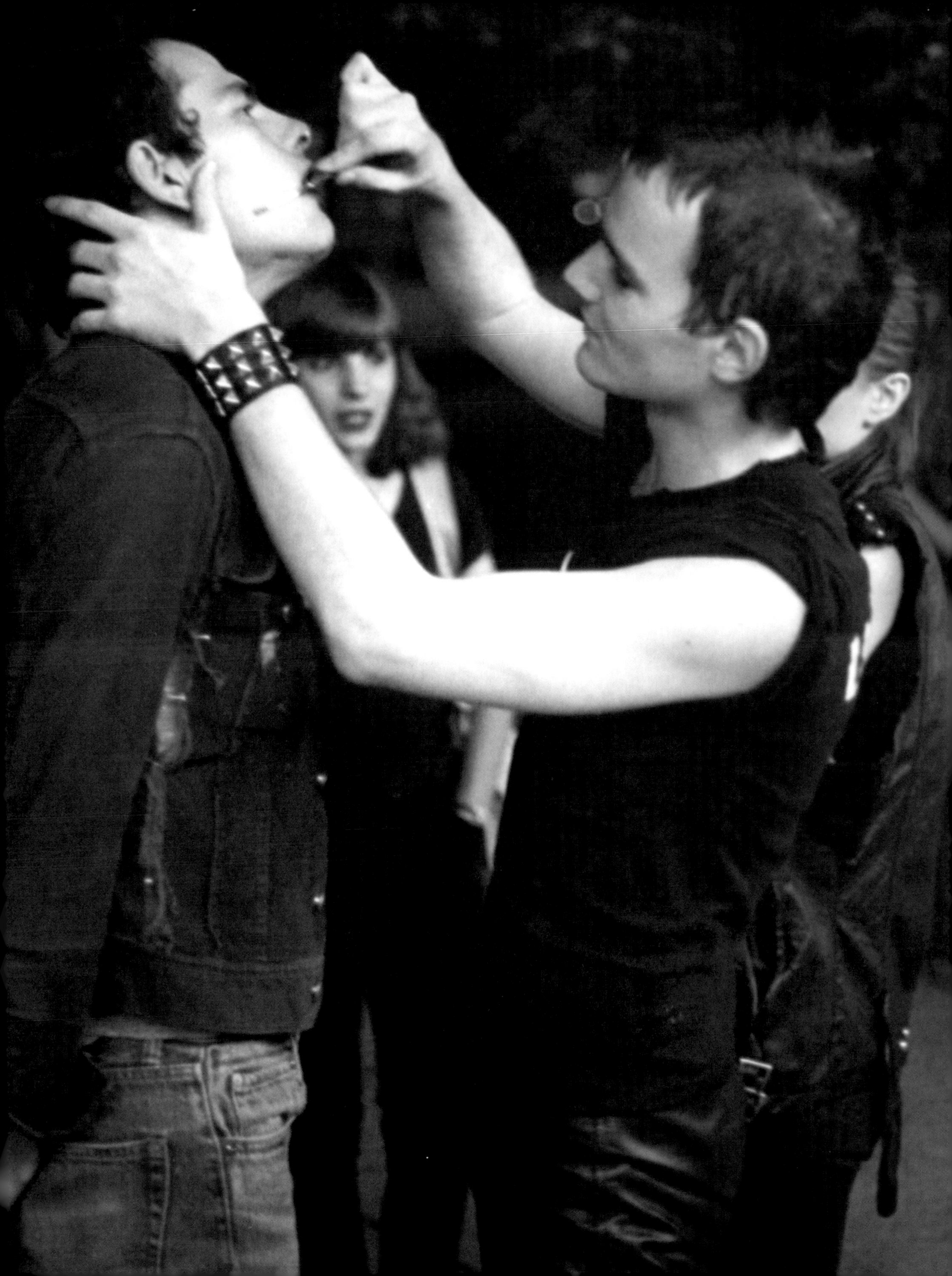

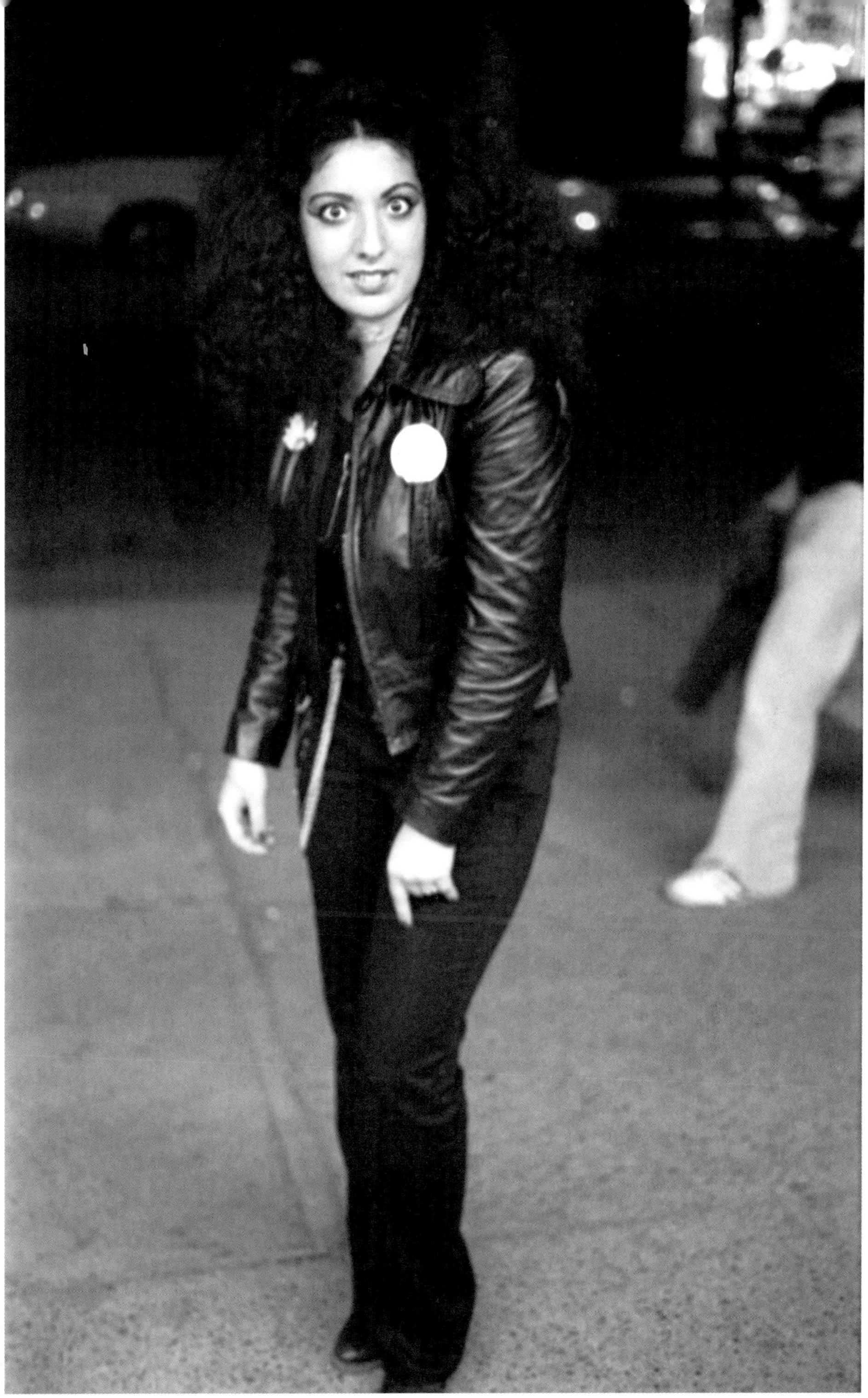

Cram, one of my best friends from this period, in front of the Horseshoe

Brian "Slash Booze" Baird, credited on Teenage Head albums as being their "inspiration," and Steven Leckie on the street in front of the Horseshoe

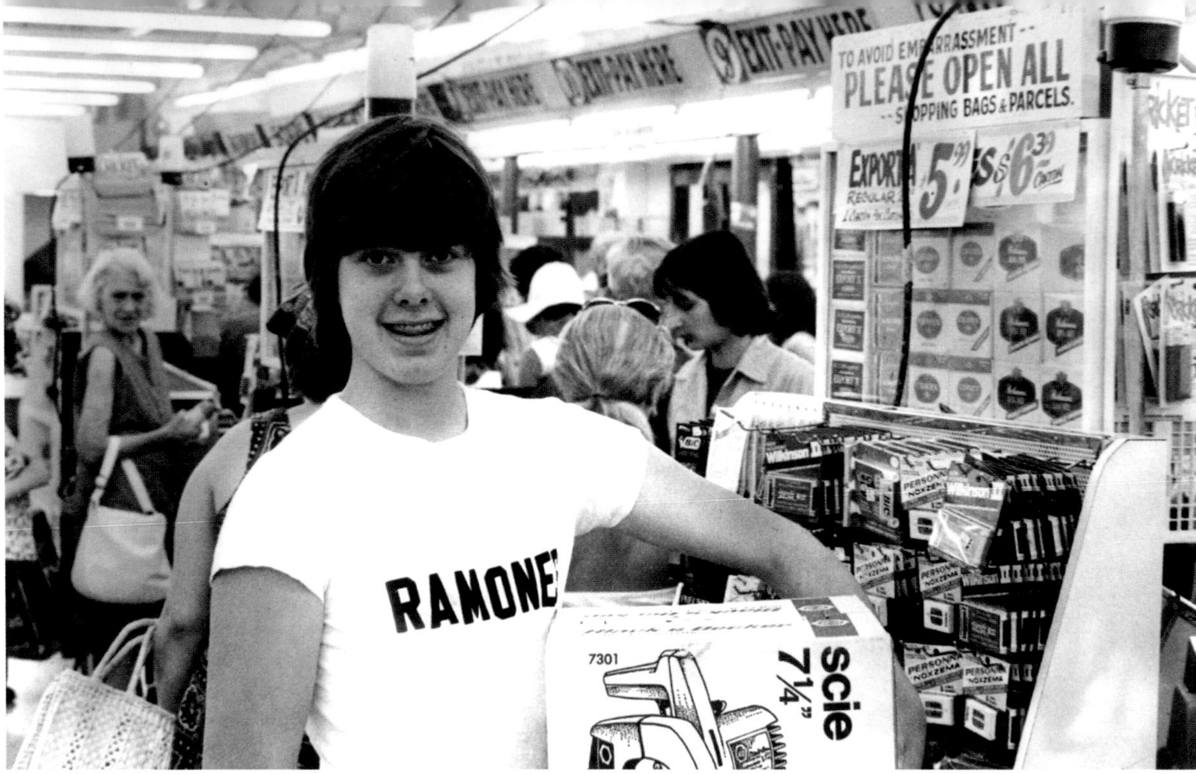

Roger, buying a birthday saw for his dad at Honest Ed's

Gerri, singer of the band Offbeat, Rojer and Gambi with the Horseshoe's "wood-paneled" windows in the background

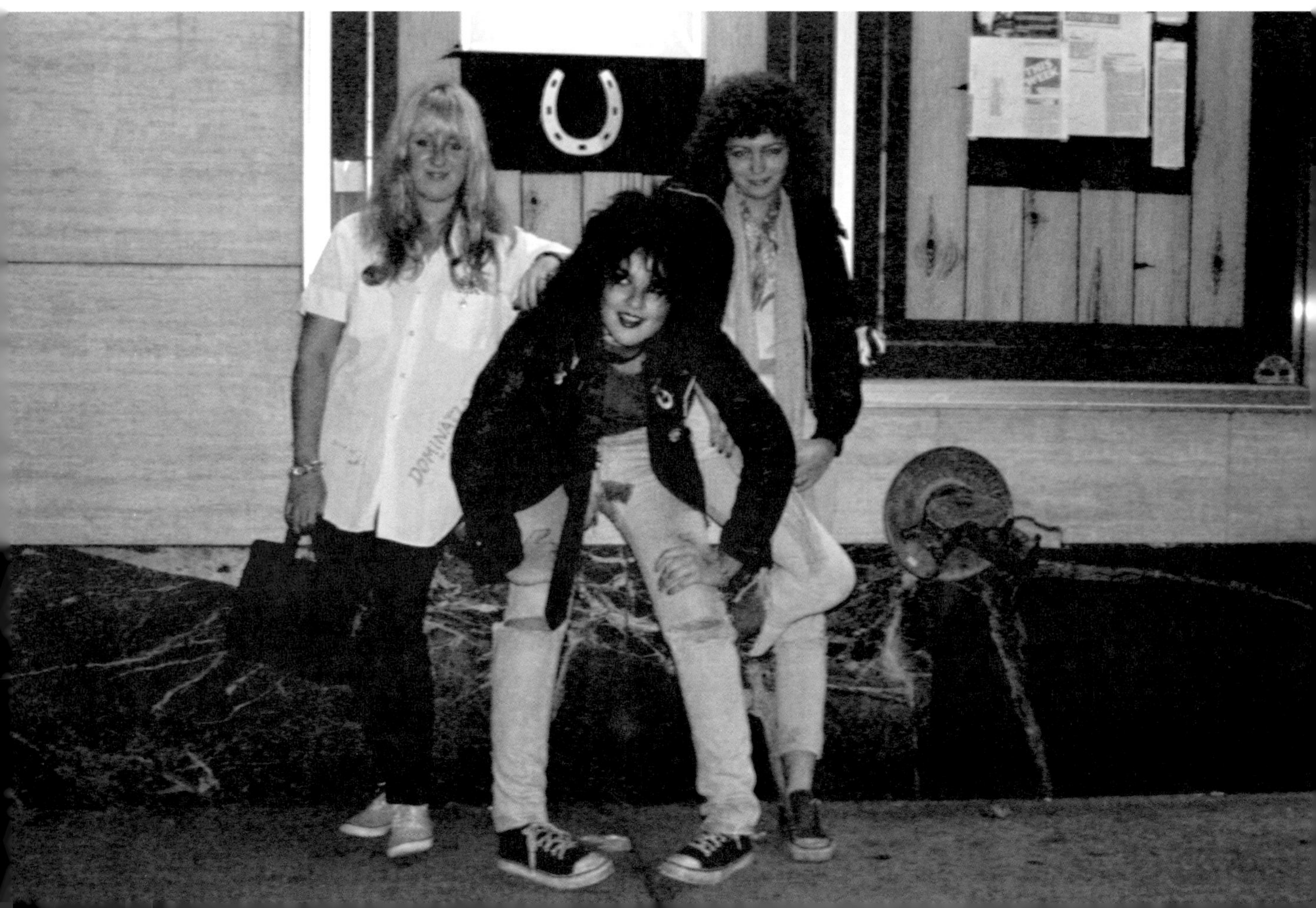

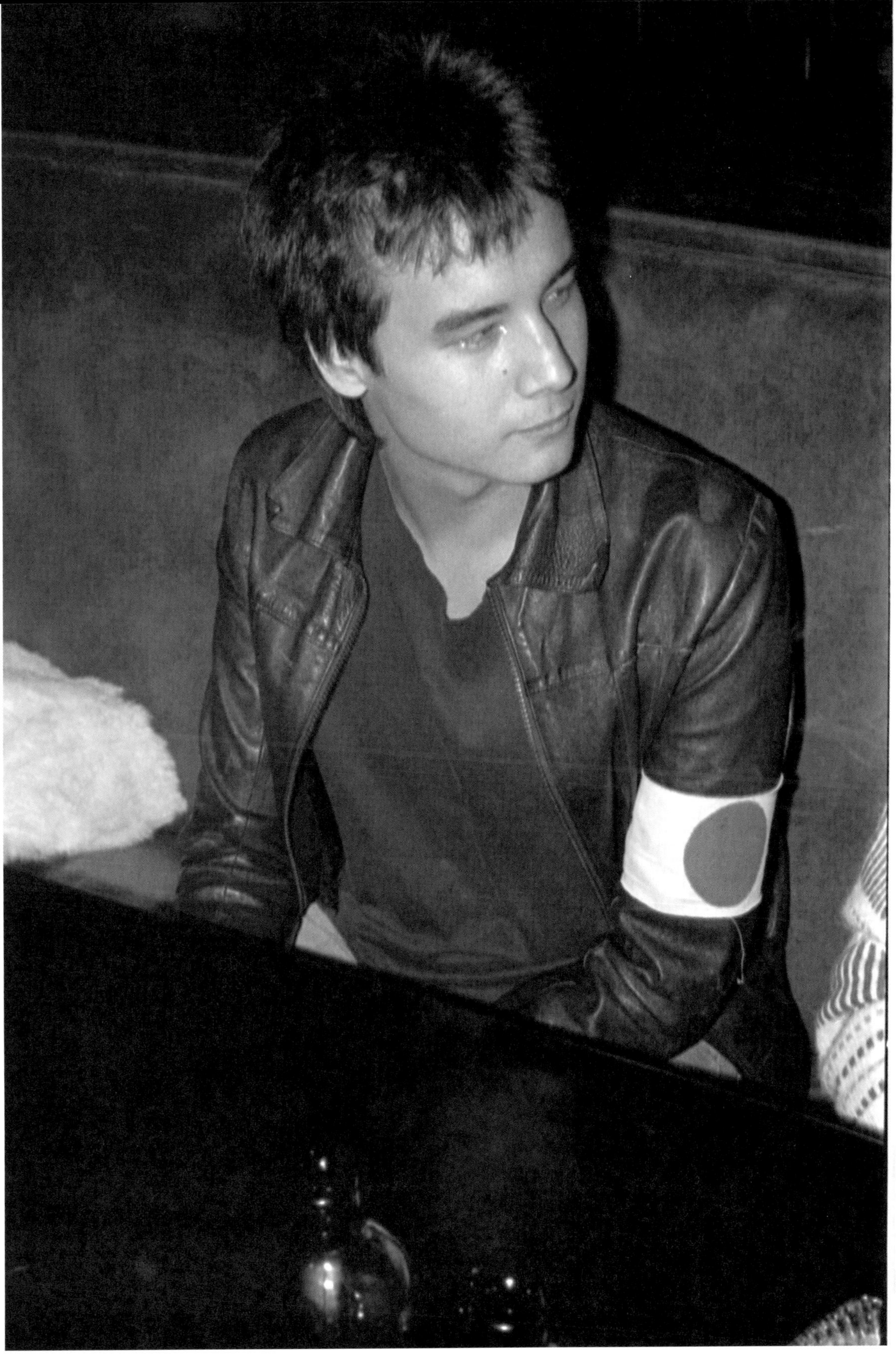

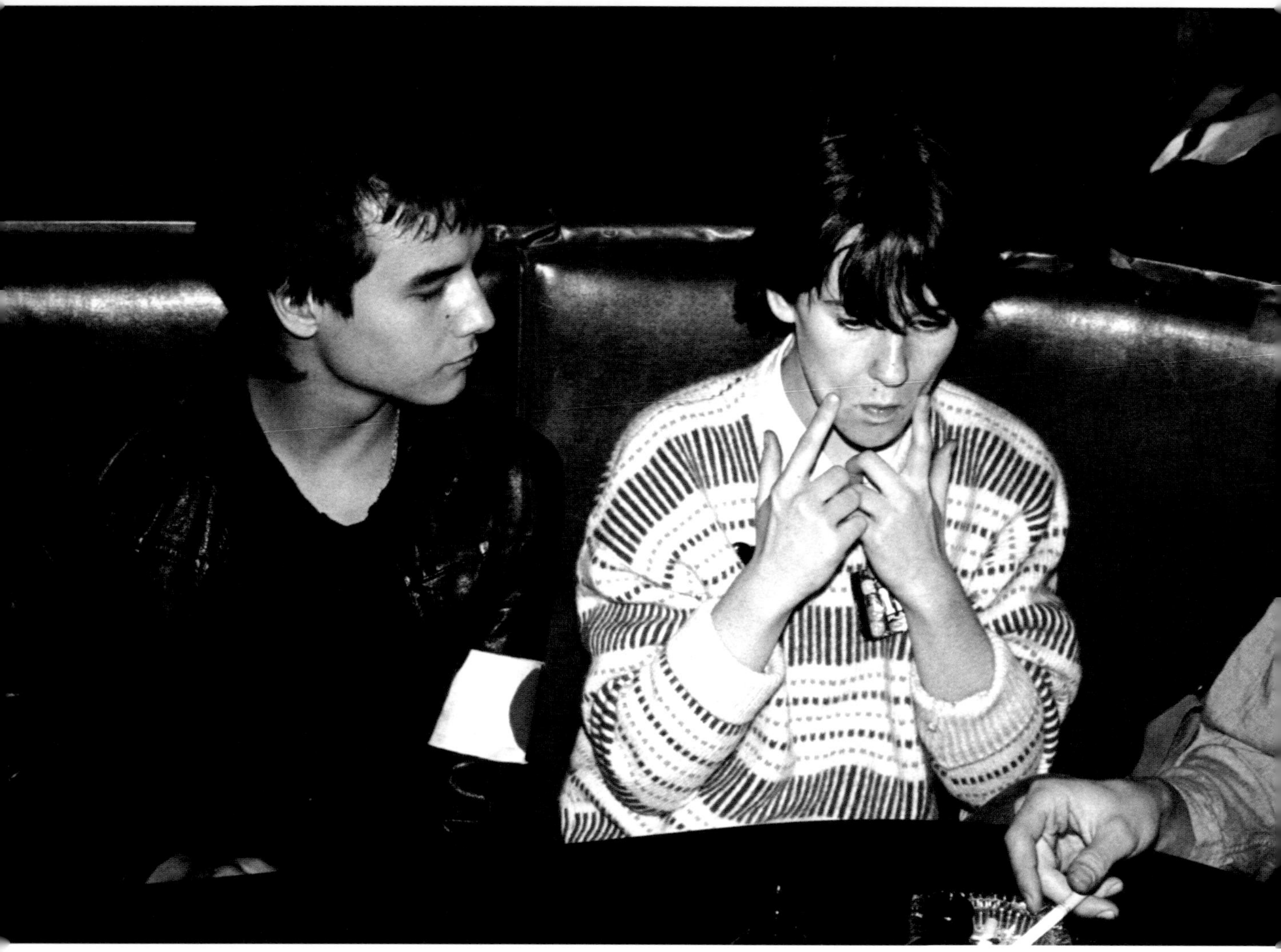

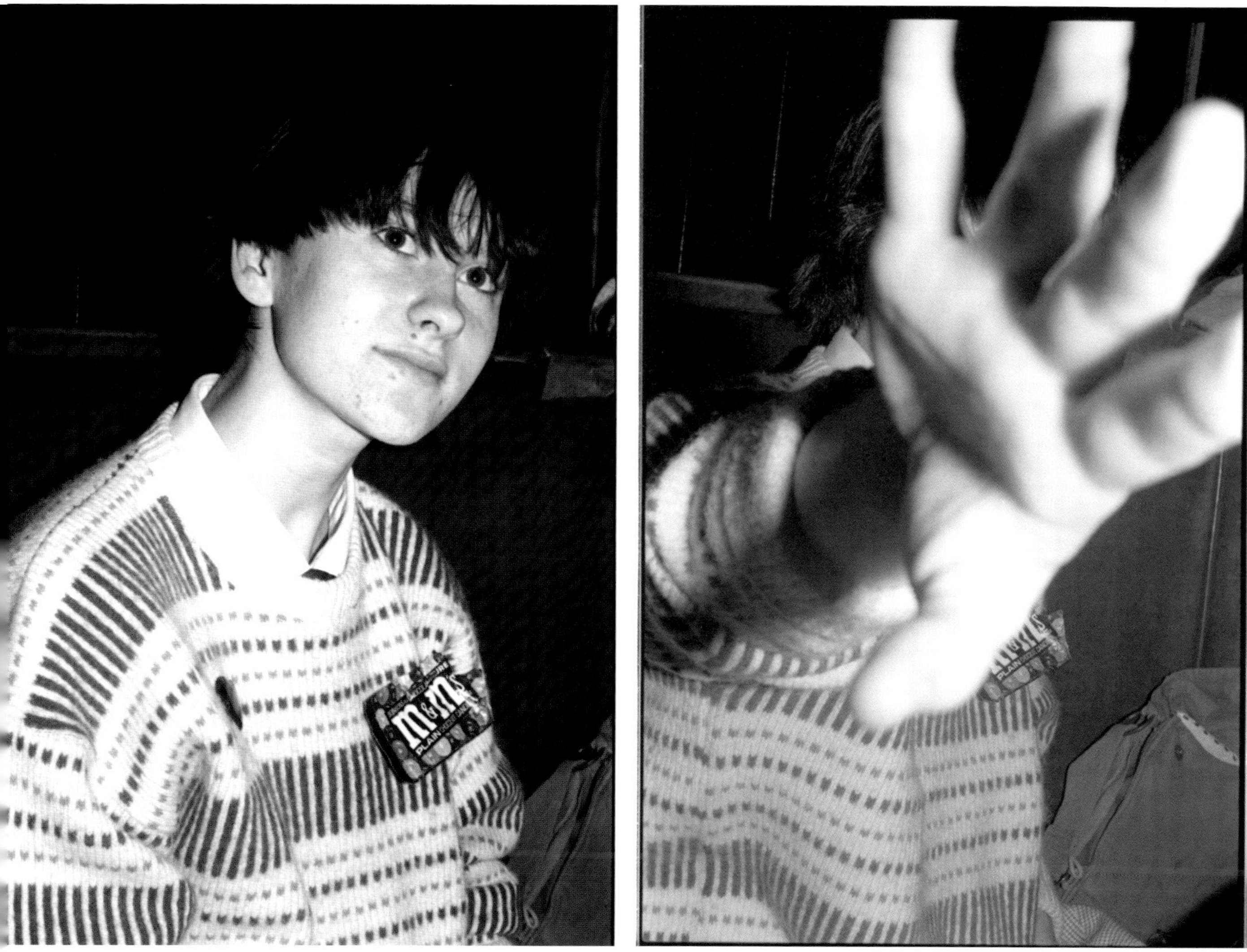

Nip Kicks, sort-of bodyguard to the Viletones, and Draga in one of the Horseshoe's back booths, before a large chunk of the venue was hacked off and made into a furniture store, eliminating the booths. Draga and I instantly became friends upon meeting, being the same age and two of the youngest people on the scene

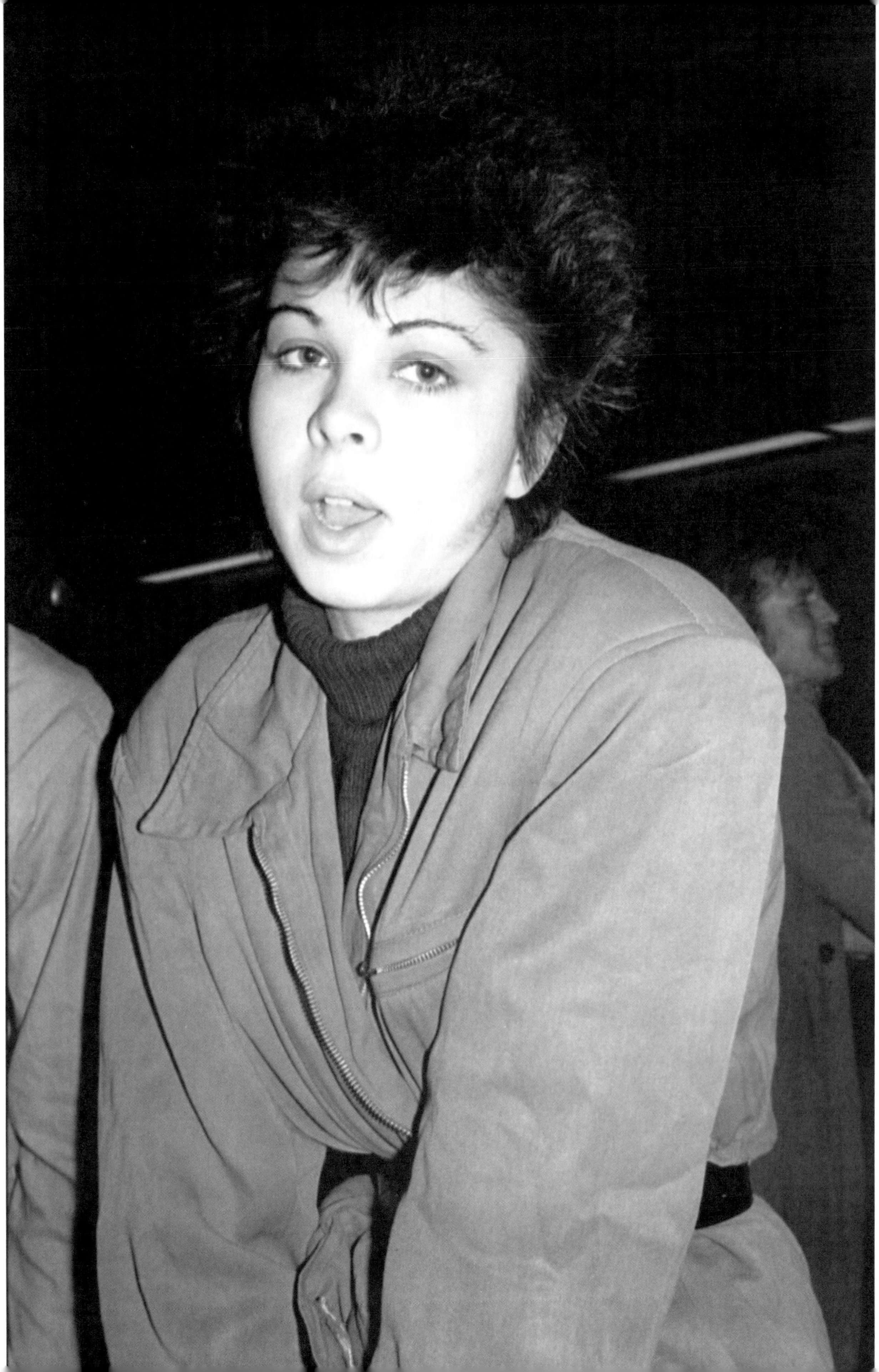

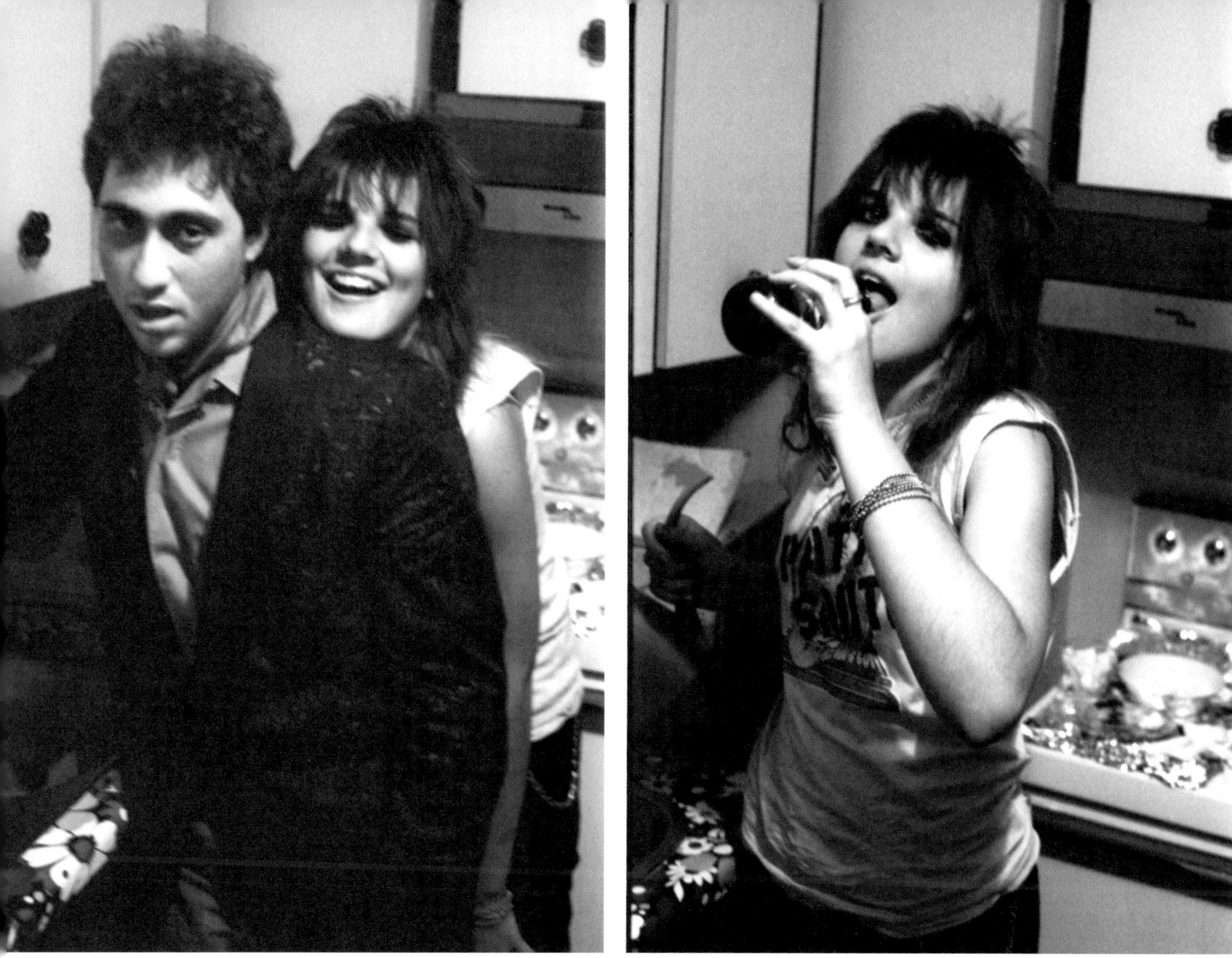

Evan (aka Mel Torment of Swollen Members) and Rojer in the Parliament Street apartment kitchen

Rojer was the other punk in my high school. Rotating classrooms for the various subjects, we met by writing band names and eventually "Who are you?" on our common desks in a ballpoint pen dialogue. Living on the same street, we formed a friendship that she would instantly turn cold if someone mistook me for her boyfriend. We rode the all-night bus home together many times and the first apartment she shared with Cram and Virlana became a gathering place for our group of friends to drink and socialize before going to gigs.

Suzanne in a Horseshoe booth

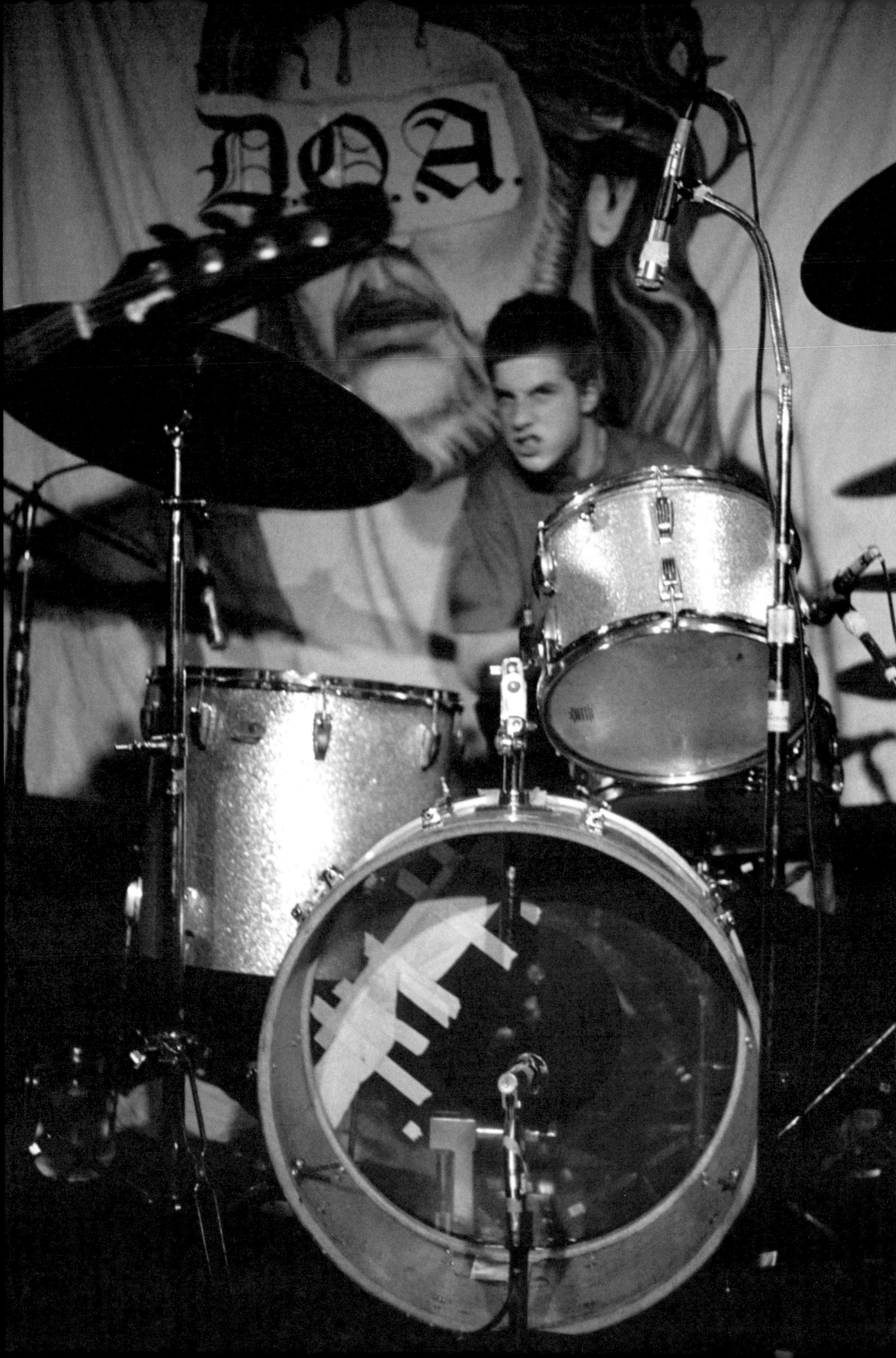
D.O.A.

D.O.A., The Edge, 1978

Chuck Biscuits

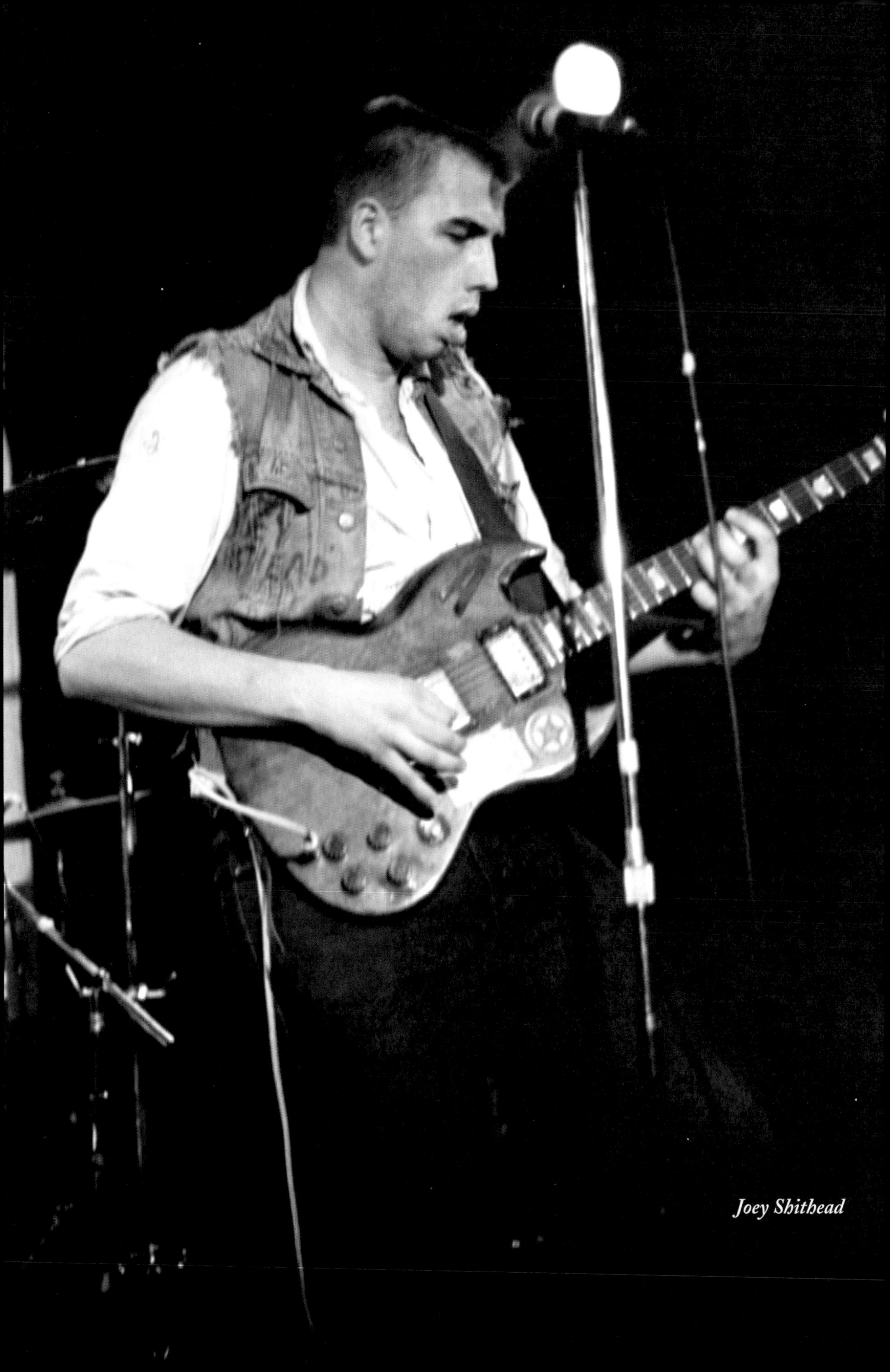

Joey Shithead

THE
SKULLS
SHOCK THEATRE
565 college st
SAT.
JAN. 7
$ 2.99
9:00 P.M.
WITH
SPECIAL
GUESTS
WIMPY
AND THE
BLOATED
COWS
FROM LONDON, ENG

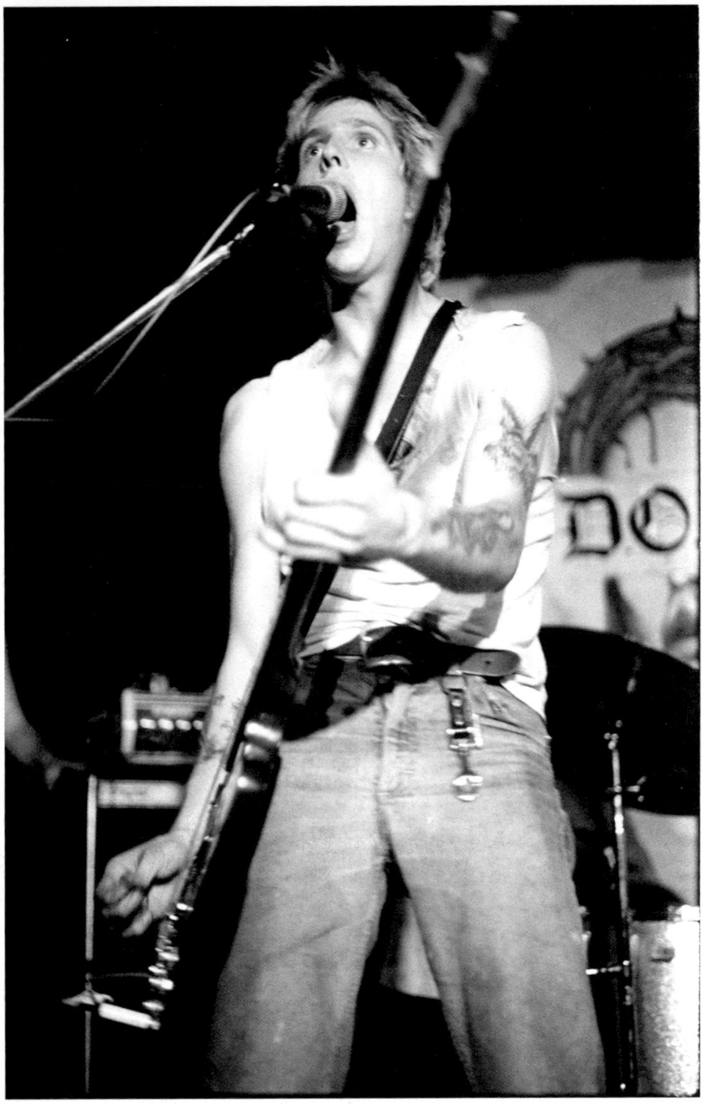

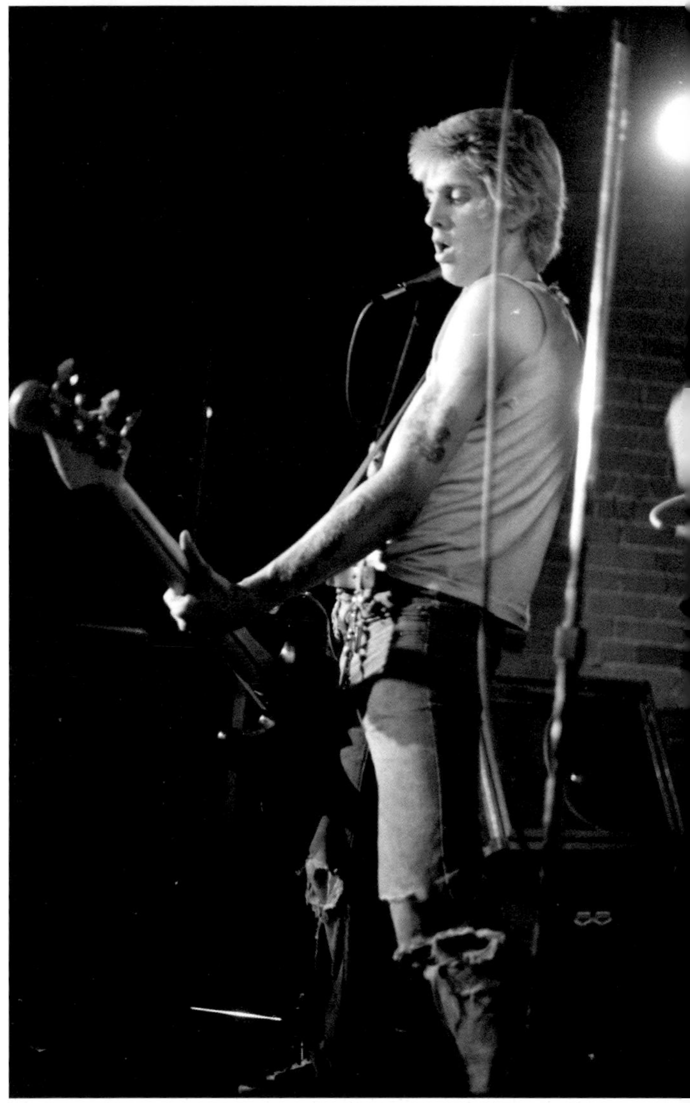

Randy Rampage

It was normal for regional music to remain regional; audiences in Toronto rarely got to see bands from Vancouver, but D.O.A. predecessors The Skulls, and Wimpy and the Bloated Cows were the first visitors, maybe even living here briefly at some point. After this D.O.A. gig, the band stayed with friends. Reid Diamond was staying on their living room floor at the time and told us how he awoke the morning after to the sight of a naked Joey Shithead lying on the floor next to him, eating cold hot dogs from a package.

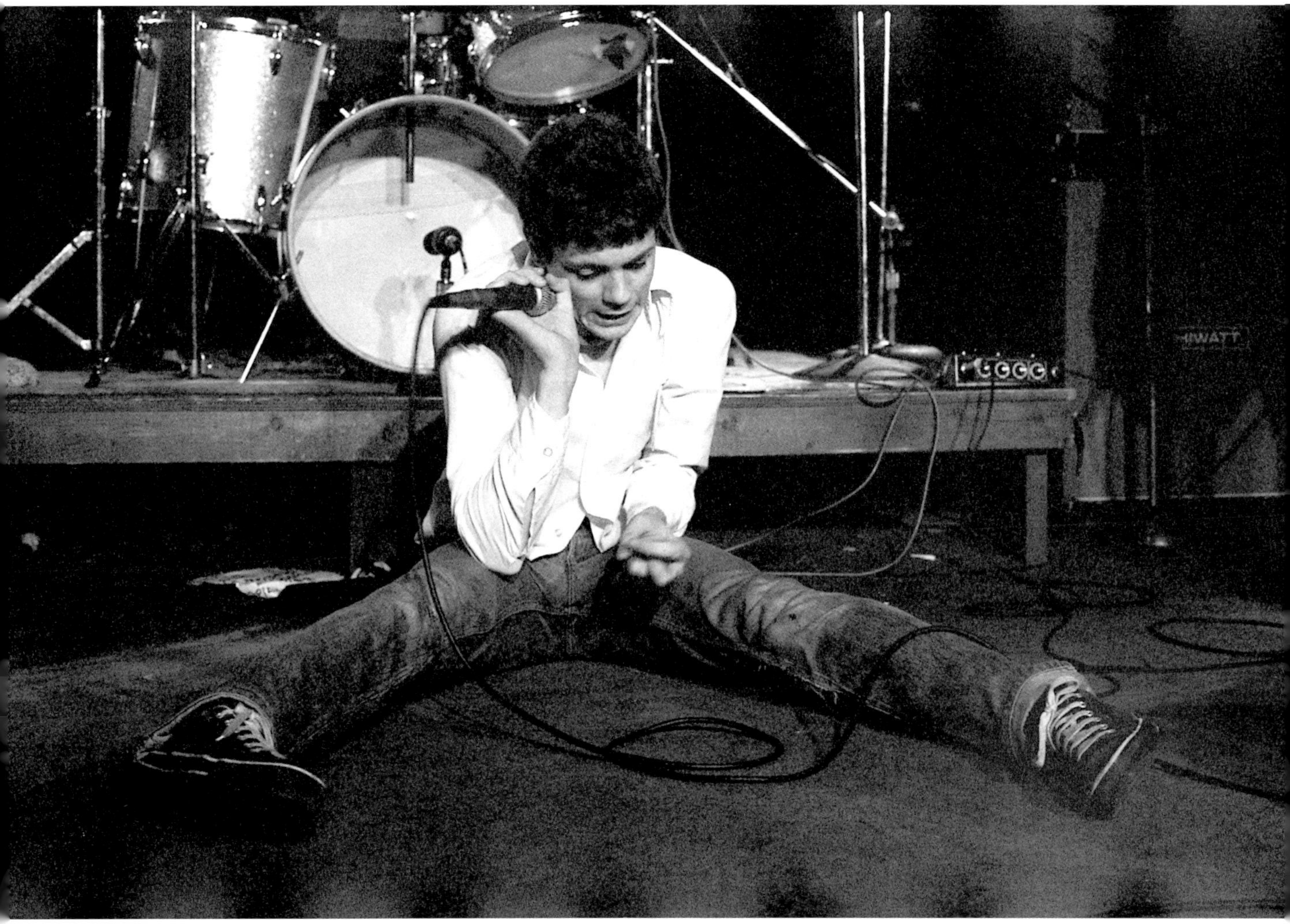

Teenage Head,
Horseshoe Tavern,
1978

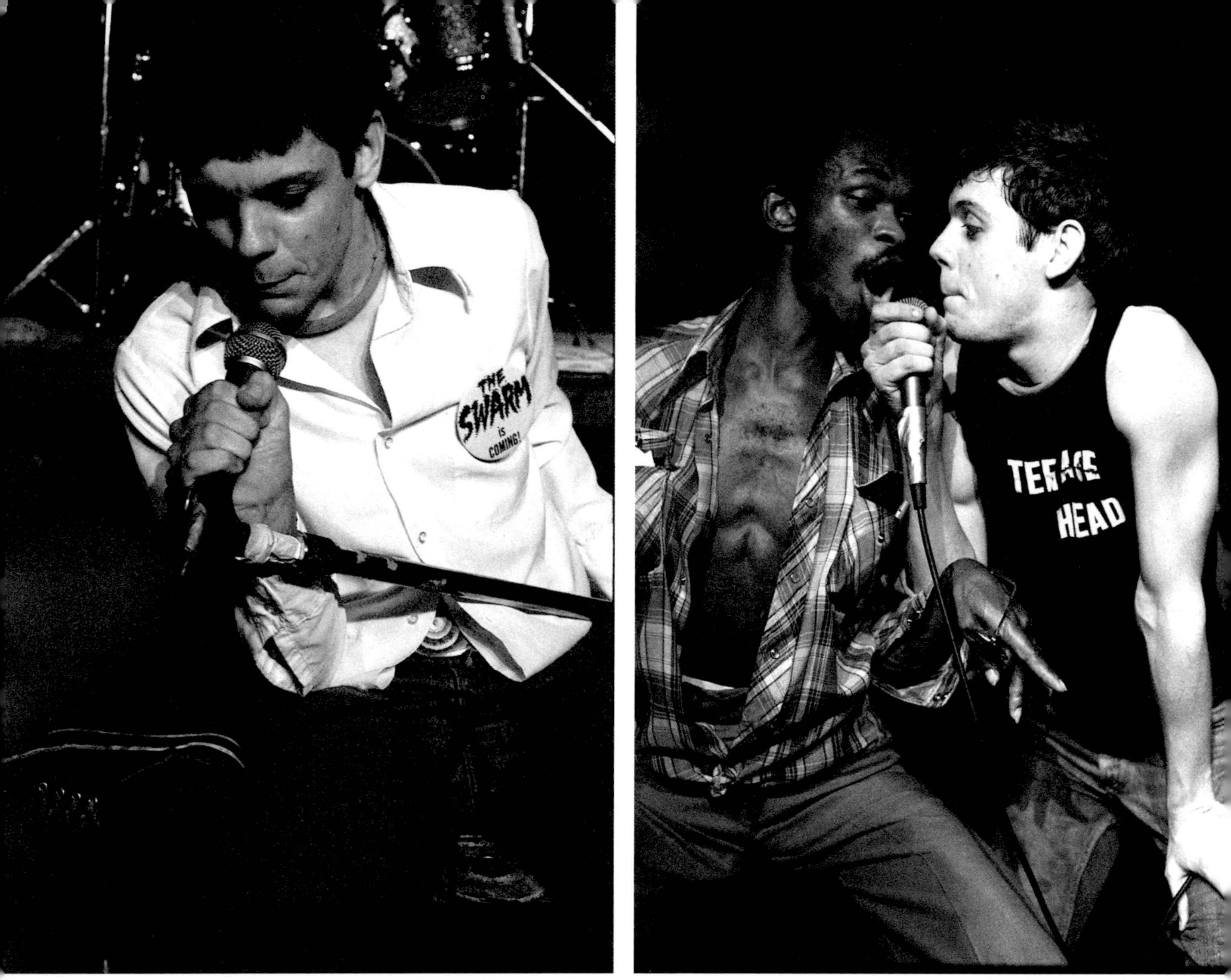

The guy pictured with Frankie was getting down on the dance floor in front of the stage, sometimes squawking on a harmonica. Frankie invited him up for their cover of Bo Diddley's "Pills," and the guy stylishly faked his way through a song he clearly didn't know

To me, Teenage Head were true rebels for no other reason than they always had long hair after everyone else had cut theirs off. This notion seems preposterous now, but the length of your hair would sometimes mean the difference between acceptance or not, of getting beaten up or not. Fabulously coiffed bassist Steve Mahon channeled the New York Dolls' Arthur Kane, with his hairsprayed and tousled do. Before settling into being a straight-up party band, Teenage Head electrified with blistering, crisp and catchy amphetamine rock and roll.

A couple of times Rojer and I took the bus to see them in their hometown, Hamilton, where they'd play longer shows than in Toronto. One Hamilton gig was at this dreadful square bar where I was refused entry because of a no-jeans policy.

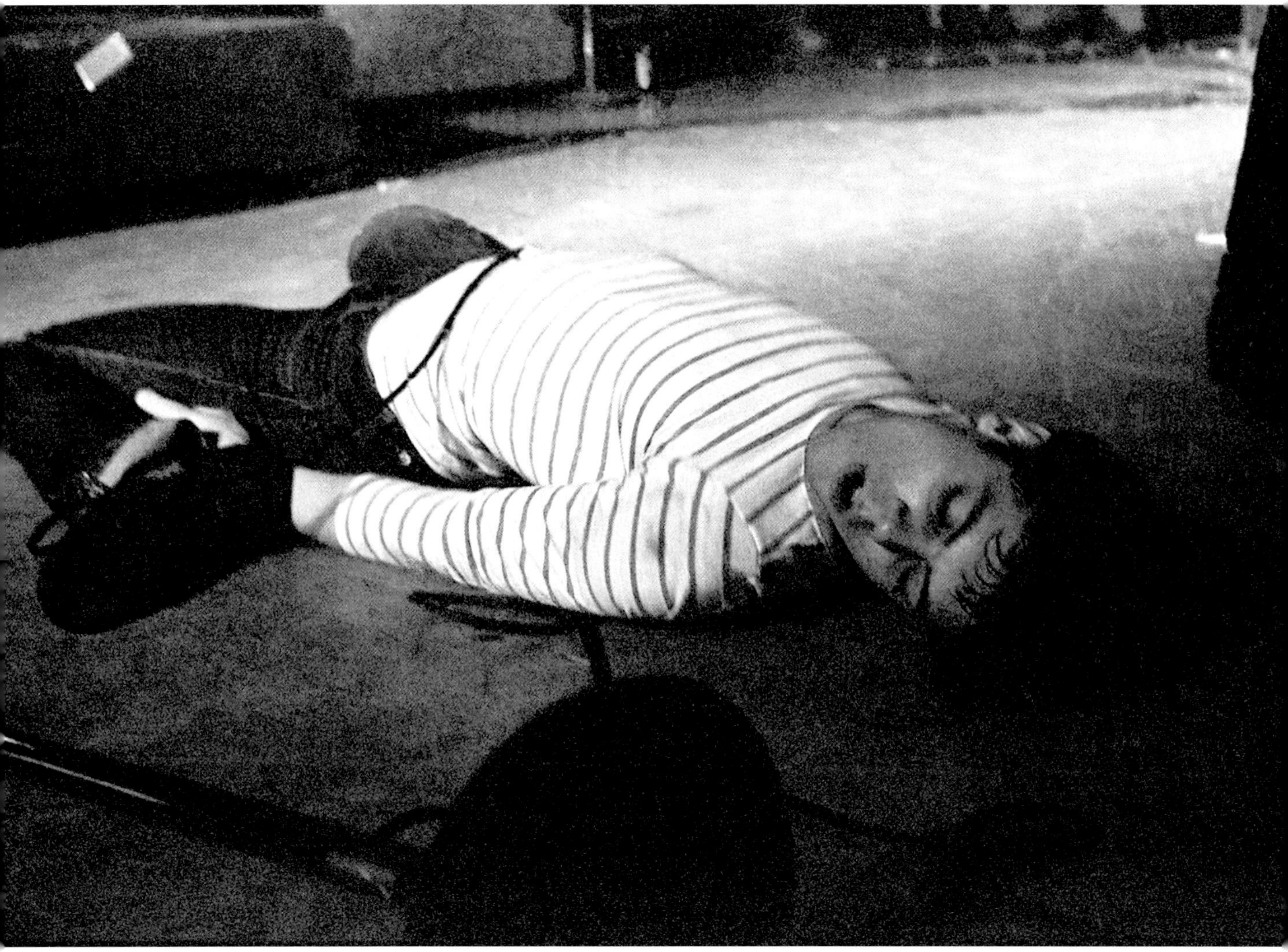

Masonic Temple, 1977

Their manager Paul Koback, who knew most of the people who came to all their Toronto shows, and who knew we had bussed from Toronto, argued with the door people about their stupid dress code and then told me to go outside by the men's washroom. His brown corduroy pants appeared through the open window and I took off my forbidden blue jeans and passed them back for him to wear. Dress codes enforced by the majority of live music venues were one the many dumb things that "punk" helped kill in Toronto. We went from a party after the show to the bus terminal where we waited a couple more hours for the first Sunday morning bus back to Toronto.

The three front men always looked supremely cool, with Frankie a dynamic presence and fearless acrobat. At one Horseshoe gig, Frankie twitched and writhed in fast-motion, absorbing and redistributing energy, then hung upside down by his feet, toes curled around the pipes above the stage. He tried trying to monkey himself down, but he lost grip and fell, knocking the wind out of himself. The audience area of the Horseshoe was lit with cornball lanterns mounted on wagon wheels and suspended from the ceiling. Before they were trashed at the Last Pogo show, I saw Frankie swing from those too.

At a speakeasy party on a Queen Street West rooftop after a Teenage Head show, Frankie passed around a baggie of Black Beauties, cheap speed we hardly needed at 2 a.m. but took anyway.

All of these shots are from before Teenage Head's first album.

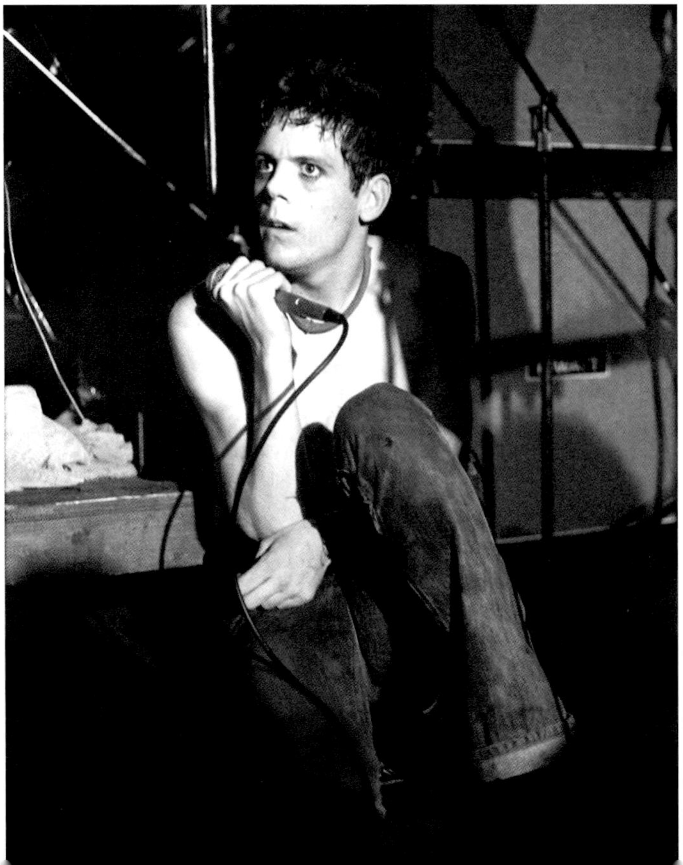

Frankie Venom

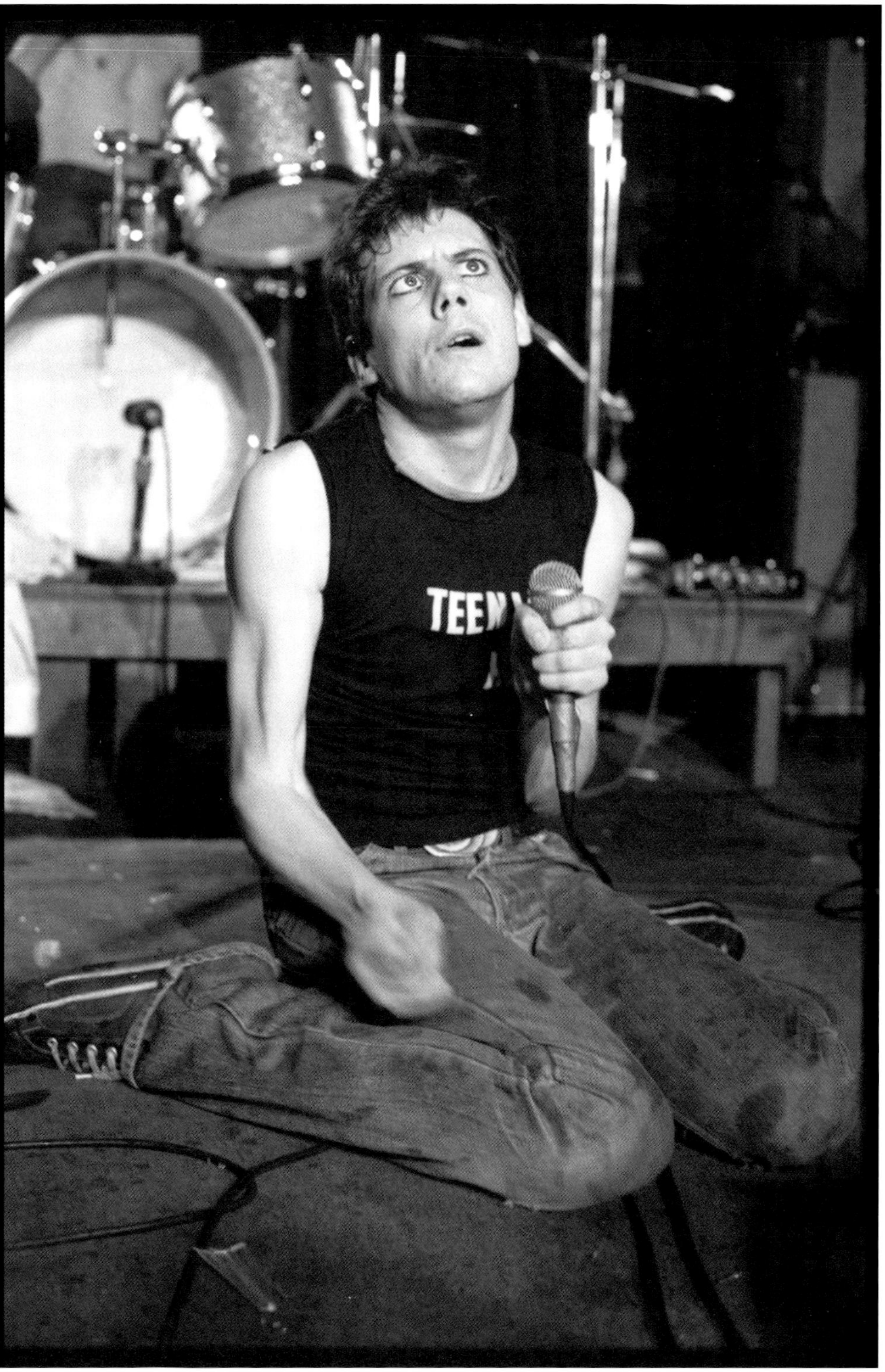

I gave Frankie a copy of this photo right after I took it and asked him to sign my copy of the same. On it, he wrote, "Don't forget me," something I thought quite odd and even then that I knew I would never do.

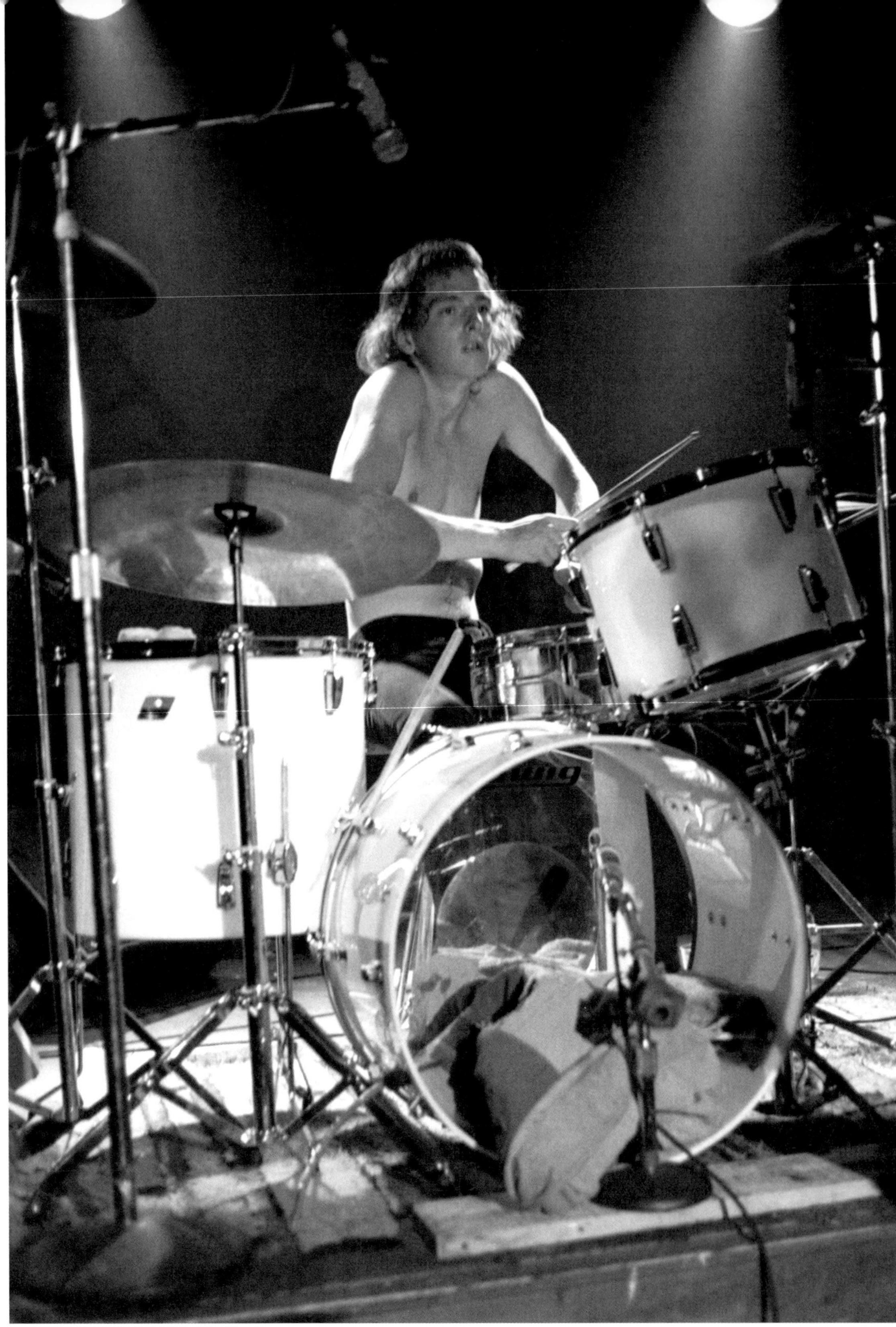

Nick Stipanitz

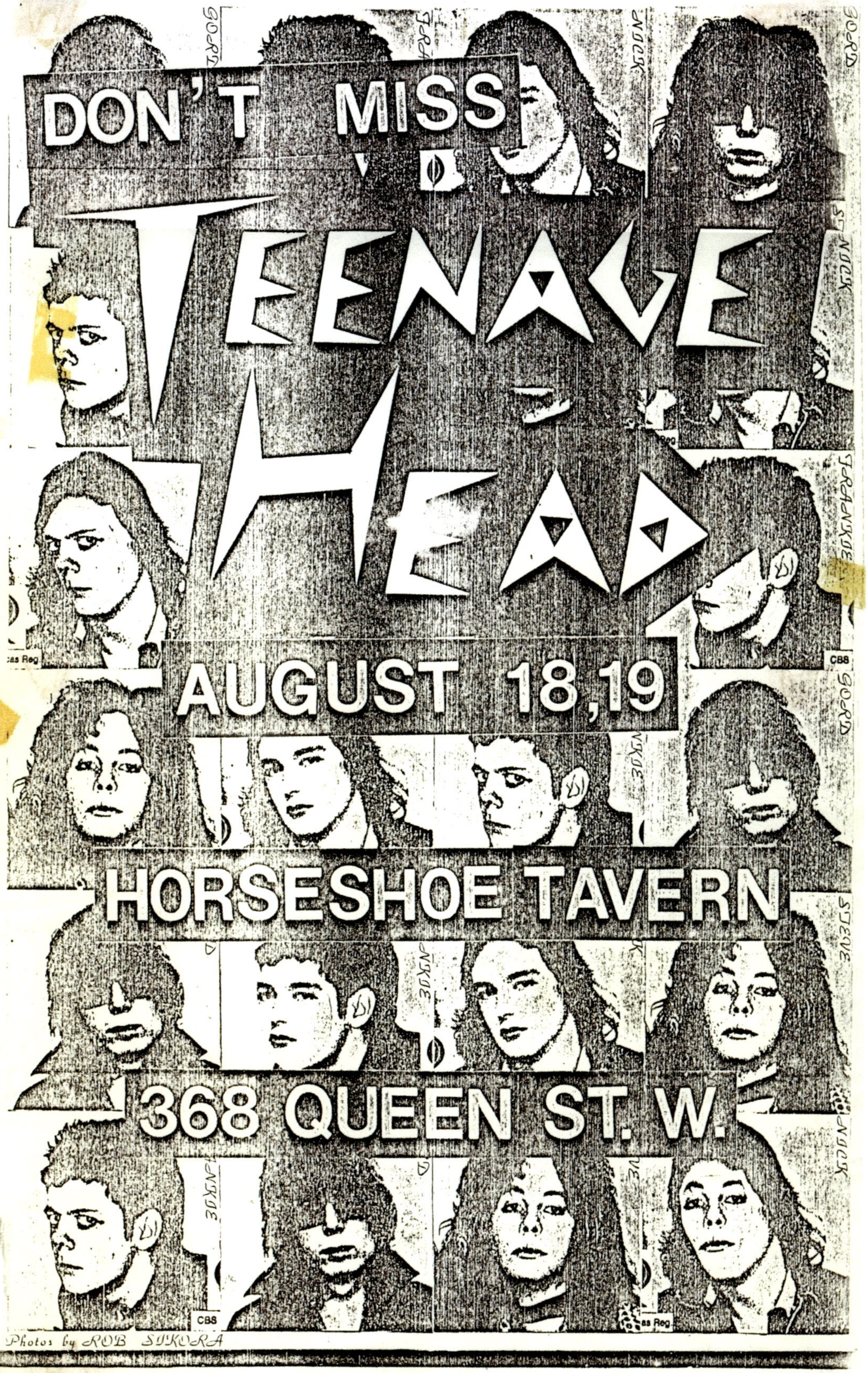
DON'T MISS
TEENAGE HEAD
AUGUST 18,19
HORSESHOE TAVERN
368 QUEEN ST. W.
Photos by ROB SIKORA

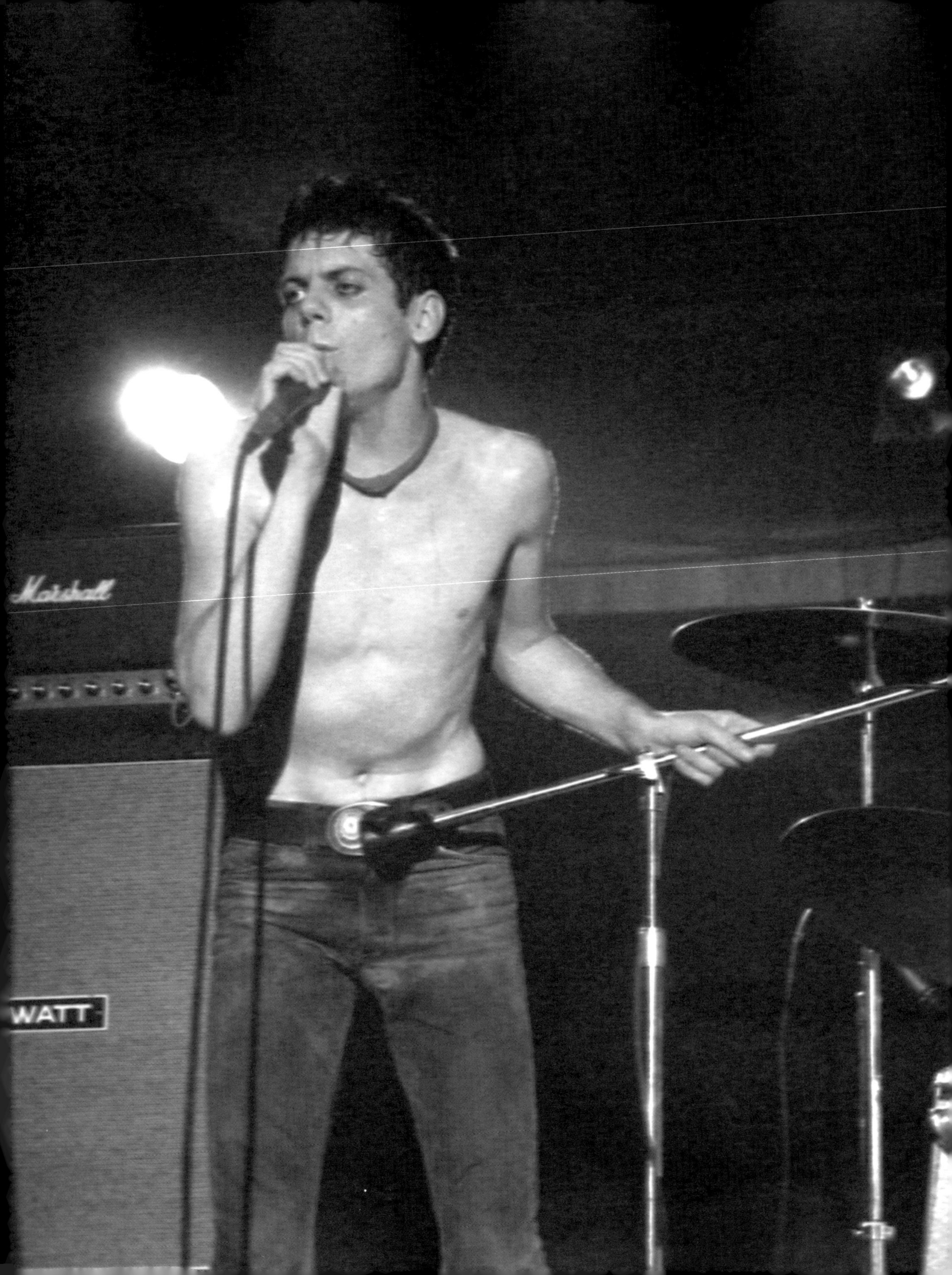
Marshall
WATT

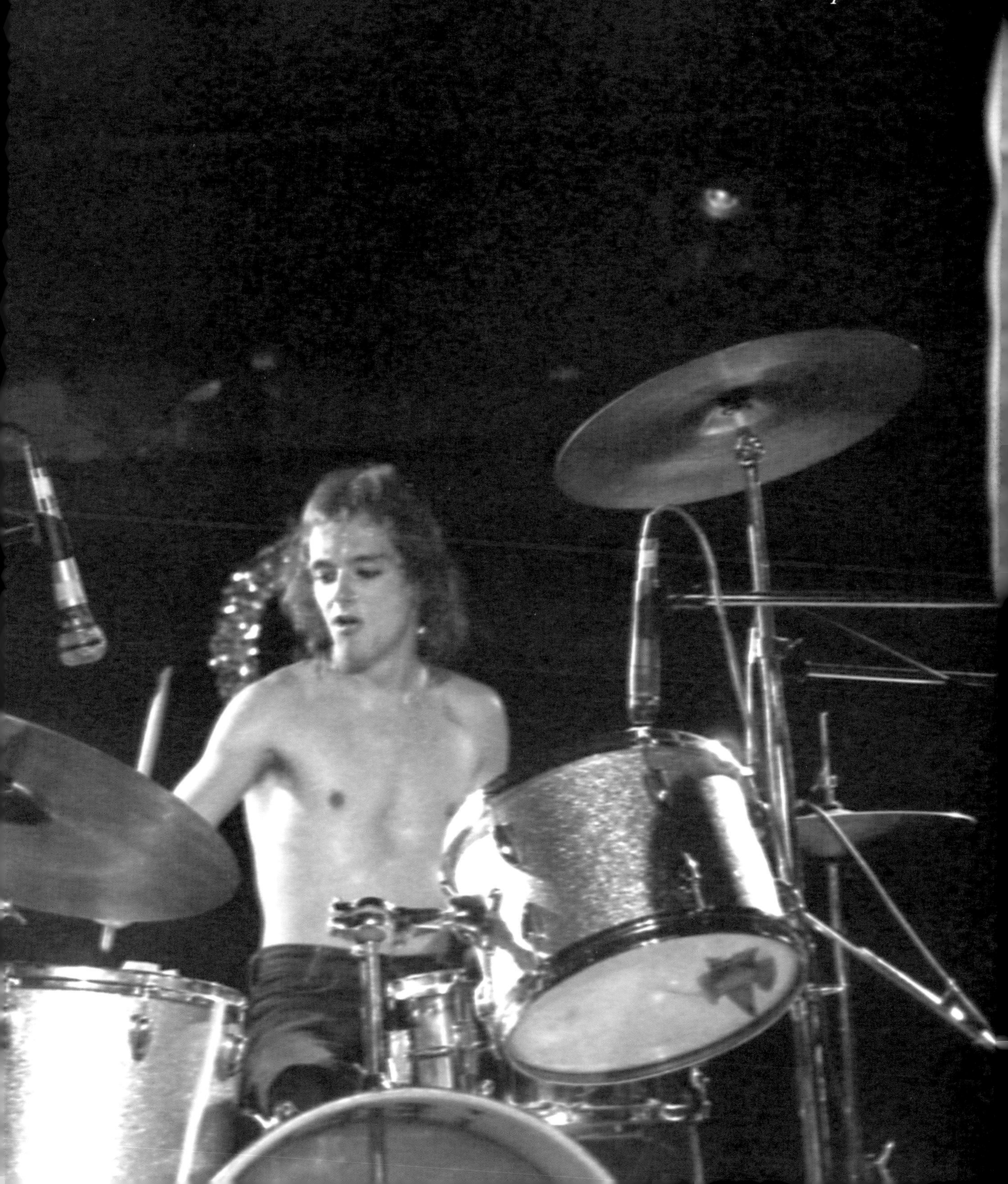

Frankie Venom, Nick Stipanitz

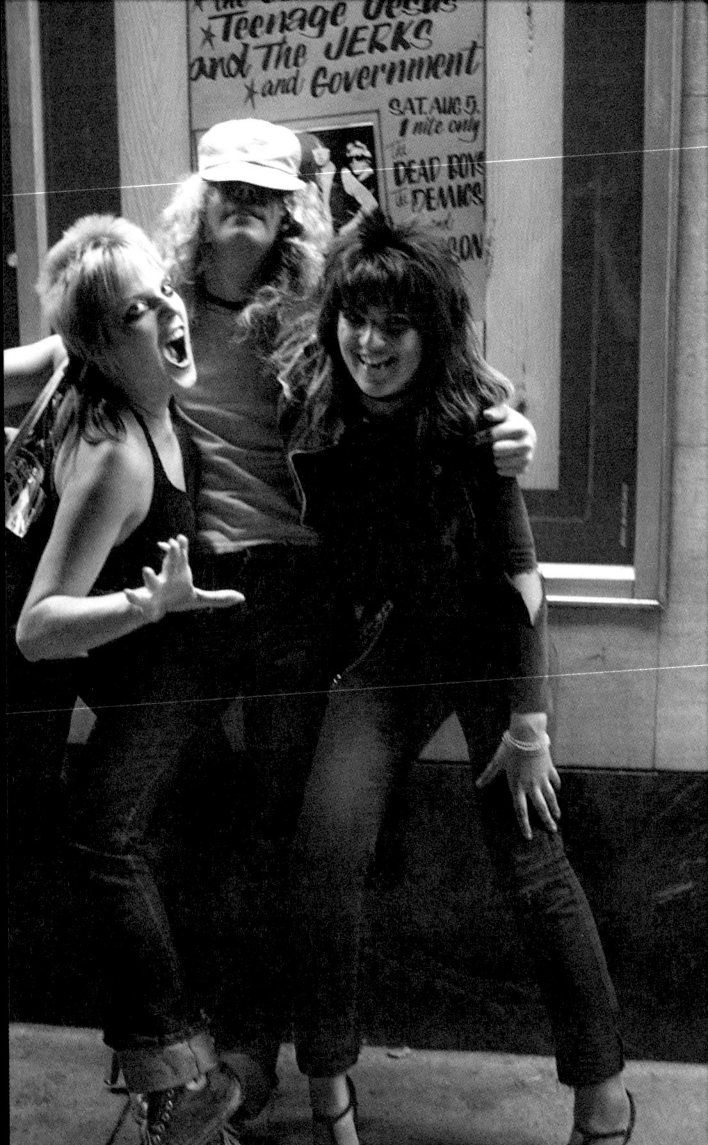

Vera, Steve Mahon, Rojer in front of the Horseshoe after a gig

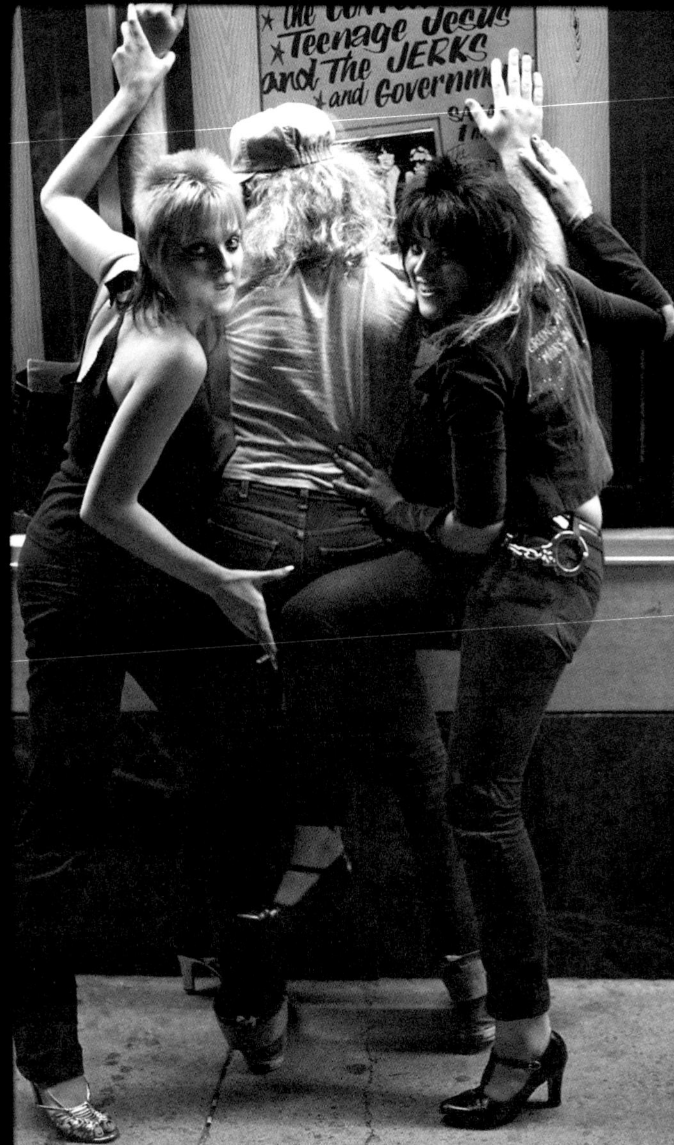

Slash Booze (aka Brian Baird), Frankie Venom

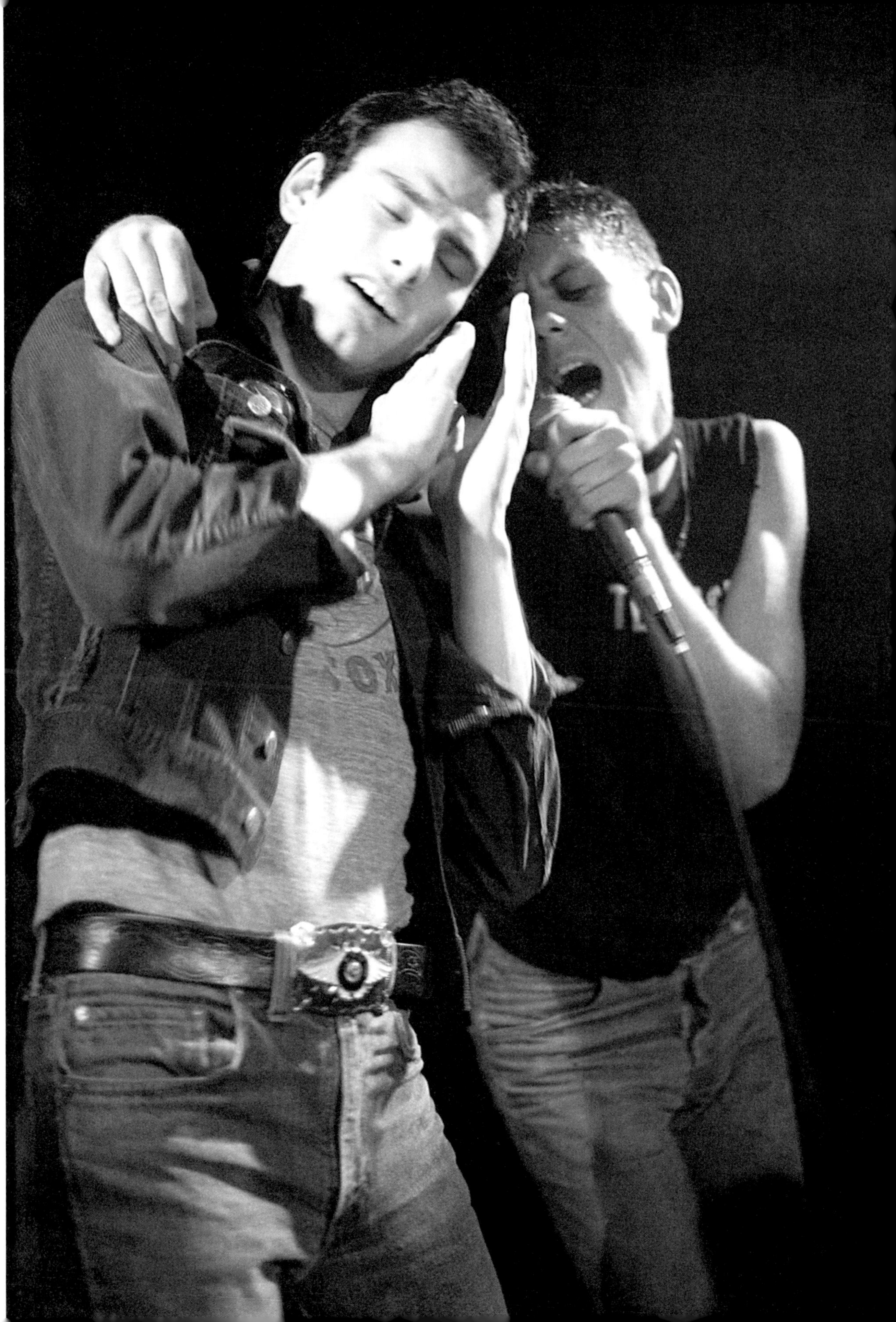

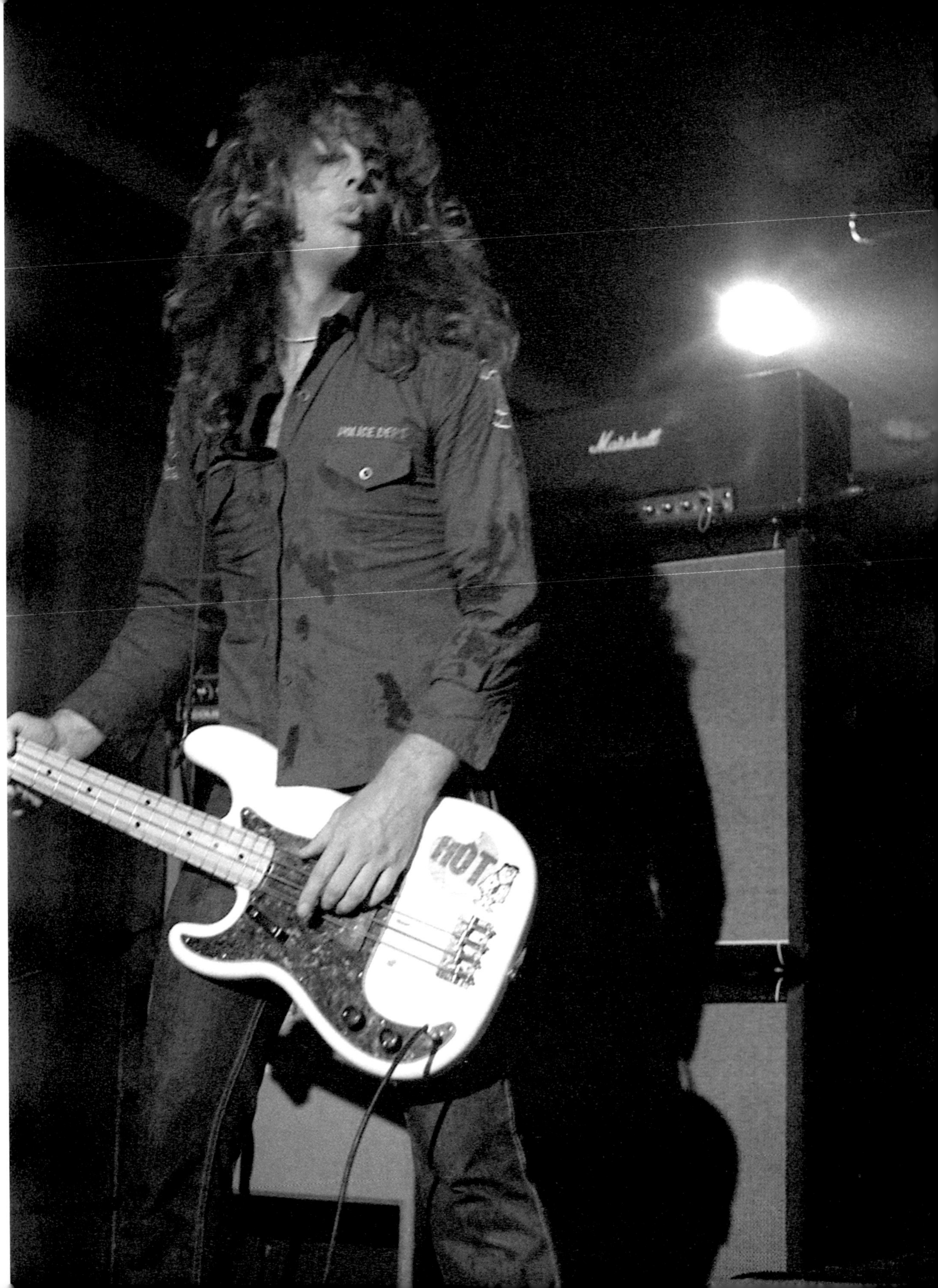
POLICE DEPT
Marshall
HOT

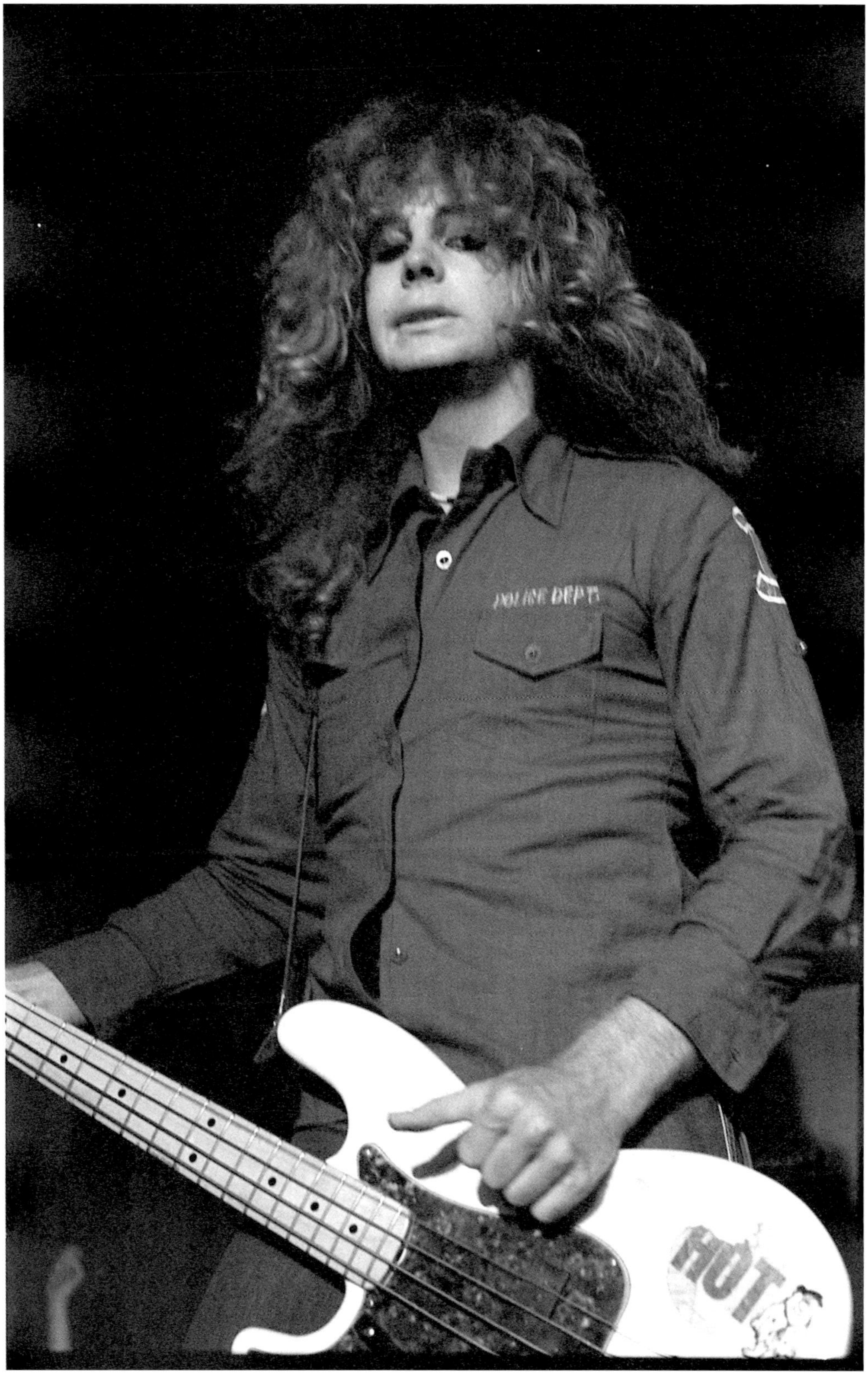

Steve Mahon

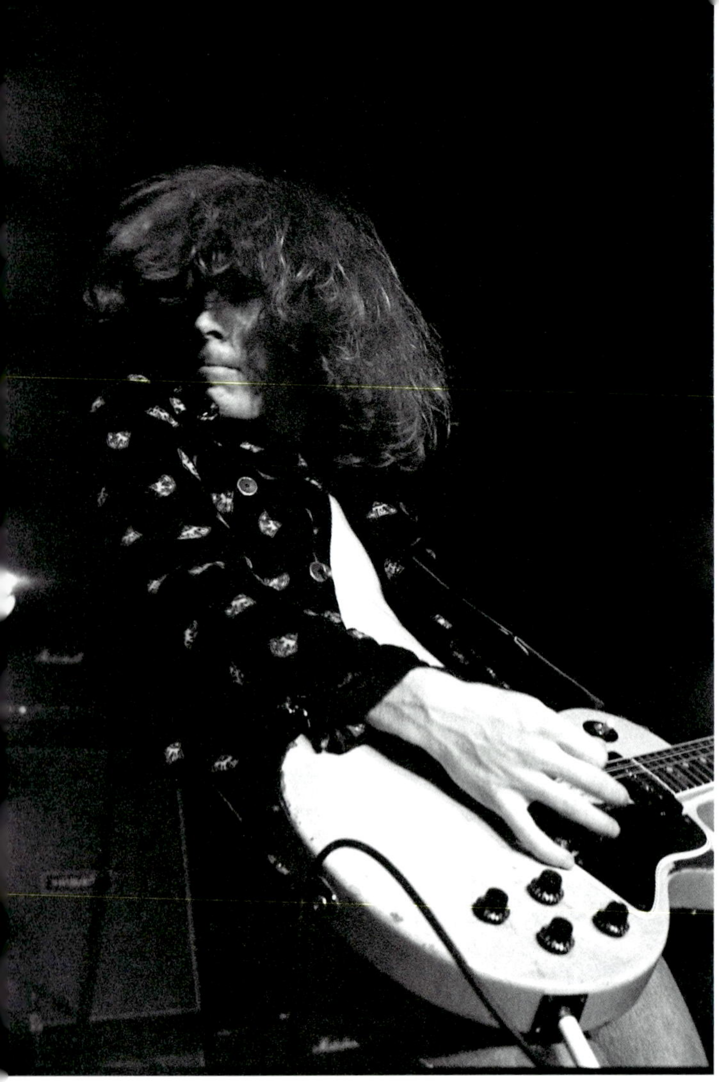

Gord Lewis

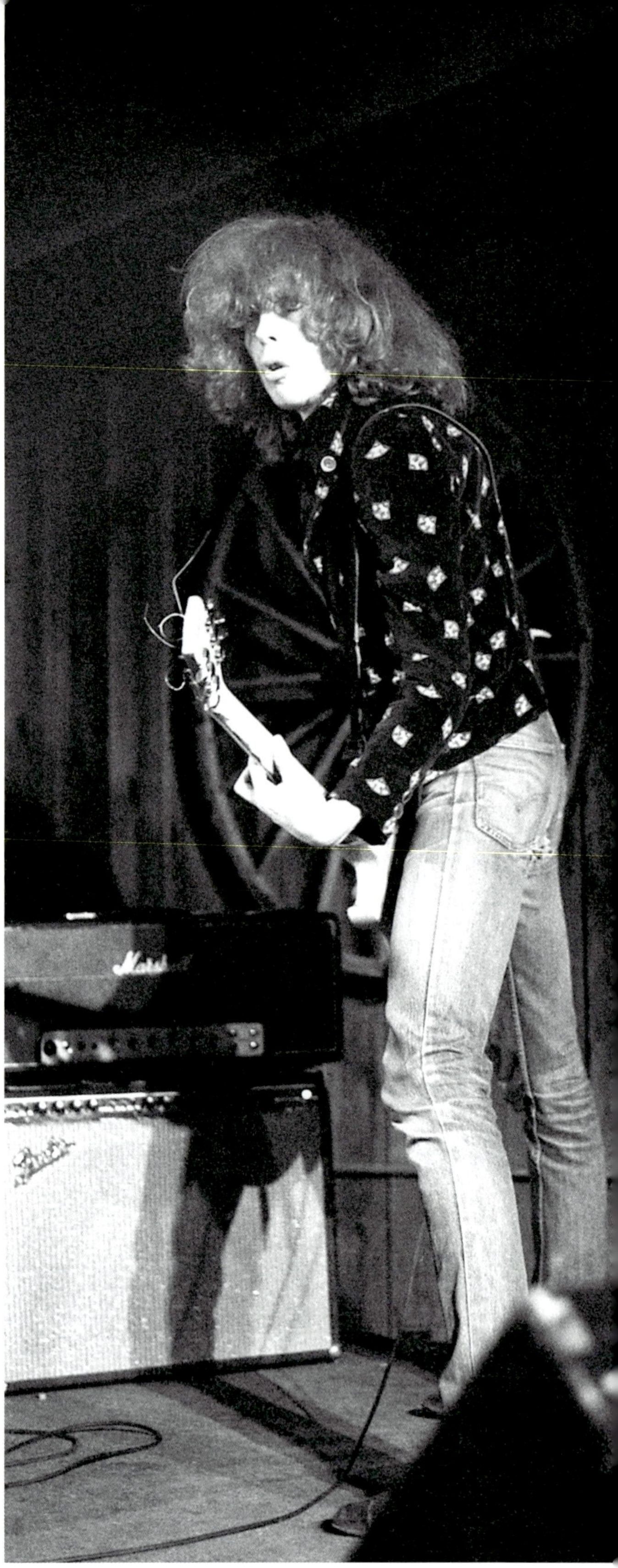

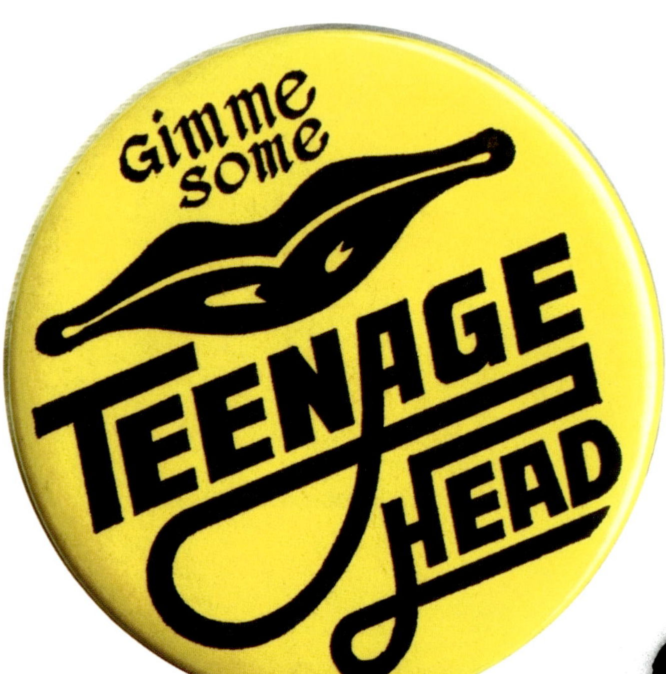

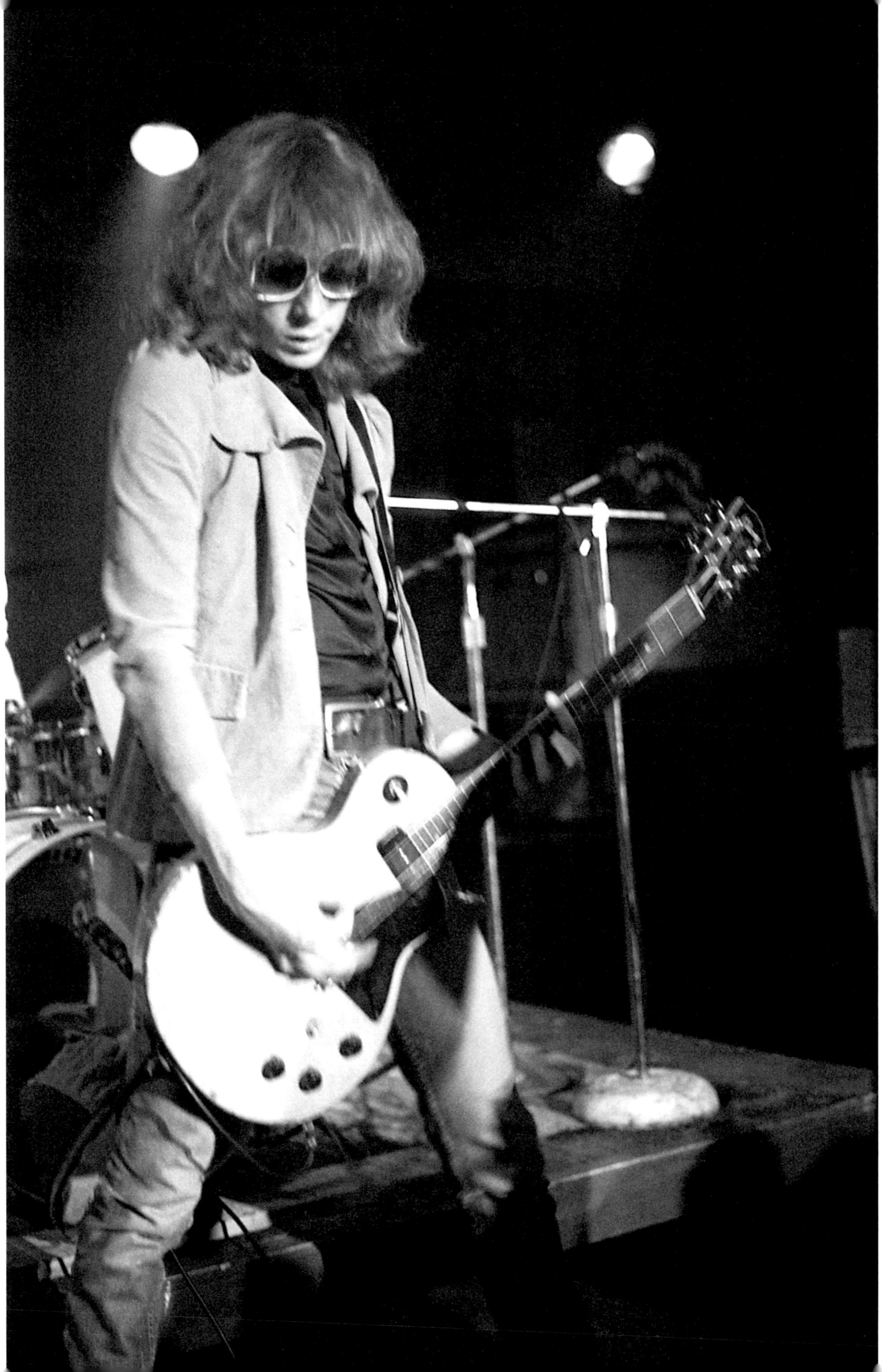

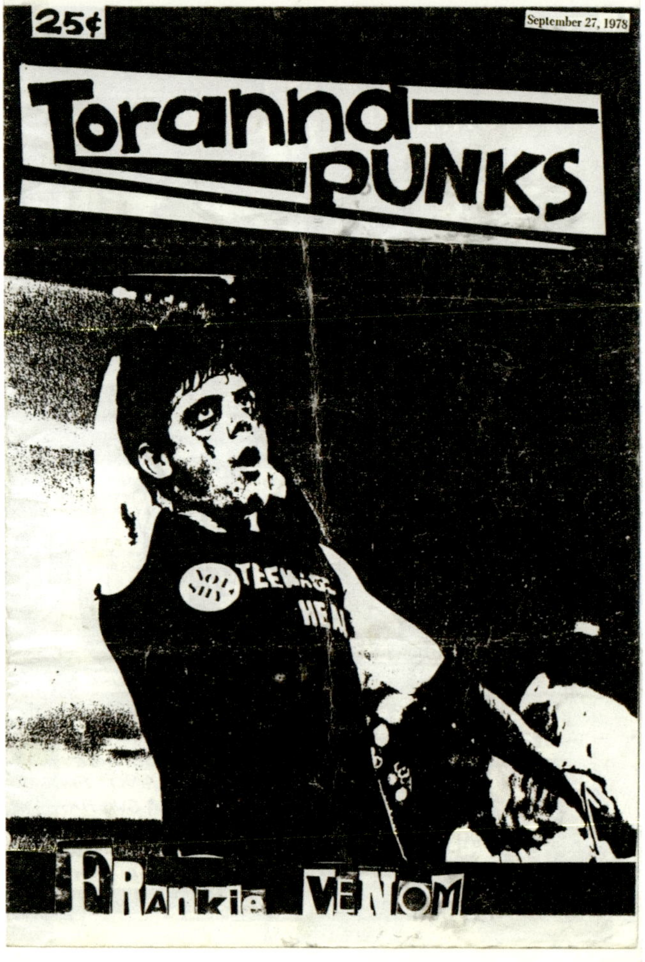

Toranna Punks *newsletter fanzine made by The Ugly's soundman/manager, Johnny Garbagecan*

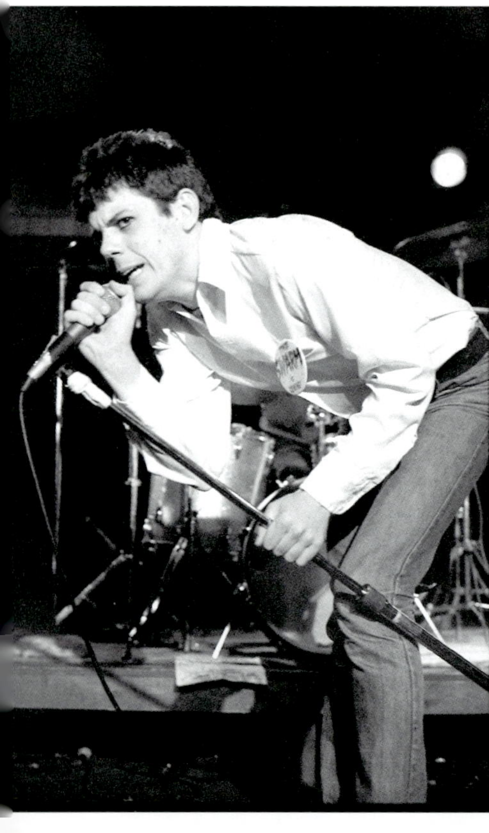

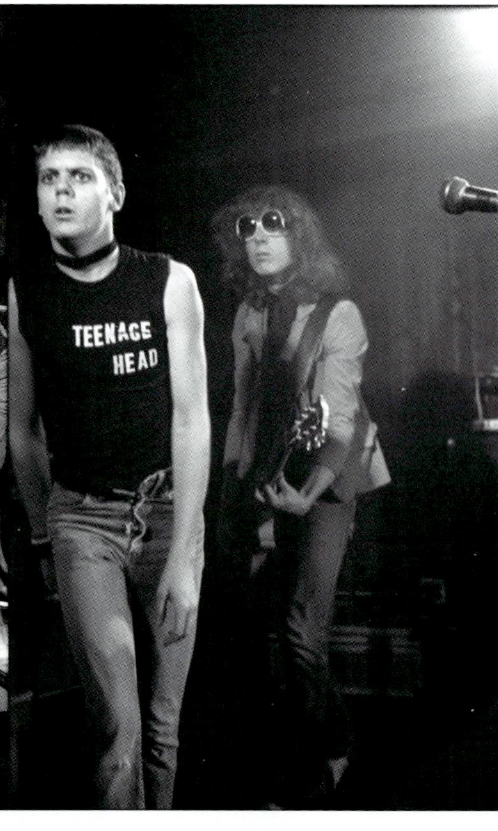

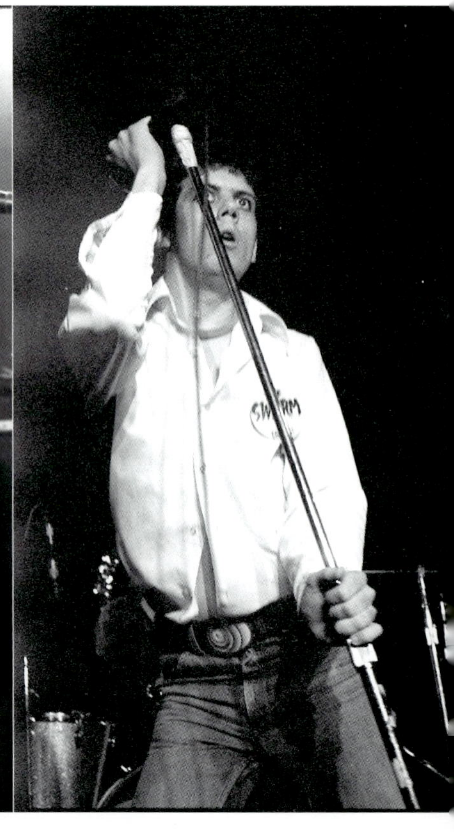

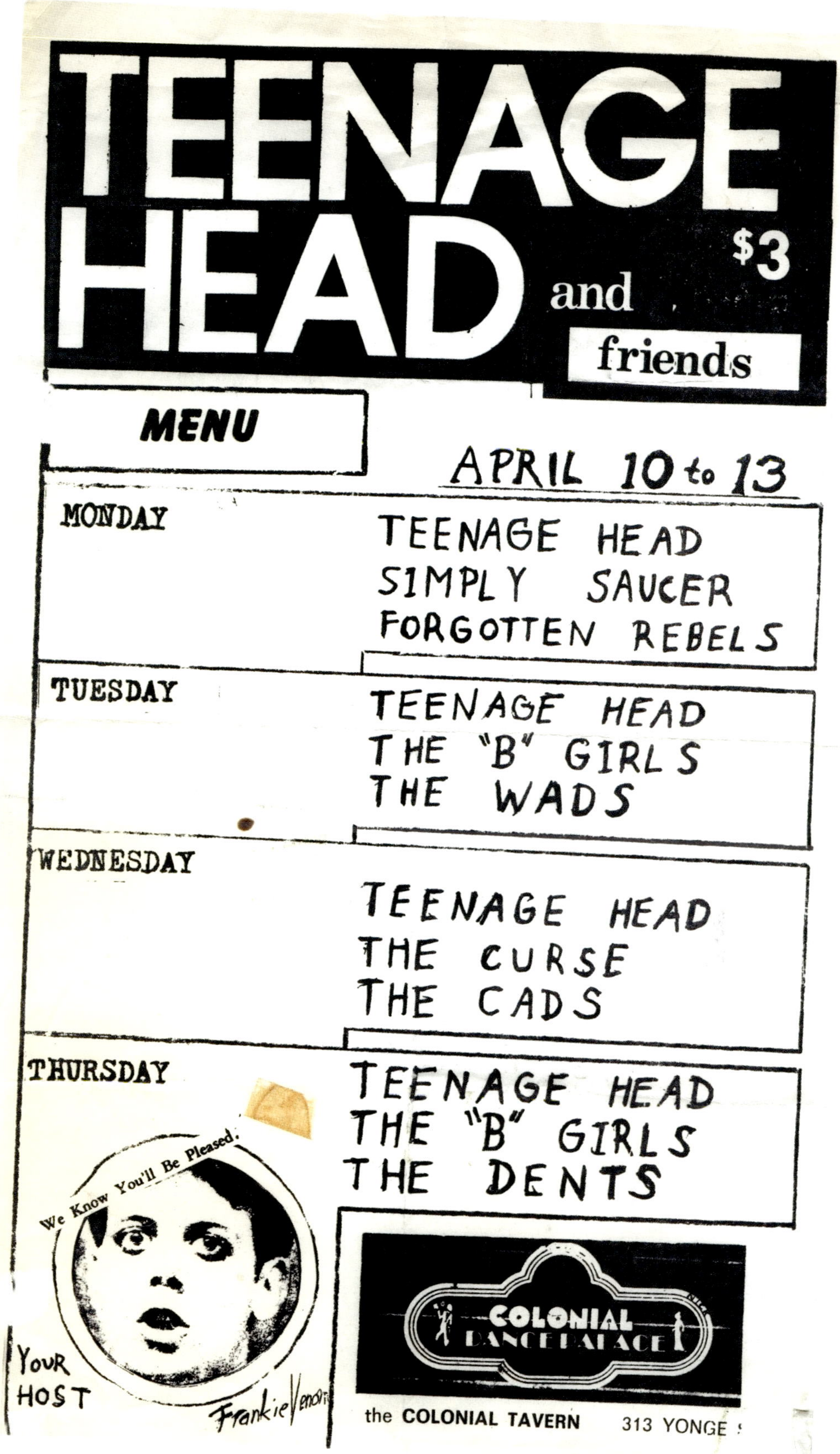
TEENAGE HEAD
$3
and
friends
MENU
APRIL 10 to 13
MONDAY
TEENAGE HEAD
SIMPLY SAUCER
FORGOTTEN REBELS
TUESDAY
TEENAGE HEAD
THE "B" GIRLS
THE WADS
WEDNESDAY
TEENAGE HEAD
THE CURSE
THE CADS
THURSDAY
TEENAGE HEAD
THE "B" GIRLS
THE DENTS
We Know You'll Be Pleased.
YOUR HOST
Frankie Venom
COLONIAL
DANCE PALACE
the COLONIAL TAVERN
313 YONGE

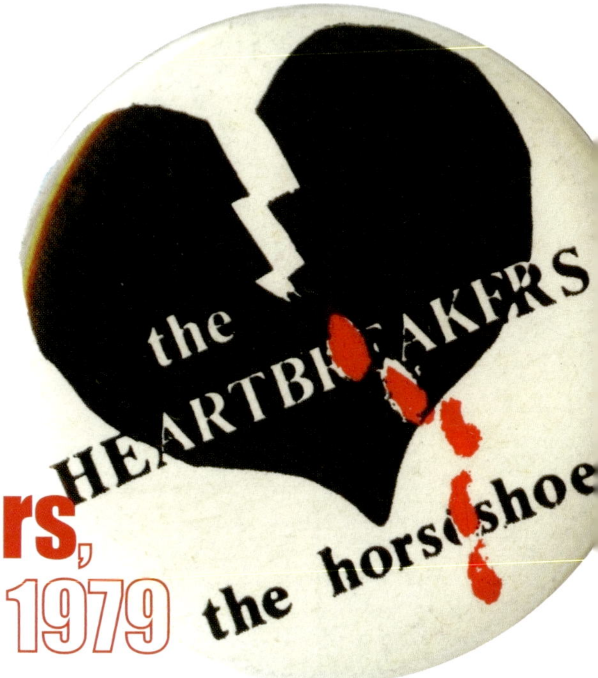

The Heartbreakers, Horseshoe Tavern, 1979

Jerry Nolan and Johnny Thunders had left the New York Dolls only a few years previous to this show, but The Heartbreakers were already breaking up and reforming every couple of months or so. This was their first "reunion" without Dolls drummer Nolan, but I don't think anyone even knew they'd split, it had been so recent. For years I've heard people say they saw Johnny Thunders shooting up backstage at the Horseshoe. Thunders appeared sleepy-eyed and disheveled, but stumbling around on Cuban heels was the way Thunders *always* looked.

The Heartbreakers made the audience wait in the dark for at least an hour before they entered to the blare of air-raid sirens and Nazi rally speeches. The intro that's heard on their *Live at Max's Kansas City* album was recorded around the same time. They'd obviously been putting their efforts into things other than songwriting as they only had two or three new songs — mostly covers — since their *L.A.M.F.* album a couple of years back. The other guitarist and singer, Walter Lure, and Thunders fell into each other, ripping duel-lead guitar attacks entwining and battling each other like fighting cobras.

Thunders was so exciting to watch, the embodiment of the most beautiful excessive archetypes of rock and roll stardom: great hair, preposterous outfits, totally cool-looking in every way and a fantastic guitar player. If he was a junkie, he didn't do it in a way that looked unappealing.

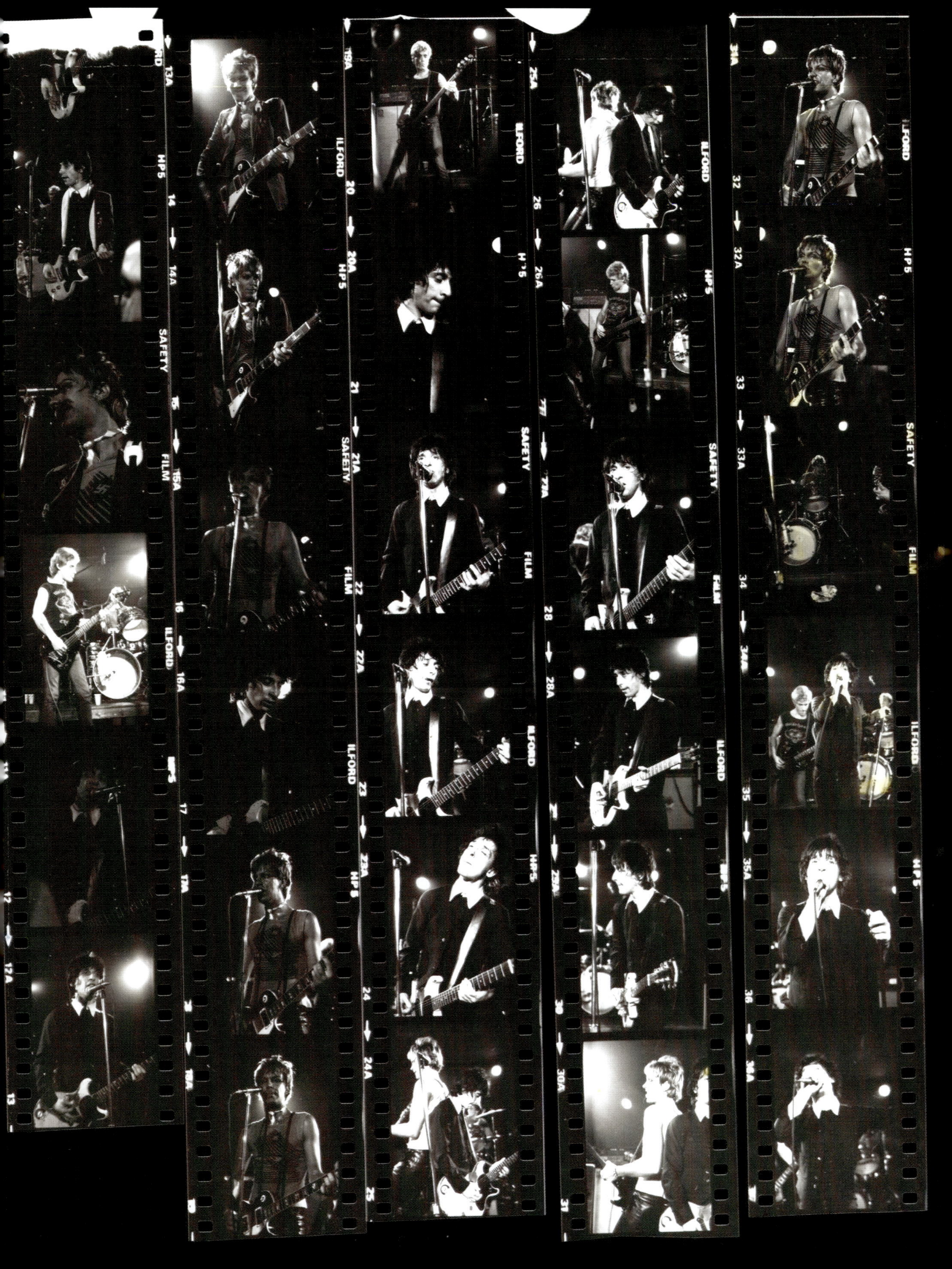

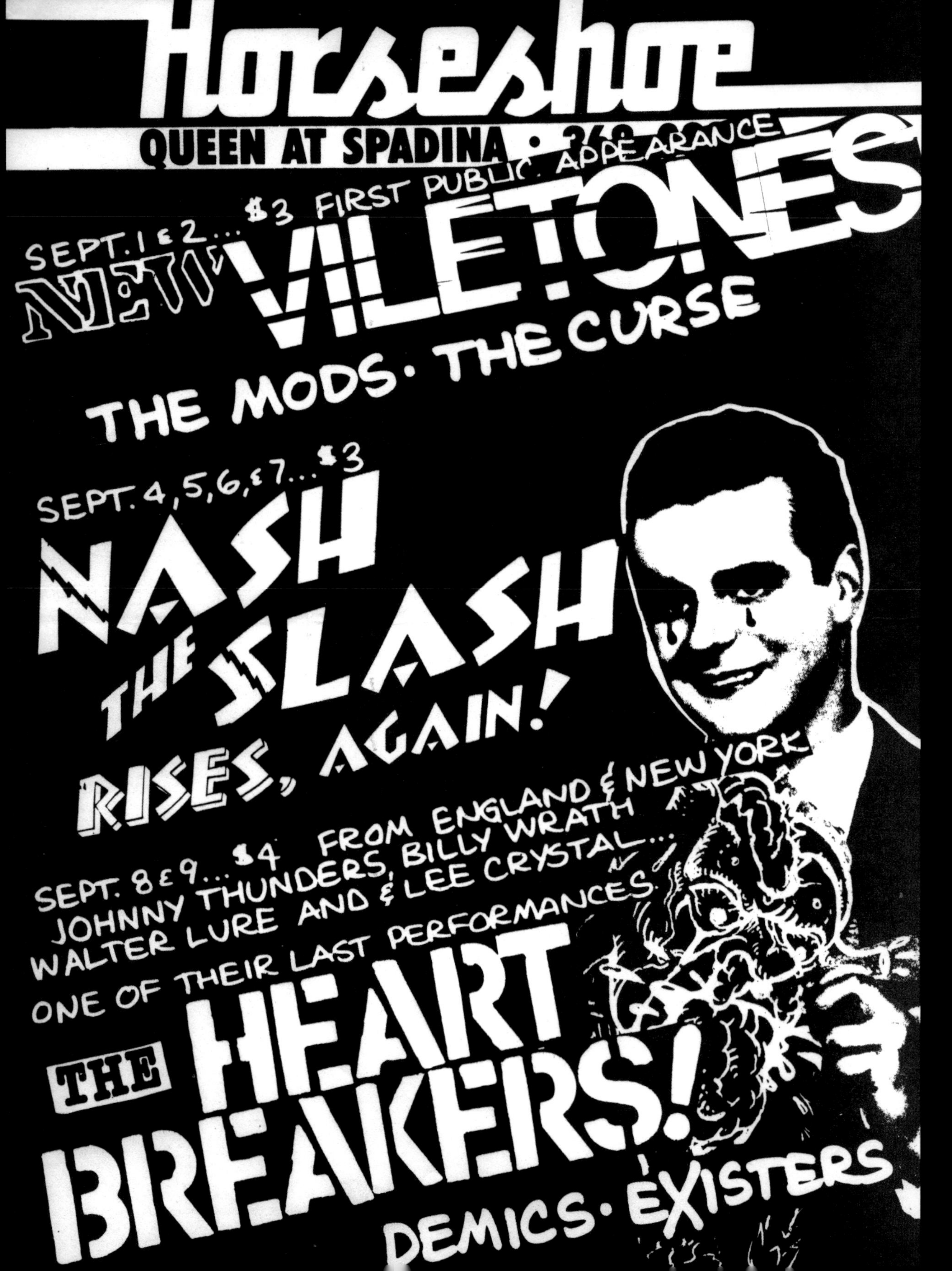
Horseshoe
QUEEN AT SPADINA •
SEPT. 1 & 2... $3 FIRST PUBLIC APPEARANCE
NEW VILETONES
THE MODS · THE CURSE
SEPT. 4, 5, 6, & 7... $3
NASH THE SLASH
RISES, AGAIN!
SEPT. 8 & 9... $4 FROM ENGLAND & NEW YORK
JOHNNY THUNDERS, BILLY WRATH
WALTER LURE AND & LEE CRYSTAL...
ONE OF THEIR LAST PERFORMANCES
THE HEART BREAKERS!
DEMICS · EXISTERS

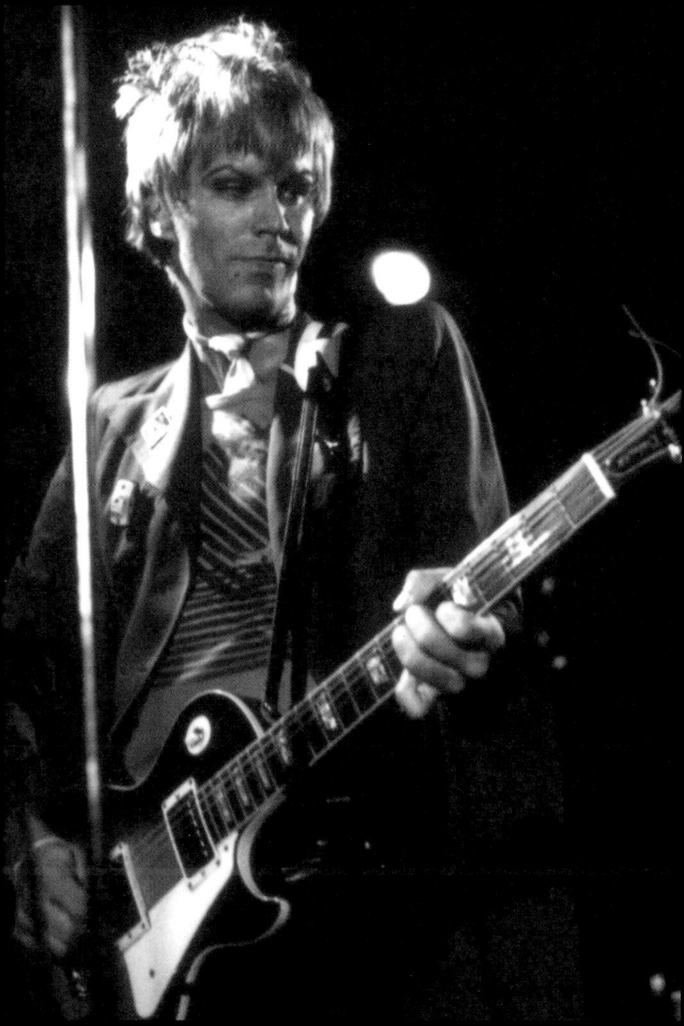

Walter Lure

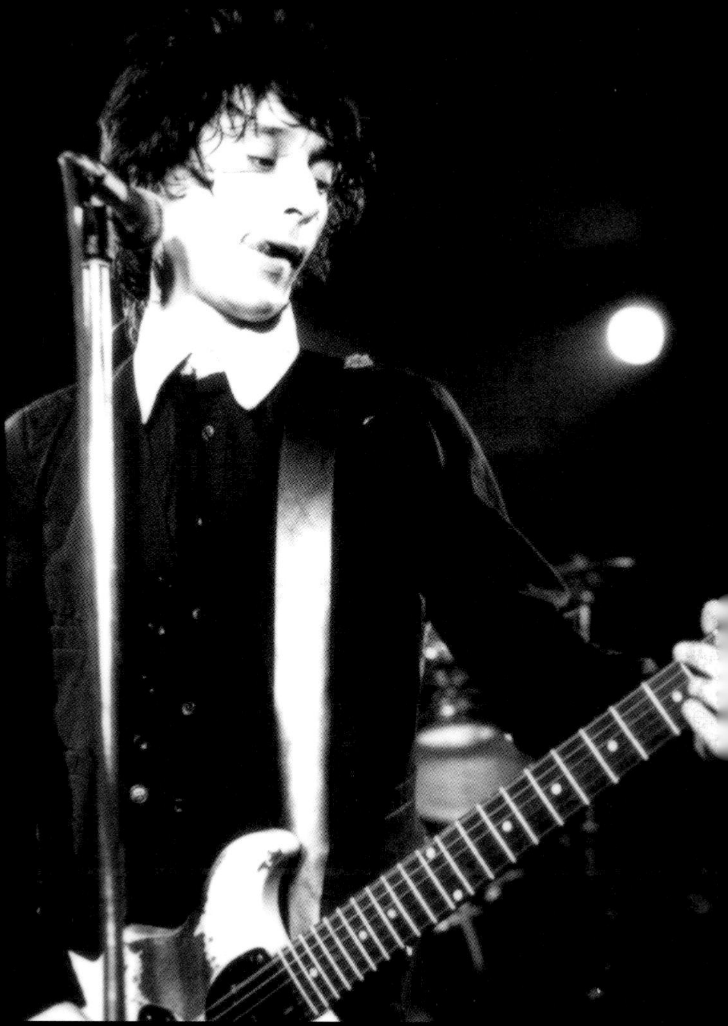

Johnny Thunders

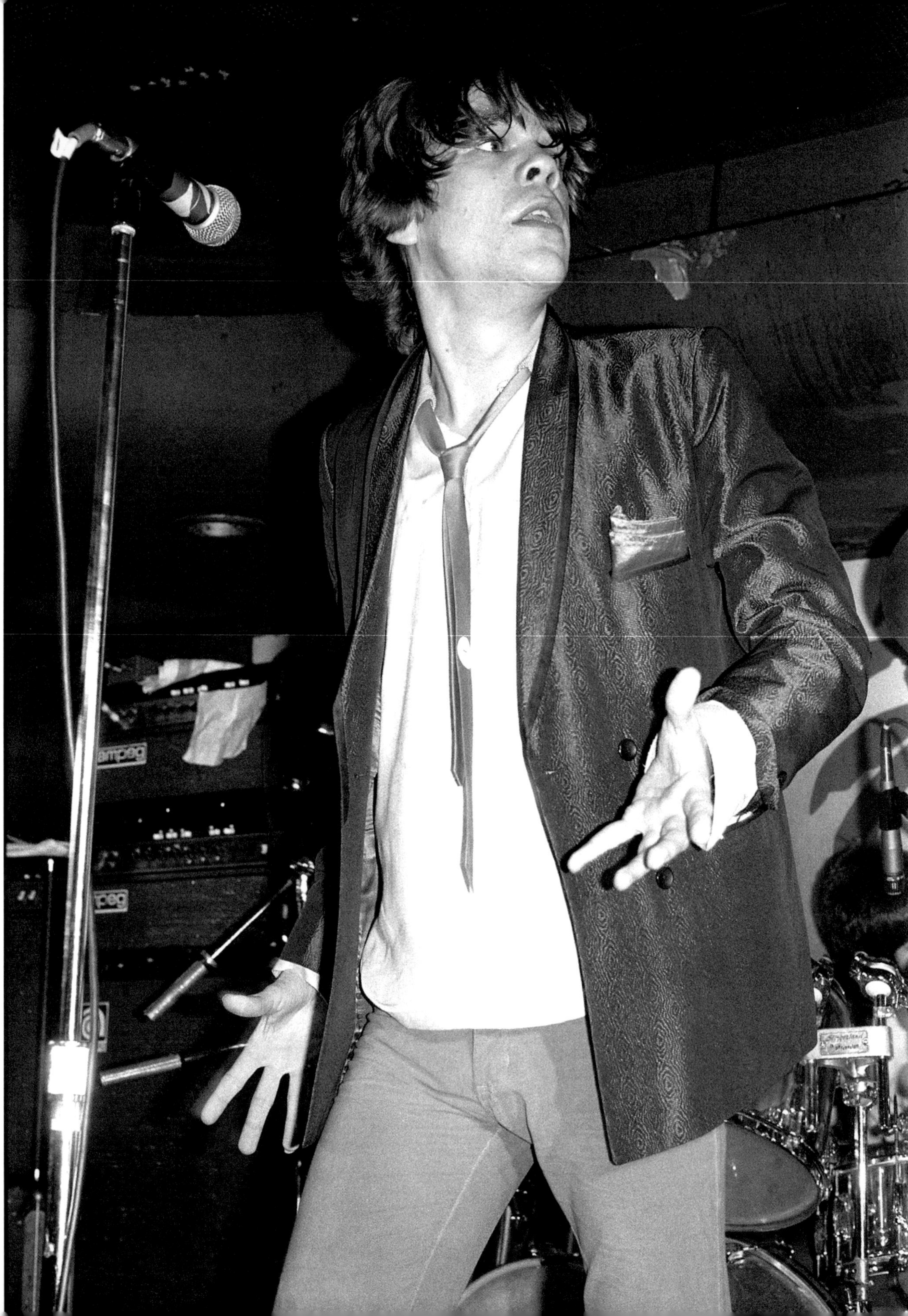
ampeg

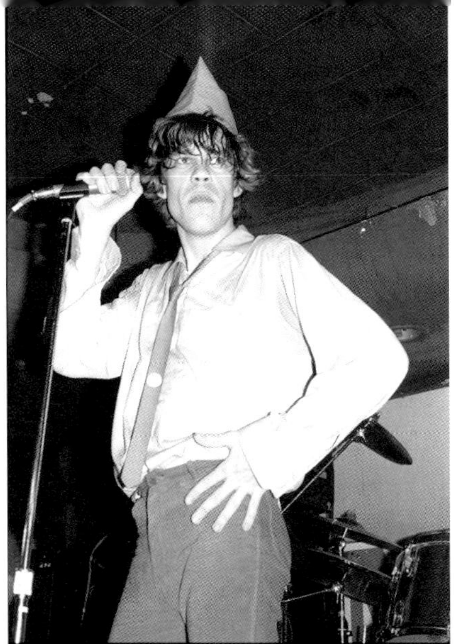

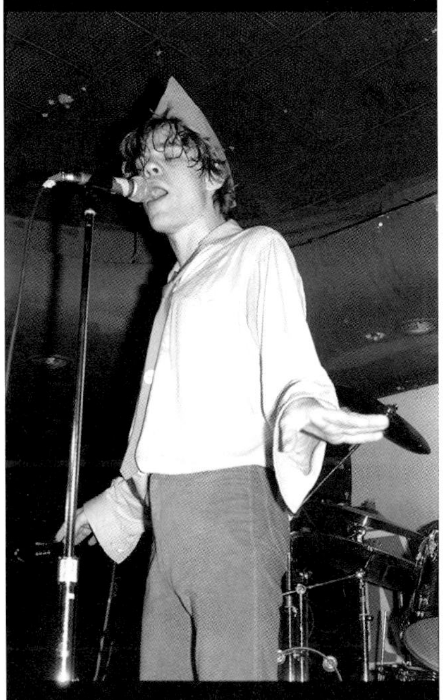

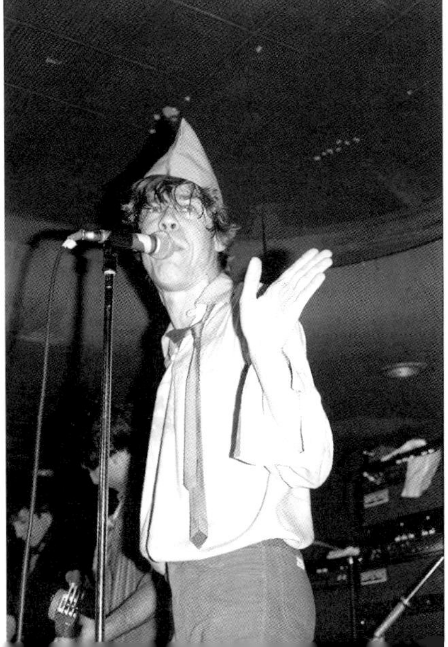

Seeing other New York Dolls members Sylvain Sylvain and David Johansen made it pretty clear who had brought the greatest sense of danger and unpredictability to the Dolls. At this El Mo show just after the release of David's first solo album, Sylvain and Johansen had a far more conventional and traditional R & B party band than either the Dolls or The Heartbreakers. Both bands played Dolls songs mixed with their own, and even though it was a thrill to see the ex-Dolls, the fantasy of indulgent and tawdry opulence had crashed into the reality of them being a hopped-up bar band.

David Johansen, El Mocambo, 1978

David Johansen, on his first post–New York Dolls tour

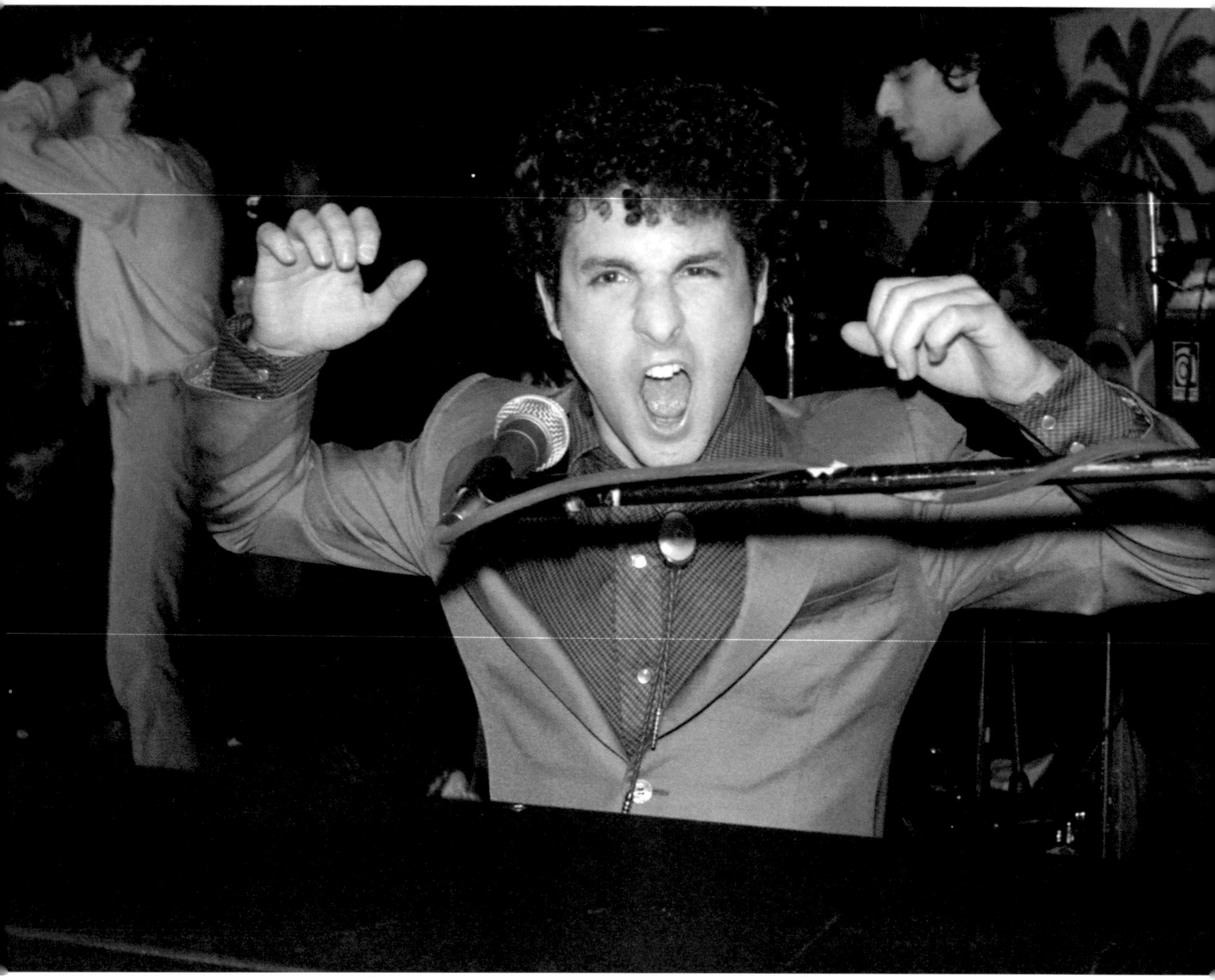

Sylvain Sylvain

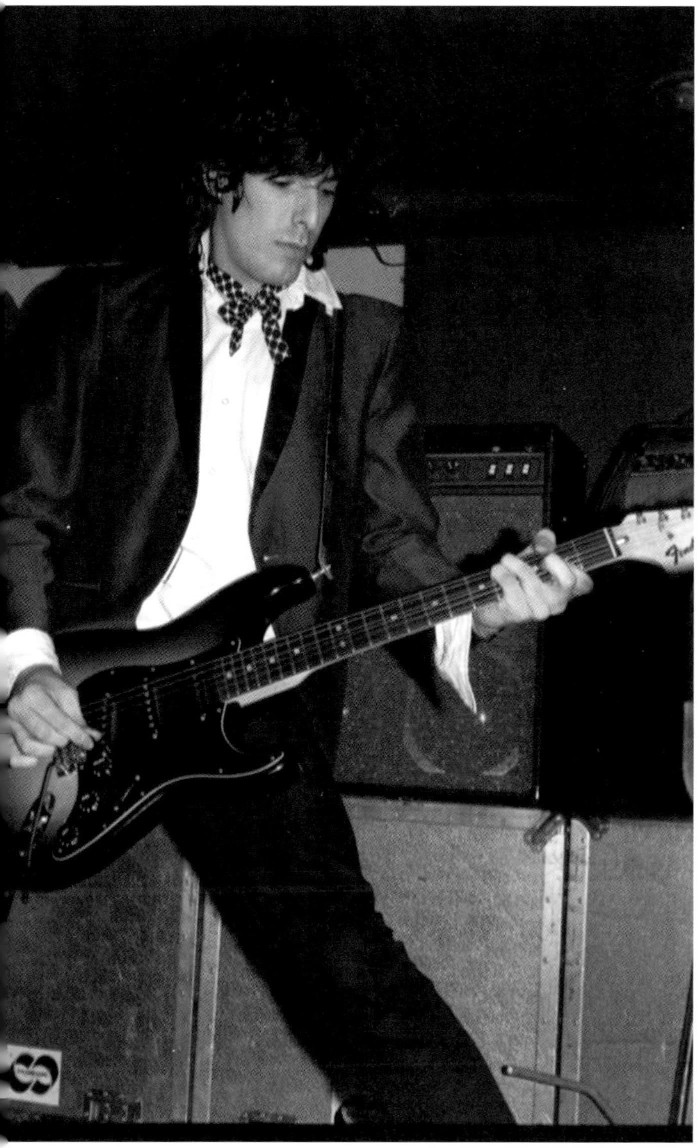

Tommy Trask

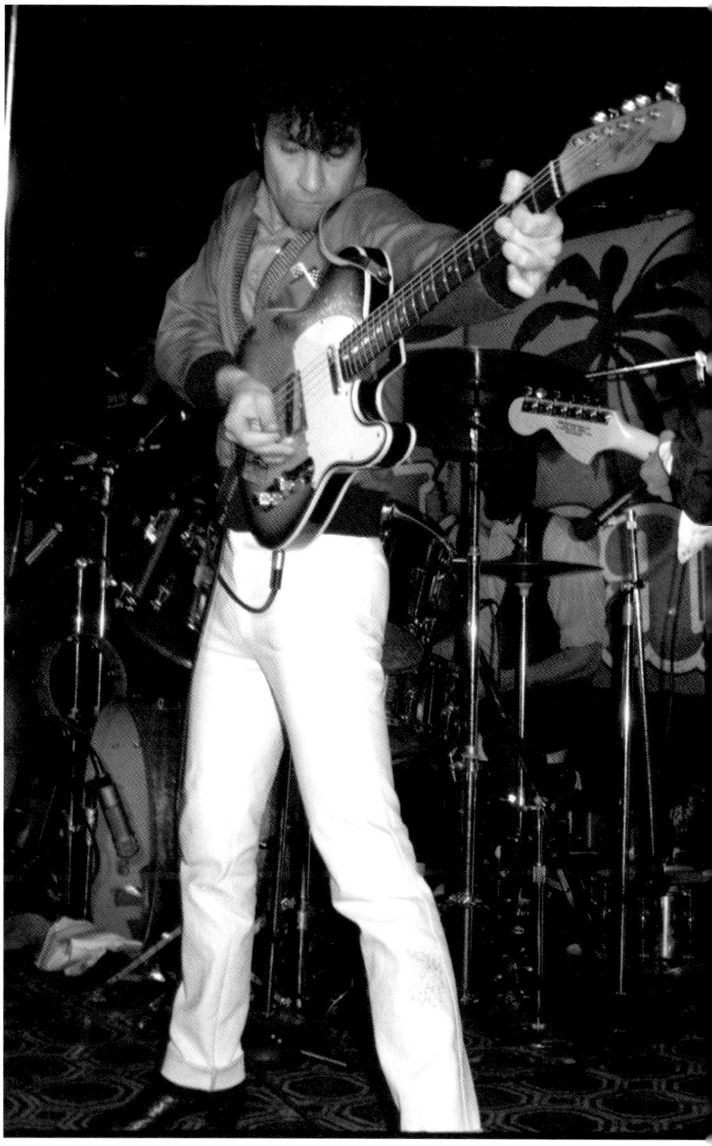

Johnny Rao

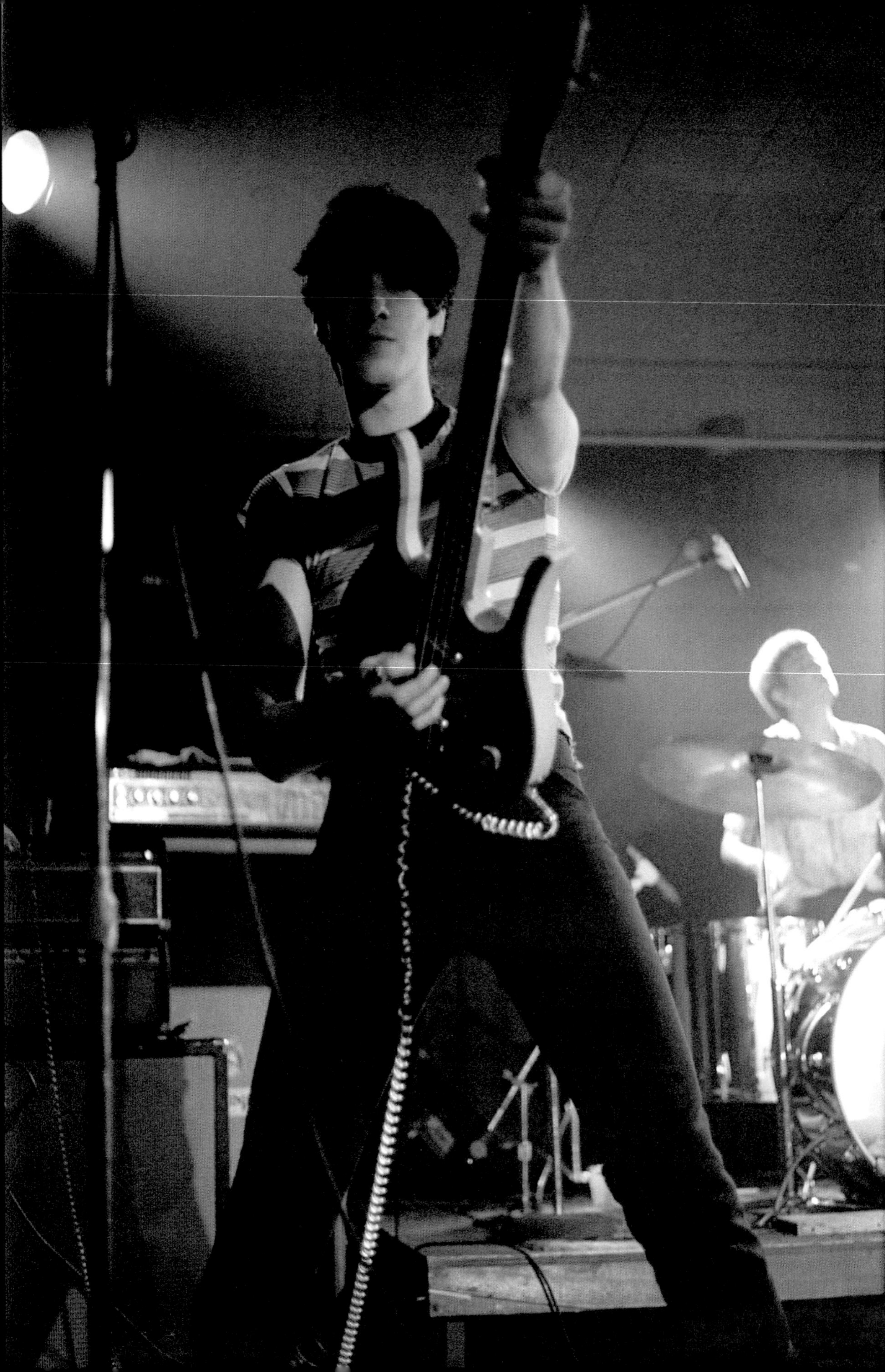

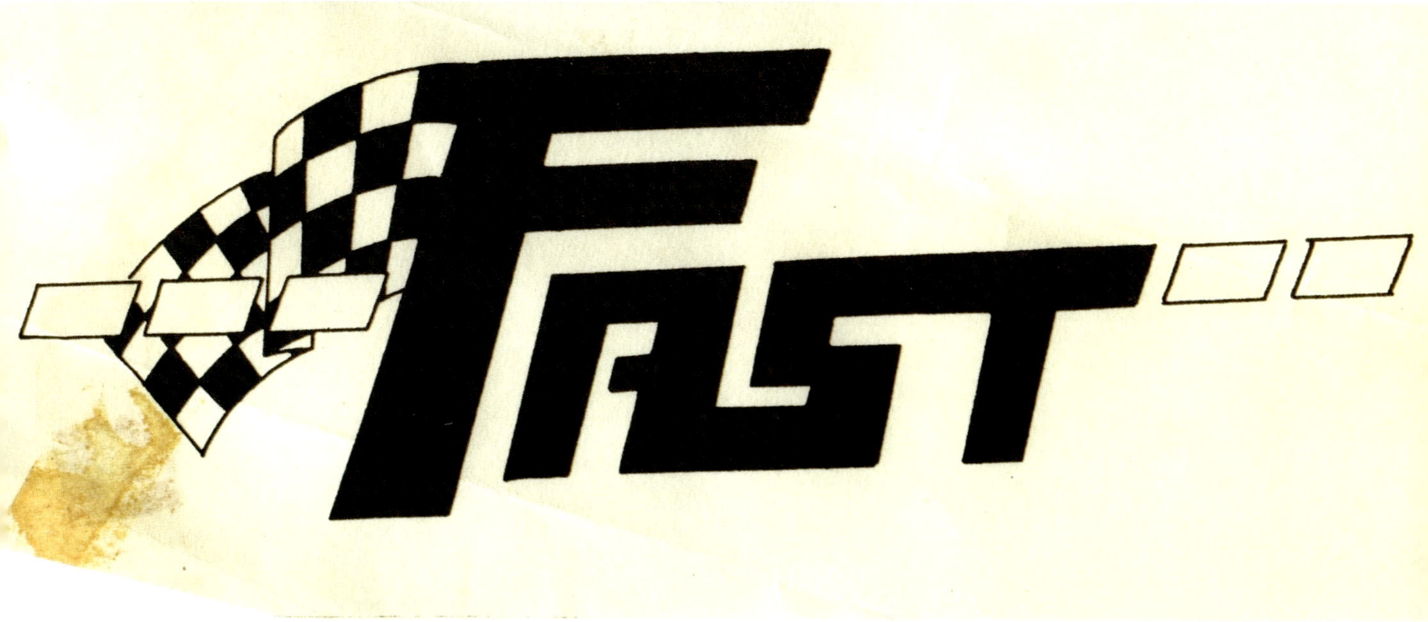

The Fast, Horseshoe Tavern, 1978, and The Edge, 1979

An underrated pre-punk pop band, real success eluded The Fast as the result of being too much, too soon. Hairspray and post-Dolls blousiness collided with skinny pants, sex and drugs, resulting in The Fast being among a handful of power pop bands like Milk N' Cookies and Lance Loud and the Mumps who were too whacked for mainstream success, too great-looking not to be anything but rock stars. Bridging the early '70s dead zone between glam and punk, their tracks on the legendary 1976 *Max's Kansas City* compilation album may have sealed the band's reputation as being forerunners of the new scene, but their recordings never captured how dynamic and exciting they were. Maybe they never took off because of the overt gayness of songs like "Boys Will Be Boys" and "Man's Favorite Sport" but it wasn't for lack of effort. The Fast played the Horseshoe, the Edge and even the Gasworks on their numerous gigs in T.O. After a brief period as Miki Zone Zoo, Paul and Miki turned out a couple of synthy club hits as running-shoed leather daddies Man2Man.

Louis Bova

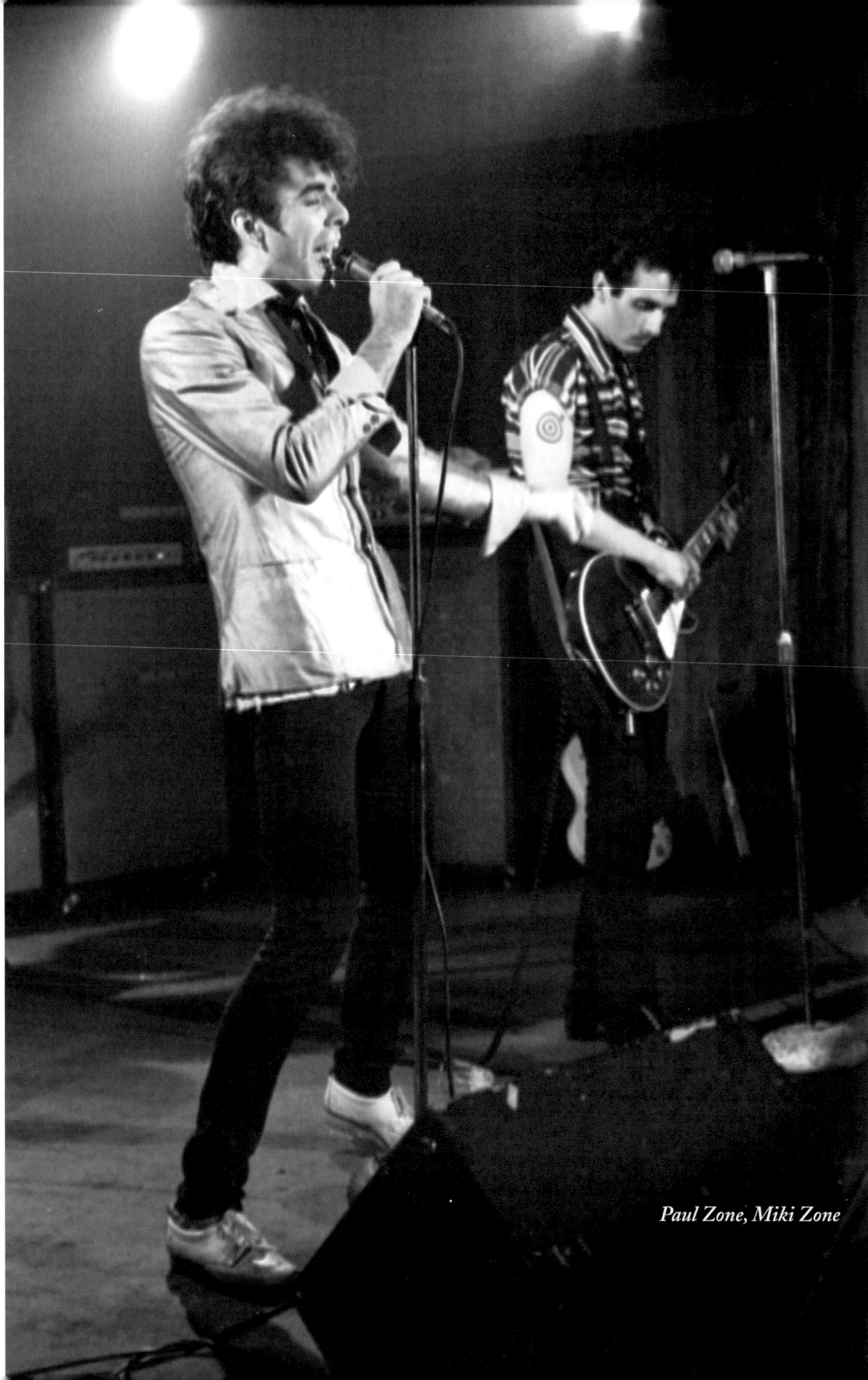

Paul Zone, Miki Zone

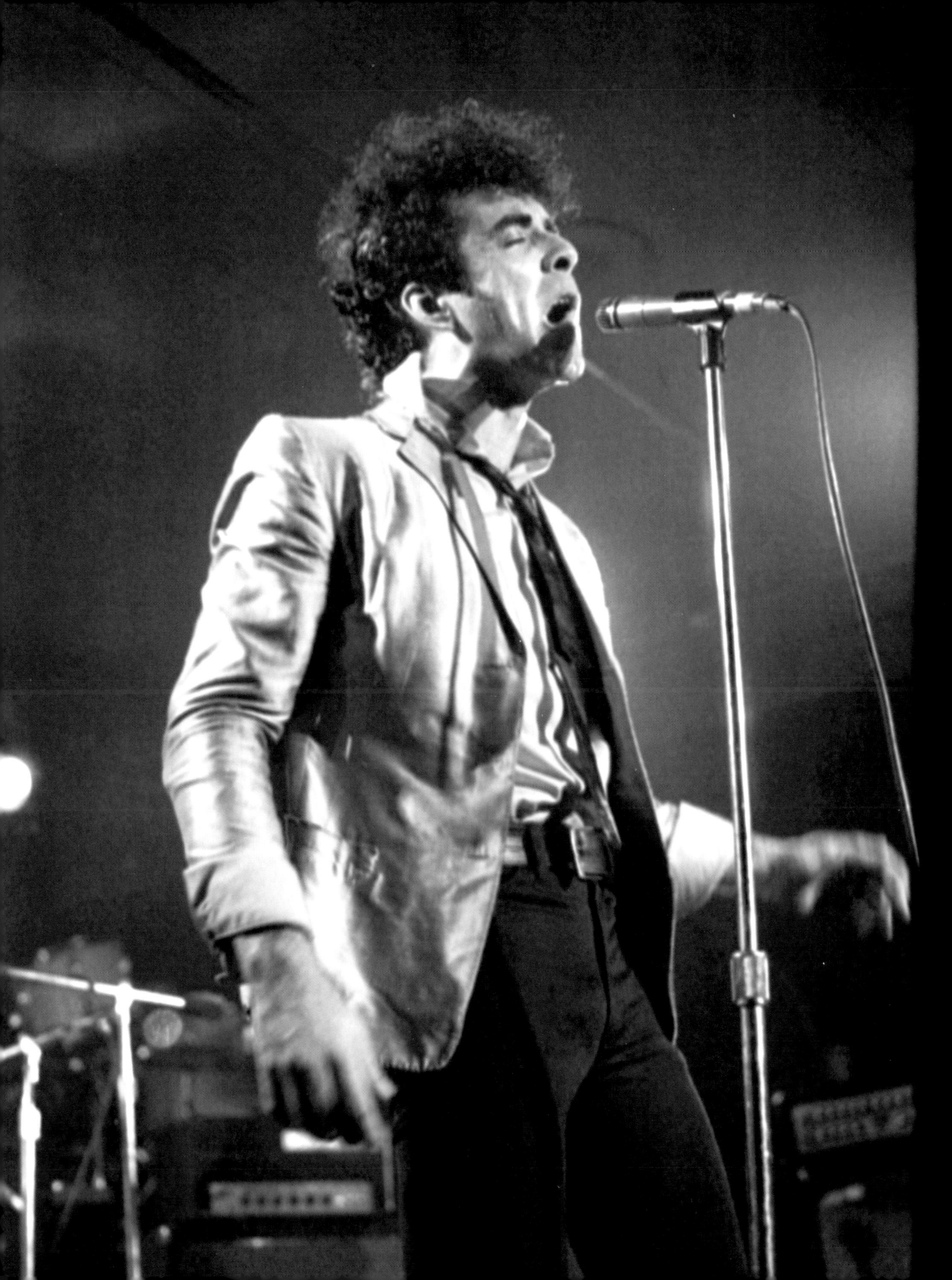

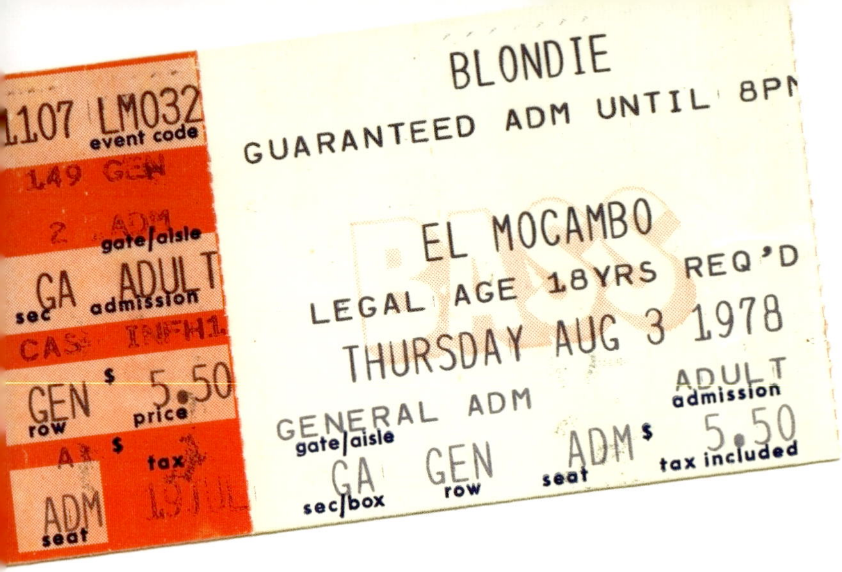

Blondie,
El Mocambo, 1978

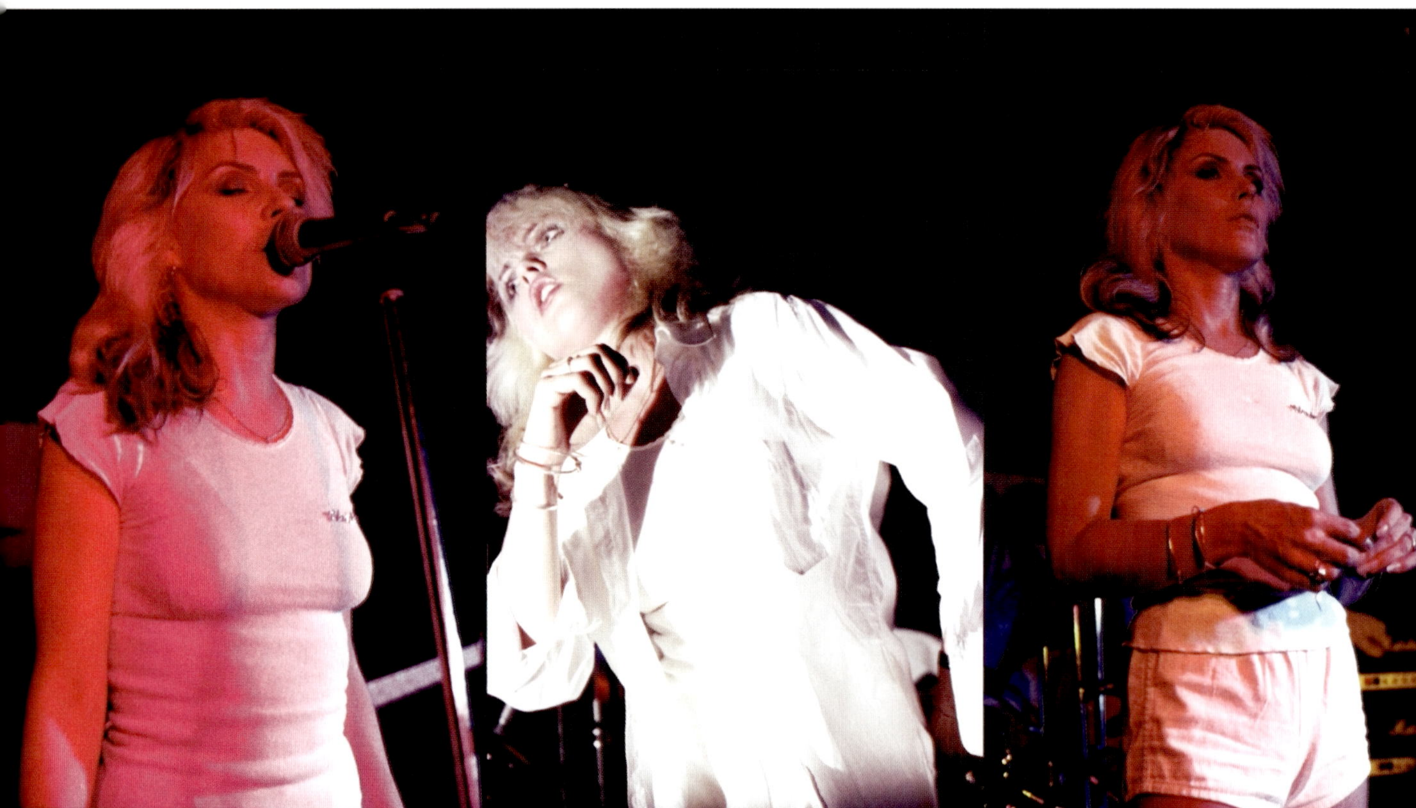

Deborah Harry

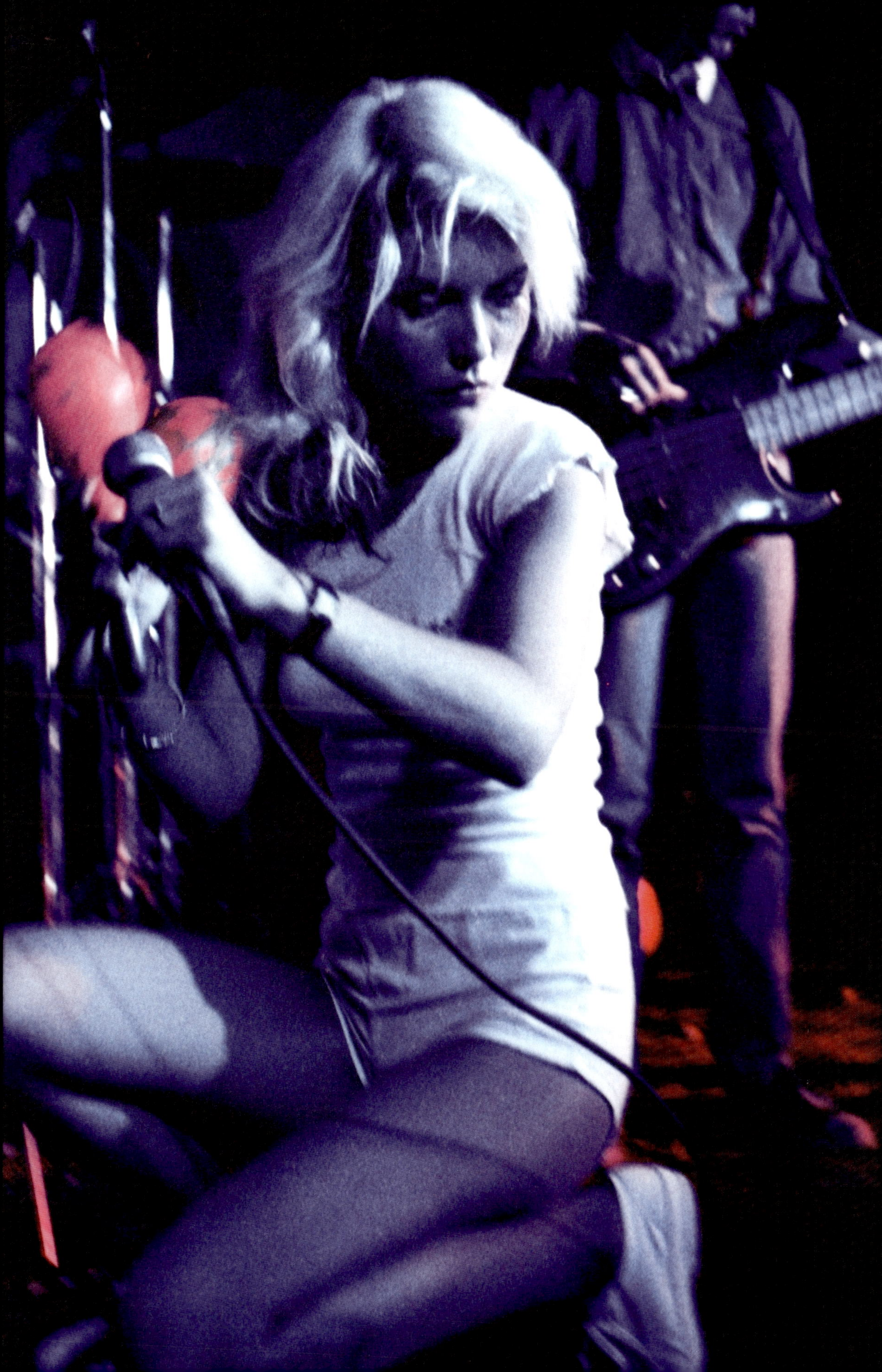

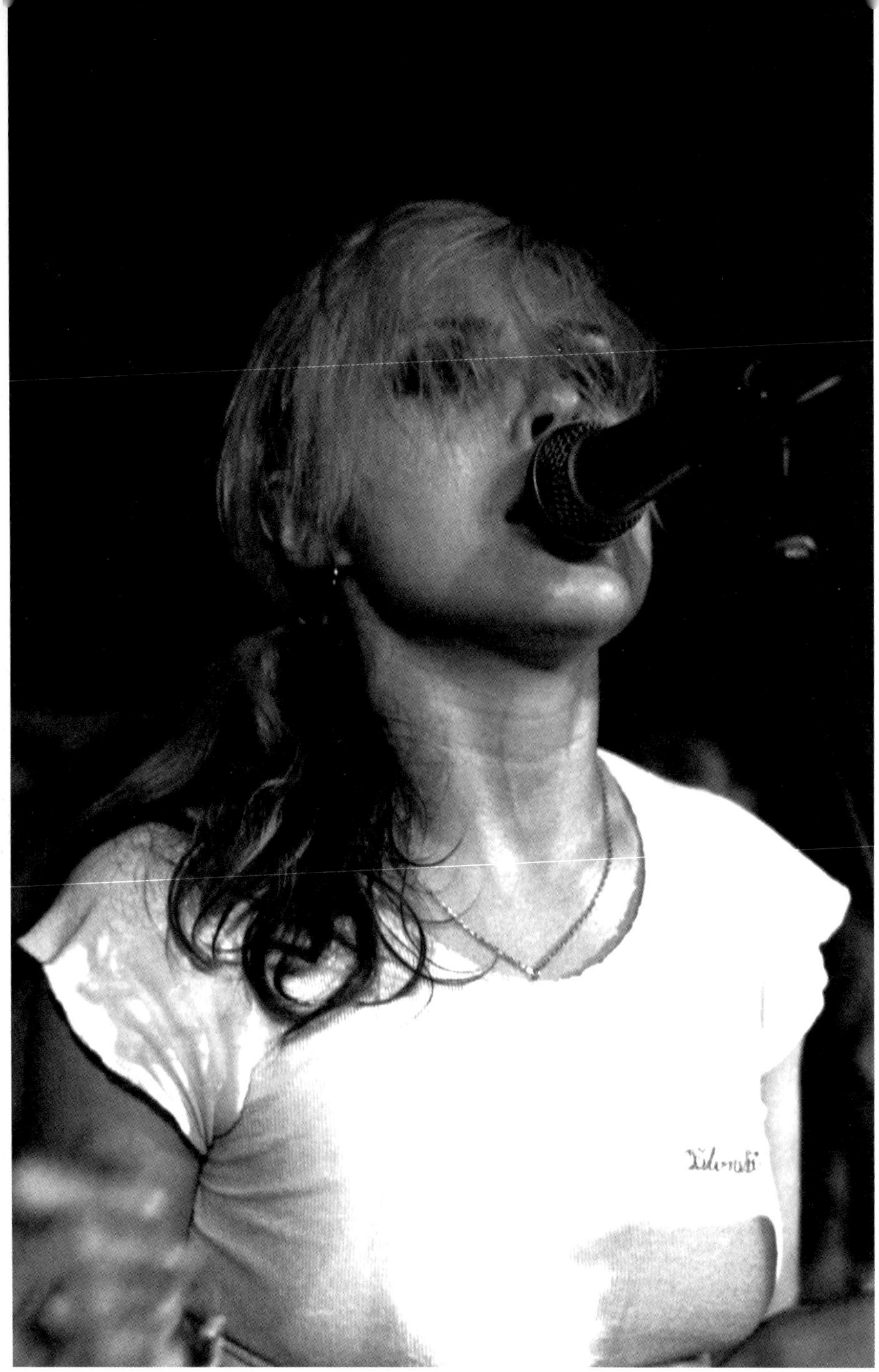

With their second album *Plastic Letters* just out, Blondie played the El Mo with a new lineup — one that would go on to record their massive third album, *Parallel Lines*. While their first LP had been a thrilling go-go and *West Side Story*–inspired '60s homage, Blondie had now begun the transformation to Top 40 juggernaut. I was so close to Deborah Harry I had to lean back to get the couple of feet distance I needed in order to focus, and she in turn leaned on my shoulder for support as she reached out to the audience.

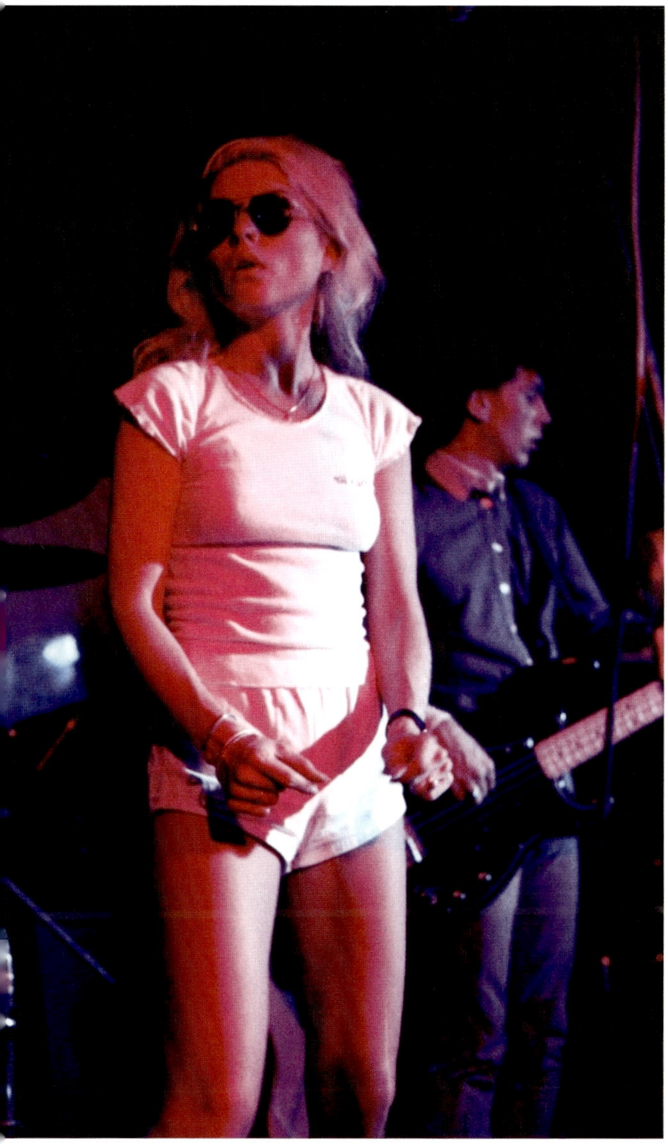

Deborah Harry, Nigel Harrison

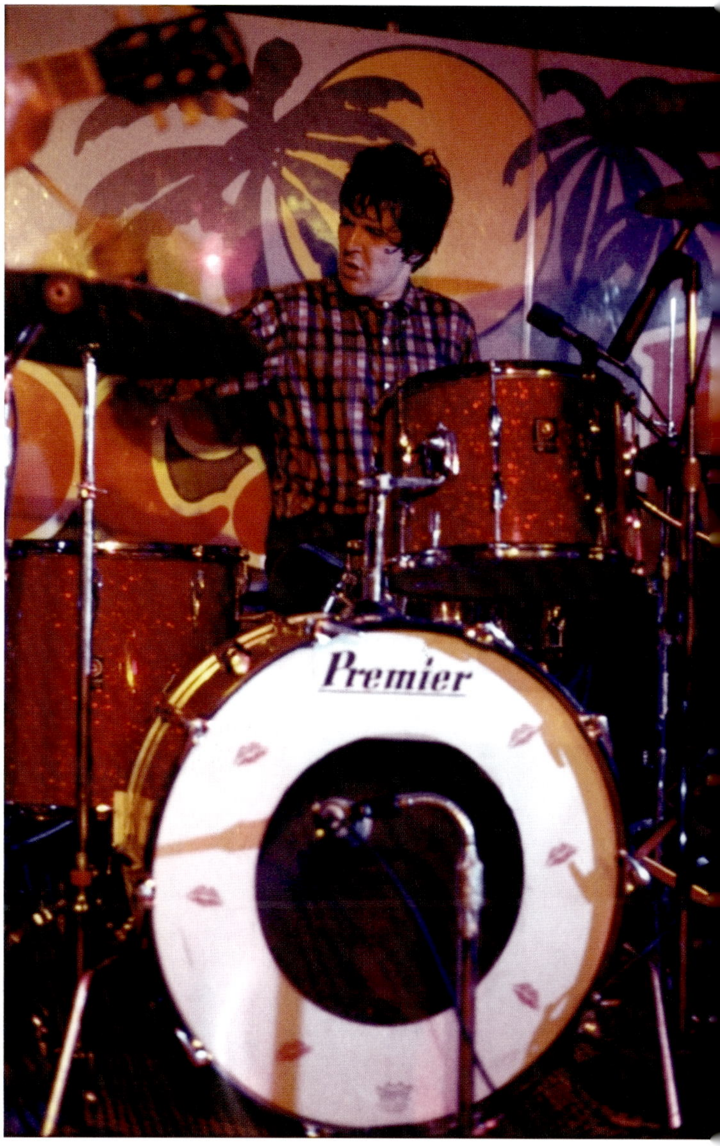

Clem Burke

The B-Girls had been playing around for maybe a year at this point and although their "Fun at the Beach" single was still a year away, their respect and affection for '60s girl groups made them the obvious opening act. Bouncy and cute, The B-Girls joined Blondie for backing vocals during their encore cover of The Shangri-Las' "Out in the Streets."

Lucasta B-Girl and Deborah Harry (next page)

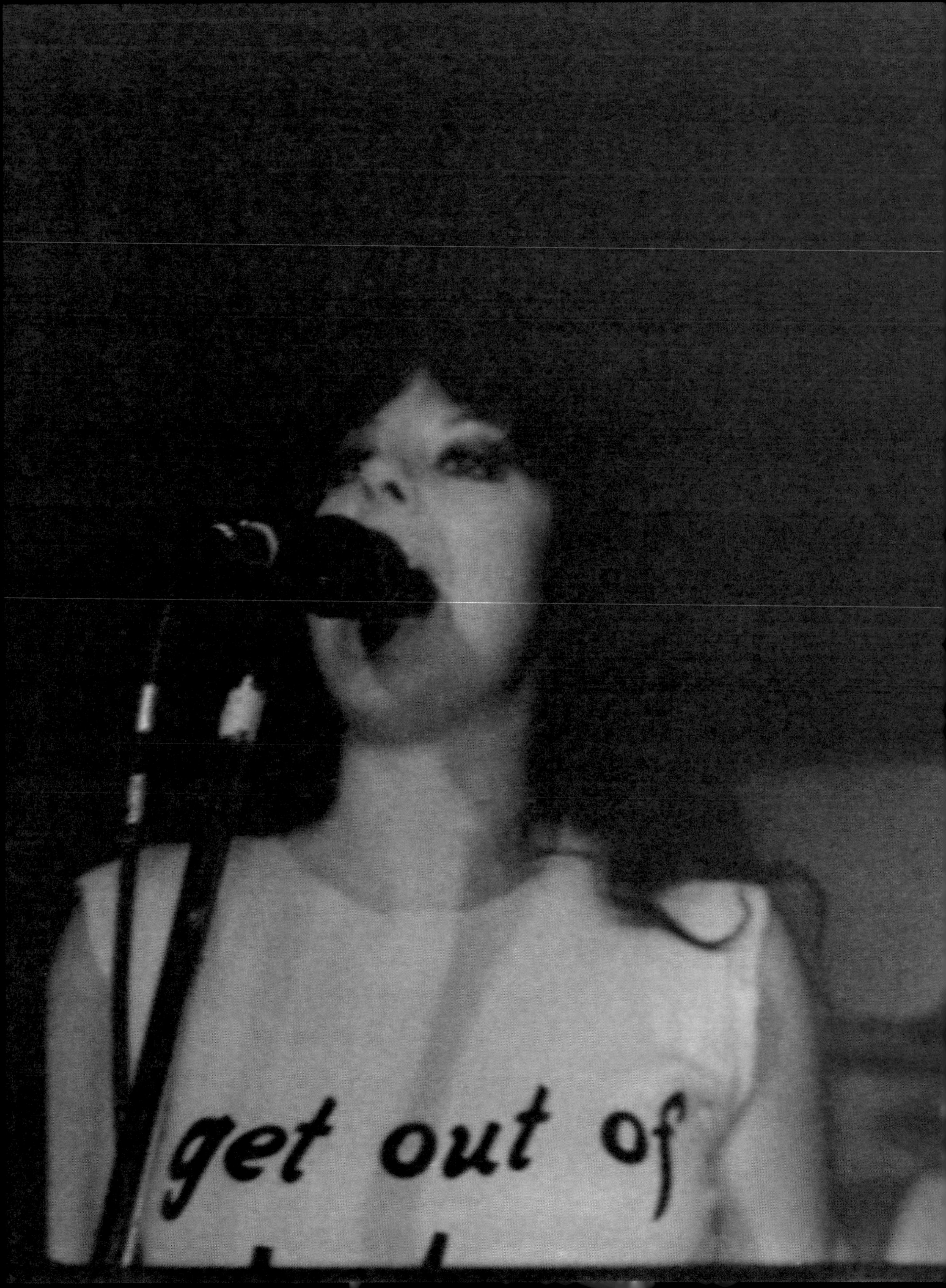
get out of

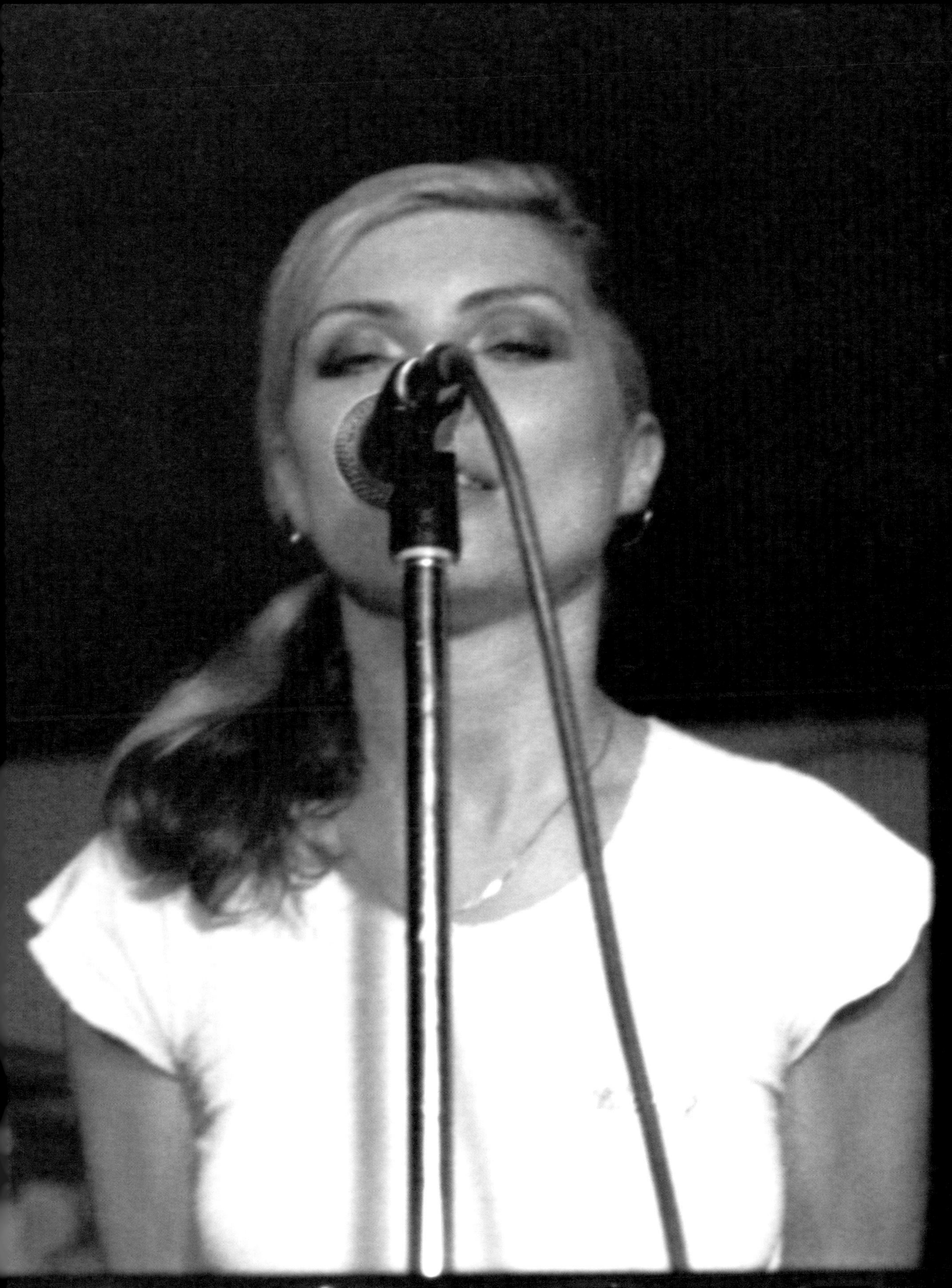

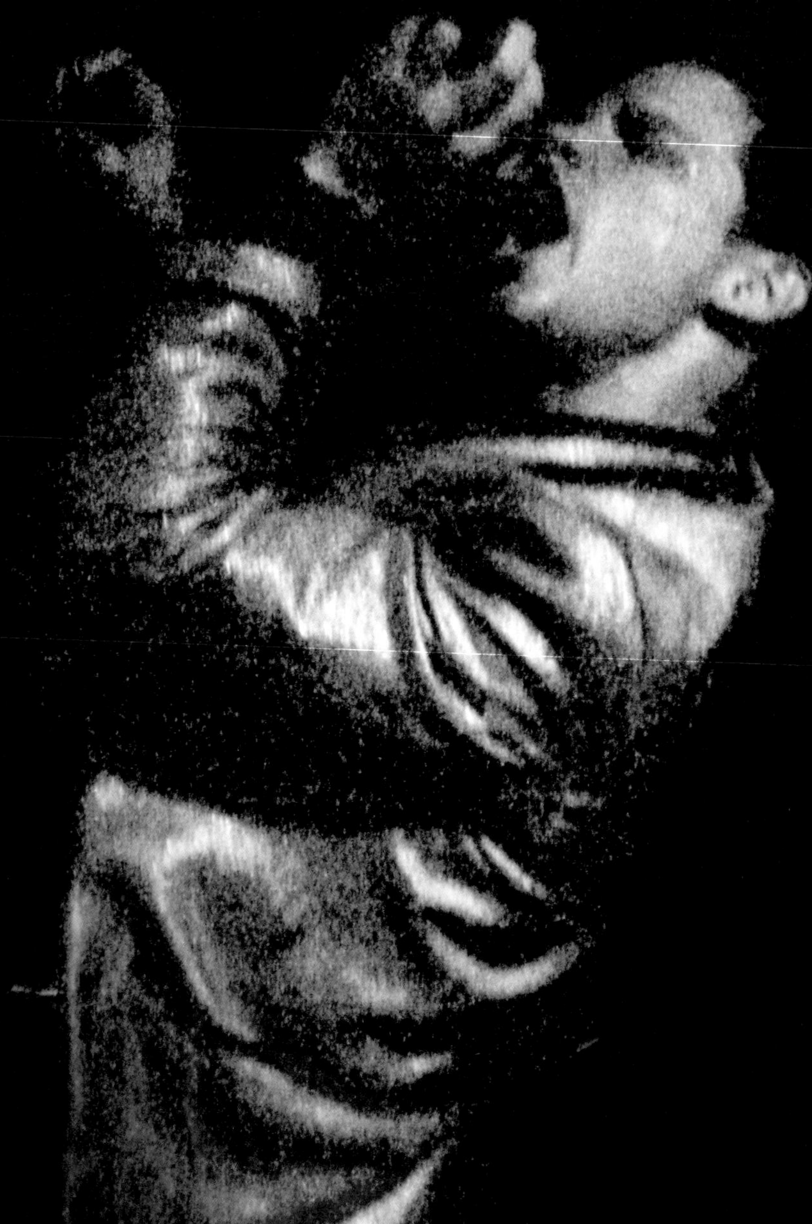

Contortions, Horseshoe Tavern, 1978

The logical extreme for music to evolve to was a complete anti-musical approach of texture, mood and the physical embodiment of antagonism. The Contortions as well as Teenage Jesus and the Jerks distilled all the negative energy that punk rock generated into a spazz-jazz attack/performance for an audience that wavered between indifferent curiosity and outright hostility. Both bands played in almost complete darkness, making photos next to impossible. The already sparse area in front of the stage cleared as soon as The Contortions began playing. Keyboardist Adele Bertei and guitarist Pat Place were compellingly memorable, creating slashes of brutal sound and pure tonal color. Place had an unhealthy physical frailty that made performing somehow look like an act of revenge, and Bertei sported shaved eyebrows that gave her a slightly crazed look as she bashed her organ with her elbows. Singer, saxophonist and leader James Chance thrashed about, throwing himself to the ground like an overamped psychostimulated James Brown. Even in their cool stillness, the rest of the musicians were riveting to watch, their creative contribution made all the more obvious in their post-Contortions bands — The Bush Tetras with Place and Bertei; The Raybeats with Jody Harris, George Scott and drummer Don Christensen.

Chance jumped to the area in front of the stage and slowly walked across the width of it with his fingers to his mouth as if pondering what to do next. Rabies, the singer of Tyranna, sat near the stage straddling a backward chair as she watched the show. When Chance reached her, he suddenly pushed the chair with all his force, sending her flailing to the floor.

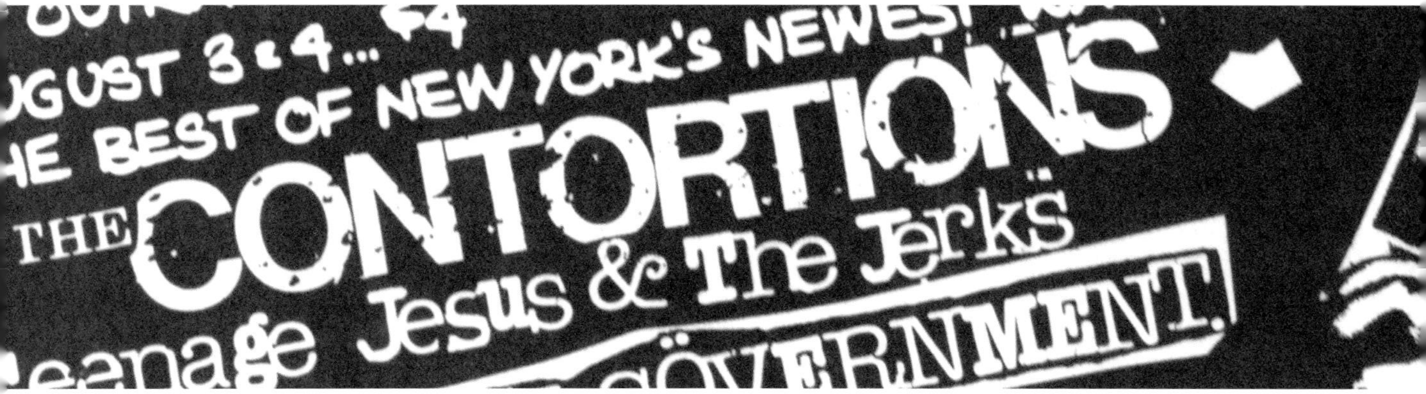

James Chance

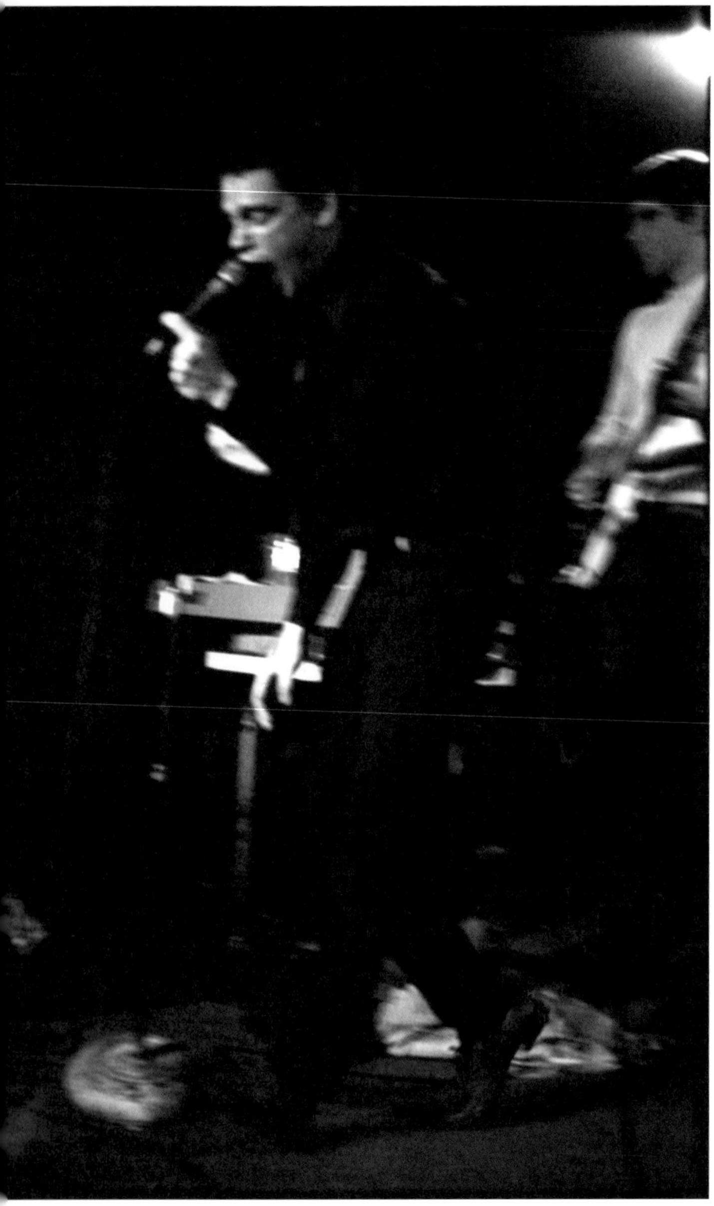

James Chance, Jody Harris

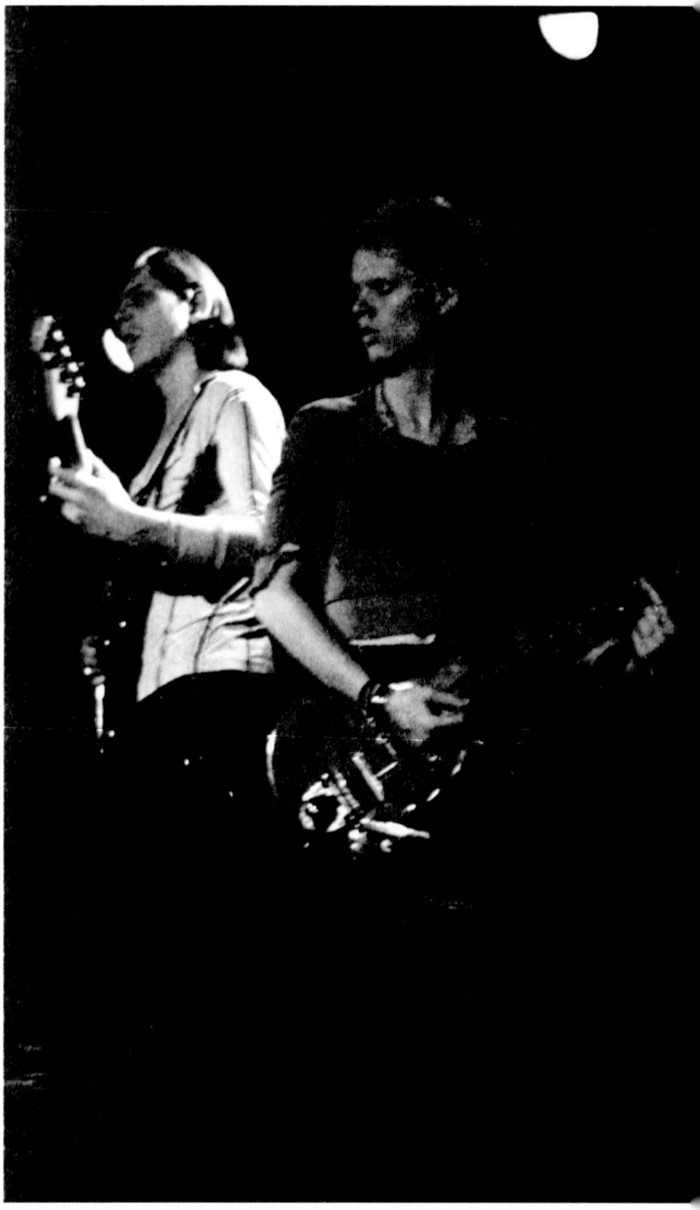

George Scott III, Pat Place

Rabies and Roger in front of the Horseshoe after the show, the hand-painted gig poster visible in the display window behind them.

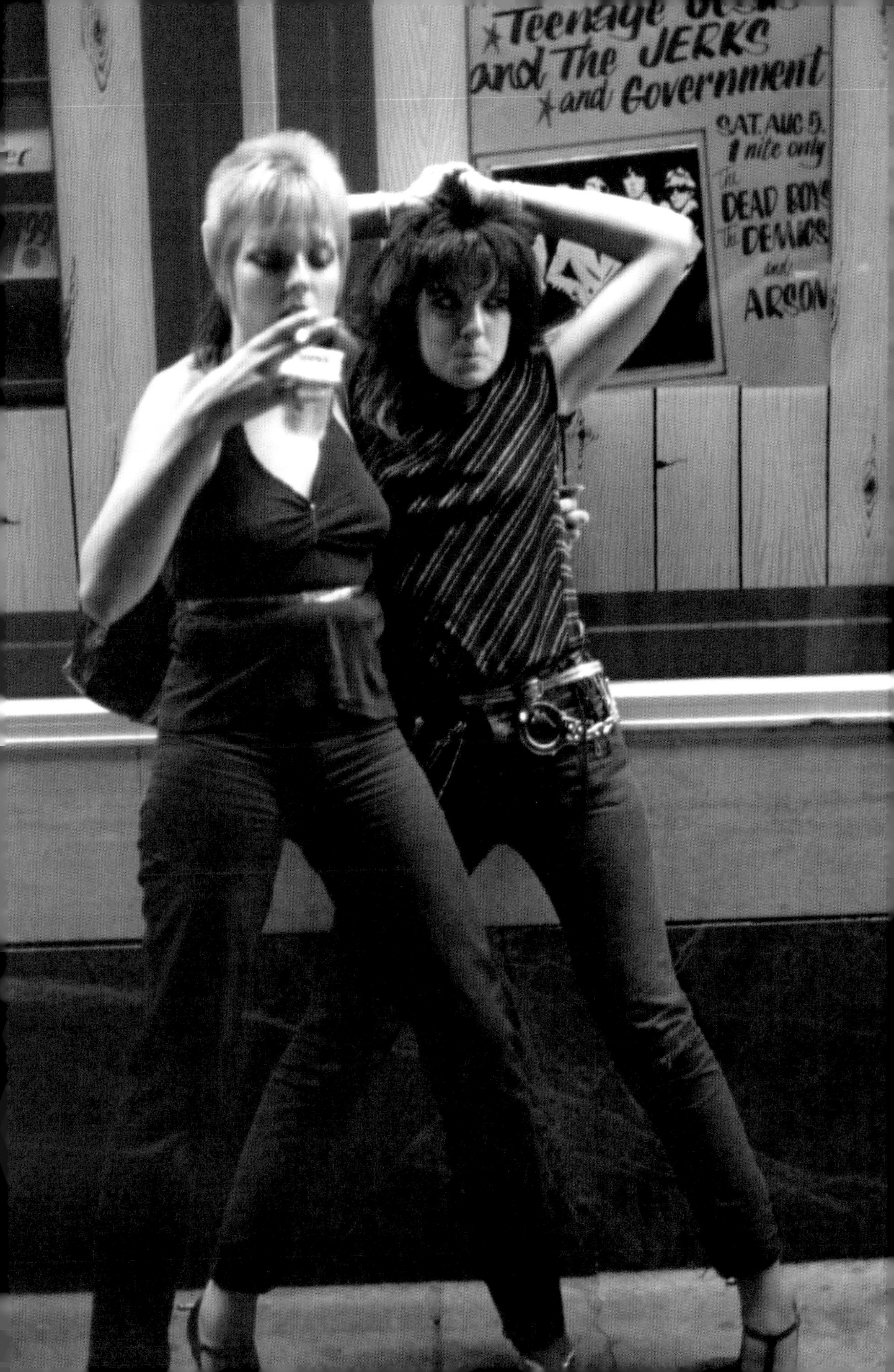
Teenage
and The JERKS
and Government
SAT. AUG 5.
1 nite only
The DEAD BOYS
The DEMICS
and
ARSON

Cheap Trick, Massey Hall, 1978

Somehow, Massey Hall was bigger in the '70s than it is now. It was always exciting to go to this spectacular late 19th-century concert hall we all knew from school field trips to see the Toronto Symphony. Even if I had tickets on the second balcony, once the lights went down, I'd try to get to the front where you might get away with a few songs or the whole show with the best view in the place. Seeing the mechanics of the curtains and the rigging offstage was always part of the thrill of being against the stage.

Cheap Trick's new album was *Heaven Tonight*, which marked the height of my interest in the band. There was probably no better time to see them live. They were totally burning — a band at its peak even though they hadn't had any hits yet and were one album away from being global stars. The pretty ones were at their prettiest and girls screamed. Rick Nielsen's hyper nerd act didn't look like an act yet, mugging as he flicked custom guitar picks to the audience. Bun E. did a drum solo with sticks the size of baseball bats and Robin Zander's perfect hair stayed in place for the whole show. I always think of them as being an anomaly like The Runaways — a rupture in the conventions of what pop music was then, too weird or different looking/sounding to have huge audiences, but too distinct to not attract attention.

Robin Zander

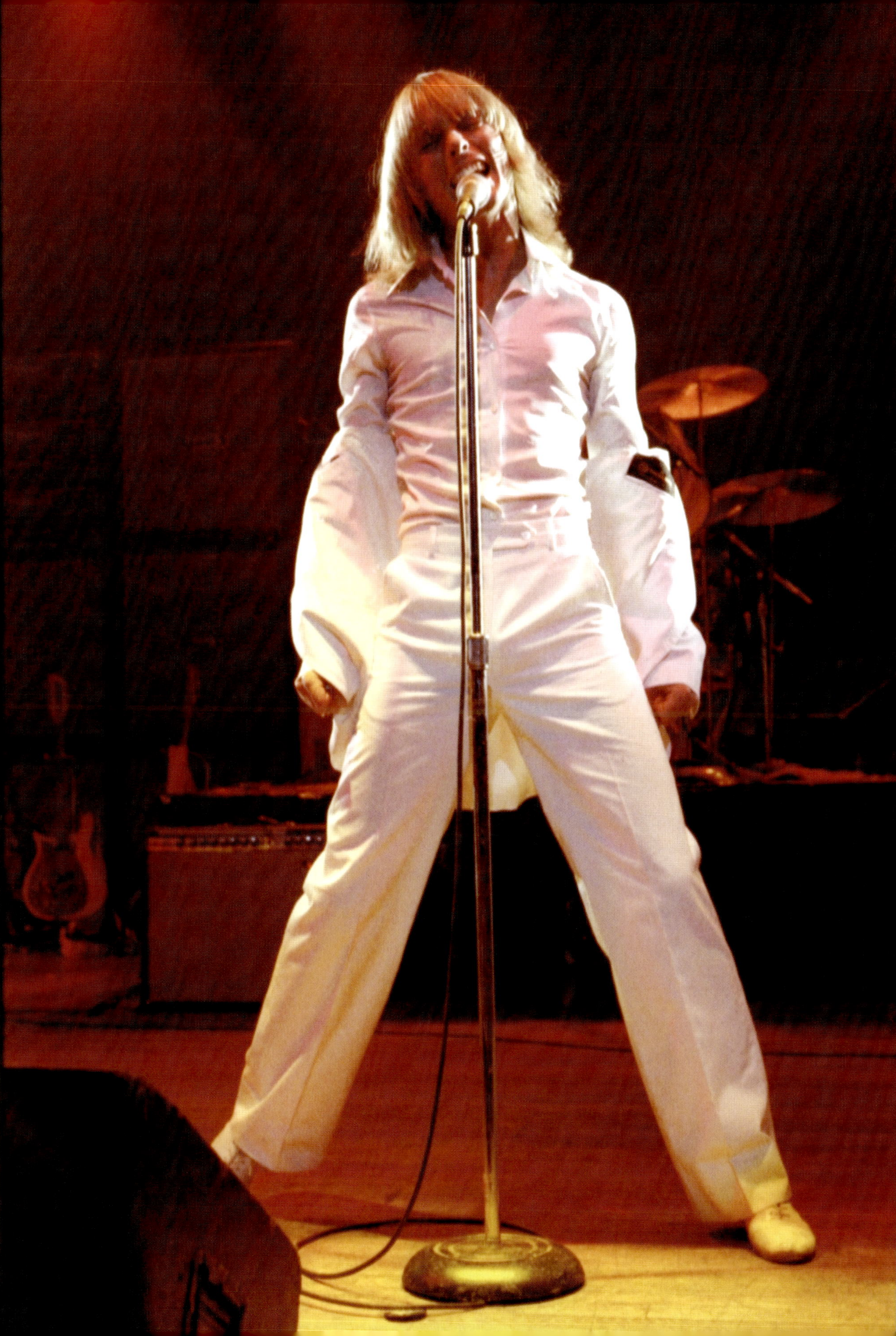

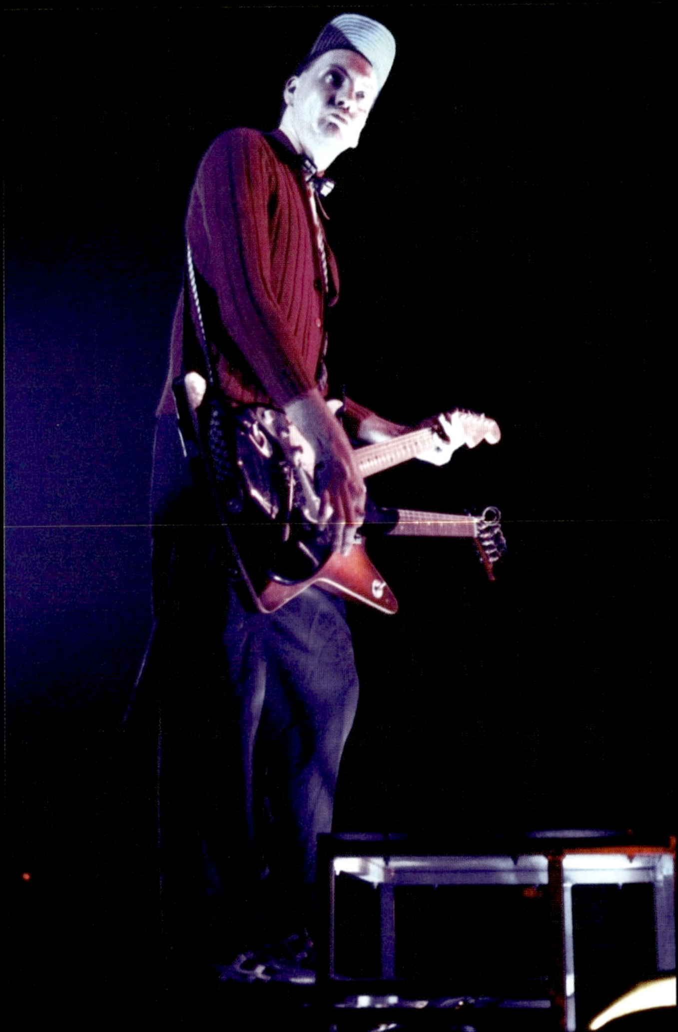

Rick Nielsen

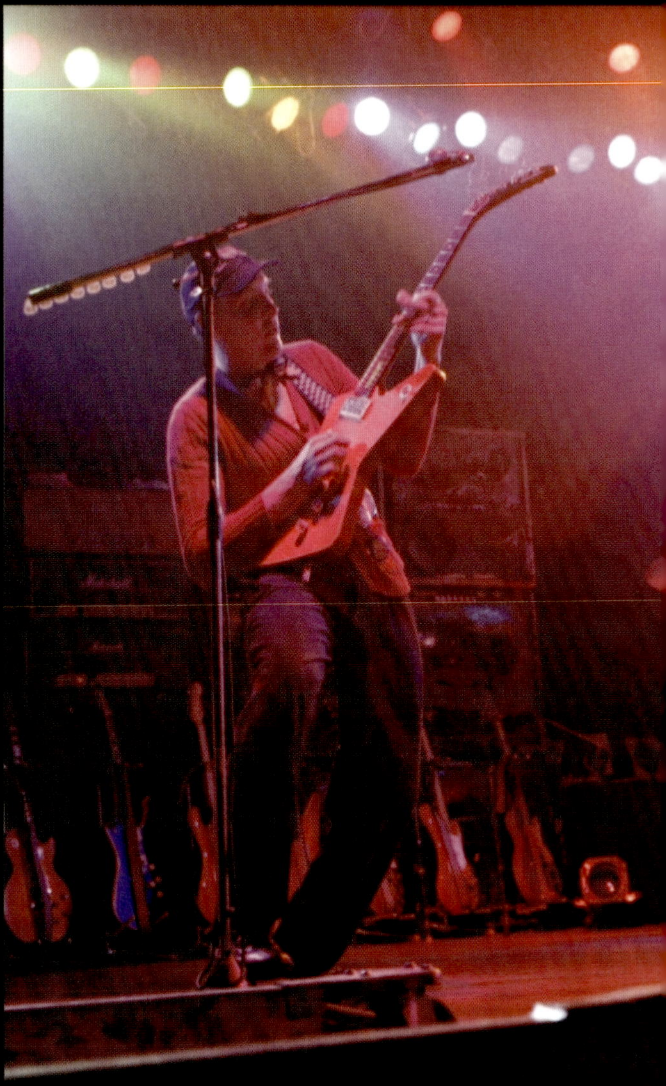

Bun E. Carlos

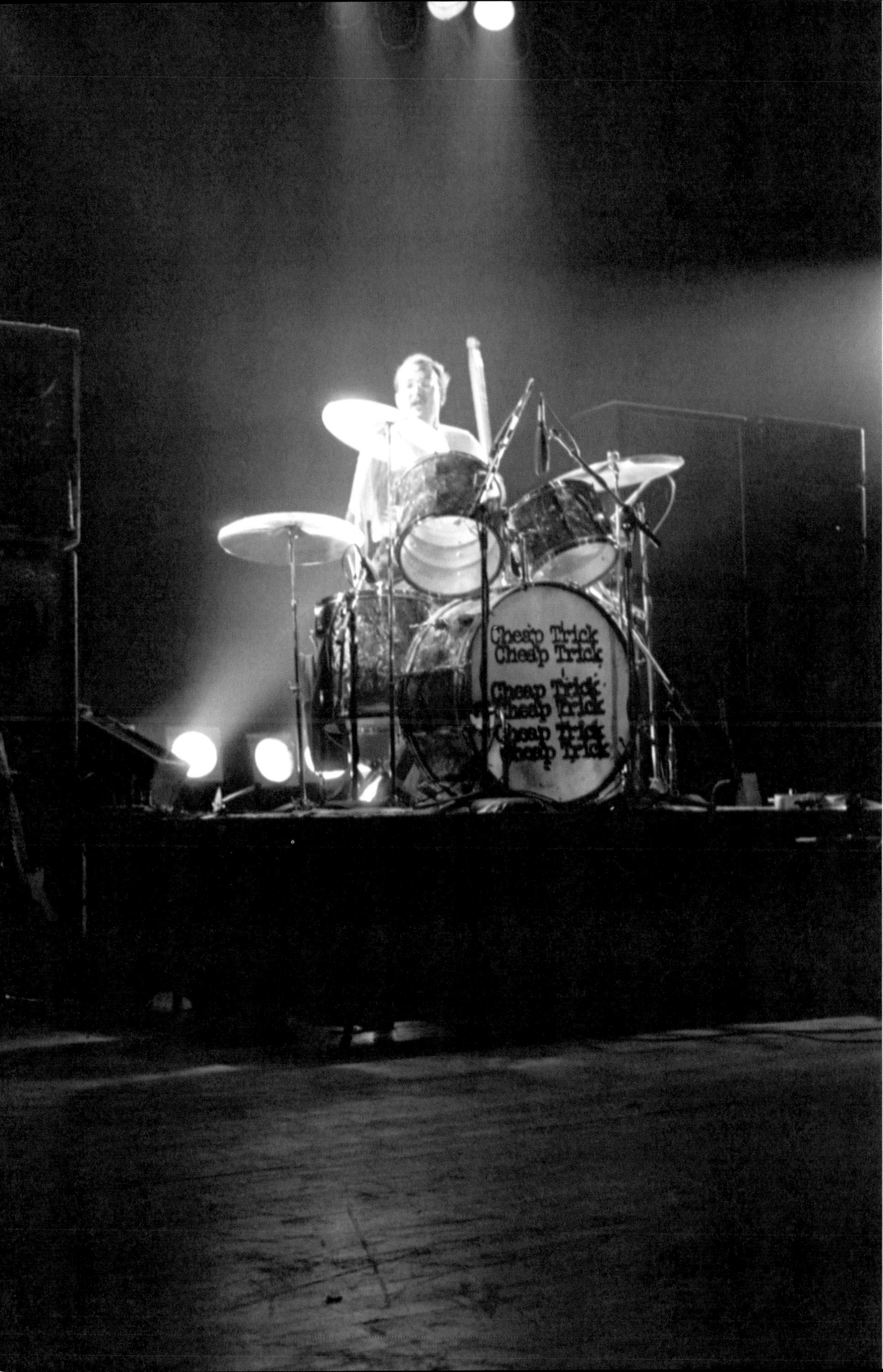
Cheap Trick
Cheap Trick
Cheap Trick
Cheap Trick
Cheap Trick
Cheap Trick

Other People

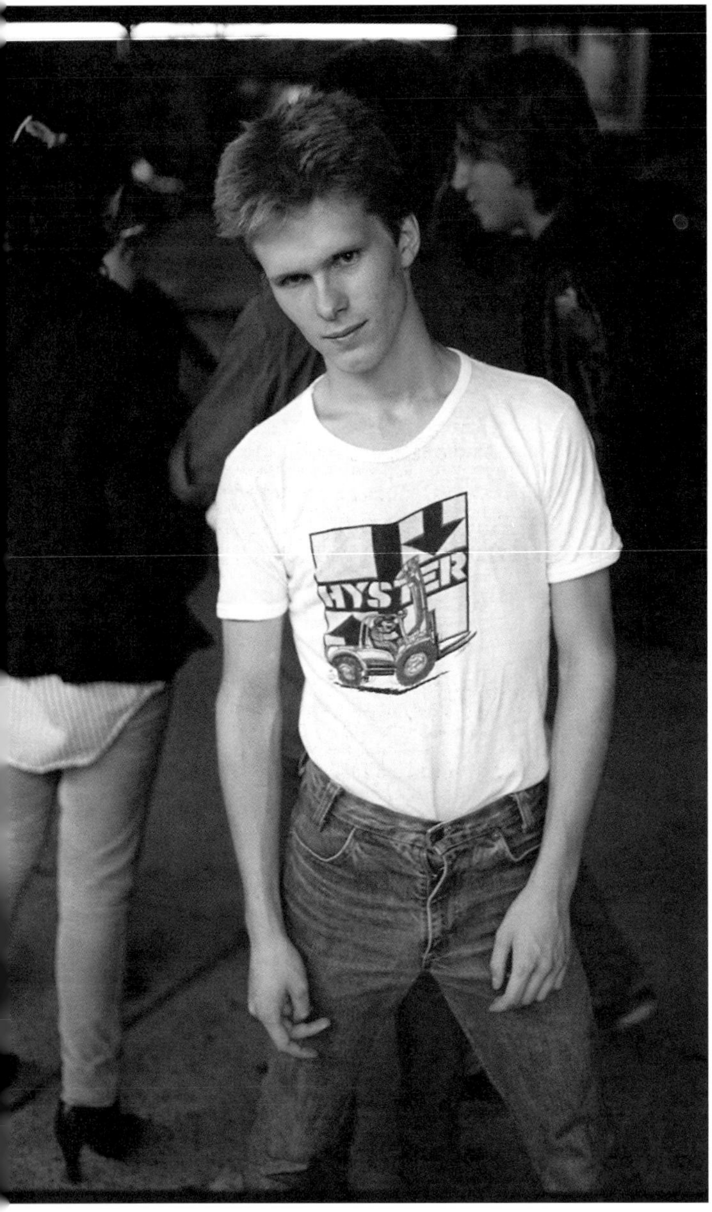

Matt on Queen Street

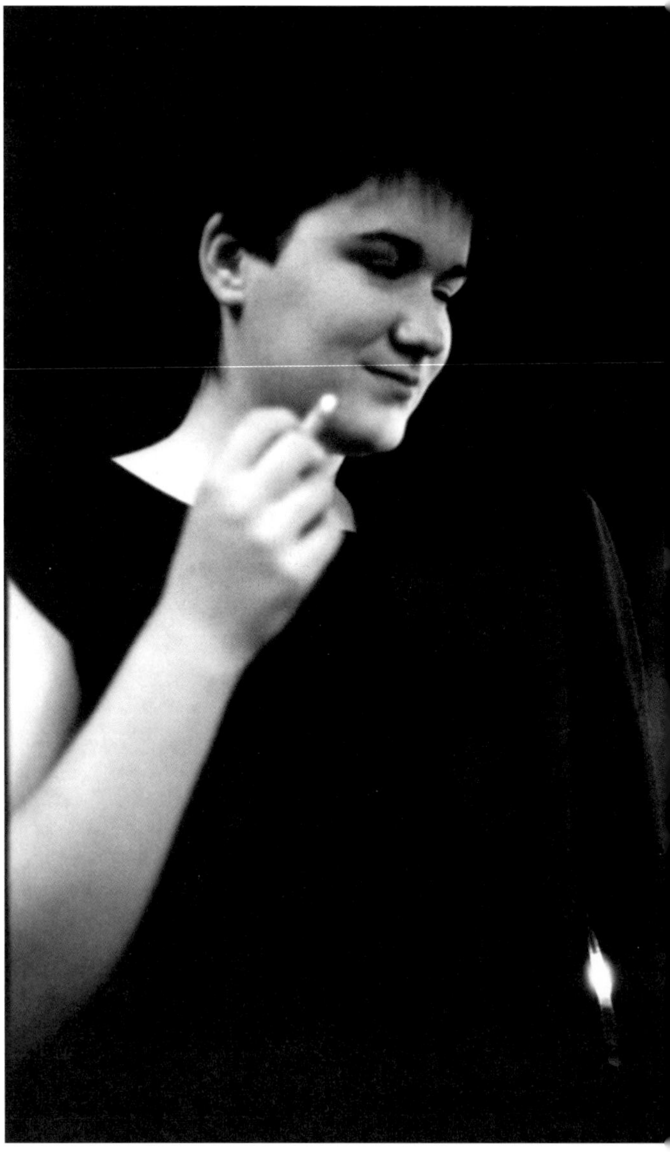

Val on Queen Street

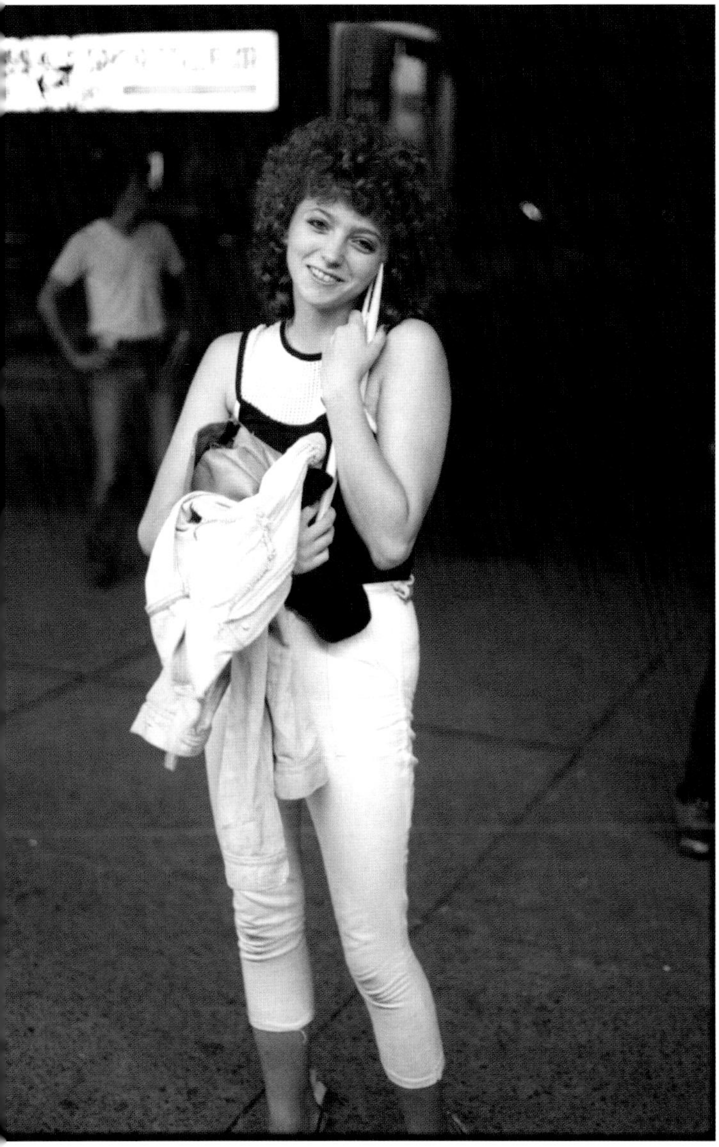

Gambi, clutching drumsticks she'd caught that were thrown from the stage

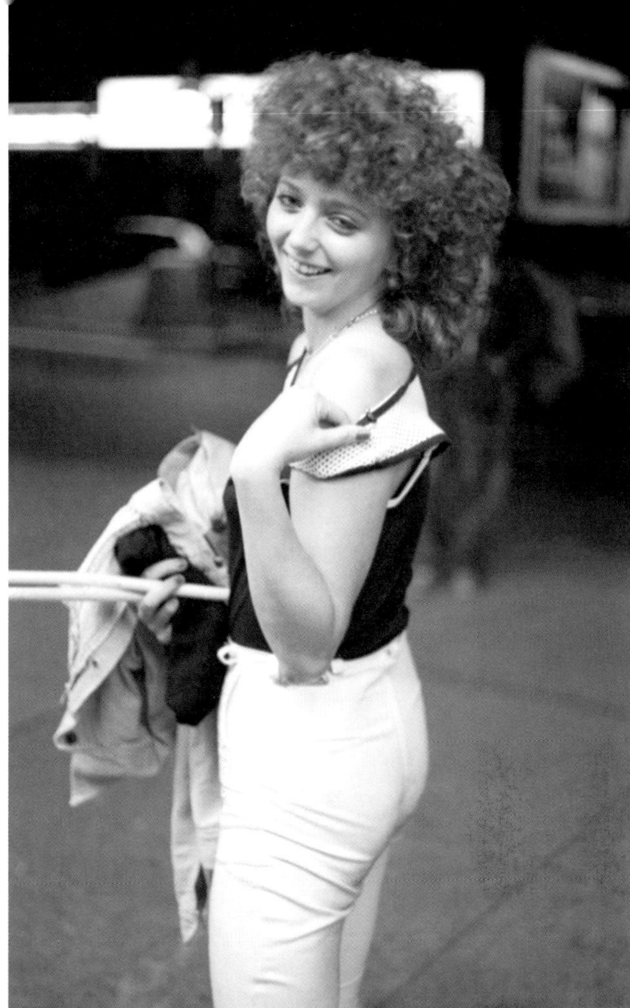

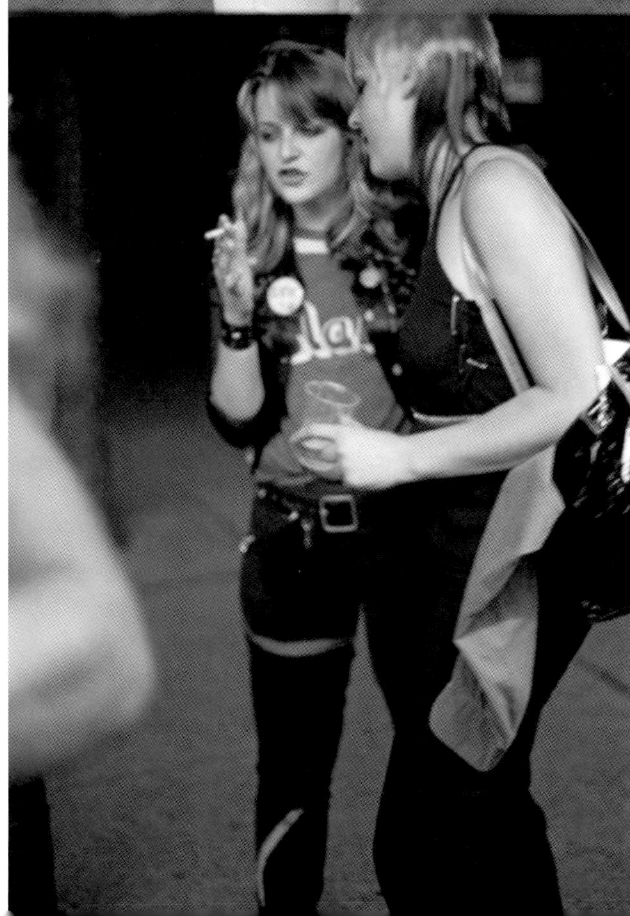

Zero of Zro4 and Rabies, in front of the Horseshoe

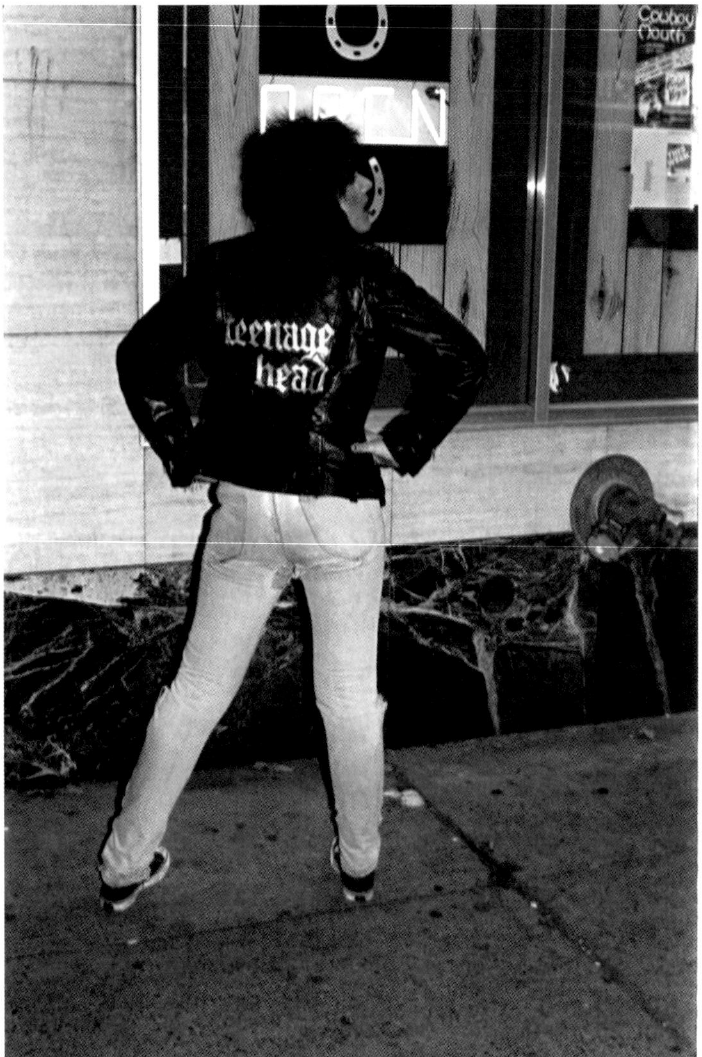

Rojer, in front of the Horseshoe

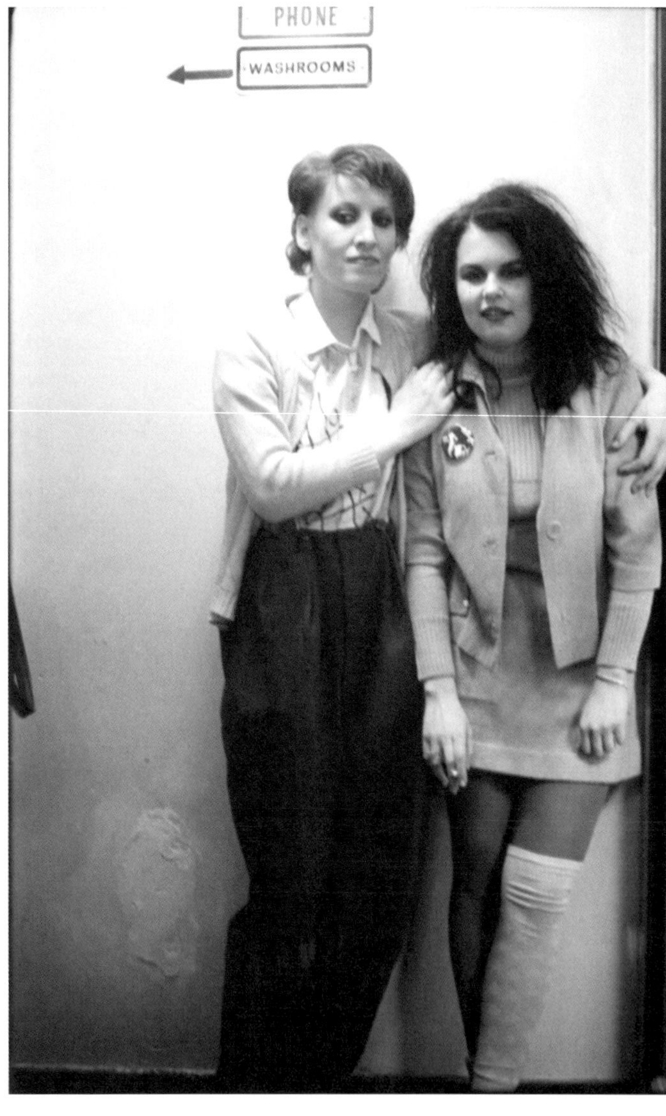

Siren and Virlana outside the bathrooms in the upstairs hall of the Edge

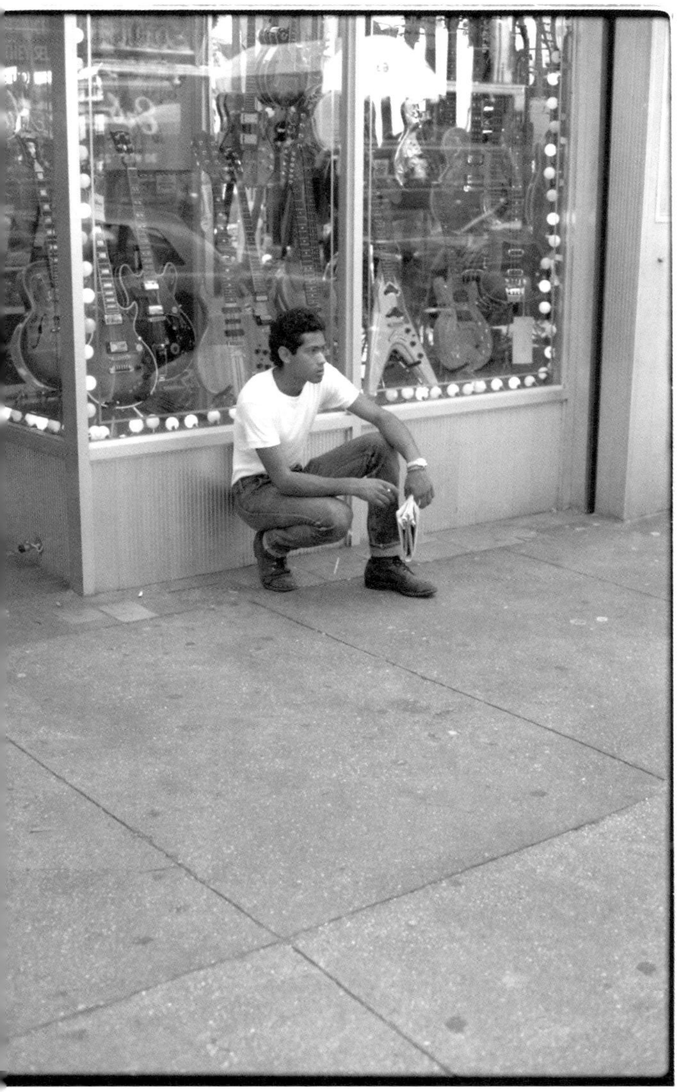

Mohamed Nagdee (aka Eddy Dent of The Dents/ Crash Kills Five) in New York City

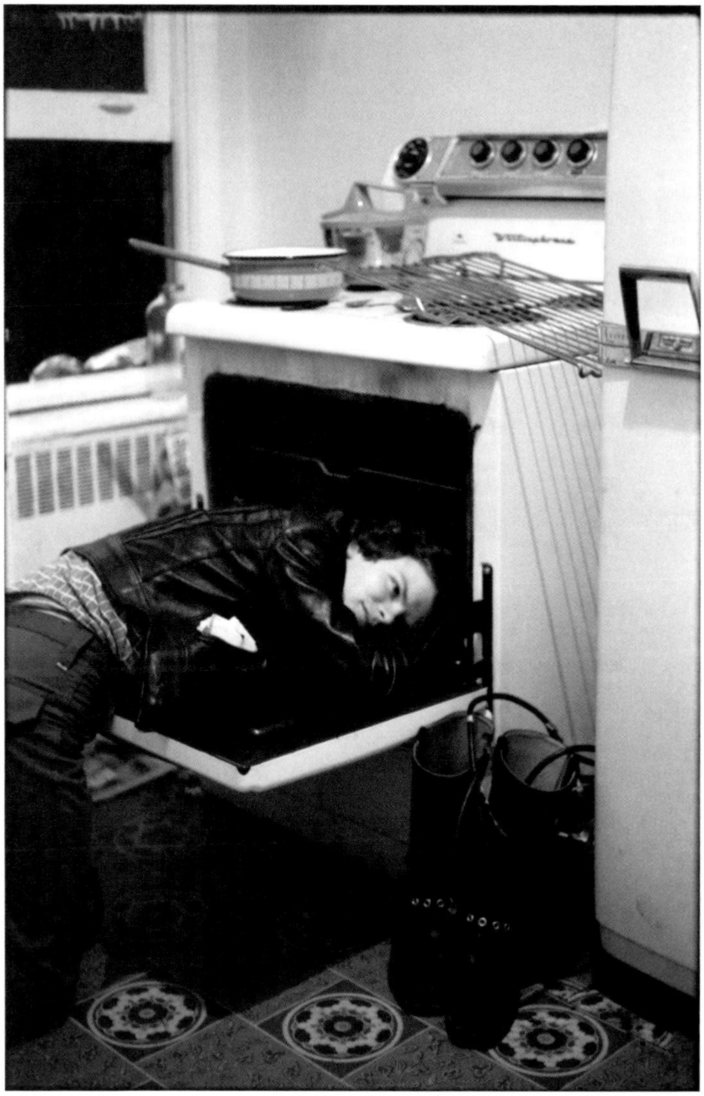

Reid Diamond, Parliament Street in Toronto

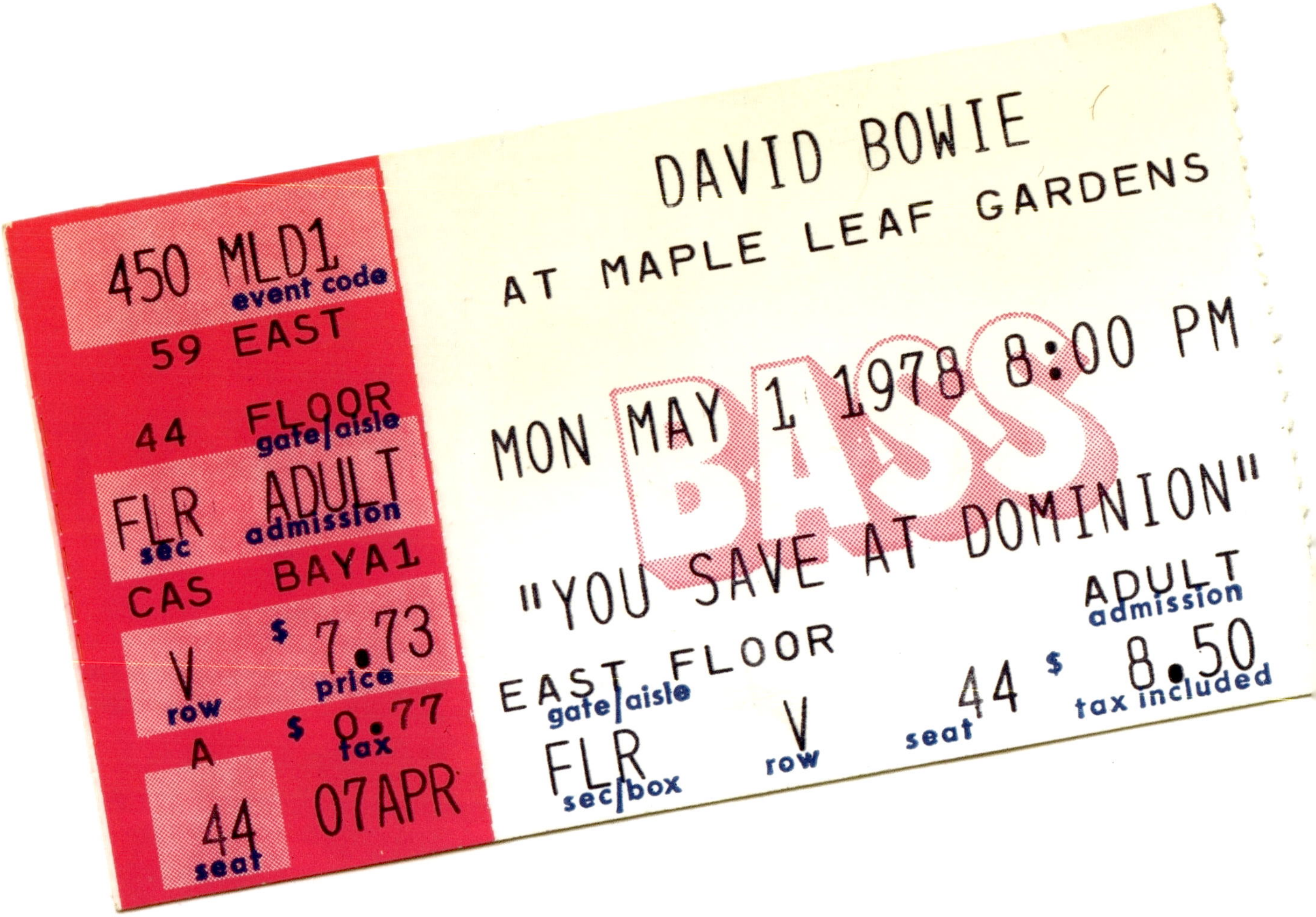

Bowie's Low/ "Heroes" tour recycled the white-light set utilized during the Station to Station tour, and would eventually appear on album as *Stage*. At this show, it appeared as though David was onstage for the first time without a persona, playing the normal "guy" who had just had a duet with Bing Crosby.

It's still shocking to me to recognize that only one year passed between *Diamond Dogs* and *Young Americans*, and only another two between *Young Americans* and this show. They felt like careers apart. David's influence on punk is undeniable; so many of the first-gen punk bands dress like him in their high school photos and before the black leather jacket, it was this style they copped the most. As "Star" on David's *Ziggy Stardust* album rings out, he says in the most casually defiant tone, "Just watch me now," a line I and thousands of others heard as a direct challenge, a call to action for all the kids who would soon form the Viletones, Generation X or The Germs.

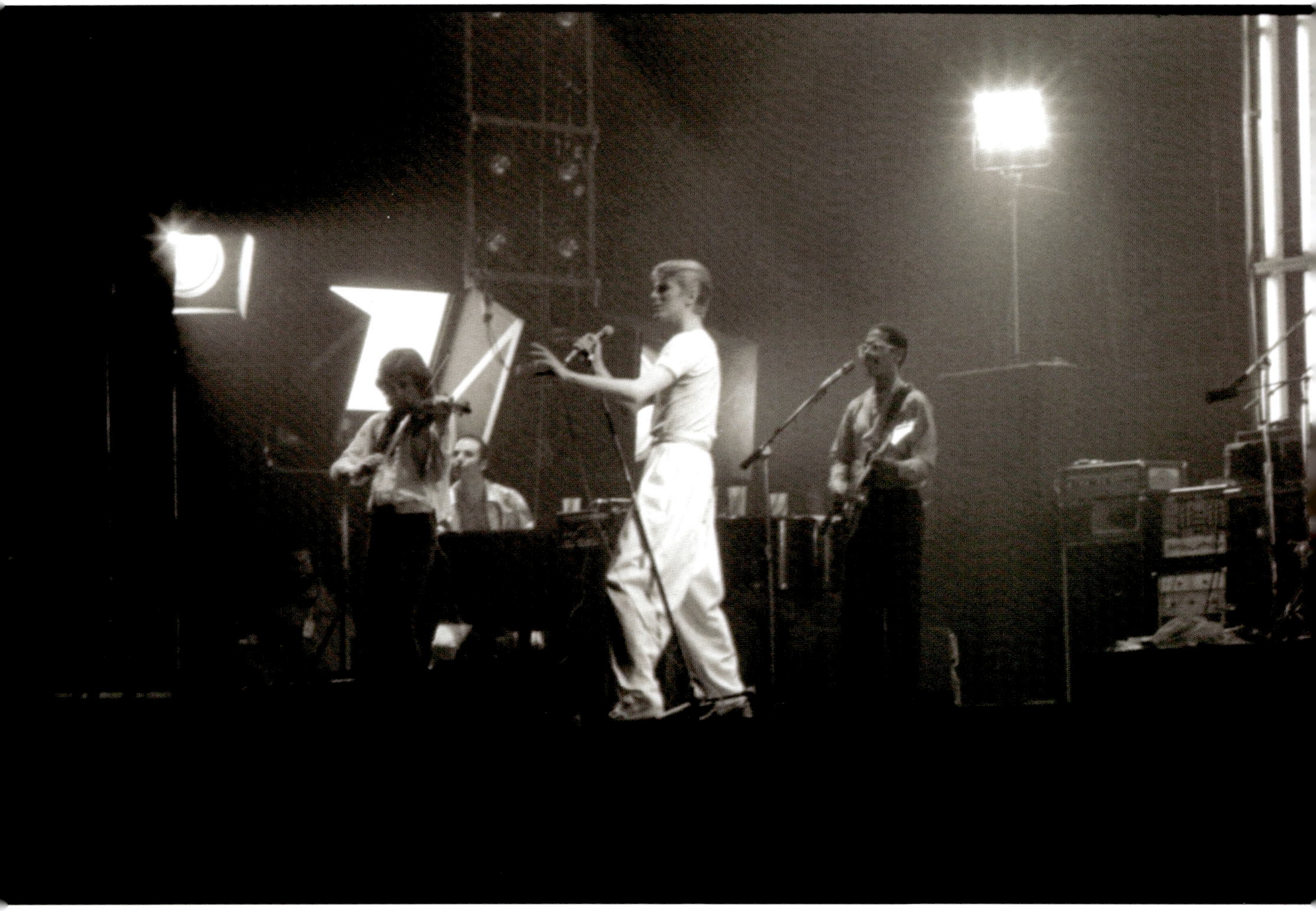

Simon House, Sean Mayes, David Bowie, Carlos Alomar

David Bowie, Maple Leaf Gardens, 1978

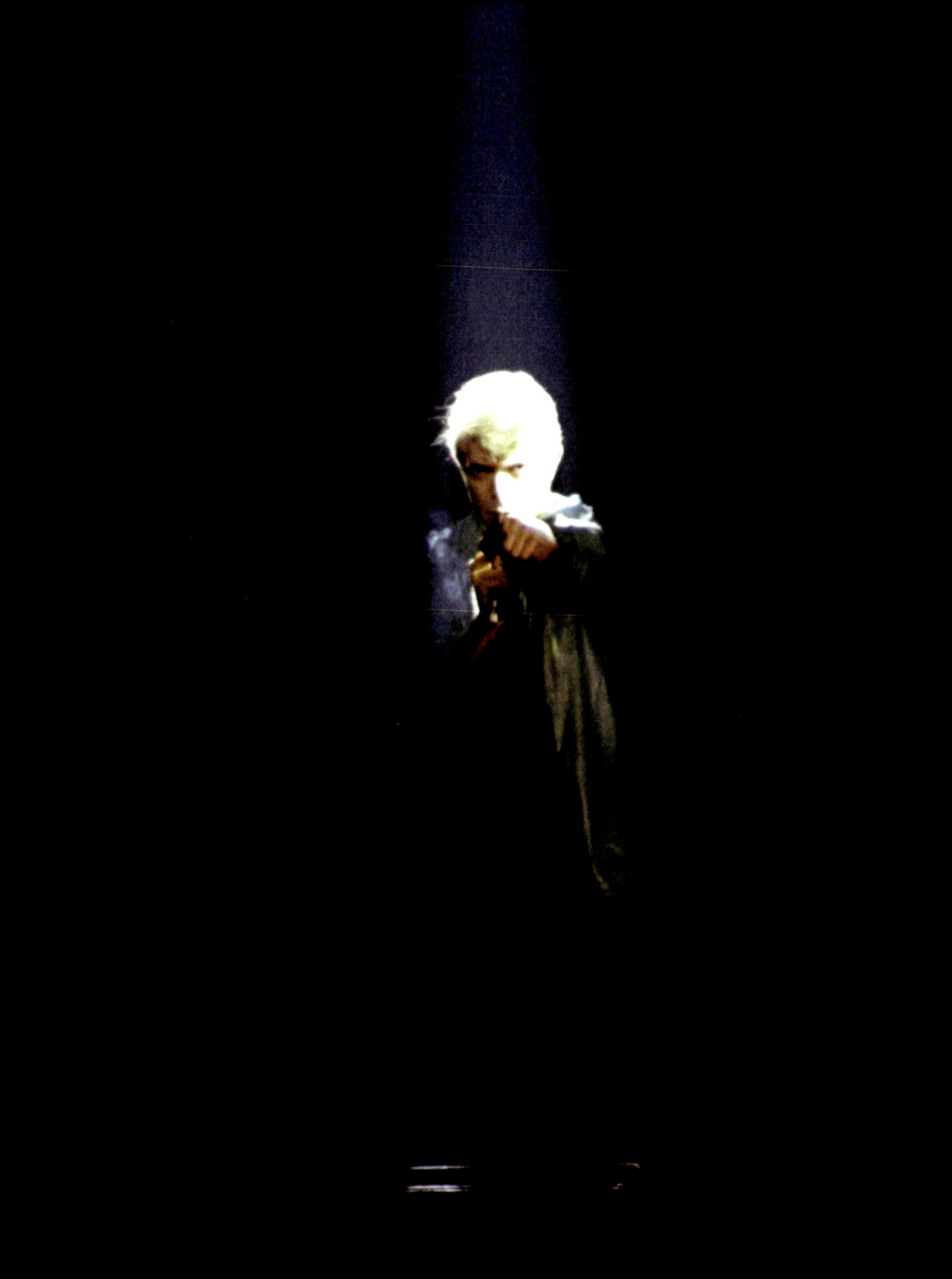

My fingers trembled to release the shutter when, at the end of "Fame," David pointed directly at me and sang, "What's your name?"

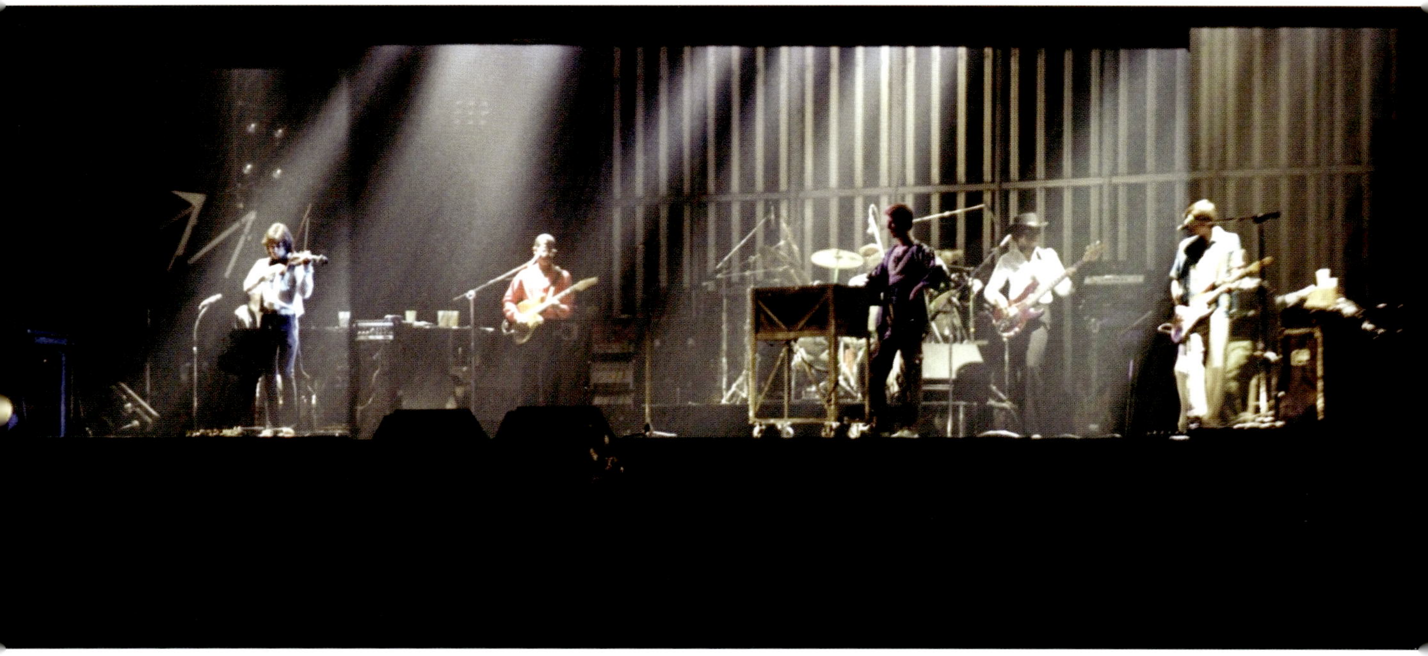

Simon House, Carlos Alomar, Dennis Davis, David Bowie, George Murray, Adrian Belew

The Concordes, Masonic Temple, 1978

These photos are from a midnight show of The Concordes opening for Eddie and the Hot Rods and Teenage Head. There had been an eight o'clock performance also scheduled but without enough audience to fill the small hall twice, people who attended the earlier show stayed for the second round.

Someone thought it was a good idea to throw a bottle at the band, encouraging sax player Ed Radford to leap from the stage and bonk the guy back. Singer Sally Cato (who had some degree of notoriety later as the vocalist of Smashed Gladys) had black electrical taped her nipples, and hid behind the curtain while the scuffle played out. In a setlist confusion, John Armstrong played a different song than the rest of the band, but all managed to end at the same time as though it were intended.

I heard a story that bassist Dave Templeton arrived for sound check with long hair and a beard. Seeing what the crowd looked like, he sneaked out to the Goodwill shop and barber, reappearing later shorn and suited.

John Armstrong

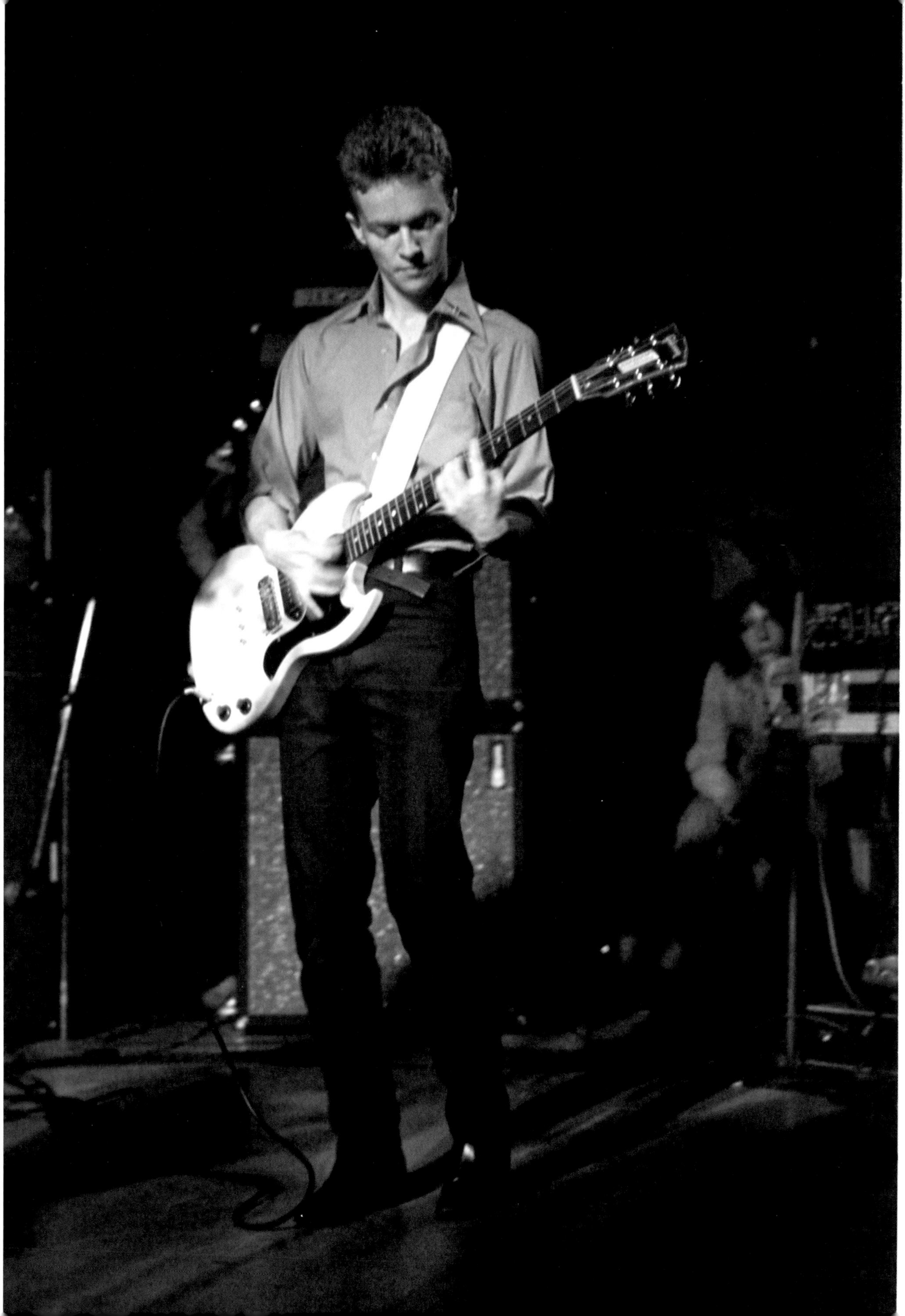

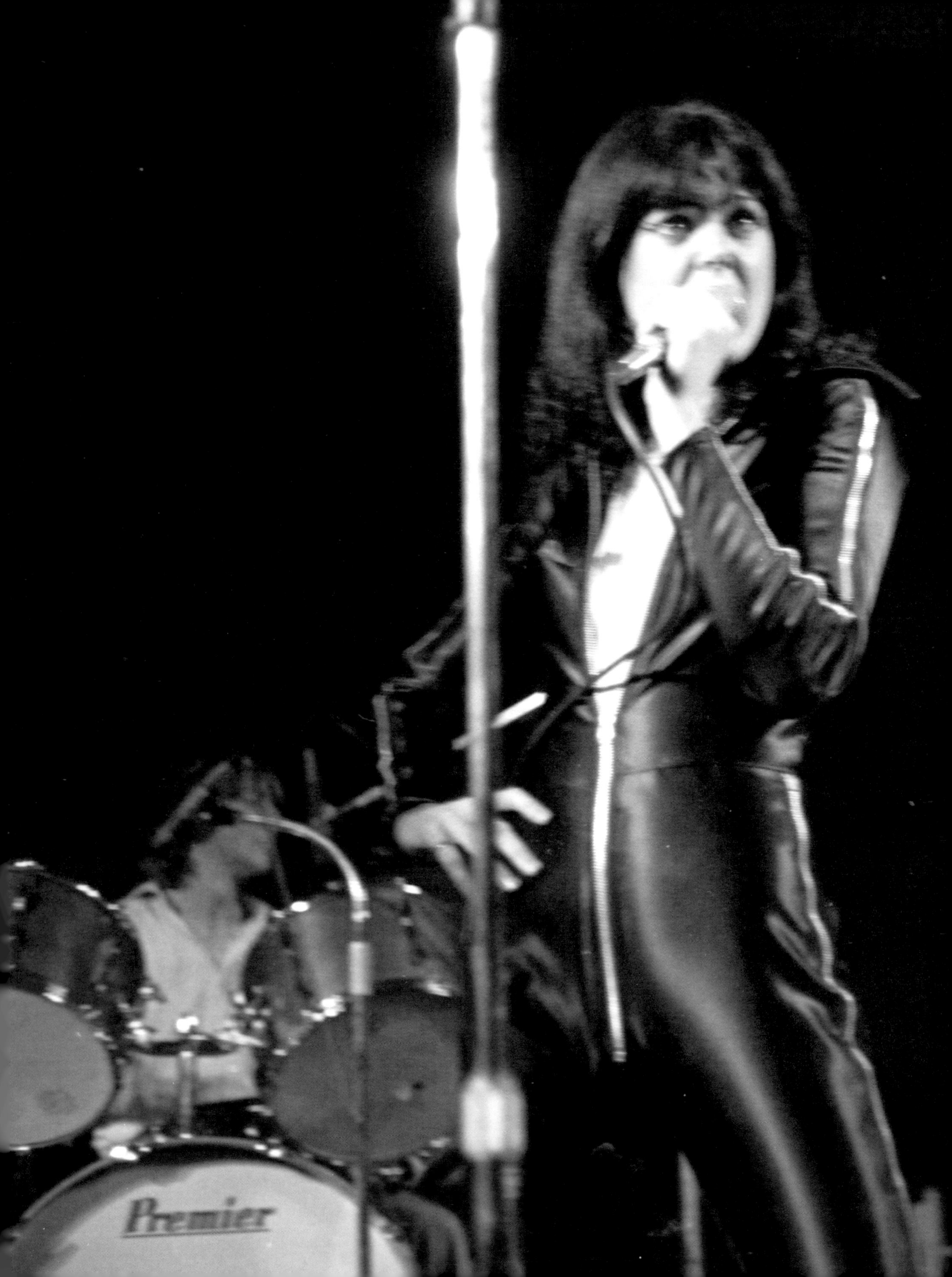
Premier

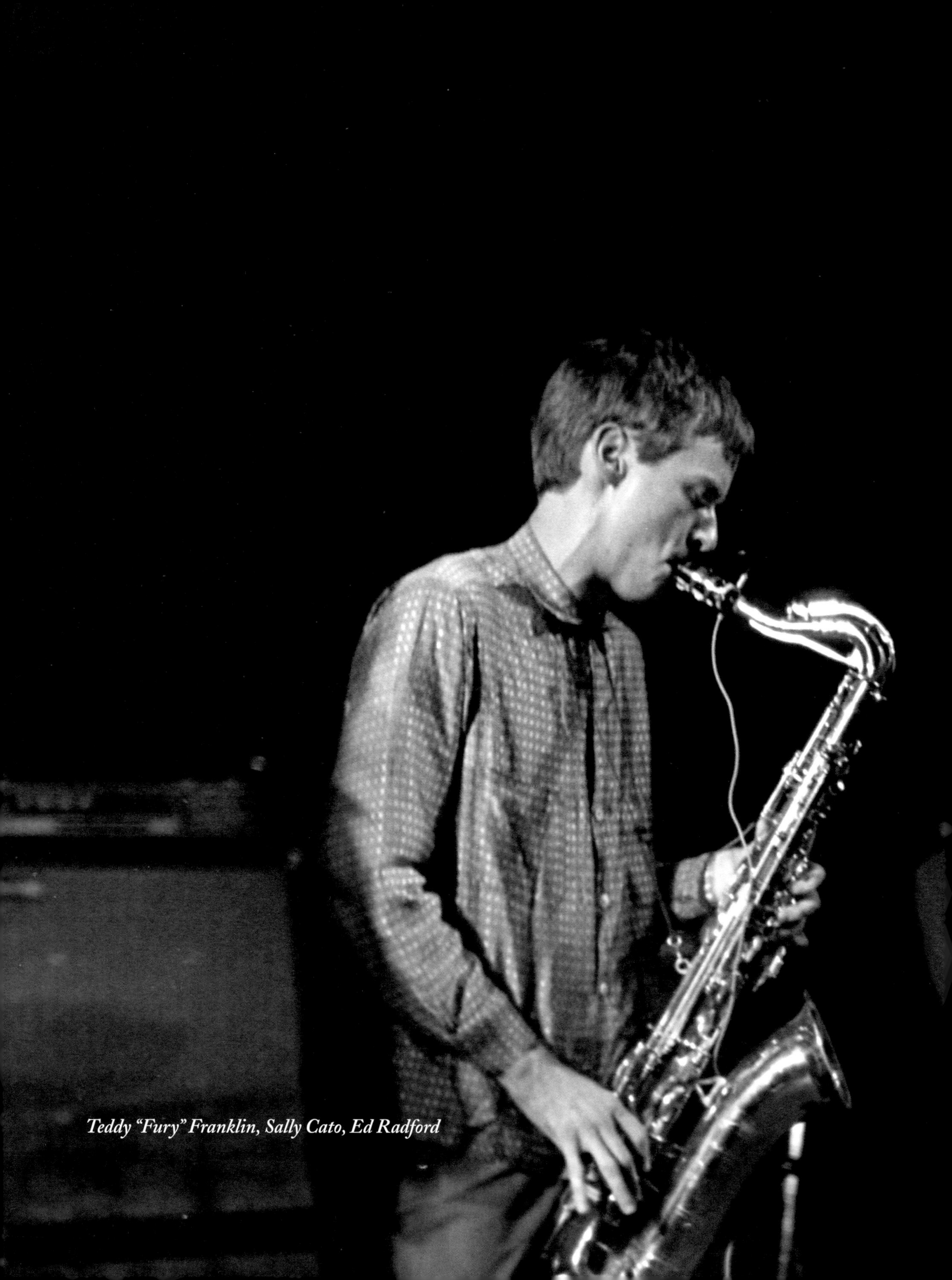

Teddy "Fury" Franklin, Sally Cato, Ed Radford

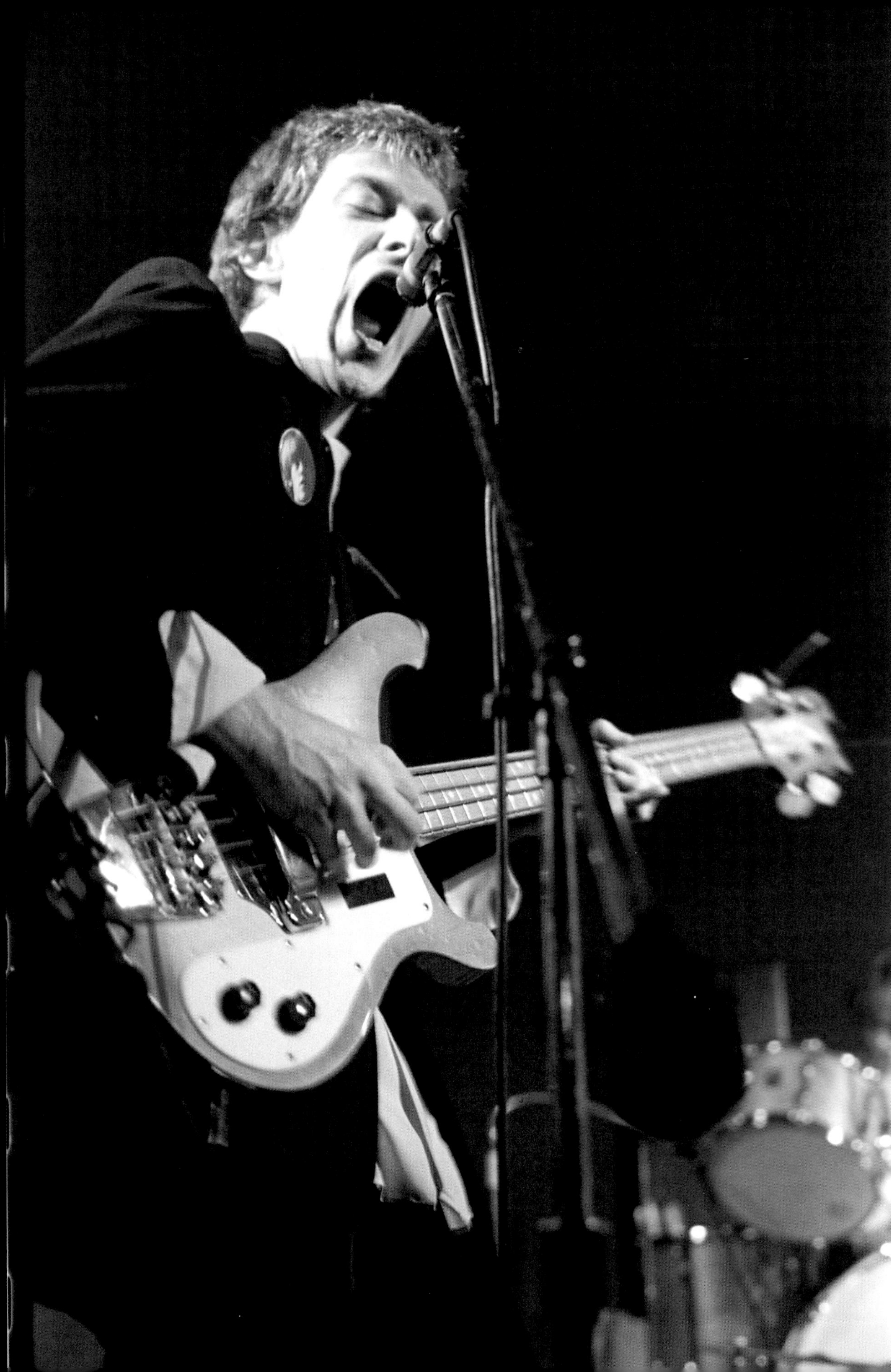

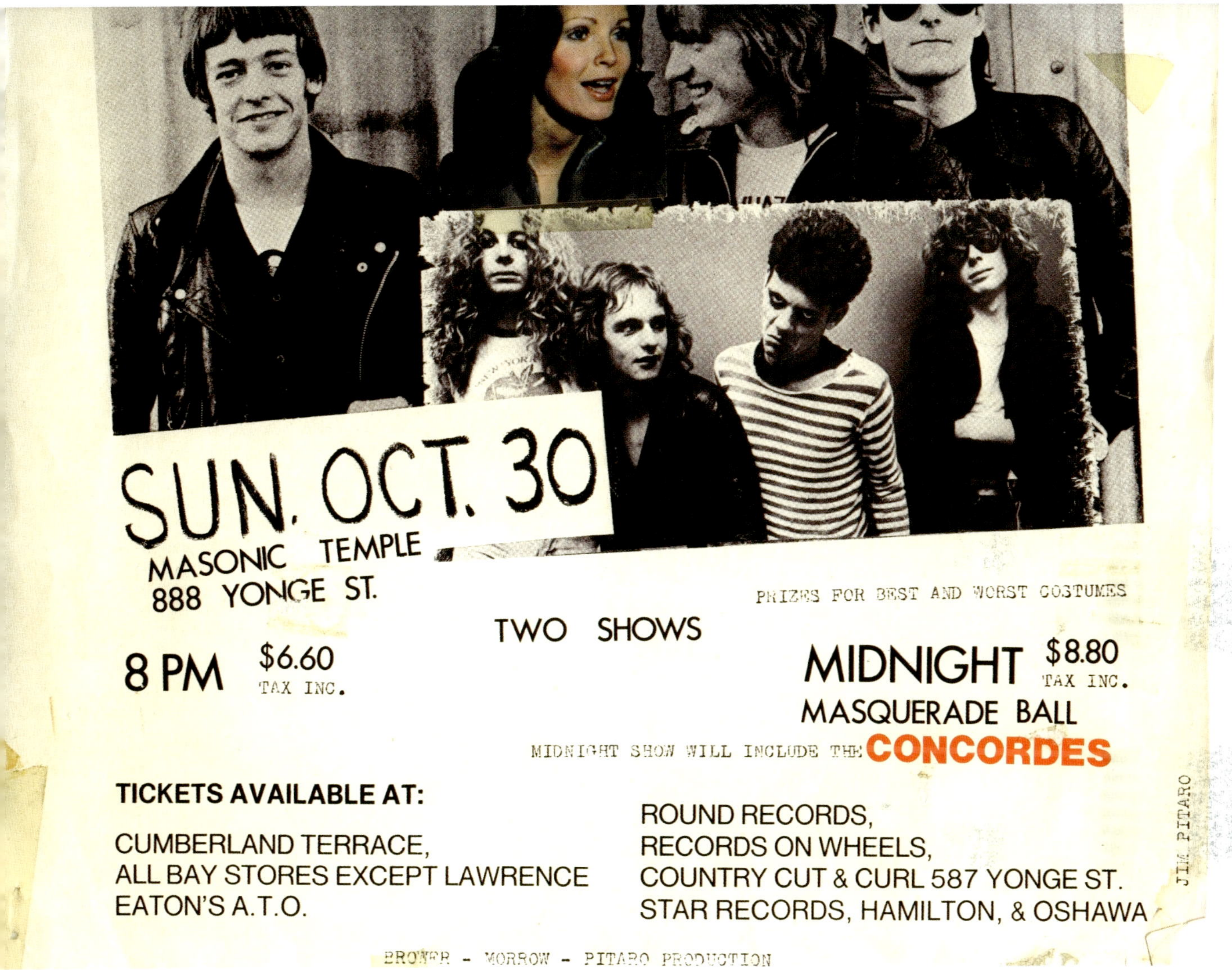

Dave Templeton

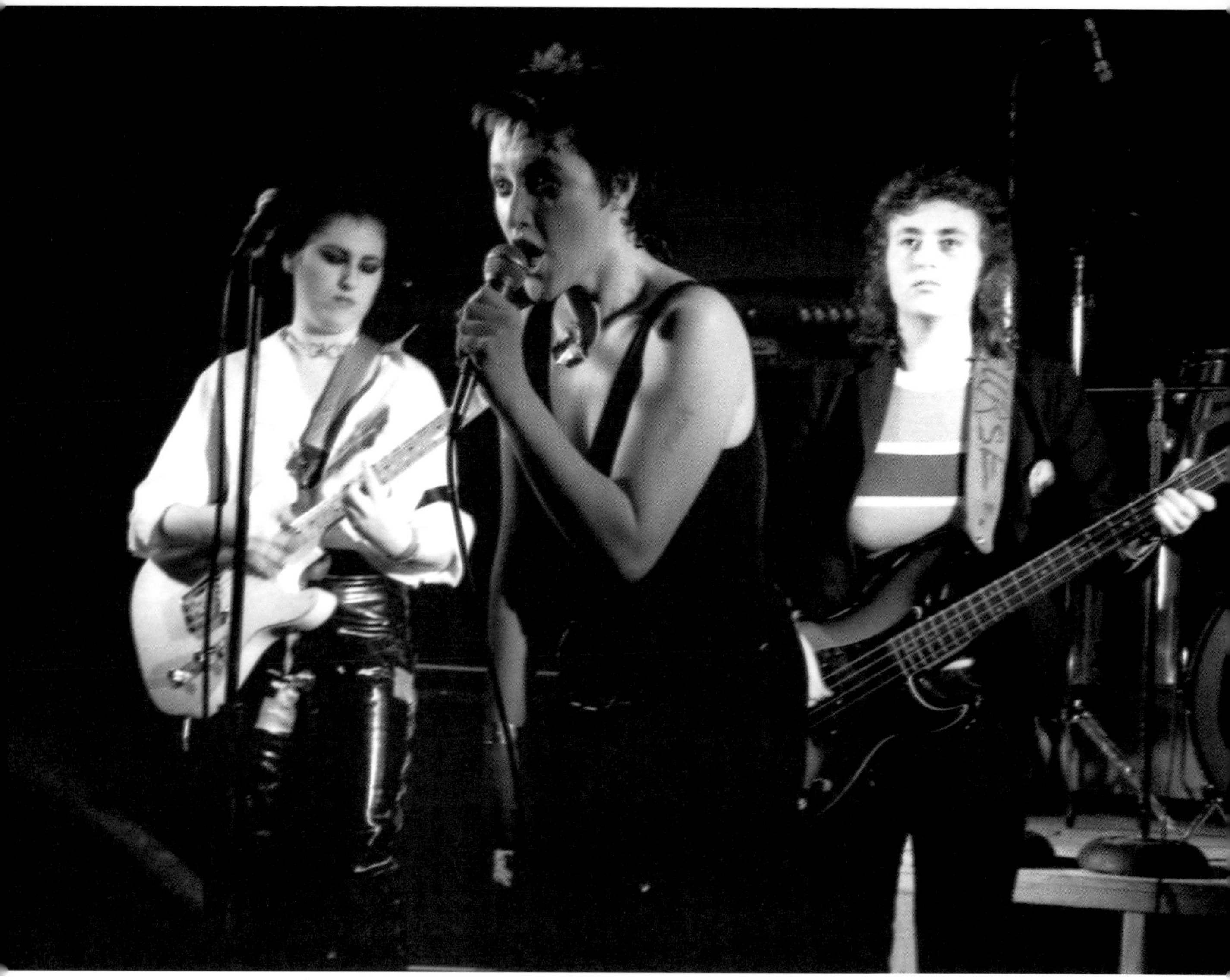

The Curse opening for The Diodes at Shock Theatre: Trixie Danger, Mickey Skin, Dr. Bourque

It was a big life, with so many different kinds of artists and artistic temperaments, art schools and schools of life, Scarborough and Don Mills, idiots and savants, the very cleverest and troglodytes. Somehow we all made it work in the very best way, albeit for a rather brief time. It was magic and everyone should get to have that much fun at least once in their life.

— Anna "Dr." Bourque

The Curse, Shock Theatre, 1978

Frequently cited as the first all-female punk group in North America, The Curse was a fantastic delinquent band of new musicians. Lead singer Mickey Skin sang in a raspy voice that sounded like cartons of cigarettes and was charmingly bratty, as she took the stage swinging an oversize tampon like a rat by its tail. You'd have to shield your eyes when Mickey came onstage because something would inevitably be flying in your direction — handfuls of mini Chiclets, whipped cream . . . anything. Drummer Patsy Poison, a fragile and distinct looking woman with massive blond curls, didn't look strong enough to bash her kit, but she did. I recognized her the first time I saw The Curse as one of the group of women who, with a couple of The B-Girls, always seemed to be talking their way backstage at bigger pre-punk gigs.

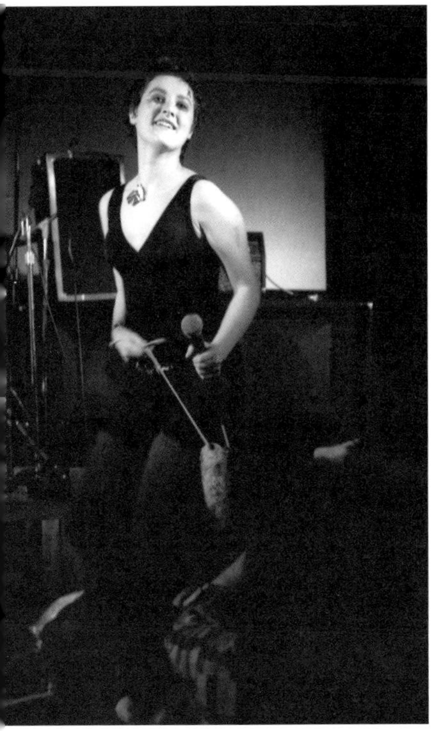

Mickey Skin

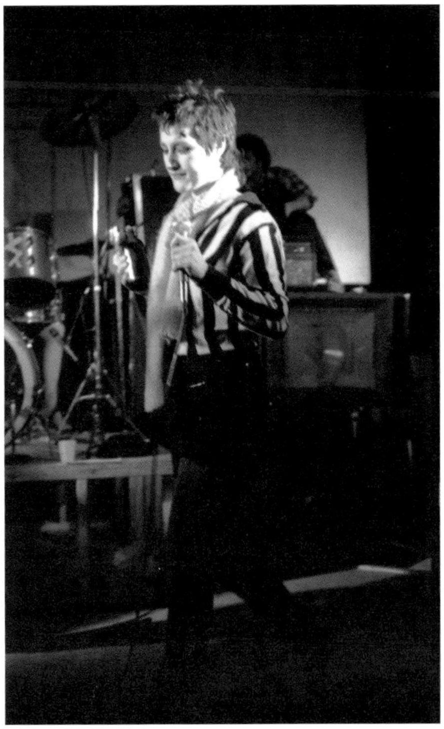

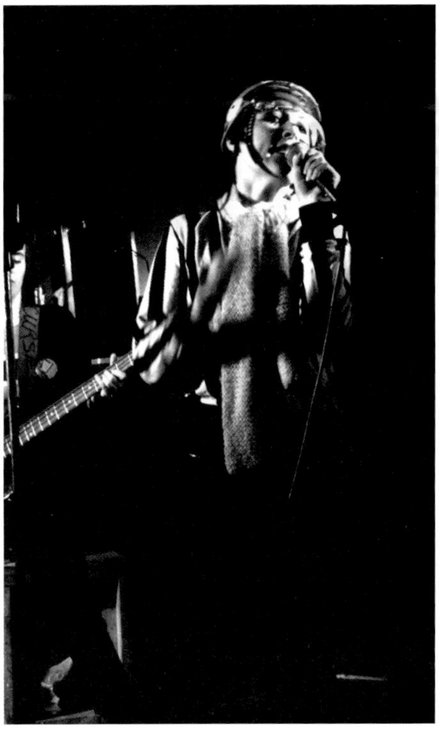

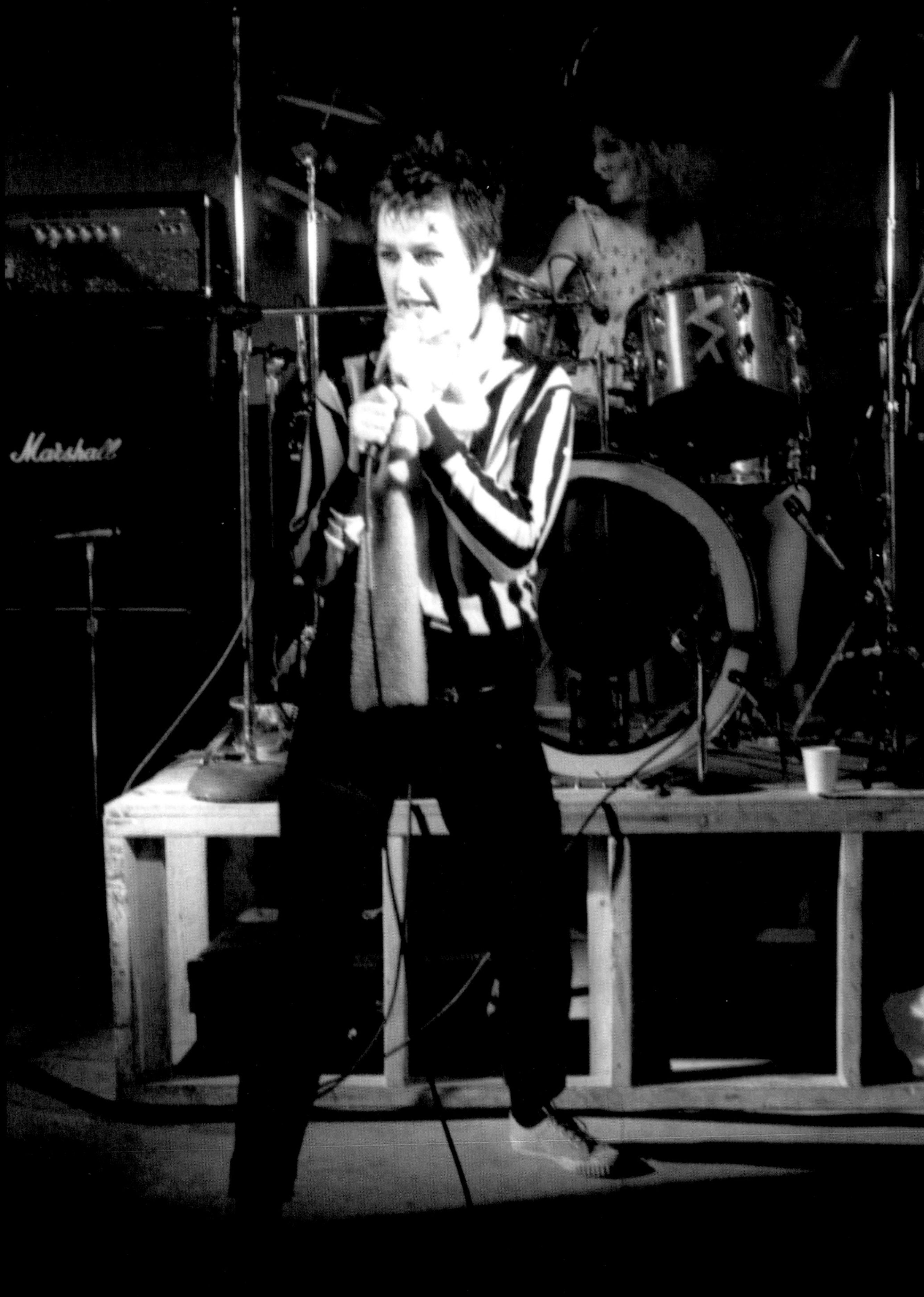
Marshall

They were quite magnificent live and I wish they'd been able to release an album to follow their stellar "Shoeshine Boy/Killer Bees" 7-inch, easily one of the greatest records produced from the Toronto scene. Given the content of The Curse 45, it seems like a case of the kettle calling the pot beige, but the media latched onto the most sensationalist aspects of punk for coverage — Sid getting arrested, violence at shows, and The Curse singing about a murdered kid and inferring he'd brought trouble on himself because of actually being a hustler. The real murder had occurred above a Yonge Street body rub parlor near Art Metropole and led to the area being "cleaned up" by the city. The B side was also "topical" — the invasion of killer bees, hot on the heels of the Irwin Allen TV movie *The Swarm*, and regular news coverage touting their imminent arrival, mostly aimed at inciting fear. Swastikas, murder and bees easily upset people, so they were used to full effect — insensitive agitation for cheap kicks. The Curse's concession to the outrage was to repackage the single with a new sleeve, relegating "Shoeshine Boy" to the B side.

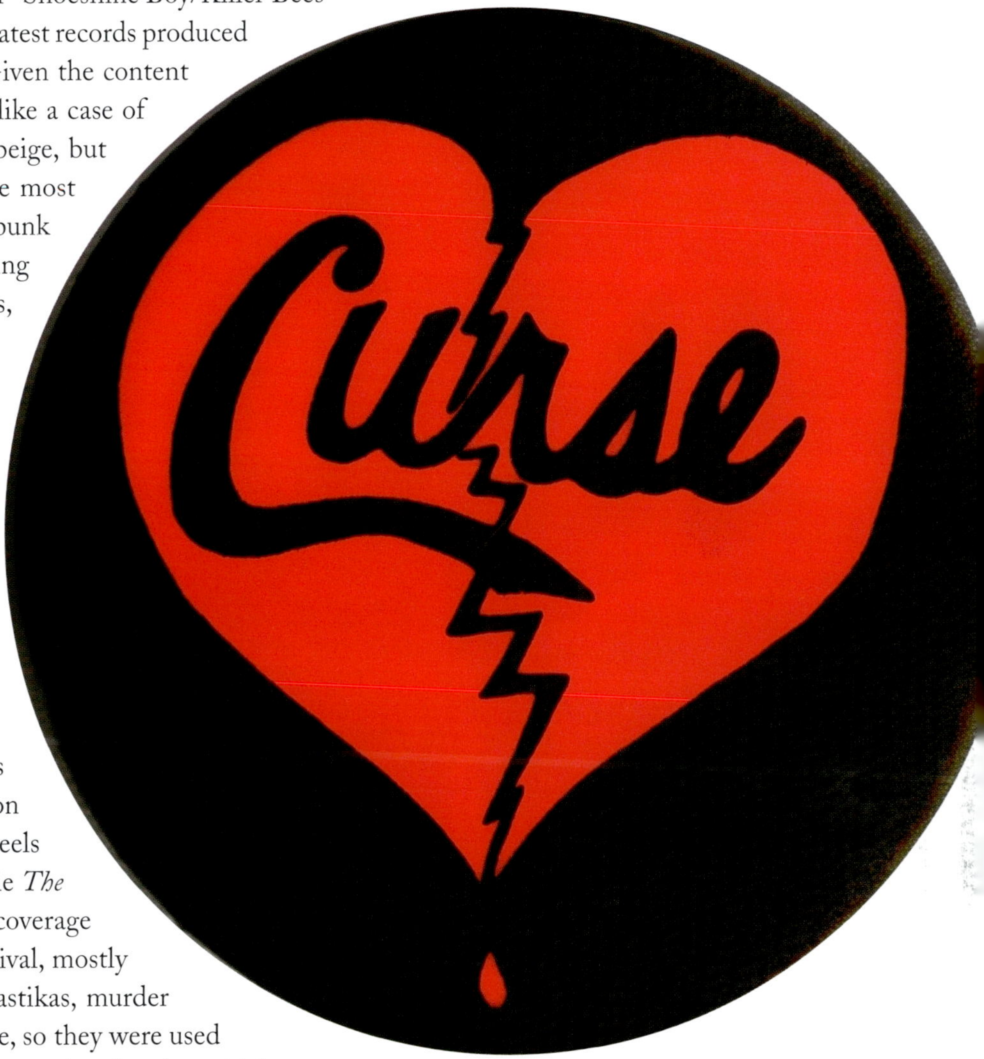

Mickey Skin, Patsy Poison

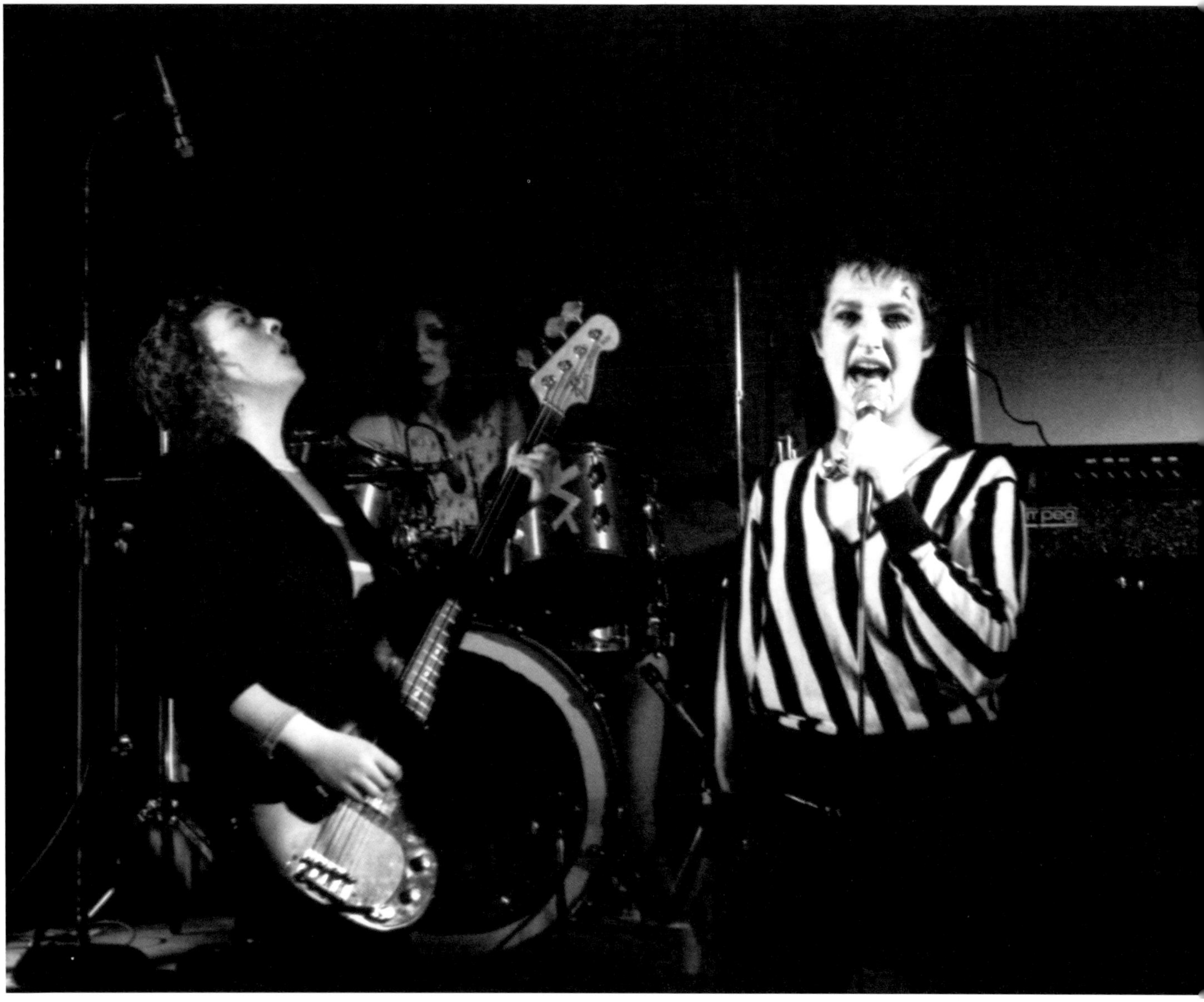

Dr. Bourque, Patsy Poison, Mickey Skin

Bass player Anna "Dr." Bourque said that when The Curse played, "something probably went terribly wrong, because something invariably went terribly wrong." It gives me a small thrill to think that the bass player of the band who sang "Shoeshine Boy" went on to work on Care Bears cartoons.

CURSE

KILLER BEES
MUMMY
AGGRAVATION
I ACCUSE YOU
FEELIN' DIRTY
HE'S MY BOY
BLUNKS
TEENAGE MEAT
OH MY GOD
SHOESHINE BOY

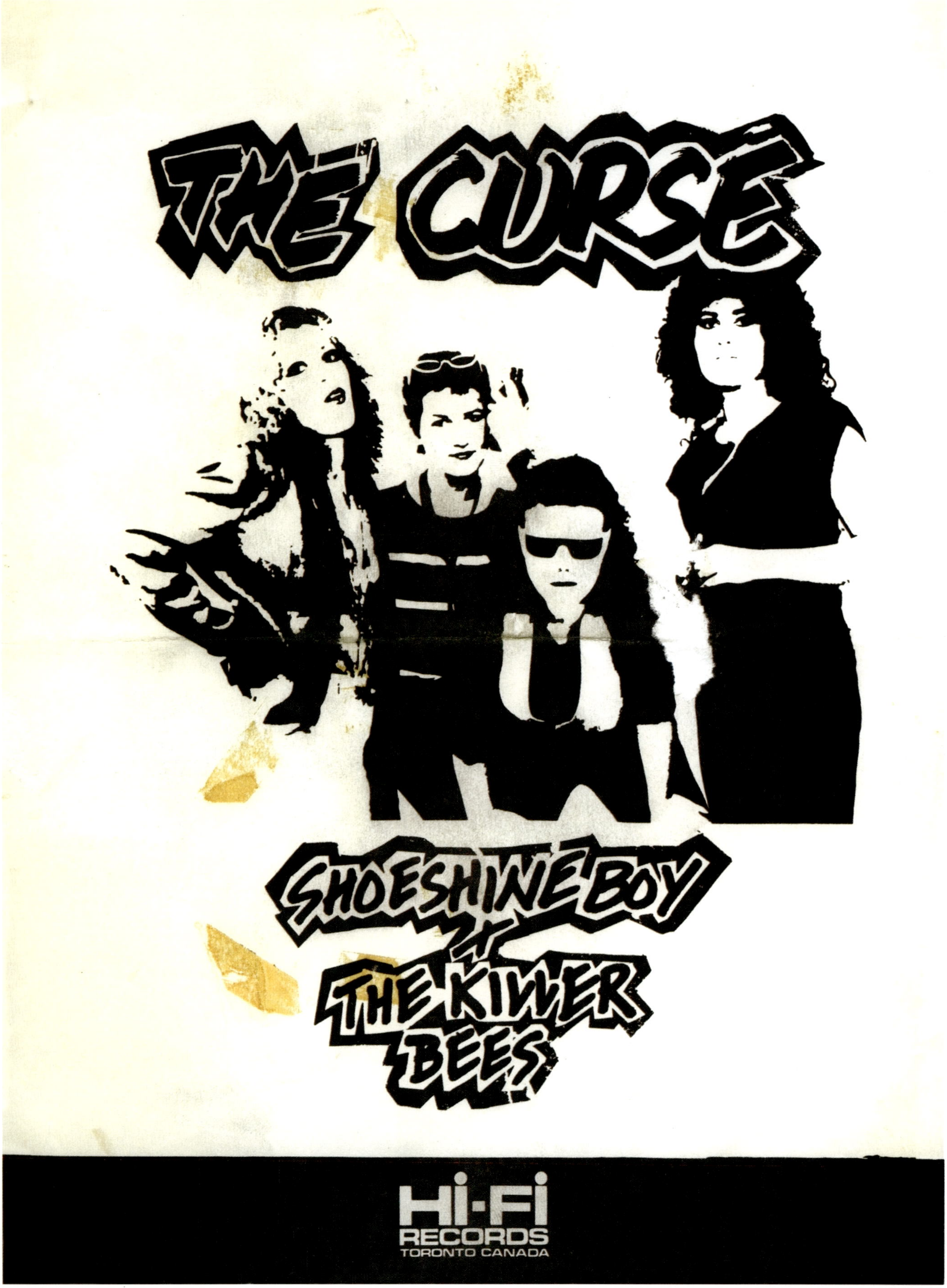
THE CURSE
SHOESHINE BOY
&
THE KILLER
BEES
HI-FI
RECORDS
TORONTO CANADA

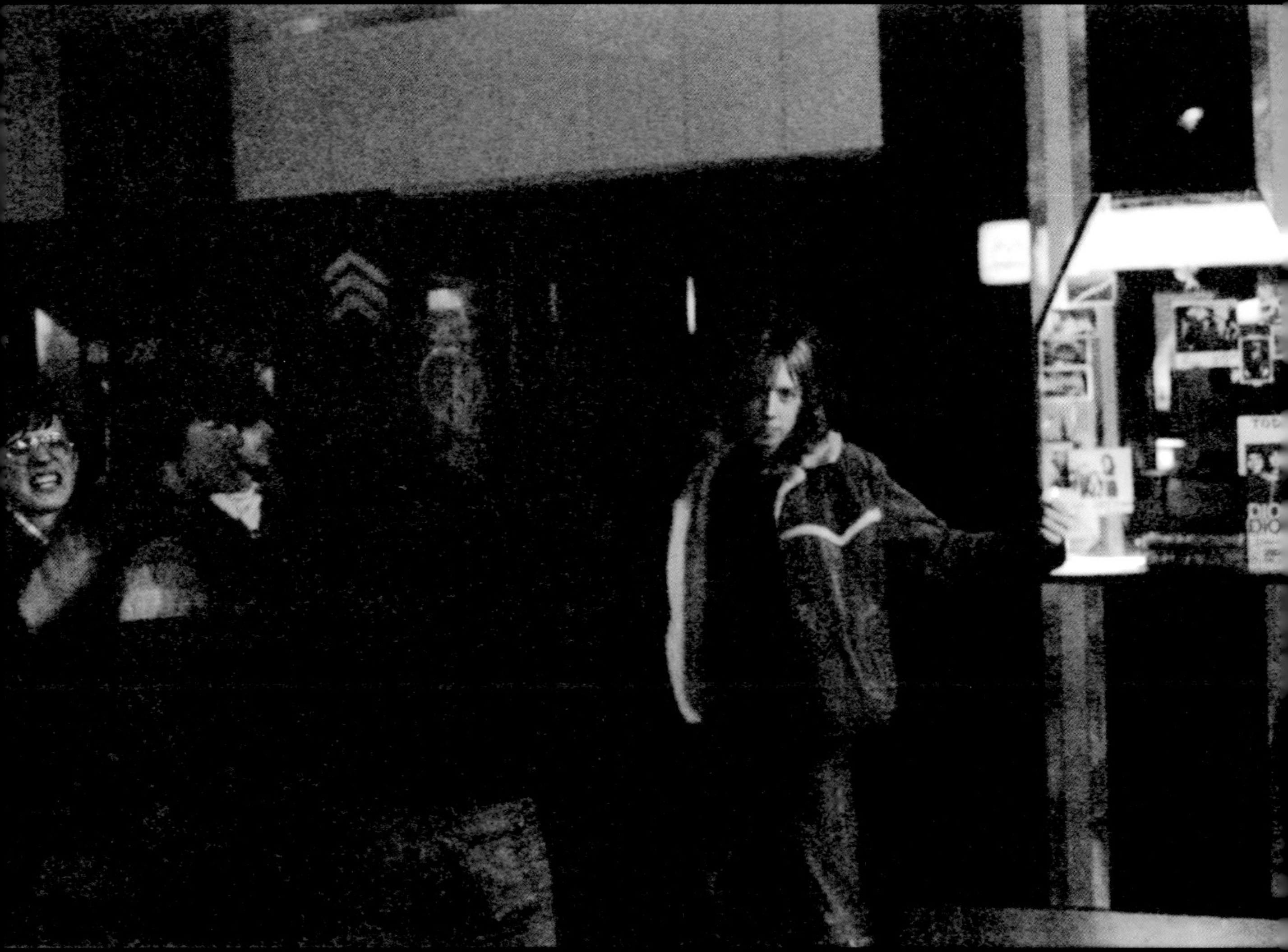

Hanging out at the Shock Theatre

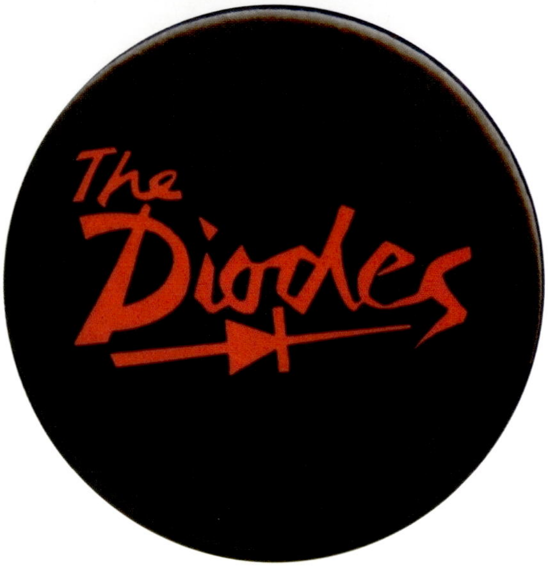

The Diodes, Shock Theatre, 1978

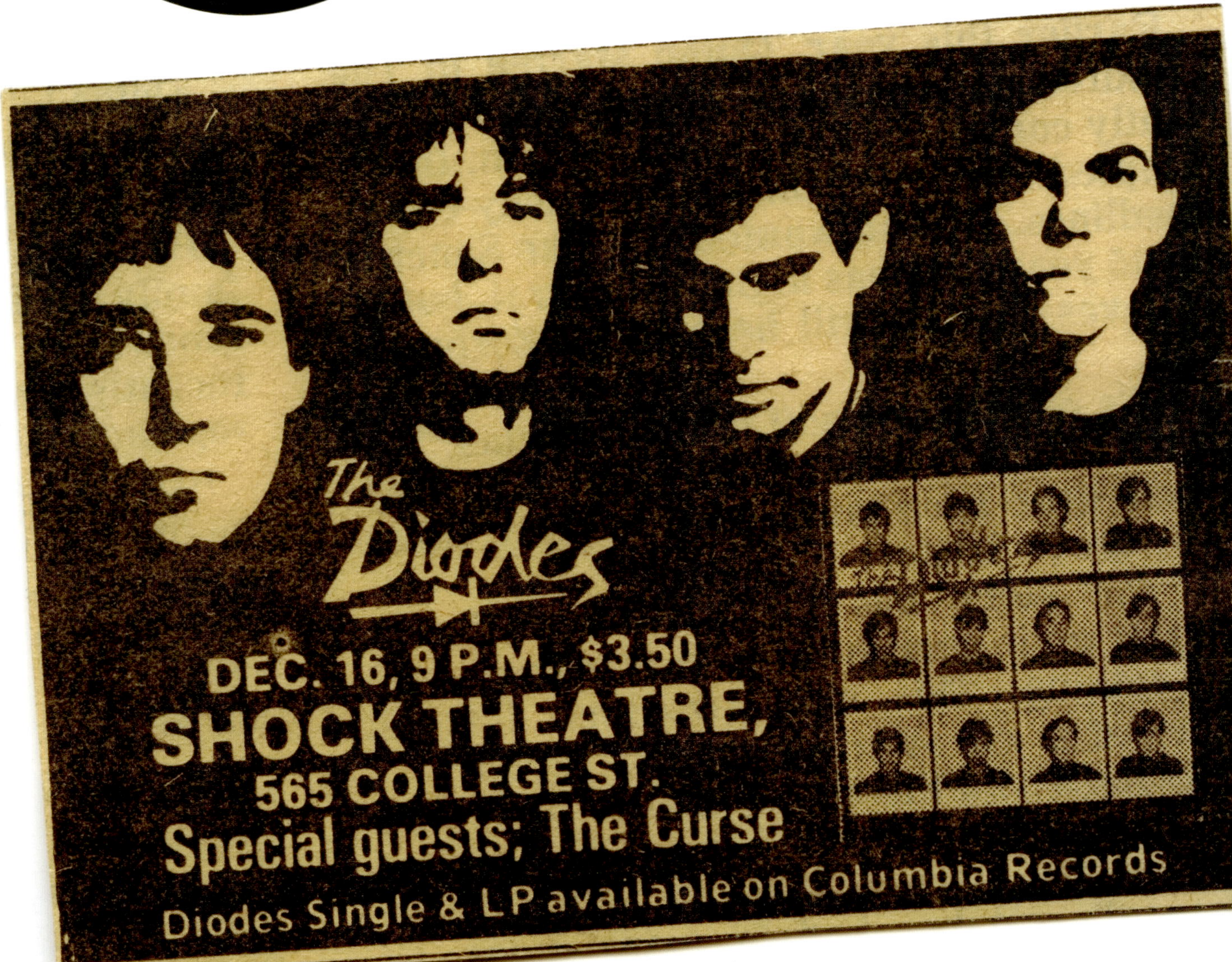

John Hamilton

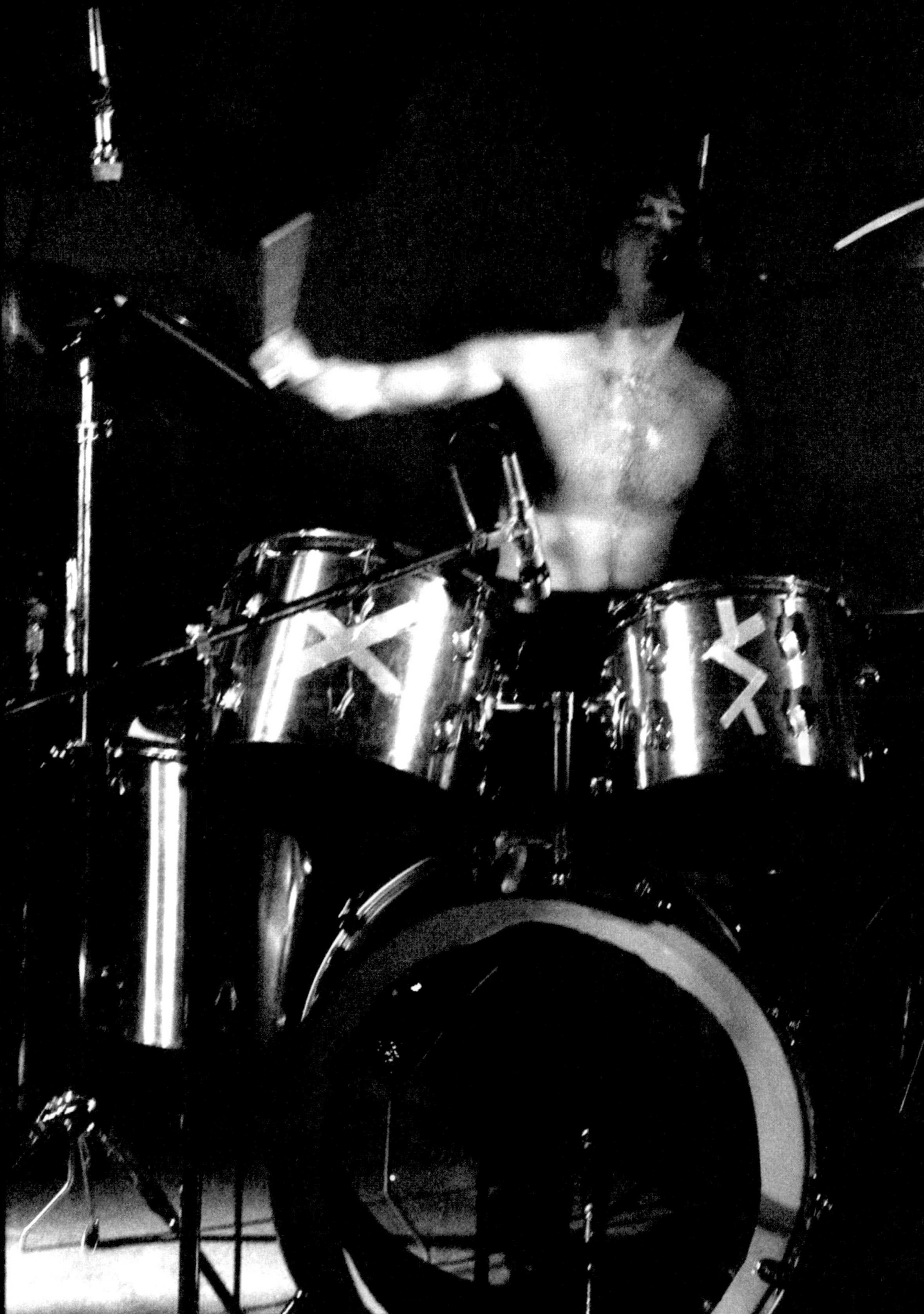

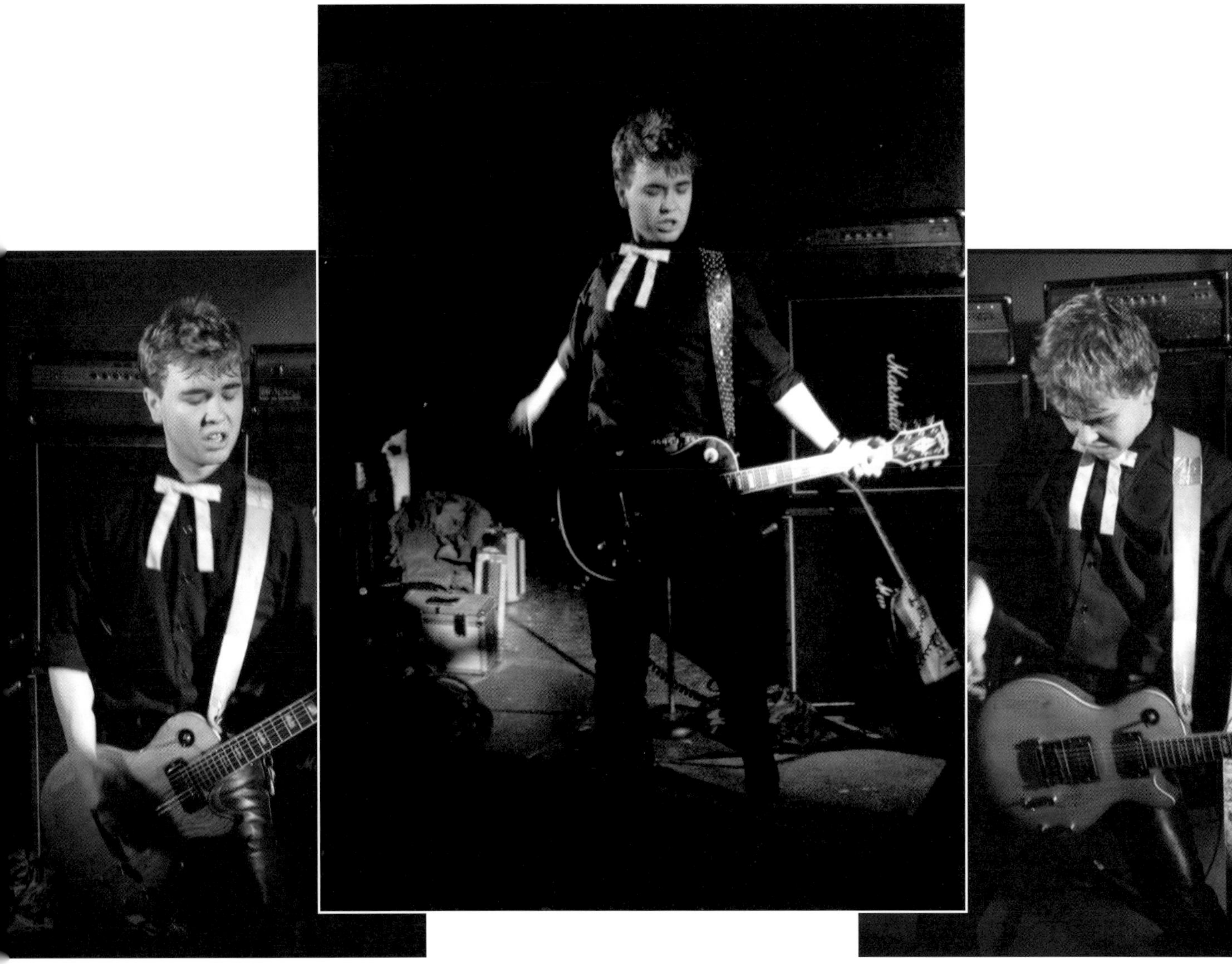

John Catto

The Shock was a short-lived venue on College Street by Bathurst — an old movie theater that alternated cheap monster movies with punk shows and had crumbling walls and chunks of plaster falling from the ceiling. I recall thinking at the time how bold it was that Diodes drummer John Hamilton wore a priest's collar, believing it was illegal to do so.

Paul Robinson, John Hamilton

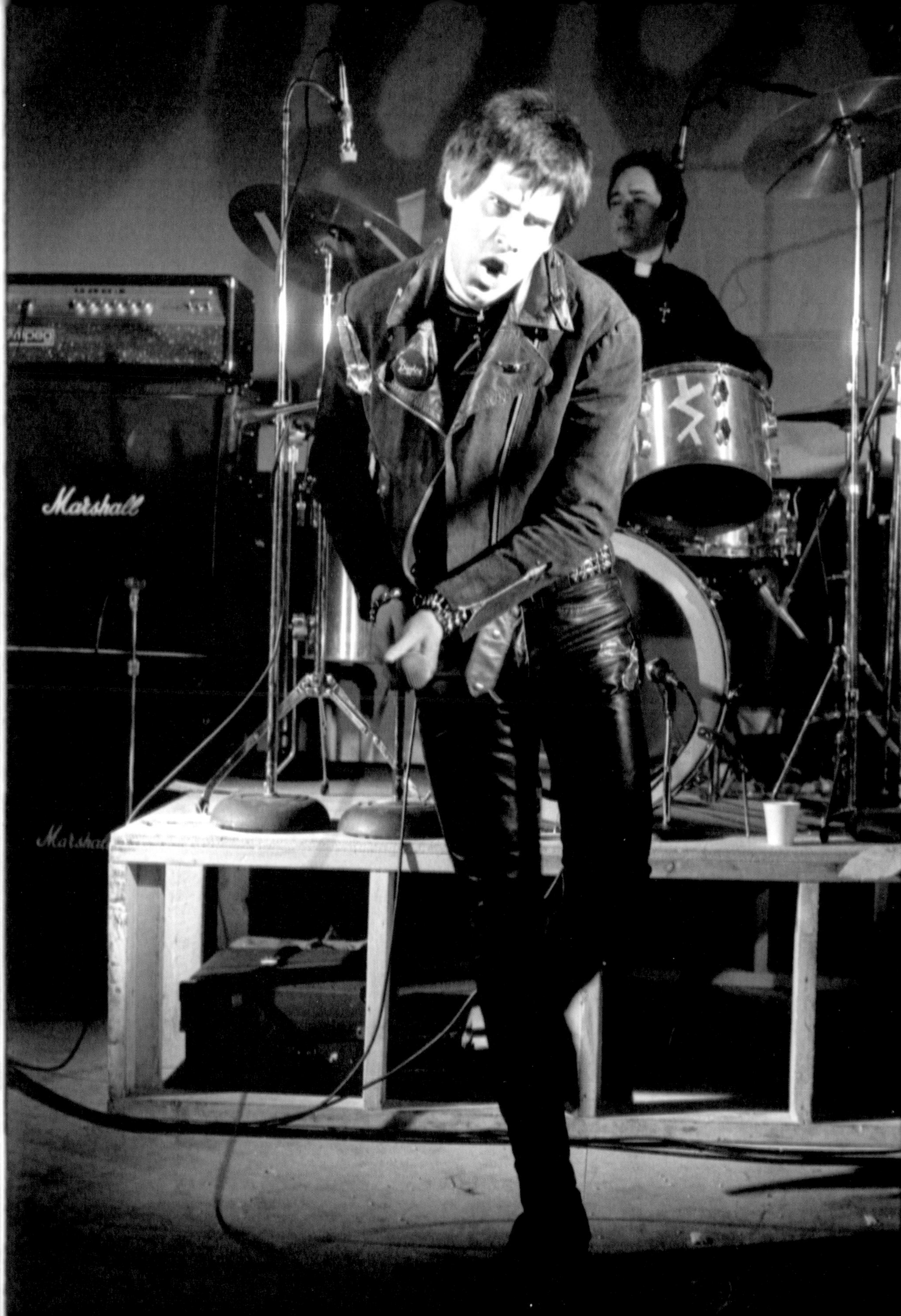
Marshall

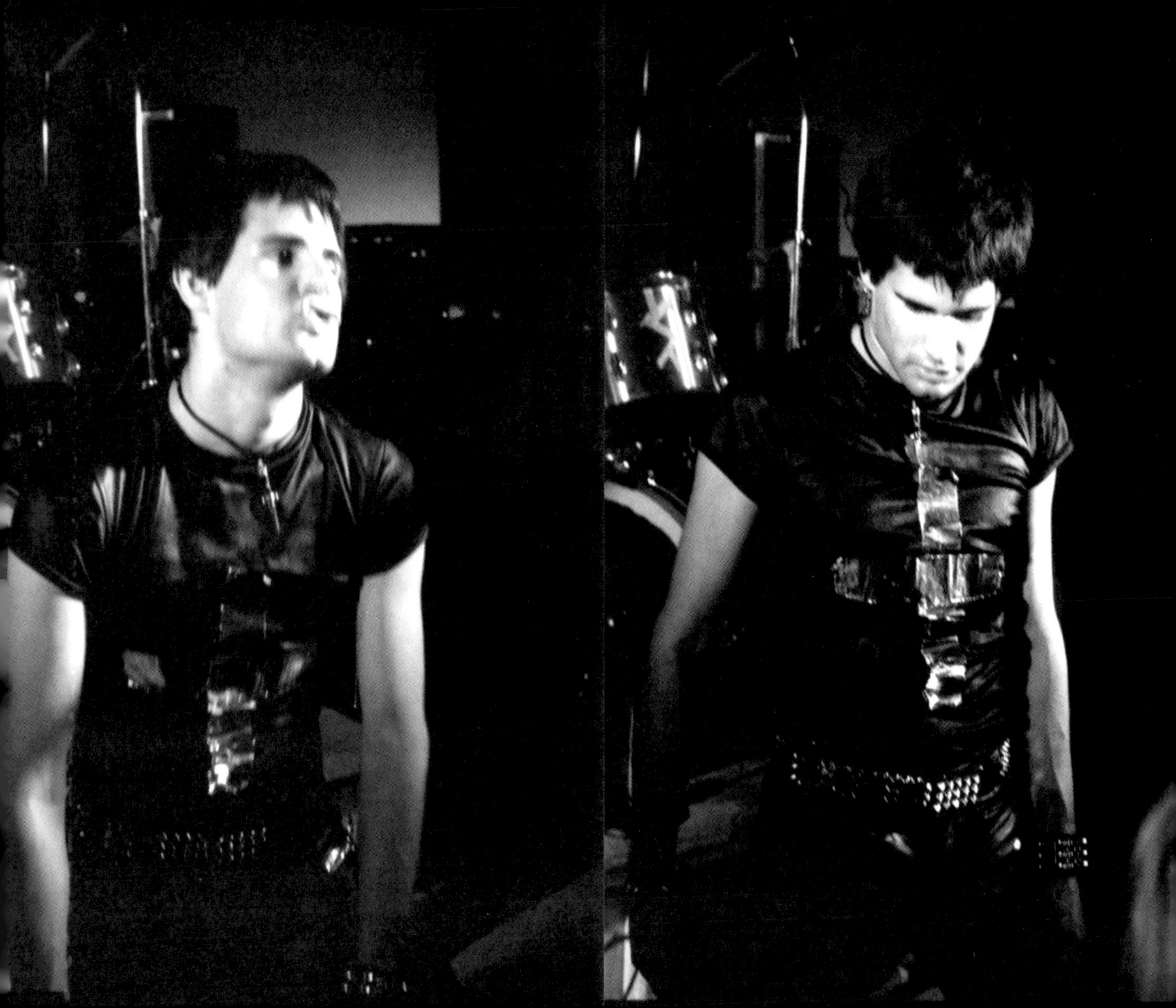

Paul Robinson

From a CBS Records archive contact sheet by John Reynolds, from the collection of Ralph Alfonso, this was taken at the same Diodes concert. I'm the 16-year-old in the white shirt with camera

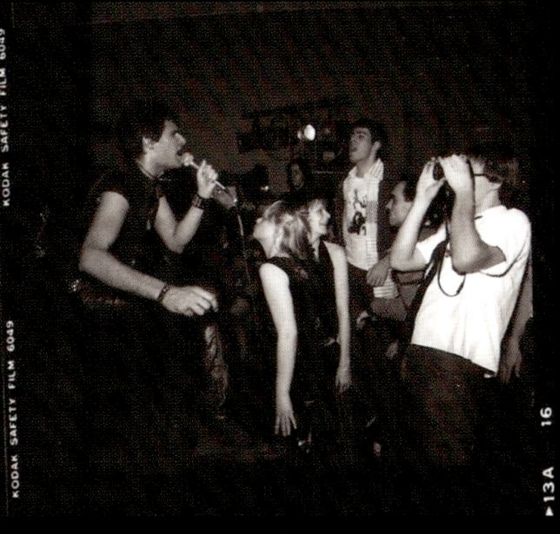

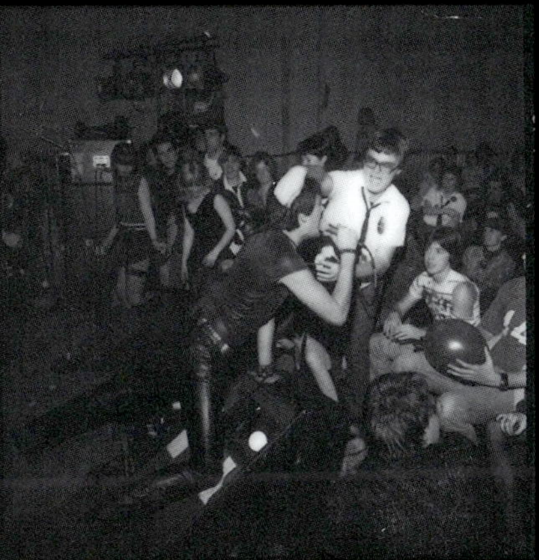

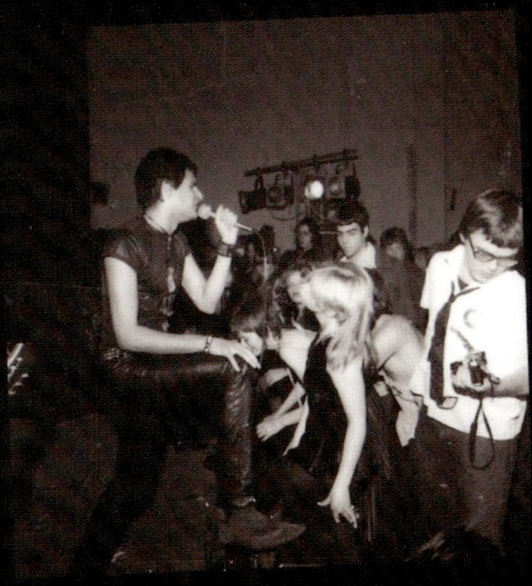

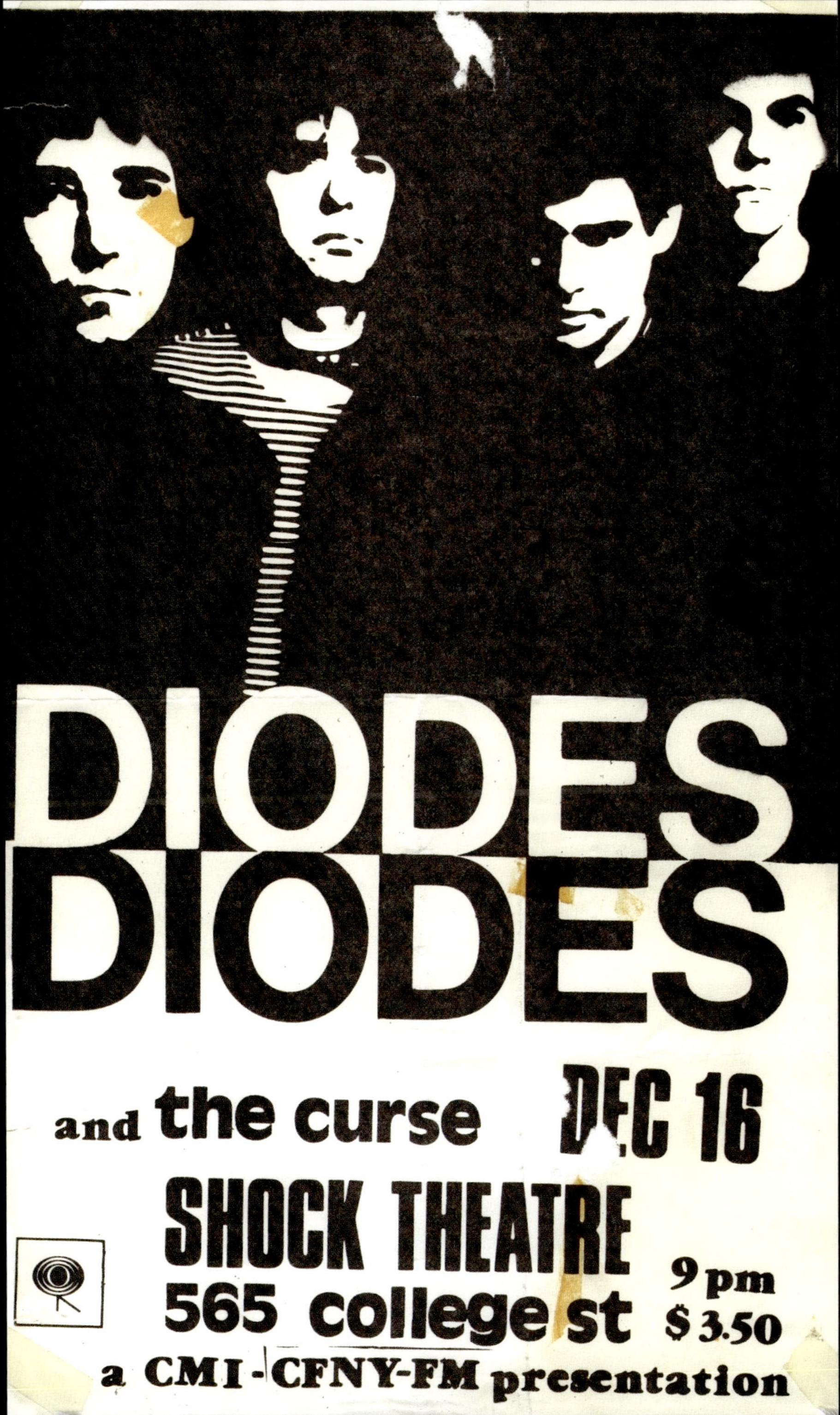
DIODES
DIODES
and the curse
DEC 16
SHOCK THEATRE
565 college st
9 pm
$ 3.50
a CMI - CFNY-FM presentation

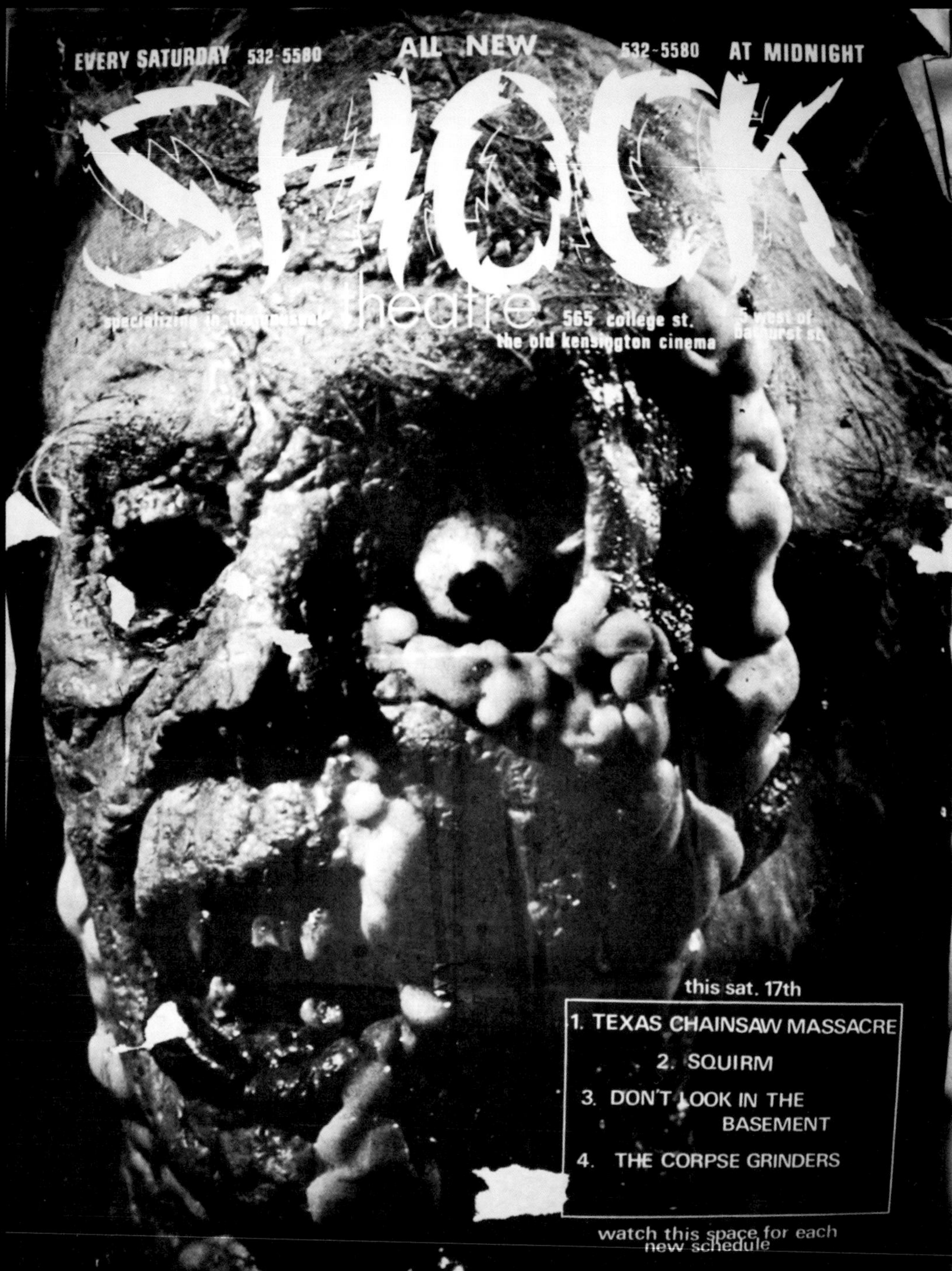
EVERY SATURDAY 532-5580
ALL NEW
532-5580 AT MIDNIGHT
SHOCK
theatre
565 college st.
the old kensington cinema
this sat. 17th
1. TEXAS CHAINSAW MASSACRE
2. SQUIRM
3. DON'T LOOK IN THE BASEMENT
4. THE CORPSE GRINDERS
watch this space for each new schedule

Tyranna, 1978, 1979

Vera and her sister lived a few blocks further down the street I grew up on — St. John's Road in the Junction area — in an old house next to the gas station. Both renamed and metamorphosed themselves with Vera becoming Rabies and her sister becoming Rojer. Rabies had several band attempts (including one with a long-haired Tony Brighton, before his tenure in Zro4 and The Ugly) before a group coalesced as Tyranna. The photo of Vera with the kids on bikes is from a walkathon that pre-Tyranna band Circuitbreaker played at, with the band set up in the parking lot to entertain the walkers.

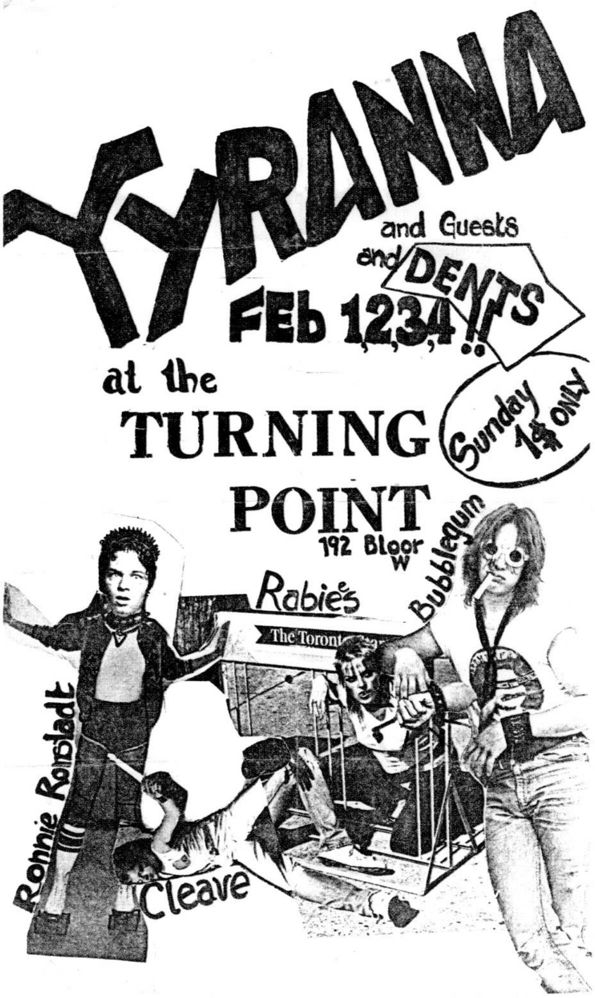

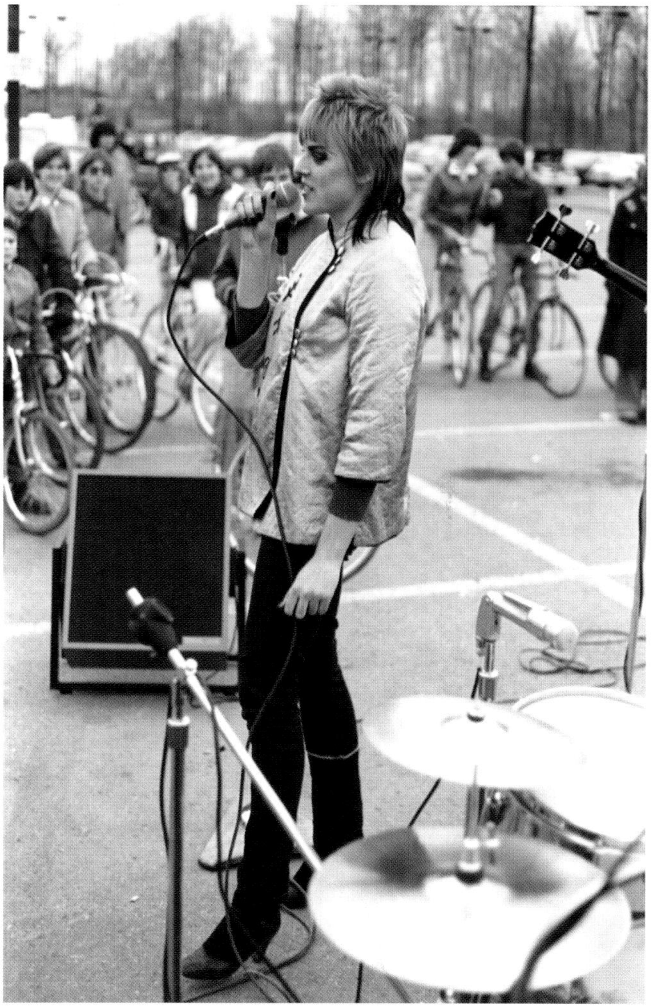

Vera/Rabies

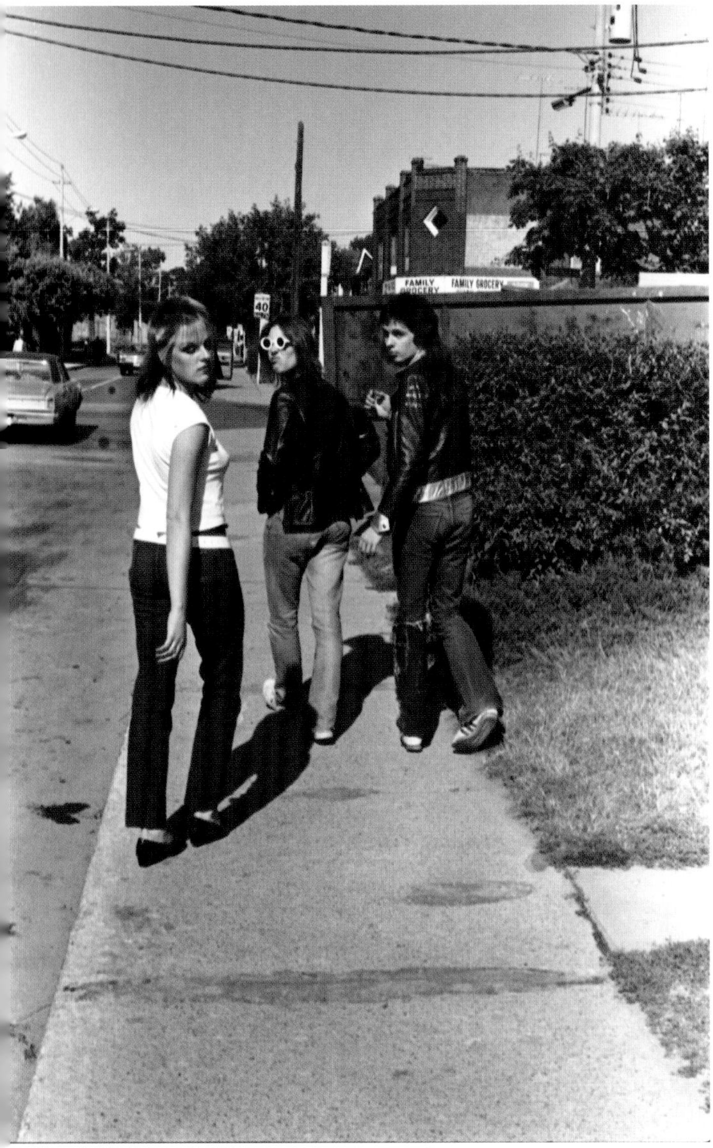

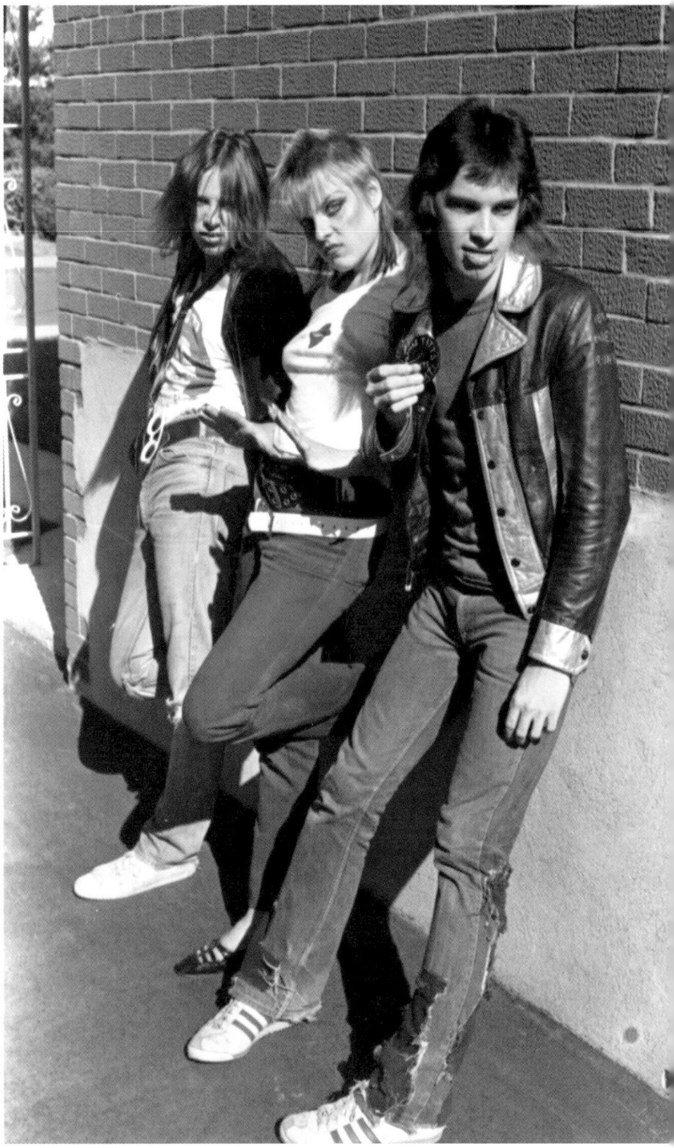

Bubblegum, Rabies, Johnny Ziegler

Vera met a bass player through a classified ad. Gerry Smith, as Johnny Bubblegum, became the first other member of Tyranna. By having photos taken before they'd even written any songs, they were able to present themselves as a band in order to find other members. Photos were a quick easy way to become the thing you wanted to be. Create it, document it and it's real. Their songs were short, sharp, high-velocity pop, and Vera was a raspy, charismatic frontperson as powerful onstage as she was uncertain of herself off.

These photos were taken on the streets of the posh west-end neighborhood Baby Point and in our own neighborhood. New drummer Cleave Anderson was fresh out of pub-rockers Battered Wives. Because of frequent member changes and instability within Tyranna, and as a consequence of Vera's ambition overriding the collective, only one song was ever released on the compilation *No Pedestrians*, until a 7-inch came out in 2008.

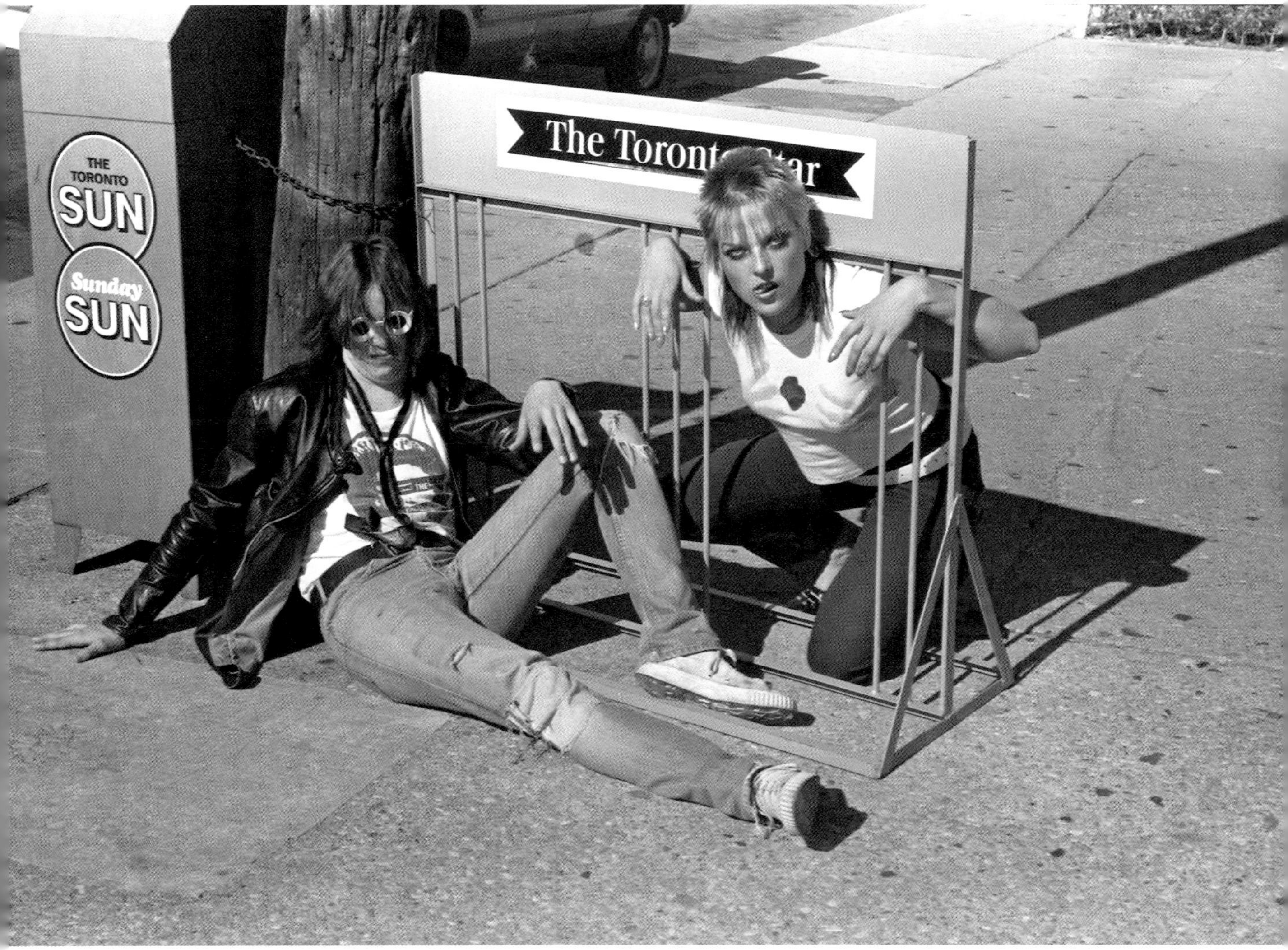

Bubblegum, Rabies

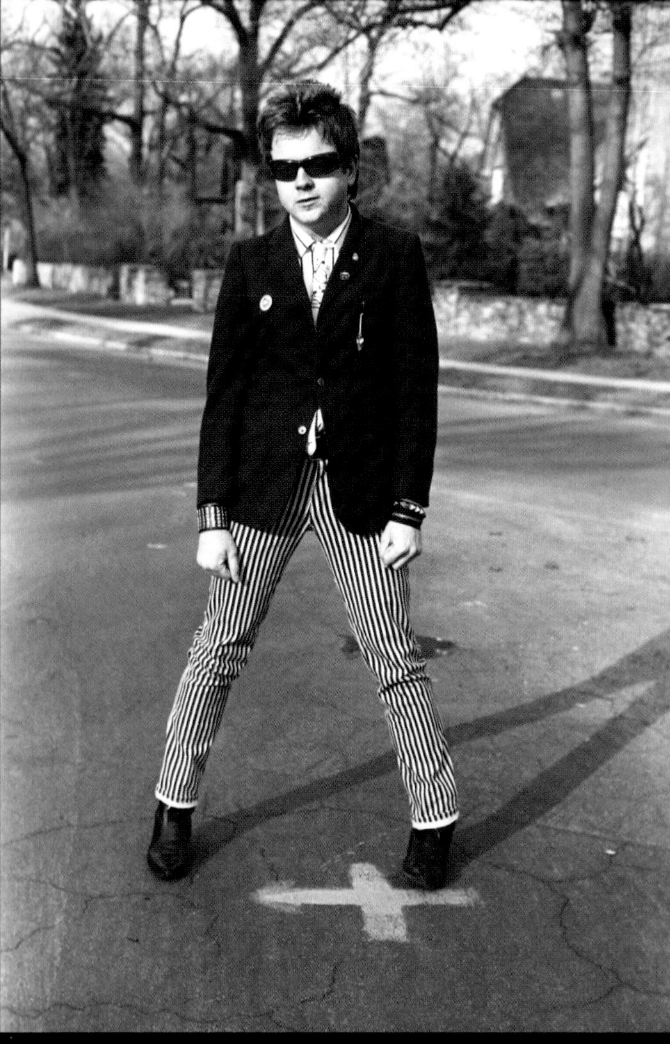

Cleave Anderson

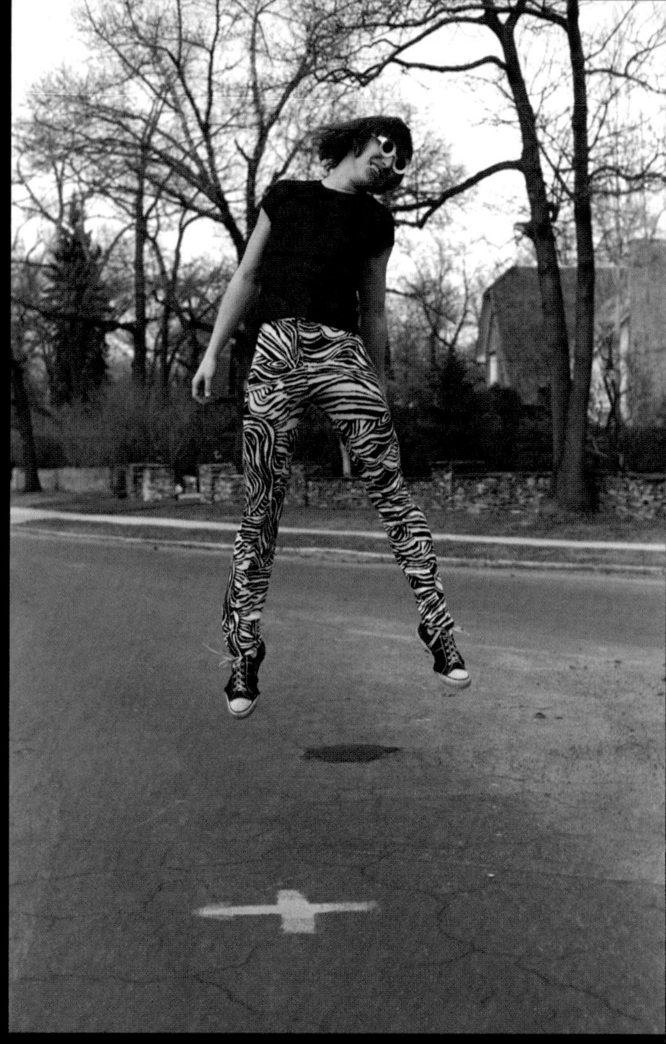

Bubblegum

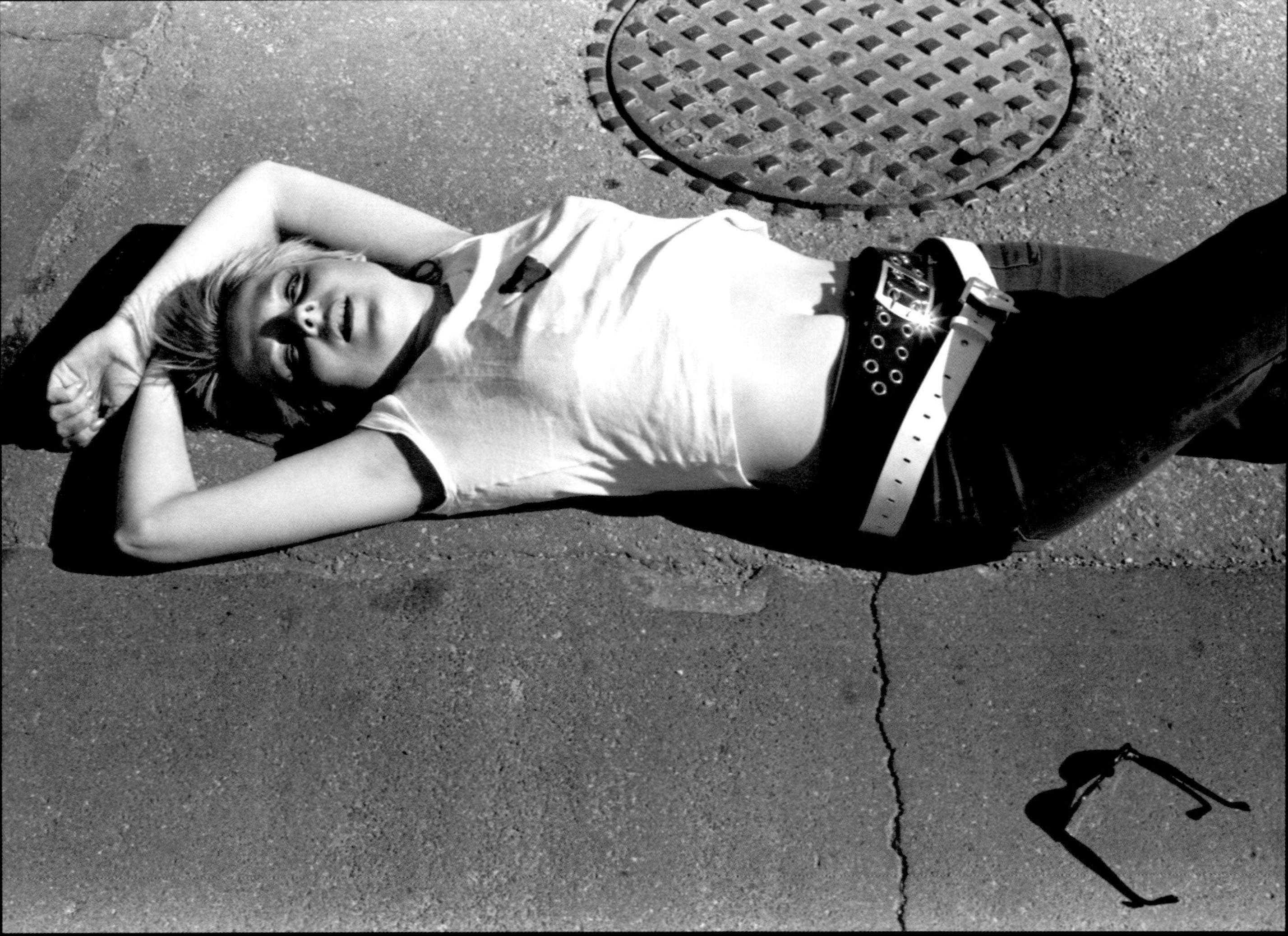

Vera Skye/Rabies

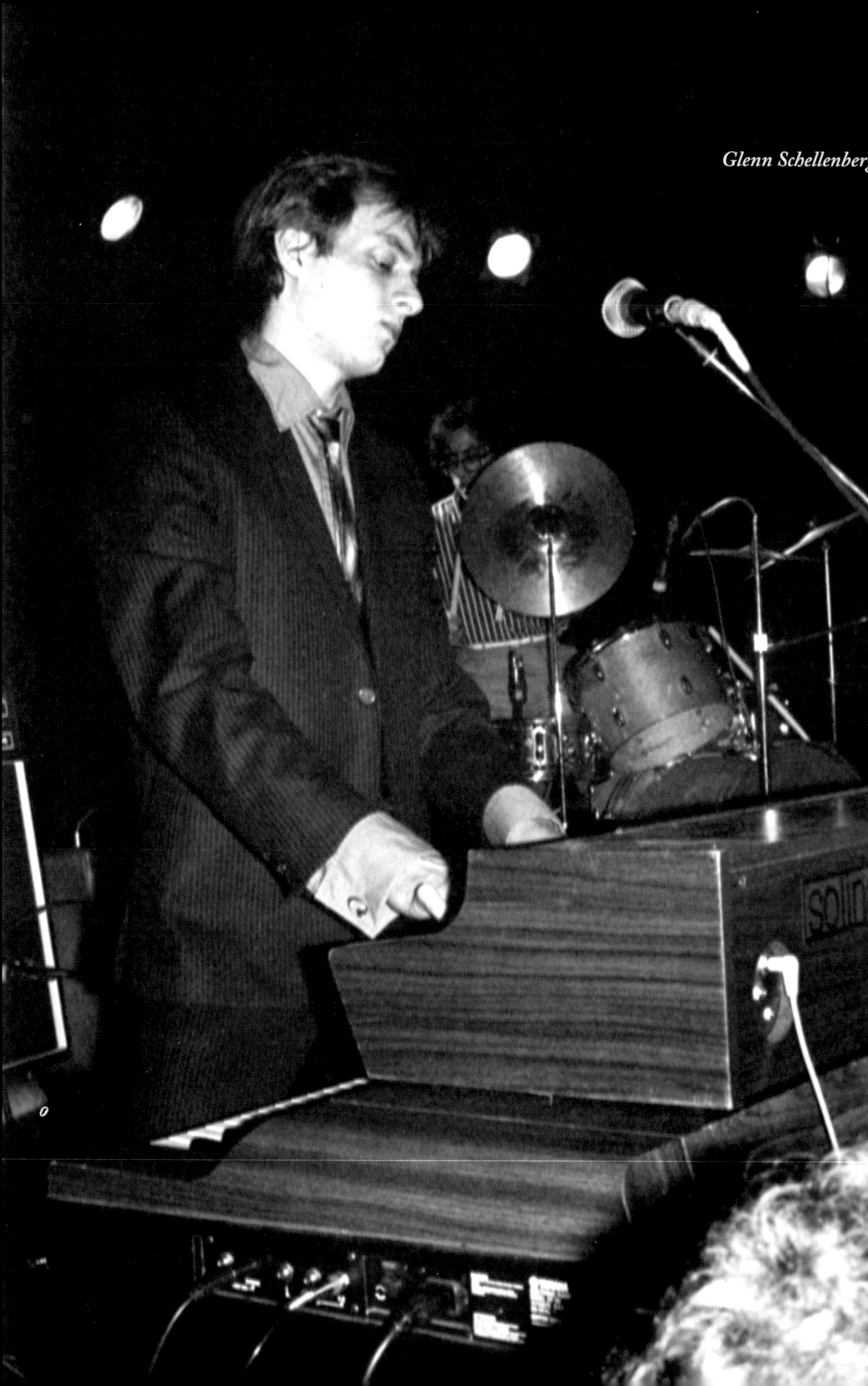

Glenn Schellenberg

Everglades, Horseshoe Tavern, 1978

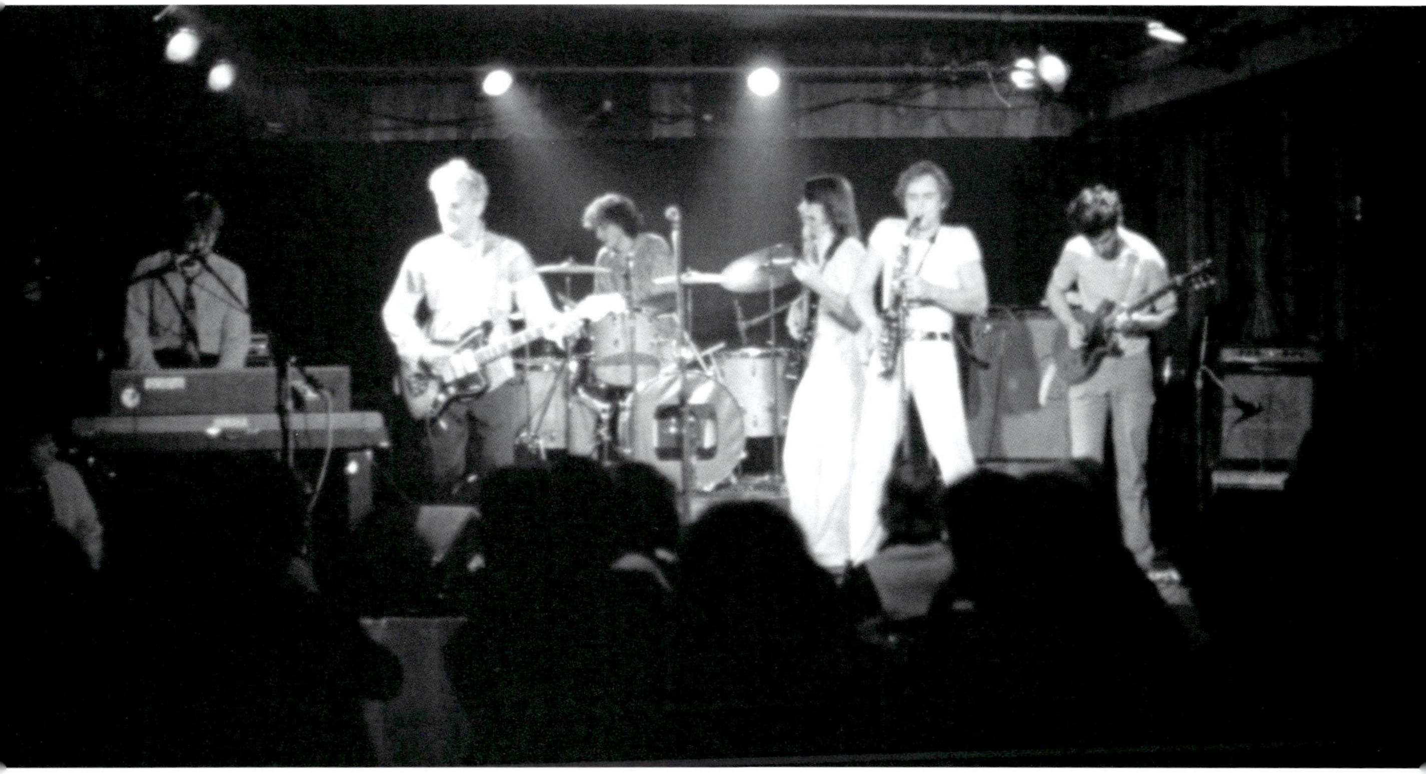

Glenn Schellenberg, Steven Davey, Steven Bock, Brad Townsend, Michael Lacroix, Michael Brook

Everglades was formed by Steven Davey with other former members of The Dishes, Glenn Schellenberg and Michael Lacroix. This shot is from one of the band's earliest gigs, before guitarist Michael Brook departed for fame as a collaborator and player with Brian Eno, Jon Hassell and artists on the Real World label. Davey, as songwriter, is certainly the only artist in Toronto to write for The Dishes, The Diodes and the Viletones. His song "I'm in a Coma," which was released by The Everglades on *The Last Pogo* album and which eventually showed up on The Diodes comp *Survivors*, is up there with The Diodes' best originals. Live, it had a tense excitement that The Diodes obviously recognized; they chose it to open their live radio broadcast from the El Mocambo on CHUM-FM, a station not known for its support of adventurous Toronto music. Most infamously Davey claims being the unequivocal writer of "Rebel Unorthodox," the song off the Viletones debut single, the credits of which claim Steven Leckie as sole writer. Despite being around for a few years, the band's only recorded output was a couple of compilation tracks.

The Mods, Horseshoe Tavern, 1978

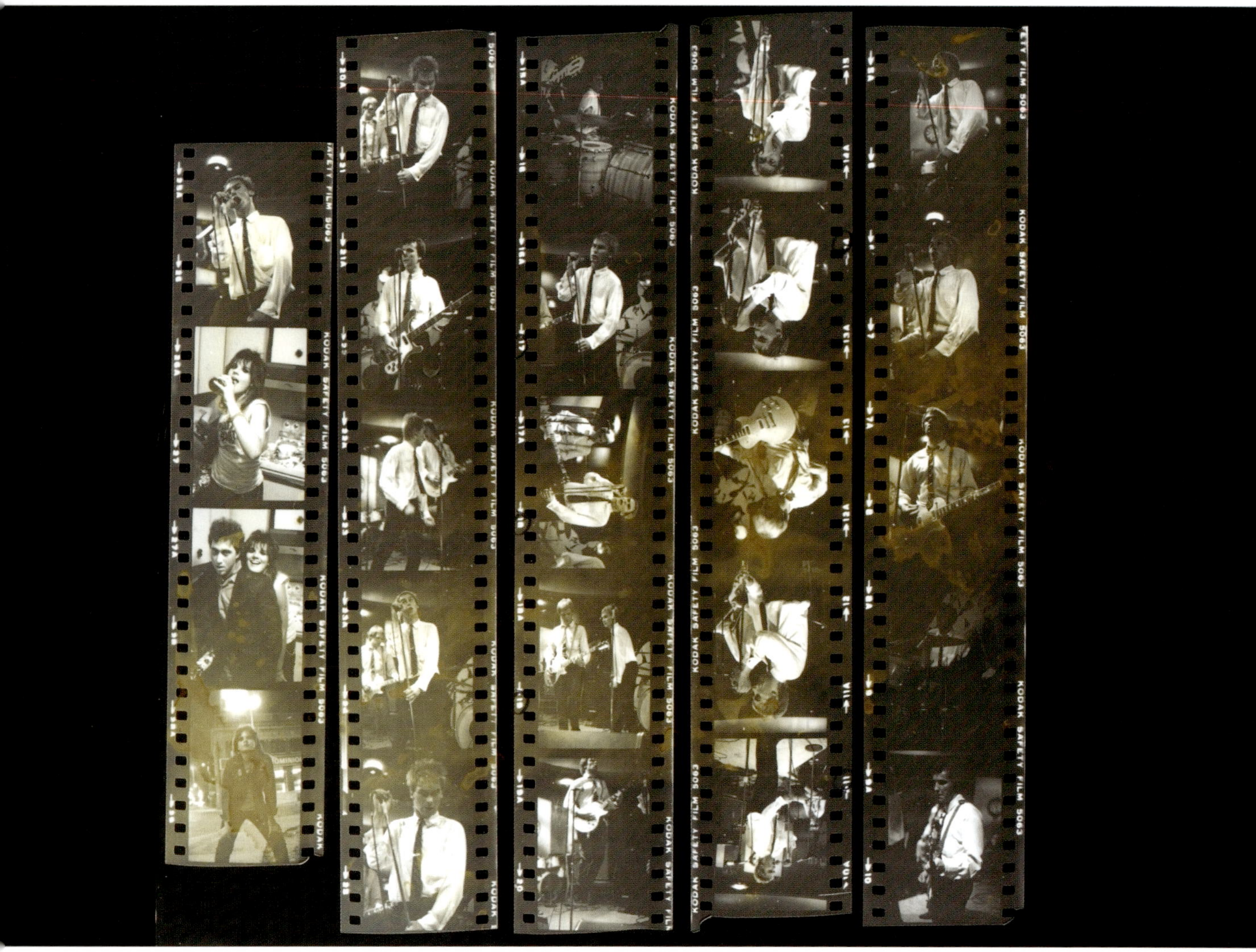

I thought I was well on a career path to being a professional photographer when The Mods noticed me taking pictures and asked if they could pay me to take some of them. They gave me $2.50 — the cost of a roll of film — to shoot their Turning Point gig. Me without a flash and the stage being lit by a couple of weak household bulbs caused the photos to come out gray and dim, unlike these earlier Horseshoe shots from their first or second gig. Despite the shoddy quality of the underexposed contact sheet I gave them, they ordered a few prints and even used one for an equally poor quality flyer. My total take for the assignment was about 10 bucks.

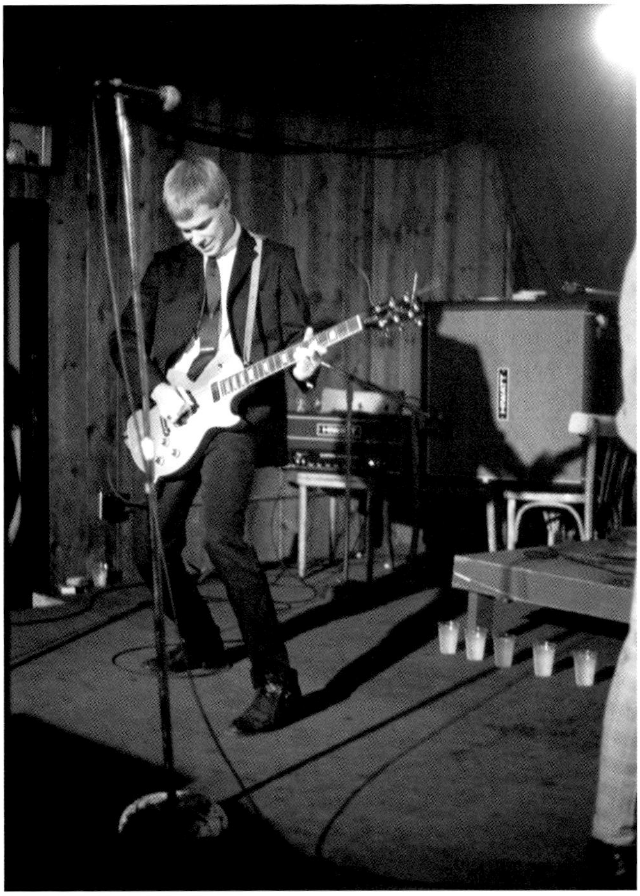

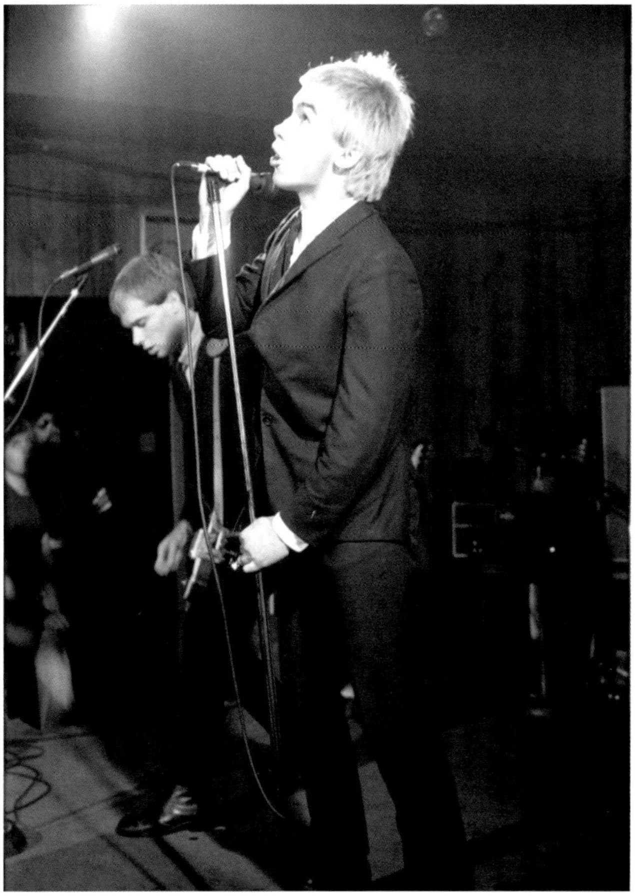

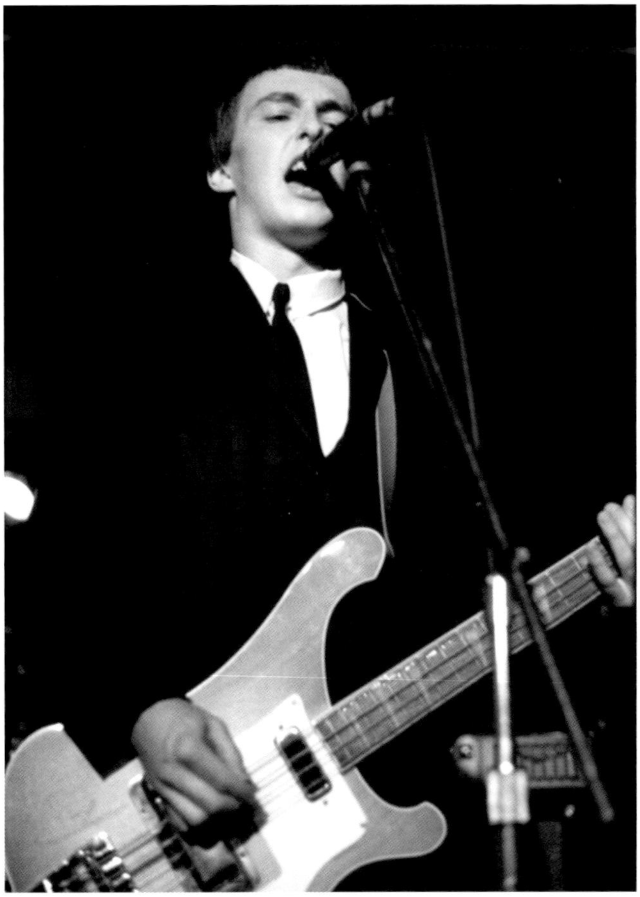

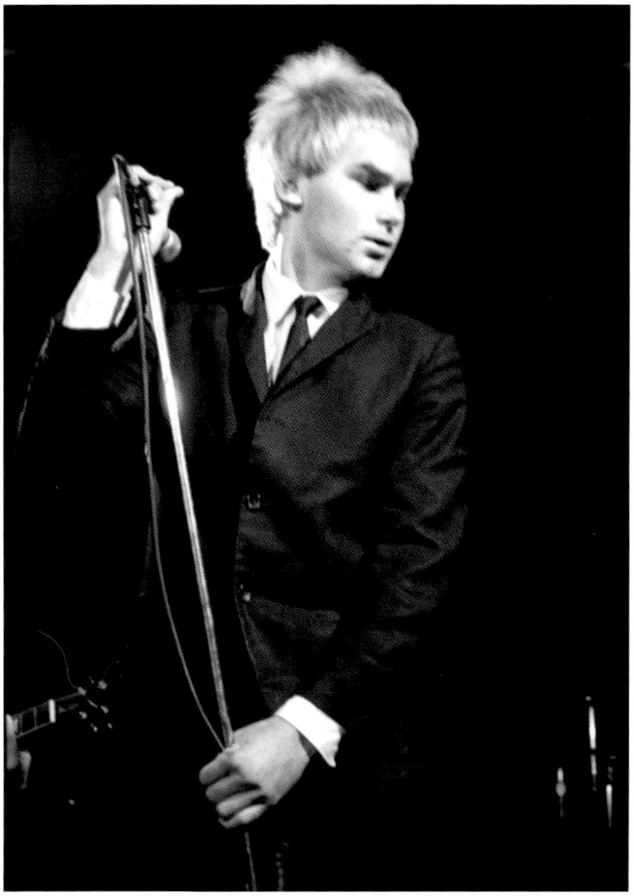

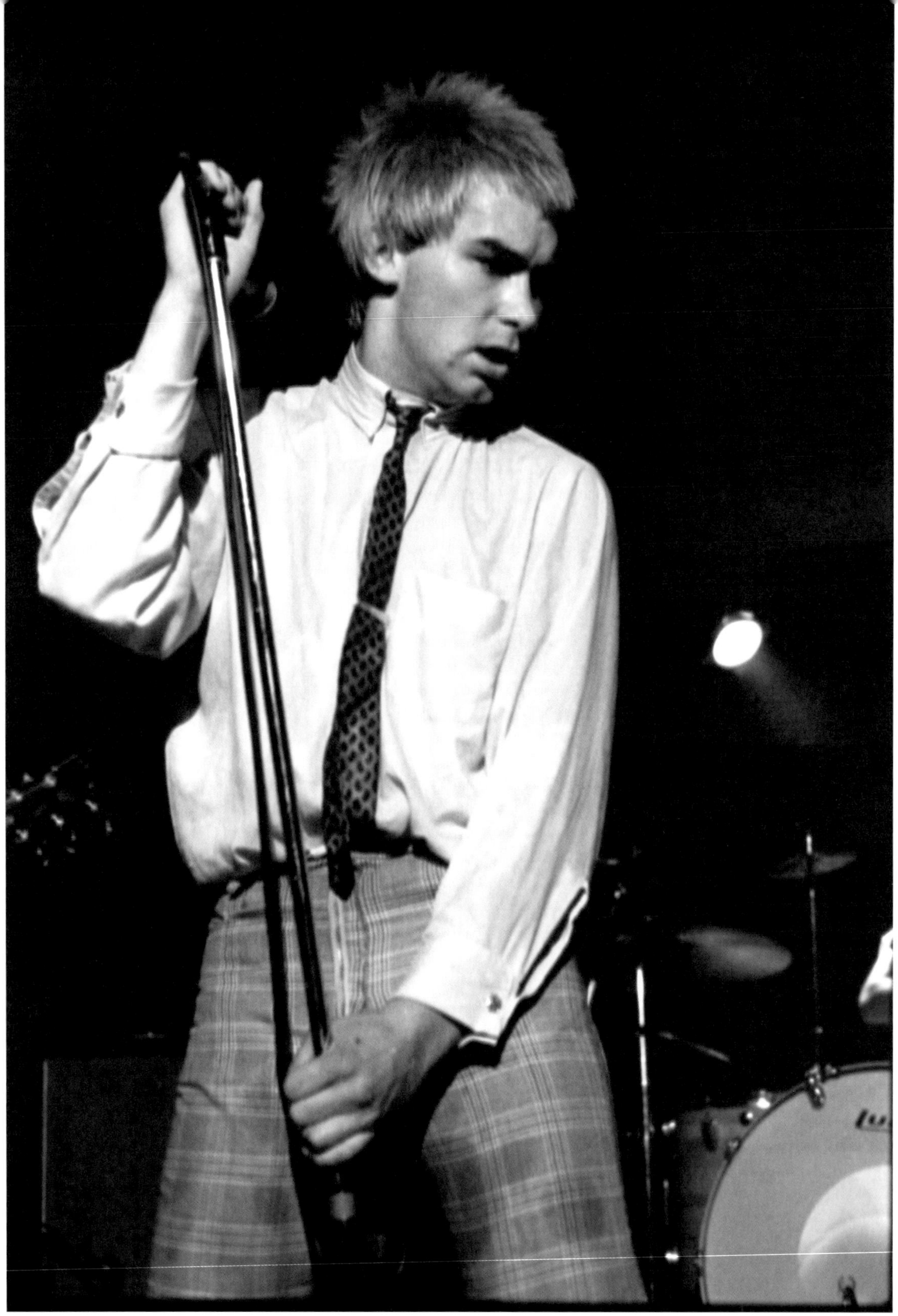

Greg Trinier

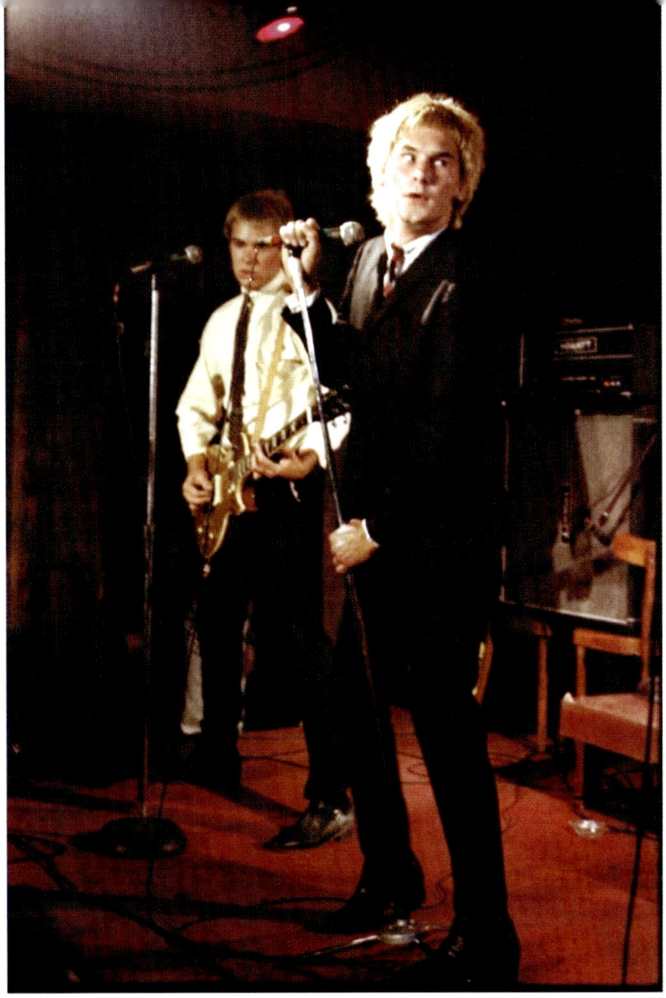

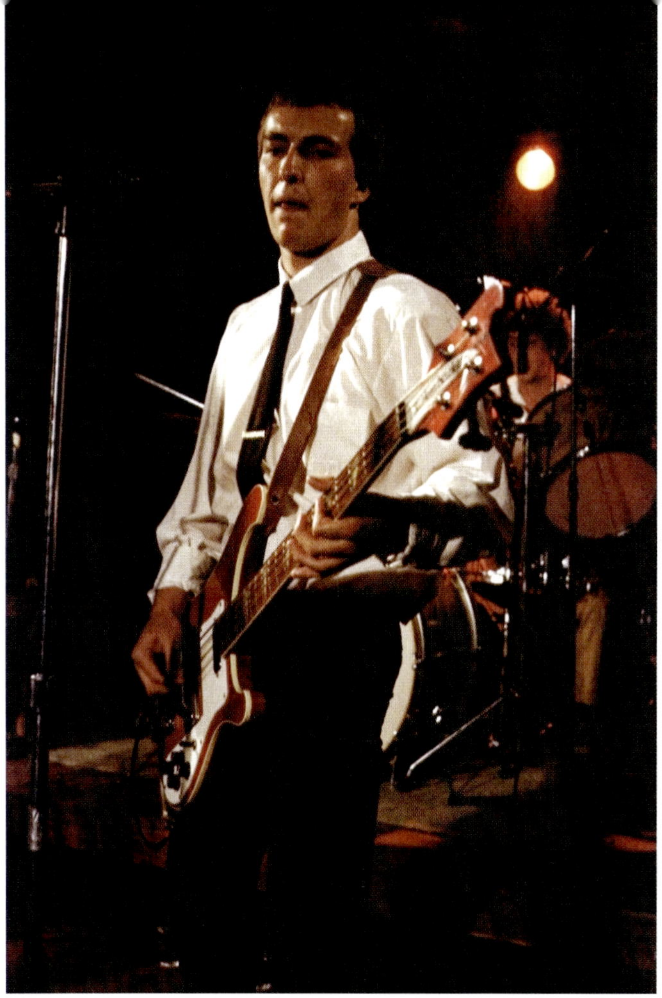

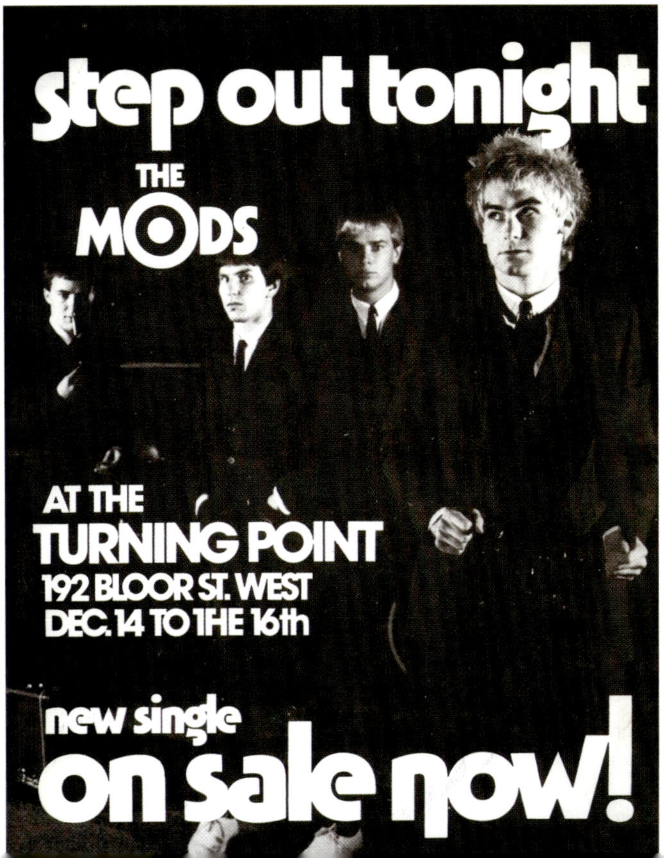
step out tonight
THE
MODS
AT THE
TURNING POINT
192 BLOOR ST. WEST
DEC. 14 TO THE 16th
new single
on sale now!

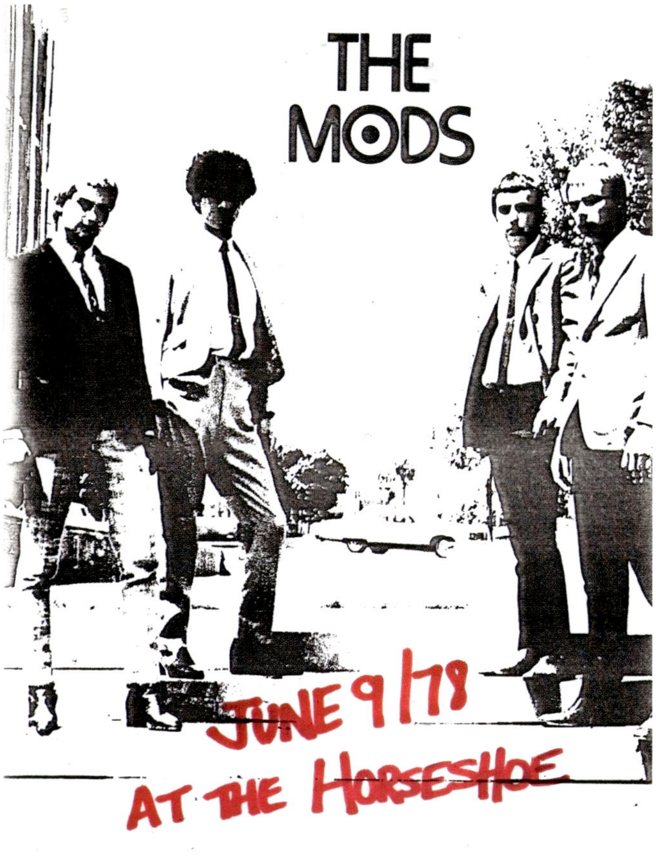
THE
MODS
JUNE 9/78
AT THE HORSESHOE

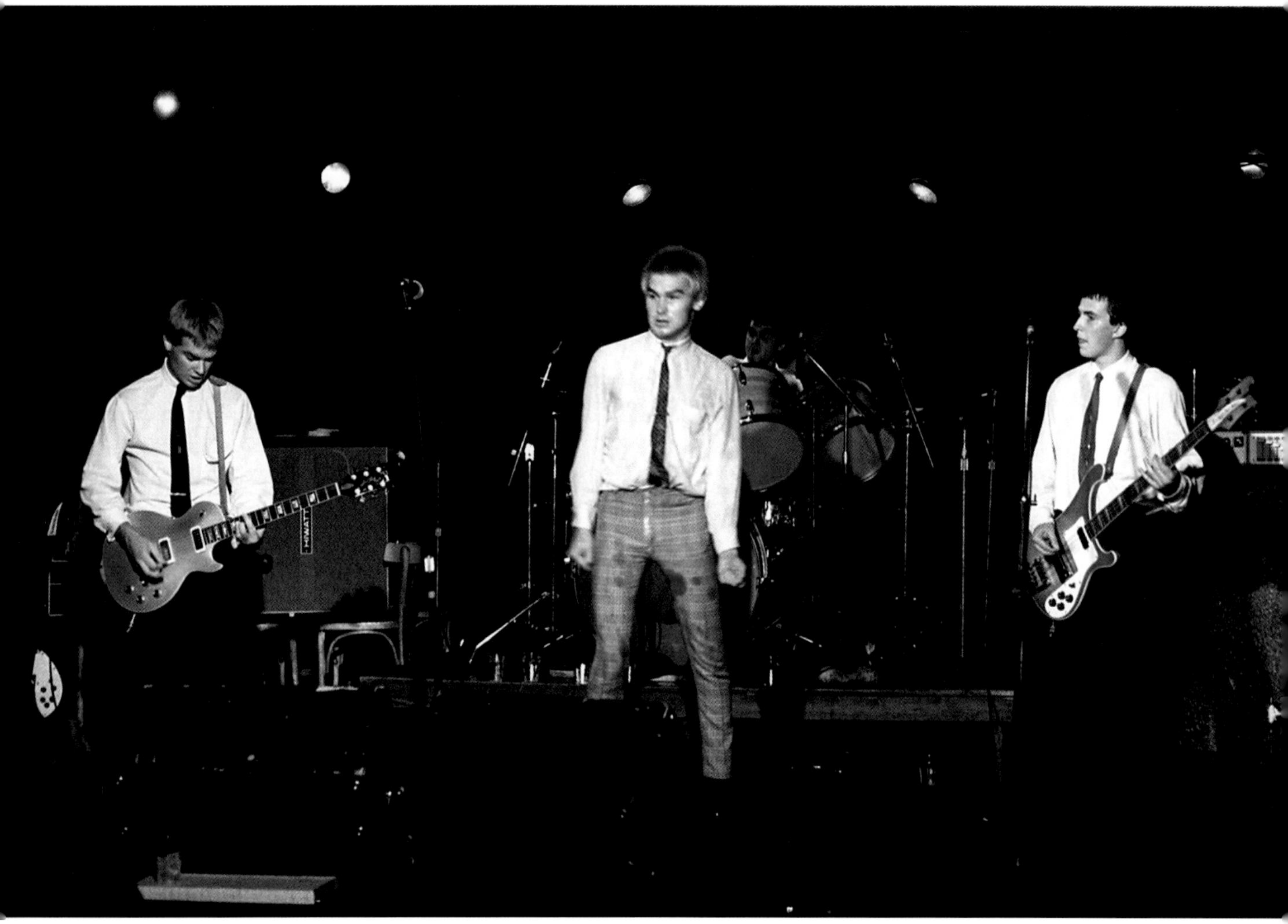

Scott Marks, Greg Trinier, Nick Catillo, Mark Dixon

Viletones, Horseshoe Tavern, 1978

This was one of the last shows before Chris Haight, Motor X and Freddy Pompeii quit to form The Secrets, their new band with Diodes' John Hamilton. They left Leckie with the Viletones name.

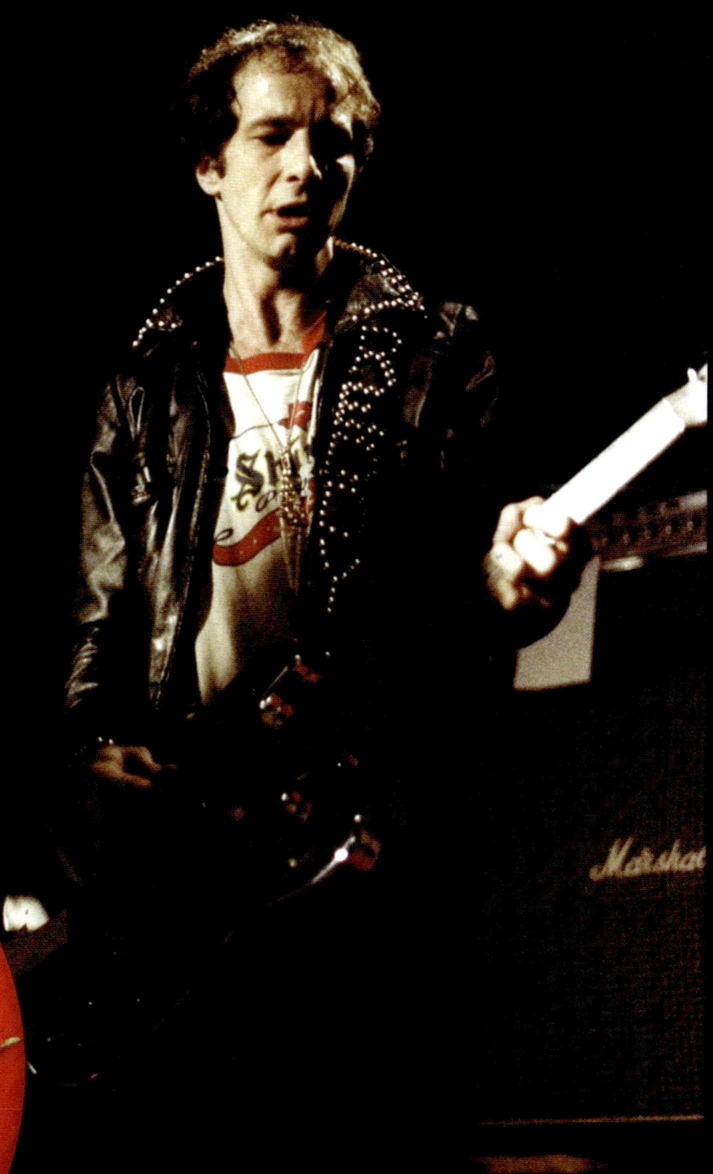

Freddy Pompeii

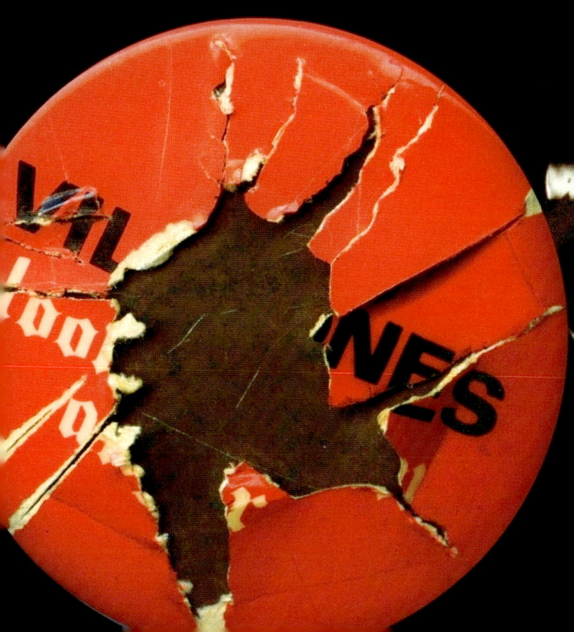

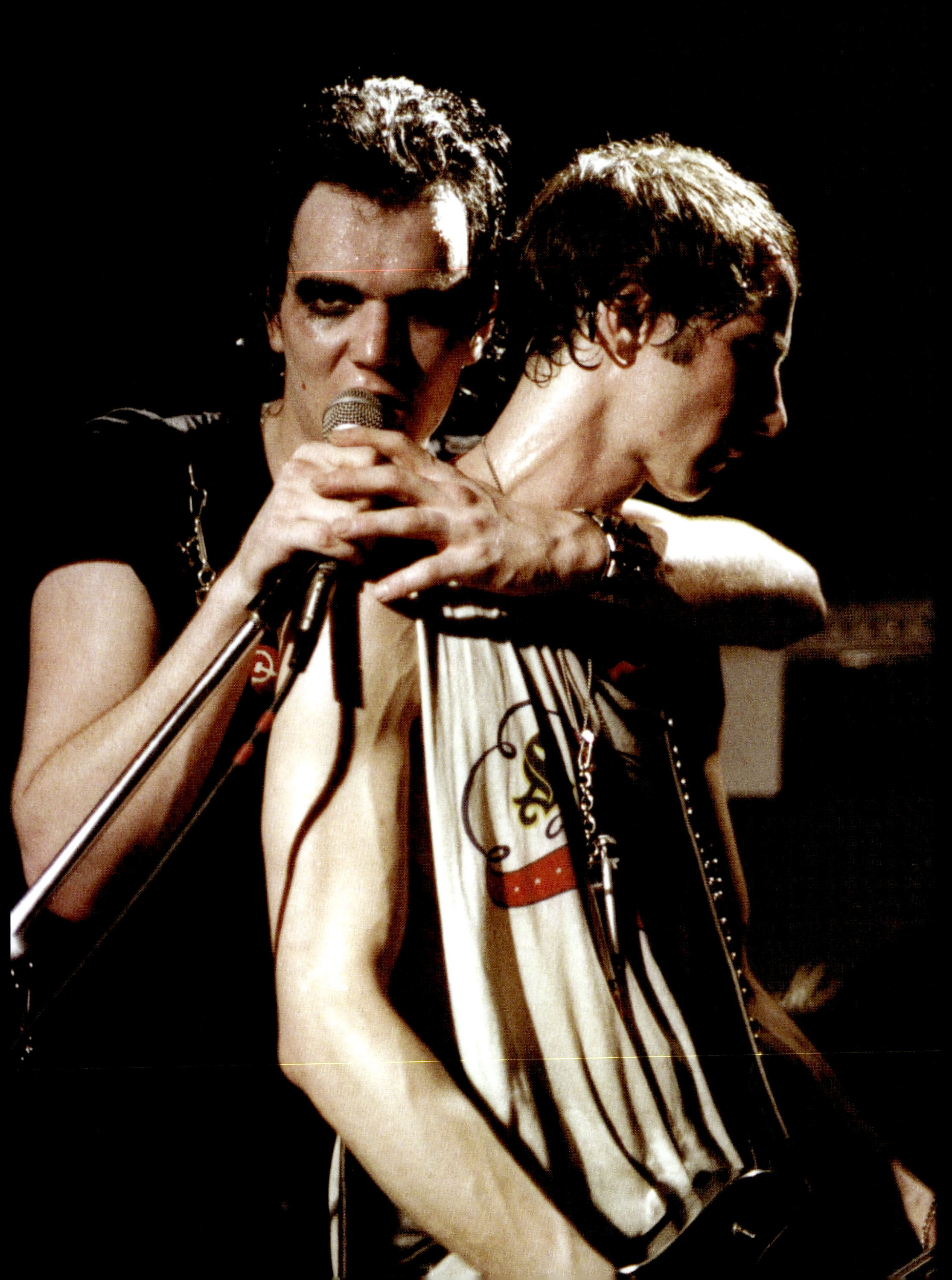

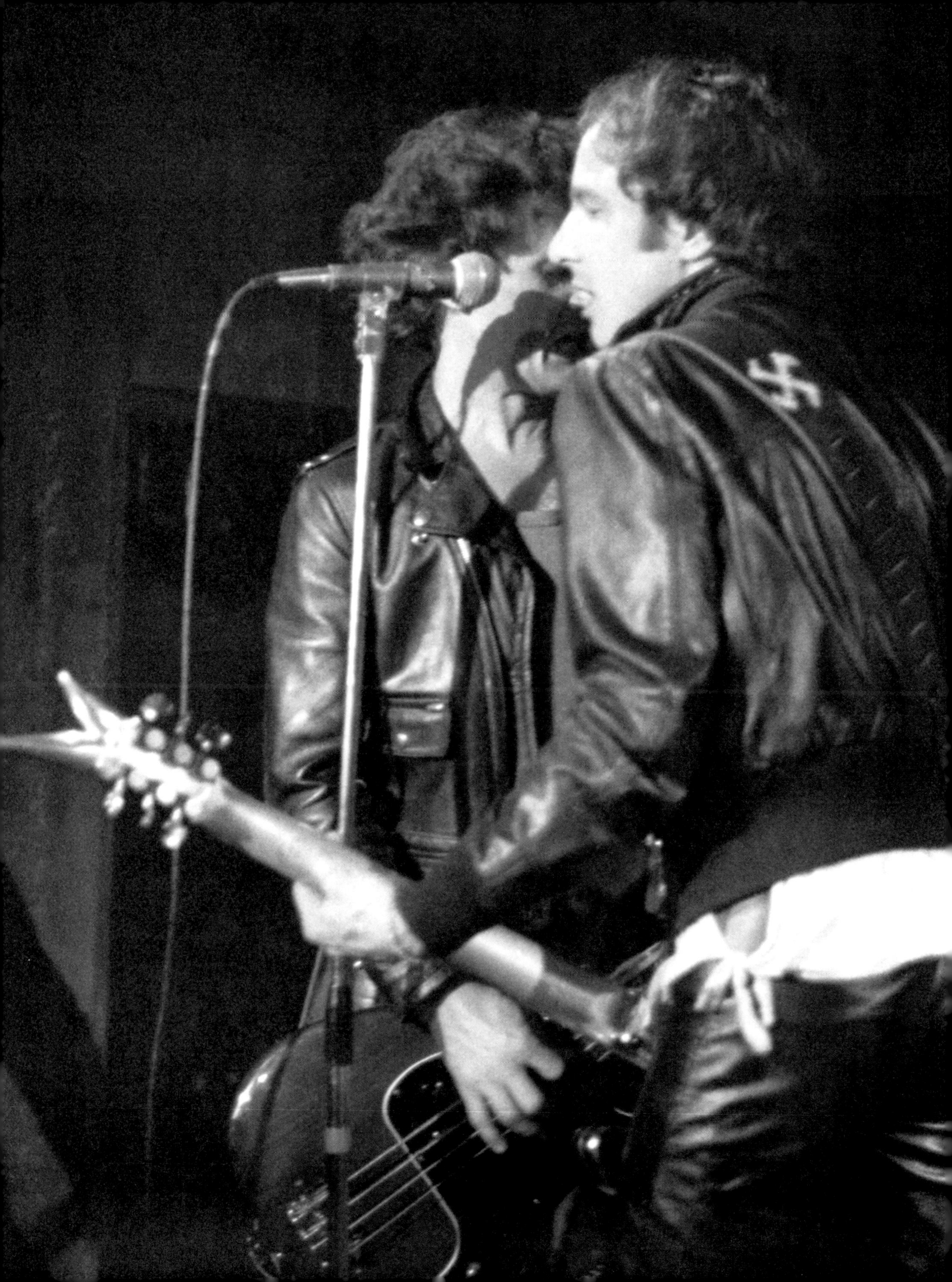

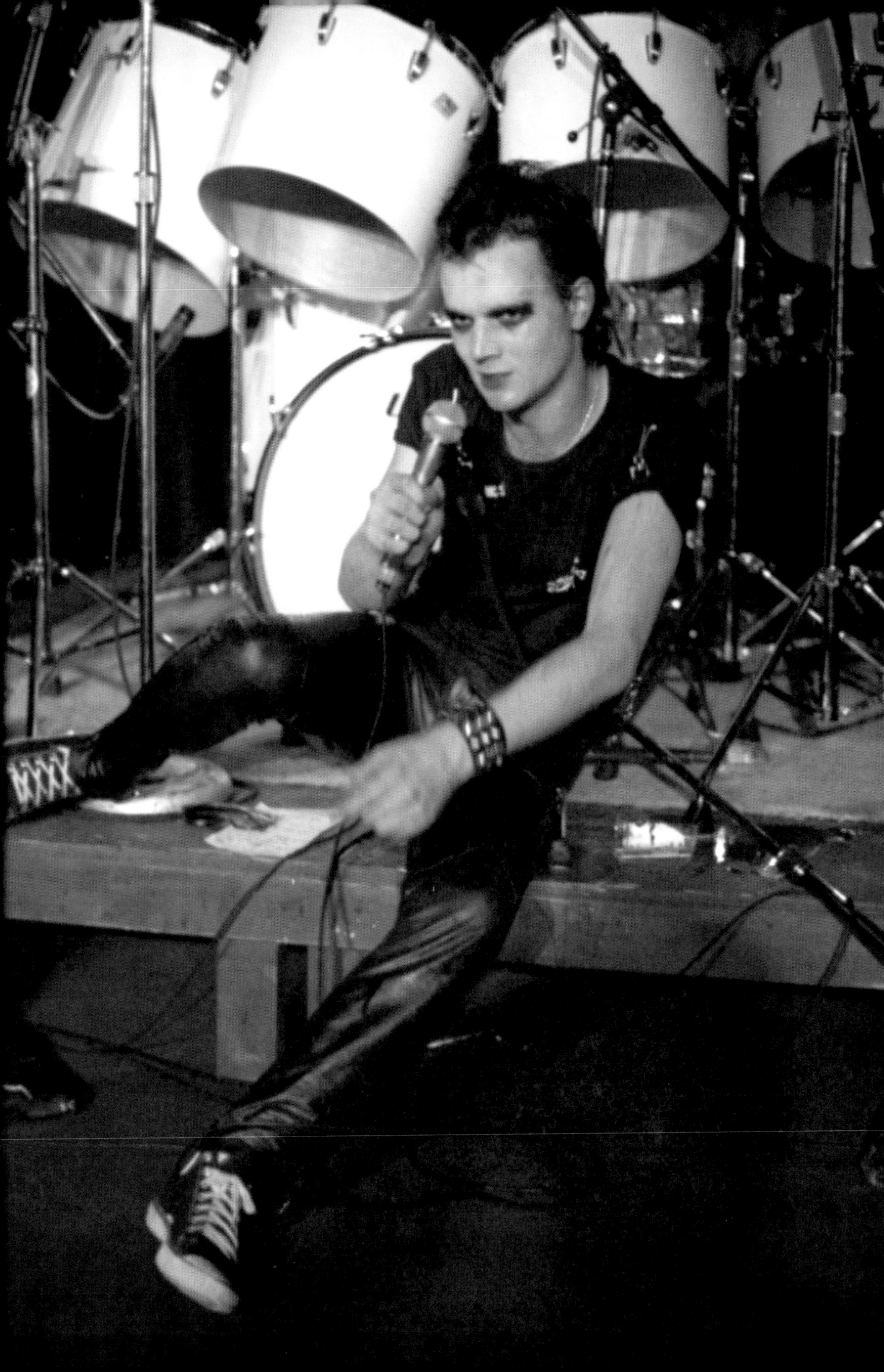

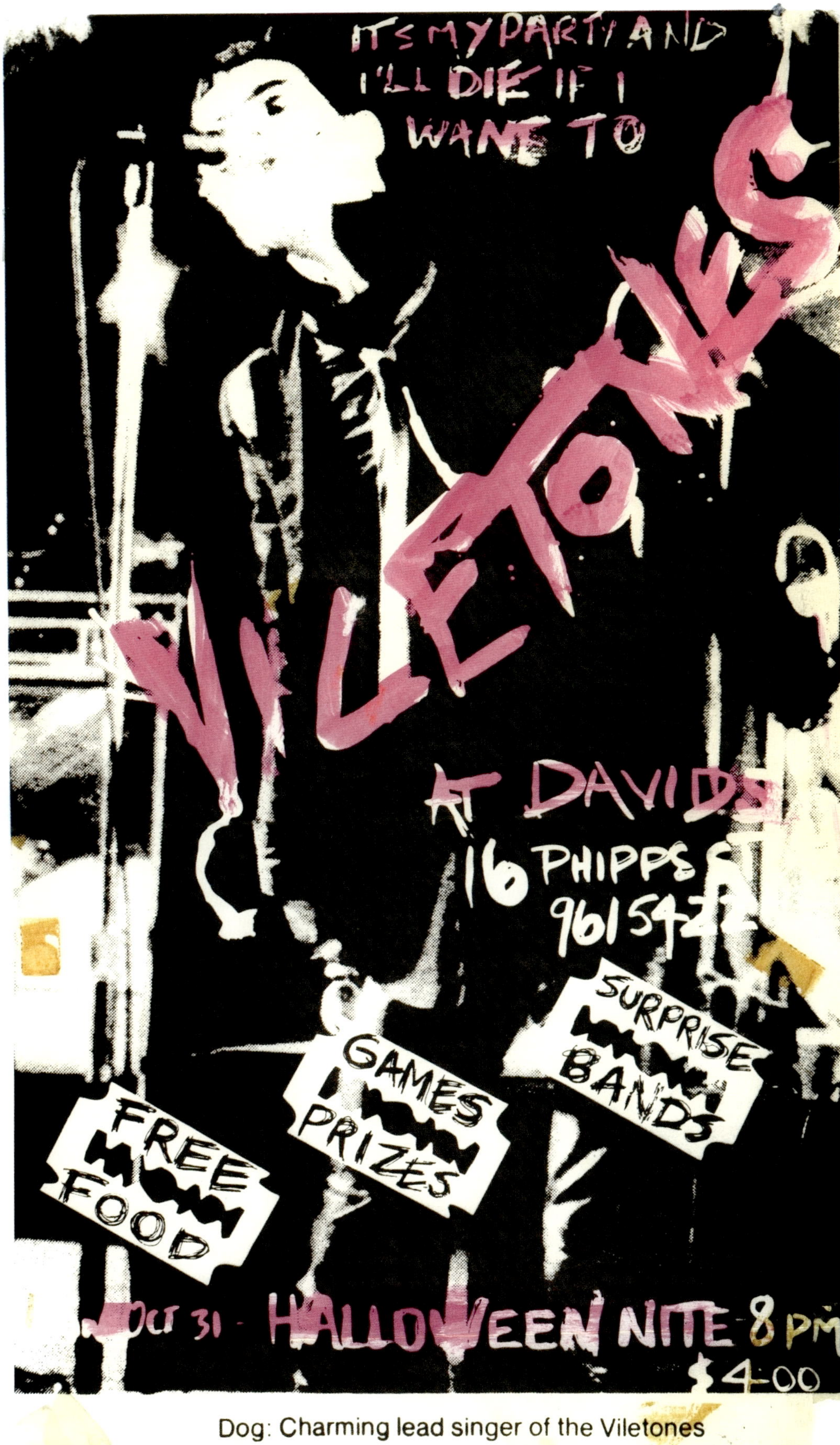

Dog: Charming lead singer of the Viletones

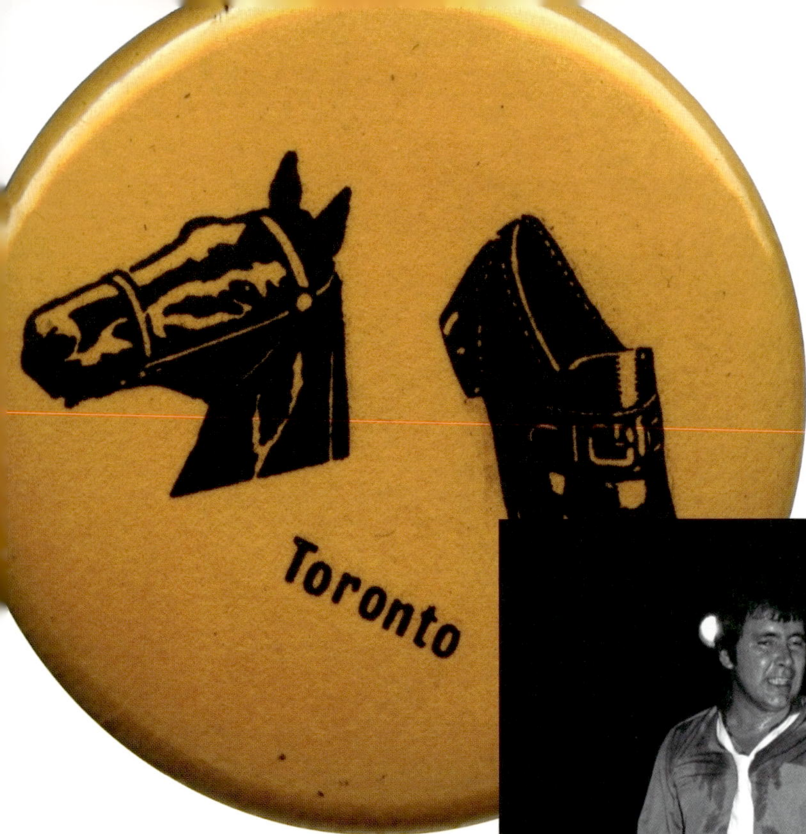

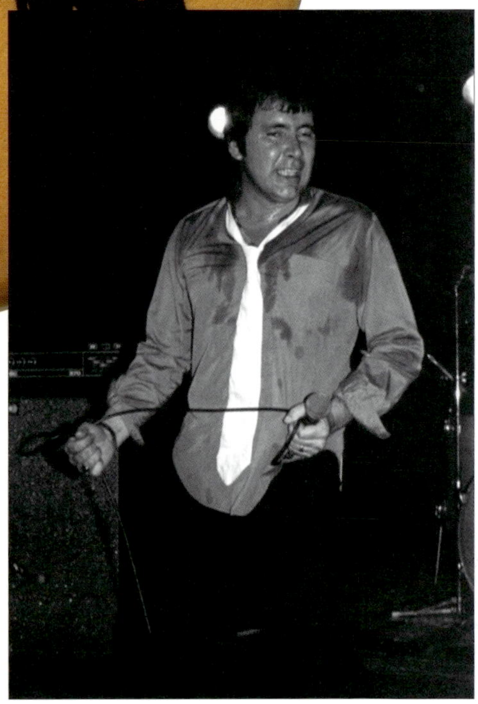

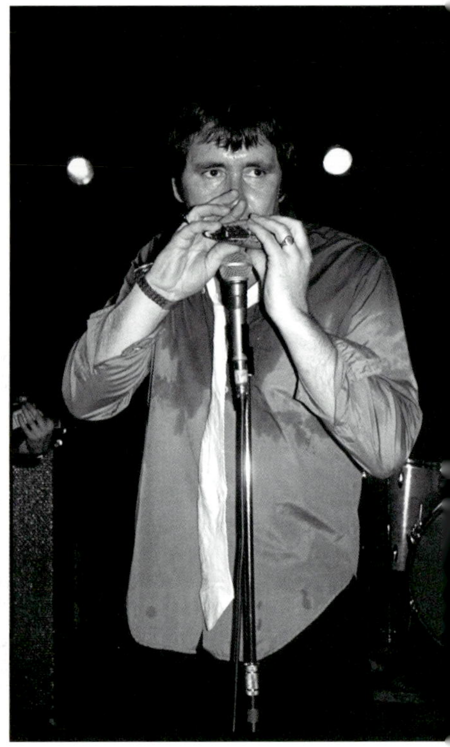

The Troggs, Horseshoe Tavern, 1978

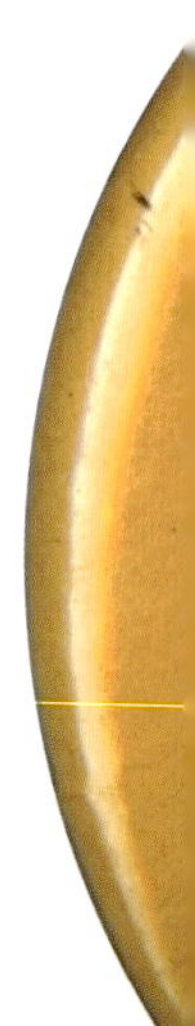

Twelve years after "Wild Thing" was released, The Troggs felt like an oldies act. The scuzzy reverb of their earliest hits and "leering uncle" Reg Presley clearly influenced some aspects of first-wave punk. The Viletones opened the show, with Leckie poking fun at the old farts whose songs were even covered by his band.

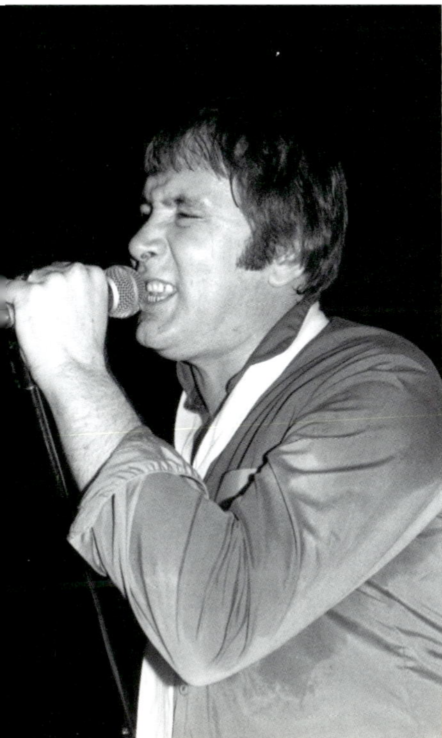

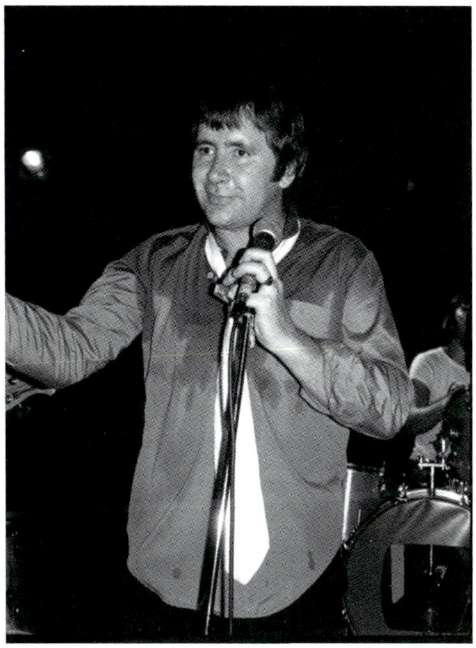

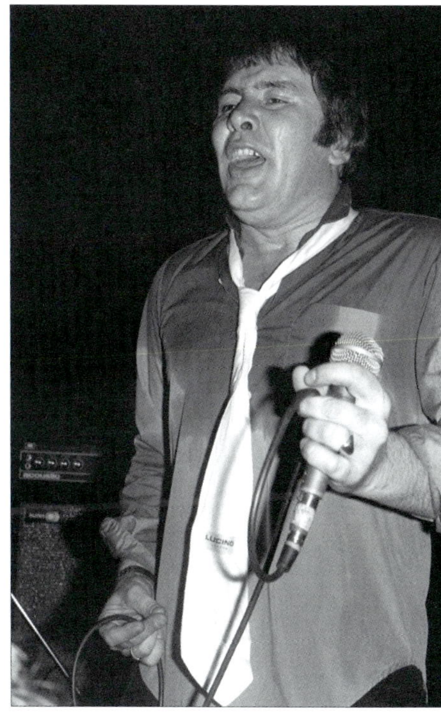

Reg Presley

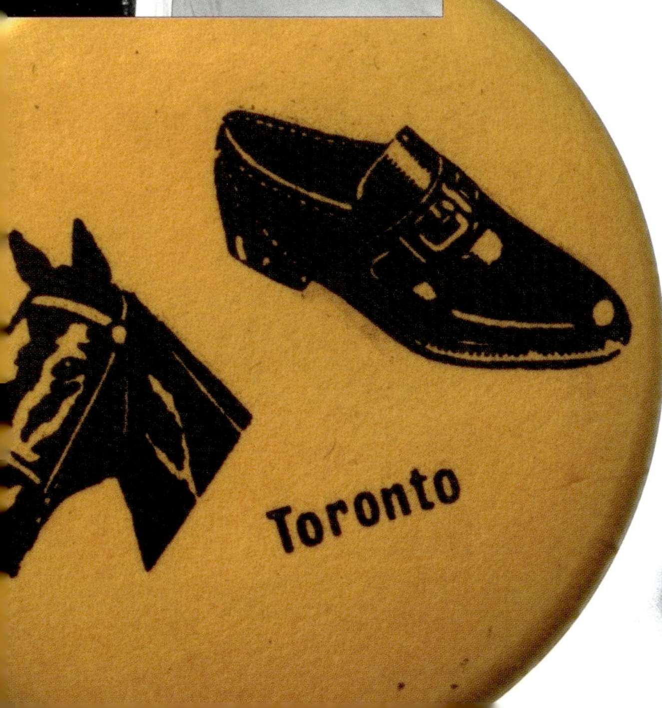

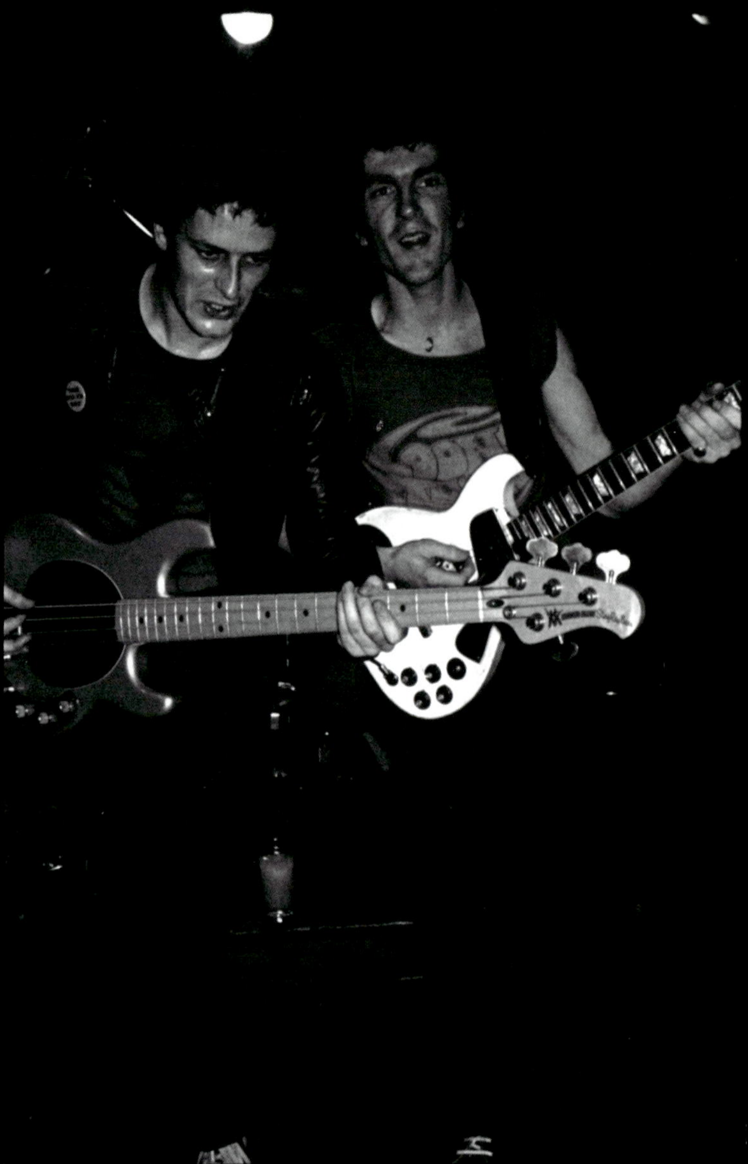

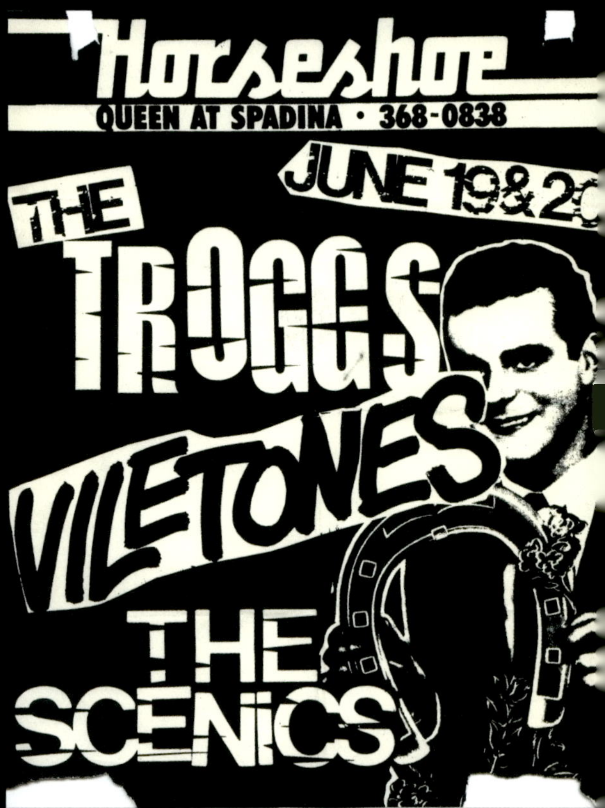

Tony Murray, Chris Britton

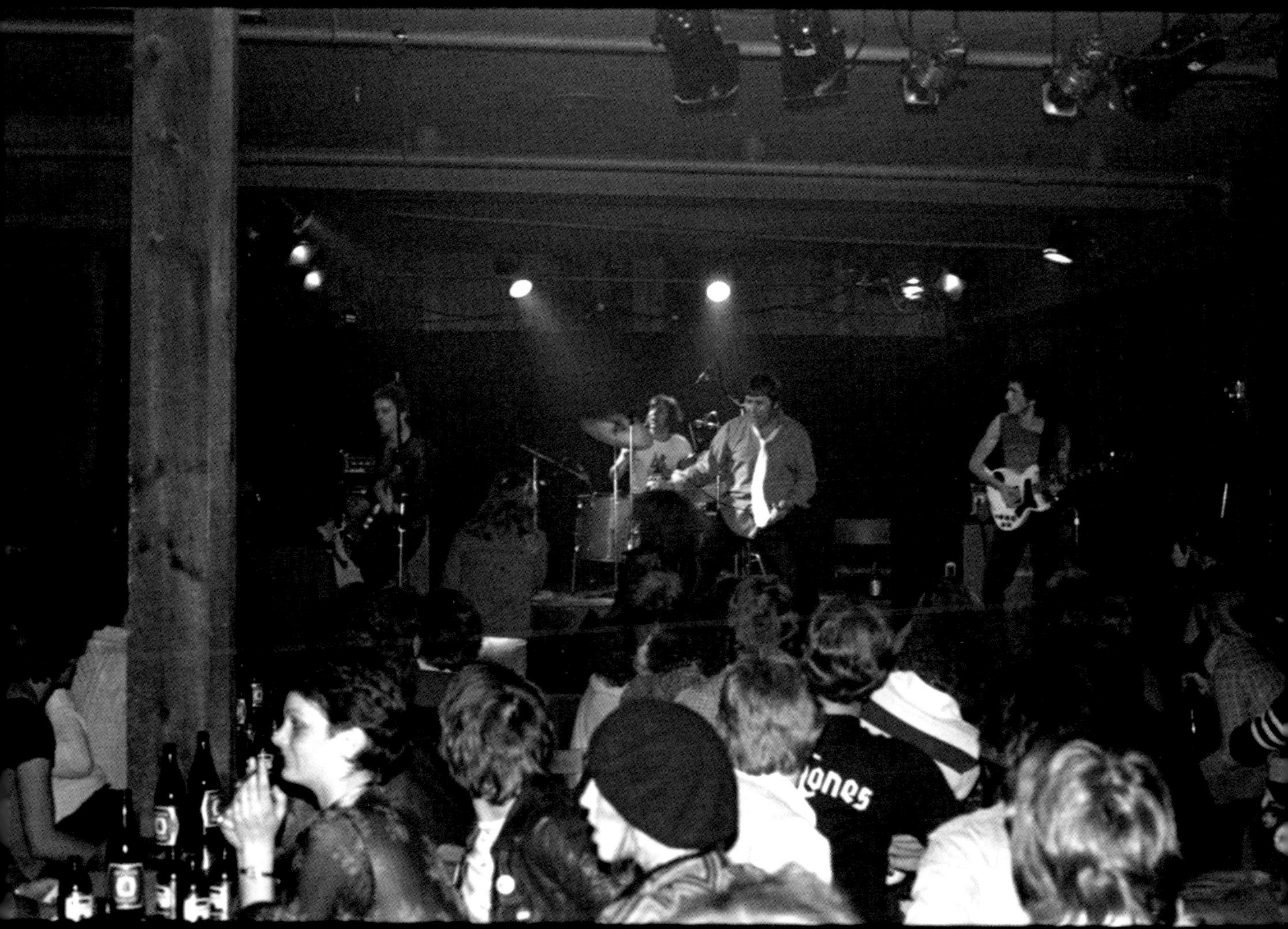

Tony Murray, Ronnie Bond, Reg Presley, Chris Britton

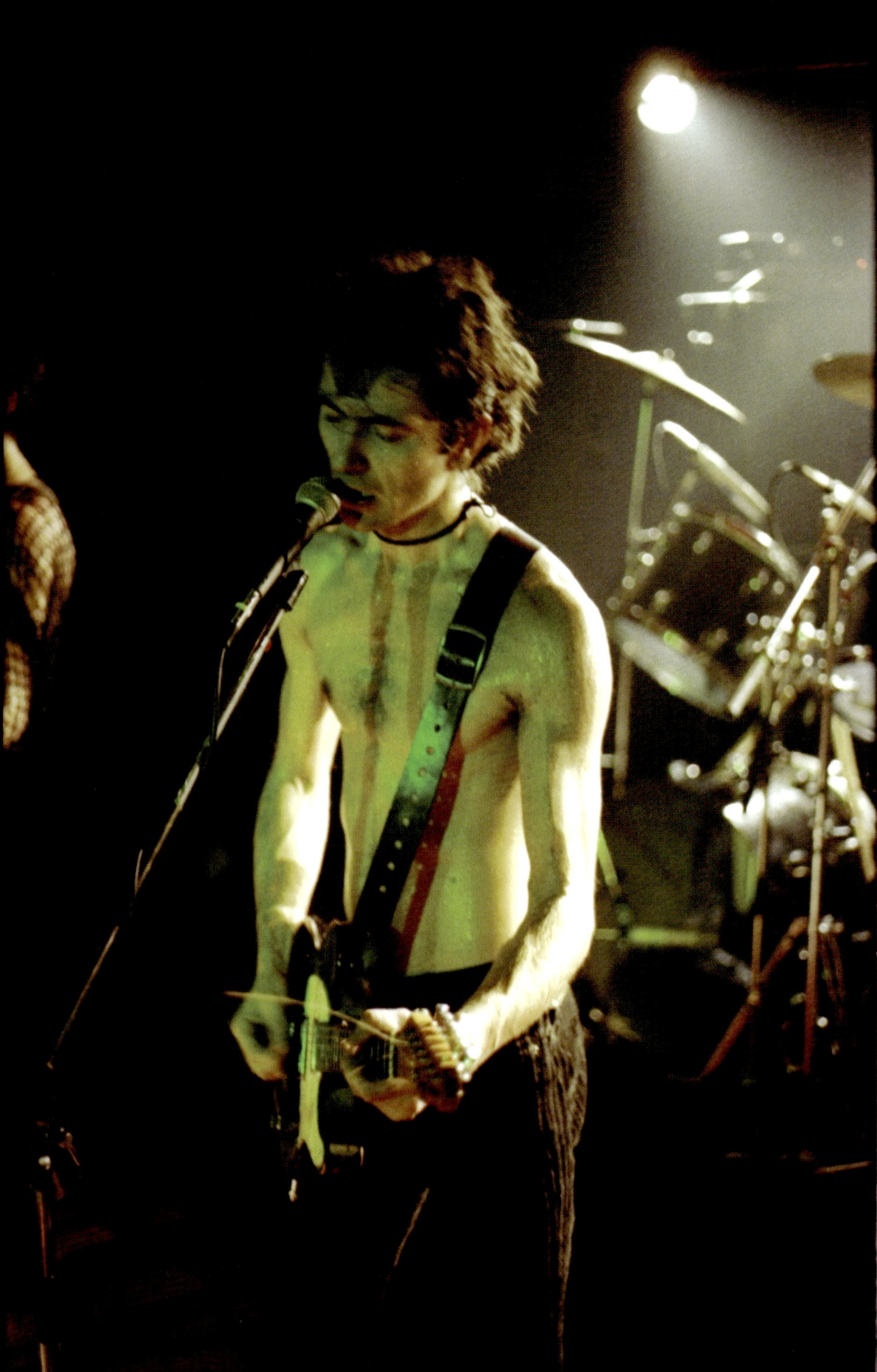

The Stranglers, Horseshoe Tavern, 1978

This show was packed mayhem. The Stranglers were in Toronto for the first time and about to release their third album, *Black and White*, and I recall the stage feeling very small, almost like it was being reshaped by the crowd filling every available inch. Pressed against the stage, we were the human barricade that prevented the surging audience from spilling onto it. Bouncer Tank pushed the audience back as my new friend Graham and I screamed along with the song on the PA, directing it back at Tank — "Little German boy! Being pushed around!" At some point, the only place for me to go if I was to move my arms to press the shutter release was up — onto the PA.

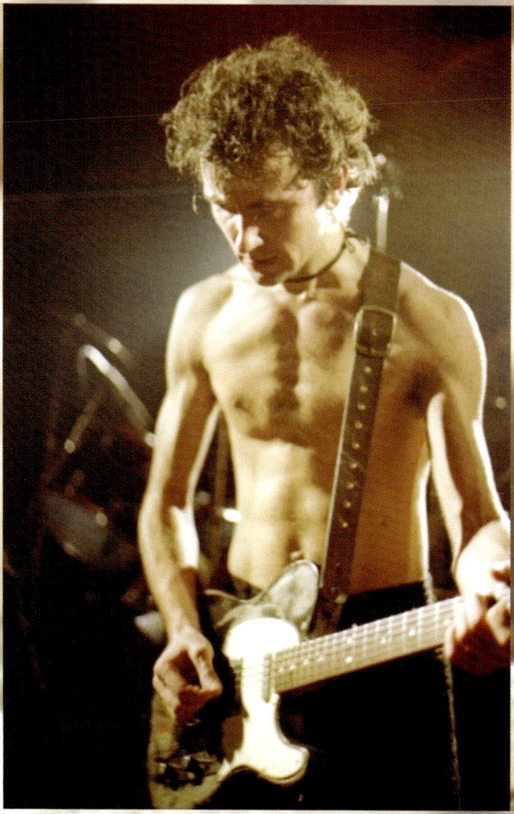

Hugh Cornwell

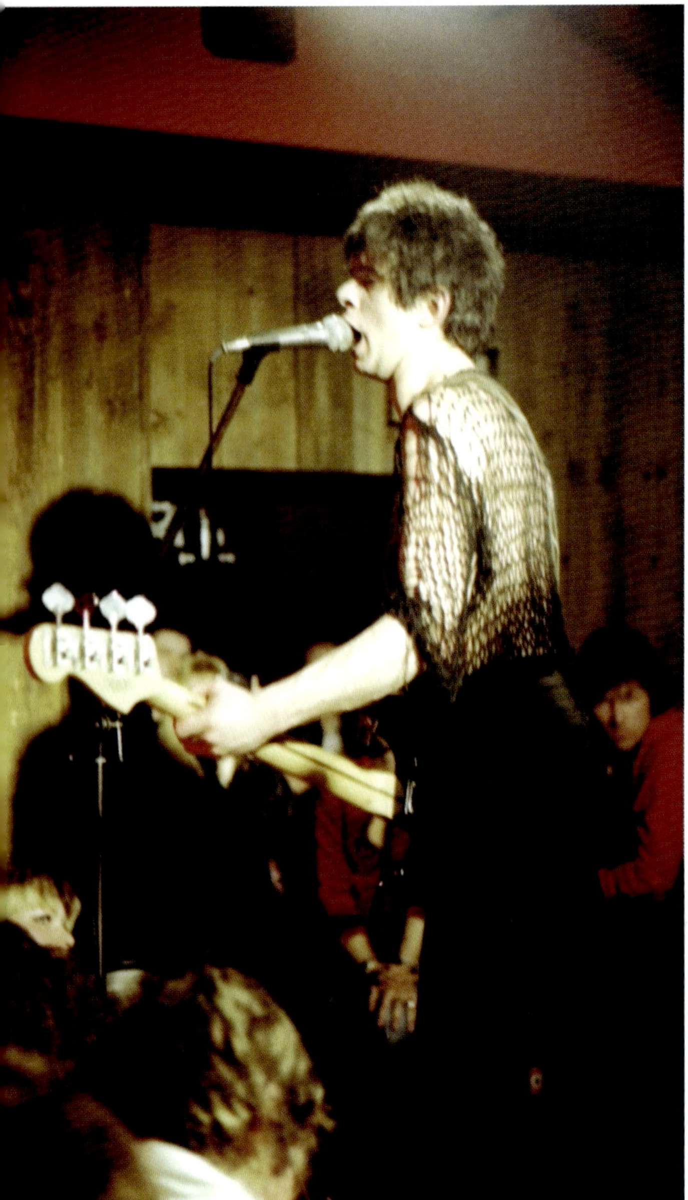

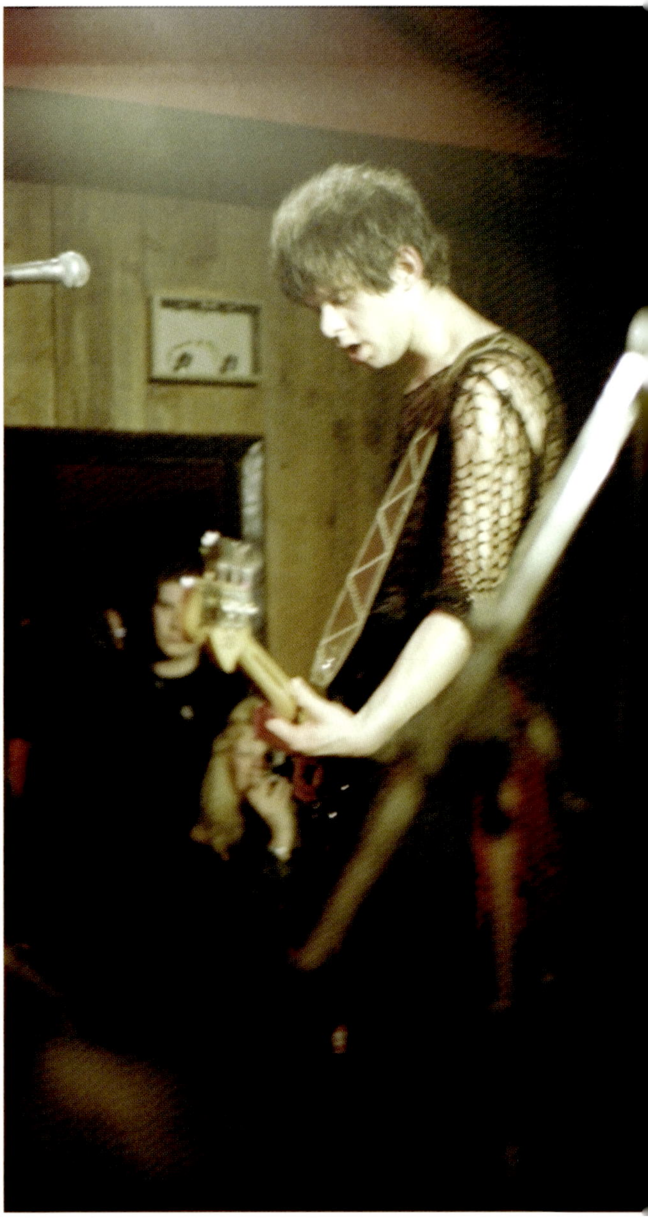

JJ Burnel

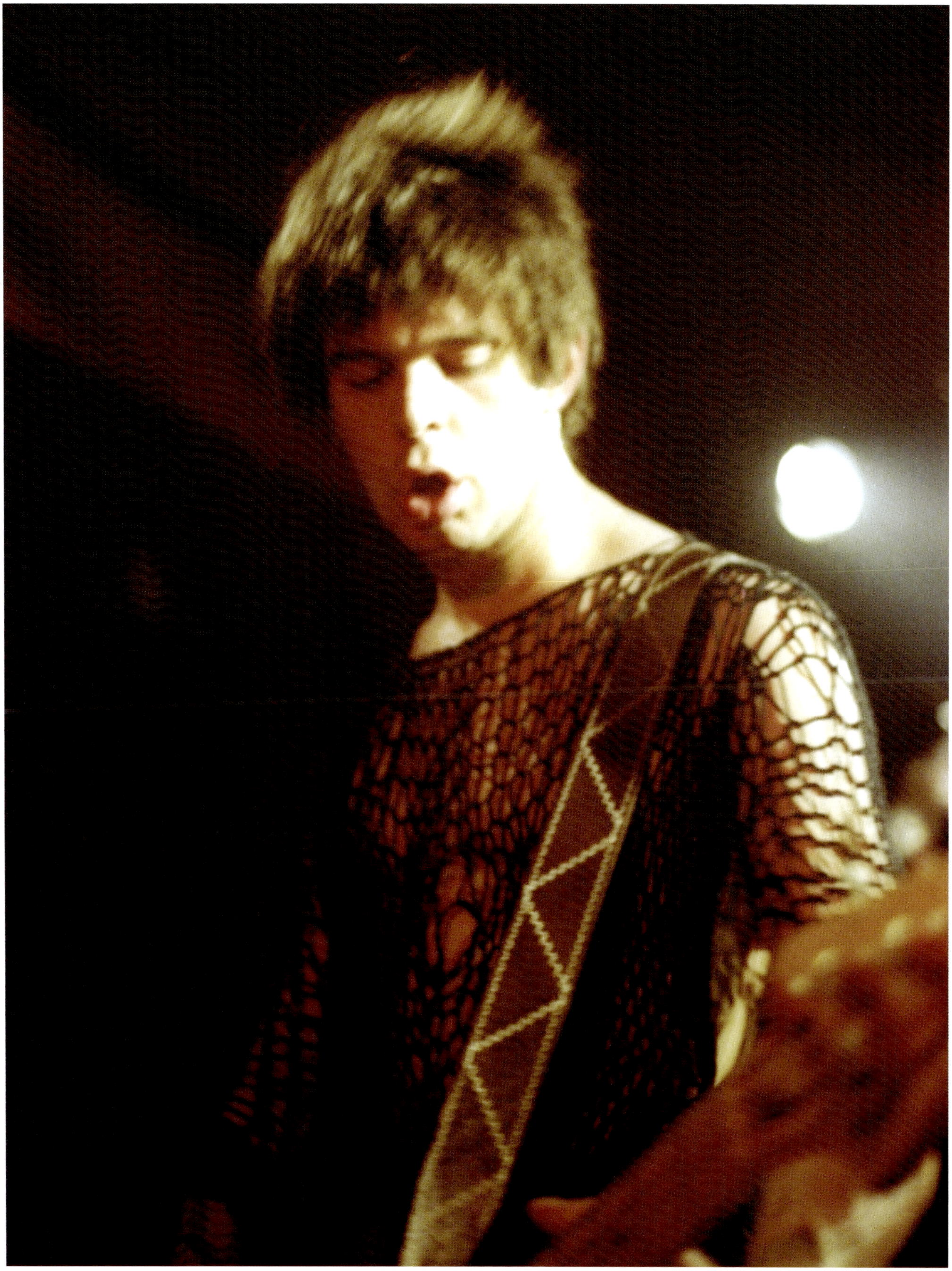

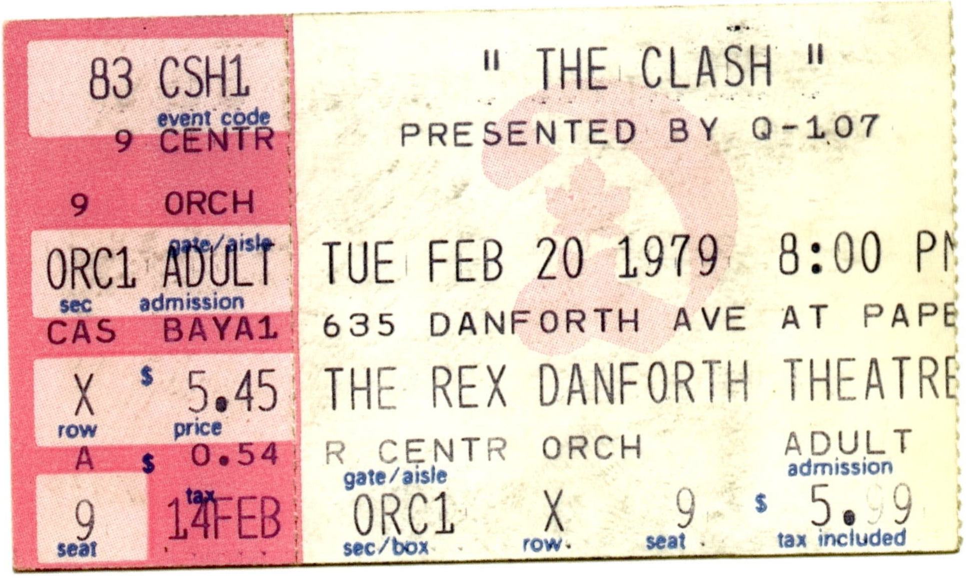

The Clash had an early foothold in Toronto by having their first album released in Canada but not in the U.S. until much later. With their second album *Give 'Em Enough Rope*, The Clash gave notice of their stadium aspirations. The contradictions apparent in The Clash made for interesting play between being "of the people" and enacting rock star fantasies.

To many factions, being a true "punk" meant following a rigid set of dress and behavioral codes, like not having long hair, wearing a black leather jacket and hating Pink Floyd. Any betrayal made you suspected of being a "poseur." When Mick Jones consorted with Ellen Foley, it brought him only one person removed from Meat Loaf, a sin even worse than making a triple album. Wearing pseudo-militaristic clothing hardly made The Clash revolutionaries, and when they played the Rex Danforth Theatre, the last-minute cancellation of the scheduled local all-boy opening band in favor of the all-girl B-Girls — one of whom was allegedly involved with one of The Clash — was but one crumbling brick in the illusory foundation of the revolution. Maybe The Clash really were just rock stars after all, and their songs against capitalism and class structure were a way to pull in chicks.

There was no denying their power as a live band when they debuted in Toronto at a Greek movie theater rarely used for rock shows. The crowd surged to the front, sardine-ing for position. As the view became more and more obstructed, I climbed up and stood with my feet straddling the arms of my theater seat, putting me at eye level with the band.

The Clash, Rex Danforth Theatre, 1979

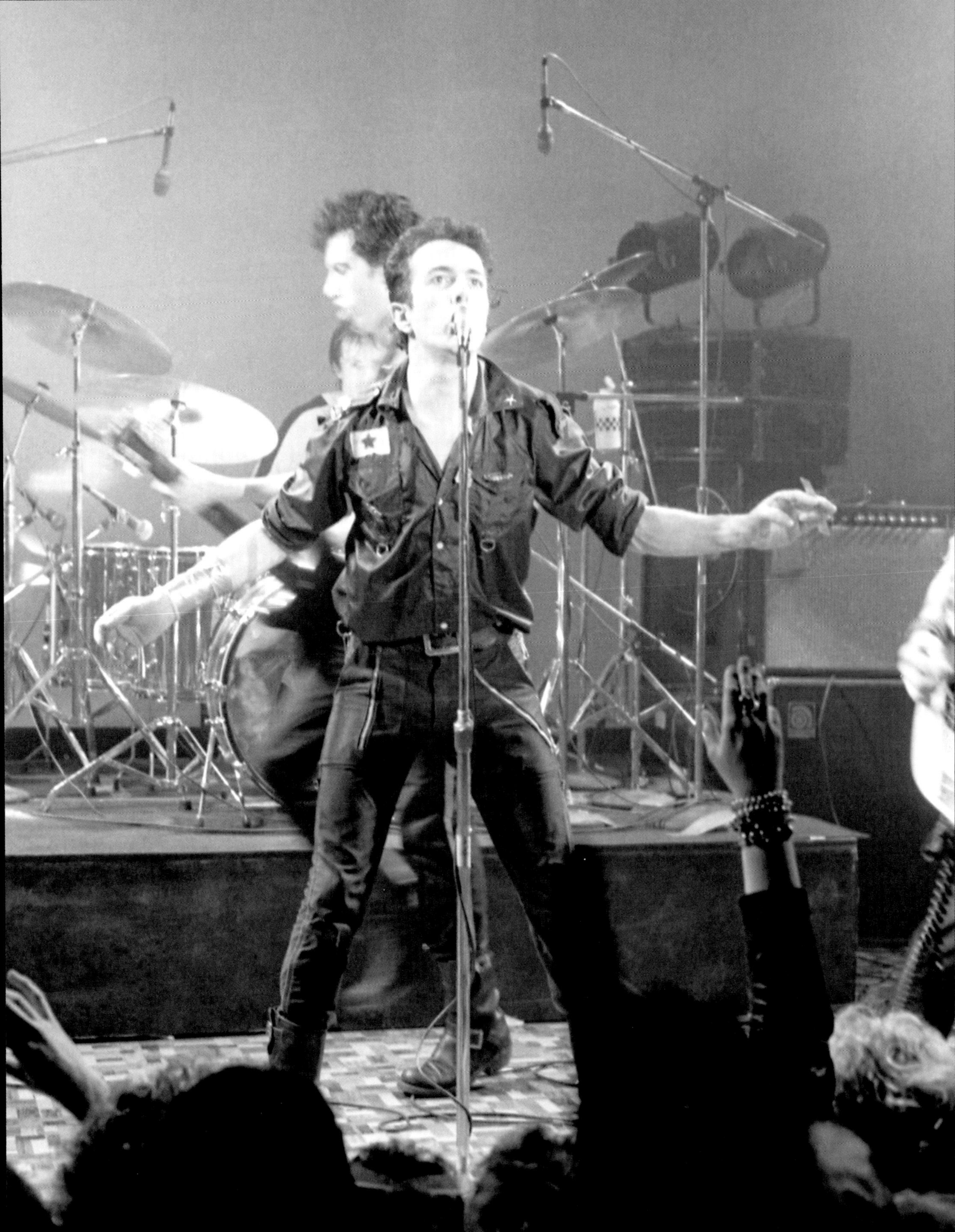

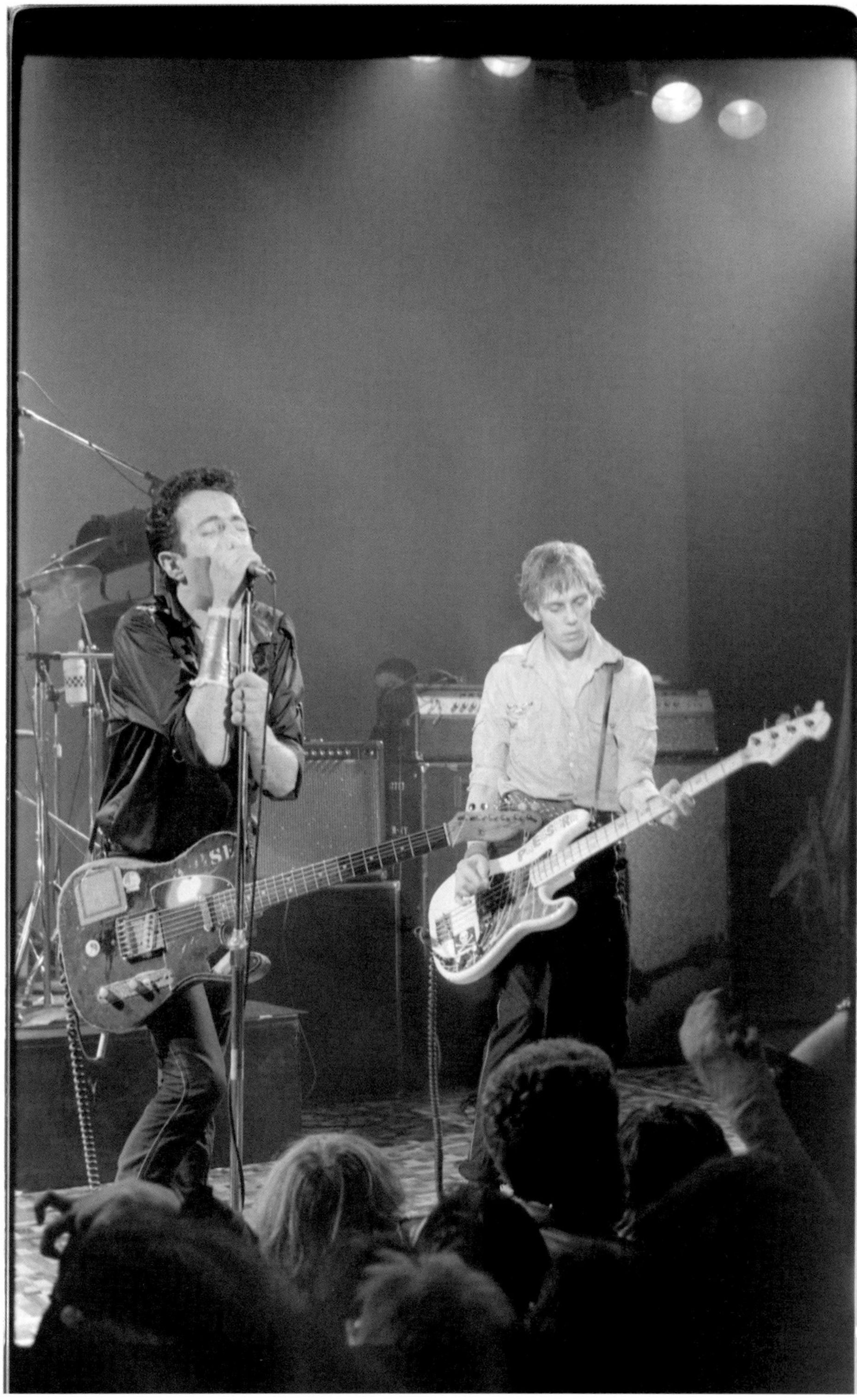

Joe Strummer, Paul Simonon

Mick Jones, Joe Strummer

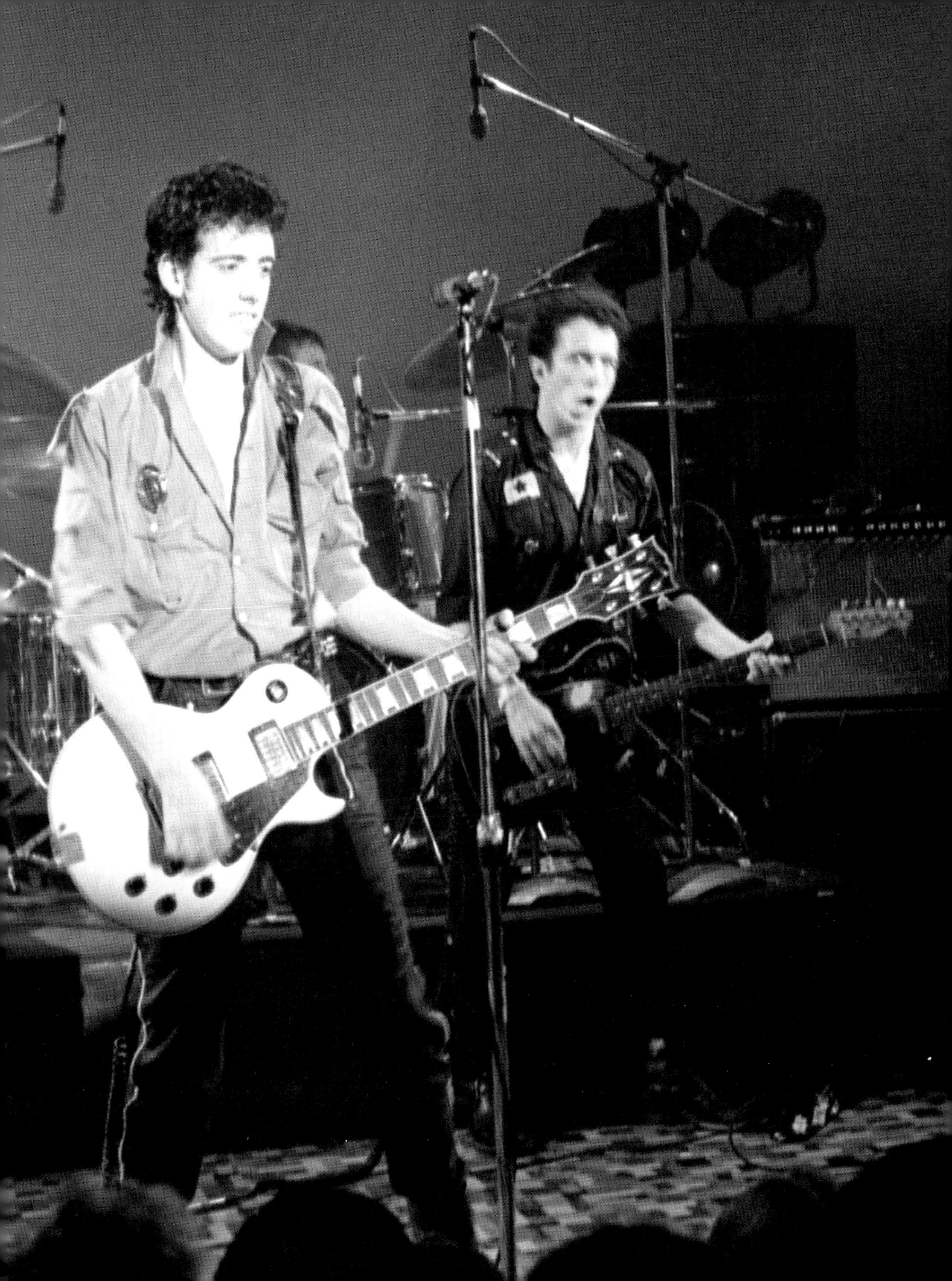

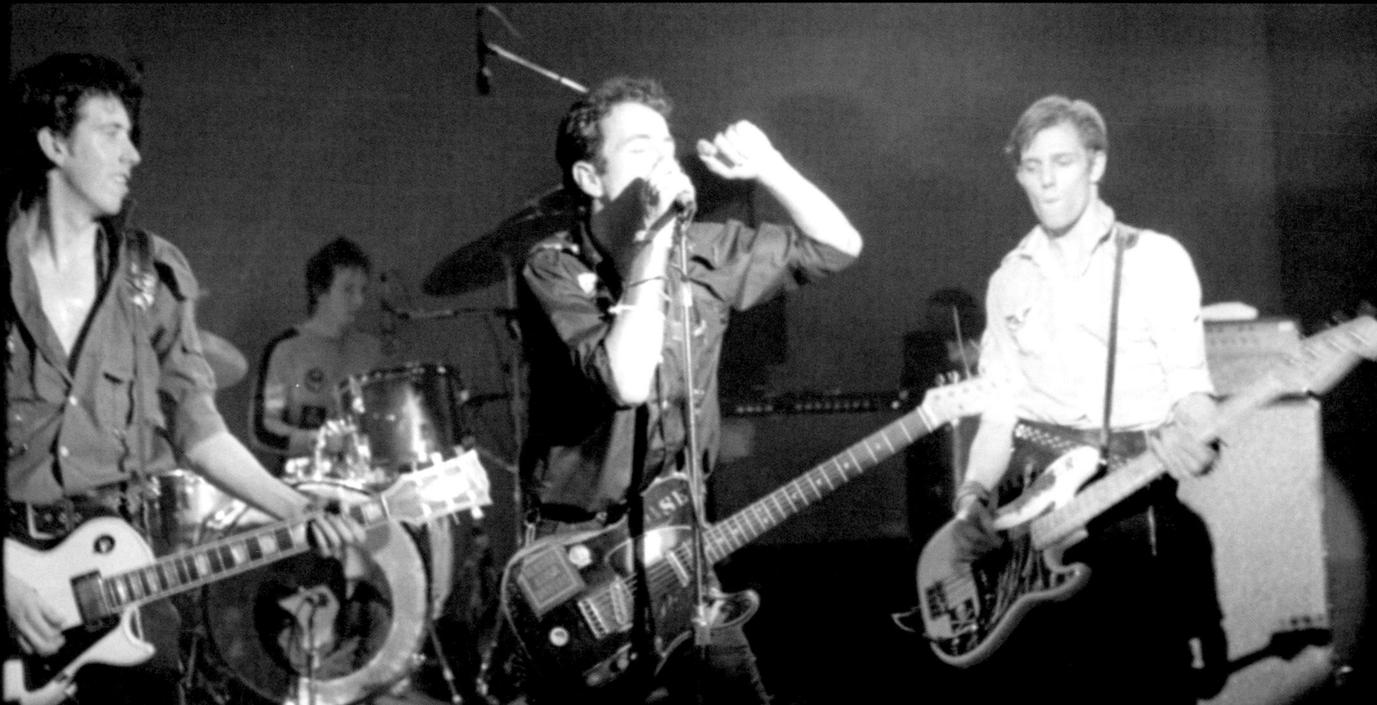

Mick Jones, Topper Headon, Joe Strummer, Paul Simonon

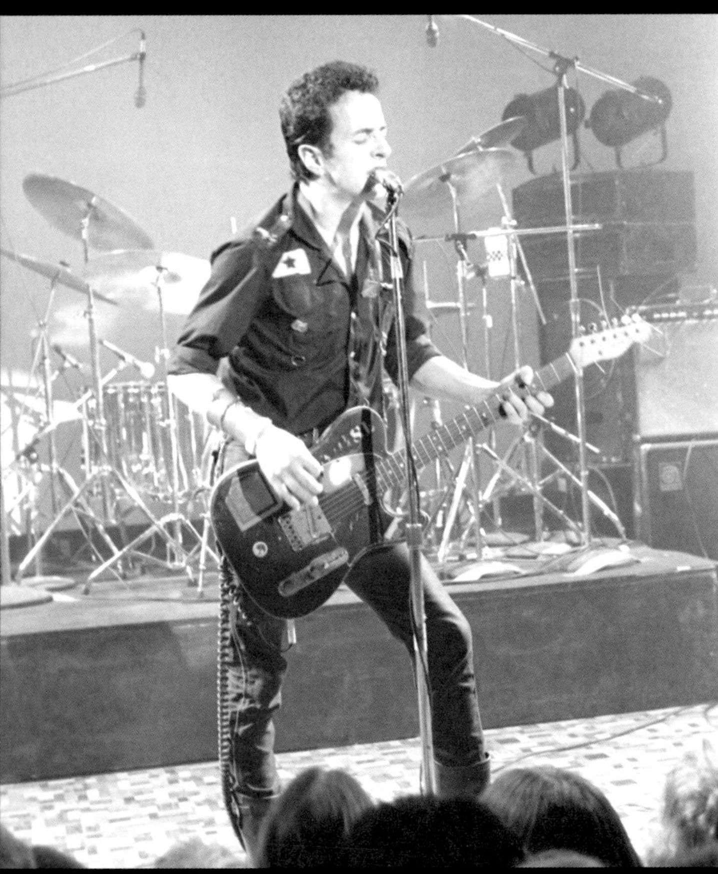

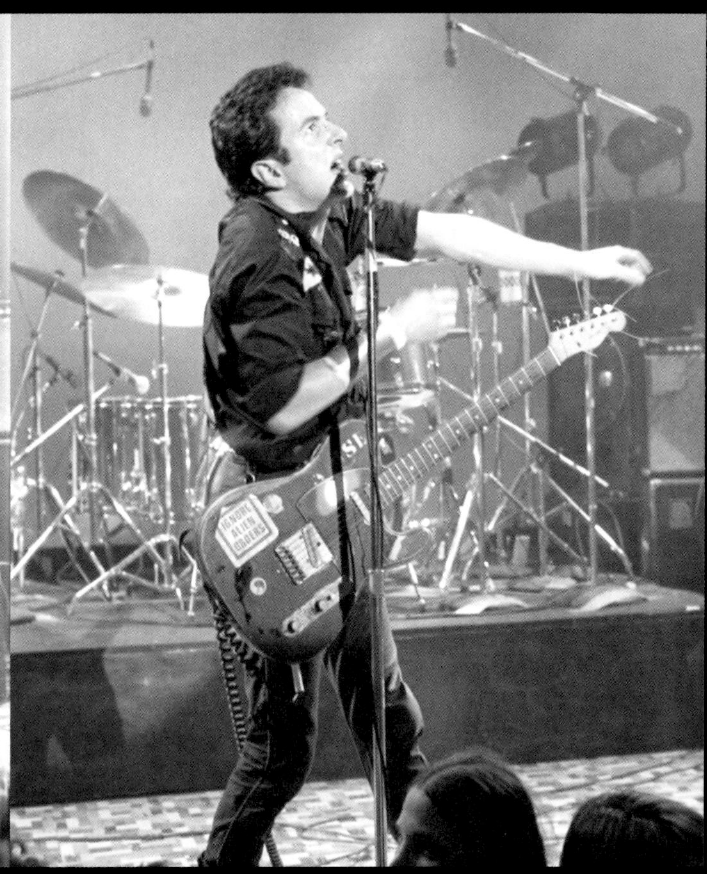

Joe Strummer

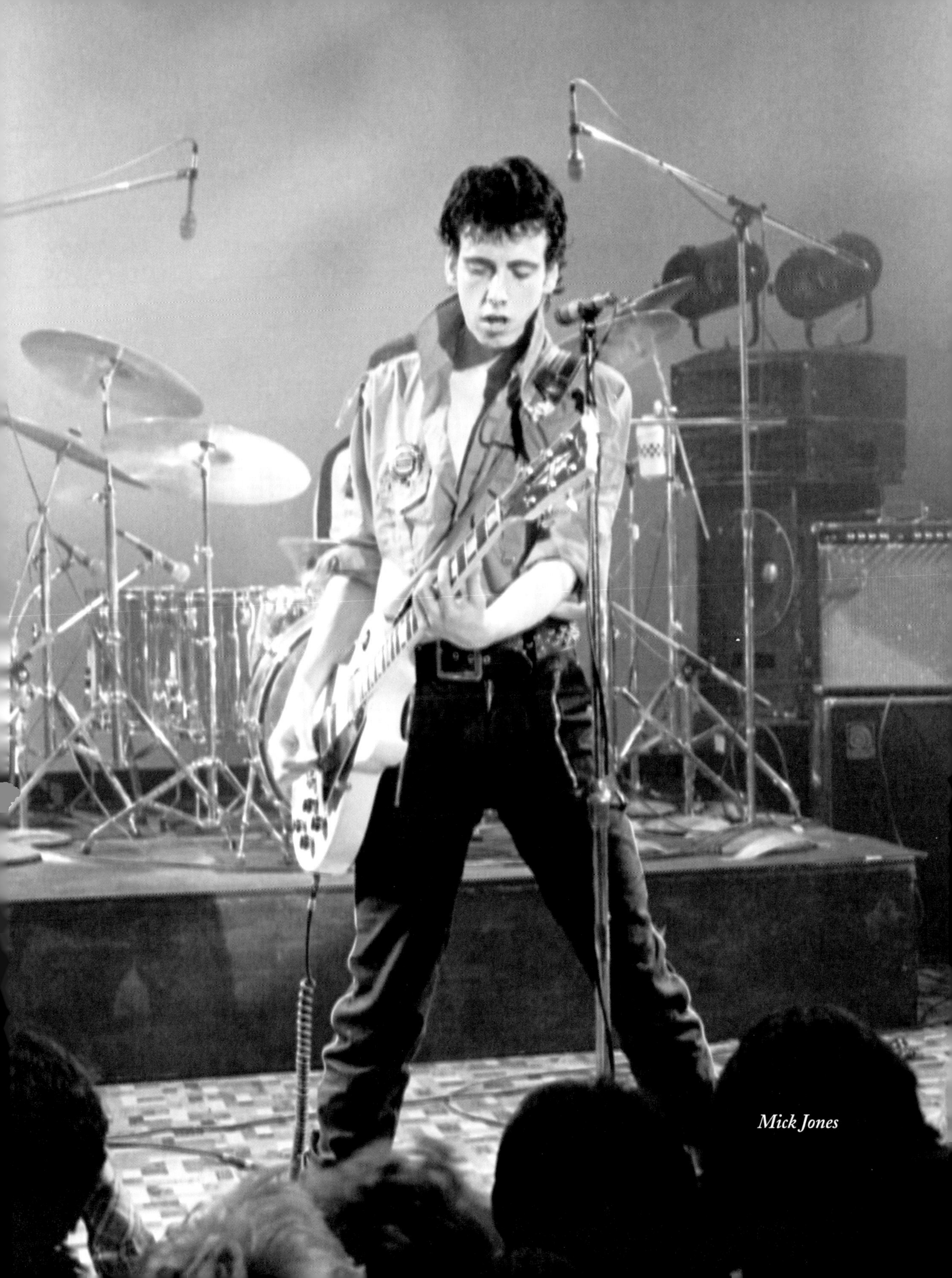

Mick Jones

The Damned, El Mocambo, 1979

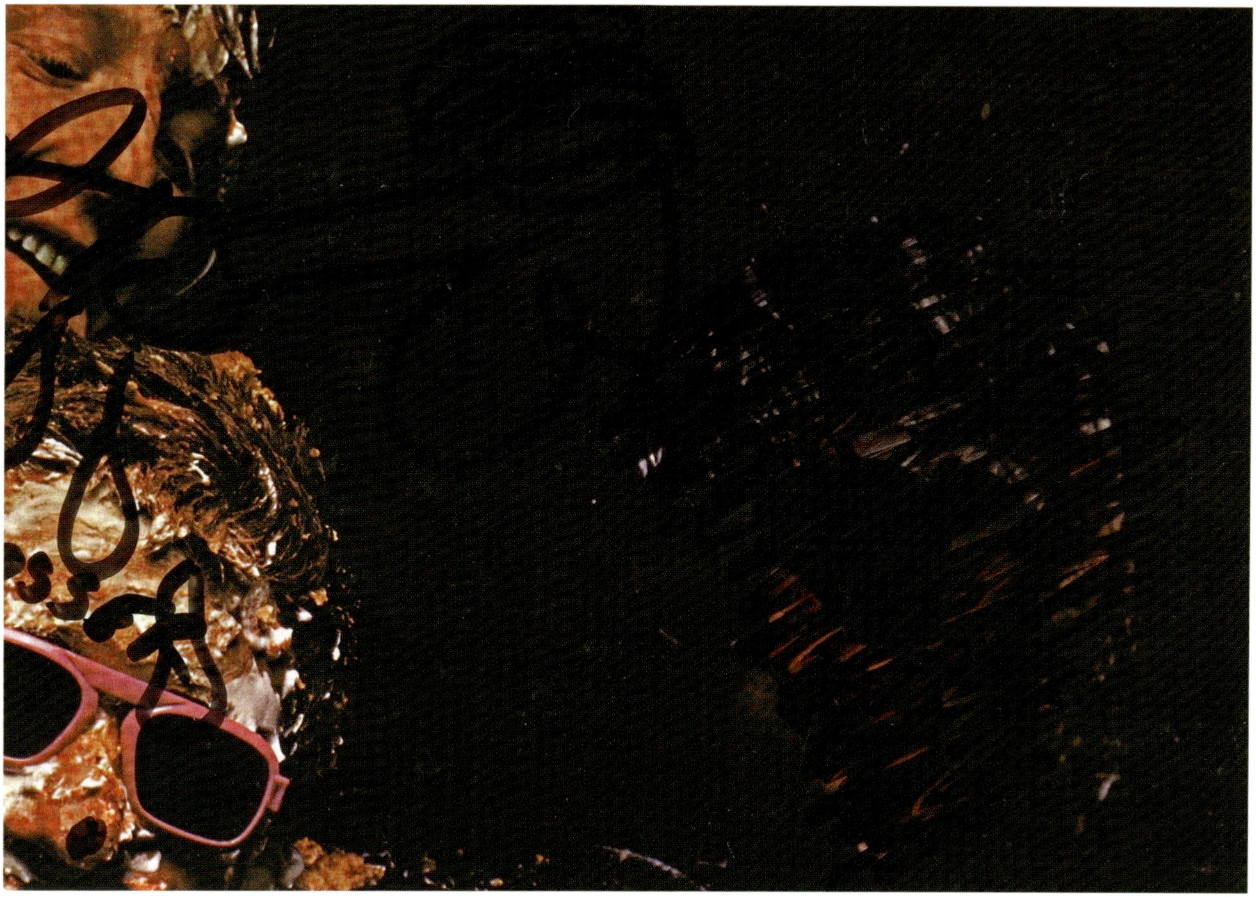

Before their set, drummer Rat Scabies was gathering drinks from fans and chatting with people in the bar. His reputation for smashing drum kits was well known so a friend asked if he was going to smash it tonight. Rat said if we gave him $50, he'd do it. We set about gathering sponsors, but gave up at about $23 and used the money for our own drinks instead.

The Damned were using some gear, including the drums, of the opening band Rex Chainbelt, a terrible pop rock band that featured some ex-members of The Poles. As Rat left the stage, we grabbed his arm and said, "But you said you were going to smash the drums!" He looked at us and mumbled, "Oh yeah," turned back to the stage and began trashing the kit. We giggled as Rex Chainbelt's drummer ran to the stage in tears, trying to stop him.

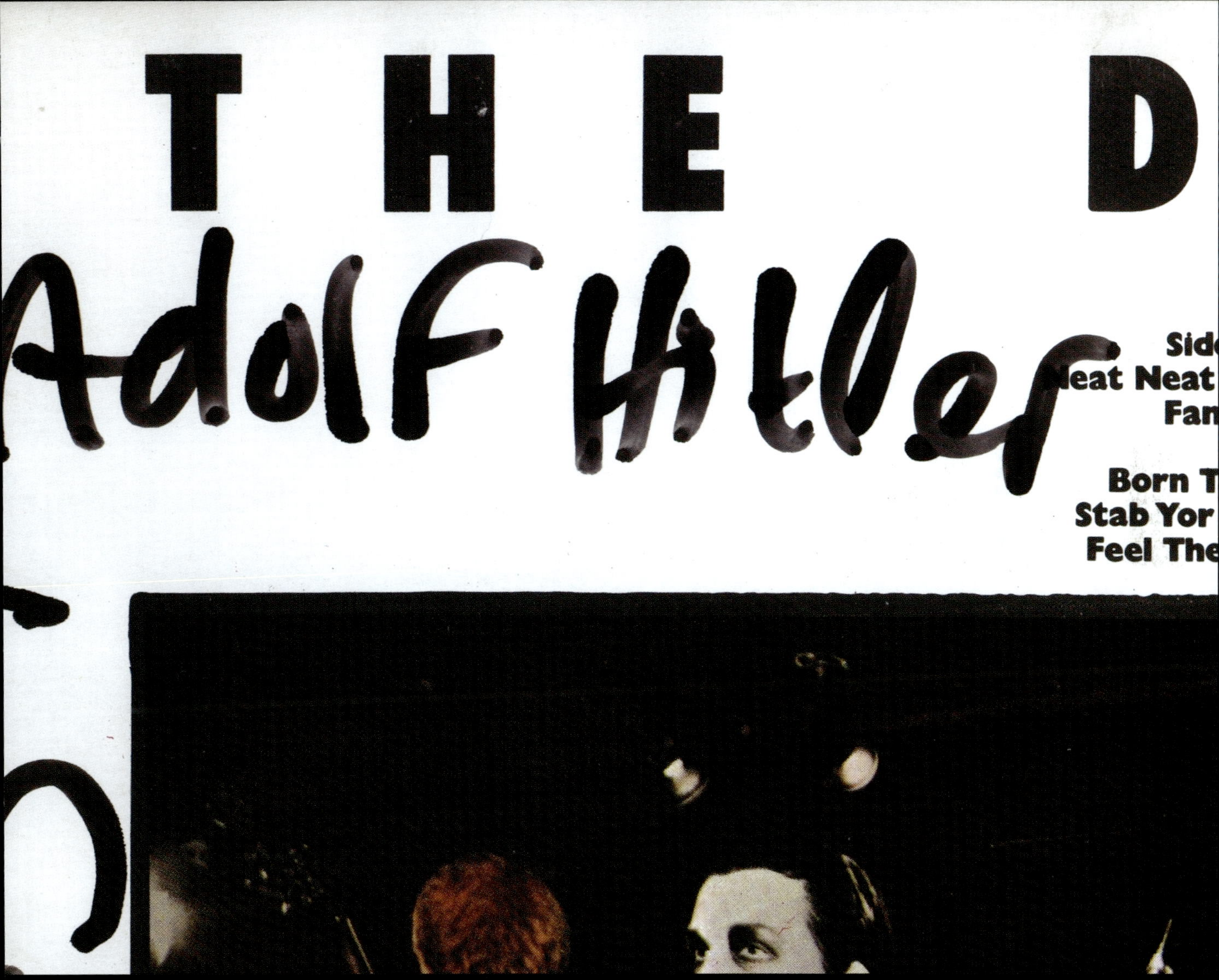
THE D
Adolf Hitler
Side
Neat Neat
Fan
Born T
Stab Yor
Feel The

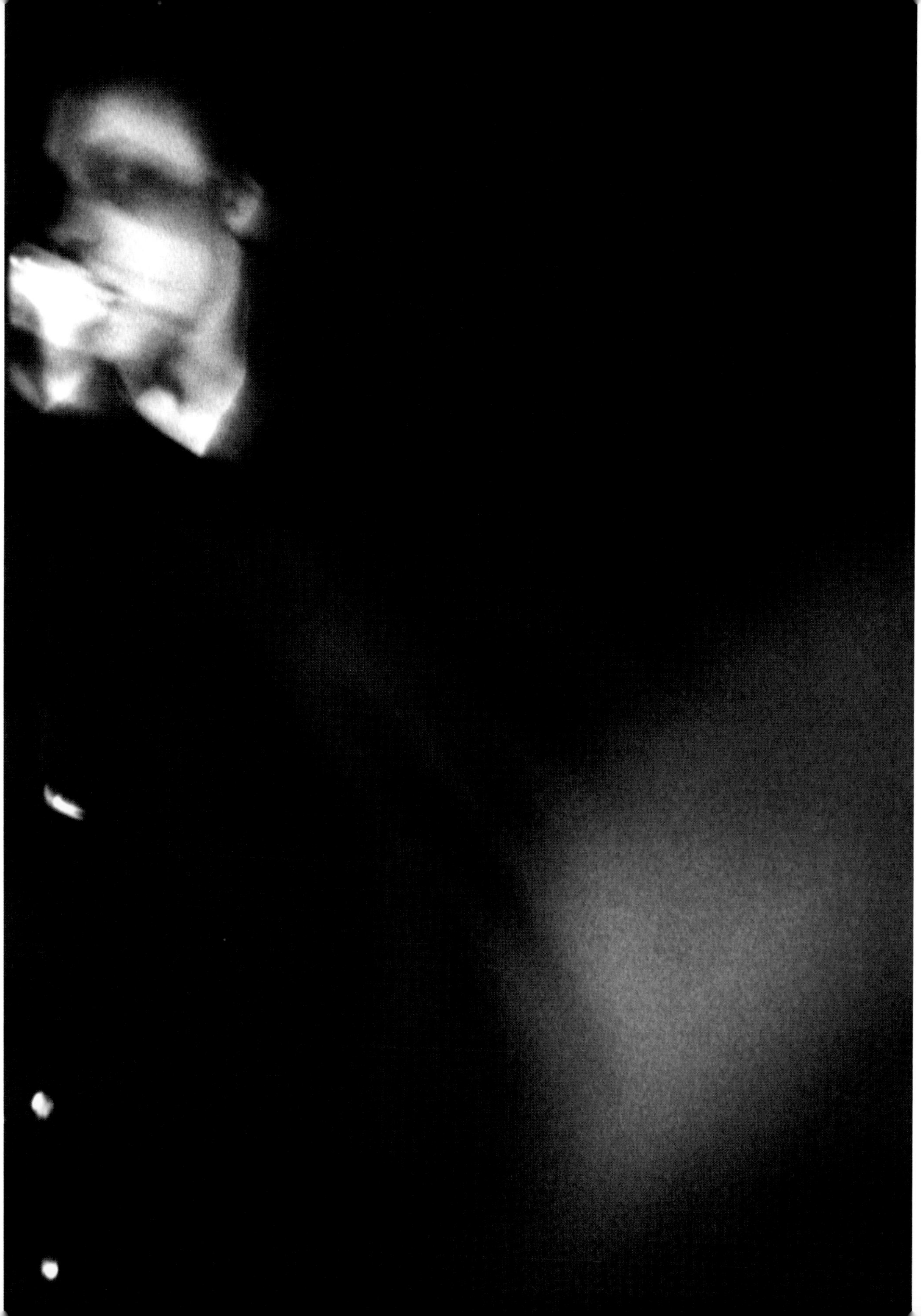

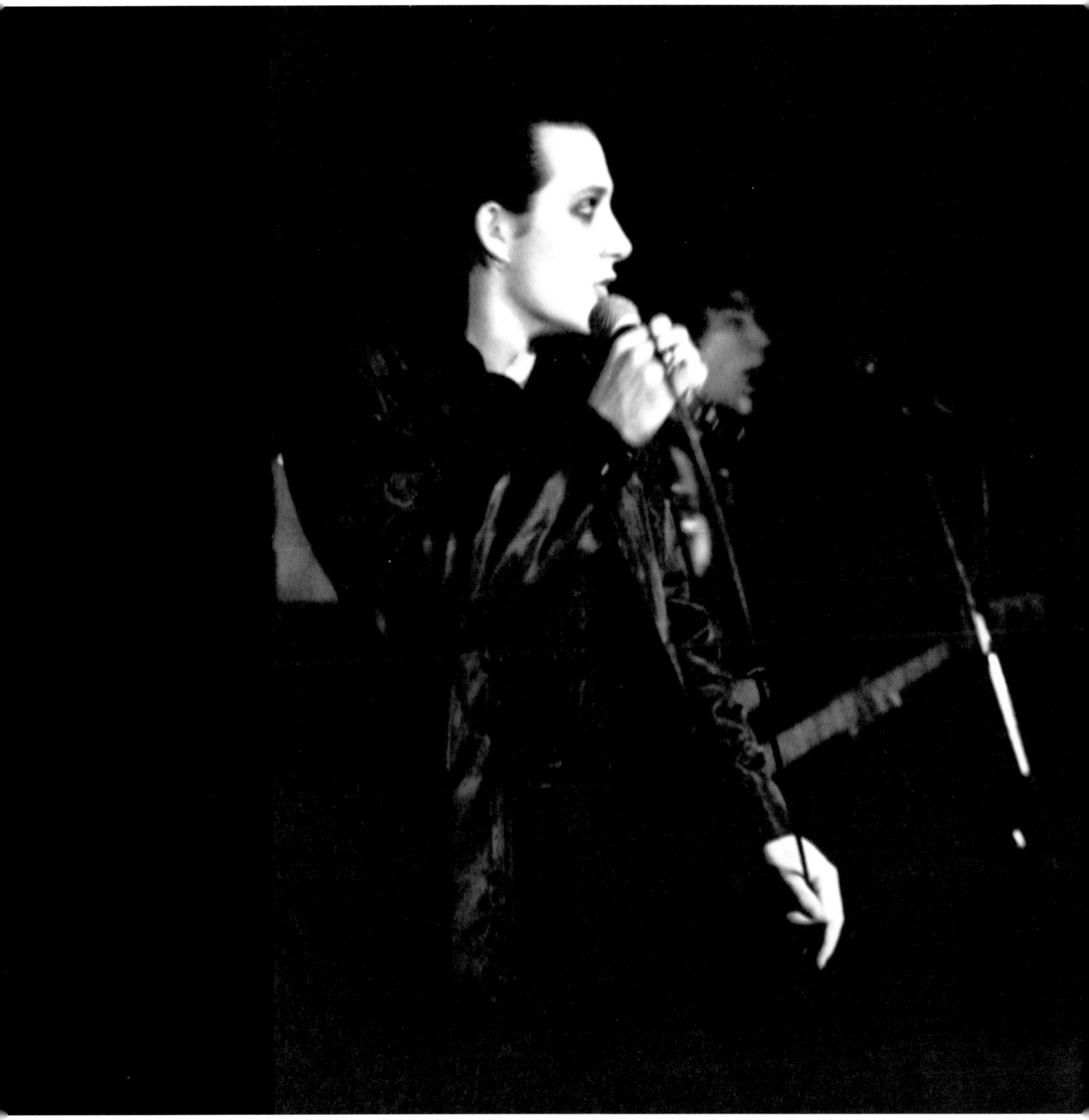

Dave Vanian, Algy Ward

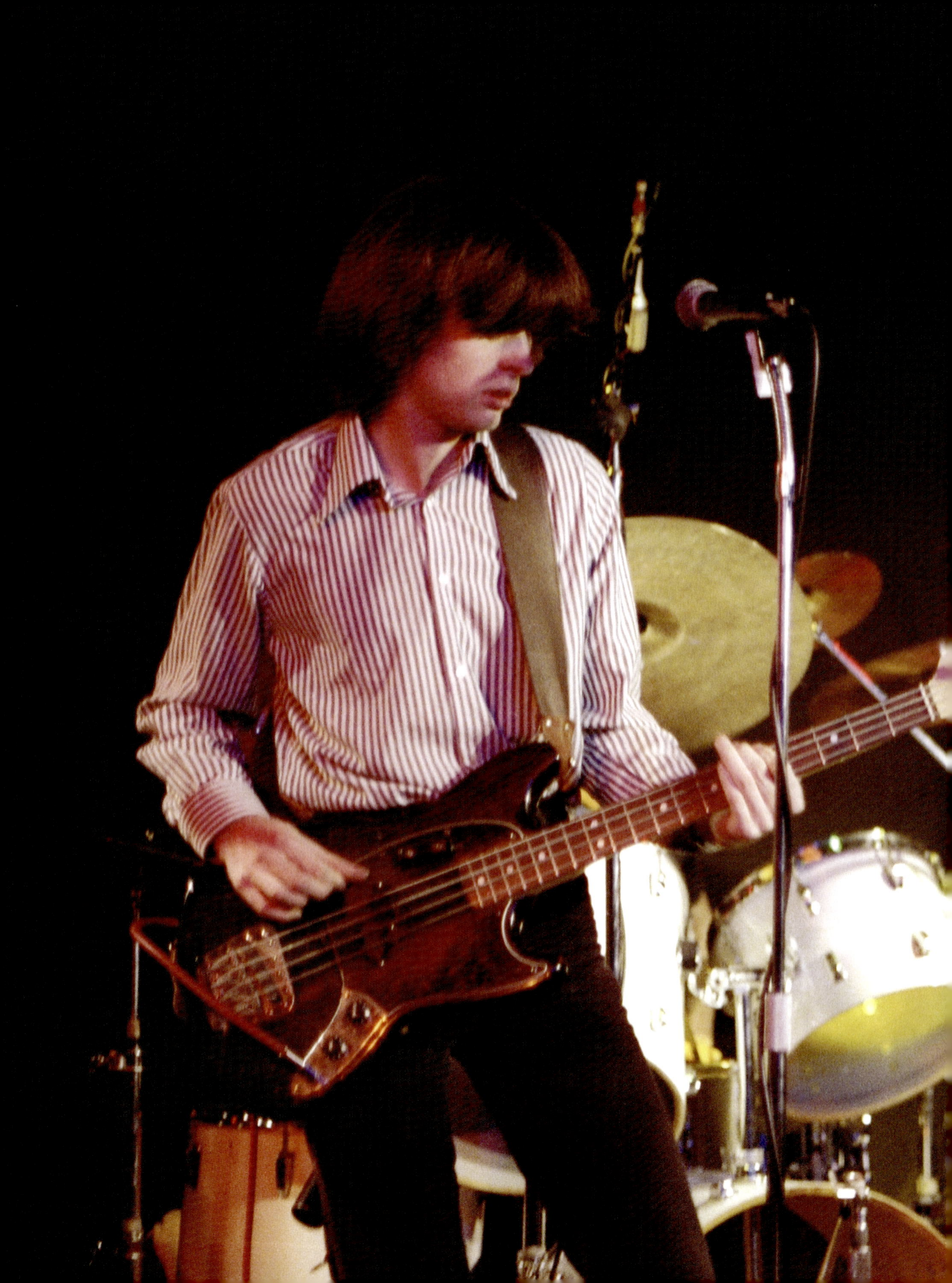

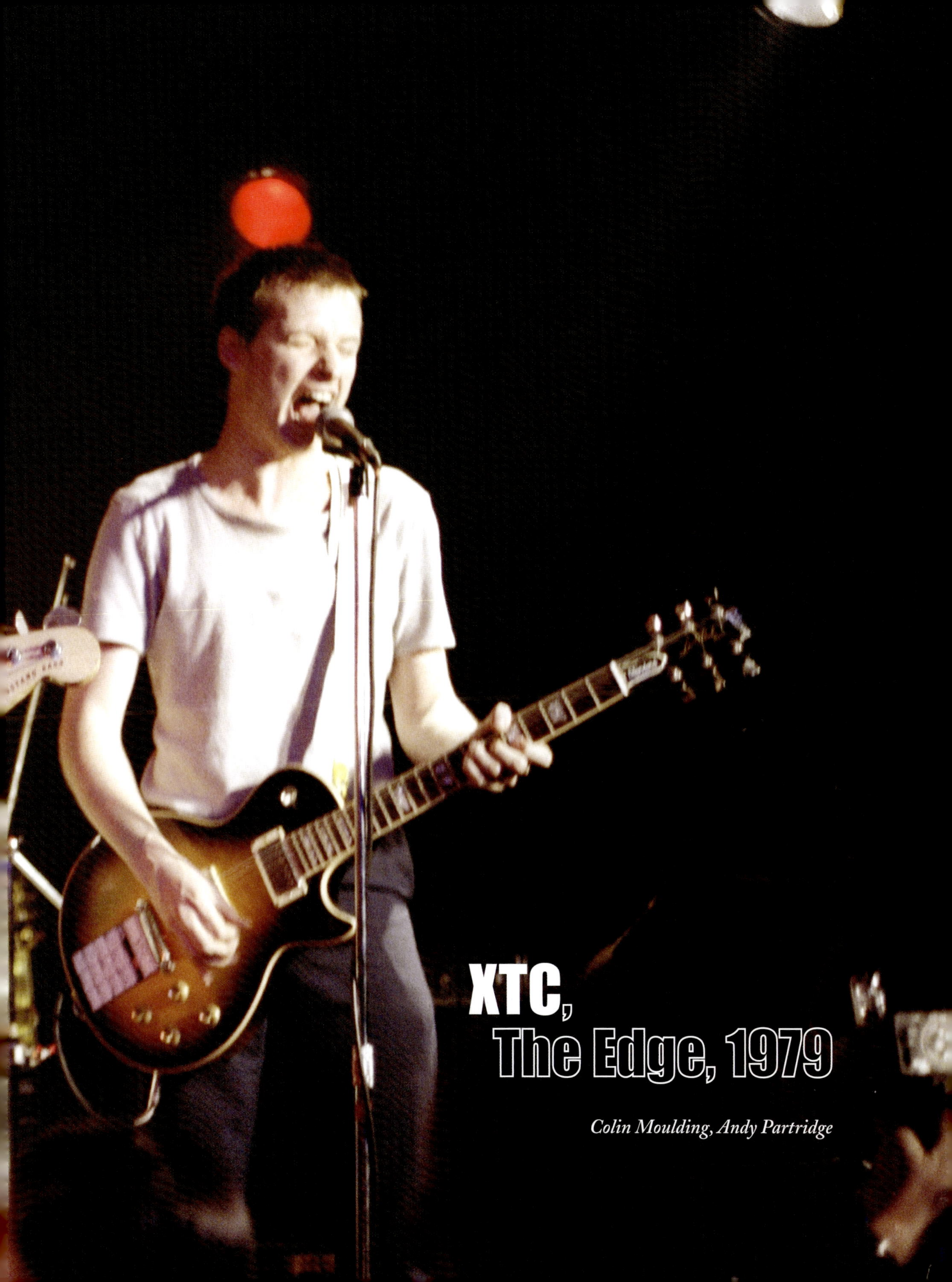

XTC, The Edge, 1979

Colin Moulding, Andy Partridge

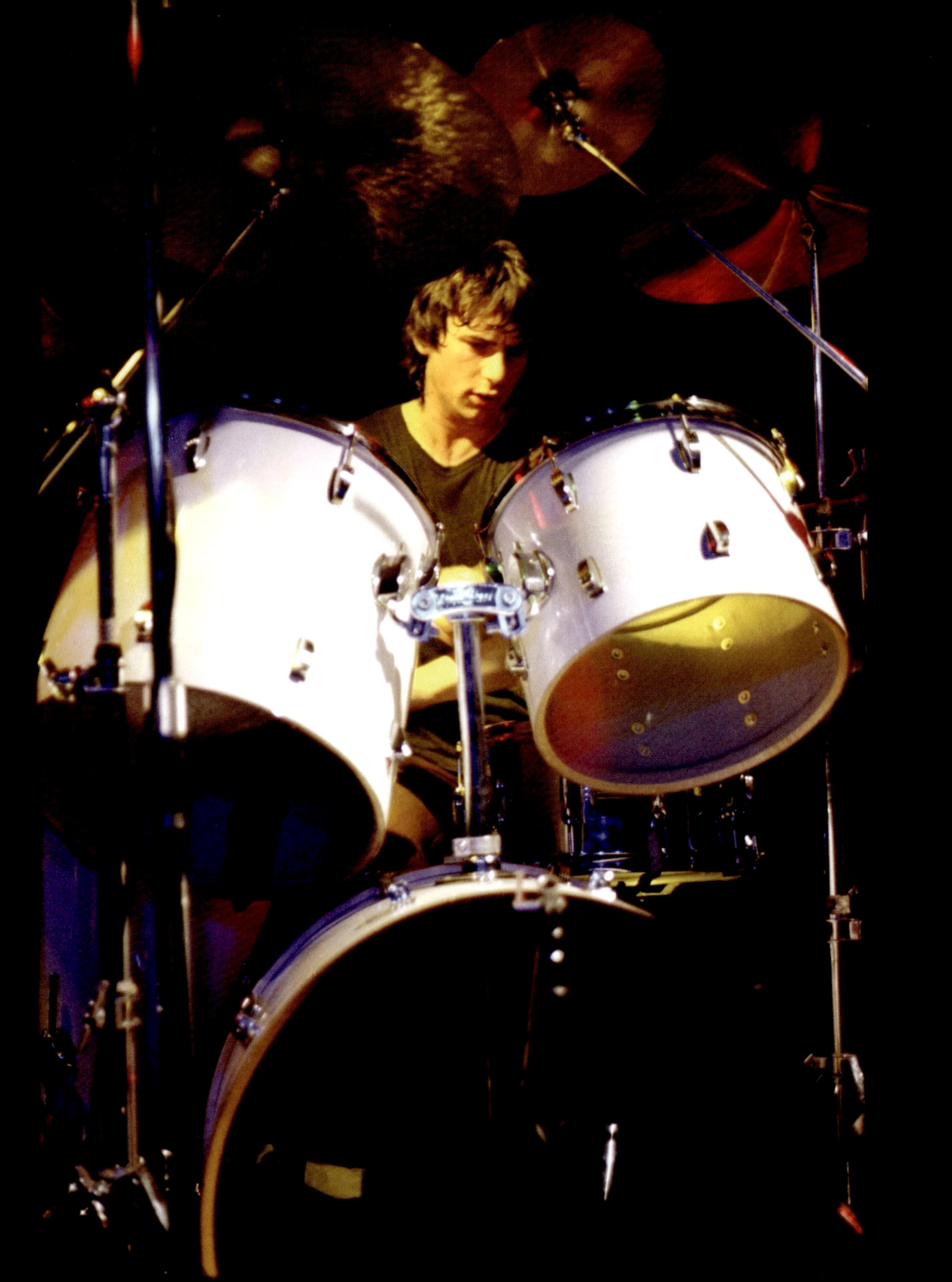

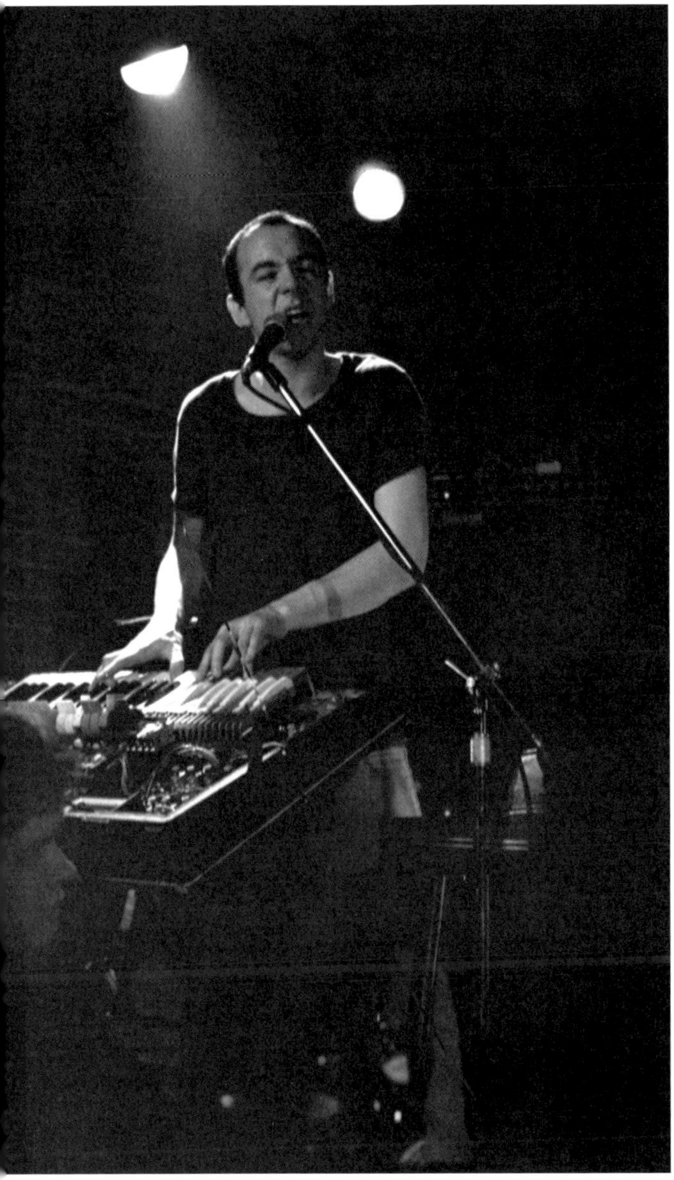

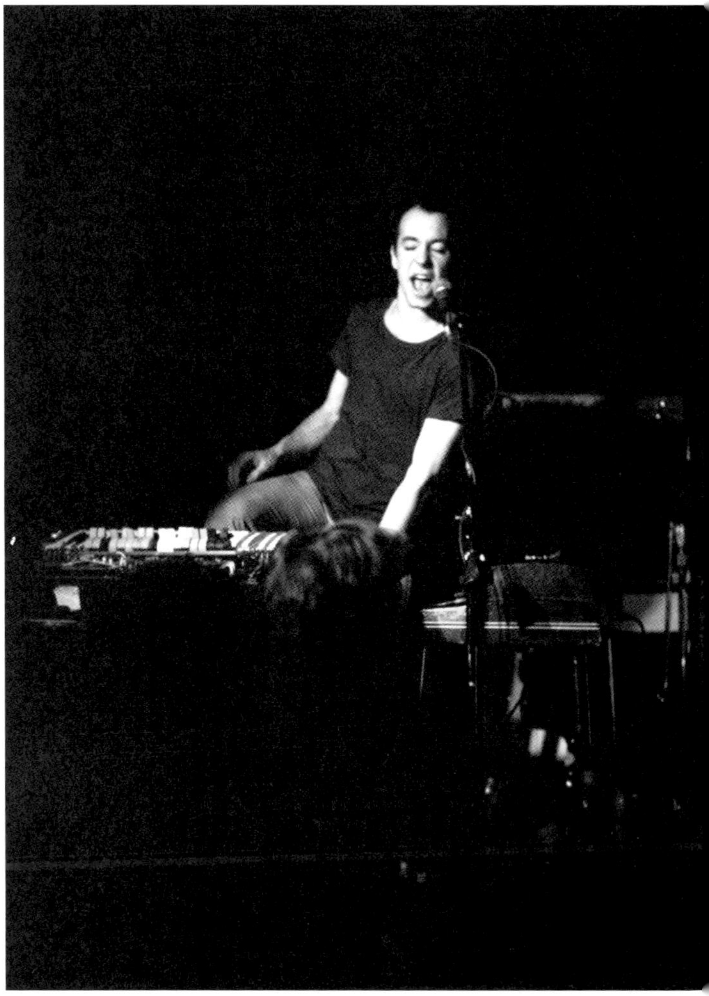

Barry Andrews

This was in their earliest incarnation, when Barry Andrews still played keyboards with them, around the time of *Go 2*. Andrews's organ had its outer body removed and throughout the set, he stuck a screwdriver inside and squeezed even more out of the squealing thing. His discordant soulful angularity was a big part of what made the band great to me at this time.

Terry Chambers

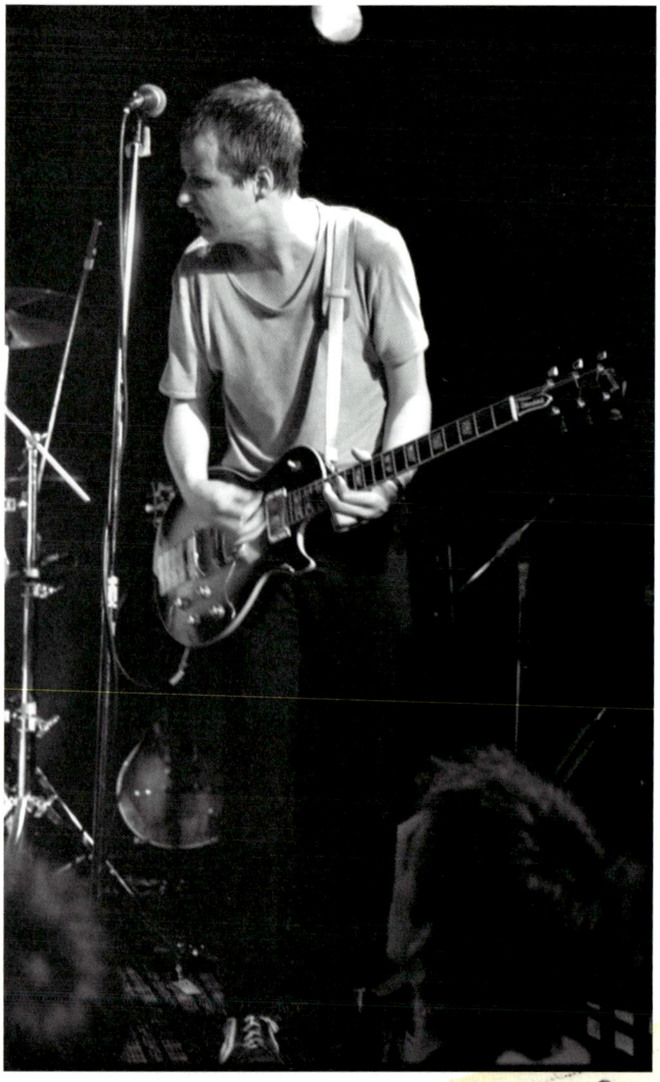

Andy Partridge

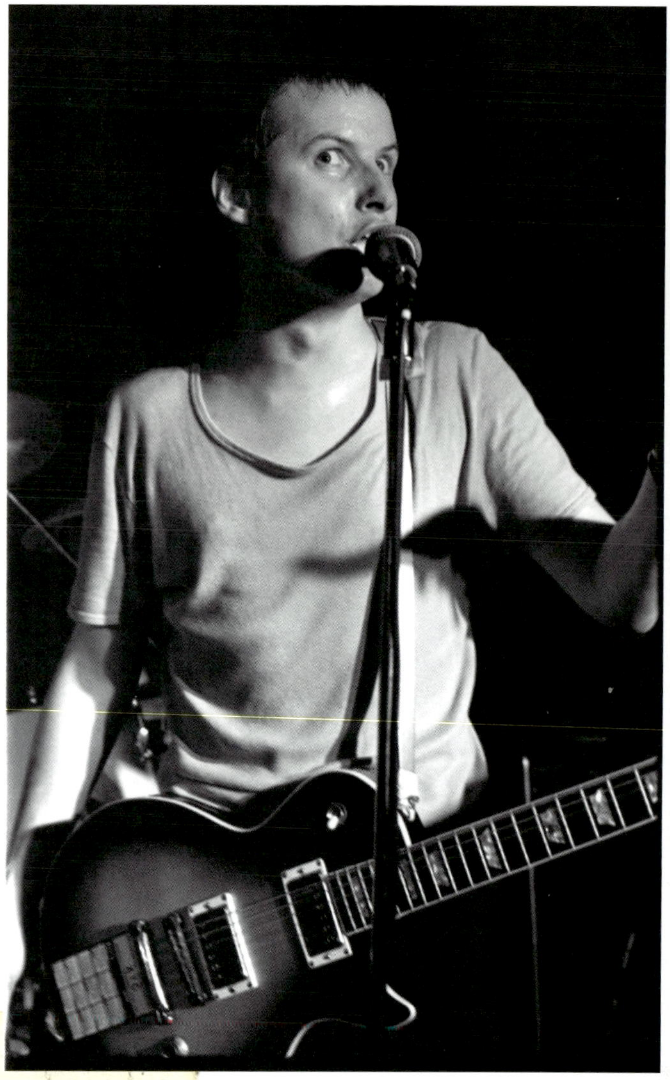

Colin Moulding

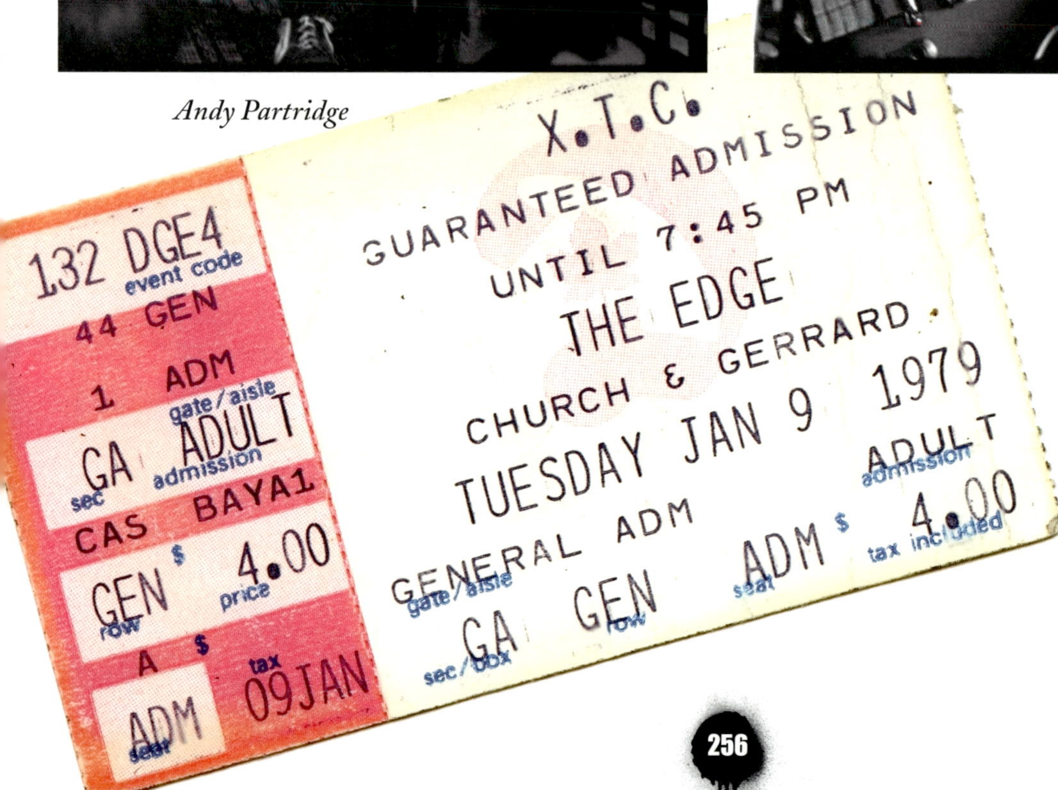

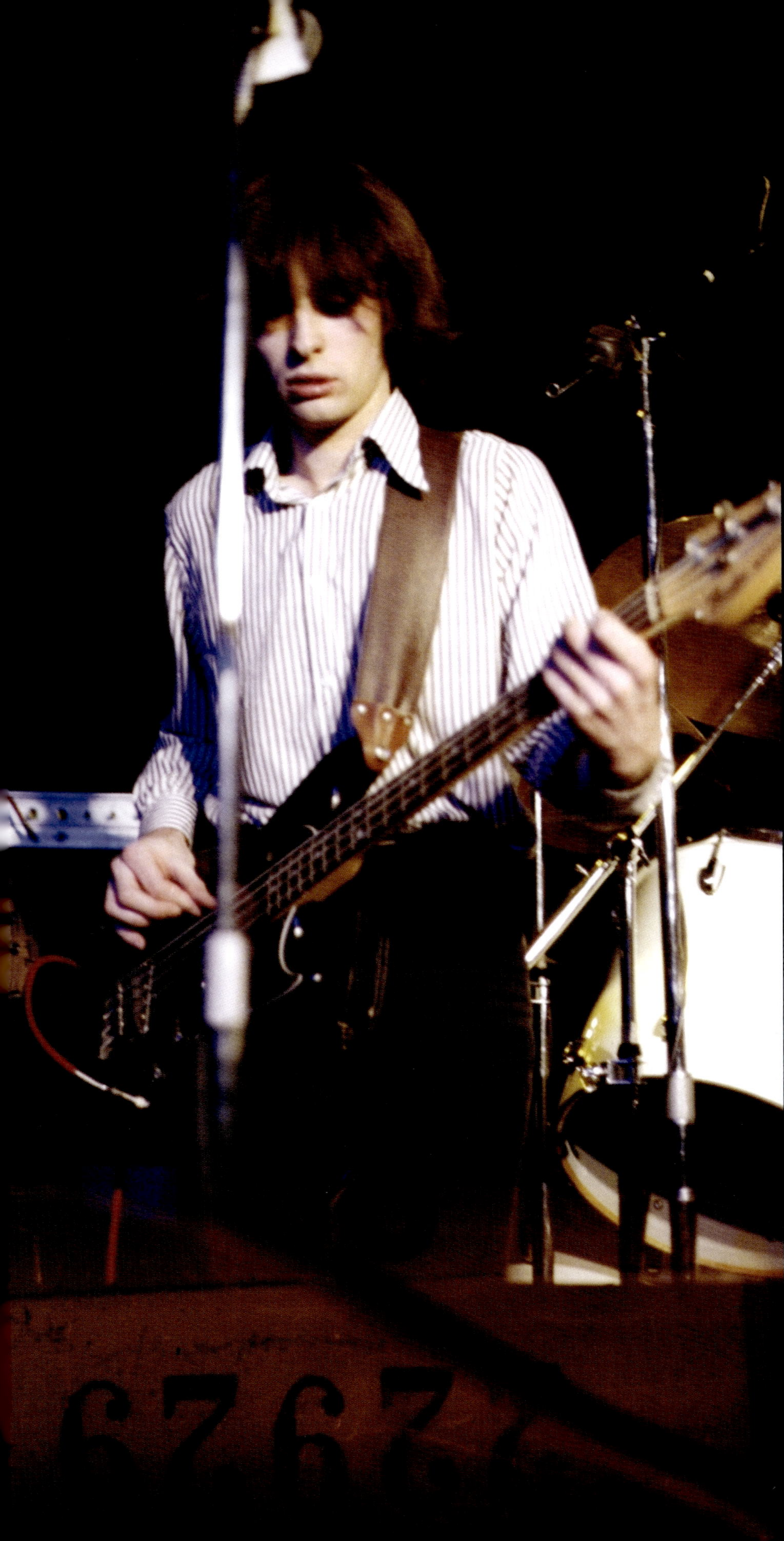

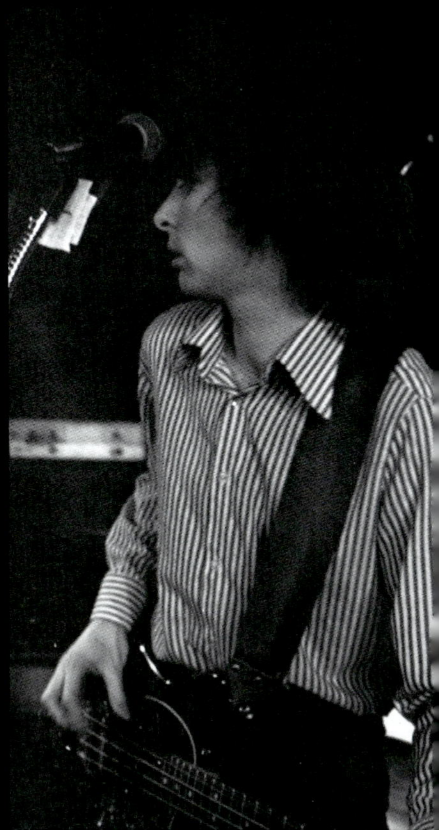

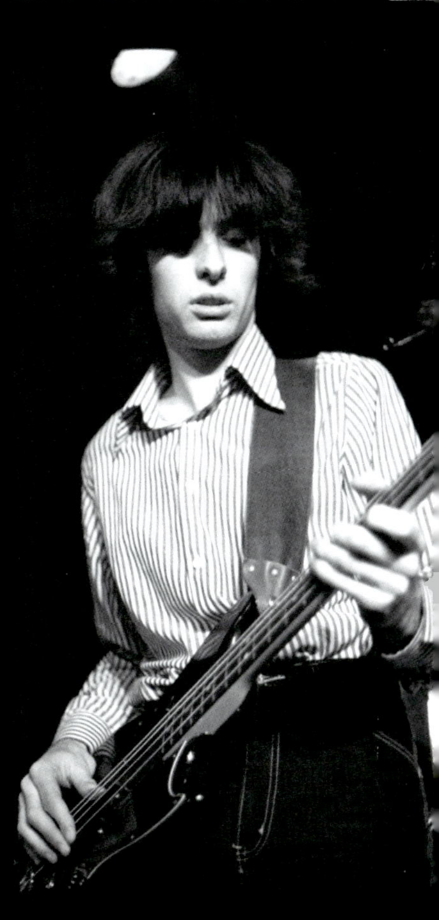

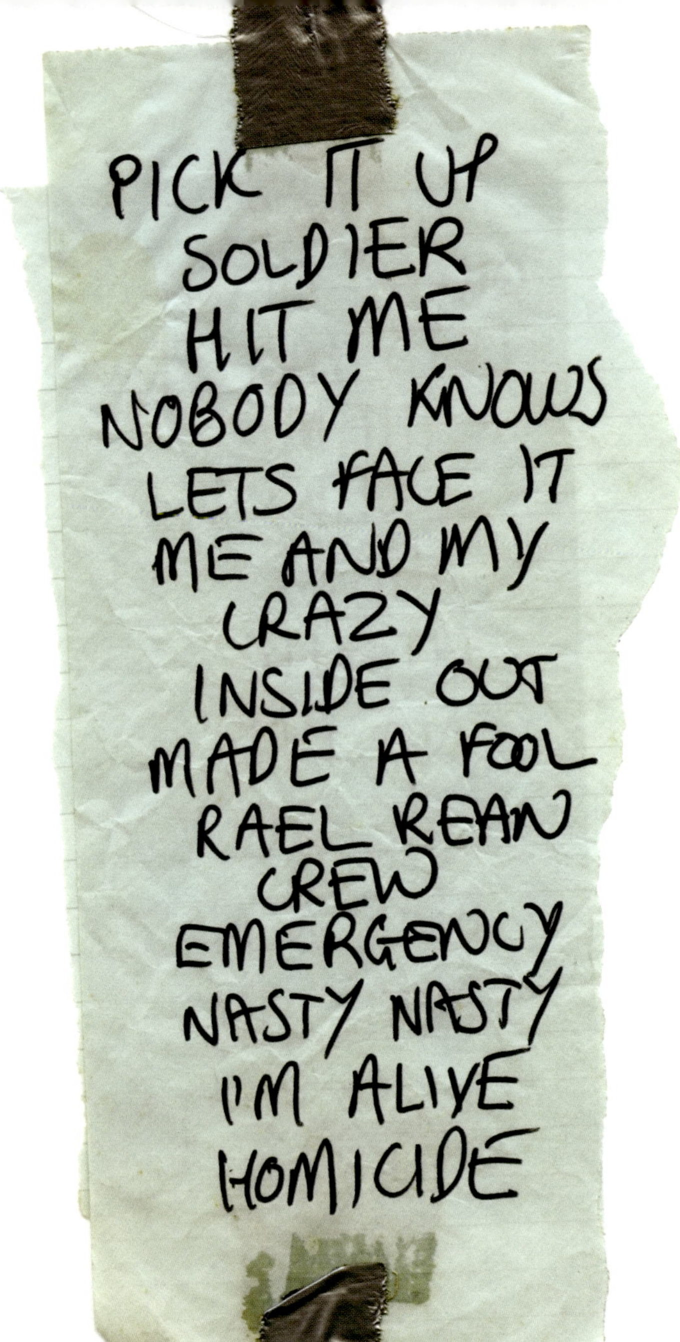

PICK IT UP
SOLDIER
HIT ME
NOBODY KNOWS
LETS FACE IT
ME AND MY
CRAZY
INSIDE OUT
MADE A FOOL
RAEL REAN
CREW
EMERGENCY
NASTY NASTY
I'M ALIVE
HOMICIDE

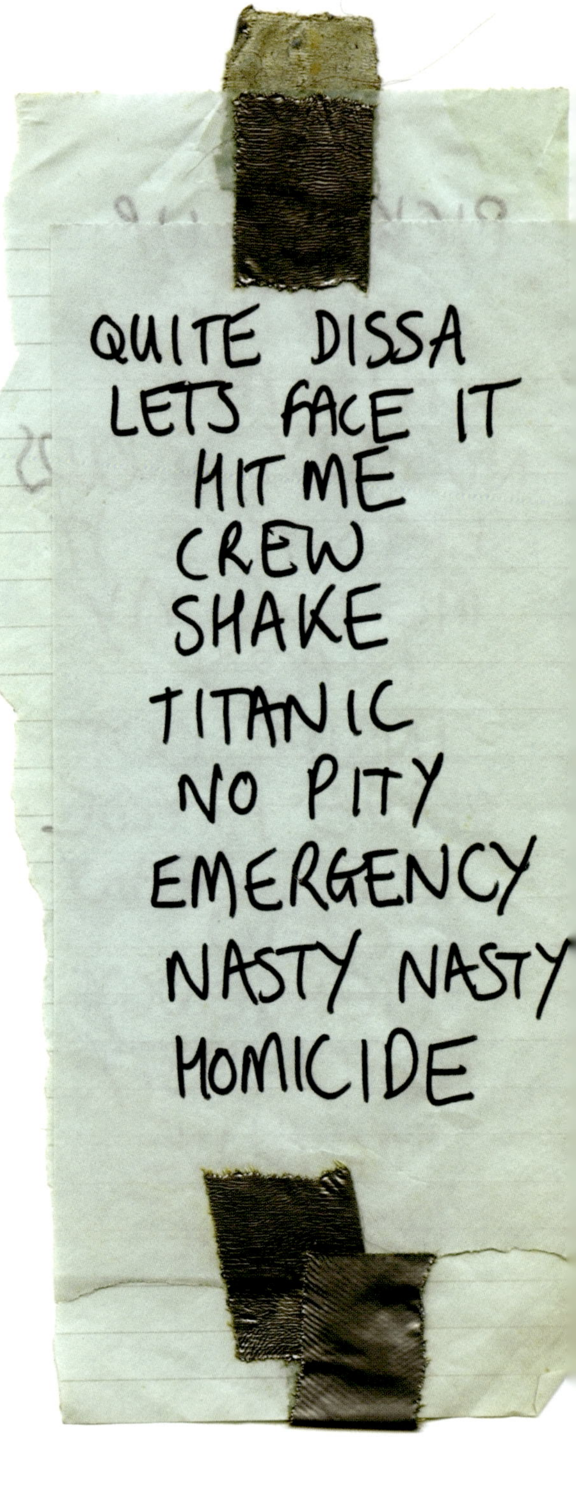

QUITE DISSA
LETS FACE IT
HIT ME
CREW
SHAKE
TITANIC
NO PITY
EMERGENCY
NASTY NASTY
HOMICIDE

999,
The Edge, 1979

Ed Case

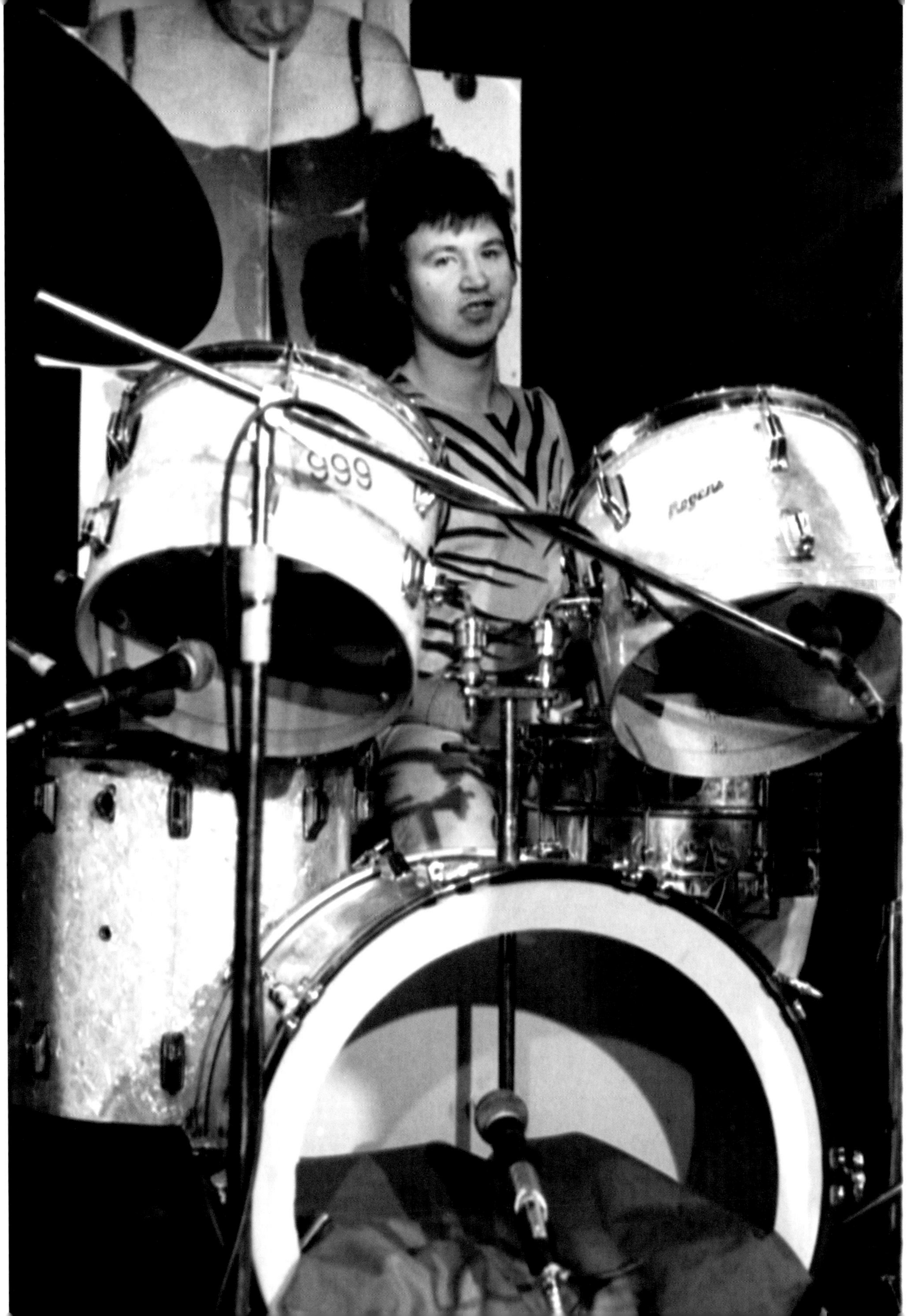
999

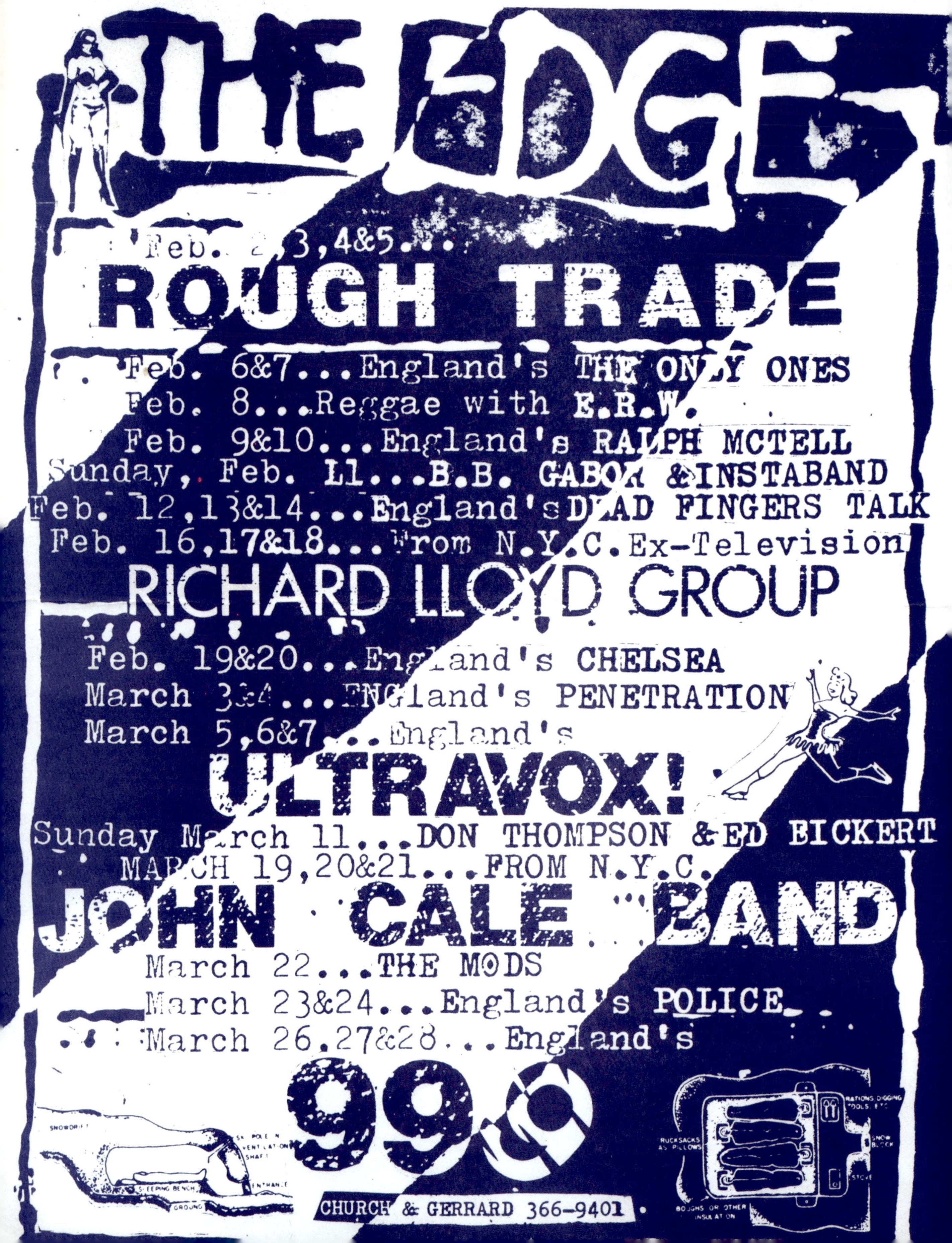
THE EDGE
Feb. 2,3,4&5...
ROUGH TRADE
Feb. 6&7...England's THE ONLY ONES
Feb. 8...Reggae with E.R.W.
Feb. 9&10...England's RALPH MCTELL
Sunday, Feb. 11...B.B. GABOR &INSTABAND
Feb. 12,13&14...England's DEAD FINGERS TALK
Feb. 16,17&18...From N.Y.C. Ex-Television
RICHARD LLOYD GROUP
Feb. 19&20...England's CHELSEA
March 3&4...ENGland's PENETRATION
March 5,6&7...England's
ULTRAVOX!
Sunday March 11...DON THOMPSON &ED BICKERT
MARCH 19,20&21...FROM N.Y.C.
JOHN CALE BAND
March 22...THE MODS
March 23&24...England's POLICE
March 26,27&28...England's
999
SNOWDRIFT
SKI POLE IN VENTILATION SHAFT
SLEEPING BENCH
ENTRANCE
GROUND
RATIONS DIGGING TOOLS, ETC.
RUCKSACKS AS PILLOWS
SNOW BLOCK
STOVE
BOUGHS OR OTHER INSULATION
CHURCH & GERRARD 366-9401

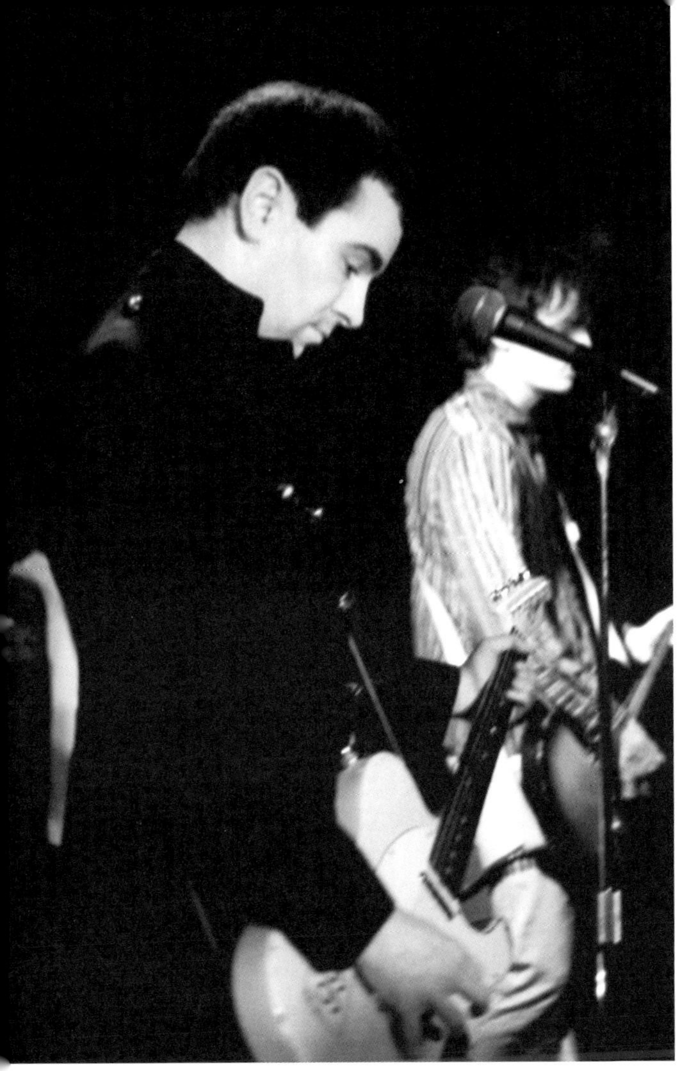

Nick Cash, Guy Days

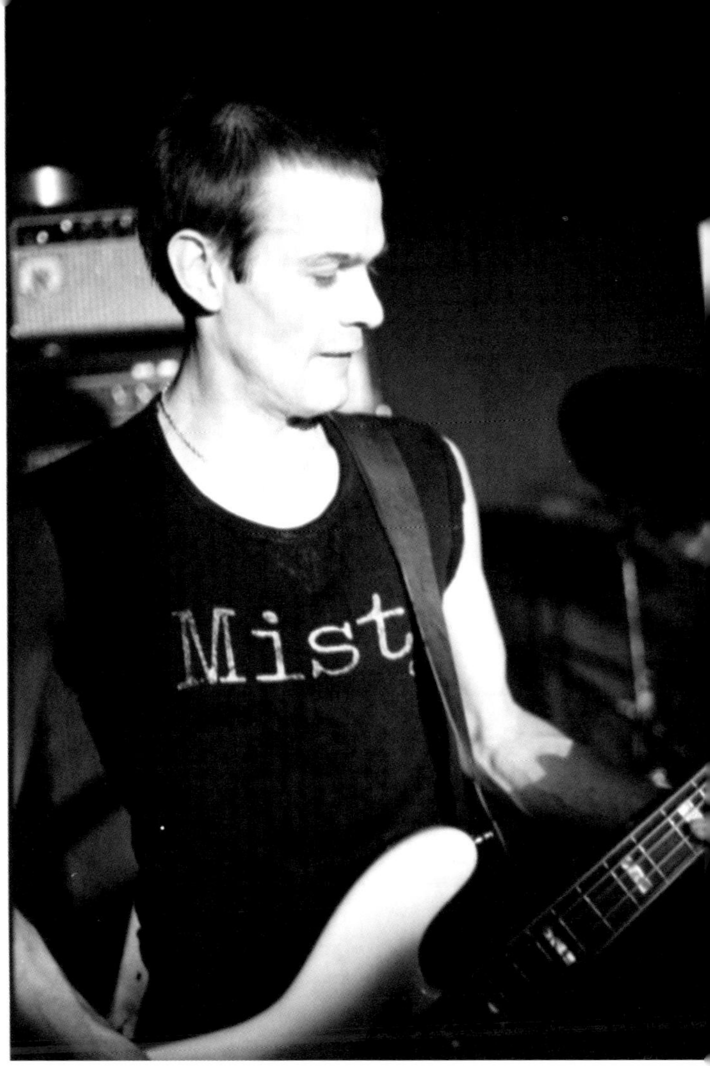

Jon Watson

Canada was still very much a colony in 1979. The motherland was England, and sometimes we benefited from this relationship by U.K. records being released to the much smaller Canadian market before the United States, if they received American release at all. Bands became huge in Canada, particularly Toronto, before they were known in the United States. One such band was 999, instantly popular and returning to the city what felt like every few months, the venues getting bigger and bigger. This image is from their first or second gig here, before a small audience at the Edge. With only one album and a few singles, the band padded their sets by performing some songs twice, ending both sets with the same crowd-rousing schtick of "Homicide." The band is still around; I've seen recent set lists and they still end with that song.

The Verbs,
Turning Point, 1979

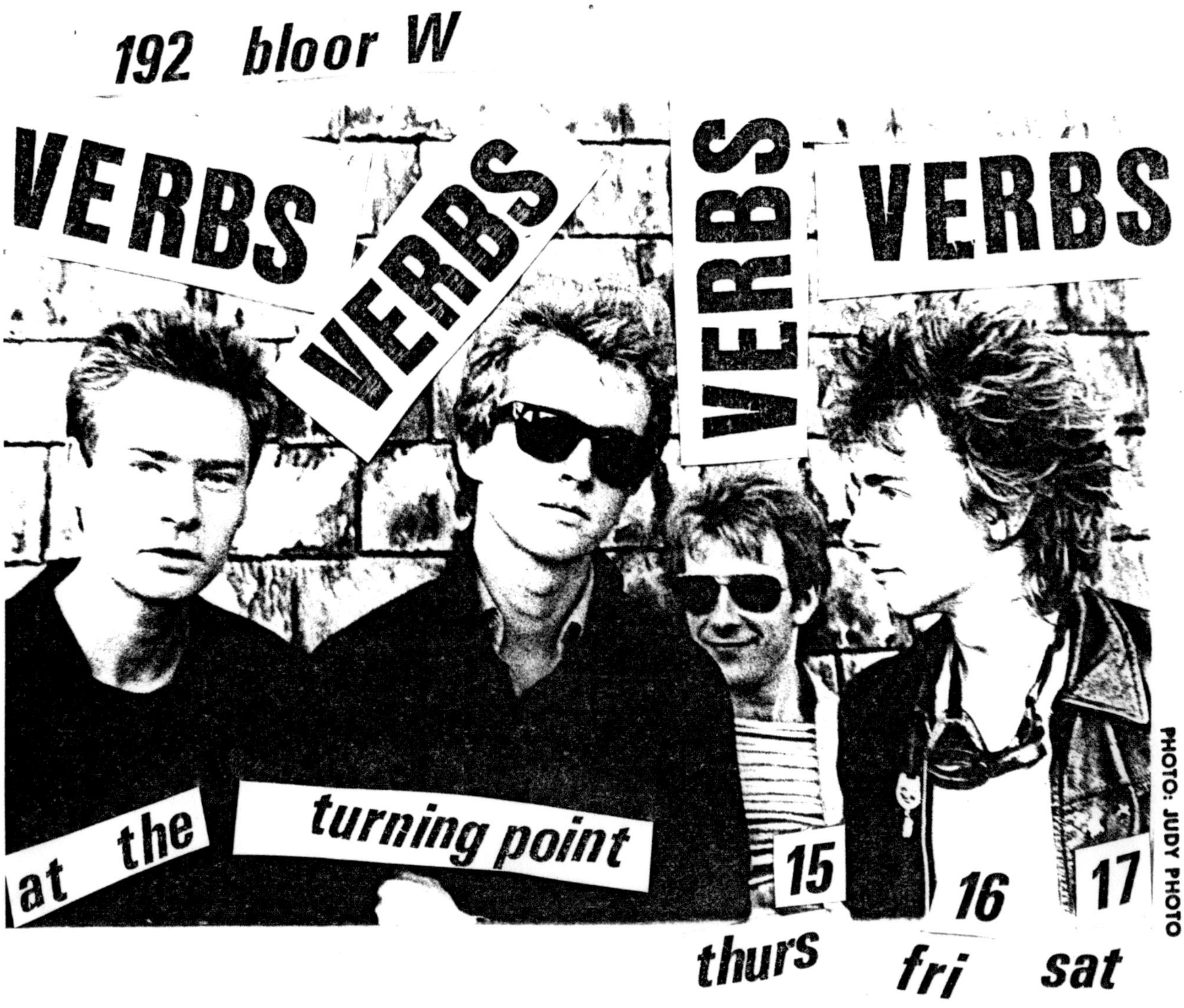

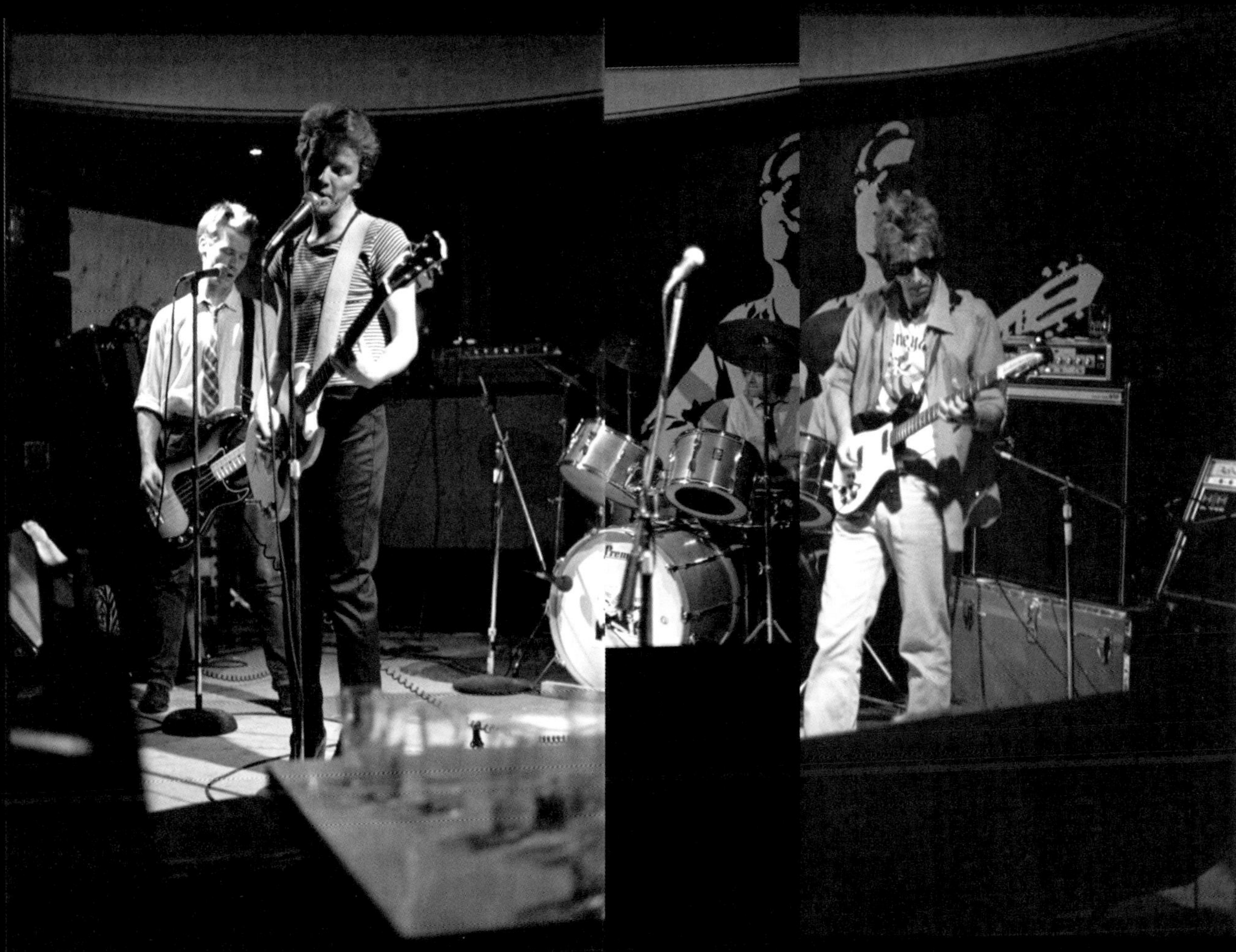

Ed Radford, John Anderson, Teddy "Fury" Franklin, Dave Templeton

The band formed out of the ashes of The Concordes.

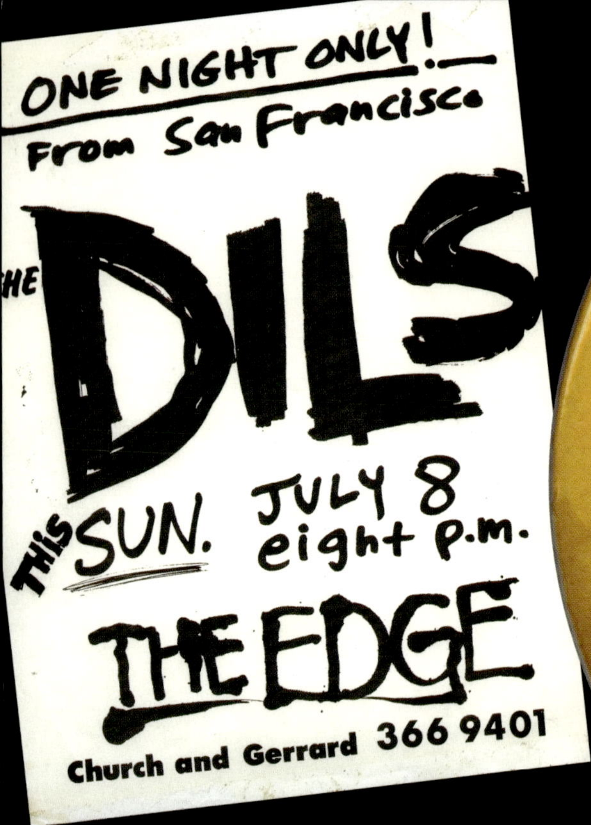

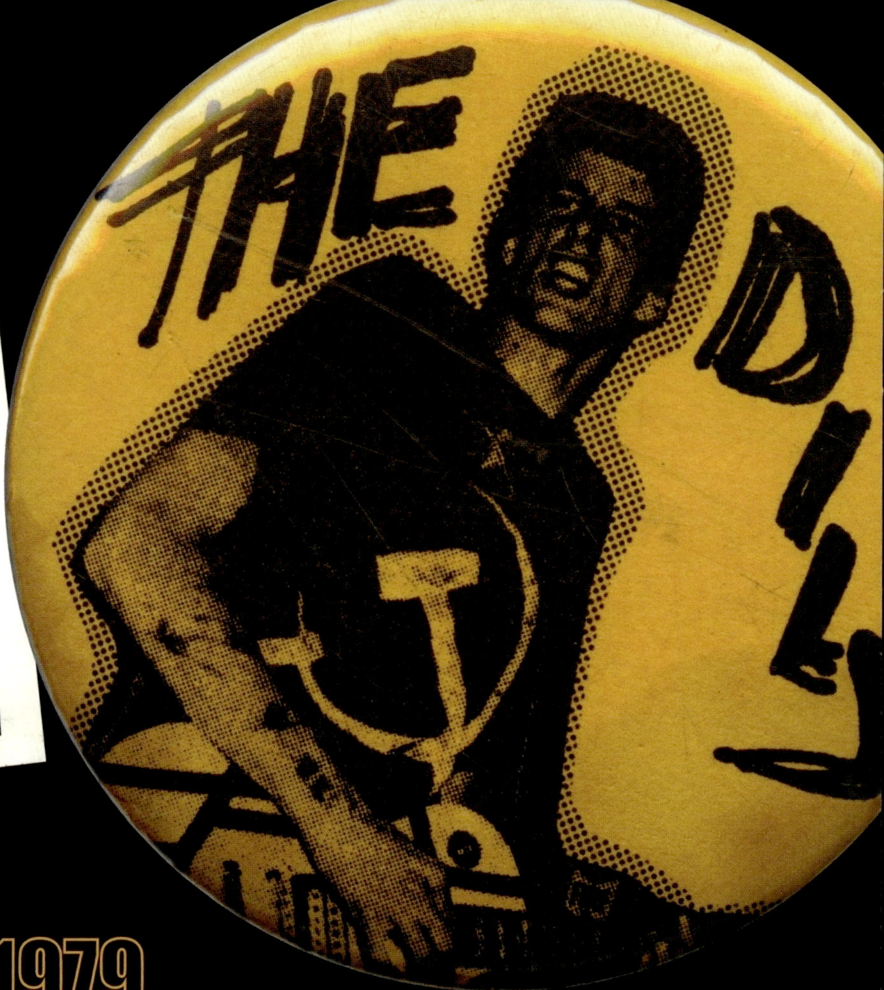

The Dils, The Edge, 1979

When the first wave of California punks put out records, I was blown away by the incredible music coming from the West Coast. The Avengers, The Weirdos, The Screamers, X and The Dils were mostly unknown in Toronto. It somehow felt like a secret underground as people clamored for music from the United Kingdom. Foreign and far away, my obsession led me to write to my favorite of them, The Dils, to ask when they were playing so I could try to coordinate a visit out there when all my faves might be performing. Their manager wrote back and told me not to come — that the band would come to me if I could book shows for them. I called Gary Topp, and he helped put together a small tour for The Dils. Two friends I'd turned on to The Dils and I had a craft afternoon, hand drawing posters for the upcoming gigs, which we pasted around town. When The Dils arrived they were slightly surprised to see a few young teenagers as their hosts, with handmade magic marker and spray paint flyers instead of the professional ones they'd been expecting. Sensing potential disaster, singer/guitarist Chip Kinman immediately made a new flyer and we set about replastering the downtown.

John Silvers

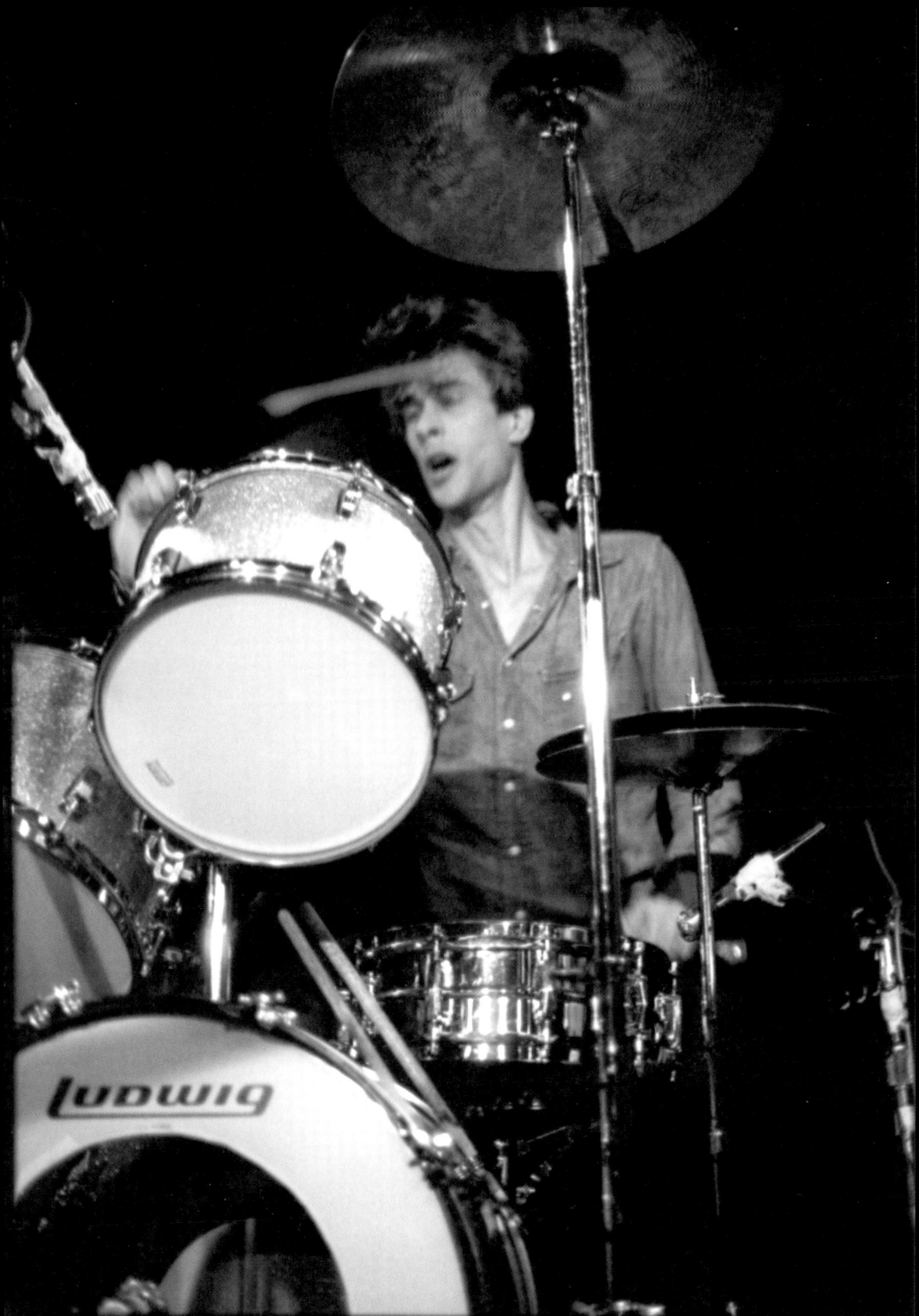
Ludwig

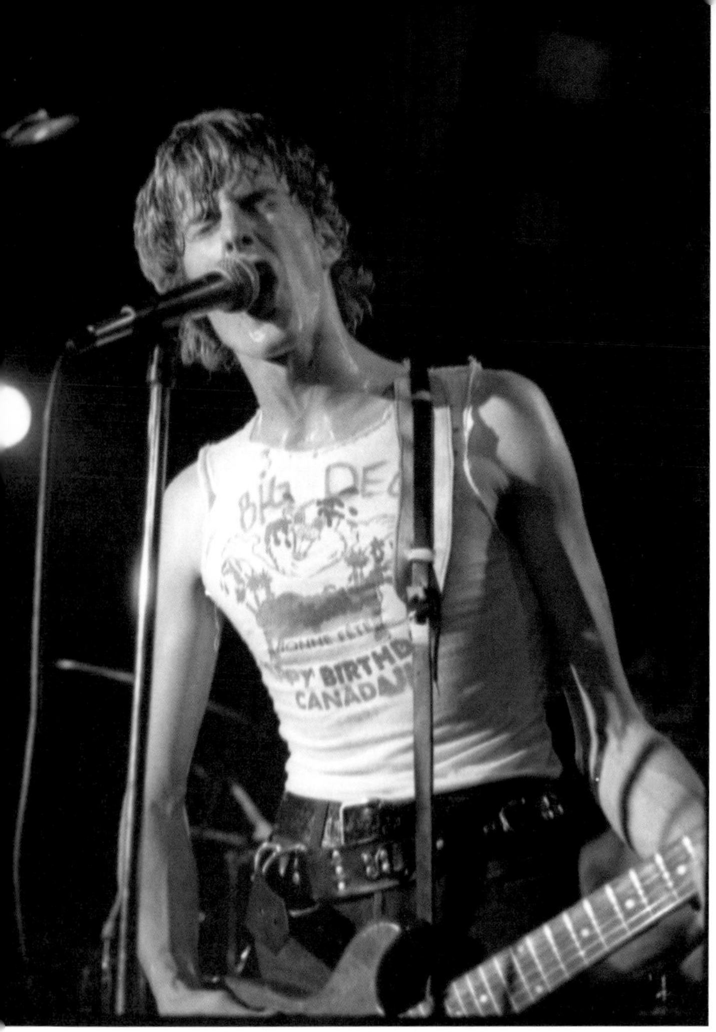

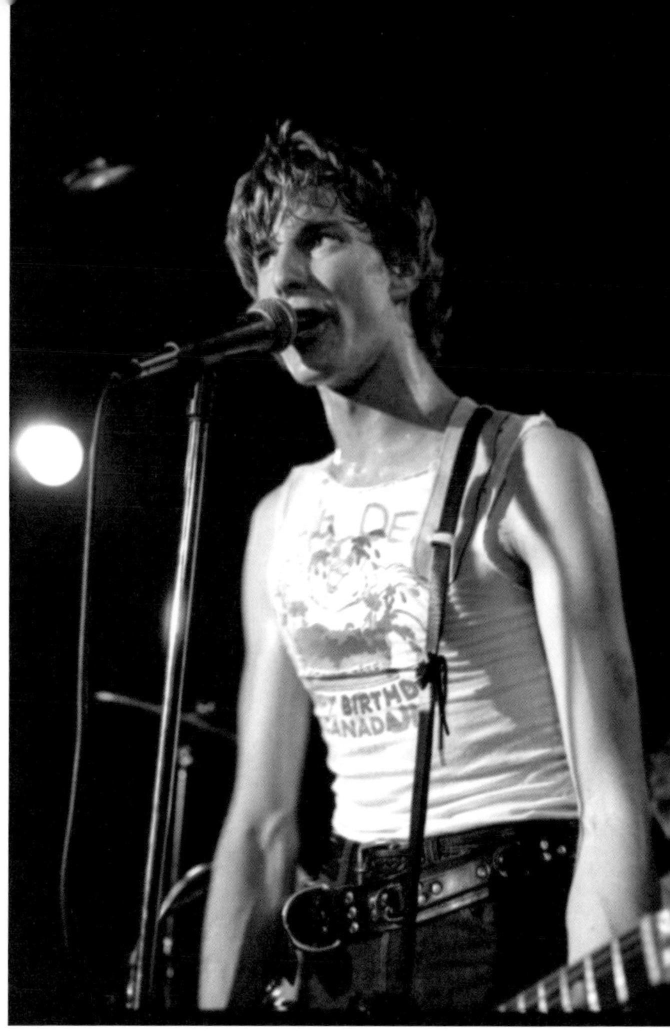

Chip Kinman

One of the gigs was at the Rotters Club in Ottawa, so a few friends and I squeezed into The Dils' van for the roadtrip. Chip and Tony invited me to sing a couple of songs with them. The club was in a basement with a low ceiling made of the type of acoustic tiles found in offices. During one of the songs, I reached up and pulled the edge of the ceiling frame, where the height of the club ceiling got even lower. The first tile came loose and slowly, one by one in a chain reaction like dominoes, the ceiling tiles fell, spilling insulation and wires onto the heads of the audience. Tony Kinman's mouth fell open and he quickly gave me the keys to their van and told me to go hide. The club manager flipped out, trying to find who had caused the damage as I cowered under blankets, laughing to myself at the fun accidental destruction.

Tony Kinman

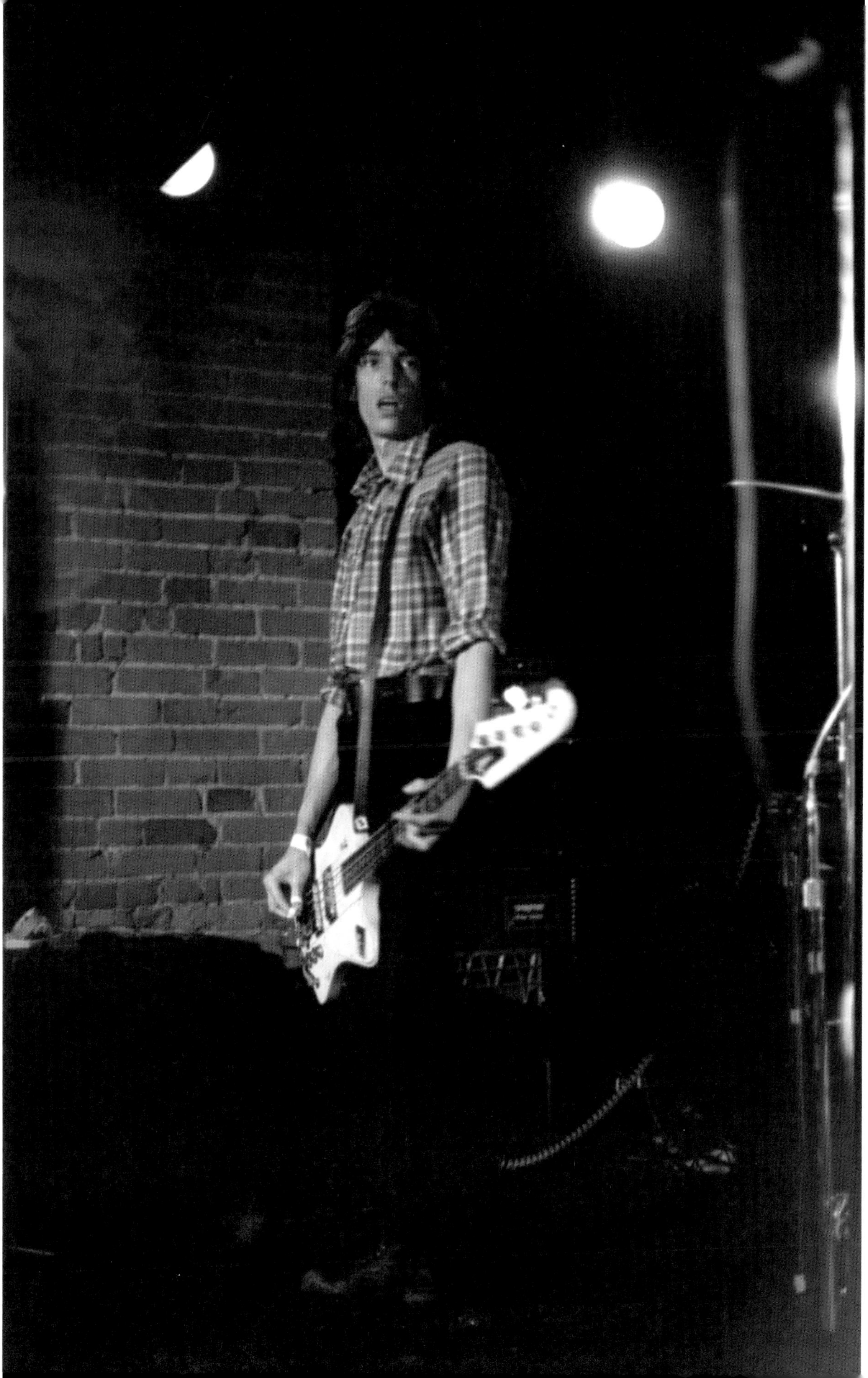

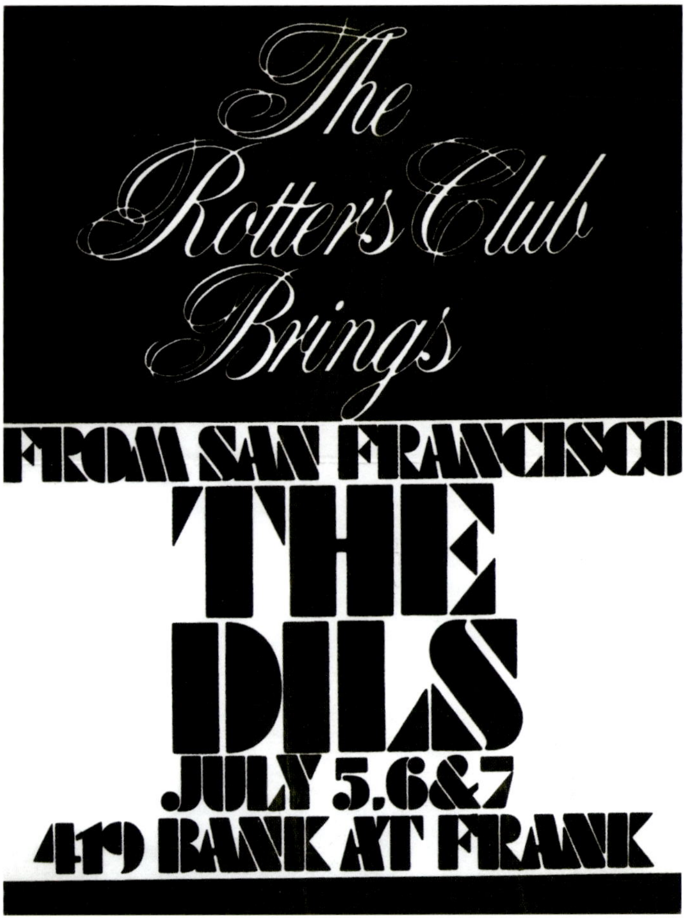

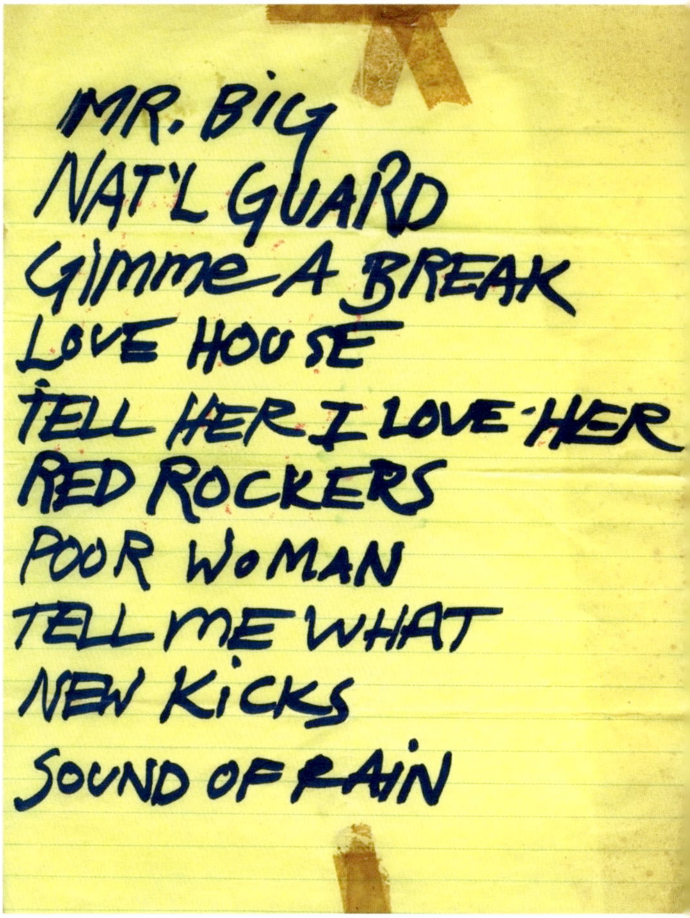

It was Dominion Day (now Canada Day) as we passed through Ottawa a couple of days before the show there, so we all took a trip to Parliament Hill, where the former U.S. Army brats were shocked to see that Canada celebrated its birthday with . . . nothing. Security guards chased us off a barren Parliament Hill after we tried to extinguish the Centennial flame, and Chip magic-markered "BIG DEAL" onto the Canada's birthday shirt he bought and wore back in Toronto.

Draga posting homemade Dils flyers for a show at the Edge

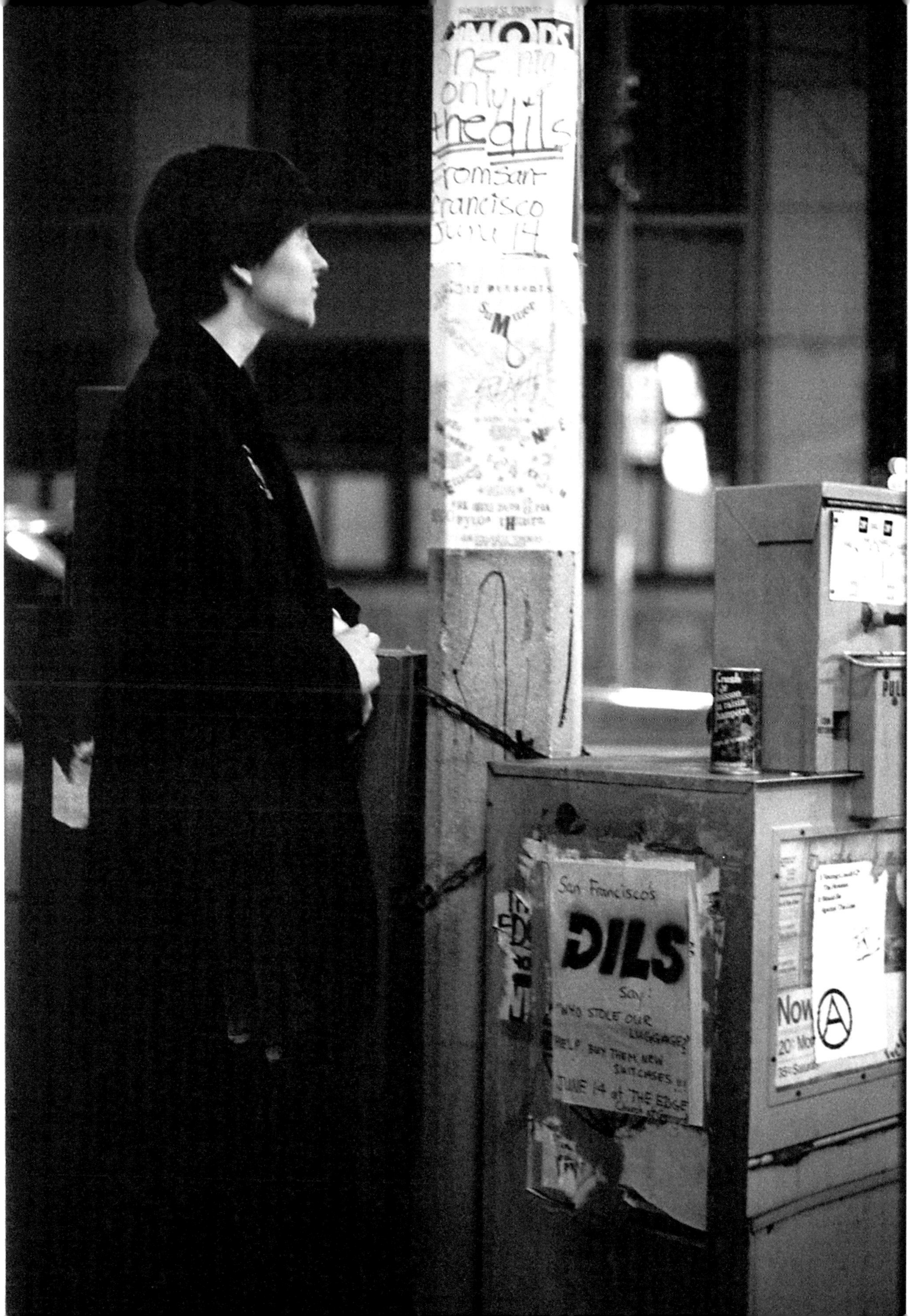
the dils
San Francisco's
DILS
say:
STOLE OUR
LUGGAGE?
BUY THEM NEW
SUITCASES
14 at THE EDGE
Now

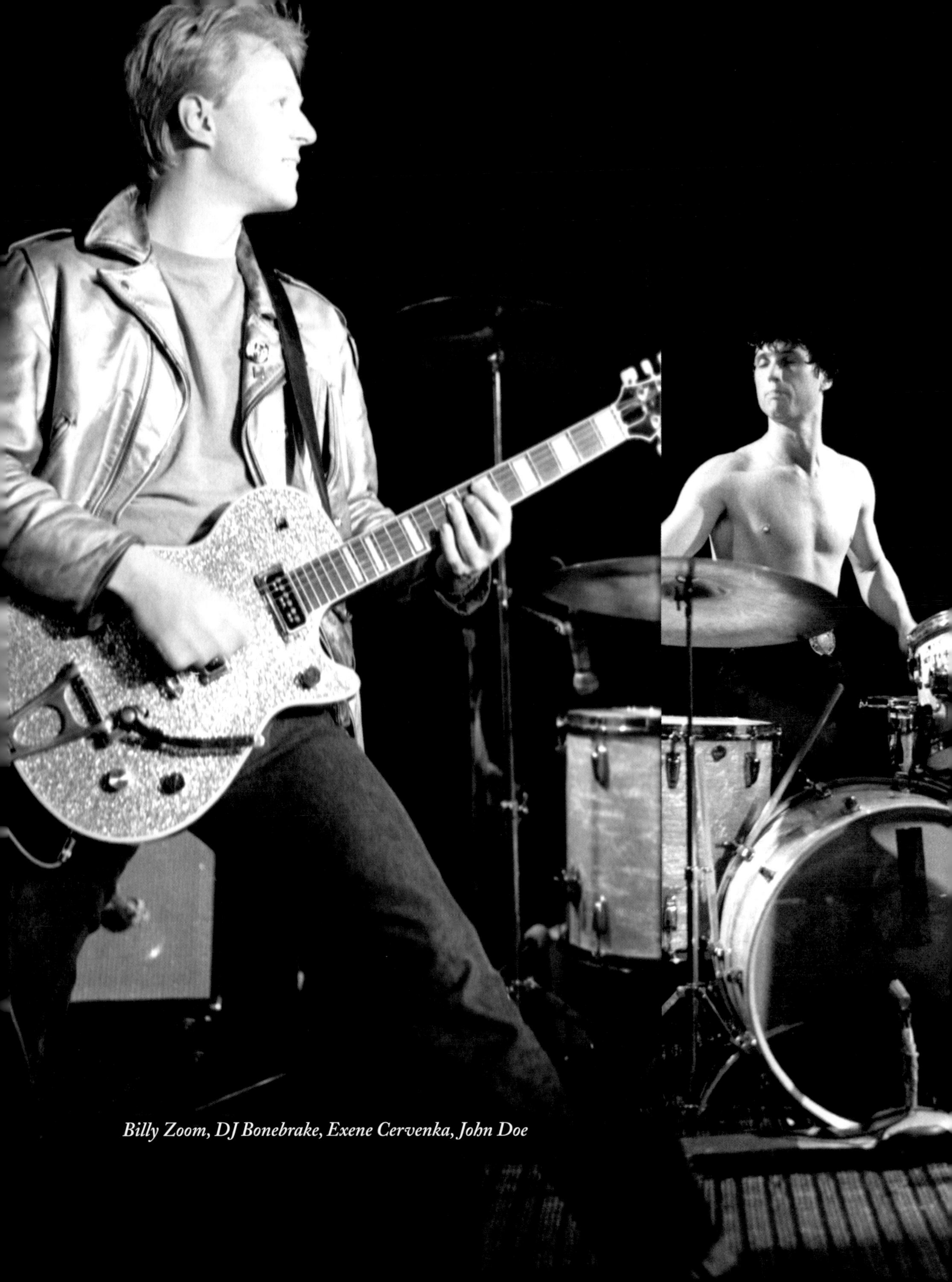

Billy Zoom, DJ Bonebrake, Exene Cervenka, John Doe

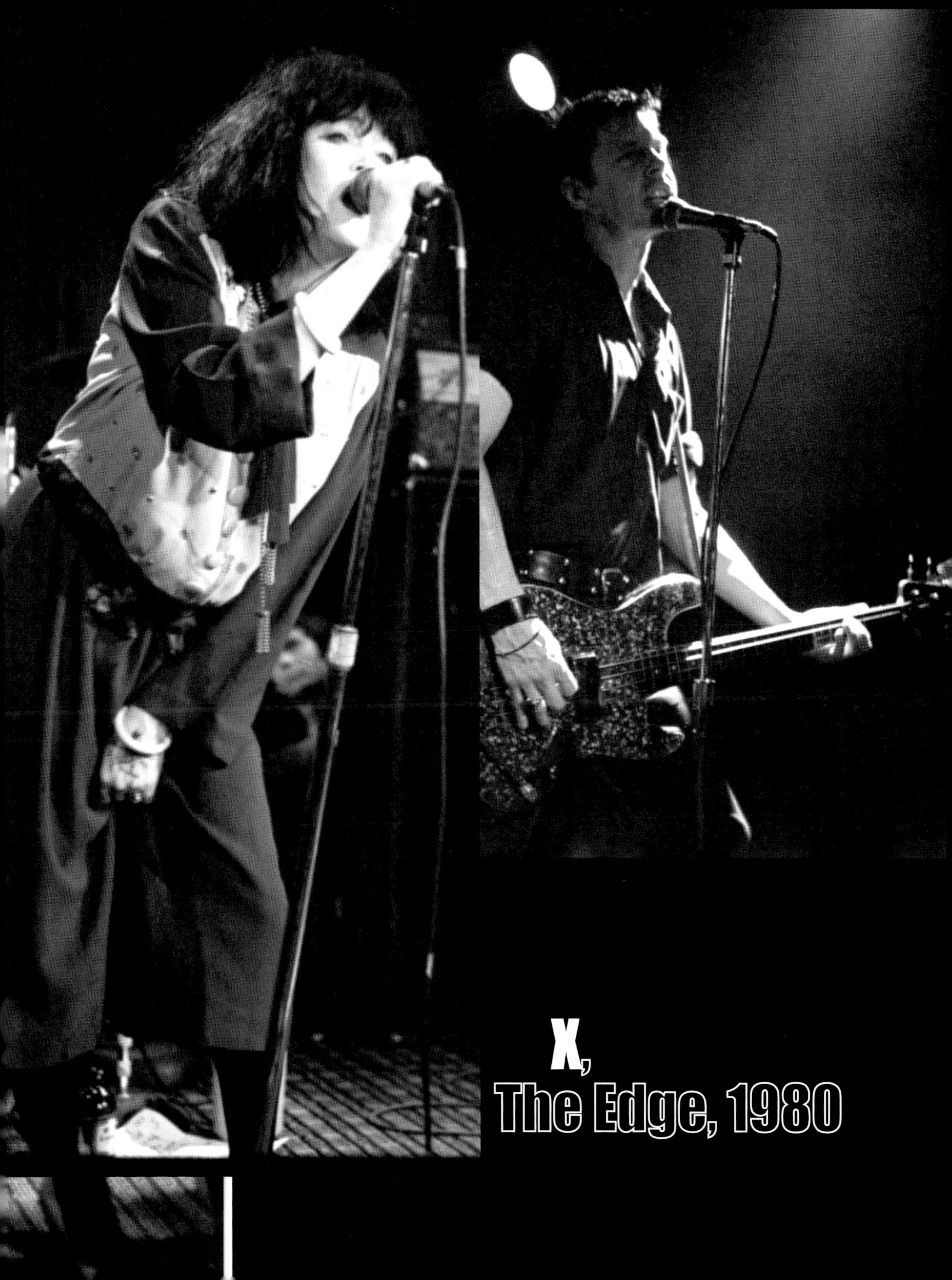

X,
The Edge, 1980

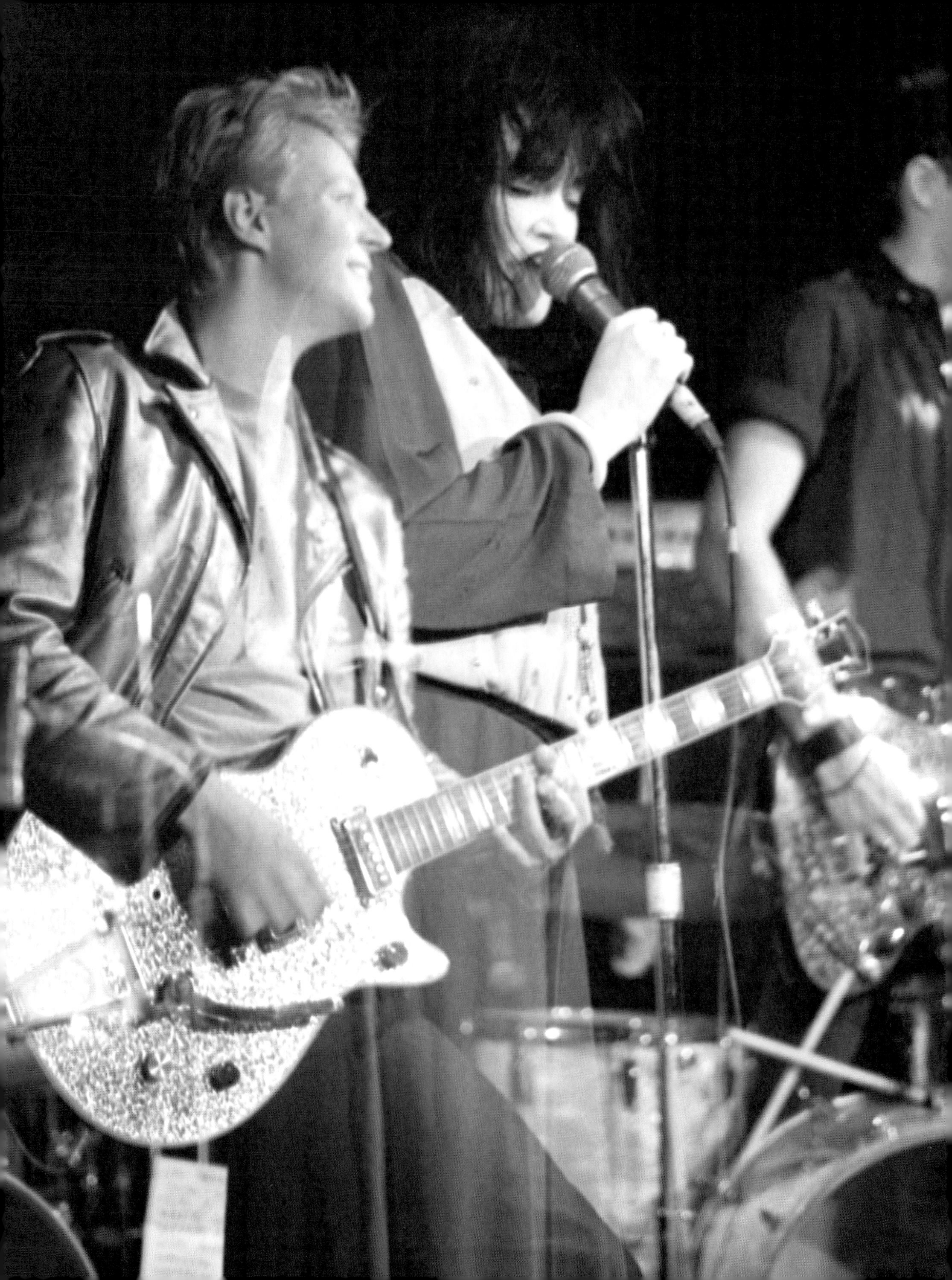

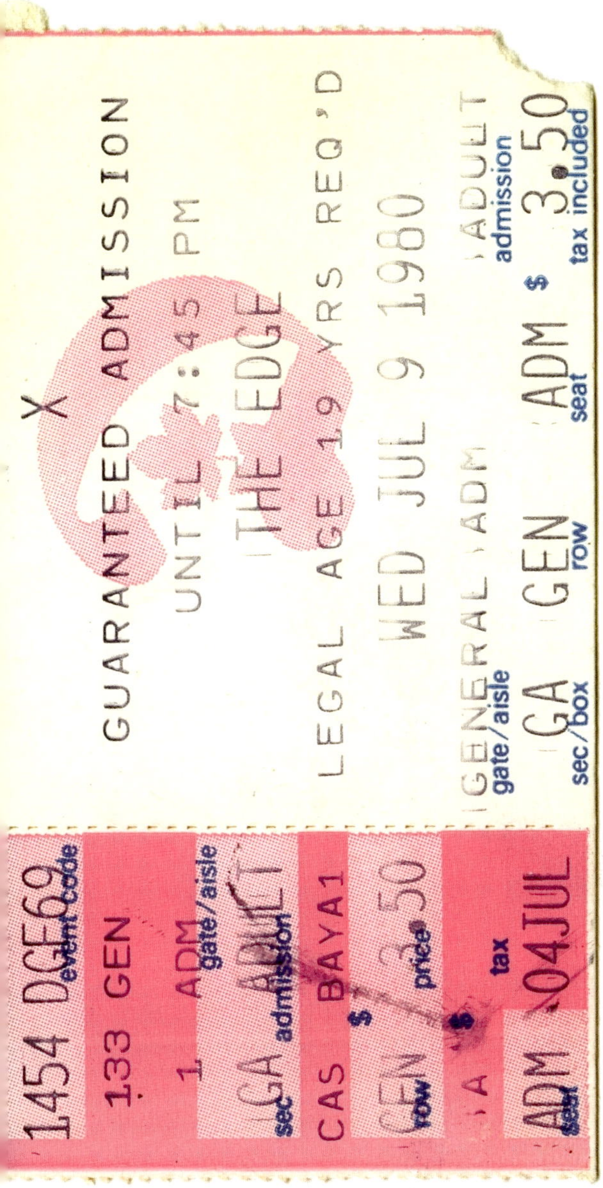

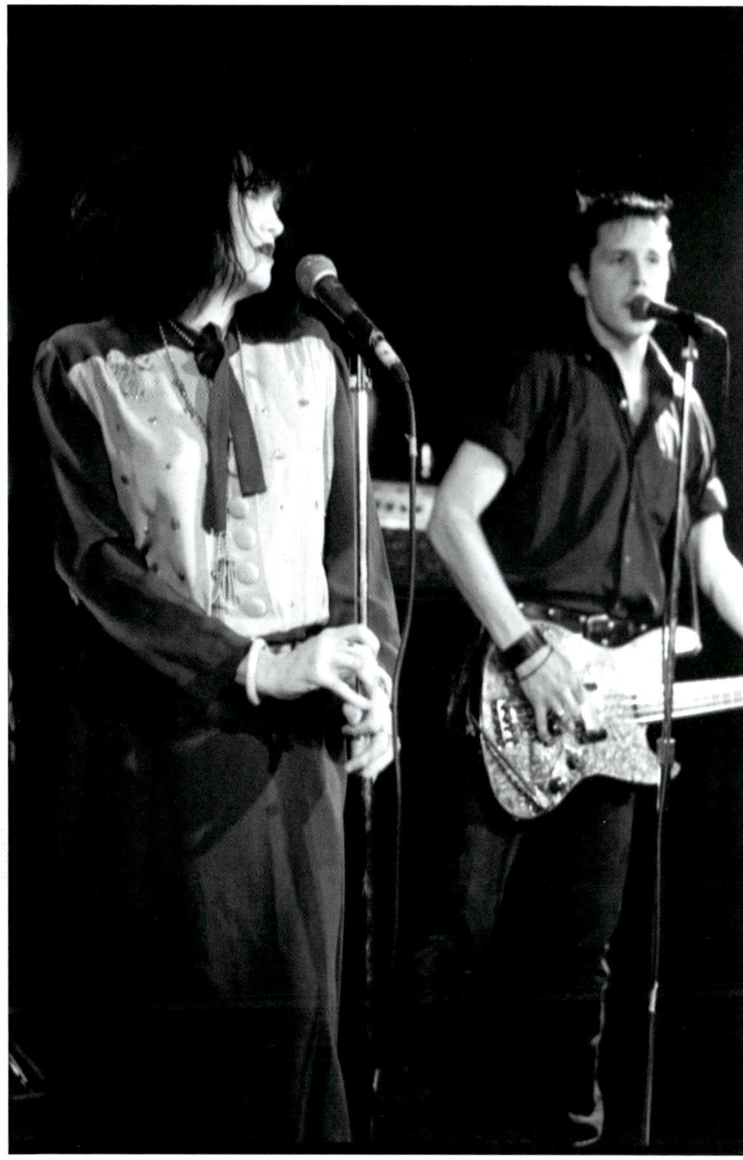

Exene Cervenka, John Doe

I was always grateful for the artists who came to town without any reason to believe there would be an audience when they arrived. Information about exciting new bands was shared by word of mouth, or through picture sleeve 45s and small press magazines like L.A.'s *Slash*, often with only a few copies reaching the city. San Francisco band Pink Section came to Toronto, as did X — with two singles out and a just-released album that hadn't yet made its way here. Guitarist Billy Zoom had a huge smile for the whole show, making his somewhat disturbing appearance rather joyful to watch.

Billy Zoom, Exene Cervenka

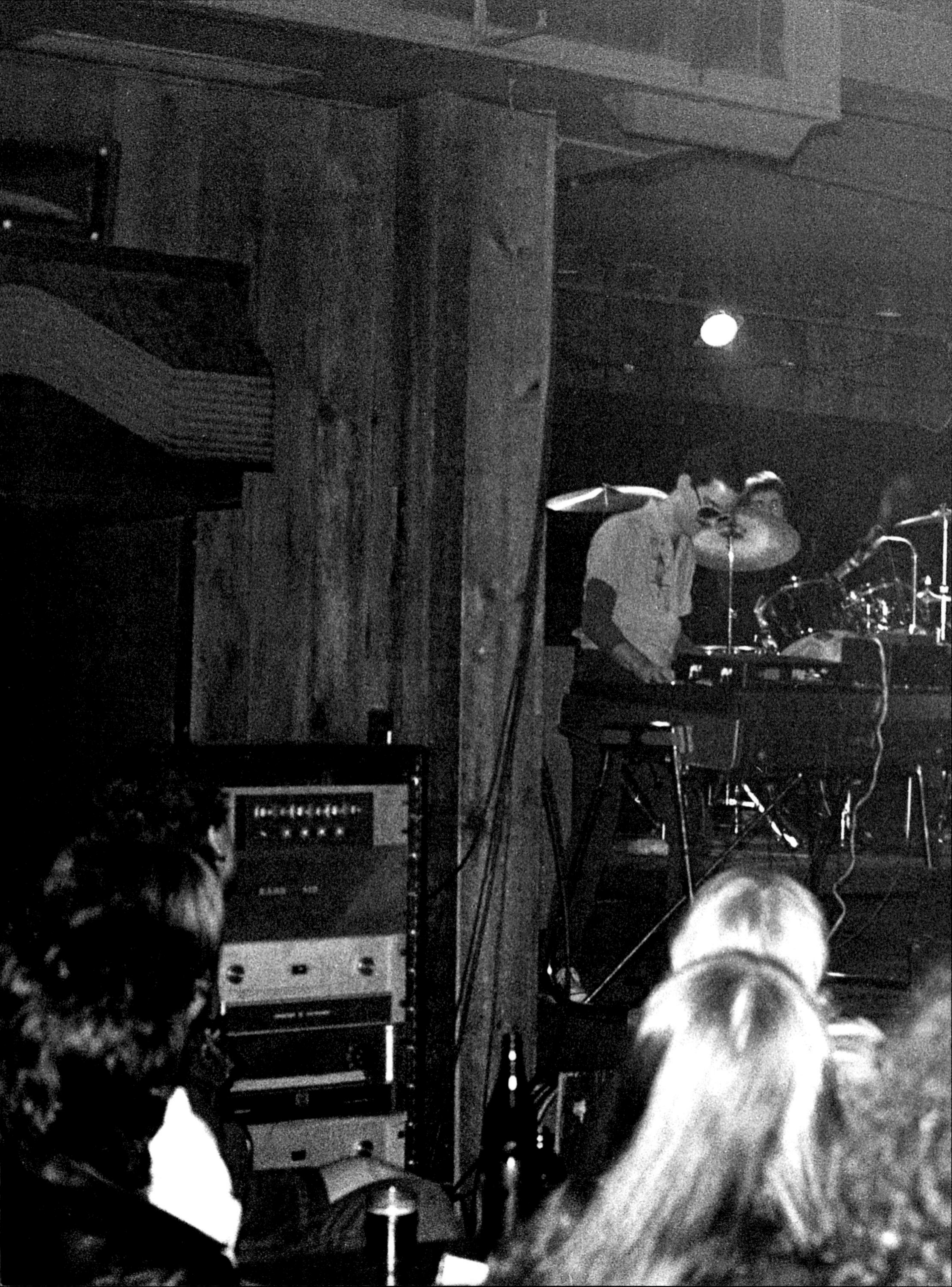

The Reds, Horseshoe Tavern, 1978

Opening for The Troggs, Philadelphia's The Reds were part of A&M's efforts at building a new wave roster. They'd go on to score Michael Mann's cult feature, *Manhunter*.

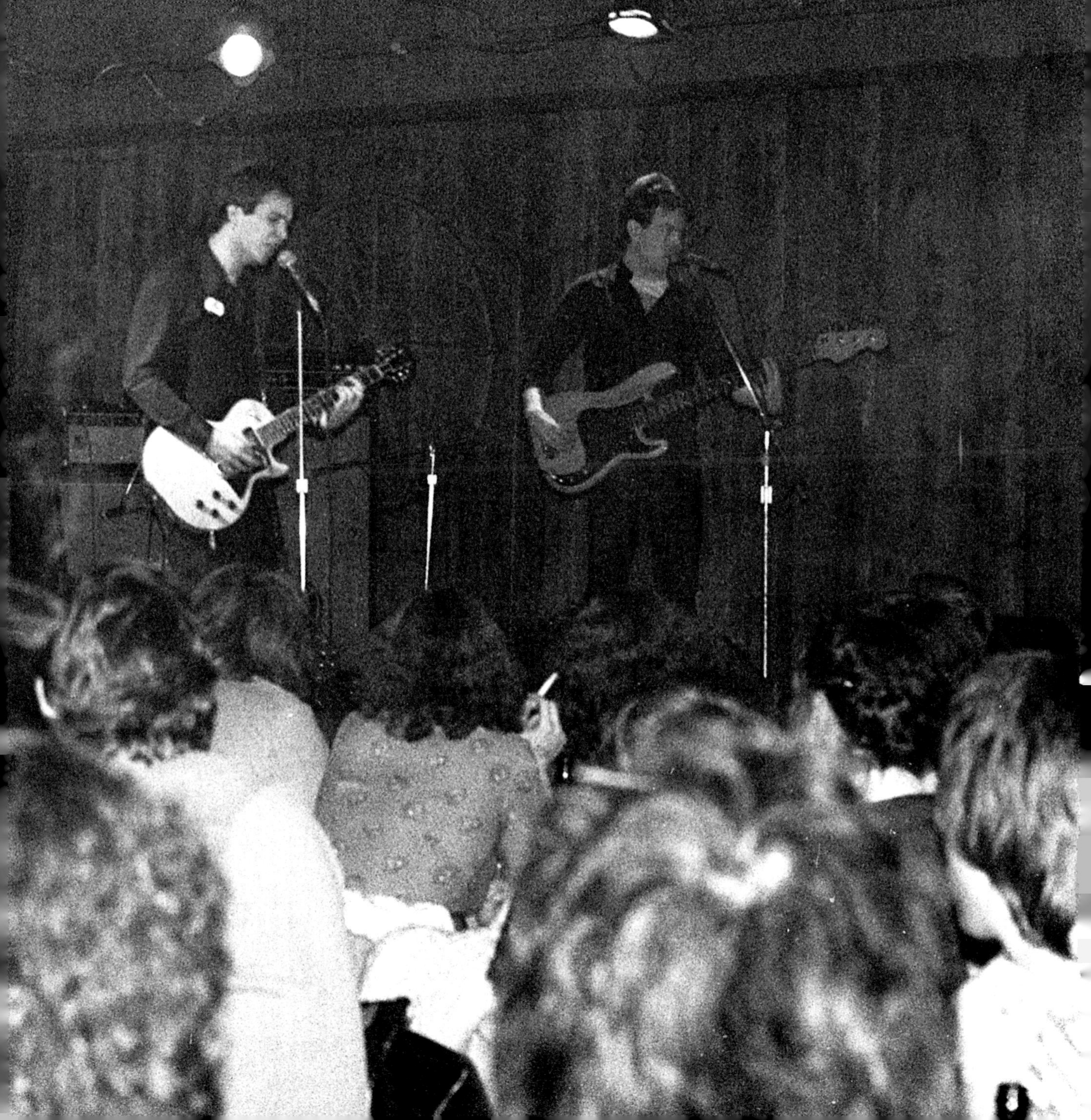

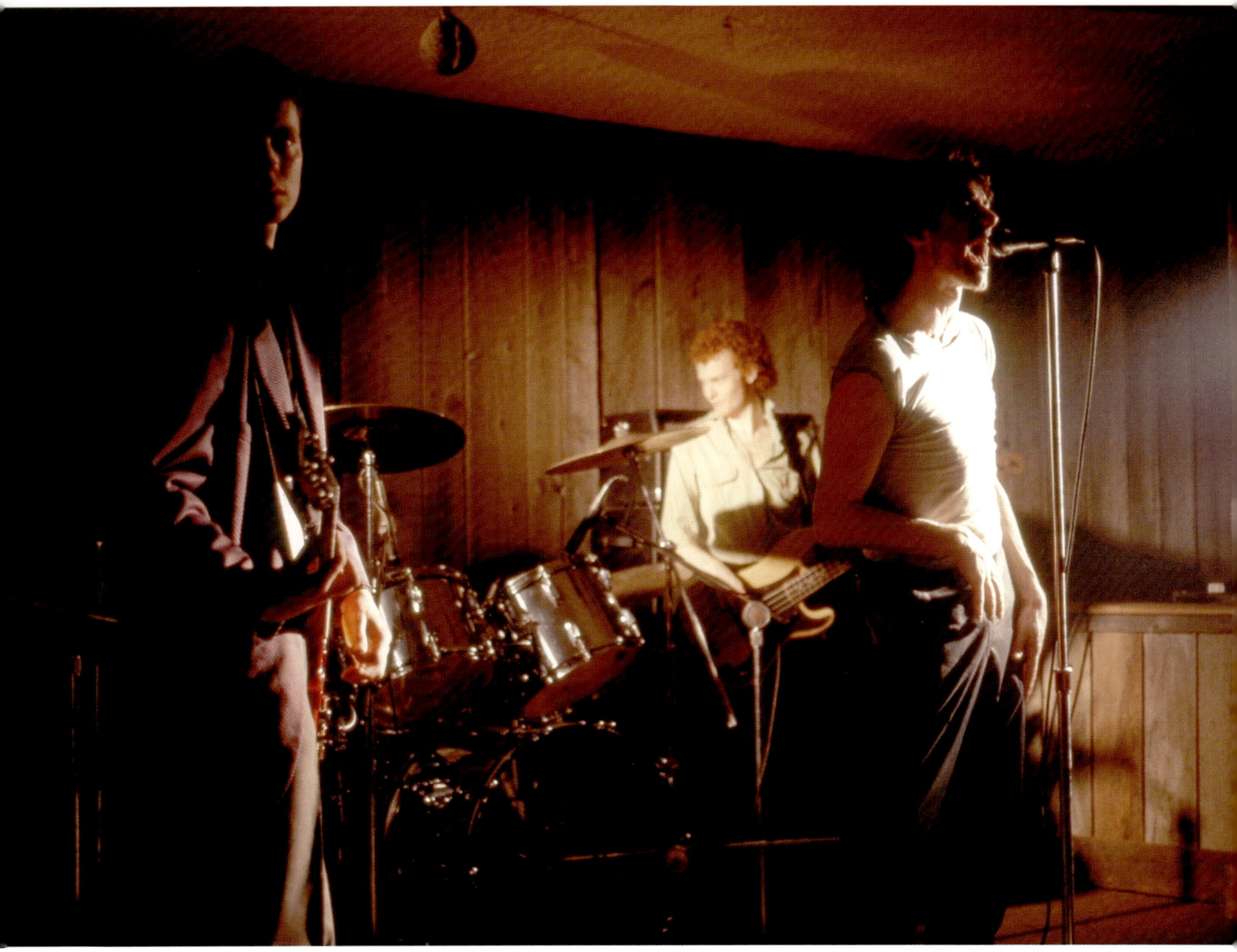

Steve Koch, Iain Atkinson-Staines, Keith Whittaker

The Demics, Trafalgar Inn, Oakville, 1980

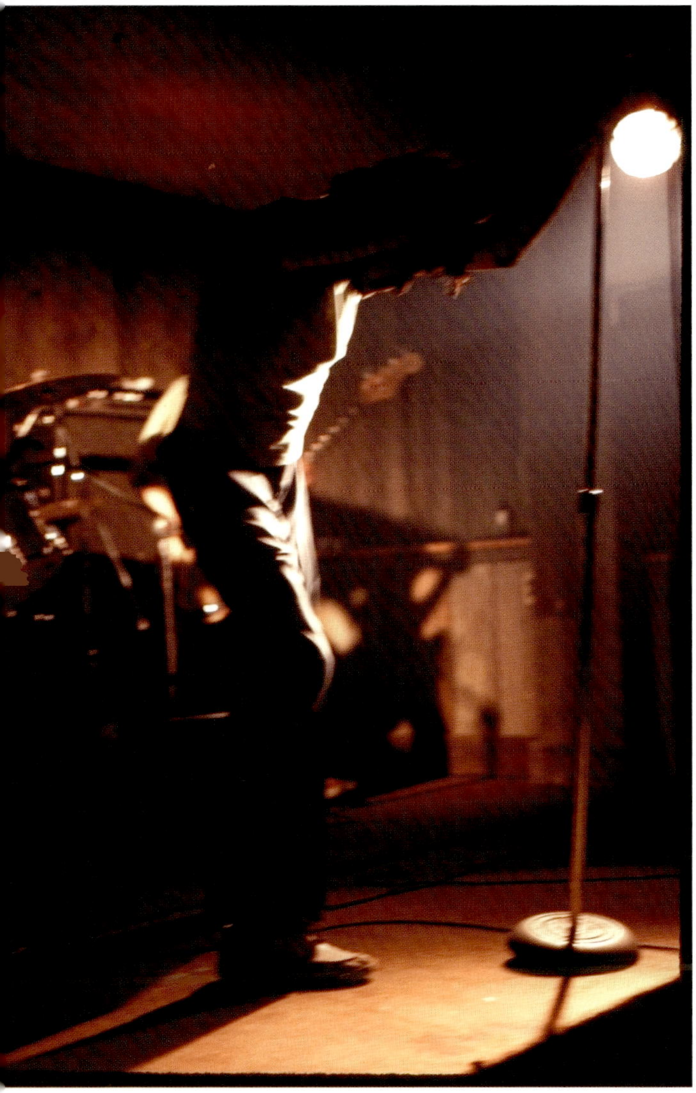

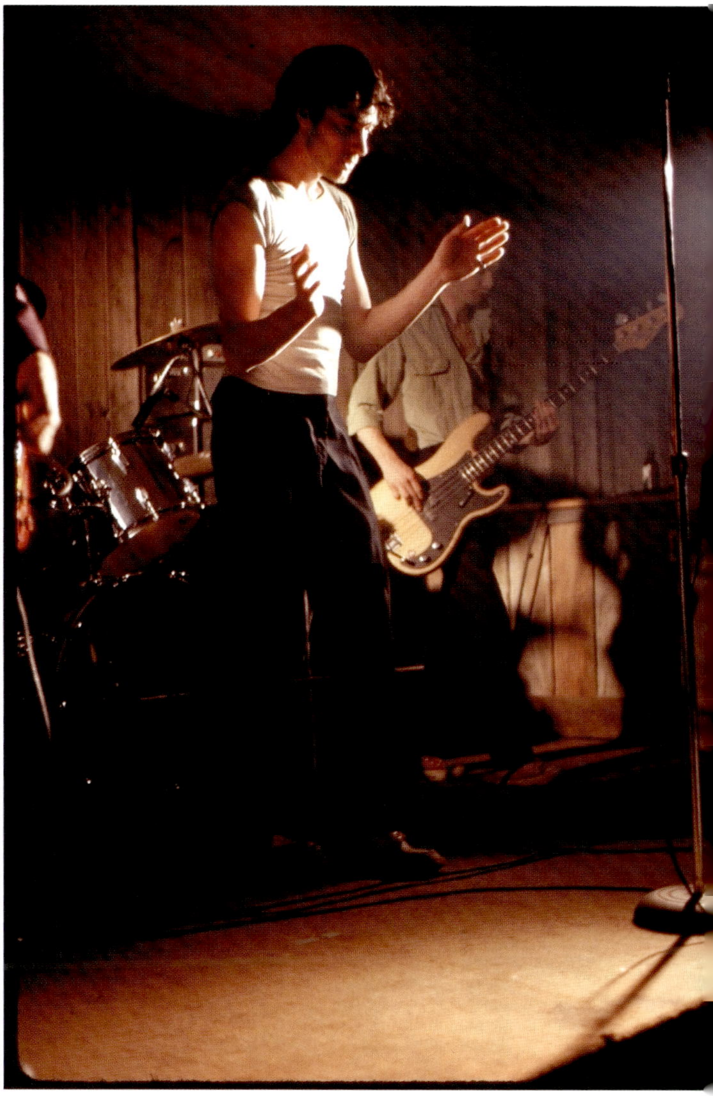

Keith Whittaker

The band I was in at this time, Crash Kills Five, shared a rehearsal space with The Demics in the basement of singer Keith Whittaker's Baldwin Street house, so we did lots of shows with them. By this time they had pretty much moved to Toronto from London, Ontario, and were just breaking in new guitarist Steve Koch, brother to CK5's drummer Alex. Twelve people and two bands' worth of equipment somehow squeezed into their van for the one-hour winter trip down the QEW to Oakville, a destination known more for Olde English fish and chips and poshly appointed lakefront homes than anything like "alternative" music. Squeezed behind a Marshall cabinet against the back doors, it was hard not to think about what would happen if we hit some ice.

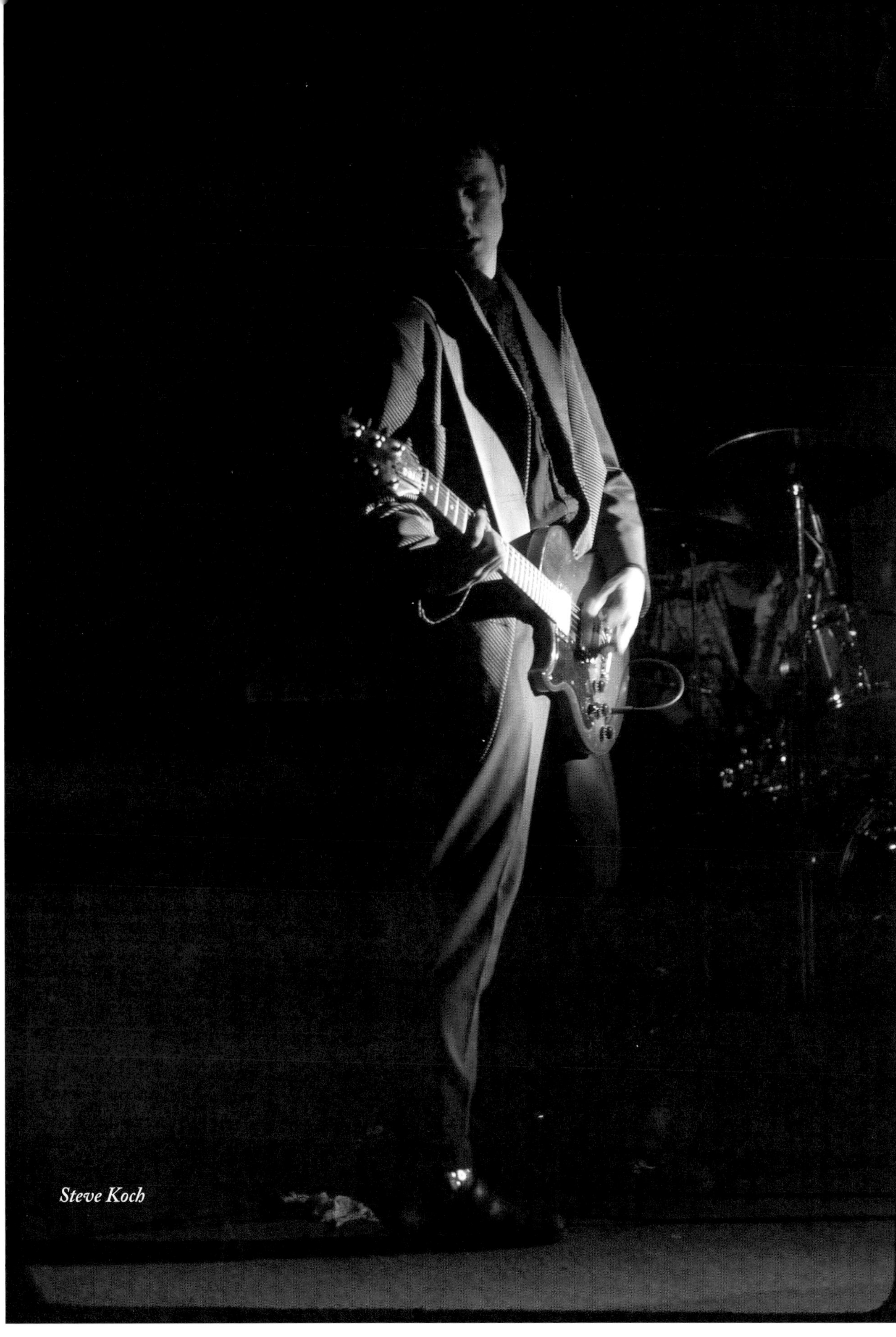

Steve Koch

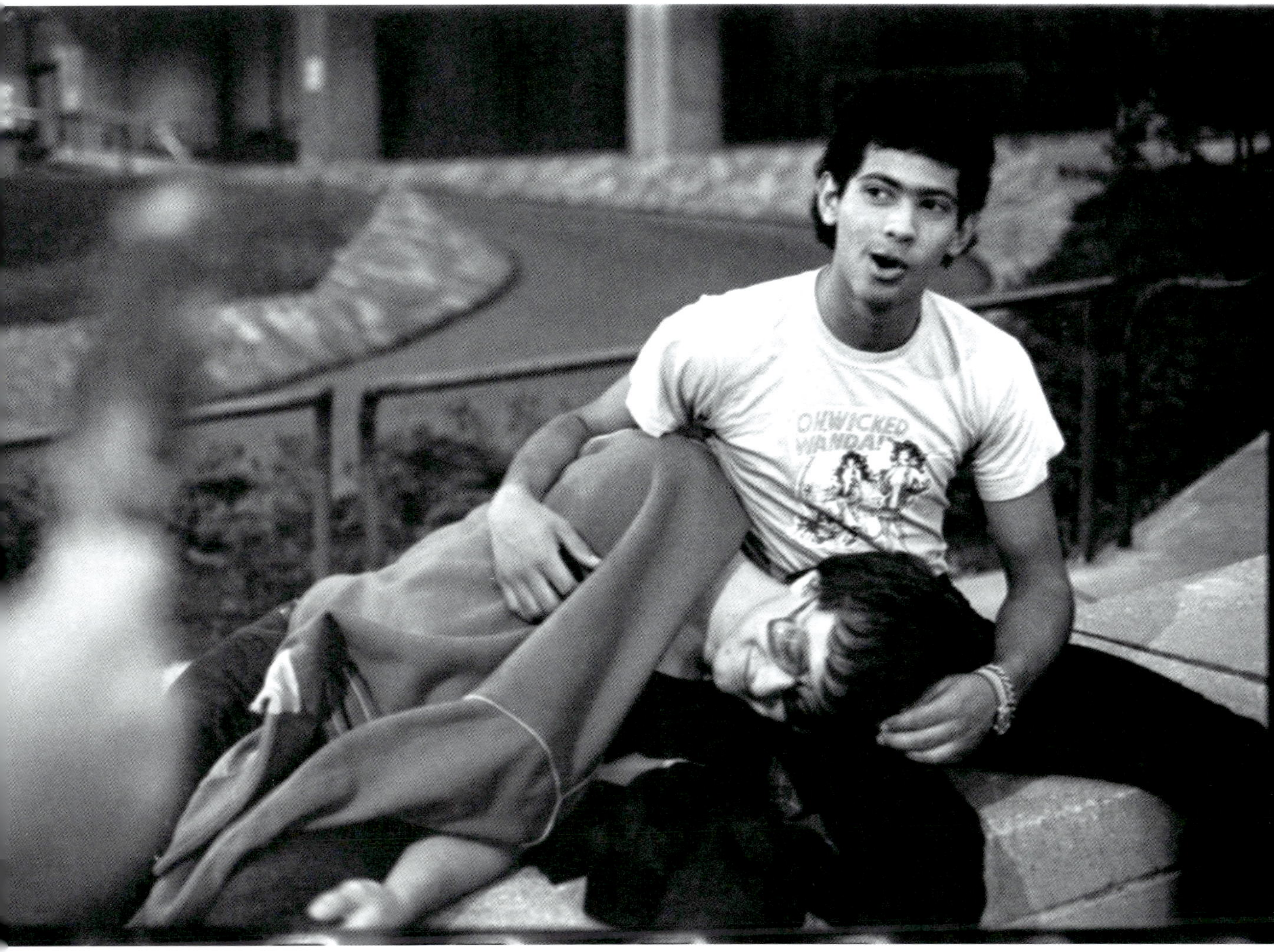

Alex Koch, Mohamed Nagdee of Crash Kills Five

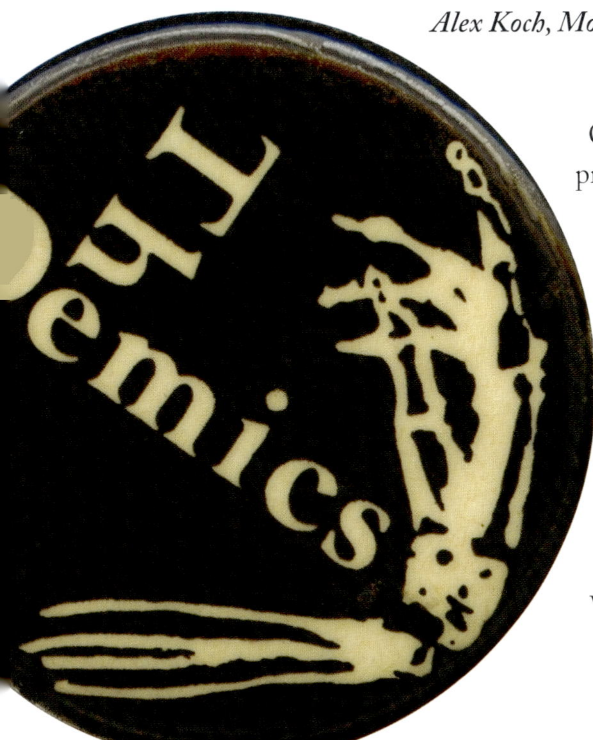

Cramming dozens of people into a vehicle for a gig was pretty common, as the one or two friends with cars would regularly be recruited as driver for a road trip to London. Besides having an opinion on everything and being an intelligent and sarcastic wit, Keith's other big asset was his English accent, not diluted in the slightest despite the years he'd lived in Canada. Many punk singers sang in fake English accents but Keith worked his real one, taking advantage of the mystique and superiority we ascribed to U.K. bands. The two words I heard out of him more than any others were "Fakkking caaaannt," applied whether he loved or loathed you. And while he was generous and supportive of other young bands, he was

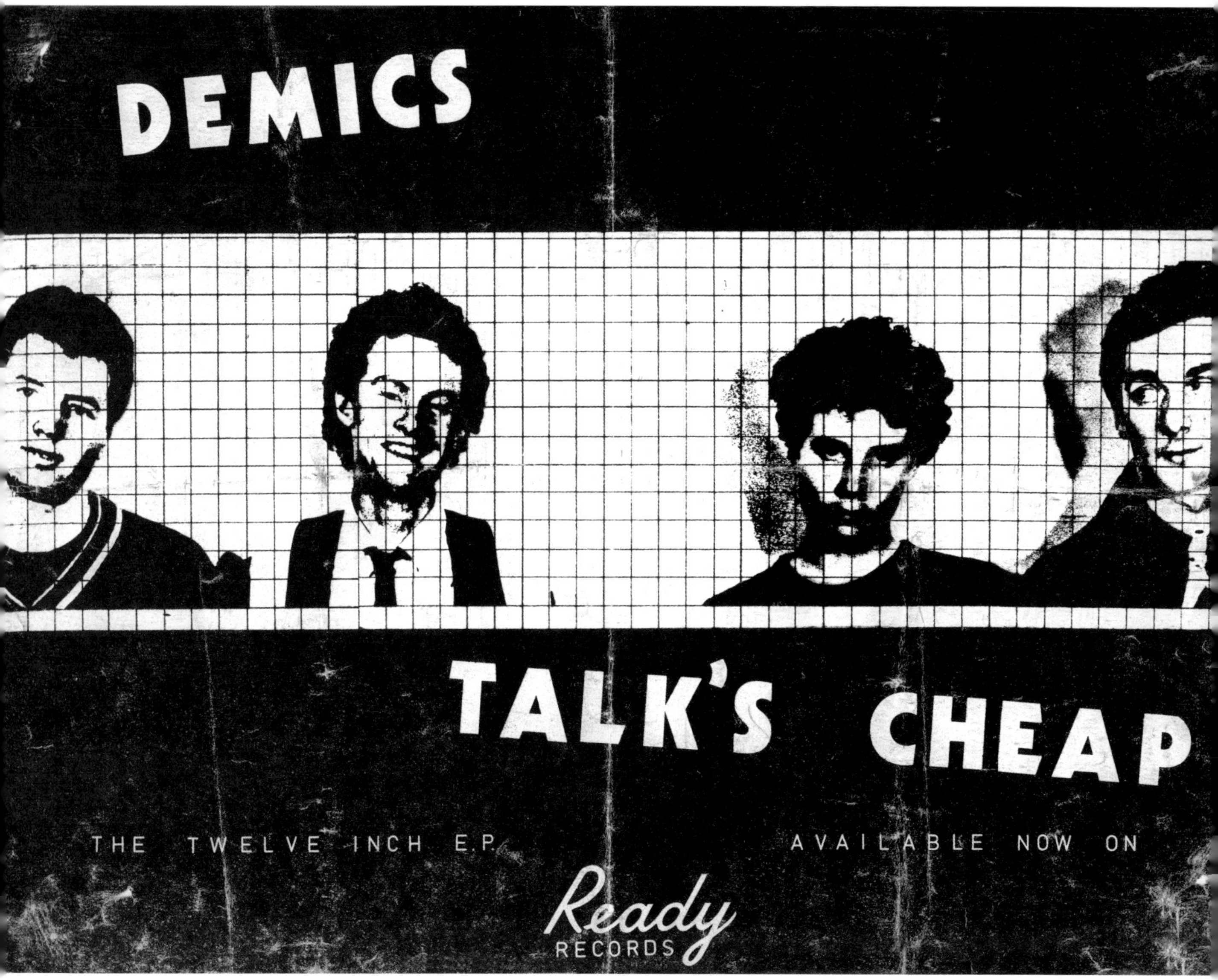

also competitive and would turn vicious after a certain point in his daily drinking.

At the time of this show, The Demics were recording their one and only album, a bloodless affair that so compromised how great the band was live that between it and Keith's erratic behavior, it was no surprise that they broke up soon after.

Psychedelic Furs, The Edge, 1980

Coming to any consensus on what "punk" is can never happen. For some, it is the current bands that fill Warped Tour bills. To me, there's a very clear through-line from the Ramones to bands like The Specials, Human League and Psychedelic Furs. Their sensibilities were unambiguously informed by the revolution and while the Furs may have destroyed their legacy (as so many artists who sustained careers beyond ground zero did) with desperate chart grabs and diminishing creative returns with each release, they briefly made beautiful and dark music on par with the best of Gang of Four, Section 25, Siouxsie and the Banshees, et al.

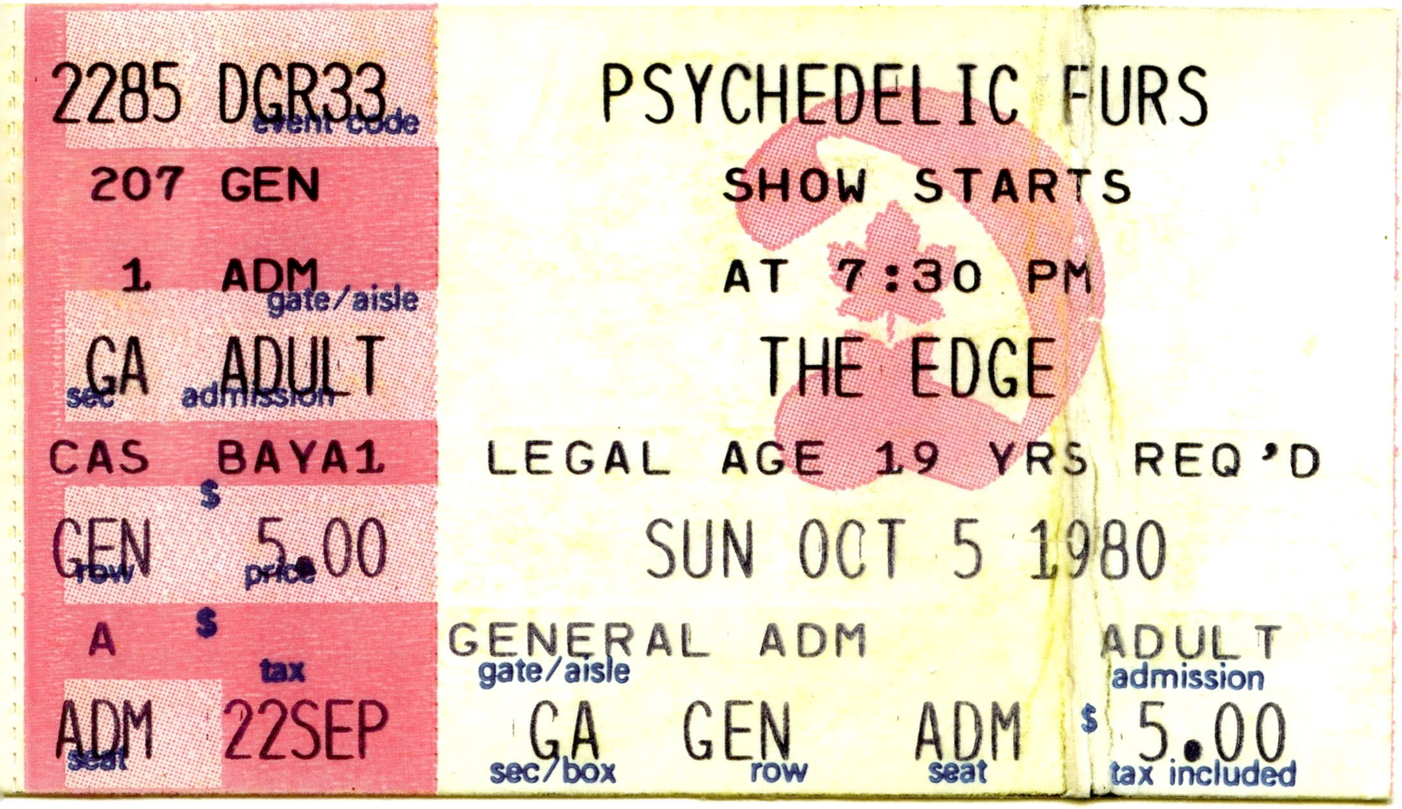

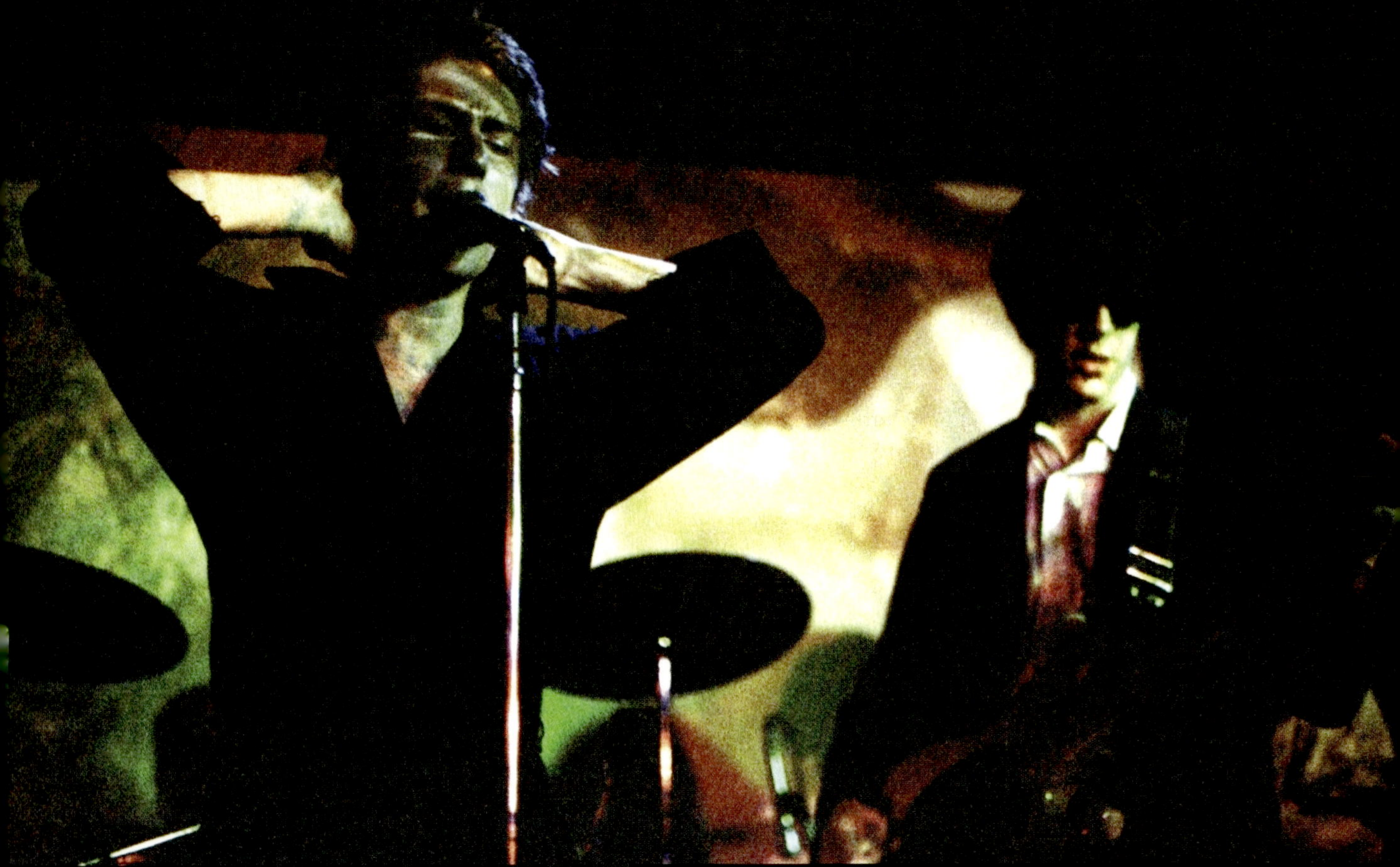

Richard and Tim Butler

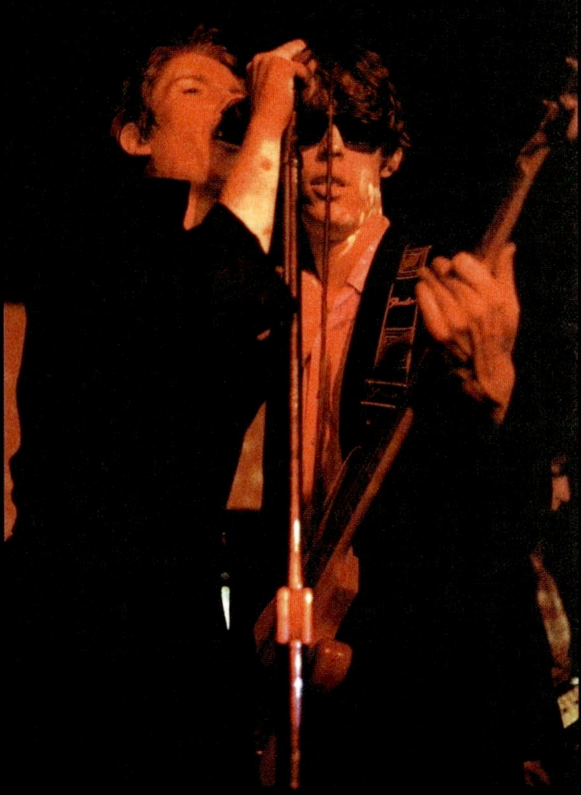

Richard Butler in the Edge dressing room

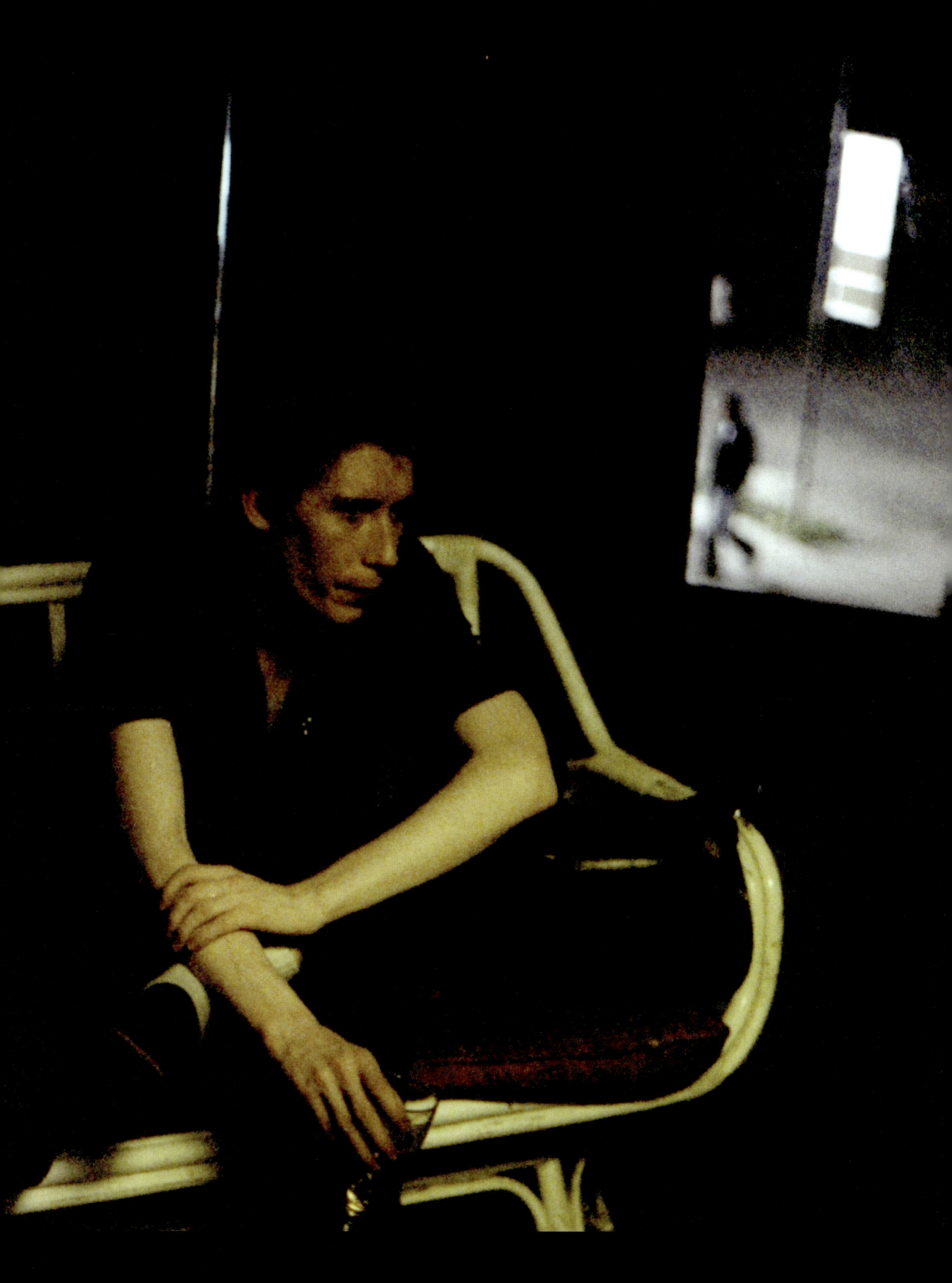

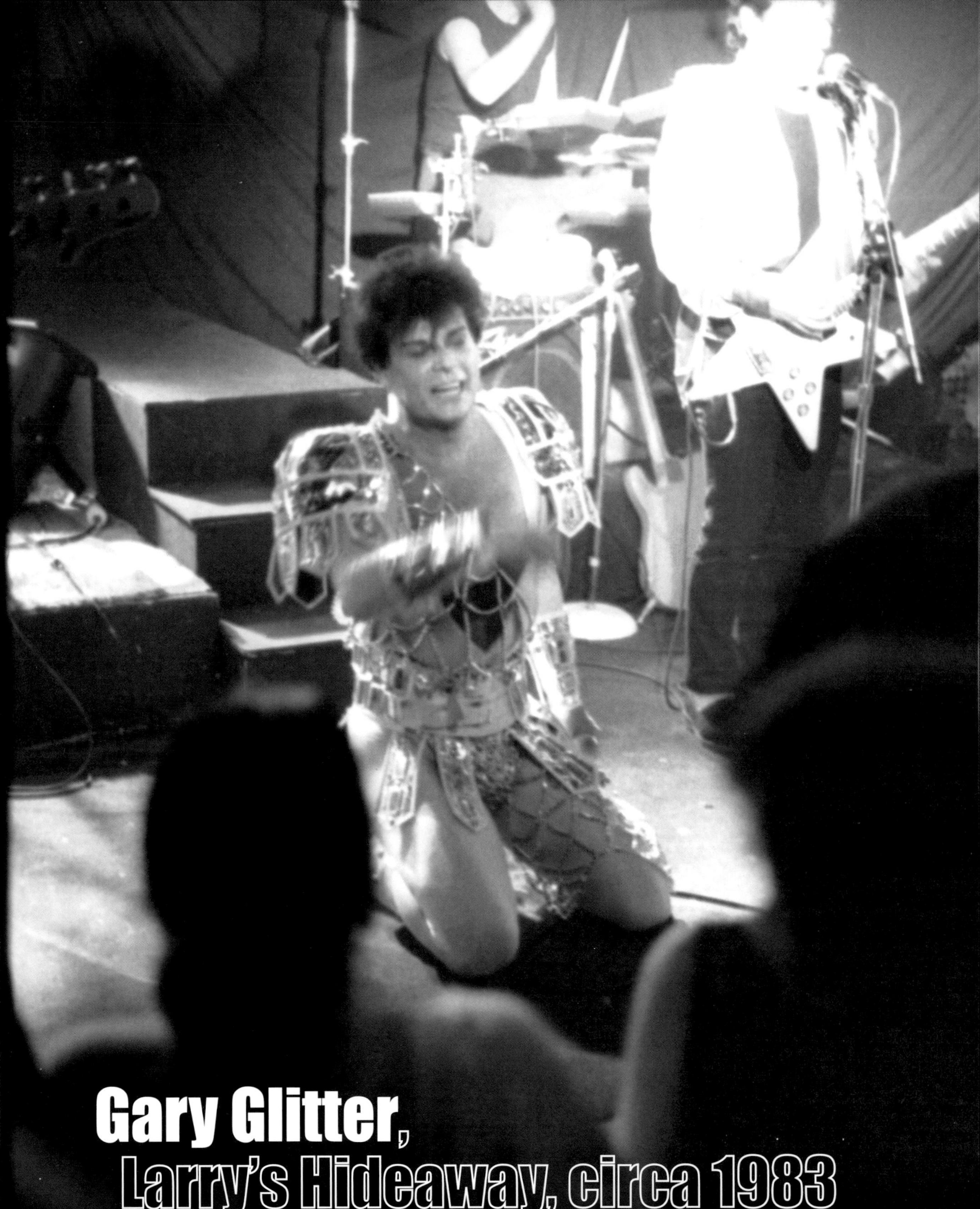

Gary Glitter,
Larry's Hideaway, circa 1983

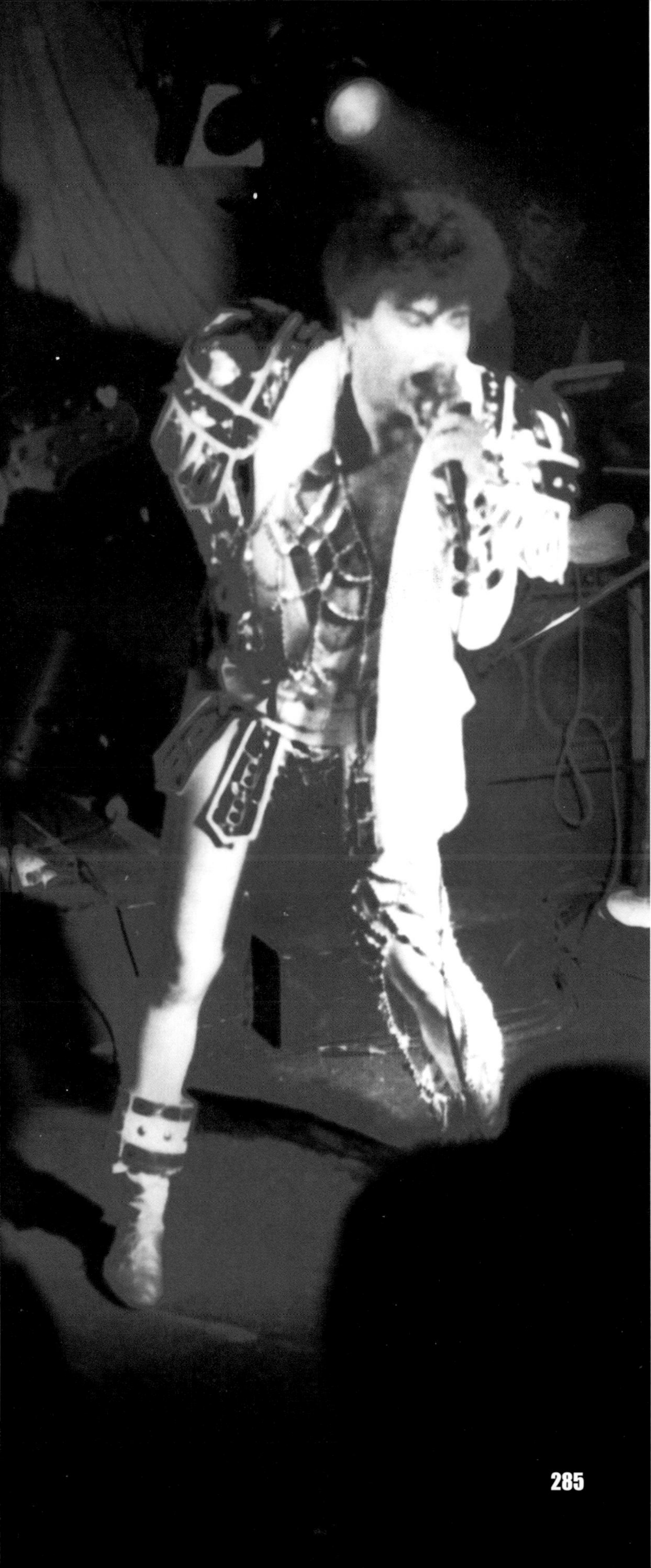

Larry's was obviously a much smaller club than those Gary Glitter was used to playing. The stage was over-crammed with equipment. Flanked by two full drum kits was a preposterous staircase pushed up against the back wall of the stage for Gary to make entrances and exits on. Behind the back wall curtain, a figure made its way, much like a cat swallowed by a python, until Gary Glitter appeared at the opening and swanned as elegantly as he could down the stairs, clutching roses and throwing them to the fans.

Glenn Branca Ensemble, Bamboo Club, 1983

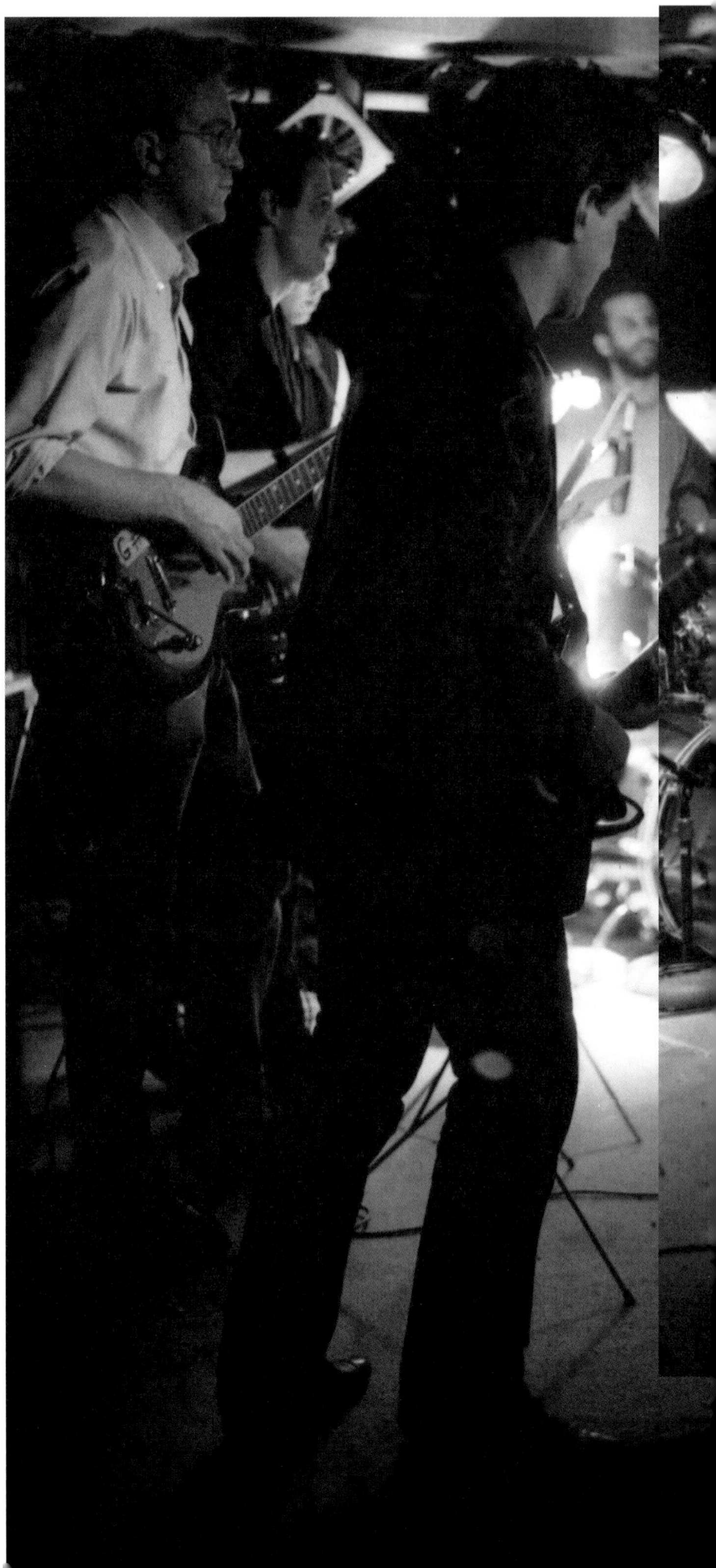

Glenn Branca

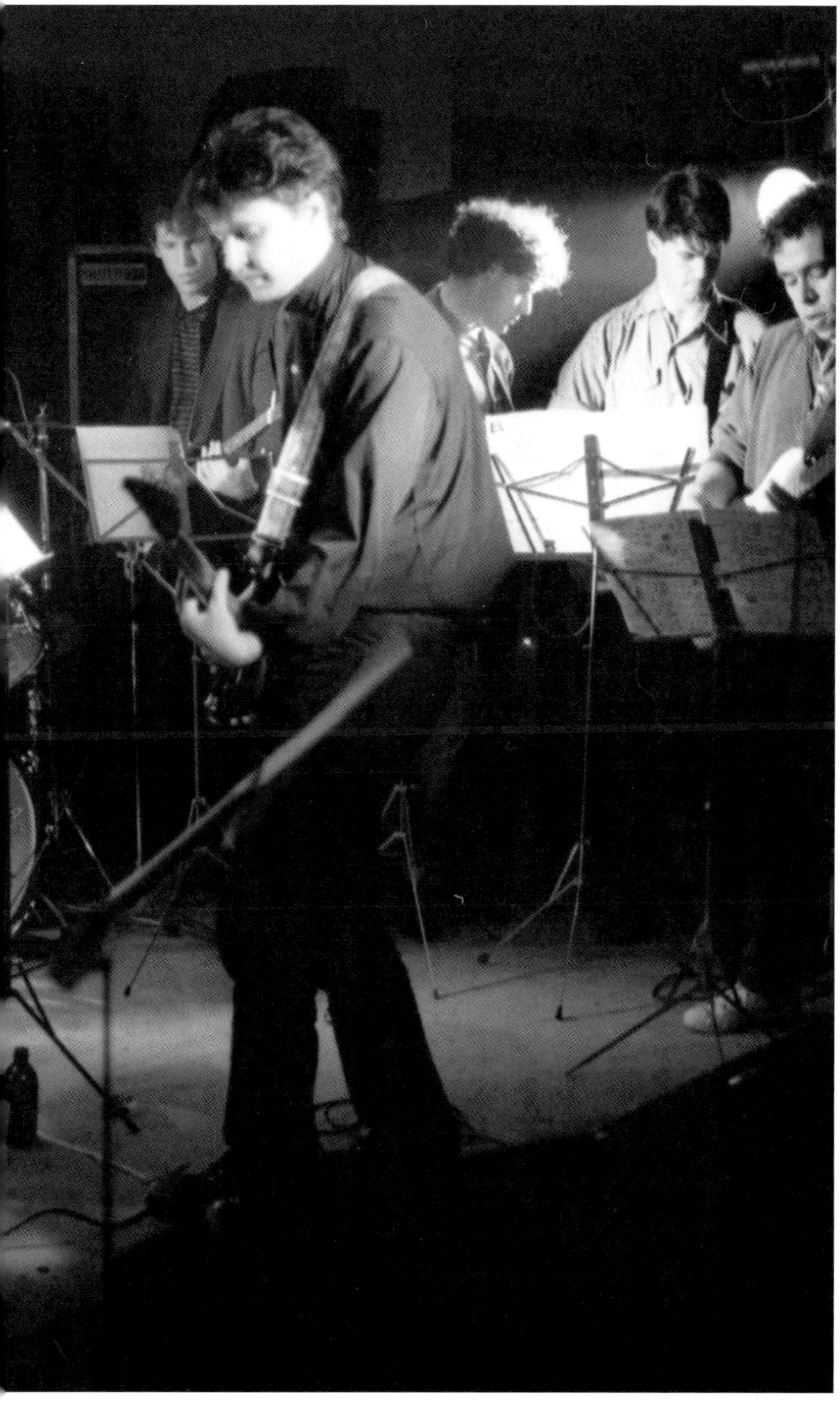

Branca's guitar orchestra at the Bamboo Club featured maybe 14 electric guitars and a drummer. After a few songs, the massed amps proved too much and the power blew. After getting it fixed, the band continued until the circuit broke again and Branca had a mini-tantrum before storming off. I heard yelling from offstage as Branca vented. After a period of negotiation, Branca and army returned for one more song, playing unamplified electric guitars to a silent audience.

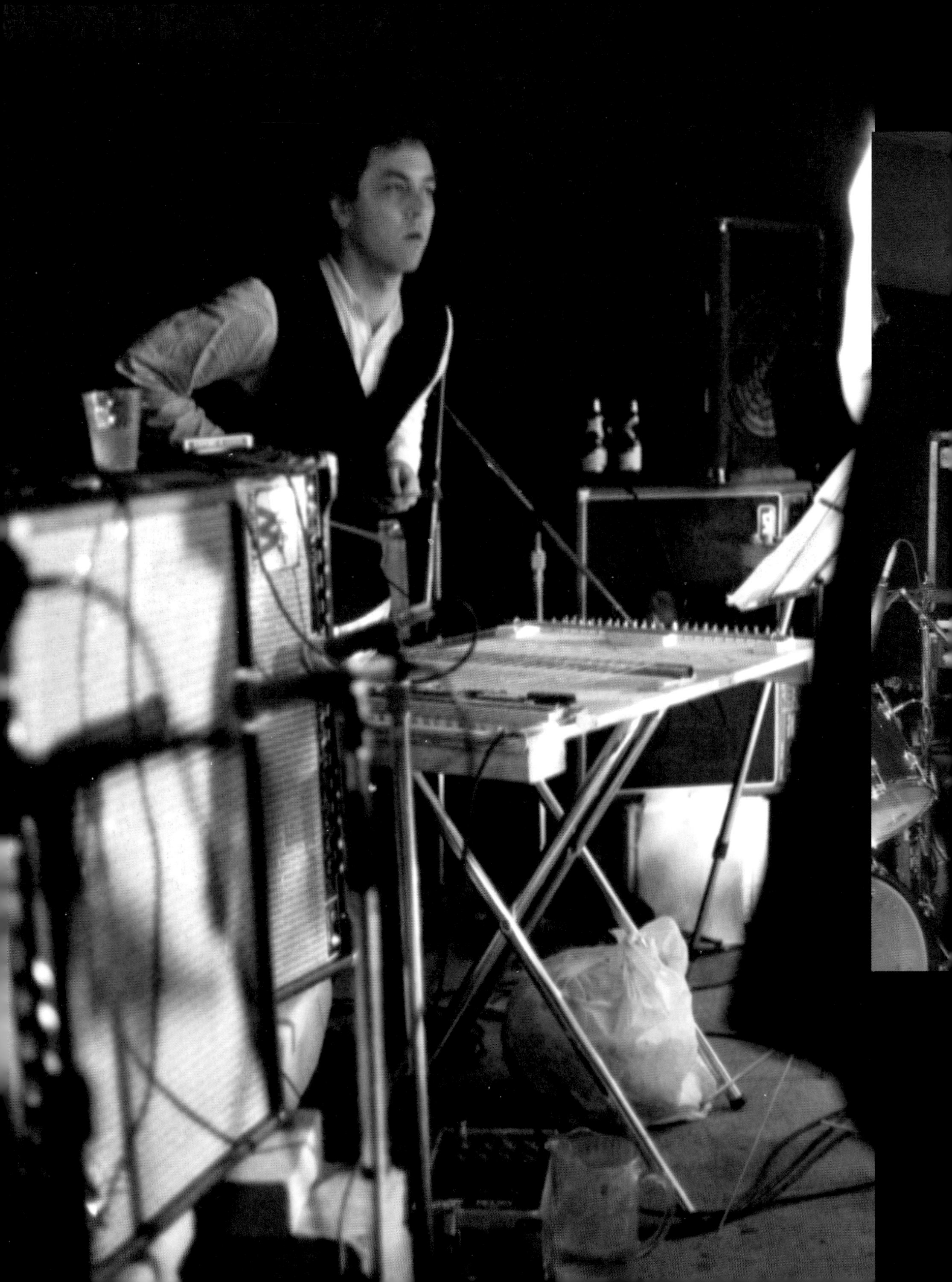

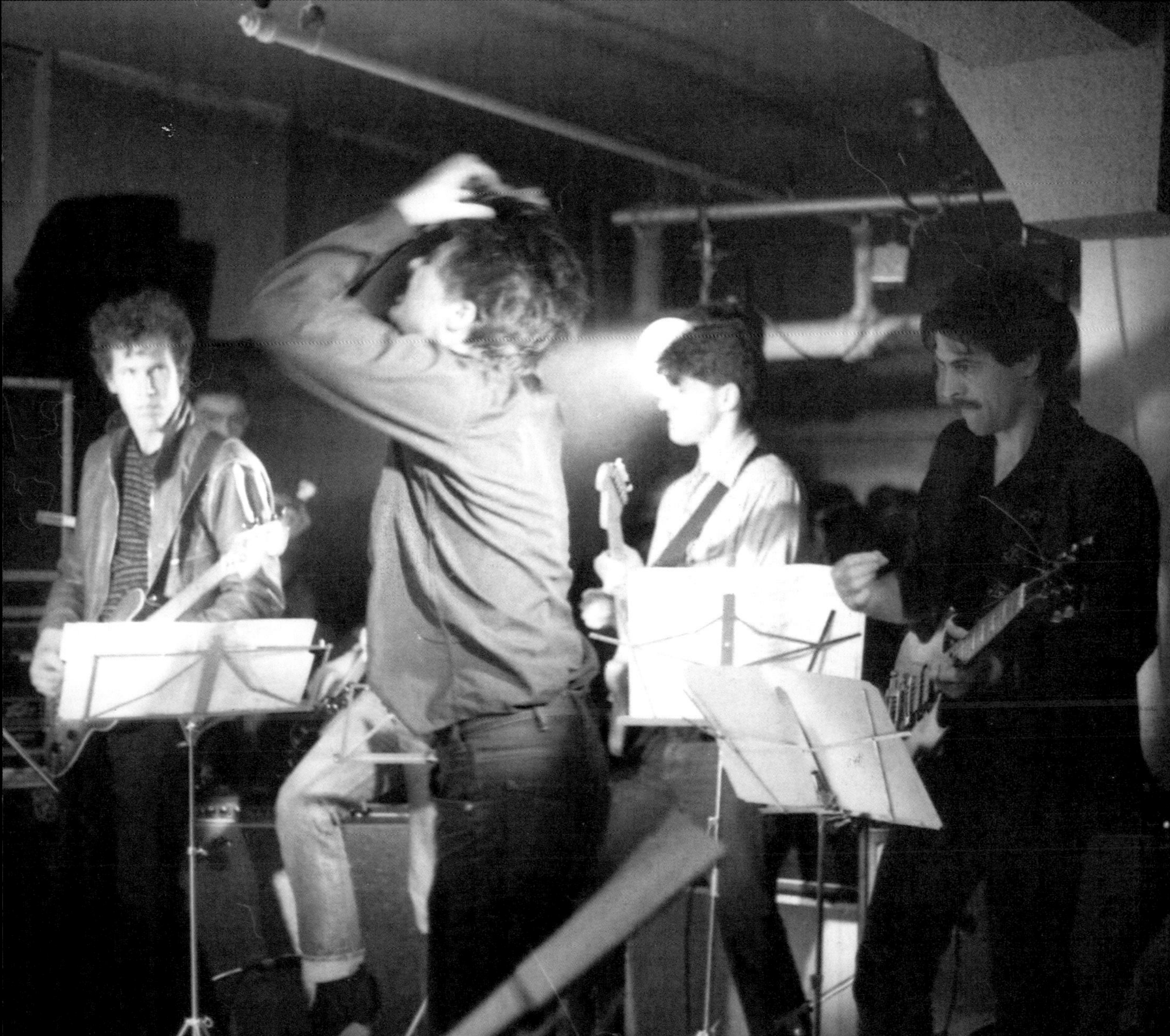

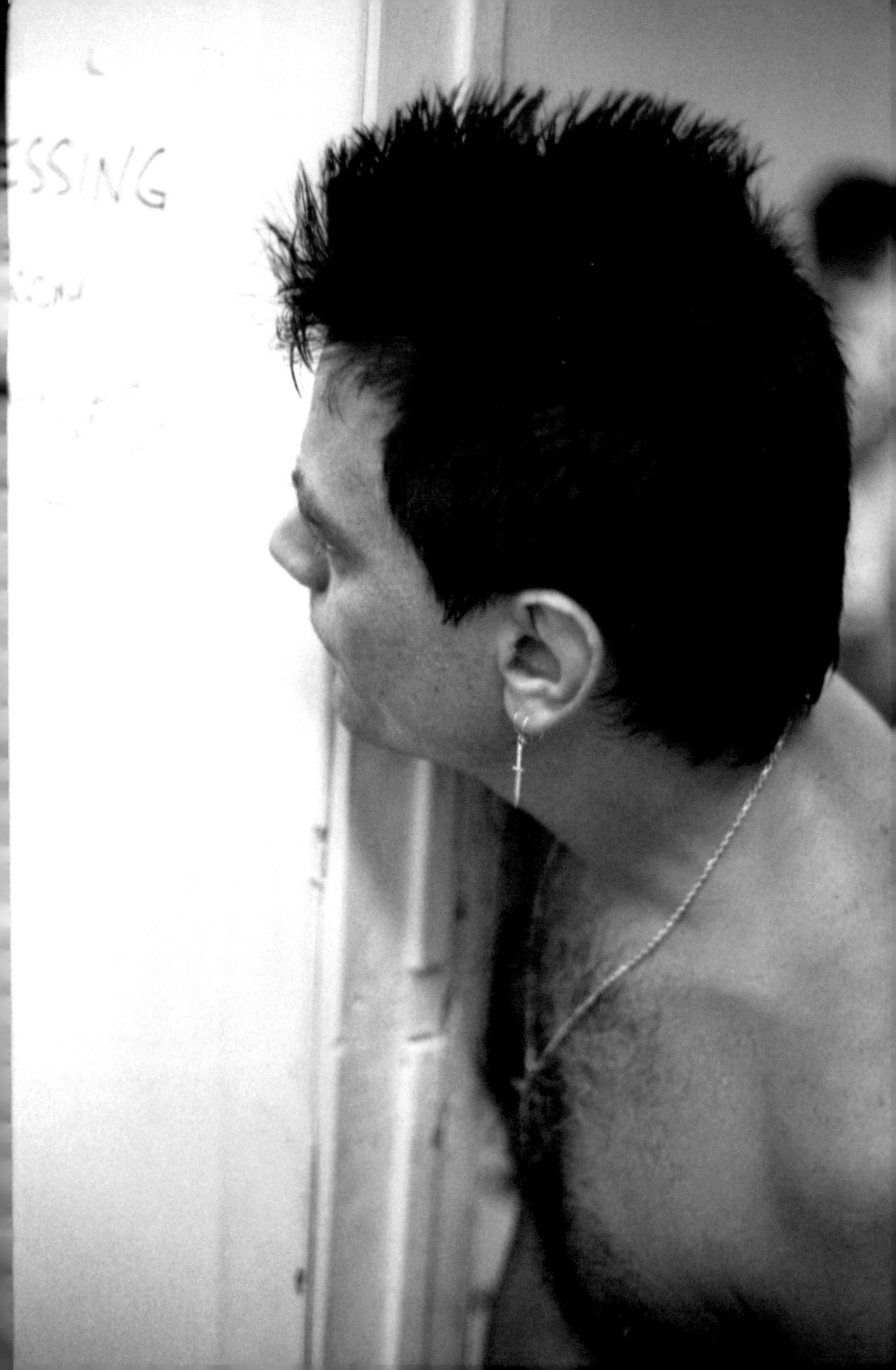

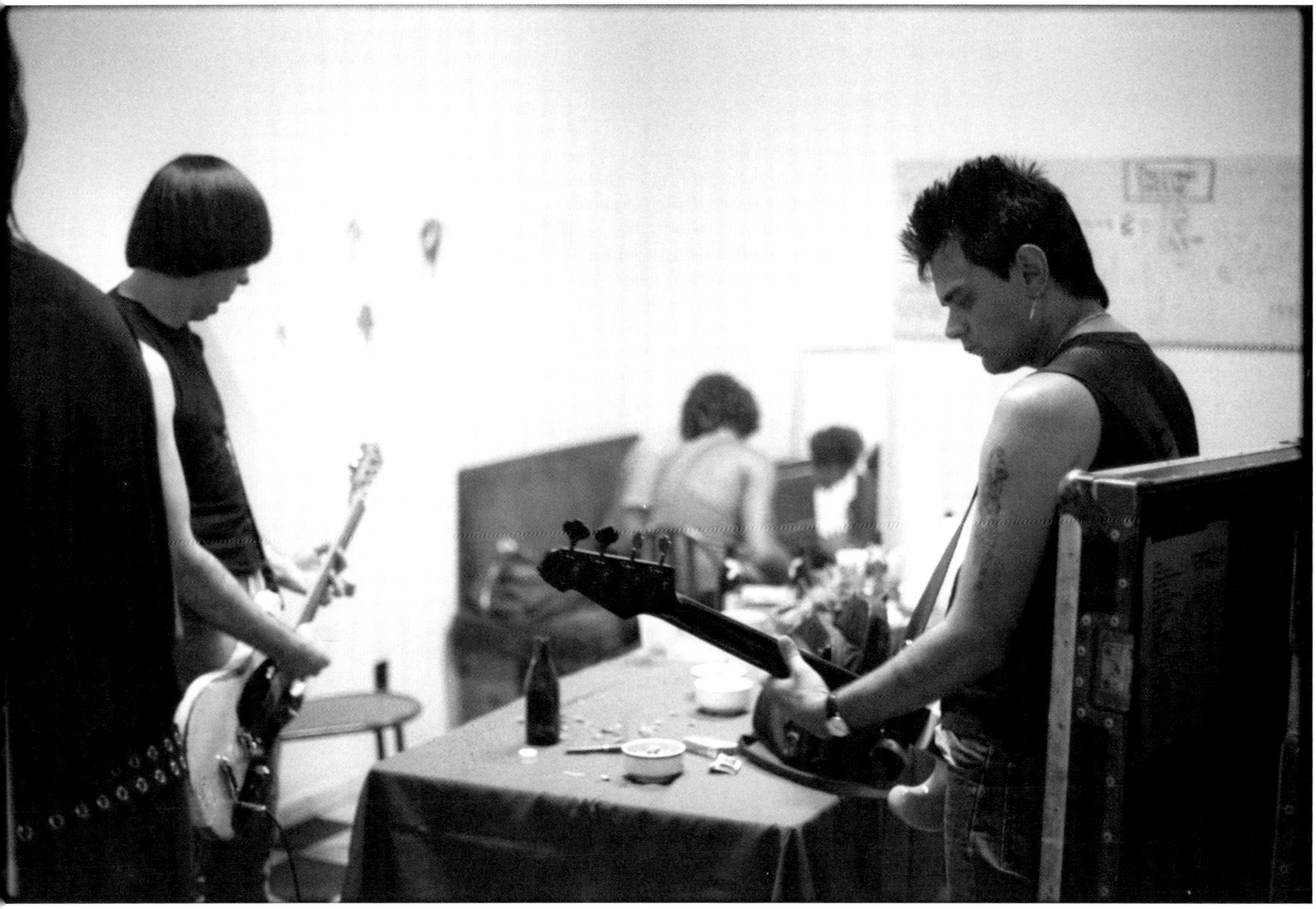

Johnny and Dee Dee

Ramones, RPM, 1987

Their repetitive and formulaic sound made audiences blasé to the Ramones to the point where the band wasn't even able to sell out the 400 or so capacity El Mocambo. For many years they didn't play Toronto, while their status as legendary innovators grew. By the time they returned, the Ramones were at the peak of their popularity and had just released *Too Tough to Die*. When Shadowy Men on a Shadowy Planet formed, we gave the Garys our first single and told them that if ever the Ramones came back, they were who we most wanted to open for. Gary Topp told me we were the only band that had asked to play with them when they were at their most unpopular, so we were given the opening spot for their three-night stint.

Dee Dee Ramone

We couldn't contain our fandom as we snuck past their dressing room, taking photos and Super 8 movies and introducing ourselves to them. I recall opening the backstage bathroom door to find Joey pre-show putting on pancake makeup to enhance his already sickly pallor. When introduced to us, the cigarette Dee Dee was holding fell from his fingers as he shook my hand, asking, "You got any valium?" After one of the nights, we also saw Joey carried out of the club for reasons unknown. He looked so fragile, thin and mantis-like.

SCHEDULE
JULY 21-23

DOORS - 8:00pm

SHADOWY MEN
9:45-10:15

RAMONES

11:00-12:30

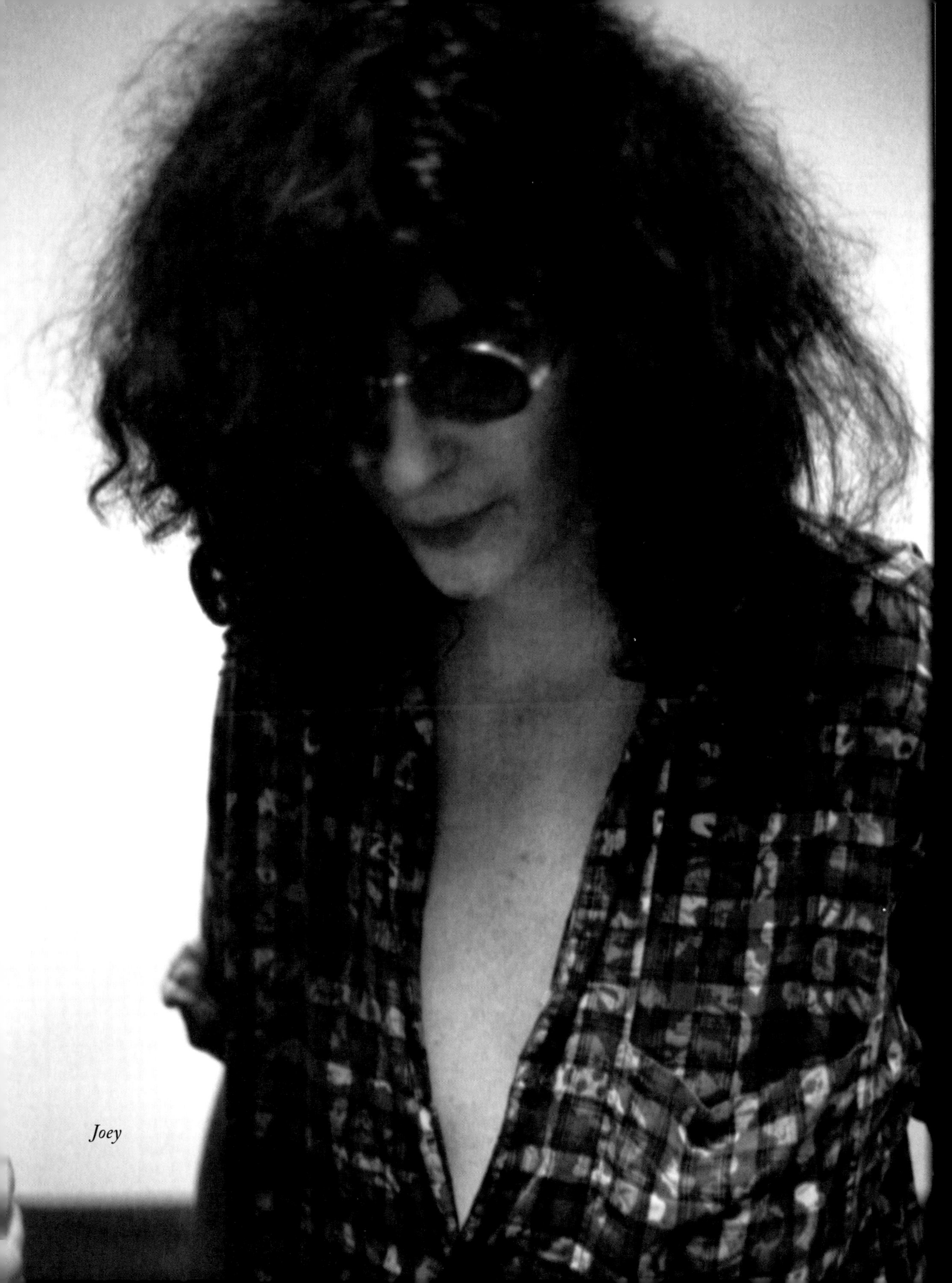

Joey

~~INTRO~~

~~LOBOTOMY~~

~~[illegible]~~

~~BLITZ 13~~

~~RR RADIO~~

~~FREAK OF N.~~

~~SHOCK~~

~~RR SCHOOL~~

~~SEDATED~~

~~KKK~~

~~[illegible] STUFF~~

~~[illegible]MOUTH~~

~~LOVE KILLS~~

~~SHEENA~~

~~GLAD TO SEE YOU~~

~~SOMETHING TO DO~~

~~TOO TOUGH~~

[illegible]

ANIMAL IS

WART

SURFIN

CRETIAN

WALK AROUN

TODAY YOUR

PIN HEAD

CHINESE ROCK

SOMEBODY

ROCK BEACH

DO YOU WANNA

CALIFORNIA

HAPPY!!

~~THE END~~

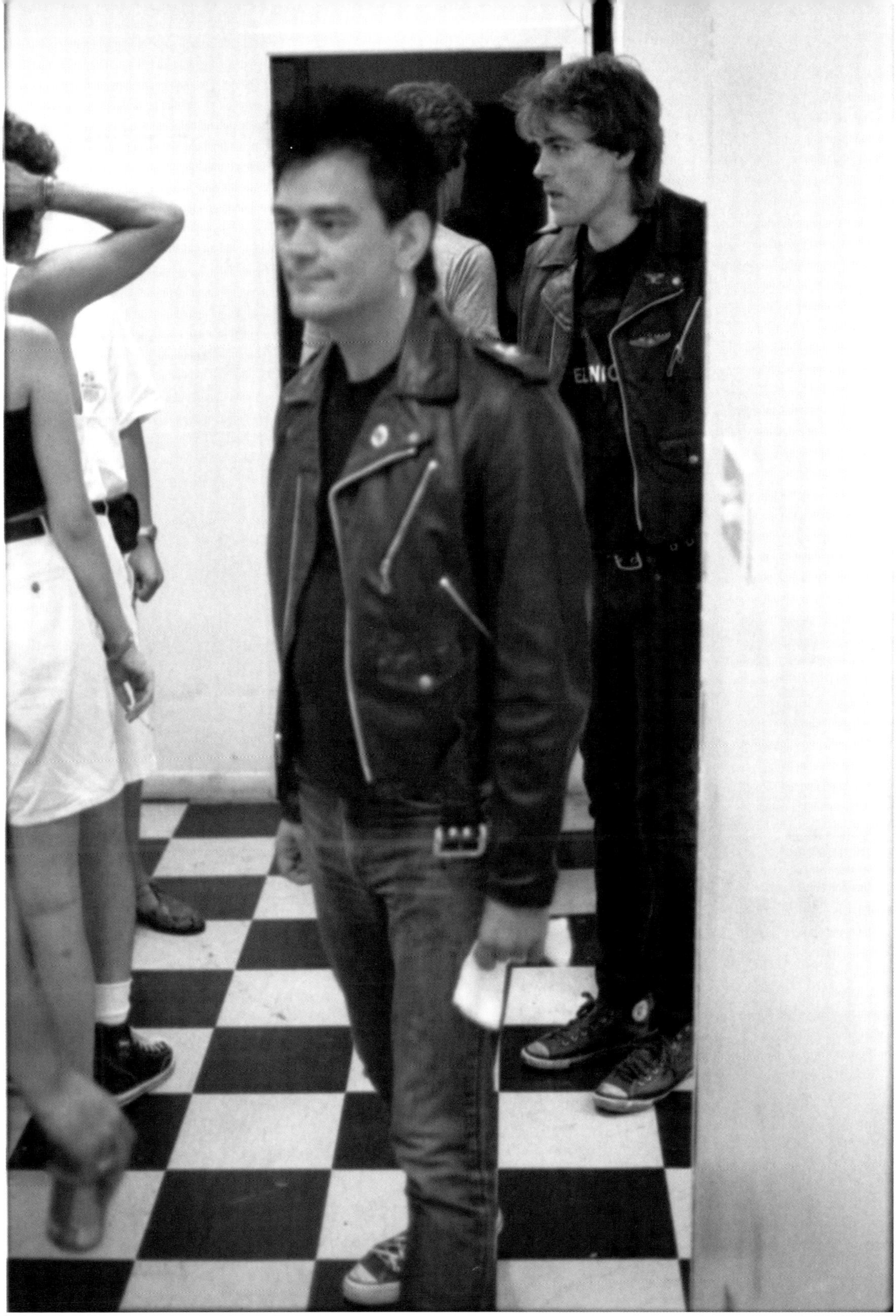

Dee Dee and Richie

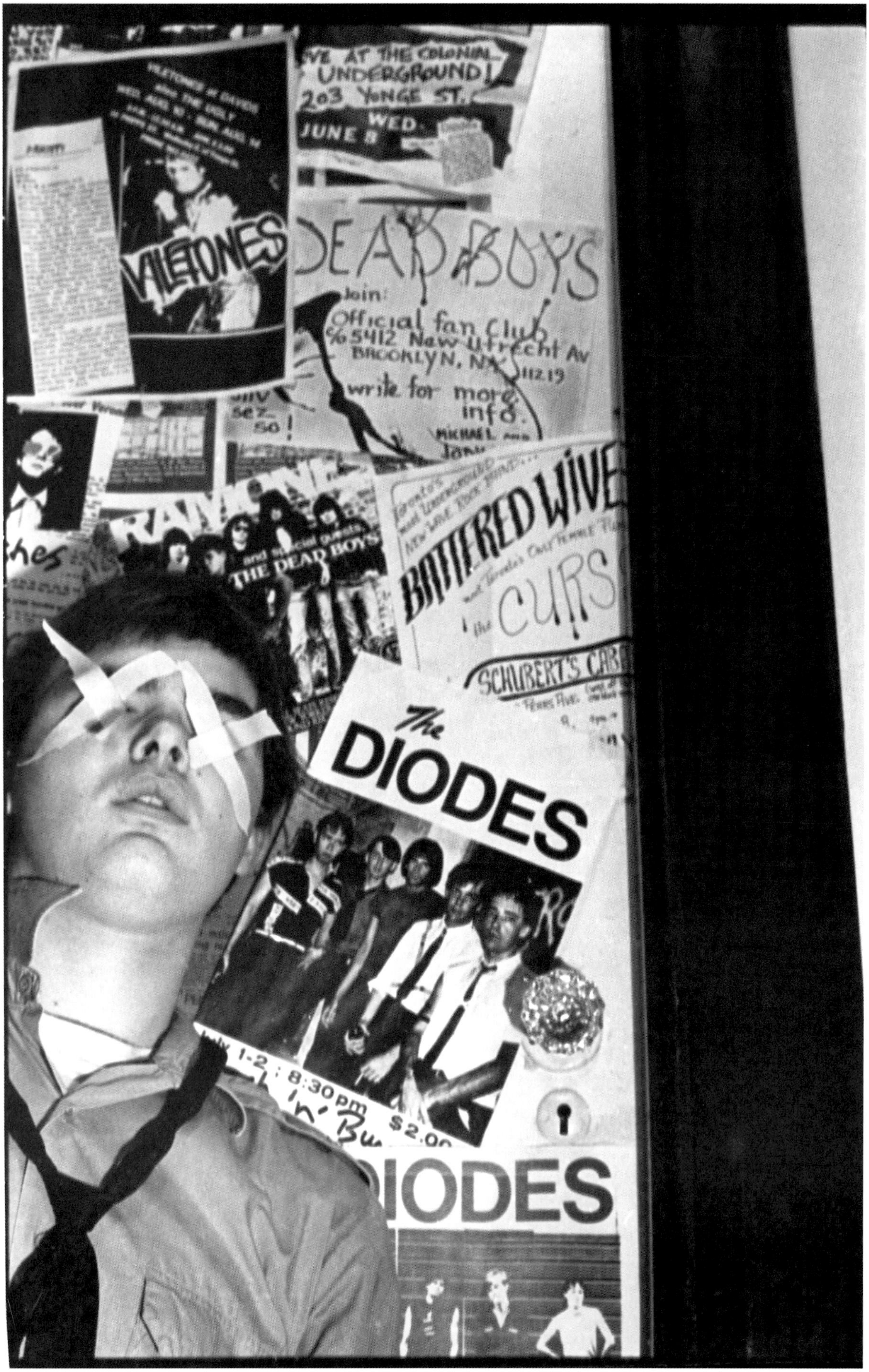

VE AT THE COLONIAL
UNDERGROUND!
203 YONGE ST.
WED.
JUNE 8
VILETONES
DEAD BOYS
Join:
Official fan Club
c/o 5412 New Utrecht Av
BROOKLYN, NY 11219
write for more
info.
BATTERED WIVE
CURS
SCHUBERT'S CAB
RAMONE
and special guests
THE DEAD BOYS
The
DIODES
8:30 pm
$2.00
DIODES

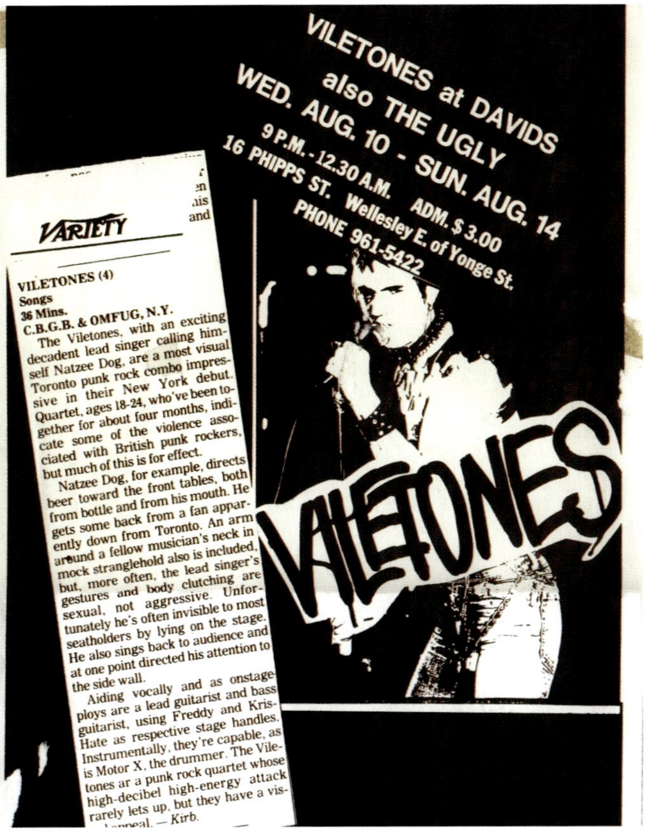

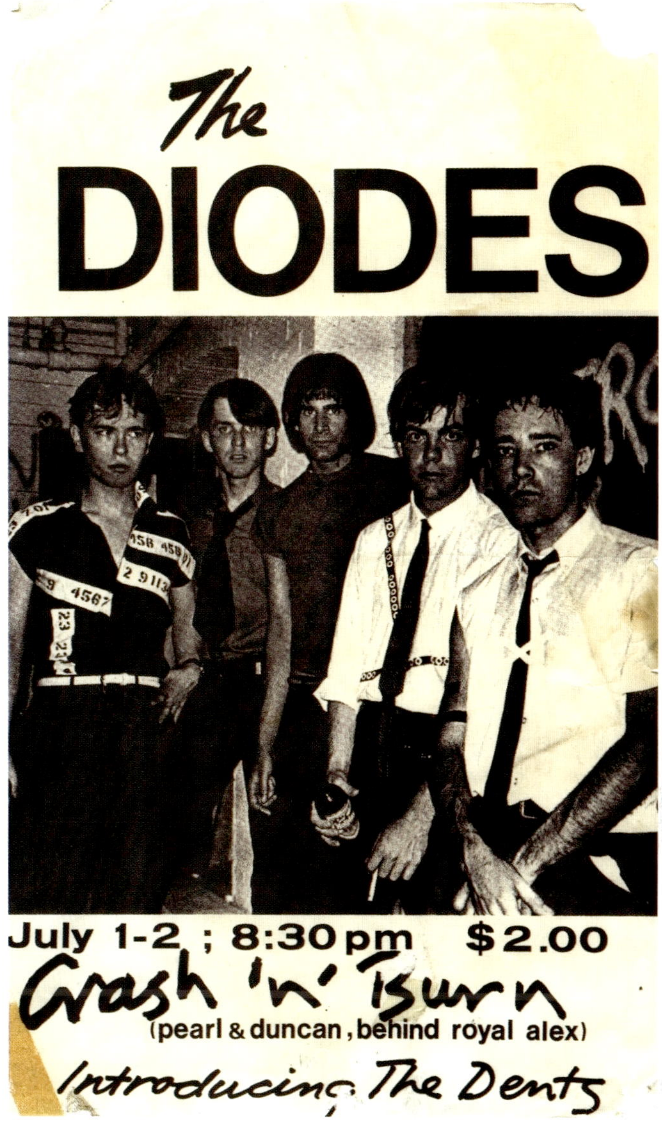

DP, 1977

It was an unusual experience seeing this for the first time 30-something years later on a roll of unprinted film as I have no memory of taking this picture of myself against my bedroom door. I do recall meticulously taping up the flyers so that they were stuck to the door and not each other, allowing them to be undamaged. Some of those same flyers are in this book.

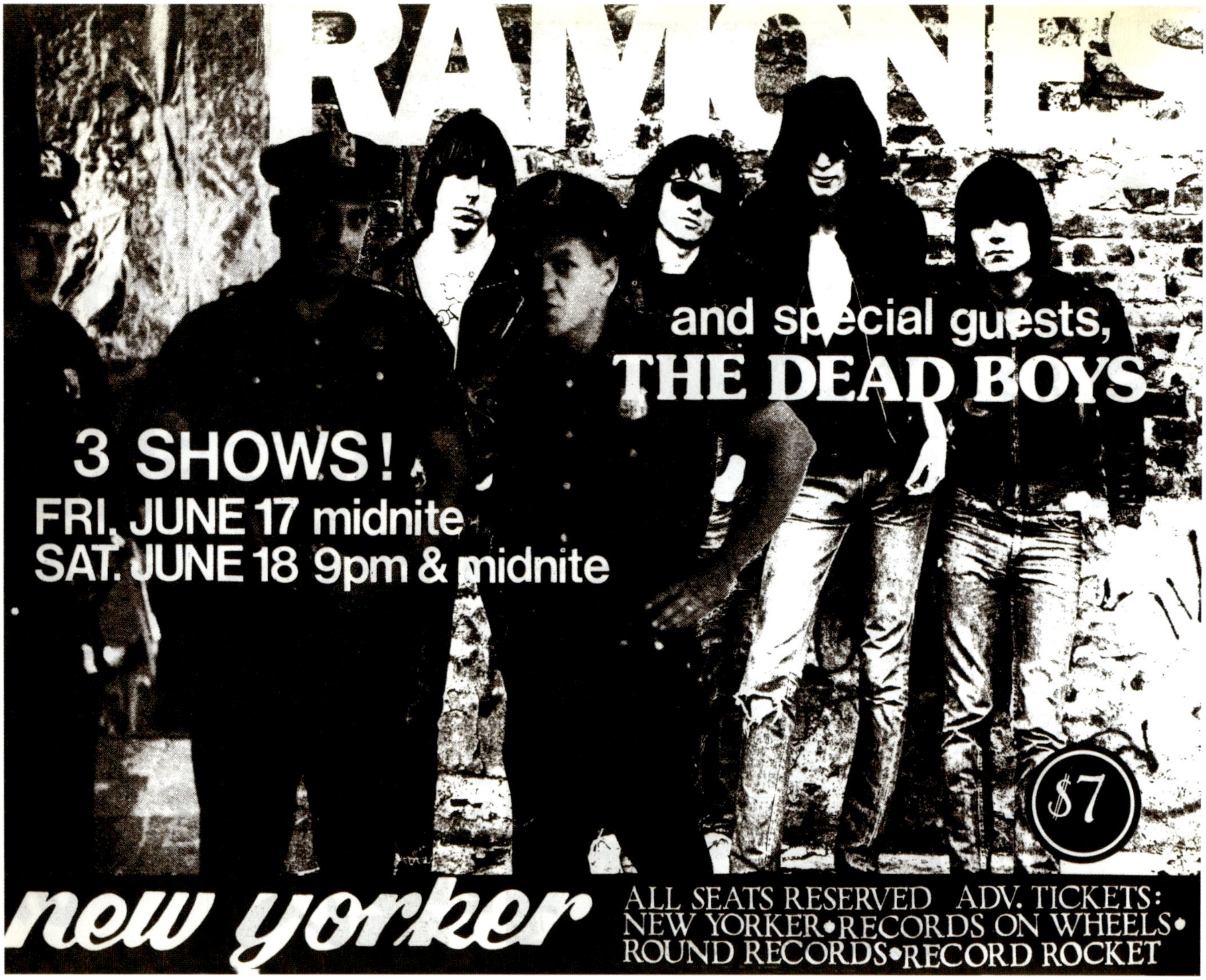
RAMONES
and special guests,
THE DEAD BOYS
3 SHOWS!
FRI. JUNE 17 midnite
SAT. JUNE 18 9pm & midnite
$7
new yorker
ALL SEATS RESERVED ADV. TICKETS:
NEW YORKER•RECORDS ON WHEELS•
ROUND RECORDS•RECORD ROCKET

Acknowledgments

Some element of this book wouldn't have happened without the following, and I thank them:

Greg Dick
Cameron Drew
Will Munro
Lynn McNeill
The Beaver
Brian and Pierre and Rotate This
Derek von Essen
Wrik Mead
Jen Hale
Michael Holmes
Rachel Ironstone
Jack David and the people of ECW Press
Mr. Kozinchuk
Alan Kennedy
Roger Logan
Rojer S.
Gary Topp and Gary Cormier
Colin Brunton
All the great people who worked with The Garys
Liz Worth
Suzanne Naughton
Dallas Good
Reid Diamond
Brian Connelly
Alex Koch
Steve Koch
Mohamed Nagdee
Anna Bourque
Linda Lee Hunter
John Armstrong
Richard Citroen
Freddy Pompeii
Steven Leckie
Viletones
Paul Robinson
Diodes
Ralph Alfonso
Teenage Head
The Demics
Everyone who taped, glued, photocopied and designed the flyers used
Jason Winkler
My family
Shirley Pyle
Everyone pictured

To Cram and Virlana and Draga and Siren and Boring Bill and Val and Matt and Thomas and Suzanne and Gambi and Bubblegum and Rabies and Cleave and Steve and Zero, thanks.

Dedicated to our friends who can't be with us today.

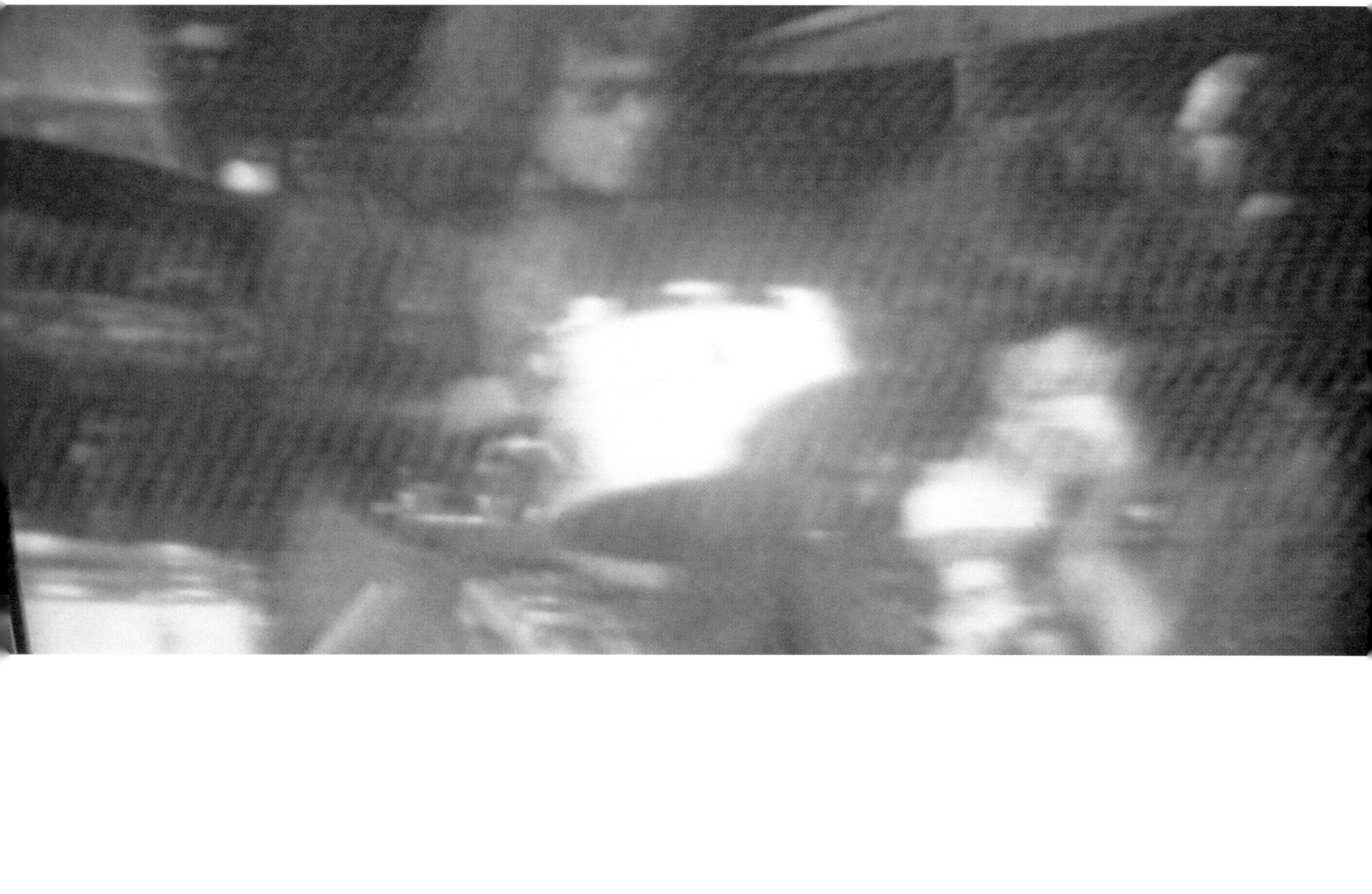